2005
Book Markets
for
Children's Writers

Published by
Institute of Children's Literature

Copyright © Institute of Children's Literature, 2004. All rights reserved.

Acknowledgments

The editors of this directory appreciate the generous cooperation of our instructor and student contributors and the children's book editors who made clear their policies and practices.

MARNI MCNIFF, Editor

SUSAN TIERNEY, Articles Editor

HEATHER BURNS-DEMELO, Assistant Editor

JANINE MANGIAMELE, Assistant Editor

SHERRI KEEFE, Research Assistant

Contributing Writers: Eileen Byrne, Barbara Cole, Vicki Hambleton, Pamela Purrone

Cover Art: Howard Munce

The material contained herein is protected by copyright. No part of it may be republished, copied, reproduced, or adapted without the express written permission of The Institute of Children's Literature, 93 Long Ridge Road, West Redding, CT 06896-0811. Printed in Canada.

International Standard Book Number 1-889715-20-4

1-800-443-6078. www.writersbookstore.com
email: services@writersbookstore.com

Contents

Step-by-Step Through the Submissions Process — 5

This section offers step-by-step instructions for compiling a submissions package.

Ready, Aim . . . Research and Prepare to Sell	6
Step-by-Step through Query Letters & Proposals	19
Query Letter Checklist	23
Sample Query Letter–Nonfiction	27
Sample Cover Letter–Nonfiction	28
Sample Cover Letter–Fiction	29
Sample Query Letter–Fiction	30
Sample Synopsis–Fiction	31
Sample Synopsis–Nonfiction	32
Sample Outline–Nonfiction	33
Sample Proposal–Nonfiction	34
Sample Bibliography	35
Sample Résumé	36
Sample Manuscript Pages	37
Manuscript Preparation	38
Picture Book Dummy	39
Picture Book Submissions	40
Step-by-Step through the Business of Publishing	41
Postage Information	47
Frequently Asked Questions	48
Publishing Terms	51

Gateway to the Markets — 55

Early Readers: Bridge the Gap Word by Word,
by Sue Bradford Edwards — 56

Editor Profiles

Rebecca Waugh, Dial Books for Young Readers	170
Anne Hoppe, HarperCollins	230
Allyn Johnston, Harcourt, Inc.	227
Shana Corey, Random House	505

Contents (Cont.)

Teens Coping with Life's Real Issues,
by *Pegi Deitz Shea*   **63**

   Editor Profiles
      Tegan Culler, Child & Family Press   **138**
      Doug Fehlen, Free Spirit Publishing   **205**
      Lori Shein, Lucent Books   **284**
      Iris Rosoff, Rosen Publishing   **366**

Step by Step through Educational Publishing,
by *Suzanne Lieurance*   **71**

   Editor Profiles
      Patience Camplair, Incentive Publications   **251**
      Matt Mulder, Upstart Books/Highsmith Press   **414**
      Lise Ragan, Course Crafters   **459**

Listings   77

How to Use the Listings   **78**
This year's directory offers 553 updated listings including 54 completely new listings

Listings of Book Publishers   **80**

Additional Listings   **438**

Selected Contests and Awards   529

Provides basic guidelines for 28 book writing contests, awards, and grants.

Indexes   545

2005 Market News   **546**
Identifies new listings and publishers not listed.

Category Index   **548**
Lists publishers under selected categories according to the type of material they are interested in acquiring.

Publisher and Contest Index   **586**
Provides page references for publishers and contests.

Step-by-Step Through the Submission Process

Ready, Aim . . . Research and Prepare to Sell

Writers are like archers. Our target is to compose the best possible work and find it a home, a market, a bull's-eye. To be a good archer, we first have to have a strong interest, a passion, for the sport. We acquire the best possible equipment, a high-quality of bow and arrows, and maintain them well. We practice our aim and technique, and train with a coach if needed. The better these requirements are followed, the more frequently we hit the bull's-eye. Now substitute the following steps and see if the simile holds for your favorite "sport"—writing.

1 - **Target the subject.** Is it of personal interest and a subject you feel passionate about? An editor isn't going to be enthusiastic about a book if you're not. What type of research will make it interesting and successful? Children's editors today require first-rate, primary research.

2 - **Target the quality.** Have you done your best writing? Practiced your skills, gone to writers' conferences, taken courses, joined critique groups, or in some way worked at your craft and gained the right "equipment"?

3 - **Target the audience.** Can you see it clearly? What is the age? Reading level? Interests? Voice?

4 - **Target the competition.** Are there other books on comparable subjects? If you're writing in one genre, what else is out there? Do you have a truly different slant to offer?

5 - **Target the market generally.** Is your book to be trade, mass-market, religious, crossover, educational?

6 - **Target the individual publisher and editor.** What is this particular company and editor most interested in, most successful with?

We will take you step-by-step through the process of hitting some of these targets. Only you can work on the quality, but we will coach you through subject, audience, competition, and market objectives and how to reach them. You'll come nearer and nearer to a bull's-eye with every arrow—every manuscript sent flying.

Target the Subject

Whether you're finding new ideas, developing a defined project, or searching for markets for your completed manuscript, you can improve the submission process by taking time to do fundamental research. The first step is to select an idea that interests you, that you believe will appeal to readers as much as it does to you, and collect information about it.

This idea and research development step is an important first measure toward selling your book. While most editors and successful writers will tell beginners to focus on writing a good book, not on worrying about what's fashionable in the market and what's not—and they're correct—a good book requires authenticity if it's fiction, and accuracy if it's nonfiction. Subject research is essential in composing the best possible manuscript, whether it's historical background for a novel or a text, geographical information on a region or city, updated data for a scientific principle, or even searches for good character names on a census or genealogical site. Finding and refining your idea with research will strengthen your work, and poise it to sell.

Research resources. Writers have a surfeit of research resources today in the Internet quiver. The Web gives writers access to libraries, research studies, museums, associations, businesses, and a seemingly endless supply of miscellaneous sites available through myriad search engines. You can do this research at your local library if you're not set up at home. Look at:

- encyclopedia sites that might provide links to more detailed pages on other sites.
- university libraries online.
- government resources like the Library of Congress, the Smithsonian, NASA.
- museum sites, such as the Metropolitan Museum of Art in

New York, the British Museum, and many other world-class museums.
- the sites of smaller, more focused museums, historical sites, even corporations (for that article on sneakers, for example).
- organizations that range from the social to the arts to sports, from the local to the universal.
- journalism and other sites that lead to "experts" for interviews.

Some sites help you to find the existence of material, but you'll need to get it physically from the library or another source. Some sites, however, provide actual content— text, photos, data—online.

Accuracy and annotations. Websites have links to other sites. Follow the trail, the links, and keep clear notes on where you go and what you learn, so you don't lose important resources or unintentionally plagiarize. Narrow your sights in on your topic, and be sure to check and recheck your information against other sources. Take every care with accuracy, since children's editors today want to see primary research sources and they want precision. Keep a running bibliography; you may need it for your submission package and even if you don't, it's a good idea for back-up and additional research, if it's needed. Be sure to check the *Book Markets for Children's Writers'* listings for indications of the kind of bibliographical or other research annotations targeted editors require. (See, for example, the bibliography on page 35.)

Fiction and research. Perhaps you're writing fiction and don't believe you need to do research. You might not, but you very well may. Is your story set in a seaside town you recall from childhood? What's the weather like there when your story is set? Are you sure? Do you need inspiration for character names for a contemporary or historical story? Check local newspapers for stories about children of a particular age and time. Remember that "local" has new meaning on the Internet. You can look up *The Columbus Dispatch* (Ohio) or *The Waterbury Republican* (Connecticut) or *The Mercury News* (San Jose, California). Check a genealogy site for names, or for story ideas, or for nonfiction research. Use all your resources, and of course, turn to print, too. Through your local library you have access to networks of other libraries that will help you borrow virtually any book you need.

Internet Research Resources

A list of possible Internet research sites that purports to be comprehensive would take up many pages, but here are broad categories and site examples to start the subject research process.

- **Search engines:** www.google.com and www.dogpile.com are effective search engines because they provide specificity and variety when searching a subject. For a different kind of search, try www.about.com, which offers expert guides to help you navigate through a subject.

- **Government sites:** The U.S. government's sites are a great place to begin research: Look for books, historical archives, photos, and much more at the Library of Congress (www.loc.gov). At NASA (www.nasa.gov), try the Strategic Enterprises sites for space, technology, exploration, earth and physical sciences, and biology. The Smithsonian site (www.smithsonian.org) is divided into Art & Design, History & Culture, Science & Technology. Go to the Government Printing Office (www.access.gpo.gov) and FirstGov (www.firstgov.gov), for everything from government operations to health to mining to special education.

- **Reference sites:** The *Encyclopedia Britannica* (www. britannica.com) site gives brief information on myriad topics, and provides helpful links; a subscriber service allows access to longer articles and more information. The Learning Network's www.infoplease.com is an almanac site with facts on topics from world events to art, architecture, biographies, holiday calendars, weather, health, weights and measures, and much more.

- **Museums:** Large and small museums across the country, and the world, can be indispensable to the writer. Through a search engine, see if local historical societies, for example, have websites. Or try the Metropolitan Museum of Art (www.metmuseum.org), British Museum (www.thebritishmuseum.ac.uk), or try the Virtual Library museums pages (www.icom.org/vlmp) to find museums around the world.

Target the Audience

Developing ideas means not only thought and research about your topic or story, but information about the readers. Audience is the meeting place of idea and market research. Who will read this story? Who is this ultimate market (assuming the editor takes the role of the intermediate, not the ultimate market)? What grabs them?

Experts. You know "experts" who can help you find out which books kids are reading at which ages, or what parents or educators are reading, if they're your projected audience. Talk to children's librarians and teachers about the kinds of stories and topics currently, or universally, appealing to young readers. Ask them about curriculum needs, especially for nonfiction. Go to bookstores and speak to managers who specialize in children's books. Online, go to library and reading sites, like those for the American Library Association (ALA) and the International Reading Association (IRA).

Developmental stages. Find out what's happening developmentally at a given age, what's being studied at school, what interests spark your audience. Talk to scout leaders, coaches, music teachers. Observe and talk to the children themselves, especially about books if you can. Go to children's websites to see the topics they cover, and watch television programming and read young people's magazines to learn more about contemporary youth culture. Go to parenting websites to see what problems and joys arise. But remember, you'll need to find your own slants on these subjects—your own way of holding your bow and releasing your arrow.

Age ranges. Use *Book Markets for Children's Writers*: Browse through the listings to look at the ages covered and review the sample titles. Or start with the Category Index (page 548) and look under "preK" or "middle grade" or "young adult," and review the publishers listed. Request their catalogues or visit their websites. Catalogues are generally free upon request with a stamped, self-addressed, 9x12 envelope. Examining the catalogues, in print or online, is a very helpful practice even at this stage of research, though it will be essential once you focus in on publishers where you'll target your specific work. See how many titles are published in what genres, for what age ranges, and give you a sense of their subjects

Age-Targeting Resources

- **American Library Association (ALA)** and **International Reading Association (IRA):** The lists of books for children compiled by these two organizations will help direct you to age-appropriate writing. (www.ala.org and www.reading.org). The ALA also lists "Great Sites!" for children, which helps writers focus in on kids' interests.

- **American Academy of Pediatrics:** Try the AAP's (www.aap.org) You and Your Family page, or the publications page.

- **Bright Futures:** Available on this organization's website (www.brightfutures.org) are downloads of tip sheets on developmental stages, and a variety of resources on juvenile and adolescent health and behavioral development.

- **National Network for Child Care (NNCC):** The website (www.nncc.org) is divided into early childhood, school age, teens, and evaluation, as well as topics such as intellectual, language, emotional/social, and an Ages and Stages series.

- **Search Institute:** This nonprofit's organization (www.search-institute.org) and website highlight 40 developmental assets for children from grades 6 to 12.

Finding Child and Teen Sites

- **KidsClick!:** A librarian-generated list of more than 600 sites for children (http://sunsite.berkeley.edu/KidsClick!). Categories include facts & reference, weird & mysterious, religion & mythology, machines & transportation, and more.

- **The Kids on the Web:** A list of sites compiled since 1994 by the author of *Children and the Internet: A Zen Guide for Parents and Educators* www.zen.org/~brendan/kids.html; ALA-recommended site.

- **Surfing the Net with Kids:** A newspaper columnist's recommendations (www.surfnetkids.com), with current topics, a calendar of interesting events, many topics.

and style. What feel do you get for the picture book illustrations, for example, if that is what you want to write, and how is the text likely to reflect that? Is this a wide-ranging publisher, or does it fill a niche?

You might need or want to buy a book to advance your research into what a segment of the children's audience is reading. Amazon.com or Barnesandnoble. com, along with other sites that help you buy books or locate out-of-print titles, have become one of a writer's best friends. Not only do they help you locate children's books you know you want, they give you information on readership ages. Reverse the process and begin your search at one of these sites with a designated age range and see what titles come up. Lots of humor? Nonfiction, but not the fiction you expected? Does this help you in thinking about what you want to write?

Target the Competition & General Markets

When you're doing your audience or subject research, you might find that two or three large publishers specialize in books for a particular age or field, but the titles they list are old. That's a beginning for your competition research— looking into titles already in the marketplace similar to your idea and finding the publishers that match.

Competitive titles. When you get to the stage of pulling together your submissions package, adding this competition information in a paragraph to your query or proposal, or in a separate one-page summary, will give you a definite advantage. It will show editors your professionalism, skills at research, and dedication to your work. If you use the research well, it will also indicate to the editor that you know what that particular company publishes and why your book will fit its list. Doing your competition research, the questions you'll need to ask are:

- What books are in print that are similar to my idea?
- Who are the publishers, and what kinds of companies are they?
- When were they published?
- How are they different in slant, format, audience, etc.,

Competition Research Form

Title	Author	Publisher	Pub. Date	Description/Differences from My Book

from mine?
- ♦ If one or more are not different, how will I reslant my idea to make my title more distinct?

This is where you'll need to strike a balance between selecting a subject or a story that is of such significant interest to the audience you're targeting that other authors have addressed it, and the challenge of giving it a new twist. The same subjects will come up over and over again, and there's a reason—a large segment of four-year-olds are always interested in trucks and always will be, for example. But how do you write another picture book on trucks and make sure it's distinct? How do you know that your book on a kindergartener's school tribulations will attract an editor's attention?

Perhaps those kindergarteners are ready for a new book on the subject, because it's been more than five years since the last one was published by one publisher, or any publisher. To find that out, once again you might go to:

- ♦ bookstores, to review the selection, put your hands on the books, and peruse them
- ♦ *Book Markets for Children's Writers,* for an overview of companies publishing possibly competitive books
- ♦ online booksellers, with subject and age searches
- ♦ libraries, whether the catalogues, or *Subject Guide to Children's Books in Print*
- ♦ publisher websites and publisher catalogues

At bookstores, ask for a list of all the books on a given subject. They should be able to print one out for you from their computer system. At the library, use the computer database to do a comparable search, or look at the *Subject Guide to Children's Books in Print.*

Market types. Use *Book Markets for Children's Writers'* Category Index to generate a list of companies that publish in the category of your book and to start you thinking about the marketplace in general. You might want to use a form like that on page 13. Are the companies with competitive titles generally educational, trade, religious, special interest? Or are they all over the map? Do they have a strong backlist of older titles that they continue to support, or are titles allowed to go out of print?

The individual publisher listings in *Book Markets for Children's Writers* also give you information on how many books a company publishes each year and how many it accepts from new authors. You're another step closer to selecting the publishers to whom you'll send your submission.

Target the Publisher & Editor

It's time to look more closely at the individual listings in *Book Markets for Children's Writers* to find out what a company has published and what its editors are currently seeking. *Book Markets for Children's Writers* can be wonderfully well used to create comparative lists of competitive titles, as above, and even better used to align your work with a publisher who is looking for it.

If you've followed the process here, you've focused in on an idea, determined your readership, and learned what books on that subject and readership are available. But editors' needs change. How do you know who wants what now? The listings in *Book Markets for Children's Writers* are updated annually, with an emphasis on finding exactly what the editor needs now.

Turn again to the Category Index on page 548, or leaf through the listings themselves, and write down those publishers with interests similar to your own, especially those you didn't find in your earlier research. You've done this in researching the field and competition as a whole, but now you need to focus on the publishers you will pursue for your book. Here's how the listings break down and how to use them best.

- **Publisher's Interests:** Does the publisher you have in mind produce hardbacks, paperbacks, or both? Is it an imprint of a larger company? Does it publish fiction and/or nonfiction? Does it have a specialization, such as history, regional subjects, educational? Is your book compatible with the publisher's profile? Don't stretch to make a match—make it a close one—but if you believe you can slant your book solidly toward a publisher's needs, work toward that in pulling together your proposal. If you've written fiction that just can't be reshaped, be honest, and don't consider a given publisher's needs a good target.

- **Freelance Potential:** How many books did the publisher produce last year? Of the books published, how many came from unpublished writers? (For an idea of your odds, compare the number of submissions the publisher received last year to the number of titles it published.) What age range does it focus on? Are there particular topics or types of books it specializes in? What genres did the company publish, in fiction or nonfiction?

- **Editor's Comments:** This section reveals a publisher's current needs, and the types of manuscripts it *doesn't* want to see. It may also give you insight into preferred style or other editor preferences. This information will be one of your best tools in deciding where to submit your work.

You can also keep up with current needs through many of the trade publications like *Children's Writer* newsletter (www.childrenswriter.com or 1-800-443-6078) and *Publishers Weekly* (http://publishersweekly.reviewsnews.com/), which has improved its regular coverage of children's publishing in recent years. *PW* also offers special feature issues on children's publishing every spring and fall. A *PW* subscription is expensive, but many libraries carry the publication.

Narrow your choices to 6 to 12 publishers, and if you have not yet requested their catalogues, do so, along with their writers' guidelines. Ask a final set of questions—those in the sidebar on page 18.

You're about to pull together your submissions package. First, review the writers' guidelines, if a company has them. Whether or not they do, read the *Book Markets for Children's Writers'* listing closely for specifications, and follow them exactly. Suppose you have completed a biography of Georgia O'Keeffe you'd like to propose to Lerner Publishing. It's ready to go, but it happens to be August. If you check the Lerner listing, and their guidelines, you'll see that the company only accepts submissions in November. Don't send your work anyway, assuming they'll hold it until October. They won't. Do exactly what the publisher directs.

Now you're ready to fire your arrow: Submit.

About Agents

Writers of books at some point face the question of whether or not to look for an agent. Some successful writers never work with an agent, while others much prefer to find a strong representative for their work to deal with the business side. Some publishers, a limited number and usually very large companies, will not accept unsolicited materials except through an agent. But a good manuscript or book proposal will find its home with or without an agent, if you are committed to finding the right publisher to match your work.

How to find an agent: Look at listings in *Literary Marketplace (LMP)*, or the *Writer's Digest Guide to Literary Agents*, or contact the Association of Authors' Representatives or go to their website (www.aar-online.org) for their members list. Identify agents who work with writers for children. Check in your agent guide or go online if the agent has a website for specific contact requirements. If not, send a well-written, professional cover letter describing your work and background, accompanied by an outline or synopsis and sample chapter.

What an agent does: An agent will review your work editorially before deciding to represent you, but the primary work of an agent is to contact publishers, market your material, negotiate for rights and licenses, and review financial statements. In a good working relationship, an agent will offer solid editorial advice on the direction your proposals and stories might take.

Fees: Be careful about agent fees. Increasingly, some will charge for readings and critiques, even without taking you on as a client. Compare the fees, and the commission if you do enter into a contract. A typical rate is 15 percent for domestic sales, 20 percent for foreign.

Take Close Aim

When you've narrowed your targeted publishers to a short list, review the individual publishers' catalogues closely or go to their websites (indicated in the listings) to find out about their overall list and specific titles—dates of publication, slant, format. With even greater focus now as you sight your target, ask:

- Is this a large house, a smaller publisher, or an independent press with 10 or fewer books published yearly?
- How many books are on its backlist?
- What audience does the publisher target?
- Are most books single titles, or does the publisher focus on series books?
- Does it aim for one or two age groups, or does it feature books for all age groups?
- Does the publisher use the same authors repeatedly, or are many different authors featured?
- Are newer authors also represented?
- Is there a mix of fiction and nonfiction books, or is there more of one than the other?
- Is there a range of subject matter? Does my book fit in their range?
- Does the publisher specialize in one or more types of books, such as picture books or easy-to-reads? Is my book one of these, or not?
- Are there books similar to yours? Too similar and too recent, so the publisher might not want duplication?
- Would your book fit in with others this house has published?
- What are the specific requirements of the writers' guidelines and how will I meet them?

Step-by-Step through Query Letters & Proposals

One publisher may prefer to receive a submission consisting of a query letter and nothing else. Another wants an extended proposal packaged in a very specific format: a cover letter, outline, résumé, samples, bibliography, competition research. A query or a cover letter is always required, but many writers find them challenging. How are query letters and cover letters different? How much information should they include? What information? What tone should they take?

Query Letters

The query letter is perhaps the most important component of a book proposal package. It should capture the editor's interest and give a sense of your treatment of the topic. It should also convince an editor that you are the person to write this book. The best advice:

- Be succinct, positive, enthusiastic, and interesting.
- Briefly describe your book proposal.
- Identify the publisher's needs by indicating your familiarity with titles on their list.
- Outline your qualifications to write the book.

Review the query letter samples on pages 27 and 30. Note each of the following elements:

Opener: A direct, brief lead that:
- captures and holds the editor's interest (it could be the first paragraph of your book);
- tells what the subject is and conveys your particular angle or slant;
- reflects your writing style, but is at all times professional; you need not be overly formal, but do not take a casual tone.

Subject: A brief description of your proposed manuscript and its potential interest to the publisher.

Specifications: If applicable, include the following:
- your manuscript's word length;
- number and type of illustrations;
- a brief indication of the research and interviews to be done; if this is extensive, include it on a separate page with a reference to it in your query;
- market information and intended audience; again, if you've done more extensive competition research, attach it separately.

Reader Appeal: A brief description of why your target audience will want to read your proposed book.

Credits: If you have publishing credits, list them briefly, including magazine credits. Don't tell the editor you've read your book to your child's class, or that several teachers have encouraged you to send it in, or that you've taken a writing course. If you have particular qualifications that helped you write the book (e.g., you run obedience classes and have written a book on dog training), say so. Many publishers request résumés. If you're attaching one in your submissions package, your query should mention relevant credits, and then refer to the résumé.

Closing: Let the publisher know if this is an exclusive or simultaneous submission.

Queries are very common for nonfiction submissions, but in the past were very uncommon in fiction. Most editors preferred to see complete manuscripts or several chapters and a synopsis for novels and early fiction. That has changed somewhat in recent years; some editors want a query for fiction before they'll read anything more. Here are some of the distinctions in the queries and packages for nonfiction and fiction:

Nonfiction Query Letter

A nonfiction package may include:

- a query or cover letter (see page 22 for which to use);
- a synopsis (see page 32);
- a detailed outline (topical or chapter) that describes each chapter's contents (see page 33);

- alternatively, a proposal that incorporates the synopsis, outline, and other information, such as the audience targeted (see page 34);
- representative chapters;
- a bibliography, consisting of the books, periodicals, and other sources you have already used to research the project, and those that you will use, including expert sources and interviews (see page 35);
- a résumé (see page 36).

Fiction Query Letters

A fiction query package may also contain any or all of the following:

- one- to two-page synopsis that briefly states the book's theme and the main character's conflict, then describes the plot, major characters, and ending;
- chapter-by-chapter synopsis consisting of one to two paragraphs (maximum) per chapter, describing the major scene or plot development of each chapter. Keep the synopsis as brief as possible. You may either single space or double space a synopsis (see pages 31 and 32);
- the first three chapters (no more than 50 pages). But check the *Book Markets for Children's Writers'* listing and publisher's guidelines carefully, as some editors prefer to see only the first chapter.

Essentials

Editors need to know from the start that you write well and that you are careful in your work. Many submissions are rejected because queries are poorly written, contain grammatical errors, or show carelessness. Since form as well as content counts, make sure your package:

- is free of spelling, typographical, and grammatical errors;
- is cleanly presented and readable, whether typewritten or computer-printed;
- includes an SASE—a self-addressed stamped envelope with correct postage, or International Reply Coupons for foreign publishers;
- is photocopied for your records.

Query Letter v. Cover Letter

When to use a query letter:

- ❏ Always when a query is the specific requirement in the publisher's writers' guidelines.

- ❏ When you are including no other attached information; the query should be specific, but not exceed a single page.

- ❏ When you are attaching some additional materials, such as a synopsis or sample chapter.

When to use a cover letter:

- ❏ When an editor has requested that you send a specific manuscript and it is attached. The cover letter is a polite, professional reminder.

- ❏ When you have had previous interactions with an editor, who will know who you are. Perhaps you've written something for the editor before, or you had a conversation at a conference when the editor clearly suggested you send your work.

- ❏ When your proposal package is comprehensive, and explains your book completely enough that a cover letter is all that is needed to reiterate, very briefly, the nature of the proposal.

Query Letter Checklist

Use this checklist to evaluate your query letter before you send it with the rest of your book proposal.

Basics:
- ☐ Address the letter to the current editor, or as directed in writers' guidelines or market listings (for example, Submissions Editor or Acquisitions Editor).
- ☐ Spell the editor's name correctly.
- ☐ Proofread the address, especially the numbers.

Opening:
- ☐ Create a hook—quote a passage from your manuscript, give an unusual fact or statistic, ask a question.

Body:
- ☐ Give a brief overview of what your book proposal is about, but do not duplicate the detailed information you give in the outline or synopsis.
- ☐ List your special qualifications or experience, publishing credits/organization memberships, and research sources.
- ☐ State whether you can or cannot supply artwork.

Closing:
- ☐ Provide a brief summation.
- ☐ Let this publisher know if this is an exclusive or simultaneous submission.

Last steps:
- ☐ Proofread for spelling and punctuation errors, including typos.
- ☐ Sign the letter.

Cover Letters

A cover letter accompanies a submitted manuscript and provides an overview of your fiction or nonfiction submission, but it does not go into the same level of detail as a query letter. A cover letter is a professional introduction to the materials attached. It's just the facts. If you are attaching a large package of materials in your submission—a synopsis, outline, competition research, résumé, for example—you don't need a full-blown query, but a cover letter.

Cover letters range from a very brief business format, stating, *"Enclosed is a copy of my manuscript, [Insert Title] for your review"* to something more. In a somewhat longer form, the letter may include information about your personal experience with the topic; your publication credits; if you have them, special sources for artwork; and, if relevant, the fact that someone the editor knows and respects suggested you submit the manuscript.

A cover letter is always included when a manuscript is sent at the request of the editor or when it has been reworked following the editor's suggestions. The cover letter should remind the editor that he or she asked to see this manuscript. This can be accomplished with a simple phrase along the lines of "Thank you for requesting a copy of my manuscript, [Insert Title]." If you are going to be away or if it is easier to reach you at certain times or at certain phone numbers, include that information as well. Do not refer to your work as a book; it is a manuscript until it is published.

Proposals

A proposal is a collection of information with thorough details on a book idea. Arguably, a query alone is a proposal, but here we'll consider the various other components that may go into a proposal package. Always consult—and follow to the letter—writers' guidelines to see what a publisher requires.

Query or cover letter. The descriptions on pages 19–24 should help you construct your query or cover letter.

Synopsis. A brief, clear description of the fiction or nonfiction project proposed, conveying the essence of the entire idea. A synopsis may be one or several paragraphs on the entire book, or it may be written in chapter-by-chapter format. Synopses should also convey a sense of your writing style, without getting wordy. See the samples on pages 31 and 32.

Outline. A formally structured listing of the topics to be covered in a manuscript or book. Outlines may consist of brief phrases, or they may be annotated with one or two-sentence descriptions of each element. See the sample on page 33.

Note that synopses are more common for fiction than outlines. Both outlines and synopses are used to describe nonfiction, but not necessarily both in the same proposal package.

Competition/market research. The importance of researching other titles in the marketplace that might be competitive to yours was discussed earlier (pages 12–15). The presentation of this information to the editor might be in synopsis form or presented as an annotated bibliography.

Bibliography. Bibliographies are important in nonfiction submissions, considerably less so with fiction, except possibly when writing in a genre such as historical fiction. A well-wrought bibliography can go a long way toward convincing an editor of the substance behind your proposal. Include primary sources, which are more and more important in children's nonfiction; book and periodical sources; Internet sources, (but be particularly careful these are well-established); expert sources you've interviewed or plan to interview. For format, use a style reference such as *Chicago Manual of Style*, *Modern Language Association (MLA) Handbook*, or one of the major journalist references by organizations such as the *New York Times* or Associated Press. See the sample on page 35.

Résumé/publishing credits. Many publishers request a list of publishing credits or a résumé with submissions. The résumé introduces you to an editor by indicating your background and qualifications. An editor can judge from a résumé if a prospective writer has the necessary experience to research and write material for that publishing house. The résumé that you submit to a publisher is different from one you would submit when applying for a job, because it emphasizes writing experience, memberships in writing associations, and education. Include only those credentials that demonstrate experience related to the publisher's editorial requirements, not all of your work experience or every membership. In the case of educational or special interest publishers, be sure to include pertinent work experience.

No one style is preferable, but make sure your name, address, telephone number, and email address (if you have one) appear at the top of the page. Keep your résumé short and concise—it should not be more than a page long. If you have been published, those credits may be included on the one page, or listed on a separate sheet. See the sample on page 36.

<u>Sample chapters or clips.</u> As well-written as a query or even a synopsis might be, nothing can give an editor as clear a sense of your style, slant, and depth of the work you are proposing, or can do, than sample chapters or clips of published work. One of the obvious dilemmas of new writers is that they may not have clips, or they may be few and not suitable to a given proposal. But sample chapters, almost always the first and perhaps one or two others that are representative, help an editor make a judgment on your abilities and the project, or determine how to guide you in another direction—and toward a sale.

Sample Query Letter – Nonfiction

Street Address
City, State ZIP
Telephone Number
Email Address

Date

Ms. Sue Thies
Perfection Learning Corporation
1000 North Second Avenue
Logan, IA 51546

Dear Ms. Thies,

Opener/Hook — Look, to your left, off the port side of our four-man dinghy. Just below the surface, a giant, black shadow tracks us. Our boat seems tiny, indeed. Salty sea spray stings your eyes. But the V-shaped dorsal fin skimming the water is easy to identify. A lump jumps up your throat. You've heard tales about orcas. Are they ferocious killer whales, all teeth and no brain? Or are they something more? You came on an orca watch to find out. Here you are. But who's watching whom?

Subject/Reader Appeal — Did you know that orcas are giant dolphins that "see" like Superman? Or that some eat only fish and never stray from their native waters, while others roam, following the small marine mammals that make up their diet? Find out more in *Orca Watch*, a real life high seas adventure for children 8-12.

Orca Watch also explores this question: Could we really "free Willy"? Would he find his family, and would they accept him as their long lost relative? With the move of Keiko, the orca who played Willy in the movie, to his native Icelandic waters, young readers will be especially interested as the world awaits his ultimate release into the wild.

Credits/Special Experience — I am a freelance writer well published in the children's market, with clips available. Having also written on an adult level for Dr. Randall Eaton, who has studied wild orcas since 1979, I am knowledgeable on the subject and have a number of beautiful photographs. Please let me know if you would like to see an outline, sample chapters, and the photographs for *Orca Watch*.

Closing — Thank you very much for your time and consideration. This is not a simultaneous submission.

Sincerely,

Ellen Hopkins

Sample Cover Letter – Nonfiction

Street Address
City, State ZIP
Telephone Number
Email Address
Date

Laura Walsh, Editor
Millbrook Press
2 Old New Milford Road
Brookfield, CT 06804

Dear Ms. Walsh,

Opener/ Subject — Please find enclosed my proposal for a book on starting seeds indoors. I've enclosed 25 pages of the text of *So You Want to Be a Dragon Farmer* and an outline of the rest of the book, plus a bibliography.

Market/ Appeal — I've focused specifically on growing snapdragons from seeds, though the principles are applicable to almost any kind of seed starting. The book is intended to fit the science curriculum. And while the text has a kind of wacky voice, the information is sound. A fourth or fifth grader might use *So You Want to Be a Dragon Farmer* to do an independent science project between mid-February and the end of school. Or the zany style might engage a young reader simply to read the book, without doing any or all of the activities.

Experience — I've gardened for years and am a committed seed starter. I've been asked to speak to garden clubs and other groups about starting seeds indoors. I've done gardening projects with kids and am currently helping a group of inner-city youths with a community garden.

Recently, I've made sales to *Guideposts for Kids, Pockets, Listen, With,* and *Flicker*. I have a Ph.D. and have taught all ages from kindergarten to college.

Submission Status/ Closing — Thank you for considering *So You Want to Be a Dragon Farmer*. This is an exclusive submission and I am willing to revise.
I look forward to hearing from you.

Very truly yours,

Sharelle Byars Moranville

SASE enclosed.

Sample Cover Letter – Fiction

Street Address
City, State ZIP
Telephone Number
Email Address
Date

Janine O'Malley, Assistant Editor
Farrar, Straus & Giroux
19 Union Square West
New York, NY 10003

Dear Ms. O'Malley,

Opener/ Subject — Ian and Cory aren't your typical high school prepsters. They lack big-family bucks, and they've both known hard times. But Cory has a plan to deliver himself from his crazy family, and that means he must succeed at Sparing, the local, posh, college-prep high school. Together, Cory and Ian stand out from their peers and find themselves forming a tight friendship. Ian's outgoing nature and class-clown routine help him fit in. But sometimes Ian doesn't know where to draw the line. When Ian gets involved with a drug dealer at his gym and goes from honor roll student and varsity basketball player to drug addict, Cory denies that anything is wrong. Denies it, that is, until it hits him where it hurts. Can he overcome his fierce anger and help his friend before it's too late?

Ms Enclosed/ Synopsis

Specifications/ Appeal — *Fighting Ian* is a young adult novel based on the story of my brother, an honor student who got involved in gangs and drugs, which ultimately ended in tragedy. The story is told by Cory, a fictional character who watches Ian's life fall apart and eventually grows as a result of all that occurs. The story includes themes of drug abuse, family dysfunction, and spiritual searching.

Credits — I am a freelance writer and editor for *Girls' Life,* where I have reviewed books since the magazine's debut in 1994. I am also a regular contributor to *Focus on the Child, The Early Years,* and *The Developing Years.*

Closing — This manuscript is not under consideration with another publisher at this time. I would be happy to revise it to meet your needs.

Thank you for your time and consideration. An SASE is enclosed for your convenience.

Sincerely,

Kim Childress

Sample Query Letter – Fiction

Street Address
City, State ZIP
Telephone Number
Email Address
Date

Chronicle Books
Children's Division
85 Second Street, Sixth Floor
San Francisco, CA 94105

Dear Sir/Madam:

Opener/Subject — Young readers are fascinated with the danger and excitement of shipwrecks. Yet there's very little material written for children on the subject of Great Lakes shipwrecks, either in fiction or nonfiction.

Synopsis — My nonfiction manuscript, *Weather-Beaten Mysteries: Great Lakes Shipwrecks*, will describe for the young reader in a lively manner many of the shipwrecks that have occurred on the five lakes since the first-known Great Lakes shipwreck, the *Griffin*, in Lake Michigan.

Included in the manuscript are maps with shipwreck positions noted and a depth chart. Pictures are available. Enclosed please find an outline and the first three chapters of my manuscript.

Also enclosed are an SASE for your convenience for a reply and an SASP for confirmation of receipt.

Experience — I have been published in *Brio* magazine, *Discoveries*, and *Wild Outdoor World*. I have also been published in an anthology of short stories, *Forget Me Knots*, from Front Porch.

Closing — This is a simultaneous submission. Thank you for considering *Weather-Beaten Mysteries: Great Lakes Shipwrecks*. Return of my submission materials is not necessary.

Sincerely,

Rita M. Tubbs
Enclosures

Sample Synopsis – Fiction

DEATH MOUNTAIN

DEATH MOUNTAIN is a fast-paced adventure survival novel for readers 10-and-up. What sets this novel apart from other adventure stories in the marketplace is that the two main characters are girls.

What begins as a day-hike in the rugged Sierra Nevada Mountains of California turns into a test of survival for Erin and her new friend Mae. The taste of freedom is soon tainted when a deadly lightning storm strikes and the girls are separated from the rest of the group.

With only each other for support, Erin and Mae are forced to face the challenges of being lost in the untamed wilderness with grit and resourcefulness. In the process, they learn to deal with unresolved personal issues and develop a life-long friendship.

The unique physical qualities of this rugged environment and its wildlife will be woven into the story. Readers will learn survival skills along with the characters:

-- Building a fire when all available wood is wet.
-- Constructing an overnight shelter from natural material.
-- Trapping fish in the style of Native Americans.
-- Using pine pitch to make torches.
-- Boiling rose hips and pine-tip tea.

This story draws on my many wilderness expeditions, including a true adventure I had while backpacking in the shadows of the highest mountain in the lower 48 states, Mt. Whitney. As in DEATH MOUNTAIN our group was caught in a deadly lightning storm on an exposed ridge. The pack horse and mule were killed and three people were airlifted off the mountain by helicopter.

Readers will sweat hour after hour as they follow Erin and Mae on their adventure.

Sample Synopsis – Nonfiction

Name   Address, Telephone, Email

<u>Storms</u>

Chapter One: How Storms Form

    Defines a storm as a mass of rapidly moving air that redistributes energy from the sun's heat. Discusses air currents, including the Jet Stream, and their patterns of movement across the Earth. Explains that storms begin when warm, moist air meets cold, dry air and discusses the role that the sharp boundary, or front, formed at this meeting place has in the creation of storms.

Chapter Two: Rainstorms, Snowstorms, and Thunderstorms.

    Provides information about about clouds and their moisture, explaining how rain, snow, and hail are produced. Describes the processes by which thunder and lightning are created. Talks about weather forecasting and storm watches and warnings. Discusses how winds influence the severity of storms, identifying the terms gale, blizzard, and cyclone.

Chapter Three: Hurricanes and Typhoons

    Explains that hurricanes and typhoons are tropical cyclones. Talks about the formation of hurricanes and typhoons as well as "the eye of the storm." Discusses the effects of these storms on the environment. Gives examples of major hurricane damage and reports on scientists' attempts to study and predict the severity of hurricanes. As part of this discussion, provides information about the hurricane naming system, the Saffir-Simpson Damage-Potential Scale, hurricane watches and warnings, and hurricane safety.

Chapter Four: Tornadoes

    Defines the term tornado and reports that they are the product of middle-latitude storms as opposed to tropical storms. Describes the formation of a tornado and mentions some of the most significant tornadoes in history. Discusses scientists' attempts to study and predict the severity of tornadoes, providing information about storm chasers, the Fujita Tornado Intensity Scale, tornado watches and warnings, and tornado safety.

Sample Outline – Nonfiction

Outline of <u>Off-the-Wall Soccer for Kids</u>

I. Introduction

II. History and size of competitive youth indoor soccer

III. How indoor soccer differs from outdoor soccer
- A. size of playing surface
- B. number of players
- C. out of bounds
- D. substitutions
- E. uninterrupted play
- F. using the boards as another teammate
- G. quick transitions between offense and defense
- H. speed of play

IV. Basic skills for offense

V. Using the boards on offense

VI. Basic skills for defense

VII. Using the boards on defense

VIII. Drills for offense

IX. Drills for defense

X. Situation strategies for offense

XI. Situation strategies for defense

XII. Handling parents and pressure

XIII. Conditioning requirements for a faster, more exhausting game

XIV. Appendix: Official Rules of Indoor Soccer

Sample Proposal – Nonfiction

Name
Address
City, State, ZIP
Date

Proposal for Millbrook Press
"Invisible Invaders: New and Dangerous Infectious Diseases"

By the middle of the 20th century, it seemed like most infectious diseases were a thing of the past. However, over the past 30 years, nearly three dozen new or re-emerging infectious diseases have started to spread among humans. Each year, 1,500 people die of an infectious disease, and half of those people are children under five years old. In the United States alone, the death rate from infectious disease has doubled since 1980.

Invisible Invaders: New and Dangerous Infectious Diseases will be an addition to The Medical Library, the Millbrook/Twenty-First Century Press series on health issues. The Center for Disease Control and Prevention, and the National Institute of Allergy and Infectious Diseases has identified 35 emerging or re-emerging diseases as serious threats to human health. The book will cover the infectious diseases with the greatest real and potential impact to Americans. It will discuss why so many infectious diseases are threatening world health and where the diseases come from. The alarming appearance of new strains of organisms that are becoming ever-more resistant to antibiotics will be covered, as will the potential use of deadly microbes and bioterrorism.

One children's book about epidemics that was published in 2000 blithely announced the eradication of smallpox in the world. Yet today, the government is making contingency plans to vaccinate millions of Americans should a bioterrorist release a deadly virus. Other books fail to mention Hantavirus, West Nile Virus, or Severe Acute Respiratory Syndrome, diseases recently threatening the health and lives of Americans. Clearly, a new children's book on the subject of infectious diseases is needed.

Invisible Invaders will consist of about 25,000 words, or approximately 115 pages of text interspersed with art. It will be written for children ages 7–10 to fit into The Medical Library series format. Each section will include information about the origin and spread of the disease, its symptoms, and treatment. With knowledge comes the power to help prevent or avoid these diseases, so the text will also cover appropriate steps that young readers can follow to decrease their risk. Case studies and pertinent sidebars enhance the text.

The author will use the latest information from prestigious organizations like the CDC, World Health Organization, National Institutes of Health, the American Public Health Association, the Infectious Diseases Society of America, and the Institute of Medicine.

Sample Bibliography

SOURCES FOR <u>DANGER ON ICE: THE SHACKLETON ADVENTURE</u>

Alexander, Caroline. "Endurance." *Natural History.* vol. 108, no. 3 (April 1999): 98-100.

_____. *The Endurance: Shackleton's Legendary Antarctic Expedition.* New York: Alfred A. Knopf, 1998.

Armstrong, Jennifer. *Shipwreck at the Bottom of the World: Shackleton's Amazing Voyage.* New York: Crown Publishers, 1998.

_____. *Spirit of Endurance.* New York: Crown Publishers, 2000.

Explorers and Discoverers of the World. Edited by Daniel B. Baker. Detroit: Gale Research, 1993.

Briley, Harold. "Sail of the Century." *Geographical,* vol. 71, no. 4 (April 1999): 48-53.

"The Furthest South." *Geographical,* vol. 68 (February 1996): 30-35.

Hammel, Sara. "The Call of the Sea: It Was a Matter of Endurance." *U.S. News & World Report.* (May 31, 1999: 67)

Kimmel, Elizabeth Cody. *Ice Story: Shackleton's Lost Expedition.* New York: Clarion Books, 1999.

Lane, Anthony. "Breaking the Waves." *The New Yorker* (April 12, 1999): 96-101.

Rogers, Patrick. "Beyond Endurance." *People Weekly,* vol. 51, no. 9 (March 8, 1999): 151-153.

"A Salute to Survival." *USA Today,* vol. 129, no. 2667 (December 2000): 8-9.

Shipwrecks. Edited by David Ritchie. New York: Facts on File, 1996): 74, 117.

Shackleton, Sir Ernest. *South: A Memoir of the* Endurance *Voyage.* (New York: Carroll & Graff, 1999 reissue of 1918 edition).

Shackleton, Sir Ernest. *Shackleton: His Antarctic Writings.* (London: British Broadcasting Corp., 1983).

"Shackleton Expedition." American Museum of Natural History website. www.amnh.org/exhibitions/shackleton

Sample Résumé

<u>Ann Purmell</u>
Address
Telephone Number
Email

<u>Experience</u>
- Writer of inspirational and children's literature.
- Freelance journalist and feature writer for *Jackson Citizen Patriot* (Michigan), a Booth Communications daily. Affiliate newspapers throughout Michigan carry my articles.
- Freelance writer for *Jackson Magazine,* a monthly business publication.
- Guest lecturer for Children's Literature and Creative Writing classes at Spring Arbor College, Spring Arbor, Michigan.
- Performs school presentations for all grade levels.

<u>Publications/Articles</u>
Published numerous articles, including:
- "Prayers to the Dead," *In Other Words: An American Poetry Anthology* (Western Reading Services, 1998).
- "Promises Never Die," *Guideposts for Teens* (June/July 1999). Ghost-written, first-person, true story.
- "Teaching Kids the Financial Facts of Life," *Jackson Citizen Patriot* (July 20, 1999). An interview with Jayne A. Pearl, author of *Kids and Money.*
- "New Rules for Cider? Small Presses Might Be Put Out of Business," *Jackson Citizen Patriot* (December 12, 1999).
- "Jackson Public Schools Prepare for Change: Technology, Ideas Shaping Education," *Jackson Magazine* (December 1999). An interview with Dan Evans, Superintendent of Jackson Public Schools.

<u>Education</u>
- B.S., Nursing, Eastern Michigan University.
- Post-B.A. work, elementary education, Spring Arbor College.
- *Highlights for Children* Chautauqua Conference, summer 1999.

Sample Manuscript Pages

Title Page

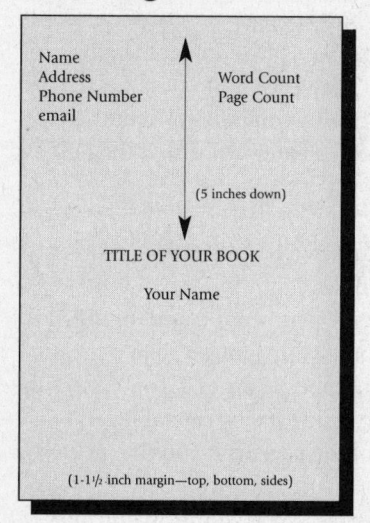

Name
Address
Phone Number
email

Word Count
Page Count

(5 inches down)

TITLE OF YOUR BOOK

Your Name

(1-1½ inch margin—top, bottom, sides)

New Chapter

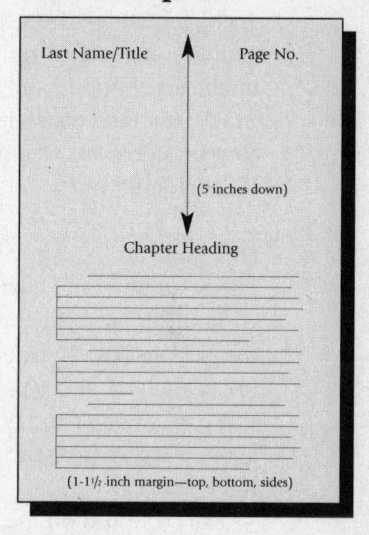

Last Name/Title   Page No.

(5 inches down)

Chapter Heading

(1-1½ inch margin—top, bottom, sides)

Following Pages

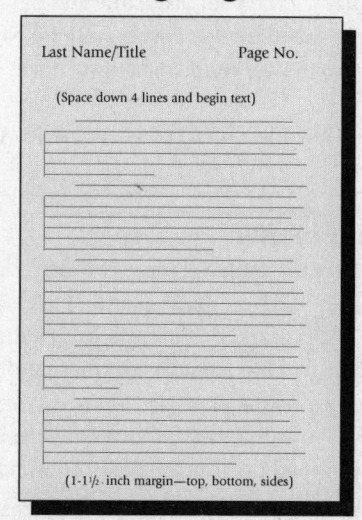

Last Name/Title   Page No.

(Space down 4 lines and begin text)

(1-1½ inch margin—top, bottom, sides)

Manuscript Preparation

Prepare and mail your manuscript according to the following guidelines:
- Use high-quality 8½x11 white bond paper.
- Double-space manuscript text; leave 1- to 1½-inch margins on the top, bottom, and sides. (See page 37.)
- Send typewritten pages, letter-quality computer printouts, or clear photocopies. You may send a computer disk if the publisher requests one.

- **Title Page.** In the upper left corner, type your name, address, phone number, and email address.

    In the upper right corner, type your word count, rounded to the nearest 10 to 25 words. For anything longer than a picture book, you may also type the number of pages. (Don't count the title page.) Center and type your title (using capital letters) about 5 inches from the top of the page with your byline two lines below it.

    Start your text on the next page. (Note: if this is a picture book or board book, see page 40.)

- **Following Pages.** Type your last name and one or two key words of your title in the upper left corner, and the page number in the upper right. Begin new chapters halfway down the page.

- **Cover Letter.** Include a brief cover letter following the guidelines on page 24.

Mailing Requirements
- Assemble pages unstapled. Place cover letter on top of title page. Mail in a 9x12 or 10x13 manila envelope. Include a same-sized SASE marked "First Class." If submitting to a publisher outside the U.S., enclose an International Reply Coupon (IRC) for return postage.
- To ensure that your manuscript arrives safely, include a self-addressed, stamped postcard the editor can return upon receipt.
- Mail your submissions First Class or Priority. Do not use certified or registered mail.

Picture Book Dummy

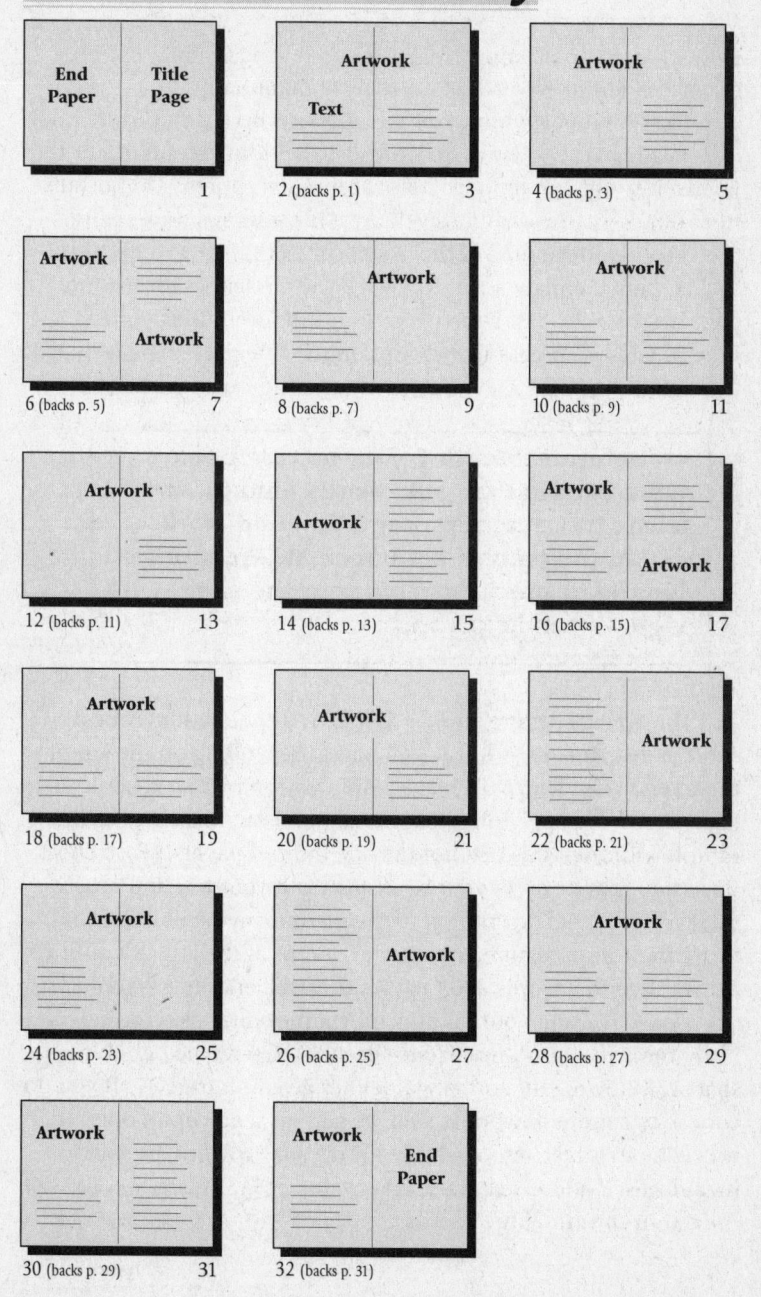

End Paper	Title Page

1

Artwork / Text

2 (backs p. 1) — 3

Artwork

4 (backs p. 3) — 5

Artwork / Artwork

6 (backs p. 5) — 7

Artwork

8 (backs p. 7) — 9

Artwork

10 (backs p. 9) — 11

Artwork

12 (backs p. 11) — 13

Artwork

14 (backs p. 13) — 15

Artwork / Artwork

16 (backs p. 15) — 17

Artwork

18 (backs p. 17) — 19

Artwork

20 (backs p. 19) — 21

Artwork

22 (backs p. 21) — 23

Artwork

24 (backs p. 23) — 25

Artwork

26 (backs p. 25) — 27

Artwork

28 (backs p. 27) — 29

Artwork

30 (backs p. 29) — 31

Artwork / End Paper

32 (backs p. 31)

39

Picture Book Submissions

Most editors will accept a complete manuscript for a picture book without an initial query. Because a picture book text may contain as few as 20 words and seldom exceeds 1,500 words, it is difficult to judge if not seen in its entirety. Do not submit your own artwork unless you are a professional artist; editors prefer to use illustrators of their own choosing.

Prepare the manuscript following the guidelines for the title page on pages 37-38. Drop down four lines from the byline, indent, and begin your manuscript on the title page. Type it straight through as if it were a short story. Do not indicate page breaks.

> **Before submitting your picture book, make certain that your words lend themselves to visual representation and work well in the picture book format. Preparing a dummy or mock-up similar to the sample on page 39 can help you.**

The average picture book is 32 pages, although it may be as short as 16 pages or as long as 64 pages, depending on the age of the intended audience. To make a dummy for a 32-page book, take eight sheets of paper, fold them in half, and number them as the sample indicates; this will not include the end papers. (Each sheet makes up four pages of your book.) Lay out your text and rough sketches or a brief description of the accompanying illustrations. Move these around and adjust your concept of the artwork until you are satisfied that words and pictures fit together as they should.

Do not submit your dummy unless the editor asks for it. Simply submit your text on separate sheets of paper, typed double-spaced, following the format guidelines given on page 37. If you do choose to submit artwork as well, be sure to send copies only; editors will *rarely* take responsibility for original artwork. Be sure to include a self-addressed, stamped envelope (SASE) large enough for the return of your entire package.

Step-by-Step through the Business of Publishing

Book Contracts

Once a publisher is interested in buying your work, he or she will send a book contract for your review and signature. While book contracts vary in length and precise language from publisher to publisher, the basic provisions of these contracts are generally similar. All writers should understand publishing contract standards, know enough to acknowledge an offer as appropriate, and recognize when there may be room to negotiate. Remember, the agreement isn't complete until you sign the contract.

In Plain English

The best advice for your first contract reading is not to let the legal terminology distract you. A book contract is a complex legal document that is designed to protect you and the publisher. It defines the rights, responsibilities, and financial terms of the author, publisher, and artist (when necessary).

Because some publishers issue standard contracts and rarely change wording or payment rates for new writers, you may not need an agent or a lawyer with book-publishing experience to represent you in the negotiation of the contract. But if you choose to negotiate the contract yourself, it is advisable that you read several reference books about book contracts and have a lawyer, preferably with book-contract experience, look it over prior to signing the agreement.

In either case, you should be familiar enough with the basic premises of the contract to communicate what items you would like to change in the document. For your protection, reread the contract at every stage of negotiation.

In the following section, you'll find a primer on the basic provisions of a book contract. If a statement in your contract is not covered or remains unclear to you, ask the editor or an attorney to "translate" the clauses into plain English.

Rights and Responsibilities
A standard book contract specifies what an author and a publisher each agree to do to produce the book and place it in the marketplace. It explicitly states copyright ownership, royalty, advance, delivery date, territorial and subsidiary rights, and other related provisions.

Grant of Rights
A clause early in the contract says that on signing, the author agrees to "grant and assign" or "convey and transfer" to the publisher all or certain specified rights to a book. You thus authorize, or license, the publisher to publish your work.

Subsidiary rights are negotiated in a contract. These rights include where a book is distributed, in what language it is printed, and in what format it is published. While most publishers want world English-language rights, some publishers will consent to retaining rights only in the United States, the Philippines, Canada, and U.S. dependencies. With the United Kingdom now part of the European Community, more and more publishers want British publication rights, in English, so they can sell books to other members of the European Community.

Other subsidiary rights often included in contracts are:

__Reprint Rights:__ These consist of publishing the work in magazines (also known as serial rights), book club editions, and hardcover or paperback versions.

__Mechanical Rights:__ These cover audio and video cassettes, photocopying, filmstrips, and other mechanical production media.

__Electronic or Computer Rights:__ More and more contracts include rights to cover potential use on software programs, multimedia packages, CD-ROMs, online services, etc.

__Dramatic Rights:__ These include versions of the work for film, television, etc.

__Translation Rights:__ These allow a work to be printed in languages other than English.

If you don't have an agent, you may want to assign a publisher broad rights since you may not have the necessary connections or experience to sell them on your own.

If possible, seek a time limit that a publisher has to use subsidiary rights. That way certain rights will revert to you if the publisher has not sold them within a specific period.

Copyright Ownership

According to the Copyright Term Extension Act of 1998, you now own all rights to work you created during or after 1978 for your lifetime plus 70 years, until you choose to sell all or part of the copyright in very specific ways. According to this law, your idea is not copyrighted; it is your unique combination of words—how you wrote something—that this law protects and considers copyrighted. A separate clause in a book contract states that you retain the copyright in your name.

Once you complete your manuscript, your work is protected. You don't need to register your work, published or unpublished, with the United States Copyright Office. In most contract agreements, a publisher is responsible for registering the published version of your work. Writers who provide a copyright notice on their submitted manuscript may be viewed as amateurs by many editors. However, registration does offer proof of ownership and a clear legal basis in case of infringement. If you decide to register your work, obtain an application form and directions on the correct way to file your copyright application. Write to the Library of Congress, Copyright Office, 101 Independence Ave. S. E., Washington, DC 20559-6000. These forms and directions are also available online in Adobe Acrobat format at: www.copyright.gov/forms. Copyright registration fees are currently $30.

If you have registered your unpublished manuscript with the Library of Congress, notify your publisher of that fact once your book is accepted for publication.

Manuscript Delivery

A book-publishing contract sets a due date by which you must complete and deliver an acceptable manuscript of the length specified in your contract. This clause allows a publisher time to request editorial changes, permits editing of the manuscript with your review and approval, establishes editorial schedules, and indicates how many author's alterations (also known as editorial changes) you may make without cost after the book has been typeset.

Warranty and Indemnification

You will be asked to ensure that the manuscript is your original work; that it contains nothing libelous, obscene, or private; and that it does not infringe on any copyright. The clause also stipulates that the author must pay the publisher's court costs and damages should it be sued over the book. This should not be an issue to the author who has exercised reasonable caution and written in good faith.

Though publishers are often reluctant to change this provision, you should still seek to limit the scope of warranty clauses. Include the phrase "to the best of the writer's knowledge" in your warranty agreement. Don't agree to pay for client's damages or attorney's fees and put a ceiling on your liability—perhaps the fee agreed upon for the assignment.

Also remember that many publishers carry their own insurance and can sometimes include writers under their house policy.

Obligation to Publish

The publisher agrees to produce and distribute the book in a timely manner, generally between one and two years. The contract should specify the time frame and indicate that if the publisher fails to publish the book within that period, the rights return to you (reversion of rights) and you keep any money already received.

Option

The option clause requires the author to offer the publisher the first chance at his or her next book. To avoid a prolonged decision-making process, try to negotiate a set period for the publisher's review of a second book, perhaps 60 or 90 days from submission of the second manuscript. Also stipulate the publisher acquire your next book on terms to be mutually agreed upon by both parties. In this way, you have room to negotiate a more favorable deal.

Payment

Calculations for the amount of money an author receives as an advance or in royalties are fairly standardized.

__Advance:__ An advance is money the writer receives in a lump sum or installments when a manuscript is accepted or delivered. It is like a loan paid "against" royalties coming from anticipated profits.

Royalty: A royalty is a percentage of sales paid to the author. It is based either on a book's retail price or on net receipts (the price actually received by the publisher), and it may be fixed or arranged on a sliding scale. Standard royalty is 10% for the first 5,000 copies, 12.5% for the next 5,000 copies, and 15% thereafter. A new author may be offered only 10% or the scale may slide at a higher number of copies. Trade paperback royalties typically are 7.5% on the first 10,000 copies and 10% on all additional copies.

Depending on the extent of artwork and who supplied it to the publisher, author and artist may divide royalties or the artist may be paid a flat fee.

Accounting Statements: The publisher must provide the author with earning statements for the book. Most companies provide statements and checks semiannually, three or more months after each accounting period ends. Be sure to determine exactly when that is. For example, if the accounting periods end June 30 and December 31, you should receive statements by October 1 and April 1.

Flat Rate: Instead of paying royalties, some book packagers and smaller publishers offer a fixed amount or flat rate in return for all rights or as part of a work-for-hire agreement. This amount is paid upon completion of the book.

Before You Sign . . .

The explanations presented here include suggestions for a reasonable and (we hope) profitable approach to your book contract. Every situation presents distinct alternatives, however. Your agreements with a publisher must be undertaken in good faith on both sides and you should feel comfortable with the deal you strike. Whenever in doubt, consult an expert for advice.

You can find additional information about copyrights and publishing law in *The Copyright Handbook: How to Protect and Use Written Words* (sixth ed.) by Stephen Fishman (Nolo Press. 2000), *The Writer's Legal Guide* (second edition) by Tad Crawford (Allworth Press, 1998), and *Every Writer's Guide to Copyright and Publishing Law* by Ellen Kozak (Henry Holt, 1997).

A Note About Self, Subsidy, and Co-op Publishing Options

When you self-publish your book, you assume the cost of and responsibility for printing and distributing your book. By contrast, subsidy presses handle—for a fee—the production and, to some degree, the marketing and distribution of a writer's book. Co-op or joint-venture publishers assume responsibility for marketing and distribution of a book, while the author pays some or all of the production costs.

A newer incarnation of self-publishing is print on demand (POD), a type of printing technology that allows companies to print and bind your book in a matter of minutes. This makes it easy and cost-effective to publish books individually or in small lots, rather than investing in print runs of hundreds of books—letting you publish your work on a shoestring. POD books, however, are more expensive to produce than books done by traditional offset printing.

Another technology that's appeared as a result of the Internet boom is electronic books. Authors can publish their work without the cost of printing and binding by distributing their books in the form of computer files—Adobe PDF files are typically used. Authors can market their work individually on their own websites or utilize services such as Booklocker.com to distribute their work for a modest fee.

Based on your own needs and expectations, you may choose to try one of these approaches. If you do, exercise caution. Be sure you understand the terms of any contract, including exactly how much you will be required to pay, the marketing and distributing services the publisher is promising (if any), and the rights you are retaining. It is advisable to consult a lawyer before entering into any arrangement.

Postage Information

When you send a manuscript to a publisher, always enclose a return SASE with sufficient postage; this way, if the editor does not want to use your manuscript, it can be returned to you. To help you calculate the proper amount of postage for your SASE, here are the U.S. postal rates for first-class mailings in the U.S. and from the U.S. to Canada based on the June 2002 increase.

Ounces	8½x11 Pages (approx pgs)	U.S. 1st-Class Postage Rate	U.S. to Canada
5	21–25	$1.26	$1.60
6	26–30	1.49	1.85
7	31–35	1.72	2.10
8	36–40	1.95	2.35
9	41–45	2.18	3.10
10	46–50	2.41	3.10
11	51–55	2.64	3.10
12	56+	2.87	3.10

How to Obtain Stamps

People living in the U.S., Canada, or overseas can acquire U.S. stamps through the mail from the Stamp Fulfillment Service Center: call 800-STAMP-24 (800-782-6724) to request a catalogue or place an order. For overseas, the telephone number is 816-545-1100. You pay the cost of the stamps plus a postage and handling fee based on the value of the stamps ordered, and the stamps are shipped to you. Credit card information (MasterCard, VISA, and Discover cards only) is required for fax orders. The fax number is 816-545-1212. If you order through the catalogue, you can pay with a U.S. check or an American money order. Allow 3–4 weeks for delivery.

Frequently Asked Questions

How do I request a publisher's catalogue and writers' guidelines?

Write a brief note to the publishing company: *"Please send me a recent catalogue and writers' guidelines. If there is any charge please enclose an invoice and I will pay upon receipt."* The publisher's website, if it has one, offers a faster and less expensive alternative. Many companies put their catalogues, or at least their latest releases and their writers' guidelines on the Internet.

Do I need an agent?

There is no correct answer to this question. Some writers are very successful marketing their own work, while others feel more comfortable having an agent handle that end of the business. It's a personal decision, but if you decide to work through an agent, be an "informed consumer." Get a list of member agents from the Association of Authors' Representatives, 3rd Floor, 10 Astor Place, New York, NY 10003 (available for $7.00 and SAE with $.60 postage).

I need to include a bibliography with my book proposal. How do I set one up?

The reference section of your local library can provide several sources that will help you set up a bibliography. A style manual such as the *Chicago Manual of Style* will show you the proper format for citing all your sources, including unpublished material, interviews, and Internet material.

What do I put in a cover letter if I have no publishing credits or relevant personal experience?

In this case you may want to forego a formal cover letter and send your manuscript with a brief letter stating, *"Enclosed is my manuscript, [Insert Title], for your review."* For more information on cover letters see page 24.

I don't need my manuscript returned. How do I indicate that to an editor?

With the capability to store manuscripts electronically and print out additional copies easily, some writers keep postage costs down by enclosing a self-addressed stamped postcard (SASP) saying, *"No need to return my manuscript. Please use this postcard to advise me of the status of my manuscript. Thank you."*

Do I need to register or copyright my manuscript?

Once completed, your work is automatically protected by copyright. When your manuscript is accepted for publication, the publisher will register it for you.

Should I submit my manuscript on disk?

Do not send your manuscript on disk unless the publisher's submission guidelines note that this is an acceptable format.

When a publisher says "query with sample chapters," how do I know which chapters to send? Should they be chapters in sequence or does that matter? And how many should I send?

If the publisher does not specify which chapters it wishes to see, then it's your decision. Usually it's a good idea to send the first chapter, but if another chapter gives a flavor of your book or describes a key action in the plot, include that one. You may also want to send the final chapter of the book. For nonfiction, if one chapter is more fully representative of the material your book will cover, include that. Send two to three but if the guidelines state "sample chapter" (singular), just send one.

How long should I wait before contacting an editor after I have submitted my manuscript?

The response time given in the listings can vary, and it's a good idea to wait at least a few weeks after the allocated response time before you send a brief note to the editor asking about the status of your manuscript. If you do not get a satisfactory response or you want to send your manuscript elsewhere, send a certified letter to the editor withdrawing your work from consideration and requesting its return. You are then free to submit the work to another publishing house.

A long time ago, in 1989, I was fortunate enough to have a picture book published. If I write a query letter, should I include that information? It seems to me that it may hurt more than it helps, since I have not published anything since that.

By all means include it, though you need not mention the year it was published Any publishing credit is worth noting, particularly if it is a picture book, because it shows you succeeded in a highly competitive field.

How do I address the editor, especially if she is female (e.g., Dear Miss, Dear Ms., Dear Mrs., Dear Editor-in-Chief, or what)?

There is no accepted preference, so the choice is really yours, but in general Ms. is used most frequently. Do use the person's last name, not his or her first. Before you decide which title to use, make sure you know if the person you are addressing is male or female.

If a publisher does not specify that "multiple submissions" are okay, does that imply they are not okay?

If a publisher has a firm policy against multiple submissions, this is usually stated in its guidelines. If not mentioned, the publisher probably does not have a hard and fast rule. If you choose to send a multiple submission, make sure to indicate that on your submission. Then it's up to the publisher to contact you if it prefers not to receive such submissions.

Publishing Terms

Advance: initial payment by publisher to author against future sales

Agent: professional who contacts editors and negotiates book contracts on author's behalf

All rights: an outright sale of your material; author has no further control over it

Anthropomorphization: attributing human form and personality to things not human, for example, animals

Backlist: list of publisher's titles that were not produced this season but are still in print

Beginning readers: children ages 4 to 7 years

Book contract: legal agreement between author and publisher

Book packager/producer: company that handles all elements of producing a book and then sells the final product to a publisher

Book proposal: see **Proposal**

Caldecott Medal: annual award that honors the illustrator of the current year's most distinguished children's book

CD-ROM: (compact-disc read-only memory) non-erasable electronic medium used for digitalized image and document storage

Clean-copy: a manuscript ready for typesetting; it is free of errors and needs no editing

Clip: sample of a writer's published work. See also **Tearsheet**

Concept book: category of picture book for children 2 to 7 years that teaches an idea (i.e., alphabet or counting) or explains a problem

Contract: see **Book contract**

Co-op publishing: author assumes some or all of the production costs and publisher handles all marketing and distribution; also referred to as "joint-venture publishing"

Copyedit: to edit with close attention to style and mechanics

Copyright: legal protection of an author's work

Cover letter: brief introductory letter sent with a manuscript

Disk submission: manuscript that is submitted on a computer disk

Distributor: company that buys and resells books from a publisher

Dummy: a sample arrangement or "mock-up" of pages to be printed, indicating the appearance of the published work

Electronic submission: manuscript transmitted to an editor from one computer to another through a modem

Email: (electronic mail) messages sent from one computer to another via a modem or computer network

End matter: material following the text of a book, such as the appendix, bibliography, index

Final draft: the last version of a polished manuscript ready for submission to an editor

First-time author: writer who has not previously been published

Flat fee: one-time payment made to an author for publication of a manuscript

Front matter: material preceding the text of a book, such as title page, acknowledgments, etc.

Galley: a proof of typeset text that is checked before it is made into final pages

Genre: category of fiction characterized by a particular style, form, or content, such as mystery or fantasy

Hard copy: the printed copy of a computer's output

Hi/lo: high-interest/low-reading level

Imprint: name under which a publishing house issues books

International Reply Coupon (IRC): coupon exchangeable in any foreign country for postage on a single-rate, surface-mailed letter

ISBN: International Standard Book Number assigned to books upon publication for purposes of identification

Letter-quality printout: computer printout that resembles typed pages

Manuscript: a typewritten, or computer-generated document (as opposed to a printed version)

Mass-market: books aimed at a wide audience and sold in supermarkets, airports, and chain bookstores

Middle-grade readers: children ages 8 to 12 years

Modem: an internal or external device used to transmit data between computers via telephone lines

Ms/Mss: manuscript/manuscripts

Newbery Medal: annual award that honors the author of that year's most distinguished children's book

Outline: summary of a book's contents, usually nonfiction, often organized under chapter headings with descriptive sentences under each to show the scope of the book

Packager: see **Book Packager**

Pen name/pseudonym: fictitious name used by an author

Picture book: a type of book that tells a story primarily or entirely through artwork and is aimed at preschool to 8-year-old children

Pre-K: children under 5 years of age; also known as preschool

Proofread: to read and mark errors, usually in typeset text

Proposal: detailed description of a manuscript, usually nonfiction, and its intended market

Query: letter to an editor to promote interest in a manuscript or idea

Reading fee: fee charged by anyone to read a manuscript

Reprint: another printing of a book; often a different format, such as a paperback reprint of a hardcover title

Response time: average length of time for an editor to accept or reject a submission and contact the writer with a decision

Résumé: short account of one's qualifications, including educational and professional background and publishing credits

Revision: reworking of a piece of writing

Royalty: publisher's payment to an author (usually a percentage) for each copy of the author's work sold

SAE: self-addressed envelope

SASE: self-addressed, stamped envelope

Self-publishing: author assumes complete responsibility for publishing and marketing the book, including printing, binding, advertising, and distributing the book

Simultaneous submission: manuscript submitted to more than one publisher at the same time; also known as a multiple submission

Slush pile: term used within the publishing industry to describe unsolicited manuscripts

Small press: an independent publisher that publishes a limited or specialized list

Solicited manuscript: manuscript that an editor has asked for or agreed to consider

Subsidiary rights: book contract rights other than book publishing rights, such as book club, movie rights, etc.

Subsidy publishing: author pays publisher for all or part of a book's publication, promotion, and sale

Synopsis: condensed description of a fiction manuscript

Tearsheet: page from a magazine or newspaper containing your printed story or article

Trade book: book published for retail sale in bookstores

Unsolicited manuscript: any manuscript not specifically requested by an editor; "no unsolicited manuscripts" generally means the editors will only consider queries or manuscripts submitted by agents

Vanity press: see **Subsidy publishing**

Whole language: educational approach integrating literature into classroom curricula

Work-for-hire: work specifically ordered, commissioned, and owned by a publisher for its exclusive use

Writers' guidelines: publisher's editorial objectives or specifications, which usually include word lengths, readership level, and subject matter

Young adult: children ages 12 years and older

Young reader: the general classification of books written for readers between the ages of 5 and 8

Gateway to the Markets

Early Readers: Bridge the Gap Word by Word

By Sue Bradford Edwards

Writers new to early reader books often think of them as *easy* readers, easily written. In reality, early readers have a specific art. "A book for beginning readers is rather like a Zen garden: It requires economy, balance, rhythm, and simplicity so that the reader may be invited to participate in filling in the details," explains author Larry Dane Brimner. "It sounds easy enough, but it's actually a challenge to do in a way that allows the new reader to tackle the book independently."

Publishers are actively looking for early readers, but this is a market segment with challenges. "Schools and libraries don't have as much money to buy books as they used to," says Harcourt Editorial Director Allyn Johnston, "and since easy readers are especially geared toward this market, selling them successfully can be more difficult these days." Despite this, Johnston and other editors still keep their eyes open for something new and wonderful that might arrive in the mail.

Sue Bradford Edwards is a full-time freelance writer with more than 120 sales to her credit. Her work has appeared in a variety of educational packages including *Children's Writer*, *Ladybug*, and the *St. Louis Post-Dispatch*, where she reviews children's books.

It's a Bird, It's a Plane, It's an Early Reader

Early readers fill the gap between picture books, illustrated books meant to be read aloud to a pre-reader, and chapter books, which are longer texts written for the newly confident reader. "Easy readers are written for a very short time in a child's life, when that child is just learning how to read," says author Anastasia Suen, author of *Subway, Raise the Roof!, Block Party, Hamster Chase,* and others. (Johnston, however, believes, "The great easy readers are also incredible readalouds to much younger children" and even appeal to "older ones—and adults.")

Because early readers are heavily illustrated, they are often confused with picture books. "An easy reader has full-color art on each page or spread," says Suen, but generally speaking, the illustration plays a supporting role, albeit sometimes an important one. In contrast, the art in picture books expands the story into something more. "Fanciful illustrations may contain information missing from the text," says HarperCollins Executive Editor Anne Hoppe. Text and art both contribute to the depth. In early readers, she says, "Illustrations present the information given in the text, serving as a means of interpreting or decoding words unfamiliar to the child." The story stands on its own, although the reader often requires the illustrations to understand the text fully.

Early readers come in several levels adjusted to the progress of the new reader, and people may confuse upper-level early readers with chapter books. "Some early readers are told in chapters," explains Brimner, "usually with each chapter being an independent, stand-alone story within the whole that helps to advance the larger tale to its conclusion. The late James Marshall's George and Martha books are examples." Brimner's own books include *Everybody's Best Friend, A Flag for All, The Sidewalk Patrol,* and many others.

Chapter books, Brimner says, handle topics with a greater "depth and breadth." The artwork also differs. "Regular chapter books," says Suen, "have black-and-white art scattered throughout the book. The art shows only a few scenes. A child cannot figure out the plot by looking at the pictures in a regular chapter book."

Early readers enable children to bridge this gap, stepping from being read to on into the world of independent reading. Building this bridge is one of the greatest challenges in writing for children.

Building Bridges One Word at a Time

Often the greatest stumbling blocks for writers new to early readers are vocabulary and reading level. While in some educational books, publishers use standardized word lists, in trade books the vocabulary for early readers is more open, and writers and editors select it more instinctively. "We don't use vocabulary lists or patterns for sentence structure, at least in my experience with books by Cynthia Rylant, Keith Baker, and Monika Bang-Campbell," says Johnston. "The way that I do it all is very intuitive and organic. To see how we do this, look at the masters—Cynthia Rylant, and the Iris and Walter series."

Word choice varies according to the levels of easy reader, from the lowest—designed for pre-readers who have just learned the alphabet—to the highest, consisting of several short chapters. "The earliest steps require single syllable words that can be sounded out," says Random House Assistant Editorial Director Shana Corey, "and have no contractions or clauses. The vocabulary and sentence structure can get more advanced with the later steps."

> **What the Editors Say about Early Readers**
>
> Read what these four editors have to say about the markets for early readers:
>
> - Rebecca Waugh of Dial Books for Young Readers, page 170.
> - Allyn Johnston of Harcourt, Inc., page 227.
> - Anne Hoppe of HarperCollins, page 230.
> - Shana Corey of Random House, page 505.

The best early readers have a smooth feel without the stops and starts often associated with forced reading. This is because, while the vocabulary is basically simple, the stress is still on choosing the right word. Elaine Marie Alphin found this when she wrote *A Bear for Miguel*. "*Guerilla* is a word that wouldn't fit in any of the reading test guides, but we had to use it," she says. "We also interspersed dialogue in Spanish, with an English translation. You use words that are accessible or you make them accessible."

To cross the bridge to independent reading, writers must also learn how sentences and the number of syllables in words influence reading level. "Some writers don't realize that they are using hard words in their manuscript," Suen says. "Short sentences aren't enough. The words themselves have to be simple too."

Brimner offers the following advice to writers trying to grasp how word choice and sentence structure affect their work: "The typical early reader sentence is no longer than 12 words or so. The structure is largely, but not entirely, *subject* followed by *predicate*. There are no convoluted dependent clauses or lengthy phrases to assist in adding variety to your text. In my early reader workshops, everyone can write these simple, straightforward sentences. But not everyone manages to achieve the *zip* factor—that snappy quality that makes the text fly."

Achieving zip and smooth reading is creatively intricate. "It's like doing an elegant word puzzle but you have to do it in a very simple and beautiful way. The flow has got to be perfect," says Alphin.

Jane Yolen, author of the Commander Toad books, *Owl Moon*, and many other books, also thinks in poetic terms. She writes her easy readers, she says, "as if they were poems—short lines and lyrical. They are written in what I call *breath spaces*; the short lines show the new readers where to pause, where an idea is finished."

Reading Level Tests

Writers can use some word processing programs to measure reading levels by typing text, making changes, and seeing how these changes affect the reading level. "In Microsoft Word, click Tools, then Spelling and Grammar. After the program finishes testing the spelling and grammar," says Suen, "it will also give you the Flesch-Kincaid [a standard reading level scale] reading level results at the bottom of the result screen." To find the Flesch-Kincaid level in WordPerfect, go into Tools, select Grammatik, then Analysis, and then Readability. Another reading level scale, Fry Readability, can be found online. Print out a graph and directions for its use at http://school.discovery.com/schrockguide/fry/fry_grades.gif.

Although they can help writers understand reading levels, note that the tests done on the different scales seldom match. "I had one book that was right on level according to Flesch-Kincaid," Suen says, "but when I sent it in and the publisher tested it the Fry reading level was much higher, resulting in a request for a rewrite."

Dialogue and Action Span the Gap

However accessible the reading level in terms of word choices or sentence length, concentration on reading level must not come at the expense of story. "It's important that the story be dramatic and have humor," says Rebecca Waugh, Editor of Dial Books for Young Readers. "Those are the two ingredients I look for because these books are meant to turn kids on to reading. If the story is dull or doesn't go anywhere, naturally a kid is going to lose interest."

Even some good stories don't work for early readers and should target to another age or genre. "Quiet, contemplative stories don't work well. Young readers struggling through each word need a compelling reason to turn every page," says Hoppe, "and the best way to achieve that is with the tension created through action and dialogue."

Remember Brimner's *zip*? This comes about through dialogue and action. "A writer wants a story to move along and the best way to have that happen is to have characters that move, that do things, that race from one place, or scene, to another. The easiest way to *show* rather than *tell* is to use dialogue." Brimner offers examples:

"Everyone try it," said Miss Morgan.
"This will be easy," said D.W.
"Who wants to be first?" asked Miss Morgan.
"I do!" said Emily.
"Very good, Emily," said Miss Morgan.
"D.W., you're next."
Whump!
"Don't worry, D.W.," said Miss Morgan.
"You will learn. It takes time."
"Lots of time," said Emily.
   D.W. Flips, by Marc Brown

Max gave Felix a present on his birthday.
"I wrapped it myself," Max said.
"I can tell," said Felix.
"It's a camera," said Max.
"I can see," said Felix. "It's just what I wanted."
"Take my picture," said Max.
"That's an idea," said Felix.
   Max and Felix, by Larry Dane BrimnerThese

Read a Good Book

To learn to write early readers, read as many as possible, but in a particular way. "Read like a kid first," says author Anastasia Suen, "and then read the book again as a writer. Take the story apart and see how it's put together." Remember that you can never read too many. Says author Elaine Marie Alphin, "I went to the library and I sat next to the I Can Read section and read my way through the section." Why not start with some of these?

Addie Meets Max, Joan Robins
Adventures of Snail at School, John Stadler
Aunt Eater's Mystery Vacation, Doug Cushman
Cat Traps, Molly Coxe
Circle City, Dana Meachen Rau
Commander Toad books, Jane Yolen
Going to the Beach, Jo S. Kittinger
Henry and Mudge books, Cynthia Rylant
Hurray for Hattie Rabbit!, Dick Gackenbach
Iris and Walter books, Elissa Haden Guest
The Outside Dog, Charlotte Pomerantz
The Poppleton books, Cynthia Rylant
Mr. Putter and Tabby books, Cynthia Rylant
Witch, Goblin, and Ghost in the Haunted Woods, Sue Alexander
World Famous Muriel, Sue Alexander

   HarperCollins I Can Read books include:

Abigail Takes the Wheel, Avi
Amelia Bedelia books, Peggy Parish
Daniel's Duck, Clyde Robert Bulla
Danny and the Dinosaur, Syd Hoff
Frances books, Russell and Lillian Hoban
Frog and Toad books, Arnold Lobel
Golly Sisters books, Betsy Byars
Harold and the Purple Crayon, Crockett Johnson
Smallest Cow in the World, Katherine Paterson
Wagon Wheels, Barbara Brenner

excerpts show clearly that short, simple sentences don't have to be boring and can serve several functions simultaneously. "You can see how dialogue and action move each story forward," Brimner says. "There is very little narration. You also get an idea of the *zip* factor, how the authors have played with the words to suggest conflict between D.W. and Emily, and between Felix and Max." This conflict keeps the new reader turning pages to find out what will happen next.

  Dialogue and action. Vocabulary and sentence. Writers who bridge the gap between pre-reader and confident reader will find editors looking for their work. Editors who work with early readers are just as passionate about them as the authors who write them. Because of their devotion to the new reader, "the author who has both an original topic and the early reader rhythm down," says Shana Corey, "will have no problem getting published."

Teens Coping with Life's Real Issues

By Pegi Deitz Shea

Electronic media aimed at teens can demonstrate how to talk, dress, dance, date, look, drink, excel at sports, make over a car, skip school, attract a mate, among other things. If you think about it, the most reliable information a teen can get about any issue comes not from their favorite pastimes. It usually comes from a printed source. Thank goodness there are authors and publishers who care, and who, of course, also need to make a living.

Consider these titles: *A Baby Doesn't Make a Man: Sources of Power and Manhood for Young Men; When Something Feels Wrong: A Survival Guide About Abuse for Young People; The Code: The 5 Secrets of Teen Success.* You'll find hundreds more simply by searching for "teen issues" on Amazon.com. Don't you wish you had books like these when you were hormonally challenged in adolescence? In the privacy of their bedrooms, today's teens can open books and gain insight without being ridiculed or punished.

The best news for writers who care deeply—and who may have personally experienced teen difficulties as a child, parent, or counselor—is that publishers want to hear from you! In general, publishers of nonfiction for young readers have always been open to new writers. Companies such as Lucent Books, Rosen Publishing, Lerner,

Pegi Deitz Shea is an award-winning children's book author specializing in multicultural stories for all ages. She has also published more than 250 poems, essays, and articles for adult readers. Pegi is a mother of two, wife of one, soccer and softball coach, gardener, and world-traveler.

Chelsea House, and Enslow invite writers to send samples. The goal is to become one of many writers publishers will assign series topics to. However, many publishers are looking for individual books or "one-offs." Just as the young adult fiction market is blooming this year, so is the YA nonfiction market.

Get Inspired & Pitch
Today's authors of books on issues for teens may take different roads to publication. Personal experience inspired Mawi Asgedom not only to write a book, but also to launch his own company, Mawi, Inc. Asgedom and his family, refugees from Ethiopia, resettled in America when he was seven. His early hardships, including the death of his brother and father, compelled him to write his memoir, *Of Beetles and Angels: A Boy's Remarkable Journey from Refugee Camp to Harvard.* He self-published it, then an agent sold it to Little, Brown. His success drove him to write *The Code: the 5 Secrets of Teen Success,* also a Little, Brown title. A follow-up, *Win the Inner Battle: The Ultimate Teen Leadership Journal,* is a motivational diary in which teens learn from other teens. "I was passionate about sharing my family's journey and helping teens become successful," Asgedom explains. "Passion is important because it's what gets you through the many rewrites you invariably have to do."

Personal experience also led author Laura Purdie Salas to write *Taking the Plunge: A Guide to Independence for Teens,* released by Child and Family Press. She moved out of her parents' home at age 16. supported herself, then worked her way through college. "This is the kind of book I wish I'd had available," Salas says. "I wanted to write this book for all the teens out there struggling to make it on their

---

What the Editors Say about Teen Nonfiction

Read what these four editors have to say about the markets for nonfiction on teen issues:

- Tegan Culler, Child & Family Press, page 138.
- Doug Fehlen, Free Spirit Publishing, page 205.
- Lori Shein, Lucent Books, page 284.
- Iris Rosoff, Rosen Publishing, page 366.

own, to give them some tools to succeed. I also wanted to weigh in with the general public, saying, 'don't dismiss these kids.' Not all minors on their own are doing drugs or committing crimes, even though that's the stereotype." Salas relates tips about finding a home, budgeting, transportation, safety, grocery shopping, and more.

Salas submitted a query to both Free Spirit and to Child & Family Press, the imprint of the Child Welfare League of America (CWLA). "Free Spirit was complimentary about the proposal, but they did not feel there was a big enough audience for it. CWLA called me shortly after that and wanted to do the book."

Professional, rather than personal, experience paved the way for psychologist Deanna S. Pledge: "I began with the age-old advice of writing what I know. My books and articles came out of working with clients or teaching. Noticing things from one's own experiences that fit a need can often be a good place to start. The writer's interest in the subject is more likely to feel authentic."

Pledge began to write professionally about five years ago. Her titles include *When Something Feels Wrong*, written for teens; and *Counseling Adolescents & Children*, written for those who deal with teens. She's contributed nonfiction to the *Gale Encyclopedia of Mental Disorders* and the *ERIC Digests* (brief educational reports for professionals), as well as articles to regional publications and broadcasts.

Summarizing her submissions practice, Pledge says that she usually submits a proposal or query that includes a chapter outline and two or three sample chapters. "Most editors do not want to see the entire manuscript for nonfiction. I don't have an agent, and it's not usually necessary when writing nonfiction." Pledge had originally written and submitted a more family-oriented book idea on abuse. After editor feedback, she refocused the book on teens, and eventually published *When Something Feels Wrong* with Free Spirit.

Also tapping his professional experience, Raymond M. Jamiolkowski, Director of Guidance at Naperville Central High School in Naperville, Illinois, began in an unlikely way. He and a friend supplemented their education salaries by writing passages for testing companies. A few years later, Jamiolkowski wanted to publish at a higher level. Having a master's degree in guidance helped Jamiolkowski market himself as an expert. He sent out 50 résumés with writing samples to nonfiction publishers.

Rosen Publishing Group liked his material. Editors wanted books on several topics in their Coping series. Jamiolkowski signed up to do *Coping with a Dysfunctional Family. Coping with an Emotionally Distant Father* followed. "It was even translated into French," says Jamiolkowski. Another title, *Drugs and Domestic Violence*, was picked up by the Hazelden Institute and reprinted in paperback.

The book that followed should have won an award for best title: *A Baby Doesn't Make a Man: Sources of Power and Manhood for Young Men*. Jamiolkowski admits that Rosen came up with the title, but he came up with the book.

Research: Not a Scary Word Anymore

One theory for the ongoing boom in nonfiction for all ages, including YA, is that the Internet has made research more fun, thorough, and efficient. Writers should not rely on Internet sources alone, however. Use the Internet to find paths to the most credible resources. Just as teens get reliable facts from the printed word, writers should still use books and articles that reek of respectability. These might include journals from professional organizations such as the American Medical Association, or international newspapers such as the *New York Times*. Your librarian can help you find the right periodicals and reference books. Ask for interlibrary loans: Almost all libraries are linked now, so any source is available, even academic ones. If you can't easily access a librarian in the flesh, try the virtual library, http://vlib.org.

Pledge first looks for the most recent articles in the professional literature, usually in psychology. "I can see how the evidence supports or refutes my perspective." When asked how she distinguishes valid Internet sources, Pledge advises, "Look at the references cited by the source. If you're unable to cross-reference or find replication of the source in other places, the website may not be valid." To writers who don't have a professional background in the content area, Pledge suggests contacting a local college professor about the validity of a source. And the professor can even become a source of primary research—an interviewee. Primary research is always the best kind.

When writing for teens, authors and editors agree: Get interviewing or surveying those teens! Teens prefer to hear or read the information straight from someone who's the same age, or from someone who has just gone through the same difficulty.

Free Spirit's catalogue includes first-person accounts, says Fehlen. "A number of our books in recent years (such as *More Than a Label* and *Boy v. Girl*) have used nationwide surveys not only to amass

Series & Singles: The Process

Many publishers want each book in a series to look like part of the whole. Most don't give authors outlines, but they send samples of other books in the series, so that the writers can conform their style. The editors assign the topic and sometimes, the actual titles. The quality of the author's outline then determines if the editor will follow through with the book. That is the process at Lucent Books. At Rosen Publishing, ideas originate in-house and are then assigned. The series guidelines are discussed with the author, who then sends in an outline, and if new to Rosen, a sample chapter.

Writing a "standalone" has its pros and cons. Author Laura Purdie Salas writes individual titles, as well as series nonfiction for Capstone Books, Steck-Vaughn, and Lerner Publishing. *"Taking the Plunge* was a completely different experience," she says, "because I controlled the content and I could choose the best structure for the book. It was also scarier because there was no series template to go by."

Author Mawi Asgedom recalls, "I split my memoir up into 13 chapters I wanted to write about, then hit it one chapter at a time. In the end, I had to cut some of the chapters and add others. With *The Code: the 5 Secrets of Teen Success*, I had to do much more outlining up front and really create a rock-solid structure early on. Even with that outline, I had to cut along the way. It went from 10 chapters to 5 pretty quickly and then I moved stuff around.

Deanna S. Pledge outlines about the same time she's beginning research on her books. "The two complement one another as I usually learn new things from the research that modify the outline."

Many successful single titles are organized as steps, guides, lists, or journals, such as Asgedom's *Win the Inner Battle: The Ultimate Teen Leadership Journal*. Salas says, "I used lots of forms, top 10 lists and little sidebars." Doug Fehlen, Acquisitions Assistant of Free Spirit, sees this trend of "short, digestible bursts" continuing.

Editors and authors realize they can get teens literally into the book with forms to fill out—exercises, quizzes. It's important that readers see their own words on the same page with the author's. It helps improve their self-esteem, validates their thoughts, and gives them more ownership of the book's ideas.

student quotes and essays, but also to help determine content. We feel it's very important that young people can find themselves within a book's pages."

Jamiolkowski uses case studies from his school district, "changing names of the students and/or getting permission from the student and parents to use the real name." If you don't happen to work in a high school, find teens at the mall, high school sports events, student theater. Hand out flyers about the book you're researching. Give all the information a parent would want in deciding to allow a child to participate. If you have a teacher friend, speak to her class and do an anonymous survey. There are many ways to reach teens.

Asgedom is a walking source-gatherer. "Any time I hear, read, or see a story I think can be inspiring I jot it down in a story database in my computer. I ask my two employees to do the same. Our goal is to come up with six stories a week. Compelling stories are vital to self-help books because stories *show* the reader your point." Asgedom also asks his readers and audiences to email him stories.

Ludent Editor Lori Shein agrees: "Anecdotes and quotes bring life to the narrative and add a sense of reality to general ideas." Shein says the quotes can come from teens or from experts in the field. Excellent quotes can come from existing books, as long as they're not YA books.

At Rosen, Iris Rosoff, Editorial Director of the YA division, says that the writer himself doesn't need to be an expert in the field, but the research must be sound. To catch errors or unsubstantiated information, "We send all of our manuscripts to expert readers and all of our books are fact-checked before they go to press."

Listen to Teen Voices, Then Write!

All writers must keep their audience in mind. When communicating to teens, nonfiction information in particular, tone is everything. "For adults, tone is important but not crucial because adults will read the book just to get the information," says Mawi. "Teens on the other hand: If they think the tone is at all preachy, they'll just drop the book."

Pledge agrees, "Authenticity has to be part of the author's voice when writing for children and teens. If readers don't feel respected by the author, they won't read any important message the book has."

Full-time guidance counselor Jamiolkowski concludes, "You need to keep it real, and offer real solutions."

Sample Outlines

A book's table of contents can show you how to outline. Many books on Amazon and Barnes & Noble let you see the table of contents and excerpts. If you don't like outlining, try writing your table of contents first! This sample is from Raymond M. Jamiolkowski's *Coping in a Dysfunctional Family,* one book in a series. Note the chapter lengths and helpful back matter.

What's Wrong with My Family?	1
Are We a Dysfunctional Family?	10
Emotional Abuse	20
Neglect	29
Overprotection	37
Sexual Abuse	46
Perfectionism	54
Substance Abuse	60
Religion or Political Fanaticism	69
Workaholic Parents	78
Depression and Other Mental Illnesses	87
Abusive Siblings	96
Physically or Mentally Challenged Siblings	103
Compulsive Gambler	112
Single Parent Families	120
What Can I Do?	129
Who Can Help?	133
Glossary	139
Where to Go for Help	141
For Further Reading	145
Index	147

Sample Outlines

Compare the preceding table of contents with that of *Taking the Plunge*, an individual title by Laura Purdie Salas. Note the snazzy chapter titles, which would appeal to the trade market (bookstores). At first glance, the chapter lengths are similar, but Salas says her forms, charts, lists, and graphics take up many pages.

Take a Deep Breath: Before you dive into independence	1
Climbing the Ladder: Reaching your goals rung by rung	11
Teamwork: Finding the people who will support you	17
Lessons: Does school train you for real life?	27
Going Pro: Choosing the right job or career	39
Home Team: Finding a place to live	51
A Ride to the Pool: The basics of transportation	61
Don't Drown in Debt: Controlling your finances	69
In Training: Taking care of your body	79
Safety Gear: Protecting yourself in a dangerous world.	93
The Commitment: Keeping up with your responsibilities	101
Freestyle: Finally, time for fun	113
Appendix A: State motor vehicle divisions	123
Appendix B: State departments of education	125

Step by Step through Educational Publishing

By Suzanne Lieurance

If you enjoy writing nonfiction and love to research topics in all sorts of different subject areas, then educational publishing just might be right for you. Many educational publishers need writers. Surprisingly, though, these publishers generally don't advertise that fact to writers' magazines or market guides. So, here's how to get started in this active market.

Develop a Focus
Educational publishing has two basic areas of focus for writers. The first is nonfiction, and some fiction, that will be used directly by children. This type of material includes reference books, early readers, remedial readers, textbooks, educational games, workbooks, and even CDs. Course Crafters, Inc., is one of many educational publishers who produces these kinds of materials.

Suzanne Lieurance is a freelance writer living in the Midwest. She writes nonfiction and fiction for children and adults and teaches children's writing. She has published 12 books for children.

The second focus is to create and develop materials that will be used by parents, librarians, and teachers. These materials include everything from books of language arts activities designed to help teachers in the classroom to books of bulletin board ideas and finger puppet patterns. Publishers who produce these kinds of materials include Barron's Educational Series, Inc., Incentive Publications, and Highsmith Press, among others.

It doesn't really matter which focus you choose. Both offer writers dozens of opportunities.

Assess Your Skills & Background

To develop a focus in educational publishing, you will need to assess your skills and background. If you have experience as a preschool or elementary school teacher or librarian, for example, you might want to try to write for imprints like Highsmith Press's Upstart Books. This publisher produces resources that aid media specialists, librarians, and teachers in their work with students in preschool through high school. While they don't advertise the fact, editors at Upstart Books do develop some titles in-house and assign these titles to outside writers, "usually to existing authors (writers who have previously been published by Upstart) or to practicing librarians and educators," says Matt Mulder, Director of Publications.

Wayne Barr, Acquisitions Editor for Barron's Educational Series, says the company also "may solicit authors to submit proposals on a particular project." He says, "advanced degrees aren't necessary to write children's fiction. Credentials are more important for educational and other nonfiction titles. Credentials include writing experience."

If you do have experience as a classroom teacher, other educational publishers, like Incentive Publications publish a variety of teacher resource materials that might be of interest. Editor Patience Camplair says a teaching background isn't absolutely necessary for writers. "We consider equally all manuscripts that we receive." Still, it is important to note that most of the writers who publish with Incentive Publications have extensive teaching experience.

Are you a teacher of ESL or a native speaker of Spanish? Then you might be able to freelance for educational publishers like Course Crafters, a developer and publisher that produces many educational materials and specializes in materials for children who are learning English as a second language (ESL). Lise B. Ragan, President and CEO, says, "We are always looking for good writers and editors of nonfiction, fiction, student, and teacher materials for preK-12."

Even if you don't speak Spanish, or any other foreign language for that matter, and you've never been a librarian or a teacher, you can still break into children's educational publishing. Many publishers don't require authors to have a background in education. They simply want good writers who know how to thoroughly research a topic and write about it in a way that children will find interesting and easy to understand. An excellent way to test your researching skills will be to research different educational publishers. Find out which ones do hire writers without teaching experience, and which ones do hire writers to develop projects they create in-house.

Develop Your Résumé or Bio

Once you develop a focus for the type of educational materials you want to create, you will need to let publishers know you're available and what you have to offer. For this you will need a brief biography or a résumé. A bio consists of a few sentences or paragraphs that describe your background and publishing experience. The back inside cover of most books (both fiction and nonfiction) usually includes information on the author. Read the bios of a few of your favorite authors until you get the hang of how one should be written. You probably won't have as much publishing experience as your favorite author, but you'll still be able to come up with a sentence or two that describes your work as a writer or educator. It might be something as simple as, "Mary Roberts is a former third-grade teacher with more than 20 years of experience in the classroom. While she was teaching, Ms. Roberts developed a wide variety of activities to use with her students."

A résumé is longer than a bio. It should include a list of your publishing credits, any writing related experience, and a list of your teaching experience (if applicable), as well as your education.

You'll also need to get good at writing cover letters. A cover letter simply introduces you to the publisher and explains that you are either looking for assignments with this publisher or you wish to submit your own ideas for publication. If you hope to submit your own ideas for publication, you'll need to learn how to write a proposal or prospectus. Many publishers have guidelines for proposals at their websites. In fact, some publishers even have a form you can complete online that will let you pitch your idea directly to an editor to see if there's any interest in your idea before you go to all the work of developing a full proposal. Generally, a proposal should include an outline or a table of contents for the book you are proposing, an introduction or overview, and enough sample pages to give editors a clear idea of the book you are proposing, as well as your writing style. If you're proposing a book with illustrations, but you're not an illustrator, don't worry about the illustrations. Simple drawings that make your ideas clear will be sufficient. Usually, the publisher has artists on staff, or will hire an outside artist, to illustrate your book if it is accepted for publication.

Study the Markets

Once you've developed a bio or résumé, it's time to start studying the markets. The *2005 Book Markets for Children's Writers* is one of the most helpful resources you will have as you begin your study. Skim through the pages to find listings for a wide array of educational book publishers that produce materials for children, parents, and educators. Many of these listings indicate the publishers' websites. Go to the sites of the companies that you are interested in writing for to see if they post manuscript submission guidelines or additional information about their current needs. Search these websites carefully. Sometimes the manuscript submission guidelines are a bit difficult to find. Look under the About Us or Contact Us pages if you don't see a link directly to submission guidelines. Once you get to the guidelines, study them carefully. Also study the kinds of books and other materials this publisher publishes by looking through their online catalogue or list of products.

> ### What the Editors Say about Educational Publishing
>
> Read what these three editors have to say about educational markets:
>
> - Patience Camplair, Incentive Publications, page 251.
> - Matt Mulder, Upstart Books, Highsmith Press, page 414.
> - Lise Ragan, Course Crafters, Inc., page 459.

Barbara and Sue Gruber are a mother and daughter team who sell their work to a variety of educational publishers. They also offer online workshops for teachers (www.bgrubercourses.com). They suggest to writers, "Go into a bookstore and study the bookshelves. If the store has five shelves dedicated to cookbooks and one shelf dedicated to parenting books, you can safely assume they are selling five times as many cookbooks as parenting books. In other words, the books that are getting the most 'real estate' on the shelves are the products that sell well. Go into a school supply store and look at the space they have allocated to reading, math, and science. Let's assume they are managing their inventory well and they know what is and is not selling. If most of their K-3 materials are about reading, that must be the subject they sell most to K-3 teachers."

Writers can also send for publishers' catalogues, then look through them to see how much space is allocated to each subject. If most of the space in a catalogue is allocated to products about science, then you will have a better chance of selling science related products to this publisher than you would materials for other subject areas.

Contact Publishers

Once you've developed a bio and résumé, and you've studied several educational publishers, you'll need to contact the publishers that interest you. If you're including a manuscript proposal for consideration, the Grubers suggest you also include a "sell sheet" instead of a letter to the editor. This sell sheet helps the editor quickly grasp your idea and the market for which it is intended.

At the top of the sell sheet, put your contact information and this sentence: "Please review this product submission for publication." Next, include the following categories in your sell sheet:

1) target market,
2) type of product,
3) working title,
4) product overview: six to eight sentences to sell editors on your proposal, and
5) who you are.

"Tell about your expertise and experience that qualifies you to develop this product," say the Grubers. "Editors are looking for products that are fresh, timely and will sell well. You must convince them that your ideas are what teachers want, need, and are willing to buy at this time."

If you don't have a manuscript you wish to submit, but would like to write for a particular educational publisher, send a cover letter asking if they hire writers to develop titles they create in-house. Include your bio or résumé, along with a few clips of articles you have published, if you have them, or some writing samples.

As you gain writing experience and acquire more writing credits, chances are you will also develop more contact with other writers. Learn to network with these people. Children's writer Lisa Harkrader has no experience as a classroom teacher, yet she has written several educational books for Enslow Publishers. She says, "I found out about opportunities with Enslow through my writer friends. Enslow didn't require teaching experience. They simply wanted writers who could research well and make information interesting and easy for kids to understand."

In the end, that's what most educational publishers want: good writers and researchers. If that describes you, then educational publishing just might be what you've been looking for to get your writing career off the ground.

Listings

How to Use the Listings

On the following pages are over 500 profiles of publishers involved in the wide range of children's publishing. Over 50 publishers are new to the directory. These publishing houses produce a variety of material from parenting guides, textbooks, and classroom resources to picture books, photo essays, middle-grade novels, and biographies.

Each year we update every listing through mailed surveys and telephone interviews. While we verify everything in the listing before we go to press, it is not uncommon for information such as contact names, addresses, and editorial needs to change suddenly. Therefore, we suggest that you always read the publisher's most recent writers' guidelines before submitting a query letter or manuscript.

If you are unable to find a particular publisher, check the Publishers' Index beginning on page 578 to see if it is cited elsewhere in the book. We do not list presses that publish over 50% of their material by requiring writers to pay all or part of the cost of publishing. While we cannot endorse or vouch for the quality of every press we list, we do try to screen out publishers of questionable quality.

To help you judge a publisher's receptivity to unsolicited submissions, we include a Freelance Potential section in each listing. This is where we identify the number of titles published in 2003 that were written by unpublished writers, authors new to the publishing house, and agented authors. We also provide the total number of query letters and unsolicited manuscripts a publisher receives each year. When possible, we list the number of books published in 2003 by category (e.g. picture books, young adult novels).

Use this information and the other information included in the listing to locate publishers that are looking for the type of material you have written or plan to write. Become familiar with the style and content of the house by studying its catalogue and a few recent titles.

Graphia

☆ — New Listing

Houghton Mifflin Co.
222 Berkeley Street
Boston, MA 02116

Senior Editor: Eden Edwards

Publisher's Interests
Graphia, a new imprint of the Houghton Mifflin Company, publishes quality paperbacks aimed at today's teens. Its first list launched in the spring of 2004. This imprint offers titles by high-profile Houghton Mifflin authors along with the works of new writers. Graphia considers submissions of fiction, nonfiction, and poetry.
Website: www.graphiabooks.com

Freelance Potential
Published 10 titles in 2004: 5 were by agented authors. Receives 180–240 queries, 240–360 unsolicited mss yearly.

- **Fiction:** Publishes young adult books, 12–18 years. Genres include contemporary, historical, and science fiction; mystery; suspense; and humorous fiction.
- **Nonfiction:** Publishes young adult books, 12–18 years. Topics include history and multicultural and ethnic issues.
- **Representative Titles:** *48 Shades of Brown* by Nick Earls (YA) is a humorous novel that centers around a teenage boy's world of calculus, roommates, birds, and love. *Zazoo* by Richard Mosher (grades 7 and up) is the story of a young Vietnamese girl, raised by adoptive parents in France, and the events that unfold when a young man arrives in her small French village.

Submissions and Payment
Guidelines available. Query with outline and sample chapters for nonfiction. Send complete ms for fiction. Responds only if interested. Publication period varies. Royalty; advance.

Editor's Comments
The name Graphia, derived from the Greek word meaning "to write," signifies the quality literature that is the hallmark of this new line of books for teen readers. We look for submissions of solid literary quality. The works of older teenage writers are of interest to us, as long as they reflect the high quality we seek.

Icon Key
☆ New Listing   🖰 E-publisher
⊗ Not currently accepting submissions

Harry N. Abrams Books for Young Readers

115 West 18th Street
New York, NY 10011

Assistant Editor: Linas Alsenas

Publisher's Interests
Abrams Books for Young Readers celebrates its fifth year in business with the introduction of a new imprint, Amulet Books. Amulet Books offers both fiction and nonfiction titles for middle-grade and young adult readers. Abrams Books for Young Readers concentrates on picture books for young readers, board books for infants, and novelty titles.
Website: www.abramsbooks.com

Freelance Potential
Published 60 titles in 2004.

- **Fiction:** Publishes early picture books, 0–4 years; easy-to-read books, 4–7 years; middle-grade books, 8–12 years; and young adult books, 12–18 years. Genres include folklore and stories about animals, nature, and the environment.
- **Nonfiction:** Publishes easy-to-read books, 4–7 years; middle-grade books, 8–12 years; and young adult books, 12–18 years. Topics include animals, natural history, and humor.
- **Representative Titles:** *The Useful Moose* by Fiona Robinson (4–8 years) shows just how useful a moose around the house can be when it comes to doing chores. *Under the Sun* by Arthur Dorros (YA) is the story of a young Balkan boy who is separated from his parents in wartime and must survive alone on a journey to a place of safety.

Submissions and Payment
Guidelines available at website. Submit cover letter and complete ms for picture books; query with sample chapter for longer works and nonfiction. Accepts photocopies and computer printouts. SASE. Responds in 6 months. Publication in 1 year. Royalty, 8–15%.

Editor's Comments
We welcome submissions for either of our two imprints but keep in mind that they are very different. Both fiction and nonfiction are welcome. If you submit a picture book, send the entire manuscript, otherwise, send a sample chapter with a query.

Absey and Company

23011 Northcrest Drive
Spring, TX 77389

Publisher: Edward E. Wilson

Publisher's Interests
Now in business for nearly a decade, Absey and Company continues to be committed to producing the best in literary fiction and nonfiction. Its list includes books for children from birth through the age of 18. The publisher also offers a limited number of resource titles for teachers.
Website: www.absey.com

Freelance Potential
Published 10 titles in 2004: all were developed from unsolicited submissions. Of the 10 titles, 9 were by authors who were new to the publishing house. Receives 1,000+ queries yearly.

- **Fiction:** Publishes story picture books, 4–10 years; chapter books, 5–10 years; and young adult books, 12–18 years.
- **Nonfiction:** Publishes educational titles, 0–18 years. Features biographies and books about religion and history. Also publishes educational activity books and poetry collections, as well as language arts resource titles for educators.
- **Representative Titles:** *Saving the Scrolls* by Mary Kerry (YA) recounts the adventures of a young Egyptian princess whose bravery helps save the library at Alexandria. *Dragonfly* by Alice McLerran tells the story of a young boy and his family who must secretly raise a young dragon.

Submissions and Payment
Guidelines available. Query with résumé, outline, and sample chapters. Accepts photocopies. No simultaneous submissions. SASE. Responds in 6–9 months. Publication in 1 year. Payment policy varies.

Editor's Comments
At this time, we are interested in reviewing quality fiction for middle-grade and young adult readers, nonfiction, poetry, and educational resources, especially related to language arts. If you are new to us, please take the time to read some of our books. You will have a better chance of acceptance if you know what works for us.

Accord Publishing

Suite 202
1732 Wazee Street
Denver, CO 80202

Editor: Ken Fleck

Publisher's Interests
This publisher specializes in educational activity books, board books, and novelty books for children up to the age of nine. Genres include adventure fiction, humor, and fantasy.
Website: www.accordpublishing.com

Freelance Potential
Published 10 titles (1 juvenile) in 2004. Of the 10 titles, 1 was by an author who was new to the publishing house. Receives 360 queries, 192 unsolicited mss yearly.

- **Fiction:** Publishes early picture books, 0–4 years; easy-to-read books, 4–7 years; story picture books, 4–9 years; and chapter books, 5–9 years. Genres include adventure, fantasy, and humor.
- **Nonfiction:** Publishes "I Can't Believe It's Science!" series for children ages 7+. Topics include insects, rocks, and weather.
- **Representative Titles:** *Frog in the Kitchen Sink* by Jim Post is a board book that follows a precocious little frog as he ends up in places that he does not belong. *Mystery in Bug Town* by William Boniface follows Inspector Cricket on his investigation in Bug Town to find out who tried to flatten Charlie Roach. *The Amazing Insect Safari* is a book and display kit that offers an exciting way to explore the insect world. Each kit includes a book, display tray, tweezers, ID labels, and magnifying lens.

Submissions and Payment
Guidelines available at website. Query or send complete ms. SASE. Response time varies. Publication period varies. Payment policy varies.

Editor's Comments
We are interested in educational board books and activity kits that make learning fun. Our material is unique as we like interactive books that are entertaining, allow children to use their imaginations, and encourage a great deal of creativity. Check our website to get an idea for what we are all about.

ACTA Publications

4848 North Clark Street
Chicago, IL 60640

Editor: Gregory Pierce

Publisher's Interests
This religious publisher concentrates on Christian materials for young adults and adults who are interested in enhancing their faith. Recently it has begun to offer some titles for younger readers (age three and older) as well. It does not publish any fiction. Audio and video resources are also part of its publishing program.
Website: www.actapublications.com

Freelance Potential
Published 20 titles in 2004: 3–5 were developed from unsolicited submissions and 3–5 were reprint/licensed properties. Of the 20 titles, 3 were by unpublished writers and 5 were by authors who were new to the publishing house. Receives 400 queries yearly.

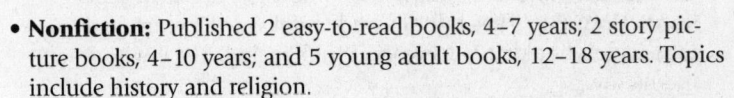

- **Nonfiction:** Published 2 easy-to-read books, 4–7 years; 2 story picture books, 4–10 years; and 5 young adult books, 12–18 years. Topics include history and religion.
- **Representative Titles:** *What You Will See Inside a Catholic Church* by Rev. Michael Keane (6–10 years) is filled with easy-to-understand text and full color photos and describes objects found in church, as well as the different parts of Mass and the major liturgies. *Getting to Know the Bible* by Rev. Melvin L. Farrell (YA-Adult) is written for those who wish to learn the basics of the Old and New Testaments.

Submissions and Payment
Catalogue available at website. Query with table of contents, sample chapter, and market analysis. Accepts photocopies. SASE. Responds in 1–3 weeks. Publication in 9–12 months. Royalty, 10%.

Editor's Comments
Everything we publish is a resource designed to enhance Christian faith in the reader. While most of what we produce targets young adults and adults, we do offer books for children age three and up. If, after reviewing our publishing program, you feel we are right for each other, send a query that includes an explanation of your proposal, a table of contents, and a sample chapter.

Action Publishing

P.O. Box 391
Glendale, CA 91209

Editor: Michael Metzler - L. A. Department

Publisher's Interests
Launched in 1996, this publisher offers creative products that motivate and involve readers. It specializes in adventure and fantasy stories for children of all ages.
Website: www.actionpublishing.com

Freelance Potential
Published 3 titles in 2004. Receives numerous queries and mss each year.

- **Fiction:** Publishes early picture books, 0–4 years; easy-to-read books, 4–7 years; story picture books, 4–10 years; middle-grade books, 8–12 years; and young adult books, 12–18 years. Genres include adventure and fantasy. Also publishes books in series.
- **Nonfiction:** Publishes middle-grade books, 8–12 years; and young adult books, 12–18 years. Topics include the environment and nature.
- **Representative Titles:** *The Secret of Gorbee Grotto* by Scott E. Sutton tells the adventures of Jetter, the curious Erf, as he sets out to discover what is causing the Grotto to glow. The book helps teach children important life values. *The Kuekumber Kids Meet the Monster of Manners* by Scott E. Sutton (3–5 years) is a story about a polite blue monster that saves a birthday party where kids are throwing cake. It is a fun and entertaining book that teaches children good manners and respect for each other.

Submissions and Payment
Guidelines available. Accepts queries and complete mss through literary agents only. SASE. Response time and publication period vary. Royalty; advance.

Editor's Comments
We publish educational and value-oriented children's books. Books that make learning fun and exciting, and teach a valuable lesson are of interest to us. Many of our titles are part of a series. Remember, we only accept manuscripts from literary agents.

Aladdin Paperbacks

Simon & Schuster Children's Publishing Division
4th Floor
1230 Avenue of the Americas
New York, NY 10020

Submissions Editor

Publisher's Interests
Aladdin is the paperback imprint of the Simon & Schuster Children's Publishing Division. It offers reprints of successful hardcover fiction and nonfiction titles for children and young adults, including historical fiction, fantasy, and biographies.
Website: www.simonsayskids.com

Freelance Potential
Published 150 titles in 2004: all were by agented authors.

- **Fiction:** Publishes story picture books, 4–10 years; middle-grade books, 8–12 years; and young adult books, 12–18 years. Genres include contemporary and historical fiction, suspense, mystery, and adventure.
- **Nonfiction:** Publishes biographies.
- **Representative Titles:** *Too Many Valentines* by Margaret McNamara (4–6 years) is the humorous story of a boy who decides he doesn't want any valentines; part of the Robin Hill School series. *The Guns of Tortuga* by Brad Strickland & Thomas E. Fuller (8–12 years) is an adventure that follows a young apprentice to a ship's surgeon; part of the Pirate Hunter series. *True Heart* by Kathleen Duey (7–10 years) is a fantasy tale of unicorns, magic armor, and gypsies; part of The Unicorn's Secret series.

Submissions and Payment
Guidelines available. Accepts submissions from agented authors only. SASE. Response time varies; publication period and payment policy vary.

Editor's Comments
We are open to queries by agented authors, but be advised that our list of original material is very small. At this time, our selective original publishing program consists, for the most part, of young nonfiction, beginning readers, and middle-grade and young adult series fiction. New writers should seriously consider their topic and audience before having their agent submit to us to avoid disappointment.

ALA Editions

American Library Association
50 East Huron Street
Chicago, IL 60611

Editorial Assistant: Emily Moroni

Publisher's Interests
ALA Editions of the American Library Association publishes titles for library professionals, library researchers, and the general library/information community. Books, as well as nonprint and electronic materials, are offered on topics relating to educating youth readers at all levels.
Website: www.ala.org./editions

Freelance Potential
Published 35 titles in 2004: 3 were developed from unsolicited submissions. Of the 35 titles, 12 were by authors who were new to the publishing house. Receives 50 queries yearly.

- **Nonfiction:** Publishes resource materials, guides, textbooks, and reference materials for teachers and librarians. Topics include children's reading programs, acquisitions, cataloguing and classification, school services, library studies, literacy, developing reading lists, and information technology.
- **Representative Titles:** *Books in Bloom* by Kimberly K. Faurot (librarians) provides scripts and instructions for bringing children's stories to life. *Hit List for Children* by Beverley C. Becker & Susan M. Stan (librarians) arms children's librarians with the information they need to fight censorship and defend children's right to read; includes information on the most commonly censored titles.

Submissions and Payment
Guidelines available at website. Query with outline/synopsis. SASE. Responds in 2-8 weeks. Publication in 7-9 months. Royalty.

Editor's Comments
If you have an idea for a book or electronic product for librarians, we're a good place to start. We're seeking original ideas and approaches to the challenges librarians face every day. Developing children's programs, media center development, and expanding young adult programs are our top priority. Most of our projects start with an author who is already involved in library or information services.

Alef Design Group

4423 Fruitland Avenue
Los Angeles, CA 90058

Submissions Editor: Jane Golub

Publisher's Interests
Well-crafted Judaica for children and adults is offered by this publisher. Alef features historical and religious fiction with Jewish themes, and nonfiction titles about Jewish life and Judaism, as well as study materials for the Torah.
Website: www.torahaura.com

Freelance Potential
Published 1 title in 2004; it was a reprint/licensed property. Receives 50 queries, 50 unsolicited mss yearly.

- **Fiction:** Publishes middle-grade books, 8–12 years; and chapter books, 5–10 years. Genres include Jewish historical and religious fiction, and adventure stories.
- **Nonfiction:** Published chapter books, 8–10 years; middle-grade books, 8–12 years; and young adult books, 12–18 years. Topics include Jewish history, holidays and celebrations, spirituality, family, self-awareness, and anti-semitism. Also publishes Torah study guides and parenting titles.
- **Representative Titles:** *Let's Talk About God* by Dorothy K. Kripke (8–10 years) simply and gently provides children with a foundation for understanding God. *Rafi's Search for the Torah Munching Monster* by Rabbi Steven L. Mills (6–8 years) is a fanciful tale about a big, green monster and a missing Torah.

Submissions and Payment
Prefers query with sample chapters. Accepts complete ms. Accepts photocopies and computer printouts. No simultaneous submissions. SASE. Responds to queries in 1–2 weeks; to mss in 3–6 months. Publication in 1–2 years. Royalty, 5–10%.

Editor's Comments
We are primarily interested in materials for the young readers that discuss Jewish themes. Everything we publish examines issues from a Jewish perspective. Children's books should reflect an open, honest assessment of Jewish life.

Alyson Publications

Suite 1000
6922 Hollywood Boulevard
Los Angeles, CA 90028

Editor

Publisher's Interests
Alyson Wonderland is the children's imprint of this leading publisher of books for children of gay and lesbian parents. Its titles explore the contemporary social issues associated with non-traditional families.
Website: www.alyson.com

Freelance Potential
Published 55 titles (4 juvenile) in 2004: 10 were developed from unsolicited submissions, 10 were by agented authors, and 3 were reprint/licensed properties. Receives 800–900 queries yearly.

- **Fiction:** Published 1 story picture book, 4–10 years; and 1 young adult book, 12–18 years. Genres include contemporary, multicultural, and ethnic fiction. Also publishes fiction for adults.
- **Nonfiction:** Published 1 story picture book, 4–10 years; and 1 young adult book, 12–18 years. Topics include gay, lesbian, and bisexual families; parenting; social issues; and self-help topics. Also publishes nonfiction titles about sexuality and parenting for adults.
- **Representative Titles:** *Heather Has Two Mommies* by Lesléa Newman is the straightforward story of a little girl with two lesbian mothers that sends a message of love and acceptance. *Daddy's Roommate* by Michael Willhoite (2–6 years) highlights the life of a young boy, his father, and the father's lover as they take part in activities familiar to all kinds of families.

Submissions and Payment
Guidelines available. Query with 1-page synopsis and available artwork. No unsolicited mss. Accepts photocopies and computer printouts. SASE. Responds in 10–12 weeks. Publication in 2 years. Advance; royalty.

Editor's Comments
We are always searching for fresh material that explains gay and lesbian lifestyles and families to children and young adults. Fiction and nonfiction books that deal with the subject sensitively, thoroughly, and thoughtfully are appreciated.

Ambassador Books

91 Prescott Street
Worcester, MA 01605

sent 3-1-06

Submissions Editor: Kathryn Conlan

Publisher's Interests
Inspirational and spiritual books for adults and children are found in this publisher's catalogue. It strives to offer material that will impact on readers' lives in a positive way. All of its titles are Christian based.
Website: www.ambassadorbooks.com

Freelance Potential
Published 7 titles (3 juvenile) in 2004: 3 were developed from unsolicited submissions. Receives 2,000 queries, 500 unsolicited mss yearly.

- **Fiction:** Publishes easy-to-read books, 4–7 years; story picture books, 4–10 years; and middle-grade books, 8–12 years. Genres include adventure, mystery, suspense, and inspirational, religious, historical, and regional fiction. Also publishes sports stories.
- **Nonfiction:** Publishes easy-to-read titles, 4–7 years; story picture books, 4–7 years; and middle-grade books, 8–12 years. Topics include self-help, religion, sports, and regional subjects.
- **Representative Titles:** *Fiona the Firefly* by Wendy Connelly (4–8 years) tells the story of a little bug with a big problem. *Survival Notes for Graduates: Inspiration for the Ultimate Journey* by Robert Stofel (YA) helps high school graduates deal with some of the fears they face as they think about the big jump to college.

Submissions and Payment
Guidelines available. Query. Accepts photocopies. Availability of artwork improves chance of acceptance. SASE. Responds in 4 months. Publication in 1 year. Royalty, 10%.

Editor's Comments
Our motto is "Spirit and Truth" and our mission is to live up to this motto. If you are new to us, we strongly urge you to read some of our published titles so you will understand this motto. We want to work with writers who also have a desire to bring readers inspiration. We publish few books each year, so please send us your very best.

Ambassador-Emerald International

427 Wade Hampton Boulevard
Greenville, SC 29609

Editor: Brenton Cook

Publisher's Interests

Established in 1995, Ambassador-Emerald is dedicated to publishing books that present the gospel as the only way of salvation and helping Christians to live in accordance with the word of God. Its children's titles are written for readers age six and older. Both fiction and nonfiction are offered by this company.
Website: www.emeraldhouse.com

Freelance Potential

Published 16-20 titles (5 juvenile) in 2004. Of the 16-20 titles, 4 were by authors who were new to the publishing house. Receives 250 queries yearly.

- **Fiction:** Publishes chapter books, 5-10 years; middle-grade novels, 8-12 years; and young adult books, 12-18 years. Genres include historical, religious, and regional fiction.
- **Nonfiction:** Publishes middle-grade books, 8-12 years; and young adult books, 12-18 years. Topics include religion, history, current events, and regional subjects. Also features biographies.
- **Representative Titles:** *The Mayflower Pilgrims* by David Beale traces the genealogical links of the pilgrims to the Baptists, Presbyterians, and Congregationalists. *Billy Sunday* by William T. Ellis tells the life story of this well-known preacher.

Submissions and Payment

Guidelines and catalogue available with 9x12 SASE ($1.29 postage) and at website. Query. Prefers email queries but will accept regular mail. Accepts photocopies and email to authors@emeraldhouse.com. SASE. Responds in 6 weeks. Publication in 1 year. Royalty, 5-15%; advance, $250-$1,000.

Editor's Comments

For the coming year, we continue to look for writers who can deliver activity books, nonfiction, and religious youth and regional fiction. Writers from South Carolina, North Carolina, Georgia, Tennessee, and Virginia have the best chance of publication.

Amulet Books

Harry N. Abrams
5th Floor
115 West 18th Street
New York, NY 10011

Editor: Susan Van Metre

Publisher's Interests
This new imprint of Abrams Books for Young Readers publishes hardcover and paperback novels and nonfiction titles for middle-grade readers and young adults. Its list includes stand-alone titles as well as books in series. Amulet Books was established in the spring of 2004.
Website: www.abramsbooks.com

Freelance Potential
Published 8–12 titles in 2004.

- **Fiction:** Publishes middle-grade books; 8–12 years; and young adult books, 12–18 years. Genres include contemporary, historical, and science fiction; fantasy; mystery; suspense; and humor. Also publishes books in series.
- **Nonfiction:** Publishes middle-grade books; 8–12 years; and young adult books, 12–18 years. Topics include multicultural and ethnic issues, nature, the environment, and history. Also publishes books in series.
- **Representative Titles:** *TTYL* by Lauren Myracle (YA) is a novel about friendship, change, and growth. *The Golden Hour* by Maiya Williams is an adventure story that weaves fantasy with history.

Submissions and Payment
Query with synopsis and first 3 chapters. SASE. Responds in 6 months. Publication period varies. Royalty; advance.

Editor's Comments
The quality of our design and our thoughtful and thorough marketing distinguish our books. Our focus is primarily on middle-grade and young adult readers, so we don't want to see submissions of picture books, easy-to-read books, or early-reader chapter books. We plan to publish the works of new writers as well as those of prominent authors, and we will continue to produce eight to twelve books each year. We accept fiction in a wide range of genres, but we're equally interested in nonfiction submissions.

Annick Press

15 Patricia Avenue
Toronto, Ontario M2M 1H9
Canada

Editors

Publisher's Interests
Readers between eight and eighteen make up the target audience of this Canadian publishing house. Annick Press offers both fiction and nonfiction titles. It was founded in 1975, and its motto is "excellence and innovation in children's literature."
Website: www.annickpress.com

Freelance Potential
Published 30 titles in 2004.

- **Fiction:** Publishes middle-grade books, 8–12 years; and young adult books, 12–18 years. Genres include contemporary fiction and humor.
- **Nonfiction:** Publishes middle-grade books, 8–12 years; and young adult books, 12–18 years.
- **Representative Titles:** *Anastasia Morningstar and the Crystal Butterfly* by Hazel Hutchins (9–11 years) features a young girl who wants to use a magical woman in her science project. *The Best of Arlie Zack* by Hazel Hutchins (9–12 years) is the story of a new kid in town as he struggles to find a place for himself.

Submissions and Payment
Guidelines available. Query with synopsis and sample chapter. Prefers email queries to annick@annickpress.com. Accepts photocopies and computer printouts. SAE/IRC. Response time, publication period, and payment policy vary.

Editor's Comments
A successful children's book is one that feels authentic and makes a child or teen feel that they belong. It poses questions, opens doors, encourages discussions, causes laughter and tears, and invites sharing of emotions. We look for authors who can deliver on these traits, and bring a sense of humor to their work, too. At this time we are interested in reviewing both fiction and nonfiction for middle-grade and teen readers. We are not currently accepting manuscripts for picture books. We are committed to publishing Canadian authors but will also consider authors from other countries.

A.R.E. Publishing, Inc.

6708 East 47th Avenue Drive
Denver, CO 80216

Editor: Steve Brodsky

Publisher's Interests
Founded in 1973, A.R.E. Publishing is known for its pamphlets about Jewish holidays, traditions, and community that are used in synagogues around the world. It has expanded its list to include educational titles for all ages, from kindergarten to adult students. Its catalogue also features Hebrew materials, teacher manuals, early childhood titles, craft books, plays, children's books, and other curriculum materials.
Website: www.arepublish.com

Freelance Potential
Published 5 titles in 2004. Receives 6 queries yearly.

- **Nonfiction:** Publishes Jewish educational titles for all ages.
- **Representative Titles:** *Jewish Every Day: The Complete Handbook for Early Childhood Teachers* by Maxine Segal Handeman (teachers) includes chapters on anti-bias, God and spirituality, Torah, Israel, Hebrew, and each of the Jewish holidays. *Like a Maccabee* by Rabbi Raymond A. Zwerin & Audrey Friedman Marcus (grade pre-K–3) brings young children the story of Chanukah and of Maccabees as role models.

Submissions and Payment
Guidelines available at website. Query. SASE. Response time and publication period vary. Royalty.

Editor's Comments
Our goal is to bring teachers and students the very best books available on subjects related to the Jewish faith and culture. As we move towards our 35th anniversary, we are looking for new ways to expand our educational materials. If you have a background in education and are familiar with Jewish culture and traditions, we invite you to send us a query. We like to think of ourselves as unique—meaning that our books are informative, fun, and beautifully illustrated. Review some of our recent titles and you'll see what we mean.

Atheneum Books for Young Readers

1230 Avenue of the Americas
New York, NY 10020

Executive Editor: Caitlyn Dlouhy

Publisher's Interests
This imprint of Simon & Schuster features original chapter books, picture books, biographies, and nonfiction titles for very young readers through adult.
Website: www.simonsayskids.com

Freelance Potential
Published 110 titles (70 juvenile) in 2004: 5 were developed from unsolicited submissions, 70 were by agented authors, and 2 were reprint/licensed properties. Receives 30,000 queries yearly.

- **Fiction:** Publishes concept books, toddler books, and early picture books, 0–4 years; story picture books, 4–10 years; chapter books, 5–10 years; middle-grade books, 8–12 years; and young adult books, 12–18 years. Genres include science fiction, historical fiction, adventure, mystery, and fantasy.
- **Nonfiction:** Publishes story picture books, 4–10 years; chapter books, 5–10 years; and middle-grade books, 8–12 years; young adult books, 12–18 years. Topics include the environment, science, nature, sports, history, and multicultural issues. Also publishes biographies.
- **Representative Titles:** *Kira-Kira* by Cynthia Kadohata (11+ years) is a first novel about a Japanese American girl who moves to the deep South in the 1950s and encounters a distinct type of prejudice. *Elena's Serenade* by Campbell Geeslin (3–7 years) is the story of a little girl determined to prove that her talents at blowing magic glass are equal to any boy's ability.

Submissions and Payment
Guidelines available. Query for nonfiction. Send 3 sample chapters with summary for fiction. Accepts photocopies and computer printouts. SASE. Responds in 3 months. Publication period varies. Royalty.

Editor's Comments
We put less emphasis on particular trends, fads, and gimmicks, and more on the qualities of craftsmanship: fine writing and originality.

Augsburg Books

Suite 700
100 South 5th Street
Minneapolis, MN 55402

Submissions Editor

Publisher's Interests
Augsburg Press is the publishing arm of the Evangelical Lutheran Church in America. Its children's list includes both fiction and nonfiction for children of all ages. The books are used in Sunday school, confirmation and youth classes, vacation Bible school, and adult Bible study classes.
Website: www.augsburgbooks.com

Freelance Potential
Published 40 titles (4 juvenile) in 2004. Receives 1,000 queries each year.

- **Fiction:** Publishes toddler and early picture books, 0–4 years; story picture and easy-to-read books, 4–7 years; middle-grade fiction, 8–12 years; and young adult novels, 10–15 years.
- **Nonfiction:** Publishes concept and toddler books, 0–4 years; and story picture books, 4–10 years. Also publishes activity books, devotionals, and educational materials. Topics include Lutheranism, family life, spirituality, prayer, parenting, and Christian education.
- **Representative Titles:** *Go Tell It on the Mountain* by Debbie Trafton O'Neal is designed to help parents teach this bedtime favorite to their children and includes related activities to make learning and singing fun. *Sleepy Jesus* by Pennie Kidd retells the story of the night Jesus was born, including the reaction of all the living things near him—animals, wise men, angels, and shepherds.

Submissions and Payment
Guidelines and catalogue available at website. Query with résumé, outline, and synopsis. Accepts photocopies, computer printouts, and simultaneous submissions if identified. SASE. Responds in 1–3 months. Publication in 2–3 years. Royalty, 5–10% of gross.

Editor's Comments
Our goal in all the materials we publish is to bring to our readers dynamic Christian ideas, values, and beliefs that will help nourish faith in their daily lives.

A/V Concepts Corporation

30 Montauk Boulevard
Oakdale, NY 11769

Editor: Laura Solimene

Publisher's Interests
This publisher is a division of the EDCON Publishing Group. It features high interest/low vocabulary books and workbooks for students in grades two through twelve. A/V Concepts also offers educational compact-disc learning materials.
Website: www.edconpublishing.com

Freelance Potential
Published 6 titles in 2004: all were by unpublished writers who were new to the publishing house. Receives 300 queries yearly.

- **Fiction:** Publishes middle-grade books, 8–12 years; and young adult books, 12–18 years. Genres include the classics, science fiction, nature and adventure stories, fantasy, and horror. Also publishes biographies, and adapted classics.
- **Nonfiction:** Publishes reading comprehension, vocabulary development, and math workbooks for grades 2–12.
- **Representative Titles:** *Sports Math* (grades 7–12) uses sports themes to focus on math concepts and provide positive reinforcement. *The Man in the Iron Mask* by Alexandre Dumas (grade 3) is a modified high interest/low readability version of the well-known classic tale about an evil king and his twin brother; includes a vocabulary and comprehension workbook.

Submissions and Payment
Guidelines and catalogue available. Query with résumé and writing samples or clips. No unsolicited mss. All work is assigned. SASE. Responds in 3–6 weeks. Publication period varies. Flat fee.

Editor's Comments
Education professionals use our products in the classroom to improve reading and math skills in their students. Focus your query to address the needs of reading specialists, early childhood educators, remedial reading teachers, and homeschooling educators and parents. We are currently seeking queries for classic children's literature for ages seven and up.

Ave Maria Press

P.O. Box 428
Notre Dame, IN 46556

Editorial Coordinator

Publisher's Interests
Ave Maria is a Catholic publisher that serves the spiritual and educational needs of individuals, families, and the church. In addition to books specifically for Catholic readers and institutions, it also offers titles for an ecumenical readership.
Website: www.avemariapress.com

Freelance Potential
Published 20 titles in 2004: 2 were developed from unsolicited submissions and 8 were by agented authors. Receives 300 queries each year.

- **Nonfiction:** Publishes educational and religious titles for Catholic families. Topics include the sacraments, prayer and spirituality, family life, Christian living, and leadership. Also publishes titles on the lives of Catholic saints.
- **Representative Titles:** *Getting Along (Almost) with Your Adult Kids* by Lois & Joel Davitz (parents) helps parents understand the dynamics of their relationships with adult children and shows parents how to achieve long-lasting bonds as their families age. *The Resilient Family* by Paul W. Power & Arthur E. Dell Orto (parents) is a comprehensive resource for families that have a child with a serious illness or disability.

Submissions and Payment
Guidelines available at website. Query with outline, table of contents, introduction, and 1 or 2 samples chapters. Accepts photocopies and computer printouts. No simultaneous submissions SASE. Responds in 4–6 months. Publication in 6 months. Payment rate varies.

Editor's Comments
As one of the oldest religious publishers in the United States, we concentrate our publishing activities in five areas: prayer and spirituality, adolescent catechesis, pastoral care and guidance, parish and ministry resources, and elementary catechetical resources. We publish no fiction, poetry, or biographies.

Avisson Press

3007 Taliaferro Road
Greensboro, NC 27408

Editor: M. L. Hester

Publisher's Interests
This small Southern publishing house publishes only nonfiction, specifically biographies, for young adult readers. The titles on its list showcase a diverse group of people from the pages of history as well as from the news of the day. It offers collective biographies as well as stand-alone titles.

Freelance Potential
Published 10 titles in 2004: 5 were developed from unsolicited submissions. Of the 10 titles, 1 was by an unpublished writer and 3 were by authors who were new to the publishing house. Receives 500 queries yearly.

- **Nonfiction:** Publishes young adult books, 12–18 years. Topics include biography, history, science, sports, and ethnic and multicultural subjects.
- **Representative Titles:** *I Dare Not Fail* by Mary Wilds (YA) focuses on the lives and accomplishments of African American women in education. *Yao Ming: Gentle Giant of Basketball* by Richard Krawiec (YA) traces the incredible life of this Chinese athlete who is now a superstar of American professional basketball.

Submissions and Payment
Query with outline, author biography, and sample chapter. Accepts photocopies, computer printouts, and simultaneous submissions if identified. SASE. Responds in 2 weeks. Publication in 1 year. Royalty, 8–10%.

Editor's Comments
We are always interested in hearing from writers with ideas for new biographies. No notable person is excluded from our consideration. We have books on American personalities, but also on individuals from countries around the world. Books that cover numerous people who have a common field are also of interest. History, sports, current events, politics, aviation, entertainment, and the arts have all been covered through our biographies.

Baker Book House Company

6030 East Fulton Road
Ada, MI 49301

Submissions Editor

Publisher's Interests
This publisher offers engaging stories that show how God interacts with children in their daily lives. Biblically based, it offers picture books, storybooks, and middle-grade titles.
Website: www.bakerbooks.com

Freelance Potential
Published 240 titles (12 juvenile) in 2004: all were by agented authors. Of the 240 titles, 1 was by an unpublished writer. Receives 100 queries yearly.

- **Fiction:** Publishes story picture books, 4–10 years. Genres include inspirational stories with a Christian theme.
- **Nonfiction:** Publishes toddler books and early picture books, 0–4 years; and middle-grade books, 8–12 years. Topics include Bible stories and stories that show the presence of God in one's life. Also publishes parenting titles and homeschooling titles for adults.
- **Representative Titles:** *Cow Makes a Difference* by Todd Aaron Smith (4–7 years) is the story of a farm cow that learns that it is better to remain at home than to search for a new life at the city zoo. *Bible Activities for Everyone* by Betty De Vries & Mary Currier (5–12 years) incorporates biblically based concepts into activities that are fun to do.

Submissions and Payment
Guidelines and catalogue available at website. Agented submissions only. No unsolicited mss. Response time varies. Publication in 1–2 years. Royalty.

Editor's Comments
We do not accept unsolicited material and will only consider work that is sent through a professional literary agent. Original, fresh, and creative stories are of interest to us. We like moral tales that show morality carried throughout the story, not just in the ending. Make sure your writing is age-appropriate and that your agent has researched our other titles to make sure that your idea has not already been published.

Baker's Plays

P.O. Box 699222
Quincy, MA 02269-9222

Managing Director: Deidre Shaw

Publisher's Interests
One-act and full-length plays, musicals, and classic dramas, as well as anthologies, audition materials, drama textbooks, and audiotapes are featured by this well-known publisher. Its material is suitable for youth, high school, and community theater groups.
Website: www.bakersplays.com

Freelance Potential
Published 20 titles (7 juvenile) in 2004. Of the 20 titles, 4 were by unpublished writers and 10 were by authors who were new to the publishing house. Receives 50–75 queries, 300+ unsolicited mss each year.

- **Fiction:** Publishes plays for children's, high school, and family theater groups. Genres include comedy, mystery, folktales, and fairy tales. Also publishes holiday plays, classics, and musicals.
- **Nonfiction:** Publishes textbooks and theater resource material. Topics include improvisation, teaching drama, acting techniques, theatrical history, and playwriting.
- **Representative Titles:** *Telling Tales Again, Sam?* by Linda M. Abbott is an amusing play that looks at favorite fairy tales as told under the direction of the Fairy Tale Kingdom PR man. *Acting Through Exercises* by John L. Gronbeck-Tedesco covers the fundamental skills of acting, and suggests means integrating voice and movement.

Submissions and Payment
Guidelines available. Query with script history, reviews, and sample pages or synopsis; or send complete ms. Accepts photocopies, computer printouts, and simultaneous submissions if identified. SASE. Responds in 1 month, to mss in 3–4 months. Publication period and payment policy vary.

Editor's Comments
Although we maintain an open submissions policy, we prefer plays that have been "production-tested." We prefer plays that have had a staged reading, workshop reading, or full production.

Bantam Books for Young Readers

1745 Broadway
New York, NY 10019

Editor

Publisher's Interests

Bantam Books is one of the juvenile literature imprints of Knopf Delacorte Dell Young Readers Group. Its list includes fiction and nonfiction titles, from board books and picture books to middle-grade and young adult novels.
Website: www.randomhouse.com/kids

Freelance Potential

Published 275 titles in 2004: most were by agented authors, and 90 were reprint/licensed properties. Of the 275 titles, some were by unpublished writers. Receives 2,000 queries yearly.

- **Fiction:** Publishes early picture books, 0–4 years; easy-to-read books, 4–7 years; story picture books, 4–10 years; chapter books, 5–10 years; middle-grade books, 8–12 years; and young adult books, 12–18 years. Genres include contemporary fiction and mystery.
- **Nonfiction:** Publishes young adult titles, 12–18 years. Topics include contemporary social issues.
- **Representative Titles:** *The Pursuit* by Lizzie Skurnick (YA) is a spin-off of the hit TV series about Agent Michael Vaughn; part of the Alias series. *Batman: The Mystery of the Batwoman* by Louise Simonson introduces a new character in the Batman and Robin series and follows her adventures of good and battling evil.

Submissions and Payment

Queries accepted through agents only. New writers may submit middle-grade novels for the Delacotre Dell Yearling Prize, and young adult novels for the Delacorte Press Contest for a First Young Adult Novel. (See the contests and award section of this directory). No simultaneous submissions. SASE. Response time varies. Publication in 2 years. Royalty; advance.

Editor's Comments

We will consider original material, but only if it is submitted by an agent. Prospective authors are invited to participate in one of our writing contests.

Beach Holme Publishing

1010-409 Granville Street
Vancouver, British Columbia V6C 1T2
Canada

Publisher: Michael Carroll

Publisher's Interests
With three imprints, Prospect Books, Sandcastle Books, and Porcepic Books, this publisher brings its audience of middle-grade and young adult readers historical fiction books. As a Canadian publisher, it publishes Canadian authors exclusively.
Website: www.beachholme.bc.ca

Freelance Potential
Published 13 titles (5 juvenile) in 2004: 5 were developed from unsolicited submissions and 8 were by agented authors. Of the 13 titles, 4 were by authors who were new to the publishing house. Receives 1,200 queries yearly.

- **Fiction:** Published 1 chapter book, 5-10 years; and 4 middle-grade books, 8-12 years. Genres include Canadian historical, contemporary, multicultural, and Native Canadian fiction.
- **Representative Titles:** *Last Days in Africville* by Dorothy Perkyns (8-12 years) follows the life of a young girl in the 1960s historic Nova Scotia community of Africville during the community relocation. *Chasing the Arrow* by Charles Reid (YA) is set in Toronto in the 1950s and follows a young boy who discovers his mother is one of a team working on the design of a new fighter jet.

Submissions and Payment
Canadian authors only. Guidelines available. Query with 3 sample chapters, market analysis, and description of intended audience. Accepts photocopies and computer printouts. SASE. Responds in 4-6 months. Publication in 1 month. Royalty; advance.

Editor's Comments
While we do publish some contemporary fiction, our focus is on historical fiction works, set in Canada. Include ideas for teachers' guides or resources and appropriate topics for a classroom situation if applicable. We are highly selective when it comes to choosing new books, and your best chance of having your novel considered is to give us as much information about marketing as possible along with your story.

Bebop Books

95 Madison Avenue
New York, NY 10016

Editor: Jennifer Frantz

Publisher's Interests
This small publishing house specializes in multicultural books for youngsters in grades K–2. It offers titles in both English and Spanish and both fiction and nonfiction are found in its catalogue. Bebop Books is an imprint of Lee & Low books. Its books are created to be used with either Reading Recovery® leveling systems or the Fountas and Pinnell's Guided Reading™.
Website: www.bebopbooks.com

Freelance Potential
Published 12 titles in 2004: 9 were developed from unsolicited submissions and 3 were reprint/licensed properties. Of the 12 titles, 1 was by an author who was new to the publishing house. Receives 600 unsolicited mss yearly.

- **Fiction:** Published 8 easy-to-read books, 4–7 years. Also features emergent and beginning readers, grades K–2. Features books in Spanish and English.
- **Nonfiction:** Published 4 easy-to-read books, 4–7 years. Also features emergent and beginning readers, grades K–2, about multicultural and ethnic subjects.
- **Representative Titles:** *Best Friends* by Tina Athaide features two best friends on an outing to the playground: published in both English and Spanish versions. *The Dashiki* by Gaylia Taylor tells the story of a father who buys himself a West African dashiki, only to have it shrink in the washing machine to his son's shirt size.

Submissions and Payment
Guidelines available at website or with SASE. Send complete ms. Only reads mss in late summer and fall. Accepts photocopies. SASE. Responds in 4 months. Publication in 1 year. Royalty; advance.

Editor's Comments
Be aware that we will only review manuscripts from late summer to early fall. We are interested in material with themes that will appeal to children while featuring familiar concepts, objects, and events.

Behrman House

11 Edison Place
Springfield, NJ 07081

Editor: Jessica Gurtman

Publisher's Interests
Behrman House publishes quality Judaic textbooks and supplementary materials for the classroom, as well as books about Judaism and Jewish life for children and adults.
Website: www.behrmanhouse.com

Freelance Potential
Published 14 titles in 2004. Of the 14 titles, 2 were by unpublished writers and 2 were by authors who were new to the publishing house. Receives 500+ queries, 50–100 unsolicited mss yearly.

- **Nonfiction:** Publishes chapter books, 5–10 years; middle-grade books, 8–12 years; and young adult books, 12–18 years. Topics include Judaism, religion, theology, prayer, holidays, the Bible, the Holocaust, history, liturgy, Hebrew, and ethics. Also publishes educational resource materials and religious instructional materials for adults.
- **Representative Titles:** *Journey of a Lifetime: The Jewish Life Cycle Book* by Rahel Lurie Musleah (grades 3–5) answers questions about significant milestones in a Jewish life. *Making a Difference* by Bradley Shavit Artson & Gila Gevirtz (grades 7–9) explains to teens both ethical and ritual mitzvot, and offers practical and creative suggestions on how to observe them.

Submissions and Payment
Prefers query with table of contents and sample chapter. Will accept complete ms with résumé and author biography. Accepts photocopies, computer printouts, and simultaneous submissions if identified. SASE. Responds in 2 months. Publication in 18 months. Royalty, 5–10%; advance, $1,500. Flat fee.

Editor's Comments
We would like to see more titles that explore Judaism and expand the reader's understanding. Topics of interest are Jewish holidays and rituals; works of the great Jewish thinkers, writers, and philosophers from ancient to modern times; and history of the Jewish people.

Benchmark Books

Marshall Cavendish
99 White Plains Road
Tarrytown, NY 10591

Editorial Director: Michelle Bisson

Publisher's Interests
This educational publisher offers a list of nonfiction titles used primarily by libraries and in classrooms to supplement the curriculum for grades K–12. All curriculum subject areas are covered including math, science, social studies, history, and literature, and all titles appear as part of series. It is a Marshall Cavendish imprint.
Website: www.marshallcavendish.com

Freelance Potential
Published 135 titles in 2004: a few were developed from unsolicited submissions and 27 were by agented authors. Of the 135 titles, 13 were by authors who were new to the publishing house. Receives 1,000 queries yearly.

- **Nonfiction:** Published 18 easy-to-read books, 4–7 years; 12 chapter books, 5–10 years; 60 middle-grade books, 8–12 years; and 45 young adult books, 12–18 years. Topics include animals, mathematics, science, social studies, history, and world culture.
- **Representative Titles:** *A Child's Day in a Ghanaian City* by Francis Provenacal and Caterine McNamara (grades 2+) explores the city through the eyes of a child and demonstrates that people living in foreign lands are really not that different from us; part of the A Child's Day series. *Carbon* by Giles Sparrow (grades 3 and up) helps students understand the basics of chemistry and how this element behaves; part of The Elements series.

Submissions and Payment
Query with 1–3 chapters and table of contents. Accepts photocopies and computer printouts. SASE. Responds in 6–8 weeks. Publication in 9–18 months. Flat fee.

Editor's Comments
Our goal is "opening new worlds for young readers." We want books that will open the reader's eyes to a new idea and leave them wanting to know more. Since many of our topics are traditional, we want to find writers who can offer a fresh or innovative point of view.

The Bess Press

3565 Harding Avenue
Honolulu, HI 96816

Editor: Réve Shapard

Publisher's Interests
Bess Press features children's fiction and nonfiction picture books relating to Hawaiian history and culture, as well as coloring and activity books. This publisher also offers textbooks and other educational materials for teachers in Hawaii and the Pacific Islands.
Website: www.besspress.com

Freelance Potential
Published 19 titles (11 juvenile) in 2004: 7 were developed from unsolicited submissions. Of the 19 titles, 1 was by a previously unpublished writer and 4 were by authors who were new to the publishing house. Receives 150 unsolicited mss yearly.

- **Fiction:** Published 4 story picture books, 4–10 years. Also publishes young adult books, 12–18 years. Genres include regional fiction, folklore, and folktales. Also publishes coloring books.
- **Nonfiction:** Published 5 concept books, 0–4 years; and 2 young adult books, 12–18 years. Topics include Hawaiian and Pacific Island culture, language, natural history, and literature. Also publishes biographies.
- **Representative Titles:** *The Story of Hula* by Carla Golembe (4–10 years) features whimsical illustrations with lyrical writing about the history, meaning, and spirit of hula. *Surfing A to Z Coloring Book* by Terry Pierce (4–10 years) combines basic information about the sport of surfing with line drawings to color.

Submissions and Payment
Guidelines available. Send complete ms. Accepts photocopies, computer printouts, and simultaneous submissions. SASE. Responds in 4–6 weeks. Publication in 6–12 months. Royalty, 5–10%.

Editor's Comments
At this time, we are interested only in story picture books for children ages four to ten about the culture and people of Hawaii. We also are interested in writers who are familiar with the Department of Education curriculum guidelines.

Bethany House

11400 Hampshire Avenue South
Minneapolis, MN 55438

Submissions Editor

Publisher's Interests
Bethany House is an evangelical publisher of books for all ages, offering fiction and nonfiction for children and young adults. It is a division of the Baker Book House company. Its books are sold in both Christian and general bookstores.
Website: www.bethanyhouse.com

Freelance Potential
Published 14 titles in 2004: 3 were by agented authors. Receives 50–75 queries yearly.

- **Fiction:** Published 1 story picture book, 4–7 years; and 8 middle-grade novels. Genres include adventure, mystery, suspense, and inspirational, contemporary, and historical fiction.
- **Nonfiction:** Published 1 early picture book, 0–4 years; 1 middle-grade title, 8–12 years; and 3 young adult books, 12–18 years.
- **Representative Titles:** *Raising Pure Kids in an Impure World* by Richard & Reneé Durfield (parents) offers strategies for helping parents keep their teens from engaging in premarital sex. *The Missing Maps of Pirate's Haven* by Sigmund Brouwer (8–12 years) follows the accidental detectives to California and a house that once belonged to pirates as they solve another mystery; part of the Accidental Detectives series.

Submissions and Payment
Guidelines available at website. Query appropriate editor by sending fax to 952-996-1304. Not currently accepting unsolicited mss. Responds in 9–12 weeks. Publication period varies. Royalty; advance.

Editor's Comments
We're seeking middle-grade and young adult fiction that is a step beyond the "traditional" series fiction. We'd like to see savvy, contemporary characters dealing with real-life issues with whom today's readers will instantly connect. We prefer shorter series and stand-alones.

Beyond Words Publishing

Suite 500
20827 NW Cornell Road
Hillsboro, OR 97124-9808

Children's Editor: Kristin Hilton

Publisher's Interests
This small West Coast publisher features a list of fiction and nonfiction titles for children age four through young adult. While it does publish fiction, its emphasis is on nonfiction titles that will inspire readers to be the best they can be. Beyond Words also publishes the work of young authors.
Website: www.beyondword.com

Freelance Potential
Published 6 titles in 2004: 4 were developed from unsolicited submissions and 2 were by agented authors. Receives 3,000 unsolicited mss yearly.

- **Fiction:** Publishes story picture books, 4–10 years; middle-grade books, 8–12 years; and young adult books, 12–18 years. Genres include fairy tales, folktales, multicultural fiction, and stories about nature.
- **Nonfiction:** Publishes story picture books, 4–10 years; middle-grade books, 8–15 years; and young adult books, 12–18 years. Also publishes middle-grade books written by young authors.
- **Representative Titles:** *Boys Who Rocked the World* (7–16 years) tells the stories of boy heroes along with writing from boys on how they will impact the world. *Better than a Lemonade Stand: Small Business Ideas for Kids* by Daryl Bernstein (9–12 years) offers unique suggestions for ways kids can earn money from their own creations.

Submissions and Payment
Guidelines available. Send complete ms with description of market and competition. Accepts photocopies, computer printouts, and simultaneous submissions if identified. SASE. Responds in 4–6 months. Publication in 1 year. Royalty, 5–10%; advance.

Editor's Comments
When we started this company we had no publishing experience, but we had faith that anything is possible. We look for writers with the same inspiration and courage, reflected in their writing.

Blackbirch Press

Suite C
15822 Bernardo Center Drive
San Diego, CA 92127

Editorial Director

Publisher's Interests
Blackbirch Press is a large publishing house specializing in educational subjects for students ages four to ten. Its list covers a wide range of subjects, including social studies, science, nature, business, sports, and geography.
Website: www.galegroup.com/blackbirch/

Freelance Potential
Published 125 titles in 2004: 54 were by reprint/licensed properties. Of the 125 titles, 4 were by authors who were new to the publishing house. Receives 100 queries yearly.

- **Nonfiction:** Publishes story picture books, 4–10 years; and middle-grade books, 8–12 years. Topics include science, nature, the environment, ecology, American history, women's history, geography, business, sports, and multicultural subjects.
- **Representative Titles:** *Maps and Symbols* (4–10 years) introduces readers to the basics of geography; part of the Geography First series. *Forensics* (grades 2–4) gives young students a look at this twenty-first century science; part of the Science on the Edge series.

Submissions and Payment
Guidelines available. Query with résumé. No unsolicited mss. Accepts photocopies and simultaneous submissions if identified. SASE. Responds in 4 months. Publication in 1 year. Advance.

Editor's Comments
All of our writers are experts on their subjects. We look for authors who can explore a subject in depth and then write about it in a way that will intrigue young readers while providing them with the latest information available. We have the ability now to expand our list considerably, now that we are part of the Gale Group, so if you have an interest in working with us, we'd like to hear from you. For the coming year we would like to see queries on the subjects of history, social studies, and other curriculum-based subjects. Remember that all our books are done on a work-for-hire basis.

A & C Black Publishers

37 Soho Square
London W1D 3QZ
United Kingdom

Submissions Editor: Clair Weatherhead

Publisher's Interests
Established in 1807, A & C Black is a British publisher offering children's curriculum-based fiction and nonfiction titles for the school and education market.
Website: www.acblack.com

Freelance Potential
Published 70 titles (20 juvenile) in 2004: 40 were by agented authors. Receives 600 queries yearly.

- **Fiction:** Publishes chapter books, 5–10 years; and middle-grade books, 8–12 years. Genres include historical fiction and humor.
- **Nonfiction:** Publishes chapter books, 5–10 years; middle-grade books, 8–12 years. Topics include literacy, math, modern languages, citizenship, science, history, geography, music, art, religion, computers, and technology.
- **Representative Titles:** *Duncan and the Pirates* by Peter Utton (5–10 years) is the tale of a soppy dog and a grumpy pirate who sail the seas to a secret island in search of treasure. *The Copper Treasure* by Melvin Burgess (8–11 years) is a historical novel of life and death set in Victorian London; part of the Flashbacks series.

Submissions and Payment
Guidelines available. Query with résumé. Accepts photocopies and email queries to childrens@acblack.com. SAE/IRC. Responds in 6–8 weeks. Publication period and payment policy vary.

Editor's Comments
Although we are well known for our Who's Who books, we also offer an extensive and varied list of educational titles for teachers, parents, and students. We are interested in original material by authors familiar with children's interests. One of our most popular fiction series, Black Cats, is written by several authors. This series of books for confident readers age eight and up includes spooky stories, silly comedies, and magical tales. Can you add a title that will grab the interest of our audience?

Bloomsbury Children's Books

Suite 712
175 Fifth Avenue
New York, NY 10010

Editor

Publisher's Interests

This medium-sized publishing house offers a list of fiction and non-fiction that includes picture books, chapter books, easy readers, middle-grade titles, and young adult books. Bloomsbury Children's Books usually publishes more fiction than nonfiction.
Website: www.bloomsburyusa.com

Freelance Potential

Published 50 titles in 2004: 25 were by authors who were new to the publishing house.

- **Fiction:** Publishes early picture books, 0–4 years; chapter books, 5–10 years; middle-grade novels, 8–12 years; and young adult books, 12–18 years. Genres include adventure, fantasy, multicultural and ethnic subjects, mystery, science fiction, and stories about sports.
- **Nonfiction:** Publishes early picture books, 0–4 years; middle-grade books, 8–12 years; and young adult books, 12–18 years. Topics include history, humor, sports, and multicultural and ethnic subjects.
- **Representative Titles:** *Clementine and Mungo* by Sarah Dyer (3–8 years) is a story about a young boy whose older sister knows everything, except how to fall asleep peacefully in the dark. *My First Day at Nursery School* by Becky Edwards (3–8 years) is a story that will help ease the worries of young children about to start school.

Submissions and Payment

Send complete ms for picture books. Query for longer works. Accepts photocopies, computer printouts, and simultaneous submissions if identified. SASE. Response time and publication period vary. Royalty; advance.

Editor's Comments

We pride ourselves on the books we publish and the authors whose writing we promote. We are always interested in hearing from new writers who have a story that will delight our readers. We consider every book on its own merit and review each submission on an individual basis.

Blue Sky Press

Scholastic Inc.
557 Broadway
New York, NY 10012-3999

Acquisitions Editor: Bonnie Verburg

Publisher's Interests
Readers of all ages enjoy the fiction books produced by this publisher, which is an imprint of Scholastic. It also offers nonfiction books on topics related to nature and history. Authors must be previously published in order to have their work considered.
Website: www.scholastic.com

Freelance Potential
Published 16 titles in 2004. Receives 5,000 queries yearly.

- **Fiction:** Publishes toddler and early picture books, 0–4 years; easy-to-read books, 4–7 years; story picture books, 0–4 years; chapter books, 5–10 years; middle-grade novels, 8–12 years; and young adult books, 12–18 years. Genres include historical and multicultural fiction, folklore, fairy tales, fantasy, humor, and adventure.
- **Nonfiction:** Publishes middle-grade books, 8–12 years. Topics include nature, the environment, and history.
- **Representative Titles:** *Whales Passing* by Eve Bunting (4+ years) is a picture book about a young boy's excitement when he sights a pod of orca whales. *How Do Dinosaurs Get Well Soon?* by Jane Yolen and Mark Teague (2+ years) is a read-aloud book about the antics of mischievous young dinosaurs who are sick. *Ricky Ricotta's Mighty Robot* by Dav Pilkey (7–10 years) tells the humorous adventure of a mouse and his powerful robot that fights off evil doers; part of the Ricky Ricotta series.

Submissions and Payment
Accepts queries from previously published authors only. No unsolicited mss. Accepts photocopies. SASE. Responds in 6 months. Publication in 2–5 years. Royalty; advance.

Editor's Comments
Please note that we only consider material from previously published writers and we look for highly unique material. We receive a large amount of queries so only send your best—and research what we have published in the past before sending us a query.

Boardwalk Books

Suite 200
8 Market Street
Toronto, Ontario M5E 1M6
Canada

Acquisitions Editor

Publisher's Interests
Boardwalk Books is an imprint of the Canadian publisher Dundurn Press. It publishes young adult fiction, specializing in mysteries, as well as biographies.
Website: www.dundurn.com

Freelance Potential
Published 5 titles in 2004: 1 was developed from an unsolicited submission. Of the 5 titles, 1 was by an author who was new to the publishing house. Receives 250 unsolicited mss yearly.

- **Fiction:** Publishes young adult books, 12–18 years. Genres include contemporary fiction, drama, and mystery.
- **Nonfiction:** Publishes young adult titles, 12–18 years. Features biographies.
- **Representative Titles:** *A Darker Light* by Heidi Priesnitz (YA) is a novel about a young photographer who learns to cope with a diagnosis of macular degeneration. *Find Me Again* by Sylvia Maultash Warsh (YA) is a historical mystery that takes place both in contemporary times and in the days of Catherine the Great; part of the Rebecca Temple Mystery series.

Submissions and Payment
Guidelines available at website. Query, cover letter, 250-word synopsis, résumé, three sample chapters, and manuscript word count, include table of contents for nonfiction; or send complete ms. Accepts photocopies and computer printouts. SASE. Responds in 3–6 months. Publication period varies. Advance.

Editor's Comments
If you wish to submit a manuscript for consideration, first ensure that your book would be a good fit for our publishing program. Please browse our website to learn more about the kinds of books we publish. We are expanding our list of mystery authors for our 12- to 18-year-old audience—take a look at our recent Castle Street Mysteries series for an idea.

Borealis Press Ltd.

8 Mohawk Crescent
Nepean, Ontario K2H 7G6
Canada

Senior Editor: Glenn Clever

Publisher's Interests
This Canadian publisher was founded in 1972 with the express purpose of publishing new Canadian writers. It specializes in Canadian oriented material and offers a catalogue of fiction and nonfiction for children of all ages.
Website: www.borealispress.com

Freelance Potential
Published 20 titles (4 juvenile) in 2004: 18 were developed from unsolicited submissions. Of the 20 titles, 2 were by unpublished writers and 8 were by authors who were new to the publishing house. Receives 50 queries yearly.

- **Fiction:** Publishes story picture books, 4–10 years; and young adult books, 12–18 years. Genres include fantasy and multicultural and ethnic fiction.
- **Nonfiction:** Publishes reference titles about Canadian history. Also offers drama, poetry, and books with multicultural themes.
- **Representative Titles:** *Albert the Talking Rooster* by A.P. Campbell is the story of an unusual rooster who uses the gift of gab when his advice is needed most by his owners. *Aka'k* by Marjorie Kendall is the story of a wolf who protects his family from human predators when oil exploration intrudes on their arctic habitat.

Submissions and Payment
Guidelines available. Query with outline/synopsis and sample chapter. No unsolicited mss. Accepts photocopies and disk submissions. No simultaneous submissions. SASE. Responds in 3–4 months. Publication in 1–2 years. Royalty, 10% of net.

Editor's Comments
We are committed to showcasing the work of Canadian authors and prefer material that has some connection to Canadian traditions, history, or nature. Most of our books also feature some connection between natural human existence, and the beauty of life in general. Please review our catalogue before sending a query.

Boyds Mills Press

815 Church Street
Honesdale, PA 18431

Manuscript Tracker: J. DeLuca

Publisher's Interests
Children's literature with lasting value is the trademark of this well-known publisher. It features titles for young children through young adult readers.
Website: www.boydsmillspress.com

Freelance Potential
Published 60 titles (46 juvenile) in 2004: 25 were developed from unsolicited submissions, 10 were by agented authors, and 6 were reprint/licensed properties. Of the 60 titles, 4 were by unpublished writers and 10 were by new authors. Receives 15,000 mss yearly.

- **Fiction:** Publishes story picture books, 4-10 years; toddler books, concept books, and early picture books, 0-4 years; easy-to-read books, 4-7 years; middle-grade books, 8-12 years; and young adult books, 12-18 years. Genres include adventure stories and multicultural and ethnic fiction.
- **Nonfiction:** Publishes concept books, toddler books, and early picture books, 0-4 years; easy-to-read books, 4-7 years; story picture books, 4-10 years; middle-grade books, 8-12 years; and young adult books, 12-18 years. Topics include history, geography, science, and nature.
- **Representative Titles:** *My Special Day at Third Street School* by Eve Bunting (5+ years) highlights a classroom visit from a well-known author who turns the experience into a book. *Steam Locomotives* by Karl Zimmermann (10+ years) is an authoritative look at the Iron Horses of the past.

Submissions and Payment
Guidelines available. Query with outline; or send complete ms. Accepts photocopies and computer printouts. SASE. Responds in 1 month. Publication period and payment policy vary.

Editor's Comments
We're looking for good middle-grade fiction with fresh ideas and subject matter, and young adult novels of real literary merit. Nonfiction should be entertaining, as well as informative.

Boynton/Cook Publishers

Heinemann
361 Hanover Street
Portsmouth, NH 03801-3912

Editorial Assistant: Melissa Wood

Publisher's Interests
Boynton/Cook Publishers is part of the Heinemann publishing company. Both imprints are devoted to producing top-quality educational products to meet the needs of English teachers and students in grades 7–12. Boynton/Cook specializes in educational texts for English teachers in high school and college and also features titles on theater arts and Third World writing.
Website: www.boyntoncook.com

Freelance Potential
Published 12 titles in 2004: 5 were developed from unsolicited submissions. Receives 1,000+ queries yearly.

- **Nonfiction:** Publishes textbooks, grade 9 and up. Also publishes professional resource materials for educators. Topics include language arts, literature, rhetoric, communication, composition, writing, style, and drama.
- **Representative Titles:** *The Subject Is Story* edited by Wendy Bishop invites students to become more aware of story—in literature, in folktales, in gossip, in their own writing and reading. *10 Easy Ways to Use Technology in the English Classroom* by Hilve Firek (grades 6–12) takes a fresh look at computers, concept mapping software, and presentation packages and demonstrates how all these tools can be valuable tools for reinforcing the study of literature.

Submissions and Payment
Catalogue and guidelines available at website. Query with project description, table of contents, sample issues, illustrations if applicable, chapter summaries, and 3 sample chapters. Accepts photocopies, computer printouts, and simultaneous submissions. SASE. Responds in 6–8 weeks. Publication in 10–12 months. Royalty.

Editor's Comments
We are constantly on the lookout for new voices and visions, and welcome proposals from previously unpublished authors. Please review our website first so you understand what kind of ideas work here.

Branden Books

P.O. Box 812094
Wellesley, MA 02482

Editor: Adolph Caso

Publisher's Interests
Brandon Books has been serving the literary and education communities since 1909. As a historic part of Boston's rich literary history, the house has always embraced both reader and writer in their efforts to document the growth of their community and beyond.
Website: www.branden.com

Freelance Potential
Published 4 titles in 2004: 3 were developed from unsolicited submissions. Of the 4 titles, 2 were by authors who were new to the publishing house. Receives 1,000 queries yearly.

- **Fiction:** Publishes story picture books, 4–10 years; and middle-grade novels, 8–12 years. Genres include historical fiction and mystery. Also publishes stories about friendship and stories with problem-solving themes.
- **Nonfiction:** Published 4 story picture books, 4–10 years. Also publishes young adult titles, 12–18 years. Topics include health, sports, and legal, ethnic, social, and multicultural subjects. Features reference books and biographies.
- **Representative Titles:** *Oh No! Steven* by Elizabeth Burton (YA) features family stories about a famous older brother. *Quiet Hero* by Rosemary Lonborg (all ages) talks about the life of Jim Lonborg, a famous Red Sox pitcher.

Submissions and Payment
Query with 2-paragraph synopsis. No unsolicited mss. Accepts photocopies and computer printouts. SASE. Responds in 1 week. Publication in 6–10 months. Royalty, 5–10%.

Editor's Comments
We have no specific needs at this time but are always interested in new writers who can bring our audience a fresh approach on a historical topic or individual that will both enlighten and entertain. Before sending your query, please research our published books.

Breakwater Books

P.O. Box 2188
St. John's, Newfoundland A1C 6E6
Canada

General Manager: Wade Foote

Publisher's Interests

Breakwater Books was founded in 1973 with the express purpose of publishing books and material that preserve the unique culture of Newfoundland and Labrador and the Maritime provinces. Many of its children's titles are developed to be used as part of the elementary and high school curricula.
Website: www.breakwater.nf.net

Freelance Potential

Published 12 titles (4 juvenile) in 2004: 6 were developed from unsolicited submissions. Of the 12 titles, 1 was by an unpublished writer and 5 were by authors who were new to the publishing house. Receives 600+ queries yearly.

- **Fiction:** Publishes early picture books, 0–4 years; and young adult novels, 12–18 years. Genres include adventure, historical fiction, and humor.
- **Nonfiction:** Publishes chapter books, 5–10 years; middle-grade titles, 8–12 years; and young adult books, 12–18 books. Topics include history, current events, religion, and social and multicultural subjects. Also publishes Canadian history anthologies.
- **Representative Titles:** *Franky Can* by Gerard Thevenet is a humorous but meaningful story about a boy who can do just about anything—except walk. *Fanny for Change* by Jean Hayes Feather shows how two young girls conspire to make changes in their small community.

Submissions and Payment

Catalogues available at website. Query with résumé and clips. No unsolicited mss. Artwork improves chance of acceptance. SAE/IRC. Responds in 8 months. Publication in 1 year. Royalty, 10%.

Editor's Comments

Our goal is to showcase writing that reveals the rich heritage and culture of Canada to children and young people of all ages. If you have an idea for a book that highlights the unique aspects of Atlantic Canada, send us a query.

Broadman & Holman Publishers

1 Lifeway Plaza
Nashville, TN 37234

Children's Team

Publisher's Interests
Although Bibles, textbooks, and reference titles for adults are the mainstay of this Christian publisher, it is expanding its line of children's and youth nonfiction titles and Christian fiction.
Website: www.broadmanholman.com

Freelance Potential
Published 25 titles in 2004: 8 were developed from unsolicited submissions and 4 were by agented authors. Of the 25 titles, 2 were by authors who were new to the publishing house. Receives 300 unsolicited mss yearly.

- **Fiction:** Publishes story picture books, 4–10 years. Genres include historical and contemporary fiction with biblical themes.
- **Nonfiction:** Publishes concept books and toddler books, 0–4 years; easy-to-read books, 4–7 years; story picture books, 4–10 years; middle-grade titles, 8–12 years; and young adult books, 12–18 years. Topics include religion, traditional and retold Bible stories, self-help, and contemporary social issues.
- **Representative Titles:** *Little One's Bible Promises* by Stephen Elkins is a book and accompanying CD that eases young ones into their faith with Bible verses and lullabies. *Secretly Do Good Deeds* by Melody Carson presents children with typical situations they may face every day, and illustrates what Jesus would have said or done.

Submissions and Payment
Guidelines available. Send complete ms for educational resources. Accepts agented submissions only for children's books. Accepts photocopies, computer printouts, and simultaneous submissions if identified. SASE. Responds in 3 months. Publication in 12–18 months. Royalty; advance.

Editor's Comments
We continue to need books for young readers that connect them with their Christian values. Fiction and nonfiction books that elaborate on basic religious themes will be considered.

Brown Barn Books

119 Kettle Creek Road
Weston, CT 06883

Editor: Nancy Hammerslough

Publisher's Interests

Brown Barn Books is a new publisher of books for young adults. Its mission is to bring readers books that make a difference; that introduce readers to new people, the places they live, and the times in which we all live. It is an imprint of the educational publisher Pictures of Record, Inc.
Website: www.brownbarnbooks.com

Freelance Potential

Published 5 titles in 2004: 2 were developed from unsolicited submissions and 1 was by an agented author. Receives 360 queries each year.

- **Fiction:** Publishes young adult books, 12–18 years. Genres include historical and contemporary fiction, adventure, mystery, suspense, and multicultural and ethnic subjects.
- **Representative Titles:** *Running Horsemen* by Dolph LeMoult (14+ years) follows the odyssey of a 14-year-old boy who goes in search of his father, who never returned home at the end of World War II. *The Secret Shelter* by Sandi LeFaucheur (10+ years) is the story of three 12-year-old children living in London who travel in time back to the London Blitz of 1940.

Submissions and Payment

Guidelines available at website. Query. Accepts computer printouts and email submissions to editorial@brownbarnbooks.com. SASE. Response time publication period, and payment policy vary.

Editor's Comments

We are looking for authors who can deliver gripping stories with great characters that will appeal to our readers. Almost any genre is acceptable, from historical fiction to fantasy. Our goal is to publish great books that our readers will remember long after they finish the last chapter and put the book down. We believe reading is a gift and we want to see material that will entertain, surprise, move, and amaze our readers.

The Bureau for At-Risk Youth

A Guidance Channel Company
135 Dupont Street
P.O. Box 760
Plainview, NY 11803-0760

Editor-in-Chief: Sally Germain

Publisher's Interests
The Bureau for At-Risk Youth, dedicated to promoting growth through knowledge and helping youth overcome life's challenges, is a source of guidance and health education materials for educators, guidance counselors, and parents who work with high-risk children. It offers curriculum materials, books, workbooks, videos, and multimedia products suitable for kindergarten through twelfth grade.
Website: www.at-risk.com

Freelance Potential
Published 12 titles in 2004.

- **Nonfiction:** Publishes curriculum and classroom material, activity books, workbooks, and reference titles, grades K–12. Topics include special needs, anger and conflict management, sexual assault, family issues, personal health, violence prevention, substance abuse, hazing and bullying, character education, career development, self-esteem, teen sexuality, and parenting.
- **Representative Titles:** *Fred Fox Learns About Smoking* (grade K–3) teaches about the dangers of smoking through activities, word searches, mazes, coloring pages, and discussion-provoking questions; part of the Pathways to Learning series. *Helping Kids Heal* includes 75 activities to help children recover from trauma and loss, manage difficult emotions, and build self-esteem.

Submissions and Payment
Query or send complete ms. SASE. Responds to queries in 1–3 months; to mss in 2–6 months. Publication in 6 months. Payment policy varies.

Editor's Comments
Most of our authors are experienced professionals in the field of youth intervention. Consider our audience—children from elementary age through high school—and make your submission suitable for their needs. We are looking for material that reinforces important life lessons about positive behavior and attitude.

Buster Books

9 Lion Yard
Tremadoc Road
London SW4 7NQ
United Kingdom

Editor: Philippa Wingate

Publisher's Interests
An imprint of Michael O'Mara Books Limited, this London publisher offers novelty books, activity books, and sets of board books for preschoolers as well as a variety of nonfiction for children ages eight to twelve.
Website: www.mombooks.com/buster

Freelance Potential
Published 40 titles in 2004. Of the 40 titles, 2 were by unpublished writers and 10 were by authors who were new to the publishing house. Receives 50 queries, 200 unsolicited mss yearly.

- **Nonfiction:** Publishes early picture books, 0–4 years; easy-to-read books, 4–7 years; and middle-grade books, 8–12 years. Topics include animals and humor.
- **Representative Titles:** *Cartooning for Beginners* by David Mostyn offers beginners a step-by-step guide to drawing successful cartoons. Exercises are easy to follow and fun. *Sassy Sleepovers* offers young girls ideas, quizzes, tests, games, and advice for creating the perfect night of fun for a sleepover party. This book encourages imagination and creativity.

Submissions and Payment
Guidelines and catalogue available at website. Query with synopsis and sample text. Accepts photocopies, and computer printouts. SASE. Responds only if interested. Publication period varies.
Flat fee.

Editor's Comments
Submissions of nonfiction ideas are welcome from illustrators, authors, and compilers. We like interactive stories that encourage creativity and provide activities to make reading fun. Synopses and sample text are more favorably welcome than complete manuscripts. Please do not send us any fiction, we do not accept it. Send us your best and if we like what we see, we will contact you.

Butte Publications

P.O. Box 1328
Hillsboro, OR 97123-1328

Acquisitions Editor

Publisher's Interests
Butte Publications was founded in 1993 to publish educational materials for students who are deaf or hard of hearing, their teachers, parents, and professionals in the field. Its list offers a mix of resource materials for professionals, skill-building language titles, and books on recreation. This publisher's books are distributed through catalogue only.
Website: www.buttepublications.com

Freelance Potential
Published 6 titles (1 juvenile) in 2004: all were developed from unsolicited submissions. Receives 30 queries yearly.

- **Nonfiction:** Publishes resource and educational books on signing, interpreting, vocabulary, reading, writing, language skills, and speech rearing. Also publishes parenting titles.
- **Representative Titles:** *Deaf Education at the Dawn of the 21st Century* by Bob Rittenhouse (professionals) looks at the field of education and chronicles the evolution of treatments and techniques. *Multiple Meanings for the Young Adult* by Dorothy McCarr (educators) offers motivational exercises on common words with many meanings.

Submissions and Payment
Guidelines available. Query with table of contents, market analysis, and sample chapters. Accepts computer printouts. Availability of artwork improves chance of acceptance. SASE. Responds in 3–6 months. Publication in 1 year. Royalty.

Editor's Comments
Our titles include time-tested, proven materials as well as exciting new innovations in deaf education. Our publishing decisions are guided by our determination to bring our audience the best information. We welcome new writers who can add to our in-depth list with an idea that will help a varied audience. Your credentials and your thoughts about who will buy your work are important factors. Successful works are written with a specific reader in mind.

Candlewick Press

2067 Massachusetts Avenue
Cambridge, MA 02140

Acquisitions: Liz Bicknell

Publisher's Interests
Outstanding children's books for readers of all ages are produced by this independent publisher. Its list includes picture books, easy readers, middle-grade and young adult fiction, nonfiction, poetry collections, and novelty and activity books.
Website: www.candlewick.com

Freelance Potential
Published 200 titles in 2004.

- **Fiction:** Publishes early picture books and toddler books, 0–4 years; middle-grade books, 8–12 years; and young adult books, 12–18 years. Genres include contemporary, multicultural, historical and science fiction; adventure; mystery; humor; fantasy; and stories about sports.
- **Nonfiction:** Publishes concept books and toddler books, 0–4 years; story picture books, 4–10 years; and young adult books, 12–18 years. Topics include animals, history, nature, the environment, and geography. Also publishes biographies for young adults.
- **Representative Titles:** *Dog Blue* by Polly Dunbar (2–5 years) is the story of a boy who loves both dogs and the color blue—and finds a creative way to make his fantasies come true. *Mr. George Baker* by Amy Hest (5–8 years) tells the tale of an elderly man and a young boy, linked by the common pursuit of learning to read. *The Once Upon a Time Map Book* by B. G. Hennessy (6–10 years) offers six comprehensive maps that lead children on a tour of their favorite magical kingdoms and introduces them to the way maps work.

Submissions and Payment
Guidelines available at website. Currently not accepting unsolicited manuscripts or queries.

Editor's Comments
At this time, we are not accepting any unsolicited queries or manuscripts. We suggest that you check our website for future changes that may be made to our submissions policy.

Capstone Press

15 Good Council Drive
Mankato, MN 56001

Editorial Director: Kay Olson

Publisher's Interests
Capstone Press publishes accurate, affordable nonfiction titles for the school and public library market. It features titles for beginning and reluctant readers, as well as ESL students.
Website: www.capstonepress.com

Freelance Potential
Published 300 titles in 2004. Receives numerous queries and unsolicited mss yearly.

- **Nonfiction:** Publishes easy-to-read books, 4–7 years; middle-grade books, 8–12 years; and young adult books, 12–18 years. Topics include social studies, geography, health, science, animals, astronomy, math, technology, sports, arts and crafts, and the human body. Also publishes biographies.
- **Representative Titles:** *Animals Building Homes* (grades 1–2) explores animals in their natural environments and the different ways they build homes. *Ethiopia* (grades 3–4) includes journals, recipes, and traditional craft ideas that give a distinctive perspective to learning about different cultures and people.

Submissions and Payment
Guidelines available at website. Query with cover letter, résumé, and 3 short writing samples. SASE. Responds in 1 month. Publication period varies. Flat fee.

Editor's Comments
Our mission is to help people learn to read and read to learn—we want to give young readers a strong foundation on which to build their reading success. Both new and reluctant readers are drawn into our easy-to-read, richly illustrated books. Our titles are curriculum-aligned for use by educators, librarians, and parents. At this time, we are looking for talented authors who can contribute their research and writing skills to cover social studies, science, and high-low topics for our various imprints. Most of our titles are produced on a work-for-hire, flat-rate basis.

Carolrhoda Books

Lerner Publishing Group
241 1st Avenue North
Minneapolis, MN 55401

Fiction Submissions Editor: Zelda Wagner

Publisher's Interests
Established in 1969 as a publisher of children's trade books, Carolrhoda Books is now an imprint of the Lerner Publishing Group. Its goal is to continue to offer young readers of all ages quality fiction, including board books, novelty books, chapter books, and young adult novels. It no longer publishes any nonfiction.
Website: www.carolrhodabooks.com

Freelance Potential
Published 14 titles in 2004: 10 were developed from unsolicited submissions. Of the 14 titles, 3 were by authors who were new to the publishing house. Receives 500 queries, 2,000 mss yearly.

- **Fiction:** Publishes story picture books, 4–10 years; and young adult books, 12–18 years. Genres include contemporary, mystery, multicultural, and historical fiction.
- **Representative Titles:** *All Year Long* by Kathleen W. Deady (grades K–2) tells the stories of the changing seasons through whimsical verse. *Almost to Freedom* by Vaunda Micheaux Nelson (grades K–2) tells the story of a young girl and her dangerous journey to freedom on the Underground Railroad.

Submissions and Payment
Guidelines available. Accepts submissions in November only. Query with outline and sample chapters; or send complete ms for shorter works. Accepts photocopies and computer printouts. SASE. Responds in 8 months. Publication period varies. Royalty; advance.

Editor's Comments
Please note that our submissions policy has changed. Effective immediately, we will only accept submissions in the month of November. We also are not interested in any nonfiction for the near future. We publish picture books for ages five to eight as well as longer fiction for ages seven and up. We like to see unique, honest stories that stay away from moralizing and overly religious themes. We are also interested in seeing science fiction and fantasy for young readers.

Carson-Dellosa Publishing Company

P.O. Box 35665
Greensboro, NC 27425

Product Acquisitions: Pam Hill

Publisher's Interests
Carson-Dellosa publishes supplementary educational resource materials for use in Pre-K through eighth-grade classrooms. It accepts submissions for teacher resource books, activity books, and student workbooks. Subject areas include language arts, math, test preparation, science, social studies, arts and crafts, and early childhood education topics. It also offers a line of Christian products.
Website: www.carson-dellosa.com

Freelance Potential
Published 100 titles in 2004: less than 5 were developed from unsolicited submissions. Of the 100 titles, less than 5 were by unpublished writers and 5 were by authors who were new to the publishing house. Receives 150 queries yearly.

- **Nonfiction:** Publishes supplementary educational materials, pre-K–grade 8. Topics include language arts, mathematics, science, arts, social studies, early childhood subjects, Christian materials, and crafts.
- **Representative Titles:** *First-Rate Reading* (grades K–3) provides activities based on popular children's literature to teach the five essential components of reading. *Daily Math Warm-Ups* (grades 1–5) is based on the NCTM standards and provides a structure for teaching and assessing students' math skills.

Submissions and Payment
Guidelines available. Query with outline and representative pages. Accepts photocopies, computer printouts, and simultaneous submissions if identified. SASE. Responds in 10–12 months. Publication in 1–2 years. Flat fee.

Editor's Comments
We welcome proposals and manuscripts for supplementary educational books for teachers and writers. Please contact us for submissions guidelines. In your proposal include a summary of your book and its objectives, as well as a description of your intended audience. We do not accept any fiction, children's storybooks, or poetry.

Cartwheel Books

Scholastic Inc.
557 Broadway
New York, NY 11105

Executive Editor: Grace Maccarone

Publisher's Interests
Cartwheel Books, a division of Scholastic Inc., publishes fiction and nonfiction titles on a variety of subjects for young children. It will only consider submissions from agented or previously published authors.
Website: www.scholastic.com

Freelance Potential
Published 100 titles in 2004: 10 were developed from unsolicited submissions, many were by agented authors, and 4 were reprint/licensed properties. Receives 800–1,000 queries, 500–800 unsolicited mss yearly.

- **Fiction:** Published 20 concept books, 20 toddler books, and 20 early picture books, 0–4 years; 20 easy-to-read books, 4–7 years; 10 story picture books, 4–10 years; and 5 chapter books, 5–10 years. Genres include humor, and stories about friendship, families, animals, and holidays.
- **Nonfiction:** Publishes concept books, toddler books, and early picture books, 0–4 years; easy-to-read books, 4–7 years; and story picture books, 4–10 years. Topics include science and math.
- **Representative Titles:** *Zoom!* by Robert Munsch (4–7 years) is a humorous story about a feisty little girl and her amazing 92-speed wheelchair. *The Passover Seder* by Emily Sper (3–7 years) is a hands-on book that introduces young children to the history and traditions of Passover.

Submissions and Payment
Accepts submissions from agents and previously published authors only. Accepts photocopies and computer printouts. SASE. Responds in 3–6 months. Publication period and payment policy vary.

Editor's Comments
We are happy to consider material suitable for preschoolers and young readers. Novelty and manipulative books for children ages four to eight continue to be a priority with us.

Cavendish Children's Books

99 White Plains Road
Tarrytown, NY 10591

Editorial Director: Margery Cuyler

Publisher's Interests
Dedicated to producing books that speak directly to children, this publisher offers a wide variety of books for readers of all levels. Its list includes picture books, chapter books, middle-grade books, and young adult books.
Website: www.marshallcavendish.com

Freelance Potential
Published 23 titles in 2004. Of the 23 titles, 2 were by unpublished writers and 3 were by authors who were new to the publishing house. Receives 500 queries and unsolicited mss yearly.

- **Fiction:** Publishes picture books, 4–10 years; chapter books, 5–10 years; middle-grade books, 8–12 years; and young adult, 12–18 years. Genres include historical fiction, folklore, mysteries, humorous stories, and contemporary fiction.
- **Nonfiction:** Publishes picture books, 4–10 years; chapter books, 5–10 years; middle-grade books, 8–12 years; and young adult books, 12–18 years. Topics include art, animals, science, and nature.
- **Representative Titles:** *Basho and the River Stones* by Tim Myers (4–8 years) tells how a tricky fox learns a lesson from a wise poet. *Down Girl and Sit* by Lucy Nolan (6–9 years) tells the hilarious adventures of two canines that become confused when a cat moves in next door. It takes a look at life in the backyard from the well-intentioned but misguided viewpoint of dogs.

Submissions and Payment
Guidelines available. Send complete ms. Accepts photocopies, and computer printouts. SASE. Responds in 3–6 months. Publication period and payment policy vary.

Editor's Comments
We have added chapter books to our line of quality books, which are perfect for readers who have outgrown picture books but aren't quite ready for full novels. Send us an engrossing story kids will love to read over and over again.

Charlesbridge

85 Main Street
Watertown, MA 02472

Submissions Editor

Publisher's Interests
Charlesbridge publishes quality books for children from birth to age 12, with the goal of creating lifelong readers. Its nonfiction titles focus on nature, science, and multicultural subjects, while its fiction list includes lively picture books.
Website: www.charlesbridge.com

Freelance Potential
Published 30 titles in 2004: 3 were developed from unsolicited submissions, 1 was by an agented author, and 6 were reprint/licensed properties. Of the 30 titles, 1 was by an unpublished writer and 4 were by authors who were new to the publishing house. Receives 2,400 unsolicited mss yearly.

- **Fiction:** Published 1 toddler book, and 3 early picture books, 0–4 years; and 3 story picture books, 4–10 years. Genres include contemporary fiction, folktales, and nature stories.
- **Nonfiction:** Published 3 concept books, 1 toddler book, and 19 early picture books, 0–4 years. Topics include animals, the alphabet, math, nature, animals, and celebrations.
- **Representative Titles:** *Grumbly Bunnies* by Willy Welch (1–6 years) is an eloquent description of the many moods of a family of bunnies. *Sir Cumference and the Dragon of Pi* by Cindy Neuschwander (5–10 years) follows Sir Cumference and Lady Di of Ameter as they seek out the magic number for circles.

Submissions and Payment
Guidelines available. Send complete ms. Accepts photocopies and computer printouts. No simultaneous submissions. SASE. Responds in 2–6 months. Publication in 2–5 years. Royalty.

Editor's Comments
We believe books for children should offer accurate information, present a positive worldview, and embrace a child's innate senses of wonder and fun. We are continually seeking new voices and new visions in children's literature.

Charles River Media

10 Downer Avenue
Hingham, AL 02043

Editorial Department

Publisher's Interests
This publisher offers books and software for graphics professionals, game developers, programmers, and IT personnel, as well as aspiring teens interested in all aspects of game programming.
Website: www.charlesriver.com

Freelance Potential
Published 50 titles (10 juvenile) in 2004: 3 were developed from unsolicited submissions and 6 were by agented authors. Receives 100 queries yearly.

- **Nonfiction:** Publishes how-to and informational books and CD-ROMs for young adults and adults. Topics include game programming, computer graphics, animation, networking, and the Internet.
- **Representative Titles:** *Elementary Game Programming and Simulators Using Jamagic* by Sergio Perez is a complete guide to building a 3-D game from the ground up; a companion CD provides tools, source codes, and games used by real developers. *Designing 3-D Games that Sell* by Luke Ahearn teaches game design using established techniques and tools, and opens the door to more complicated languages by teaching common programming concepts.

Submissions and Payment
Guidelines and catalogue available at website or with #10 SASE ($.76 postage). Query. Accepts photocopies and computer printouts. Availability of artwork improves chance of acceptance. SASE. Responds in 1 month. Publication in 4 months. Royalty, 5–15% of net; advance, $1,000–$7,500.

Editor's Comments
At this time, we are interested in books and software dealing with graphics and animation, game programming, the Internet, and networking. All material should be suitable for an audience over eleven years of age. We assume that most of our readers have some experience in the areas of computers and electronics, so you need not cover the rudiments of your topic.

Chelsea House Publishers

Suite 201
2080 Cabot Boulevard West
Langhorne, PA 19047

Editorial Assistant

Publisher's Interests
This educational publisher specializes in developing curriculum-based books that are used in school classrooms and libraries as well as in public libraries. It publishes no fiction and most of its titles appear as parts of series. Chelsea House Publishers offers books for kindergarten through high school students.
Website: www.chelseahouse.com

Freelance Potential
Published 225 titles in 2004: 2 were by agented authors and 56 were reprint/licensed properties. Of the 225 titles, 112 were by authors who were new to the publishing house.

- **Nonfiction:** Published 56 easy-to-read books, 4–7 years; 56 middle-grade books, 8–12 years; and 112 young adult books, 12–18 years. Topics include American history, world history, African American studies, the classics, criminal justice, sports, popular culture, science, travel, drug education, and Christian studies. Also publishes books about parenting, literary criticism, and reference titles for adults.
- **Representative Titles:** *Judy Blume* by Elisa Ludwig (6–12 years) chronicles the life of this famous children's writer: part of the Who Wrote That? series. *The Horse Family* (grades K–2) explores the similarities and differences between different animals belonging to the same species: part of the Animal Families series.

Submissions and Payment
Guidelines available. All books are assigned. Send résumé with clips or writing samples. No queries or unsolicited manuscripts. SASE. Publication period varies. Flat fee.

Editor's Comments
If you are an experienced author interested in writing for Chelsea House, contact our editorial staff by sending us your résumé and publishing credits. We would like to hear your ideas for an exciting new biography, an indepth look at hot issues in world cultures, or a sophisticated survey of cutting edge science or technology.

Chicago Review Press

814 North Franklin Street
Chicago, IL 60610

Editorial Director: Cynthia Sherry

Publisher's Interests
This mid-sized publisher offers a list of nonfiction titles for readers of all ages. It offers books for and about children including activity books, nature writing, parenting topics, and how-to titles. It also offers books on regional subjects, as well as books on gardening.
Website: www.ipgbook.com

Freelance Potential
Published 47 titles (9 juvenile) in 2004: 4 were developed from unsolicited submissions, 13 were by agented authors, and 10 were reprint/licensed properties. Of the 47 titles, 9 were by unpublished writers and 14 were by authors who were new to the publishing house. Receives 1,500 queries, 1,000 unsolicited mss yearly.

- **Nonfiction:** Published 8 middle-grade books, 8–12 years. Also publishes toddler books, 0–4 years; primary books, 6–9 years; and young adult titles, 12–18 years. Topics include science, mathematics, social issues, history, literature, and art.
- **Representative Titles:** *Salvador Dali and the Surrealists* by Michael Elsohn Ross (10+ years) explores Dali's life and introduces kids to the idea of surrealism through a series of activities. *More Math Games and Activities from around the World* by Claudia Zaslavsky (9+ years) appeals to children, bored by the usual math topics, with a wide range of games and activities from diverse cultures.

Submissions and Payment
Guidelines available. Query with 1–2 sample chapters or projects; or send ms with résumé. Accepts photocopies, computer printouts, and simultaneous submissions. SASE. Responds in 8–10 weeks. Publication in 18 months. Royalty, 7–10%; advance, $1,500–$5,000.

Editor's Comments
We consider our list of children's titles to be the best when it comes to covering a topic, be it history, science, or math. Our mission is to engage young readers through lively subject matter and presentation.

Children's Book Press

2211 Mission Street
San Francisco, CA 94110

Editorial Submissions

Publisher's Interests
This publisher specializes in picture books for elementary school-age children about contemporary life in Latino/Chicano, African American, Asian American, Native American, multiracial, and new immigrant communities.
Website: www.childrensbookpress.org

Freelance Potential
Published 4 titles in 2004: 1 was developed from an unsolicited submission. Receives 1,200 unsolicited mss yearly.

- **Fiction:** Publishes story picture books, 4–10 years. Genres include multicultural, ethnic, and social fiction.
- **Nonfiction:** Publishes story picture books, 4–10 years. Topics include multicultural communities, social concerns, and ethnic issues.
- **Representative Titles:** *Cooper's Lesson* by Sun Yung Shin is the story of a young biracial Korean boy caught in the cultural tension of his community. *A Shelter in Our Car* by Monica Gunning tells about a mother and child from Jamaica who must live in their car until better times come along.

Submissions and Payment
Guidelines available at website. Send complete ms. Accepts photocopies, computer printouts, and simultaneous submissions if identified. SASE. Responds in 2+ months. Publication in 12–18 months. Royalty; advance.

Editor's Comments
Our goal is to broaden the base of children's multicultural and bilingual stories that reflect the diversity and experiences of minority and new immigrant communities in the United States. We like to see children in active roles, and stories told from a child's point of view. Adult characters are fine, as long as young readers can identify with them. Stories should encourage critical thinking about social, personal, and worldy issues.

Children's eLibrary

11th Floor
24 West 25th Street
New York, NY 10010

Submissions Editor

Publisher's Interests
This publisher is dedicated to providing school and library institutions with high-quality, e-books that are based on children's books. Specializing in picture books for young readers, it offers both fiction and nonfiction titles that are published via the Internet only. It is powered by ipicturebooks.com, an affiliate of the AOL Time Warner Book Group.
Website: www.childrenselibrary.com

Freelance Potential
Published 600 titles in 2004: 90 were developed from unsolicited submissions. Receives 2,000 queries yearly.

- **Fiction:** Publishes stories about nature and the environment; humor, historical, multicultural, and ethnic fiction; fantasy; fairy tales; folklore; and folktales.
- **Nonfiction:** Publishes books about nature, the environment, animals, pets, science, technology, and multicultural and ethnic subjects. Also features biographies.
- **Representative Titles:** *A Beautiful Seashell* by Ruth Bornstein shares the memories of a great-grandmother with her great-granddaughter her life as a little girl living by the sea in another country, and how she later came to the United States. *A Kid's Guide on How to Save the Animals* by Billy Goodman teaches children about the endangered animal species in the world, and how to make a difference in helping to save them.

Submissions and Payment
Guidelines available at website. Query via email following instructions at website. SASE. Responds in 1–2 weeks. Publication in 1 year. Royalty.

Editor's Comments
Please make sure you check out our site before submitting your work as we have very specific guidelines. We seek both original and out-of-print children's books for publication.

Children's Press

Scholastic Inc.
90 Sherman Turnpike
Danbury, CT 06816

Editor-in-Chief

Publisher's Interests
This nonfiction imprint is part of the Scholastic corporation. It features nonfiction for readers of all ages, from birth through young adult. Its primary market includes schools and libraries and all of its titles have strong ties to school curriculum. Many of its books appear in a series format.
Website: www.scholasticlibrary.com

Freelance Potential
Published 300 titles in 2004: 50 were by agented authors. Of the 300 titles, 15 were by authors who were new to the publishing house. Receives 2,000 queries yearly.

- **Nonfiction:** Publishes concept books, 0–4 years; easy-to-read books, 4–7 years; story picture books, 4–10 years; chapter books, 5–10 years; and middle-grade books, 8–12 years. Topics include science, geography, sports, social studies, and career guidance. Also publishes biographies, Spanish titles, and hi/lo titles. All titles support elementary and middle school curriculum.
- **Representative Titles:** *African Elephant* by Edana Eckart (pre-K–grade 2) brings emergent readers fun facts about these giant animals: part of the Welcome Books series. *All about Light* by Lisa Trumbauer (grades 1–2) reveals the fascinating facts about how light works: part of the Rookie Read About Science series.

Submissions and Payment
Query with outline/synopsis and sample chapters. No unsolicited mss. SASE. Responds in 2–6 months. Publication in 1–2 years. Royalty. Flat fee.

Editor's Comments
We publish titles on a wide array of subjects and are always interested in writers who can bring us a new subject, or a unique way of looking at an old subject. Keep in mind that we only accept queries; unsolicited manuscripts are not reviewed. Send us a query that explains the purpose of your book and why it is right for us.

Childswork/Childsplay

A Guidance Channel Company
135 Dupont Street
P.O. Box 760
Plainview, NY 11803-0760

Editor: Karen Schader

Publisher's Interests

Geared toward the needs of therapists, teachers, and parents, this publisher offers educational resources that address the social and emotional needs of children and young adults.
Website: www.childswork.com

Freelance Potential

Published 7 titles in 2004: 1 was developed from an unsolicited submission. Of the 7 titles, 1 was by an unpublished writer and 1 was by an author who was new to the publishing house. Receives 200 queries yearly.

- **Nonfiction:** Publishes workbooks, therapeutic games, activity books, and audio and video cassettes, 6–12 years. Topics include anger control, conflict resolution, behavioral problems, social skills, ADD/ADHD, play therapy, teen sexuality, bullying, self-esteem, cooperation, substance abuse, and special education. Also publishes parenting resources for family-based issues.
- **Representative Titles:** *The Rabbit Who Lost His Hop* (4–8 years) teaches specific social, emotional, and behavioral skills to young, impulsive readers; part of the Early Prevention series. *Teaching Teens to Create Their Own Solutions* by Lawrence E. Shapiro (12+ years) provides practical activities to help teens deal with depression, social rejection, and family problems.

Submissions and Payment

Guidelines available with SASE. Query with clips or writing samples. Accepts photocopies and computer printouts. SASE. Responds in 2 months. Publication period varies. Flat fee.

Editor's Comments

Although our target audience is primarily adult, our products must also be fun to read and do by the children who use them. Your ideas should have a clear therapeutic value, be carefully thought-out, and useful. Let us know how your product differs from others on the market.

Mission-Driven Publishers
Tegan Culler
Child & Family Press/Child Welfare League of America

Child & Family Press is the publishing arm of the Child Welfare League of America (CWLA). Founded in 1920, it is the oldest and largest membership-based child welfare organization in the country. More than 1,100 public and private child-serving agencies belong to CWLA, including adoption agencies, child and foster care providers, physical and mental health professionals, and substance abuse counselors.

From its beginning, CWLA has provided print resources to its members. The publications range from pamphlets and issue briefs to reports on research. These kinds of material are either written in-house or by solicited experts. In 1993, Child & Family Press came out with its first picture book, the extremely successful *The Kissing Hand*, and began to sell books in the trade market as well.

Tegan Culler, Assistant Director of Publications, says, "We now publish about six books a year, two or three of them about parenting. We're *mission-driven* publishers." Culler says Child & Family Press is open to unsolicited submissions, and receives about 700 a year. The picture book or nonfiction manuscript must speak to issues children face today. Culler says she is also open to books that have been previously published as long as the author still has the copyright. *A Look in the Mirror: Freeing Yourself from the Body Image Blues* was originally self-published by author Valerie Rainon McManus. McManus is a licensed clinical social worker, specializing in child- and women-focused areas.

Unlike most nonprofit organizations, Child & Family Press enters into royalty contracts with authors. The editorial staff prefers complete manuscript submissions.

Child Welfare League of America

3rd Floor
440 1st Street NW
Washington, DC 20001

Assistant Director of Publications: Tegan Culler

Publisher's Interests
The goal of this publisher is to offer relevant and timely books and materials that encourage improved welfare services to children and their families. Its list includes informational books for welfare professionals and parents, as well as children's titles.
Website: www.cwla.org/pubs

Freelance Potential
Published 6 titles (5 juvenile) in 2004. Of the 5 titles, 3 were by unpublished writers and all were by authors who were new to the publishing house. Receives 500+ unsolicited mss yearly.

- **Fiction:** Publishes story picture books, 4–10 years; chapter books, 5–10 years; and middle-grade books, 8–12 years. Genres include contemporary fiction about social issues.
- **Nonfiction:** Publishes titles for professionals in the fields of social work, human services, child welfare, and child care. Topics include adoption, foster care, child abuse and neglect, teen pregnancy, special needs, and learning disabilities. Also publishes books on parenting and family issues.
- **Representative Titles:** *ADD Not BAD* by Audrey Penn (5–10 years) helps young children understand other children with attention deficit disorder. *Achieving Excellence in Special Needs Adoption* by Madeline Freundlich & Ann Sullivan (welfare professionals) features articles on key issues surrounding special-needs adoption.

Submissions and Payment
Send complete ms. Accepts photocopies, computer printouts, email submissions to tculler@cwla.org, and simultaneous submissions if identified. SASE. Responds in 6–7 months. Publication in 2 years. Royalty.

Editor's Comments
We are looking for children's books that provide young readers with the age-appropriate resources they need to handle certain situations. Material must be original and engaging.

Christian Ed. Publishers

P.O. Box 26639
San Diego, CA 92196

Assistant Editor: Janet Ackelson

Publisher's Interests
Focusing on the Bible, this publisher offers curriculum materials and crafts for children and youth. It aims to provide educational material that teaches children about God, how to grow in their Christian lives, and share their faith with others.
Website: www.christianedwarehouse.com

Freelance Potential
Published 84 titles (11 juvenile) in 2004: 6 were by unpublished writers and 10 were by authors who were new to the publishing house. Receives 300 queries yearly.

- **Fiction:** Publishes religious fiction, pre-K–grade 12. All work is on assignment only.
- **Nonfiction:** Publishes Christian educational titles, Bible-based curriculum, and Bible club materials, grades K–12.
- **Representative Titles:** *Cubby Bears for Jesus* (4–5 years) helps teach children love and respect for God, and helps form the basis for faith in Jesus. *Teaching Children to Pray* (grades 3–4) offers different prayers and engaging activities to teach children how and why we talk to God.

Submissions and Payment
Guidelines and catalogue available with 9x12 SASE (4 first-class stamps) All work by assignment only. Publication in 12–18 months. Flat fee, $.03 per word.

Editor's Comments
We are always eager to work with quality writers who are active members of a church, and relate well to the age group they are writing for. Currently we are only accepting preschool-age curriculum materials. Easy-to-use crafts are of interest to us and we look for activities that make it simple to teach God's word, while being fun for youngsters to learn. We want children to apply what they have learned to their everyday lives.

Christian Focus Publications

Geanies House, Fearn by Tain
Ross-shire IV20 1TW
Scotland

Children's Editor: Catherine Mackenzie

Publisher's Interests
Located in Scotland, Christian Focus publishes books that bring glory to God and help readers remain faithful to God's word. Its list includes biblically accurate, non-denominational, evangelical books for adults and children.
Website: www.christianfocus.com

Freelance Potential
Published 100 titles (35 juvenile) in 2004: 2 were developed from unsolicited submissions and 1 was by an agented author. Receives 360 queries, 240 unsolicited mss yearly.

- **Fiction:** Publishes chapter books, 7–10 years; middle-grade books, 9–12 years; and young adult books, 12+ years. Genres include contemporary Christian fiction.
- **Nonfiction:** Publishes Christian biographies, Bible story books, devotionals, puzzle books, and activity books.
- **Representative Titles:** *Arabella Finds Out* by Jacqueline Whitehead is about a rich and spoiled child who discovers that possessions are not the only valuable things in life. *A Girl of Two Worlds* by Lorna Eglin tells about a young Maasai girl who learns to juggle the Christian world with her Maasai life at a missionary boarding school.

Submissions and Payment
Guidelines available at website. Query with author information sheet, synopsis, chapter headings, and 3 sample chapters. Send complete ms for works shorter than 10 chapters. Accepts email submissions to Catherine.Mackenzie@christianfocus.com. SAE/IRC. Does not return ms to authors outside the UK. Response time, publication period, and payment policy vary.

Editor's Comments
Our aim is to help children find out about God and get them enthusiastic about reading the Bible. Our children's books are bright, fun, and full of biblical concepts, making them an ideal way to help children discover Christ for themselves.

Christopher-Gordon Publishers

Suite 12
1502 Providence Highway
Norwood, MA 02062

Sr. Vice President: Susanne F. Canavan

Publisher's Interests
Christopher-Gordon was established to provide educational materials for administrators, teachers, school staff developers, and curriculum coordinators. It concentrates on topics of universal interest to educators at all grade levels.
Website: www.christopher-gordon.com

Freelance Potential
Published 16 titles in 2004: 4 were developed from unsolicited submissions. Receives 150 queries, 50 unsolicited mss yearly.

- **Nonfiction:** Publishes professional enrichment materials for educators. Topics include literacy, administration, classroom management, general education, teaching skills, self-development, mathematics, science, technology, supervision, literature, education law, and cognitive thinking.
- **Representative Titles:** *Developing Effective Assessments to Improve Teaching and Learning* by Loyde W. Hales & Jon C. Marshall (educators) is a comprehensive guide for integrating assessment methods into the curriculum. *Inquiry, Literacy, and Learning in the Middle Grades* by Lauren Freedman & Holly Johnson (educators) emphasizes cognitive strategies for literacy development across the curriculum.

Submissions and Payment
Guidelines and catalogue available with #10 SASE ($.57 postage) or at website. Query with table of contents, sample chapters, and market analysis; or send complete ms. Accepts photocopies. SASE. Response time varies. Publication in 18 months. Royalty; advance.

Editor's Comments
Our materials are used most frequently by educators for professional enrichment. Our overall strategy is to publish a controlled number of outstanding projects each year. We work carefully and thoughtfully with our authors to develop a manuscript for its intended market, and we pride ourselves on our willingness to accept new ideas and alternative ways of doing things.

Chrysalis Children's Books

The Chrysalis Building
London W10 6SP
England

Publisher: Sarah Fabiny

Publisher's Interests
Books for children from birth to age 13 are included on the list of this British publisher. It publishes more than 100 fiction, trade nonfiction, and educational titles each year.
Website: www.chrysalisbooks.co.uk

Freelance Potential
Published 179 titles in 2004: 1 was developed from an unsolicited submission, 15 were by agented authors, and 4 were reprint/licensed properties. Of the 179 titles, 1 was by an unpublished writer and 3 were by authors who were new to the publishing house. Receives 200 unsolicited mss yearly.

- **Fiction:** Published 4 toddler books, 0–4 years. Genres include humor and animal stories.
- **Nonfiction:** Published 10 concept books, and 10 toddler books, 0–4 years; 15 story picture books, 4–10 years; 100 middle-grade books, 8–12 years; and 40 young adult books, 12–18 years. Topics include science, geography, math, history, citizenship, special needs, sports, languages, and religion. Also offers reference materials for students, and resources for teachers.
- **Representative Titles:** *Floating and Sinking* by Jack Challenger (6–9 years) introduces simple science concepts through facts, experiments, and activities; part of the Start-Up Science series. *Space Dramas* (8+ years) offers an insight into the history of space exploration; part of the Space Busters series.

Submissions and Payment
Send complete ms with résumé. Accepts photocopies and Macintosh disk submissions. SAE/IRC. Responds in 2 months. Publication period varies. Flat fee.

Editor's Comments
We like to see books that educate and entertain young children. Titles for older readers should introduce educational concepts while capturing a student's imagination.

Clarion Books

Houghton Mifflin Company
215 Park Avenue South
New York, NY 10003

Editorial Director/Associate Publisher: Dinah Stevenson

Publisher's Interests
This publisher, who is an imprint of Houghton Mifflin, offers active picture books, lively fiction, and nonfiction for infants through young adult readers.
Website: www.hmco.com

Freelance Potential
Published 60 titles in 2004: 30 were by agented authors, and 5 were reprint/licensed properties. Of the 60 titles, 10 were by authors who were new to the publishing house. Receives 500 queries, 2500 unsolicited mss yearly.

- **Fiction:** Publishes picture books, 3-8 years; chapter books, 7-10 years; middle-grade novels, 8-12 years; and young adult novels, 12-18 years. Genres include adventure, folktales, fairy tales, and historical and science fiction.
- **Nonfiction:** Publishes picture books, 3-6 years; middle-grade books, 8-12 years; and young adult books, 12-18 years. Topics include nature, ecology, biography, science, history, holidays, and multicultural and ethnic issues.
- **Representative Titles:** *Dinah!* by Kae Nishimura (3-6 years) is the story of a cat's adventure in the outside world and discovery of the meaning of family and home. *Dust to Eat* by Michael L. Cooper (YA), offers a look at the tumultuous period in the 1930s during the Great Depression and Dust Bowl disaster in the Midwest.

Submissions and Payment
Guidelines available. Query or send complete ms for chapter books and novels; send complete ms for picture books. Accepts photocopies and computer printouts. SASE. Responds in 4 months. Publication in 2 years. Royalty.

Editor's Comments
We receive a high volume of queries and mss. Send us something that is well-written, new, and exciting. We are looking for picture books that deal honestly with children's emotions.

Clear Light Publishers

823 Don Diego
Santa Fe, NM 87505

Publisher: Houghton Harmon

Publisher's Interests
All of the books found on this publisher's list relate to one of the following areas: American Indian culture, religion, or history; Western Americana; Eastern philosophy and religion; U.S. and world history. Its list includes titles for young readers between the ages of four and eighteen.
Website: www.clearlightbooks.com

Freelance Potential
Published 15 titles (6 juvenile) in 2004. Receives 200 mss yearly.

- **Fiction:** Publishes story picture books, 4–10 years; and young adult books, 12–18 years. Genres include historical, regional, multicultural, and inspirational fiction.
- **Nonfiction:** Published 6 middle-grade books, 8–12 years. Also publishes young adult titles, 12–18 years. Topics include animals, nature, history, religion, multicultural subjects, social issues, health, and fitness. Also publishes biographies.
- **Representative Titles:** *Always the Heart* by Jim Sagelo (grades 7 and up) is a coming-of-age story about a young Navajo girl, loosely based on the legend of the Changing Woman. *Baby Learns to Count* by Jessie Ruffenach is written in both Navajo and English.

Submissions and Payment
Send complete ms. Accepts photocopies, computer printouts, and simultaneous submissions if identified. Availability of artwork improves chance of acceptance. SASE. Responds in 3 months. Publication in 1 year. Royalty.

Editor's Comments
We welcome manuscript submissions for books in any of the categories listed above; however we encourage you to review our catalogue to help you determine whether your book may be appropriate for us. In general, we are on the lookout for books that can be published in a bilingual format. Retold legends and folktales are always of interest.

Concordia Publishing House

3558 South Jefferson Avenue
St. Louis, MO 63118-3968

Editorial Assistant: Brandy Overton

Publisher's Interests
Founded in 1869 to preserve the German Lutheran heritage in the U.S., Concordia Publishing House provides resources that meet the needs of Christians at all stages of life, from birth to death. Supplementing its adult list are books for children and teens, as well as catechisms, resource programs, and devotionals. It does not accept freelance manuscripts but will consider assigning work to writers who submit queries or résumés.
Website: www.cph.org

Freelance Potential
Published 50 titles (32 juvenile) in 2004. Of the 50 titles, 1 was by an unpublished writer and 4 were by authors who were new to the publishing house. Receives 1,000–1,500 queries yearly.

- **Nonfiction:** Publishes early picture books, 0–4 years; easy-to-read books, 4–7 years; story picture books, 4–10 years; middle-grade books, 8–12 years; and young adult books, 12–18 years. Topics include religious issues. Also publishes devotionals and books for families.
- **Representative Titles:** *A Surprise in Disguise* by Jeffrey E. Burkart retells the Bible story of the disciples' encounter with Jesus on the road to Emmaus. *Soup Kitchen Suspicion* by Dandi Mackall (6–9 years) is a mystery that demonstrates how God helps the characters in the story live out Christian values; part of the Cinnamon Lake Mysteries series.

Submissions and Payment
No unsolicited mss. All work is done on assignment only. Query or send résumé.

Editor's Comments
Everything we publish is meant to strengthen our readers' Christian faith and encourage them in their discipleship. Our books for very young children introduce them to Jesus, while our books for teens offer a Christian perspective on the real-life issues they face.

Contemporary Drama Service

Meriwether Publishing Ltd.
885 Elkton Drive
Colorado Springs, CO 80907

Associate Editors: Theodore Zapel & Arthur Zapel

Publisher's Interests
One-act plays, oral interpretations, prevention plays, speech contest materials, and full-length royalty plays are among the types of drama available from Contemporary Drama Service. Its catalogue also includes acting textbooks, how-to speech and theater textbooks, scenes for students, and improvisation and theater games.
Website: www.contemporarydrama.com

Freelance Potential
Published 50–60 titles (45 juvenile) in 2004. Of the 50–60 titles, 5 were by unpublished writers and 30 were by authors who were new to the publishing house. Receives 1,500 queries yearly.

- **Fiction:** Publishes middle-grade plays, 8–12 years; and young adult plays, 12–18 years. Publishes musicals, folktales, and fantasies. Also offers skits, adaptations, novelty plays, parodies, and social commentaries.
- **Nonfiction:** Publishes young adult books, 12–18 years. Features books about improvisation, theater games, speech, acting techniques, and theater arts.
- **Representative Titles:** *Bethlehem P. D.* by Daniel Wray is a mystery with a Christmas theme that spoofs the television show, *Dragnet*. *Comedy Improvisation* by Delton T. Horn includes performance tips and exercises for young actors interested in mastering the elements of successful improvisation.

Submissions and Payment
Guidelines available. Query with outline/synopsis. Accepts photocopies, computer printouts, and simultaneous submissions if identified. SASE. Responds in 6 weeks. Publication in 6 months. Royalty. Flat fee. Special projects, negotiable.

Editor's Comments
Plays for students in the middle grades through college are a specific need this year. Please provide a list of your publishing credits with your query, and tell us about your theatrical experience.

Cook Communications Ministries

4050 Lee Vance View
Colorado Springs, CO 80918-7100

Editorial Assistant: Laura Riley

Publisher's Interests
Committed to helping Christians embrace wholeness of life in Christ and develop the gifts God has given them, Cook Communications Ministries offers books for preschool through middle-school children. In addition to their adult list, it also provides resources for teachers in children's ministry.
Website: www.cookministries.com

Freelance Potential
Published 75 titles (30 juvenile) in 2004: 5 were developed from unsolicited submissions and 49 were by agented authors. Of the 75 titles, 1 was by an unpublished writer and 5 were by authors who were new to the publishing house. Receives 1,500 queries yearly.

- **Fiction:** Publishes concept books, toddler books, and early picture books, 0–4 years; easy-to-read books, 4–7 years; chapter books, 5–10 years; and middle-grade books, 8–12 years. Also publishes books in series, 8–12 years. Genres include inspirational and religious fiction.
- **Nonfiction:** Publishes concept books and early picture books, 0–4 years; story picture books, 4–10 years; and middle-grade books, 8–12 years. Topics include religion and social issues. Also publishes self-help titles and reference books for adults.
- **Representative Titles:** *What Do You See When You See Me?* by Jeannie St. John Taylor (4–7) tells of a girl who gets a glimpse of the young spirit inside an elderly woman. *Baby Bible Animals* by Robin Currie introduces toddlers to 22 Bible stories that feature animals.

Submissions and Payment
Guidelines available. Query with clips. Accepts photocopies and simultaneous submissions if identified. SASE. Responds in 2 weeks. Publication in 2 years. Payment policy varies.

Editor's Comments
If you're interested in writing for our Sunday school papers, please see the specific guidelines at our website. If you'd like to write for our Bible-in-Life™ curriculum, first fill out our online questionnaire.

Cornell Maritime Press

P.O. Box 456
Centreville, MD 21617

Managing Editor: Charlotte Kurst

Publisher's Interests
Established in 1938, this regional publisher specializes in instructional books on the maritime arts and sciences, and titles about the Chesapeake Bay area of Maryland. Its small children's list includes both fiction and nonfiction for young readers.
Website: www.cornellmaritimepress.com

Freelance Potential
Published 12 titles (4 juvenile) in 2004: all were developed from unsolicited submissions. Receives 500 queries yearly.

- **Fiction:** Published 2 early picture books, 0–4 years; and 1 middle-grade book, 8–12 years. Genres include regional fiction, contemporary fiction, and mystery.
- **Nonfiction:** Published 1 chapter book, 5–10 years. Topics include maritime history and seamanship. Also publishes titles on nautical knowledge, boating and marine lore for adults, as well as books on topics relating to Maryland.
- **Representative Titles:** *Secret of Belle Meadow* by Mary McVicker (grades 4 and up) is a mystery about a young Virginia girl who finds an old diary hidden during the Revolutionary War, and seeks to discover the treasure it tells about. *Majesty from Assateague* by Harvey Hagman (grades 4–8) is a lesson of courage, will, and persistence as a determined boy and a special pony learn to adjust to life together.

Submissions and Payment
Guidelines available. Query with synopsis and sample chapters. Accepts photocopies and computer printouts. SASE. Responds in 1 month. Publication in 7 months. Royalty.

Editor's Comments
We are interested in queries for children's books that relate to Maryland and the Chesapeake Bay. Titles that relate to boating and the sea are also welcome. Writers interested in submitting to us should be able to write for young readers and convey the unique qualities that are found in Maryland's history.

Corwin Press

2455 Teller Road
Thousand Oaks, CA 91320

Editorial Director: Robert D. Clouse

Publisher's Interests
Corwin Press publishes materials for kindergarten through grade twelve educators, as well as administrators, specialists, and principals. Its list includes practical manuals and research-based books that offer solutions to educational issues.
Website: www.corwinpress.com

Freelance Potential
Published 120 titles in 2004: 10-15 were developed from unsolicited submissions, 1-2 were by agented authors, and 3-5 were reprint/licensed properties. Of the 120 titles, 90-120 were by unpublished writers and 114 were by authors who were new to the publishing house. Receives 100+ queries yearly.

- **Nonfiction:** Publishes books for educators in grades K-12. Topics include administration, assessment, evaluation, professional development, curriculum development, classroom practice, special education, gifted and talented education, bilingual learning, counseling, school health, and educational technology.
- **Representative Titles:** *Reading Strategies for Elementary Students with Learning Difficulties* by William N. Bender & Martha J. Larkin (educators) presents a variety of instructional techniques for the classroom. *What's So Funny about Education?* by Lou Fournier & Tom McKeith (educators) is a satirical look at the current state of American education.

Submissions and Payment
Guidelines available. Query with outline and prospectus, including alternative titles, rationale, prospective market, and competitive analysis. SASE. Response time varies. Publication in 7 months. Royalty.

Editor's Comments
Our goal is to provide practical, hands-on resources to help educational professionals work better, and advance the field of education for all levels of learners. We are looking for material that is based on theory and research but drawn from real-world examples, and also immediately applicable to the classroom.

Coteau Books

401-2206 Dewdney Avenue
Regina, Saskatchewan S4R 1H3
Canada

Managing Editor: Nik L. Burton

Publisher's Interests
This Canadian publisher, founded in 1975, offers a list that includes poetry, fiction, drama, children and young adult chapter books, and quality nonfiction. It only publishes the work of Canadian authors.
Website: www.coteaubooks.com

Freelance Potential
Published 19 titles in 2004: 2 were developed from unsolicited submissions and 1 was by an agented author. Of the 19 titles, 9 were by unpublished writers and 9 were by authors who were new to the publishing house. Receives 1,000+ queries, 500+ mss yearly.

- **Fiction:** Published 4 chapter books, 5–10 years; 4 middle-grade novels, 8–12 years; and 4 young adult books, 12–18 years. Genres include historical, regional, and contemporary fiction, mystery, suspense, and humor.
- **Representative Titles:** *The International Polly McDoodle* by Mary Woodbury (YA) sees Polly and her friend, Kyle, off on a trip to Italy where they find themselves in the middle of a mystery; part of the Polly McDoodle mystery series. *Dinosaur Breakout* by Judith Silverthorne (9+ years) finds a 12-year-old boy sent back in time millions of years on a journey from which he may never return.

Submissions and Payment
Canadian authors only. Guidelines available with 9x12 SASE ($.90 Canadian postage). Query with summary, writing samples, and curriculum vitae. Or send complete ms. Accepts photocopies and computer printouts. No simultaneous submissions. SASE. Responds in 3–6 months. Publication in 1–2 years. Royalty, 10%.

Editor's Comments
We cannot stress enough that we only publish Canadian authors! Many of our titles have won awards, and our mission continues to be to find and develop the best talents and to bring readers works of the highest literary merit.

Covenant Communications

Box 416
American Fork, UT 84003-0416

Managing Editor: Shauna Humphries

Publisher's Interests
All of the books from this publisher promote the faith of members of The Church of Jesus Christ of Latter-day Saints. The children's titles from Covenant Communications range from beginning prayer books for young children to inspirational works for young adults.

Website: www.covenant-lds.com

Freelance Potential
Published 80 titles in 2004: 15 were developed from unsolicited submissions and 4 were reprint/licensed properties. Of the 80 titles, 12 were by unpublished writers and 17 were by authors who were new to the publishing house. Receives 600 mss yearly.

- **Fiction:** Publishes early picture books, 0–4 years; story picture books, 4–10 years; and young adult books, 12–18 years. Genres include adventure, humor, suspense, romance, science fiction, and inspirational and historical fiction.
- **Nonfiction:** Publishes concept books and toddler books, 0–4 years; easy-to-read books, 4–7 years; and story picture books, 4–10 years. Topics include history, religion, and regional subjects. Also publishes biographies, activity books, novelty and board books, photo essays, and reference titles.
- **Representative Titles:** *Long Road Home* by Cheri Crane (YA) teaches the importance of personal testimony. *The Miracles of Jesus* by Val Bagley introduces young children to the miracles Jesus performed.

Submissions and Payment
Guidelines available at website. Send ms with summary. Accepts photocopies, computer printouts, disk submissions, and email to shaunah@covenant-lds.com. SASE. Responds in 3 months. Publication in 6–12 months. Payment policy varies.

Editor's Comments
You must be knowledgeable about LDS doctrine and values if you wish to submit your work to us. Visit our website for more details.

Creative Bound

P.O. Box 424
151 Tansley Drive
Carp, Ontario K0A 1L0
Canada

Editor: Gail Baird

Publisher's Interests

A nonfiction publisher, Creative Bound specializes in books that deal with the broad topic of personal growth. Issues covered include stress management, life balance, leadership, family life, reaching one's potential, and relationships. Although most of its titles have targeted adult readers, Creative Bound resumed reviewing submissions of children's material in 2004.
Website: www.creativebound.com

Freelance Potential

Published 4 titles in 2004: 1 was developed from an unsolicited submission. Of the 4 titles, 2 were by unpublished writers and 2 were by authors who were new to the publishing house. Receives 120 queries yearly.

- **Nonfiction:** Publishes informational and self-help books. Topics include parenting, personal growth, health, fitness, spirituality, recovery, healing, business, motivation, and teaching.
- **Representative Titles:** *The Wisdom of Oma* by Karen Vos Braun is a tribute to the author's grandmother that features 23 of Oma's "gifts of advice." *Bringing Your Work to Life* by William J. Mills provides practical ways to discover one's purpose in life and to transform a job into a meaningful and rewarding experience.

Submissions and Payment

Guidelines available with 6x9 SAE/IRC. Accepts photocopies and IBM disk submissions. SAE/IRC. Responds in 1 month. Publication in 6–12 months. Royalty.

Editor's Comments

Please consult our guidelines before preparing your submission. They are available by mail and at our website, where you may also download a copy of our manuscript submission form. We require you to complete this form in full, following the instructions carefully. We will not consider any submission unless it is accompanied by this form.

The Creative Company

123 South Broad Street
Mankato, MN 56001

Editor: Aaron Frisch

Publisher's Interests
A small publisher, The Creative Company specializes in nonfiction books for children in the elementary grades. Most titles are of an educational nature, and most are organized into series of four to eight books. Picture books, though very few, also appear on its annual list, along with some titles for older readers.

Freelance Potential
Published 100 titles in 2004: 8 were developed from unsolicited submissions and 4 were by agented authors. Of the 100 titles, 1 was by an unpublished writer and 4 were by authors who were new to the publishing house. Receives 200 unsolicited mss yearly.

- **Fiction:** Publishes story picture books, 4–10 years; and young adult books, 12–18 years.
- **Nonfiction:** Publishes story picture books, 4–10 years; chapter books, 5–10 years; and young adult books, 12–18 years. Topics include science, sports, music, history, zoology, architecture, geography, nature, the environment, animals, astronomy, the arts, literature, humanities, world history, and explorers. Also publishes poetry.
- **Representative Titles:** *Mountains* by Charles Rotter explores these geographic wonders through words and photographs; part of the LifeViews series. *Mimicry and Camouflage* by Mary Hoff describes how some creatures use these devices as protection from predators or as a means of finding food; part of the World of Wonder series.

Submissions and Payment
Guidelines available. Send complete ms. Accepts photocopies. SASE. Responds in 10–12 weeks. Publication in 2 years. Flat fee.

Editor's Comments
If you would like to propose a nonfiction series, keep in mind that the series should include four to eight titles, with each title running 700–3,000 words in length. We have no restrictions on subject matter. Our picture books target a sophisticated audience of readers and may be stories, poetry, or biographical tributes.

Creative Learning Press

P.O. Box 320
Mansfield Center, CT 06250

Editor: Kris Morgan

Publisher's Interests

For the past 25 years, this publisher has provided teachers and parents with high quality educational products, resources, and programs. It offers a variety of curriculum areas such as language arts, history, science, and math. In addition, it offers activity books and manuals for teachers working with gifted children.
Website: www.creativelearningpress.com

Freelance Potential

Published 50 titles in 2004: 5 were developed from unsolicited submissions. Receives 100 queries, 100 unsolicited mss yearly.

- **Nonfiction:** Publishes textbooks, educational materials, how-to titles, teaching resources, and audio cassettes, grades K–12. Topics include science, mathematics, language arts, geography, history, research skills, business, fine arts, and leadership. Also offers materials for gifted students.
- **Representative Titles:** *Engineering the City* by Matthys Levy & Richard Pnachy (grades 4–9) tells the fascinating story of how infrastructure from power lines, bridges, sewers, and tunnels are built, work, and affect the environment of the city and land around them. *Skyscrapers* by Carol A. Johmann (grades 3–8) lets students plan a model city and try out the roles involved in its construction. It includes activities that will involve building decisions and solving design problems.

Submissions and Payment

Query with sample pages; or send complete ms with résumé and artwork. Accepts photocopies, computer printouts, and email to clp@creativelearningpress.com. SASE. Responds in 1 month. Publication period varies. Royalty.

Editor's Comments

We are always on the lookout for exciting hands-on books and activities that engage students, and develop creative thinking skills. If you have an idea for a book that goes beyond the basics that is fun and intriguing, send us a query.

Creative Teaching Press, Inc.

15342 Graham Street
P.O. Box 2723
Huntington Beach, CA 92649

Director/Assistant: Rebecca Cleland

Publisher's Interests
This educational publisher offers a wide range of materials for use in classrooms for grades preK–8, including resource books, charts, borders, and bulletin boards. It also offers a few books for emergent readers, but these make up only a small part of its offerings. Much of their material is produced by teachers.
Website: www.creativeteaching.com

Freelance Potential
Published 80+ titles in 2004: 4 were by unpublished writers and 20 were by authors who were new to the publishing house. Receives 30 queries, 300 unsolicited mss yearly.

- **Fiction:** Publishes easy-to-read books, 4–7 years. Genres include ethnic and multicultural fiction, fantasy, and folktales.
- **Nonfiction:** Publishes easy-to-read books, 4–7 years. Topics include history, social issues, arts and crafts, and mathematics. Also features special education and multicultural titles.
- **Representative Titles:** *Creative Puzzles to Challenge the Brain* (grades 1–5) offers creative puzzles that will help students develop their critical thinking and problem-solving skills; part of the Critical Thinking Series. *Figuratively Speaking* (grades 5–8) uses classic literature to illustrate 40 basic literary terms.

Submissions and Payment
Guidelines available. Prefers complete ms; accepts query with outline. Accepts photocopies, computer printouts, and simultaneous submissions if identified. SASE. Responds in 1–2 months. Publication period and payment policy vary.

Editor's Comments
We are teachers ourselves and continue to be committed to providing teaching materials that make a difference in the lives of children, teachers, and parents. We are always interested in reviewing new ideas developed by teachers and successfully tested and used in the classroom. Remember, we publish very few works of fiction.

Creative With Words Publications

P.O. Box 223226
Carmel, CA 93922

Editor & Publisher: Brigitta Geltrich

Publisher's Interests
This independent publisher offers thematic anthologies, both fiction and nonfiction, for readers of all ages. Some of the themes recently showcased in anthologies include school, folklore, friends, and love. This house publishes a small list each year, but receives nearly one thousand queries and unsolicited manuscripts yearly.
Website: http://members.tripod.com/CreativeWithWords

Freelance Potential
Published 6-8 titles in 2004: all were developed from unsolicited submissions. Of the 6-8 titles, 2 were by unpublished writers and 4 were by authors who were new to the publishing house. Receives 500-800 queries, unsolicited mss yearly.

- **Fiction:** Publishes anthologies for all ages. Genres include fairy tales, folktales, romance, and humor as well as stories about sports, the environment, animals, holidays, and school issues.
- **Nonfiction:** Publishes educational anthologies for all ages. Topics include animals, pets, nature, sports, and humor.
- **Representative Titles:** *Animals Our Friends* investigates the numerous ways animals touch our lives. *Human Emotions* explores the wide range of emotions we experience over a lifetime.

Submissions and Payment
Guidelines available. Query or send complete ms. Accepts photocopies and computer printouts. SASE. Responds to queries in 1-4 weeks, to mss 1 month after anthology deadline. Publication in 1 month. No payment; 20-40% discount on 10+ copies purchased.

Editor's Comments
Remember that we are only interested in seeing submissions that will fit into one of our planned anthologies. Prose manuscripts should be no longer than 800 words and poetry cannot exceed 20 lines. We are not a paying market and so our publications are ideally suited for new writers who want to see their work in print. We suggest you review some of our publications before you send your work.

Cricket Books

Suite 1100
332 South Michigan Avenue
Chicago, IL 60604

Submissions Editor

Publisher's Interests
High-quality picture books, chapter books, middle-grade books, and young adult novels are published by this imprint of the Cricket Magazine Group. It also offers nonfiction for children of all ages.
Website: www.cricketbooks.net

Freelance Potential
Published 6 titles in 2004: 4 were by agented authors, and 1 was a reprint/licensed property. Receives 1,500 queries yearly.

- **Fiction:** Published 2 chapter books, 5–10 years; and 2 middle-grade books, 8–12 years. Genres include fantasy and contemporary, historical, and multicultural fiction. Also publishes poetry, bilingual and picture books, and humor.
- **Nonfiction:** Published 1 chapter book, 5–10 years; 1 middle-grade book, 8–12 years. Topics include history, mathematics, science, technology, social issues, and sports.
- **Representative Titles:** *One Hungry Monster* by Susan Heyboer O'Keefe (6 months–2 years) follows a young boy on a hilarious romp through the house as he tries to control his naughty but lovable guests. *Bug Girl* by Carol Sonenklar (6–9 years) tells the story of a girl who changes into a superpower of the insect world to save her friend who was transformed into an exotic beetle.

Submissions and Payment
Guidelines and catalogue available. Only accepting agented submissions at this time; check website for updates in submissions policy. SASE. Responds in 4–6 months. Publication in 18 months. Royalty; up to 10%; advance, $2,000+.

Editor's Comments
We are primarily interested in chapter books, middle-grade fiction, young adult novels, and nonfiction for all ages. Currently, we are only accepting agented submissions. Please check our website for updates in our submissions policy.

Critical Thinking Company

P.O. Box 1610
Seaside, CA 93955

Director of Book Development: Cheryl Block

Publisher's Interests
For more than 25 years, this educational publisher has offered fun, easy-to-use books and software that develop thinking skills and improve standards-based learning in kindergarten through grade-twelve classrooms. Its products can also be used by students in an independent setting.
Website: www.CriticalThinking.com

Freelance Potential
Published 24 titles in 2004. Of the 24 titles, 2 were by unpublished writers and 4 were by authors who were new to the publishing house. Receives 25–30 unsolicited mss yearly.

- **Fiction:** Publishes concept books, 0–4 years; and activity books, 8–18 years. Features reading series that develop critical thinking skills.
- **Nonfiction:** Publishes concept books, early picture books, 0–4 years; easy-to-read books, 4–7 years; and chapter books, 5–10 years. Topics include critical thinking skills, language arts, writing, reading comprehension, mathematics, science, and U.S. history.
- **Representative Titles:** *Mind Building Math* (grade K) offers puzzles, story problems, and activities to reinforce math concepts and skills. *Mind Benders Warm Up* (grades K–2) develops real-life problem solving skills through deductive thinking.

Submissions and Payment
Guidelines available. Send complete ms. Accepts photocopies, computer printouts, and Macintosh and DOS disk submissions. SASE. Responds in 6–9 months. Publication in 1–2 years. Royalty, 10%.

Editor's Comments
Our products do not teach through drill and memorization, nor do we "teach to the tests." Our goal is to empower the mind for higher grades, top test scores, and problem-solving skills that meet life's challenges. We want fresh material that requires more cognitive involvement than the usual study guides.

Crossway Books

Good News Publishers
1300 Crescent Street
Wheaton, IL 60187

Editorial Administrator: Jill Carter

Publisher's Interests
Crossway Books is an evangelical publisher that offers fiction and nonfiction titles written from a Christian perspective. Its list includes titles for young children, middle-grade readers, and young adults as well as reference materials and Bible study guides.
Website: www.crosswaybooks.org

Freelance Potential
Published 73 titles (13 juvenile) in 2004: 2 were developed from unsolicited submissions, 3 were by agented authors, and 1 was a reprint/licensed property. Of the 73 titles, 9 were by authors who were new to the publishing house. Receives 1,000 queries yearly.

- **Fiction:** Published 2 toddler books, and 3 story picture books, 4–10 years; and 8 middle-grade books, 8–12 years. Genres include contemporary and historical fiction, and adventure stories with Christian themes.
- **Nonfiction:** Publishes educational resources for parents and teachers. Topics include home and family life, Christian living, homeschooling, health, the Bible, and church issues.
- **Representative Titles:** *A Hat for Ivan* by Max Lucado describes a town where everyone wears a hat that shows what they do best. *Will Northway & the Quest for Liberty* by Susan Olasky follows a young boy from London who begins a new life in Boston; part of the Young American Patriots series.

Submissions and Payment
Guidelines available. Accepts submissions from agented authors only. Responds in 6–8 weeks. Publication in 12–18 months. Payment policy varies.

Editor's Comments
We want books that provide a deeper understanding of Christian truth and its application to daily life. Our youth audience is interested in lively adventure/action stories, historical fiction, and novels that deal with contemporary issues.

Crown Books for Young Readers

1745 Broadway
New York, NY 10019

Submissions Editor

Publisher's Interests
A division of Random House Children's Books, Crown Books for Young Readers publishes hardcover nonfiction titles for preschool children through young adults. Its list includes books on science, nature, history, and sports.
Website: www.randomhouse.com/kids

Freelance Potential
Published 30 titles in 2004: 11 were by agented authors, and 4 were reprint/licensed properties. Receives 500 queries, 1,000 unsolicited mss yearly.

- **Nonfiction:** Publishes concept books and toddler books, 0–4 years; story picture books, 4–10 years; chapter books, 5–10 years; middle-grade books, 8–12 years; and young adult books, 12–18 years. Topics include science, nature, sports, history, and social issues.
- **Representative Titles:** *Ice Age Cave Bear* by Barbara Hehner (7–10 years) tells the story of these formidable creatures, offering detailed drawings, maps, and accurate information. *Happy, Happy Chinese New Year* by Demi (4–8 years) looks at how the Chinese celebrate their new year.

Submissions and Payment
Guidelines available. Accepts submissions from agented authors only. Accepts photocopies, computer printouts, and simultaneous submissions if identified. SASE. Responds in 3 months. Publication period varies. Royalty; advance.

Editor's Comments
Although we accept only agented submissions, we continue to receive hundreds of queries for books that are not suitable for our publishing program. We publish hardcover nonfiction books for children from birth to young adulthood. Please take a look at a recent catalogue or our website to see the type of work we have done in the past—we don't want material that duplicates what we have already done. Check our guidelines before your agent submits your work.

CSS Publishing Company

P.O. Box 4503
517 Main Street
Lima, OH 45802-4503

Acquisitions Editor: Stan Purdum

Publisher's Interests
CSS Publishing Company is an ecumenical resource center that serves clergy and congregations interested in promoting an active Christian lifestyle. Its list includes books for pastors, educators, and Sunday school students.
Website: www.csspub.com

Freelance Potential
Published 180 titles in 2004: 100 were developed from unsolicited submissions, 2 were by agented authors, and 10 were reprint/licensed properties. Of the 180 titles, 25 were by unpublished writers and 80 were by authors who were new to the publishing house. Receives 1,000 unsolicited mss yearly.

- **Nonfiction:** Publishes story picture books, 4–10 years; and young adult books, 12–18 years. Topics include religious education, prayer, worship, and family life. Also publishes resource materials, program planners, newsletters, and church supplies for Christian educators.
- **Representative Titles:** *When You Run out of Soap* by Mary Rose Pearson (teachers) suggests games and activities that encourage the spiritual and physical growth of children while teaching Bible stories and promoting Christian values. *Bible Stories, Food, and Fun* by Michele Howe (teachers) makes Bible learning fun by offering ideas for snacks and activities that relate to specific Bible lessons.

Submissions and Payment
Guidelines and catalogue available at website. Send complete ms with résumé. Accepts photocopies, computer printouts, and simultaneous submissions if identified. SASE. Responds in 6 months. Publication in 6 months. Royalty. Flat fee.

Editor's Comments
We are looking for practical, proven, ready-to-use materials, including children's lessons and youth resources, lectionary-based resources for group study, and parish-tested material for education, youth ministry, and church growth.

Dandy Lion Publications

Suite L
3563 Sueldo
San Louis Obispo, CA 94301-7331

Editor: Dianne Draze

Publisher's Interests
For 27 years, Dandy Lion Publications has been providing teachers with the resources they need to effectively challenge students in mainstream, special, and gifted classrooms. Its materials are suitable for students in kindergarten through junior high school.
Website: www.dandylionbooks.com

Freelance Potential
Published 10-12 titles in 2004: 6 were developed from unsolicited submissions and 6 were by agented authors. Receives 50 queries each year.

- **Nonfiction:** Publishes reference books, activity books, and workbooks for grades K-8. Topics include math, grammar, public speaking, literature, reading, critical and creative thinking, research and report writing, social studies, and personal growth. Also publishes poetry.
- **Representative Titles:** *The Great Chocolate Caper* (grades 5-8) teaches logical thinking through eight fun mysteries. *Famous People Puzzles* (grades 5-8) uses inference and research to discover the identities of famous people.

Submissions and Payment
Guidelines available. Accepts queries from practicing teachers only. Query with sample chapter. No unsolicited mss. Accepts photocopies, computer printouts, and simultaneous submissions if identified. SASE. Responds in 2-4 weeks. Publication in 6-9 months. Royalty; advance.

Editor's Comments
Please note that we will only consider material from practicing teachers. As a leading educational publisher, we look for grade-specific activities, games, exercises, and instructional procedures that supplement the basic curriculum. As a teacher, you know what your students need to strengthen their skills in the areas of creative and critical thinking. Send us an idea for materials and books that are helpful in your classroom.

Darby Creek Publishing

7858 Industrial Parkway
Plain City, OH 43064

Submissions Editor

Publisher's Interests
Established in 2002, this publisher features a small list of children's books that cover contemporary topics from an unusual angle. Titles cover sports, science, and history of interest to middle-grade readers.
Website: www.darbycreekpublishing.com

Freelance Potential
Published 10 titles in 2004: 3 were developed from unsolicited submissions, 2 were by agented authors, and 3 were reprint/licensed properties. Of the 8 titles, 1 was by an unpublished writer and 3 were by authors who were new to the publishing house. Receives 720 queries and 500 mss yearly.

- **Fiction:** Published 2 chapter books, 5–10 years; 2 middle-grade books, 8–12 years; and 2 young adult books, 12–18 years. Genres include contemporary fiction, humor, romance, and sports stories.
- **Nonfiction:** Published 2 middle-grade books, 8–12 years. Topics include animals, history, humor, science, and sports. Also publishes biographies.
- **Representative Titles:** *Dinosaur Mummies* by Kelley Milner Halls (10+ years) discusses the world's most amazing dinosaur discoveries, including dinosaur mummies. *Venus and the Comets* by Erika Tamar (8+ years) is the story of a young girl being groomed to be a supermodel, but who yearns to be a soccer superstar.

Submissions and Payment
Guidelines available with SASE or at website. Query with summary and 2 sample chapters; or send complete ms. Accepts photocopies and simultaneous submissions if identified. SASE. Responds to queries in 2–6 weeks, to mss in 4–8 weeks. Publication in 12–18 months. Royalty; advance.

Editor's Comments
We are especially interested in nonfiction works for children ages 8 to 14, with themes they can relate to. Take a topic that's not too obscure and make your readers say "Ah ha!"

May Davenport, Publishers

26313 Purissima Road
Los Altos Hills, CA 94022

Publisher & Editor: May Davenport

Publisher's Interests
May Davenport Publishers is a family-owned publishing house that produces a small number of fiction titles for young adult readers. Although it does not plan any new titles for 2004, it will consider submissions for future lists, but only of contemporary teen fiction.
Website: www.maydavenportpublishers.com

Freelance Potential
Published no titles in 2004. Receives 1,000 queries yearly.

- **Fiction:** Publishes young adult books, 12–18 years. Genres include historical fiction, mystery, humor, and adventure.
- **Representative Titles:** *Driver's Ed Is Dead* by Pat Delgado (YA) is a humorous novel about a school that drops drivers' ed classes from its curriculum, and the students who devise a plan to reinstate it. *Making My Escape* by David Lee Finkle (4–12 years) tells the story about a young boy who escapes from his problems into a world of fantasy.

Submissions and Payment
Guidelines available. Query. SASE. Responds in 1–2 weeks. Publication in 1–2 years. Royalty, 15%. Flat fee.

Editor's Comments
At this time we regret that we have enough children's color-and-read stories, juvenile novels, and young adult novels. For the next few years we will primarily be reprinting material from our back list. In general we are interested in publishing-inspired authors who write purposefully for today's teens. Many of our writers are in fact teachers who have created stories themselves to help their students deal with a specific topic or issue, and to acquire better reading skills. If you feel your story is truly unique and will make a strong impact on teens and their teachers, you may still send a submission. It may be a long time before we get back to you, but in the meantime, we suggest you visit our website and review the titles selected above to understand what works best for us.

Jonathan David Publishers

68-22 Eliot Avenue
Middle Village, NY 11379

Editor-in-Chief: Alfred J. Kolatch

Publisher's Interests
Nonfiction titles emphasizing Judaica are the mainstay of this publisher. Its children's titles explore the customs and history of Judaism and Jewish holidays.
Website: www.jdbooks.com

Freelance Potential
Published 15 titles (1 juvenile) in 2004: 11 were developed from unsolicited submissions and 4 were by agented authors. Of the 15 titles, 6 were by authors who were new to the publishing house. Receives 1,200 queries yearly.

- **Fiction:** Publishes easy-to-read books, 4–7 years; and story picture books, 4–10 years. Genres include folktales and stories of Jewish culture and heritage.
- **Nonfiction:** Publishes easy-to-read books, 4–7 years; and middle-grade books, 8–12 years. Topics include religion, Judaica, history, culture, and multicultural issues.
- **Representative Titles:** *Let's Celebrate Our Jewish Holidays* by Alfred J. Kolatch (6+ years) teaches how each holiday in the Jewish calendar originated, how each is celebrated, and the message each offers today. *My Brother's Bar Mitzvah* by Sylvia Rouss (6+ years) is a delightful story about a girl whose brother ignores her during his studies for his upcoming Bar Mitzvah.

Submissions and Payment
Guidelines available. Query with résumé, table of contents, synopsis, and sample chapter. No unsolicited mss. Accepts photocopies and computer printouts. No simultaneous submissions. SASE. Responds in 1–2 months. Publication in 18 months. Royalty; advance. Flat fee.

Editor's Comments
For more than 50 years we have offered nonfiction material for young Jewish readers. We continue to need books that deal with Jewish traditions in contemporary times.

DAW Books

375 Hudson Street
New York, NY 10014

Associate Editor: Peter Stampfel

Publisher's Interests
DAW Books specializes in science fiction and fantasy novels. Its readership includes young adults and adults. While it rarely publishes first-time authors, it is always willing to consider a first book if it is of professional quality. This publisher does not offer any nonfiction.
Website: www.dawbooks.com

Freelance Potential
Published 48 titles (10–15 juvenile) in 2004. Of the 48 titles, 1 was by an unpublished writer and 2 were by authors who were new to the publishing house. Receives 1,000+ unsolicited mss yearly.

- **Fiction:** Publishes science fiction and fantasy novels for young adults and adults.
- **Representative Titles:** *The War of the Flowers* by Tad Williams (YA–Adult) is the story of a young man who is drawn into a parallel world where his presence will determine the outcome of a war. *Broken Crescent* by S. Andrew Swann (YA–Adult) is about a computer hacker who is kidnapped and taken to an alien world where he becomes a pawn in a dangerous game of power.

Submissions and Payment
Guidelines available. Send complete ms. Accepts photocopies and computer printouts. No simultaneous submissions. SASE. Responds in 3 months. Publication in 8–12 months. Royalty, 6%; advance.

Editor's Comments
We publish science fiction and fantasy novels, period. You will not find short story collections, novellas, or poetry listed anywhere in our catalogue. We stress this because we frequently get material that is not suitable for our specific publishing needs. All of the books we publish are at least 80,000 words in length. If you are a new writer, we won't turn away, but make sure your work is really top-notch and in keeping with the high-quality work we offer. The best way to do this is to take the time to read some of the titles found in our catalogue.

Dawn Publications

12402 Bitney Springs Road
Nevada City, CA 95959

Editor: Glenn Hovemann

Publisher's Interests
Dawn Publications focuses on books whose subject matter relates to nature awareness. While it features a number of titles for adult readers, it is increasingly concentrated on material that will teach children about the wonders of nature. Many of its books are used in the classroom as supplementary materials.
Website: www.dawnpub.com

Freelance Potential
Published 6 titles in 2004: 3 were developed from unsolicited submissions and 3 were by agented authors. Of the 6 titles, 3 were by unpublished writers and 3 were by authors who were new to the publishing house. Receives 2,500+ queries, unsolicited mss yearly.

- **Nonfiction:** Publishes story picture books, 4–12 years. Topics include the environment, conservation, ecology, family relationships, personal awareness, and multicultural and ethnic issues.
- **Representative Titles:** *Okomi Enjoys His Outings* by Helen and Clive Dorman (2–5 years) is published in association with the Jane Goodall Institute and introduces young children to a baby chimpanzee; part of the Okomi series. *Where Does the Wind Blow?* by Cindy Rink (4–10 years) explores the wind and where it comes from.

Submissions and Payment
Guidelines available at website. Query or send complete ms. Accepts photocopies, computer printouts, and simultaneous submissions if identified. SASE. Responds in 2–3 months. Publication in 18–24 months. Royalty; advance.

Editor's Comments
At Dawn Publications we are committed to teaching each new generation to respect and appreciate the nature and wildlife of the world. While all of our stories are engaging, they also teach respect for harmony of life. We are interested in seeing submissions that reflect these qualities through an engaging story line.

Denlinger's Publishers

P.O. Box 1030
Edgewater, FL 32132-1030

Acquisitions Editor: Elizabeth-Anne Rogers

Publisher's Interests

Established as a traditional publisher in 1926, Denlinger's is now an electronic book publisher that offers e-books and print-on-demand paperbacks. Its juvenile list includes fiction titles for children ages five to twelve.
Website: www.thebookden.com

Freelance Potential

Published 24 titles (4 juvenile) in 2004: all were developed from unsolicited submissions and 3 were by agented authors. Of the 24 titles, most were by unpublished writers and 12 were by authors who were new to the publishing house. Receives 1,700 unsolicited mss yearly.

- **Fiction:** Publishes chapter books, 5–10 years; and middle-grade books, 8–12 years. Genres include adventure, fantasy, folklore, and historical and inspirational fiction.
- **Representative Titles:** *The Orb* by Hasko Starrenburg (8–12 years) is a fantasy tale about a mystical Orb and the strange beings that protect it. *Monsoons and the Wicked Witch of the West* by Diane Lee Horwood (8–12) is a fiction/nonfiction mix of historical sites in Arizona, real Morgan horses, and a magical witch of the desert.

Submissions and Payment

Guidelines and catalogue available at website. Send complete ms with market analysis and biography. Accepts disk submissions (WordPerfect), and email submissions to acquisitions@thebookden.com. SASE. Responds in 3–6 months. Publication in 6–8 months. Royalty.

Editor's Comments

We plan to remain at the forefront of electronic publishing by expanding into new formats and finding better ways to bring content to the customer, while giving new authors a venue for their work. If you are interested in joining our team of writers who are having their works electronically published, please review our submissions policy.

Exceptional Stories: Please Apply Within
Rebecca Waugh
Dial Books for Young Readers

Publishing only three or four young readers a year, Dial Books is select. "One thing to know about early readers is that we take on very few of them because they are financially difficult to publish in hardcover. They tend to do better in paperback," explains Editor Rebecca Waugh. "When we sign something up, it means we feel it's a really strong manuscript with something fresh and unique about it."

Waugh looks for strong plots. "An early reader master is someone who knows how to take an interesting story idea and find ways to tell only as much as needs to be told, keeping it simple," Waugh says. "It's a delicate balance because you don't want the story to sound choppy or confusing by leaving out anything important."

Vocabulary lists are absent from Dial's Easy-to-Read line. "Common sense will tell you what words and sentence structure might not be clear to a beginning reader," Waugh says. "As long as the writer seems to have a good feel for the early reader genre, a few complicated words do not make me stop reading a submission. If there are a few words that are too difficult, that can be fixed in the editing stage."

Waugh encourages writers to submit their finest work. "I don't like query letters," she says. "I prefer to see at least the first few pages of the work or the whole manuscript and an SASE." Only the best need apply, but isn't that what new readers deserve?

Dial Books for Young Readers

Penguin Group (USA) Inc.
345 Hudson Street
New York, NY 10014

Submissions Coordinator

Publisher's Interests
This popular, award-winning imprint of Penguin Young Readers Group features fiction and nonfiction titles for preschoolers and young students, as well as novels and nonfiction titles for middle-grade and young adult readers.
Website: www.penguin.com

Freelance Potential
Published 41 titles (40 juvenile) in 2004: 25 were developed from unsolicited submissions, 16 were by agented authors, and 3 were reprint/licensed properties. Receives 2,000+ queries, 1,000+ unsolicited mss yearly.

- **Fiction:** Publishes concept books, toddler books, and early picture books, 0–4 years; easy-to-read books, 4–7 years; story picture books, 4–10 years; chapter books, 5–10 years; middle-grade novels, 8–12 years; and young adult books/novels, 12–18 years. Genres include contemporary and literary fiction.
- **Nonfiction:** Publishes concept books and early picture books, 0–4 years; easy-to-read books, 4–7 years; story picture books, 4–10 years; middle-grade books, 8–12 years; and young adult books, 12–18 years. Topics include humor, science, and social issues.
- **Representative Titles:** *Pearl and Wagner: Three Secrets* by Kate McMullan (5+ years) is a charming story about secrets, surprises, and friendship. *Too Big a Storm* by Marsha Qualey (14+ years) is a moving portrait of a young woman's journey of self-discovery and the healing power of family during the Vietnam era.

Submissions and Payment
Guidelines and catalogues available with SASE. Query with up to 10 pages; send complete ms for picture books. SASE. Response time, publication period, and payment policy vary.

Editor's Comments
Lively stories with memorable characters stand the best chance for a second look from our editors.

Didax

395 Main Street
Rowley, MA 01969

Vice President: Martin Kennedy

Publisher's Interests

A supplier of educational products for over 30 years, Didax offers manipulatives, software, and printed material that address diverse student needs and learning styles. Its products cover the curriculum areas of math, language arts, and social studies.
Website: www.didax.com

Freelance Potential

Published 50 titles in 2004: 10 were developed from unsolicited submissions and 3 were by agented authors. Of the 50 titles, 2 were by unpublished writers and 8 were by authors who were new to the publishing house. Receives 100 queries, 80 unsolicited mss each year.

- **Nonfiction:** Publishes reproducible activity books and teacher resources, grades pre-K–12. Topics include basic math, fractions, geometry, algebra, probability, problem-solving, the alphabet, pre-reading, phonics, word study, spelling, vocabulary, writing, reading comprehension, and social studies.
- **Representative Titles:** *Cloze Encounters: Space* by Rik McGuinness (grades 5–6) includes reproducible activities that build language skills such as note taking and word study. *Ancient Greece* by George Moore (grades 4–7) covers the geography, agriculture, domestic life, culture, society, and religion of this ancient civilization.

Submissions and Payment

Guidelines available. Query with résumé and outline; or send complete ms. Accepts photocopies, computer printouts, disk submissions (Microsoft Word), email submissions to development@didaxinc.com, and simultaneous submissions if identified. SASE. Responds to queries in 2 weeks, to mss in 1 month. Publication in 1 year. Royalty; advance.

Editor's Comments

If you are a teacher with an idea you'd like us to consider, send us your query. Nearly all our products come directly from teachers.

Discovery Enterprises

31 Laurelwood Drive
Carlisle, MA 01741

President: JoAnne Weisman-Deitch

Publisher's Interests

Founded in 1990, this publisher offers reproducible plays on topics in American history that target grades four through twelve, and history books based on primary-source documents.
Website: www.ushistorydocs.com

Freelance Potential

Published 10 titles (6 juvenile) in 2004: 2 were developed from unsolicited submissions. Of the 10 titles, 1 was by an unpublished writer and 3 were by authors who were new to the publishing house. Receives 50–60 queries yearly.

- **Fiction:** Publishes plays, grades 4–12. Also publishes middle-grade novels, 8–12 years; and young adult books, 12–18 years. Genres include historical fiction.
- **Nonfiction:** Published 1 easy-to-read book, 4–7 years; 2 chapter books, 5–10 years; 6 middle-grade books; and 1 young adult book, 12–18 years. Features educational books about American history.
- **Representative Titles:** *Seaman's Adventure with Lewis and Clark* by Duncan Brown (grades 1–4) takes readers on a journey of discovery with Lewis and Clark and their dog, Seaman, who went along on their adventures. *The Underground Railroad* by Karin Luisa Badt (grades 4–8) is a play that follows the escape of three young adults and a baby from Virginia. The group rests at the home of a family who is a stop on the Underground Railroad.

Submissions and Payment

Guidelines available. Query with résumé, outline, and nonfiction clips. No unsolicited mss. Accepts photocopies and simultaneous submissions if identified. SASE. Responds in 3 months. Publication in 2–8 months. Royalty.

Editor's Comments

We are seeking plays that focus on American history. We strive to make students aware of the exciting and compelling history of the United States through the study of primary-source documents.

DiskUs Publishing

P.O. Box 43
Albany, NY 47320

Submissions Editor: Holly Janey

Publisher's Interests
Established in 1995, this e-publisher features children's fiction and nonfiction that may be downloaded or purchased on disks. Its website includes toddler books, middle-grade novels, and young adult books of all genres.
Website: www.diskuspublishing.com

Freelance Potential
Published 60–70 titles (10 juvenile) in 2004: 30 were developed from unsolicited submissions. Receives 12,000 queries yearly.

- **Fiction:** Publishes concept and toddler books, 0–4 years; easy-to-read books, 4–7 years; middle-grade books, 8–12 years; and young adult books, 12–18 years. Genres include science fiction, fantasy, horror, mystery, Western, action, adventure, and mainstream fiction.
- **Nonfiction:** Publishes concept and toddler books, 0–4 years. also publishes puzzle books, religious titles, and adult self-help books.
- **Representative Titles:** *Freezie the Snowman* by Cia Leah is the story of Snowman Village, the evil Thawer Snowman who seeks to destroy the village, and the good Weather Snowman who saves them all. *The Easter Village Twins* by Cia Leah is a humorous tale about mischievous twin bunnies who manage to put Easter in jeopardy.

Submissions and Payment
Guidelines available at website. Query with résumé, word count, synopsis, and first 3 chapters. Accepts email queries to editors@diskuspublishing.com. Responds in 3–6 months. Publication in 5 months. Royalty.

Editor's Comments
We are a royalty-paying publisher of works in electronic format. Our titles are a variety of fiction and nonfiction, and occasionally poetry, in electronic bindings. We ask for no payment from our authors, and we pay no advances, but we do offer a higher royalty than traditional publishers. Our standard contract is for one year, with the option for renewal.

Dorchester Publishing

200 Madison Avenue
New York, NY 10016

Editor: Kate Seaver

Publisher's Interests
Founded in 1971, Dorchester Publishing specializes in fiction for young adult and adult readers. It is best known for its romance titles and its young adult audience is primarily female.
Website: www.dorchesterpub.com

Freelance Potential
Published 225 titles (12 juvenile) in 2004: 12 were developed from unsolicited submissions and 112 were by agented authors. Of the 225 titles, 18 were by unpublished writers and 27 were by authors who were new to the publishing house. Receives 3,000 unsolicited mss yearly.

- **Fiction:** Publishes young adult books, 12–18 years. Genres include contemporary fiction.
- **Representative Titles:** *Princesses Don't Sweat* by Kaz Delaney follows the story of an American teen who moves to Australia with her mother after her mother meets a new man online. *Chloe, Queen of Denial* by Naomi Nash follows the adventures of two girls who go on an archaeological dig.

Submissions and Payment
Guidelines available. Query with first three chapters. Accepts photocopies. SASE. Responds in 6–8 months. Publication in 9–12 months. Royalty; advance.

Editor's Comments
Our niche is mass-market, paperback genre fiction. While most of our titles are written for adults, we are expanding our list of young adult titles. We are interested in hearing from writers who can deliver a query that is fun and contemporary. Our young adult books run about 45,000 words. If you are unfamiliar with our books please take the time to review our catalogue and read some of our titles. While romance plays a major role in our teen books, the plots should also focus on one of the many issues that teens face today in dealing with family, friends, and school.

Dorling Kindersley

375 Hudson Street
New York, NY 10014

Submissions: Beth Sutinis

Publisher's Interests
Dorling Kindersley is best known for its innovative picture books for all ages. Its catalogue also offers interactive titles as well as CD-ROMS and parenting books. This publisher offers both fiction and nonfiction.
Website: www.dk.com

Freelance Potential
Published 250 titles in 2004: 3 were by agented authors and 50 were reprint/licensed properties. Receives 1,000 queries yearly.

- **Fiction:** Publishes concept books, toddler books, and early picture books, 0–4 years; chapter books, 5–10 years; middle-grade novels, 8–12 years; and young adult books, 12–18 years. Genres include contemporary and historical fiction, science fiction, fairy tales, folktales, humor, mystery, stories about nature, and romance.
- **Nonfiction:** Publishes concept books and toddler books, 0–4 years; easy-to-read books, 4–7 years; middle-grade titles, 8–12 years; and young adult books, 12–18 years.
- **Representative Titles:** *Escape from Earth* by Peter Ackroyd (8+ years) covers the thrilling history of human exploration into space. *Baby Love: Baby Animals* (0–3 years) is a padded board book featuring things babies like to see, touch, and feel.

Submissions and Payment
Guidelines available. Accepts queries through agents only. No unsolicited mss. SASE. Responds in 6 months. Publication in 2 years. Royalty, 10%; advance, varies.

Editor's Comments
If you are a new writer, we will accept your query only if it is presented through an agent. As an international publisher of note, we receive far more submissions than we can ever use, and this is one way we narrow the field. Generally, most of the books on our list come from established writers with a number of published books to their credit. Carefully review our catalogue before submitting.

Dover Publications

31 East 2nd Street
Mineola, NY 11501-3582

Editor-in-Chief: Paul Negri

Publisher's Interests
Established more than 60 years ago, Dover Publications features books for children of all ages, including coloring, activity, and sticker books. Titles for elementary school students in the areas of mathematics, music, and science also appear regularly in its catalogue.
Website: www.doverpublications.com

Freelance Potential
Published 650 titles (140 juvenile) in 2004. Receives 400 queries, 400 unsolicited mss yearly.

- **Fiction:** Publishes reprints of children's classics and storybooks. Genres include foktales, fantasy, and fairy tales. Also publishes animal stories.
- **Nonfiction:** Publishes educational titles, anthologies, and biographies. Topics include Native Americans, ancient history, animals, dinosaurs, science, mythology, American history, needlework, fashion, languages, literature, hobbies, adventure, and fine art.
- **Representative Titles:** *Cars and Trucks Dot-to-Dot* by Barbara Soloff Levy is an activity book filled with connect-the-dot pictures about motorized vehicles. *Life in a Bucket of Soil* by Alvin & Virginia Silverstein introduces grade-school children to industrious ants, tunnel-building earthworms, snails, and slugs, and other creatures inhabiting the world beneath our feet.

Submissions and Payment
Catalogue available at website. Query or send complete ms. SASE. Response time and publication period vary. Flat fee.

Editor's Comments
Submissions for young children that are well-written, accurate, and original are always needed. We welcome ideas from new writers who can fit the bill with an idea that will intrigue our audience, while introducing them to something educational. Most of our books are printed in paperback format.

Down East Books

P.O. Box 679
Camden, ME 04843

Managing Editor: Michael Steere

Publisher's Interests
As a small, regional publisher, Down East specializes in books with strong Maine and New England themes. Its list includes fiction and nonfiction titles for children and young adults. 2% self-, subsidy-, co-venture, or co-op published material.
Website: www.downeastbooks.com

Freelance Potential
Published 28 titles (5 juvenile) in 2004: 5 were developed from unsolicited submissions, 2 were by agented authors, and 3 were reprint/licensed properties. Of the 28 titles, 3 were by unpublished writers and 4 were by new authors. Receives 1,000 queries, 500 unsolicited mss yearly.

- **Fiction:** Published 2 easy-to-read books, and 1 young adult book, 12–18 years. Also publishes early picture books, story picture books, chapter books, and middle-grade books. Genres include contemporary fiction, adventure, mystery, and humor.
- **Nonfiction:** Published 2 easy-to-read books, 4–7 years. Also publishes story picture books and biographies. Topics include natural history, ghosts, ecology, nautical subjects, and travel.
- **Representative Titles:** *What the Sea Left Behind* by Mimi Gregoire Carpenter (4+ years) describes fascinating things children can find in tidal pools. *My Brother's Keeper: A Civil War Story* by Nancy Johnson (9+ years) follows a young medic during the Civil War.

Submissions and Payment
Guidelines available. Query with clips or writing samples; or send complete ms. Accepts photocopies, computer printouts, and simultaneous submissions. No email. SASE. Responds in 2–8 weeks. Publication in 1 year. Royalty, 9–12%; advance, $300–$600.

Editor's Comments
Regional settings and subjects are mandatory for our children's titles. The New England setting must be integral to the work; a story that could take place in another region does not meet our requirements.

Dramatic Publishing

311 Washington Street
Woodstock, IL 60098

Acquisitions Editor: Linda Habjan

Publisher's Interests
Founded in 1885, this publisher is committed to showcasing exciting new plays and musicals from both new and established authors. Its catalogue includes comedies and dramas in the form of one-act plays, scenes, and full-length dramas. While many of its plays are produced in high schools, they are also popular with community theater groups, professional companies, children's theater groups, and stock companies.
Website: www.dramaticpublishing.com

Freelance Potential
Published 50 titles (25 juvenile) in 2004. Of the 50 titles, 25 were by authors who were new to the publishing house. Receives 250 queries, 600 unsolicited mss yearly.

- **Fiction:** Publishes full-length and one-act plays, musicals, and anthologies.
- **Nonfiction:** Publishes books about the theatre arts and production guides. Topics include stagecraft, audition techniques, and directing.
- **Representative Titles:** *Salt & Pepper* by José Cruz González explores family, friendship, and illiteracy and is written for production by a young cast. *Mask of the Unicorn Warrior* by Y. York is a mythic tale of love and deception inspired by the unicorn tapestries that hang in the Cluny Museum in Paris.

Submissions and Payment
Guidelines available. Send complete ms with résumé, synopsis, production history, reviews, cast list, and set and technical requirements; include audiocassette for musicals. Accepts photocopies and computer printouts. SASE. Responds in 10–12 weeks. Publication in 18 months. Royalty.

Editor's Comments
Our needs remain the same—to bring our audience new plays that can be easily produced by amateur theater groups as well as school students. Short, contemporary plays are especially needed at this time.

Dutton Children's Books

Penguin Young Readers Group
14th Floor
345 Hudson Street
New York, NY 10014

Queries Editor

Publisher's Interests
Dutton Children's Books is one of the best-known publishers of books for young readers. Because of the great volume of submissions it receives, it has a query-only submission policy that is strictly adhered to. It offers fiction and nonfiction for readers of all ages.
Website: www.penguin.com

Freelance Potential
Published 100 titles in 2004: 6 were developed from unsolicited submissions, 29 were by agented authors, and 30 were reprint/licensed properties. Of the 100 titles, 12 were by unpublished writers and 16 were by authors who were new to the publishing house. Receives 3,500 queries yearly.

- **Fiction:** Publishes concept books, toddler books, and early picture books, 0–4 years; easy-to-read books, 4–7 years; story picture books, 4–10 years; middle-grade books, 8–12 years; and young adult books, 12–18 years. Genres include adventure, mystery, fantasy, and humor.
- **Nonfiction:** Publishes story picture books, 4–10 years; middle-grade books, 8–12 years; and young adult books, 12–18 years. Topics include history and nature.
- **Representative Titles:** *Mary Margaret and the Perfect Pet Plan* by Christine Kole MacLean (8+ years) is the story of a young girl who thinks a pet will make her life perfect. *The Song of an Innocent Bystander* by Ian Bone (14+ years) is about a girl who must relive a harrowing experience of her childhood.

Submissions and Payment
Guidelines available. Query with brief synopsis, sample pages (up to 10 for novels, up to 5 for picture books), and publishing credits. No unsolicited mss. SASE. Responds in 2–3 months. Publication in 1+ years. Royalty; advance.

Editor's Comments
If you query, please include a few lines that will give us a feel for your writing style. You may also explain what your book will accomplish.

Eakin Press

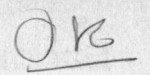

Sunbelt Media, Inc.
P.O. Box 90159
Austin, TX 78709-0159

Publisher: Virginia Messer

Publisher's Interests
This independent regional publishing house has been in business for more than 25 years. Its focus is on the history and culture of the Southwest, especially Texas and Oklahoma. It publishes little fiction other than children's fiction. It is interested in books tailored to a mainstream audience, rather than a regional one.
Website: www.eakinpress.com

Freelance Potential
Published 200–300 titles (80 juvenile) in 2004. Receives 2,500 queries yearly.

- **Fiction:** Publishes picture books, 4–10 years; easy-to-read books, 4–7 years; chapter books, 5–10 years; and middle-grade fiction, 8–12 years. Genres include historical and multicultural fiction, folklore, and stories about animals.
- **Nonfiction:** Publishes easy-to-read titles, 4–7 years; story picture books, 4–10, years, chapter books, 5–10 years; and middle-grade books, 8–12 years. Features biographies and books about regional history subjects.
- **Representative Titles:** *The Rachel Resistance* by Molly Levite Griffis follows the adventures of an aspiring spy who is convinced there are traitors and spies in her hometown. *Katherine Stinson: The Flying Schoolgirl* by Debra L. Winegarten is a true story about a girl who, in 1912, was a pioneer in flying, and an inspiration to male and female pilots.

Submissions and Payment
Guidelines available. Query with résumé, sample chapter, and clips or writing samples. Accepts photocopies, computer printouts, and simultaneous submissions if identified. SASE. Responds in 6 months. Publication in 1–2 years. Royalty.

Editor's Comments
We are interested in picture books and chapter books for preschool through third grade readers; fiction and nonfiction for grades four through seven; and young adult fiction and nonfiction.

Ebooksonthe.net

Write Words, Inc.
2934 Old Route 50
Cambridge, MD 21613

Publisher: Constance Foster

Publisher's Interests

"Pure reading pleasure" is the motto of this e-publisher, whose list includes books for readers of all ages, adults as well as children. It is open to submissions of fiction of any genre and nonfiction on a wide variety of topics.
Website: www.ebooksonthe.net

Freelance Potential

Published 30 titles (8 juvenile) in 2004: 1 was developed from an unsolicited submission, 1 was by an agented author, and 8 were reprint/licensed properties. Of the 30 titles, 1 was by an unpublished writer and 10 were by authors who were new to the publishing house. Receives 150 queries, 30 unsolicited mss yearly.

- **Fiction:** Published 1 early picture book, 0–4 years; 2 easy-to-read books, 4–7 years; and 2 middle-grade books, 8–12 years. Genres include mainstream, experimental, historical, Western, and science fiction; adventure; horror; and mystery.
- **Nonfiction:** Publishes nonfiction for all ages. Topics include psychology, money, and business. Also publishes self-help and inspirational titles, how-to books, and biographies.
- **Representative Titles:** *Torpedo Roads* by Roger Vaughan Carr (YA) is a full-length novel that tells of a U-boat crew forced to seek sanctuary with the residents of Abel Island during World War II. *The Ghost Who Lived on Jefferson Street* by Rebecca J. Zarrinnegar is a tale of the supernatural featuring a boy and the ghost he is asked to help.

Submissions and Payment

Guidelines available at website. Query or send complete ms. Accepts disk submissions and email submissions to publisher@ebooksonthe.net (RTF attachments). SASE. Responds to queries in 1 day, to mss in 3 months. Publication in 3 months. Royalty, 40%.

Editor's Comments

Keep in mind that we reach a global audience, and therefore we seek books that have an international appeal.

Educational Ministries

165 Plaza Drive
Prescott, AZ 86303-5549

Submissions Editor: Linda Davidson

Publisher's Interests
Christian educators turn to this publisher for its teaching resources and curricula. It produces nonfiction activity books, educational fiction, educational journals, parenting material, and videos for religious education.
Website: www.educationalministries.com

Freelance Potential
Published 2–3 titles (1 juvenile) in 2004: 1 was developed from an unsolicited submission. Receives 190 unsolicited mss yearly.

- **Fiction:** Publishes toddler books, 0–4 years. Features books with Christian themes, educational themes, educational fiction, and adult fiction.
- **Nonfiction:** Publishes educational resource materials for use by Protestant denominations.
- **Representative Titles:** *Dictionary of Biblical Crafts* by Phyllis Wezeman (teachers) provides easy-to-use instructions for 52 biblical themes. It is designed in a dictionary format so the user can find a definition as well as directions for a variety of projects. *Children and Anger* by Elaine Ward offers methods for helping children understand their anger and ways to deal with it. *Journaling* by Elaine Ward is designed to initiate an interest or support one in keeping a journal, and attending or leading a workshop.

Submissions and Payment
Guidelines available. Send complete ms. Accepts photocopies, computer printouts, and simultaneous submissions if identified. SASE. Responds in 6–8 weeks. Publication in 1–4 months. Flat fee.

Editor's Comments
We are always on the lookout for new, creative resources for church educators and worship leaders. Material must be easy-to-read with step-by-step instructions, and provide a lot of how-to suggestions for teachers. Topics related to teaching the Bible and using the latest technology in the classroom are of interest to us.

Educators Publishing Service

P.O. Box 9031
Cambridge, MA 02139-9031

Vice President, Publishing: Charlie Heinle

Publisher's Interests
This publisher offers educators materials that support students' diverse abilities in classrooms. It publishes a variety of materials in the reading and language arts areas for the general classroom, as well as for students with learning disablities.
Website: www.epsbooks.com

Freelance Potential
Published 40 titles (10 juvenile) in 2004: 2 were developed from unsolicited submissions. Of the 40 titles, 5 were by unpublished writers and 5 were by authors who were new to the publishing house. Receives 250 queries yearly.

- **Fiction:** Publishes easy-to-read books, 4–7 years; and chapter books, 5–10 years.
- **Nonfiction:** Publishes reading, writing, vocabulary, grammar, and comprehension workbooks, grades K–8. Also publishes educational materials for students with learning disabilities.
- **Representative Titles:** *Wordly Wise 3000* by Kenneth Hodkinson and Sandra Adams (grades 2–12) provides systematic vocabulary development including word lists, nonfiction narratives, and other vocabulary exercises. *The Paragraph Book* by Diane Tucker-LaPlount (grades 5–8) is specially designed for the reluctant writer; offers a step-by-step approach to help students write clear, interesting material.

Submissions and Payment
Query with résumé, outline, sample chapter, and table of contents. Accepts photocopies, computer printouts, and simultaneous submissions if identified. SASE. Responds in 2–3 months. Publication in 1 year. Royalty.

Editor's Comments
We are interested in materials following pedagogical restraints that we can incorporate into ongoing or future projects, such as decodable tests and leveled readers. We are also interested in research-based programs in any of the language arts areas.

Edupress

208 Fabricante, #200
San Clemente, CA 92675

Product Coordinator: Kathy Rogers

Publisher's Interests

Innovative products for pre-K through eighth-grade students, teachers, and homeschoolers is the specialty of this educational publisher. Its catalogue includes workbooks, activity books, and classroom materials to help educators create a sound learning environment.
Website: www.edupressinc.com

Freelance Potential

Published 30 titles in 2004: 3 were developed from unsolicited submissions. Receives 30 queries yearly.

- **Nonfiction:** Publishes books and resource materials for educators, pre-K–grade 8. Topics include social studies, science, curriculum coordination, language arts, early learning, math, holidays, arts and crafts, and classroom decor.
- **Representative Titles:** *Ancient Egypt* (grades 2–6) is an activity book loaded with historic and cultural arts, crafts, games, and recipes that help children learn about other cultures; part of the Hands-On Heritage series. *Photo History Activities* (grades 5–8) is a set of photo charts depicting important historical events and people; each set includes related activities and discussion topics.

Submissions and Payment

Guidelines available. Query with outline and sample pages. Accepts photocopies and computer printouts. SASE. Responds in 4–5 months. Publication in 1 year. Flat fee.

Editor's Comments

At Edupress, we create products that help children learn. If students can be successful in what they learn, if they are stimulated by their classroom environment, and if they participate in creative and interactive learning experiences, they will become better students. Send us teaching tools and workbooks that explain concepts in a new way. Take a look at our website and catalogue for an idea of what we do—we have many series on various subjects that need more material for every grade.

Eerdmans Books for Young Readers

255 Jefferson Avenue SE
Grand Rapids, MI 49503

Editor-in-Chief: Judy Zylstra

Publisher's Interests
This publisher offers books that nurture children's faith, help them rejoice in the wonders and joys of life, and prepare them to deal with life's challenges. It publishes picture books, nonfiction, and middle reader and young adult fiction.
Website: www.eerdmans.com/youngreaders

Freelance Potential
Published 15 titles in 2004: 5 were developed from unsolicited submissions, 10 were by agented authors, and 2 were reprint/licensed properties. Of the 15 titles, 2 were by unpublished writers and 7 were by authors who were new to the publishing house. Receives 500 queries, 3,000 unsolicited mss yearly.

- **Fiction:** Published 2 early picture books, 0–4 years; 4 easy-to-read books, 4–7 years; 6 story picture books, 4–10 years; 2 middle-grade books, 8–12 years; and 2 young adult books, 12–18 years. Genres include multicultural and religious fiction. Also publishes retellings of classic tales.
- **Nonfiction:** Publishes early picture books, 0–4 years; and middle-grade books, 8–12 years. Also publishes biographies.
- **Representative Titles:** *A Chick Called Saturday* by Joyce Dunbar (3+ years) tells the story of a young chick who wants to do what all the other farm animals do. *Maggie in the Morning* by Elizabeth Van Steenwyk (9+ years) reveals a young, small town girl's self-discovery and growth during a summer.

Submissions and Payment
Guidelines available. Send complete ms for picture books. Query with 3–4 sample chapters for longer works. Accepts photocopies, computer printouts, and simultaneous submissions if identified. SASE. Responds in 3–4 months. Publication period varies. Royalty.

Editor's Comments
We seek stories that celebrate the wonders of our physical and spiritual world, as well as stories that will simply delight us.

Egmont Children's Books

239 Kensington High Street
London W8 6SA
United Kingdom

Submissions: Jo Spooner

Publisher's Interests
Egmont Books is one of the largest children's book publishers in the United Kingdom, offering titles for all age groups from babies to teens. Its catalogue includes an extensive list of picture books, award-winning fiction, and nonfiction.
Website: www.egmont.co.uk

Freelance Potential
Published 20–30 titles in 2004.

- **Fiction:** Publishes concept books, toddler books, and early picture books, 0–4 years; easy-to-read books, 4–7 years; story picture books, 4–10 years; chapter books, 5–10 years; middle-grade books, 8–12 years; and young adult books, 12–18 years. Genres include adventure; drama; fairy tales; fantasy; mystery; horror; humor; multicultural, inspirational, and historical fiction; and stories about nature and the environment. Also publishes activity books and novelty and board books.
- **Nonfiction:** Publishes concept books, toddler books, and early picture books, 0–4 years; easy-to-read books, 4–7 years; story picture books, 4–10 years; chapter books, 5–10 years; middle-grade books, 8–12 years; and young adult books, 12–18 years. Topics include history and humor. Also publishes activity books and novelty and board books.
- **Representative Titles:** *Just a Boy* by Maeve Henry (10+ years) is the story of a boy who is trying to discover his family's secret. *Five Little Ducks* (0–3 years) is a book of action rhymes; includes a plush toy.

Submissions and Payment
Guidelines available. Query with outline/synopsis and 2 sample chapters. Accepts photocopies. SAE/IRC. Response time varies. Payment policy varies.

Editor's Comments
We aim to introduce creative new formats that will intrigue children and motivate them to learn. Above all, we aim to entertain them.

Eldridge Publishing

P.O. Box 14367
Tallahassee, FL 32317

Editor: Susan Shore

Publisher's Interests
In business for over 98 years, this publishing company offers plays and musicals that are suitable for performances by junior and high school seniors, as well as community theaters. In addition, it produces a smaller line of religious plays.
Website: www.histage.com or www.95church.com

Freelance Potential
Published 70 titles in 2004: 2 were by agented authors. Receives 500+ unsolicited mss yearly.

- **Fiction:** Publishes full-length plays, skits, and musicals, grades 6–12. Genres include contemporary and classical drama, humor, folktales, melodrama, Westerns, and Bible stories. Also publishes plays about holidays and adult drama for community theater.
- **Representative Titles:** *A Substantial Risk* by Joe Rizzo tells the story of a student body president who staged a phony shooting at his school to make a point about school safety. *Toys-R-Alive* by Regina Ballard is a humorous fantasy about adventurous dolls who come alive after a toy store closes.

Submissions and Payment
Send complete ms stating play length and age ranges for actors and audience. Include cassette and sample score with musical submissions. Accepts photocopies, computer printouts, and simultaneous submissions if identified. SASE. Responds in 2 months. Publication in 6–12 months. Royalty, varies. Flat fee for religious plays.

Editor's Comments
We publish a variety of material and are open to new ideas. Please make sure that the age range for actors in plays is not younger than junior high. We are always looking for holiday plays and children's plays for our religious catalogue. Keep in mind that we prefer work to be performed before it is submitted.

Encore Performance Publishing

Suite 200
2181 West California Avenue
Salt Lake City, UT 84104

President: Michael Perry

Publisher's Interests
This publisher specializes in books for all ages that are related to the theater and plays. Its titles are used in school classrooms and by community and church theater groups. Full-length plays, musicals, one-act plays, skits, and monologues are found in its catalogue.
Website: www.encoreplay.com

Freelance Potential
Published 8–15 titles in 2004: 2 were by agented authors. Of the 8–15 titles, 2 were by unpublished writers and 6 were by new authors. Receives 100+ queries yearly.

- **Fiction:** Published 2 easy-to-read books, 4–7 years; 6 middle-grade books, 8–12 years; and 10 young adult books, 12–18 years. Features dramas with multicultural, religious, and ethnic themes, as well as educational, bilingual, and humorous plays.
- **Nonfiction:** Publishes books about theater arts for all ages. Topics include acting, auditions, improvisation, stage management, set design, lighting, and makeup.
- **Representative Titles:** *Elephans* by Jeff Goode is a musical set on the lonely planet of Eleph, where language was never invented and its people learn to communicate without words. *The Glint of Gold* by Gawen Robinson is written specifically for young voices and is set in Egypt at the discovery of the tomb of Tutankhamun.

Submissions and Payment
Guidelines available. Query with résumé, synopsis, and production history. Accepts photocopies and computer printouts. SASE. Responds in 2 weeks. Publication in 2 months. Royalty, 50% performance, 10% book.

Editor's Comments
While we welcome a wide variety of material, we are especially interested in plays that will broaden the talents of young performing actors. When you write, keep in mind that many of our plays must be produced with minimal sets and need a large number of characters.

Enslow Publishers, Inc.

Box 398
40 Industrial Road
Berkeley Heights, NJ 07922-0398

Vice President: Brian Enslow

Publisher's Interests

Enslow Publishers, Inc., is a large publishing house with a list of more than 200 titles. All its books are curriculum-based nonfiction geared towards children between the ages of four and eighteen. Topics covered include multicultural subjects, the environment, health, and social issues. It offers stand-alone titles as well as books in series.
Website: www.enslow.com

Freelance Potential

Published 225 titles (75 juvenile) in 2004: 25 were developed from unsolicited submissions. Of the 225 titles, 25 were by unpublished writers and 75 were by authors who were new to the publishing house. Receives 1,000 queries yearly.

- **Nonfiction:** Publishes easy-to-read books, 4–7 years; chapter books, 5–10 years; middle-grade books, 8–12 years; and young adult books, 12–18 years. Topics include social issues, health, history, the environment, science, and multicultural and ethnic subjects.
- **Representative Titles:** *Land Mines* by Elaine Landau (6+ years) takes an in-depth look at these killers hidden underground, waiting to detonate on unsuspecting civilians; part of the Issues in Focus series. *Mary Cassatt* by Carolyn Casey (grades 3–4) looks at the life of this famous American painter—one of the few women of the Impressionist period; part of the Artist Biographies series.

Submissions and Payment

Guidelines available. Query with outline and market analysis. Accepts photocopies and computer printouts. SASE. Responds in 1–6 months. Publication in 1 year. Royalty; advance. Flat fee.

Editor's Comments

Our needs remain the same as they have always been. Our mission is to publish the best educational, curriculum-based books out there. The topics of science and history and biographies head our list of needs at this time.

Evan-Moor Educational Publishers

18 Lower Ragsdale Drive
Monterey, CA 93940

Editorial Assistant: Lisa Mathews

Publisher's Interests
This educational publisher meets the needs of teachers working with students in pre-kindergarten through grade six. Its curriculum-based titles cover a wide range of subject matter including math, social studies, science, language arts, writing, and arts and crafts. The bulk of its titles target primary school students.
Website: www.evan-moor.com

Freelance Potential
Published 40 titles in 2004: 2 were by authors who were new to the publishing house. Receives 350 queries, 250 unsolicited mss yearly.

- **Nonfiction:** Publishes classroom and homeschooling resources, teaching materials, and activity books, pre-K–grade 6. Topics include social studies, mathematics, science, technology, reading, writing, language arts, early learning, and arts and crafts. Also publishes thematic units.
- **Representative Titles:** *Daily Paragraph Editing* (grades 2–6) is a series of five books that presents passages aimed at teaching grammar and punctuation. *Continents and Oceans* (pre-K–grade 2) contains materials and projects to help children become familiar with the continents and major bodies of water on Earth; part of the Beginning Geography series.

Submissions and Payment
Guidelines available at website. Query with outline and sample pages; or send complete ms. Accepts photocopies and computer printouts, and simultaneous submissions if identified. SASE. Responds in 3 months. Publication in 1–2 years. Flat fee.

Editor's Comments
At this time, we are interested in receiving résumés and writing samples from authors who can write preschool activities across all subject areas. Keep in mind that most of the books we publish appear as parts of series. Because the market for curriculum resources is so large, we strongly urge you to research your area of expertise carefully to determine whether your titles will bring new ideas to the field.

Facts On File

17th Floor
132 West 31st Street
New York, NY 10001

Editorial Director: Laurie Likoff
Senior Editor, Young Adult: Nicole Bowen

Publisher's Interests
Established in 1940, Facts On File is one of the best-known reference publishers catering to the school and library markets. Its books are written for students in grades three through twelve. All curriculum subjects are covered, including social studies, history, language and literature, and science.
Website: www.factsonfile.com

Freelance Potential
Published 250 titles in 2004: 5 were developed from unsolicited submissions, 60–70 were by agented authors, and 15 were reprint/licensed properties. Of the 250 titles, 60 were by unpublished writers. Receives 150 queries yearly.

- **Nonfiction:** Publishes chapter books, 5–10 years; middle-grade books, 8–12 years; and young adult books, 12–18 years. Topics include history, social issues, current affairs, politics, multicultural subjects, mathematics, science, and the environment.
- **Representative Titles:** *Life on Earth* (grades 4–8) answers questions about how life on Earth began and developed on land. *Adventure Heroes* by Jeff Rovin (grades 6 and up) investigates such legendary characters as Odysseus and James Bond.

Submissions and Payment
Query with outline, sample chapter, description of audience, competitive titles, and marketing ideas. Accepts photocopies, computer printouts, and simultaneous submissions if identified. SASE. Responds in 2 months. Publication in 1 year. Royalty; advance.

Editor's Comments
Our goal is to bring our audience the very best and most up-to-date reference materials on a wide range of curriculum subjects. We look for writers who can deliver reference material in a balanced, complete, and forthright manner. To better understand what works best for us, visit our website or review our catalogue to see if your material is appropriate, and has not been addressed by another book.

Faith Kidz

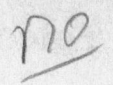

4050 Lee Vance View
Colorado Springs, CO 80918

Editorial Assistant

Publisher's Interests
Faith Kidz is an imprint of Cook Communications Ministries. Its books share the same mission: equipping kids for life through faith. Its catalogue contains interactive books, toys, and games that develop strong character in children. Books for birth through age 12 are found on its list.
Website: www.cookministries.com/faithkidz

Freelance Potential
Published 120 titles (31 juvenile) in 2004. Of the 120 titles, 5 were by authors who were new to the publishing house. Receives 1,000+ queries yearly.

- **Fiction:** Publishes easy-to-read books, 4–7 years; chapter books, 5–10 years; and middle-grade novels, 8–12 years. Genres include religious and inspirational fiction.
- **Nonfiction:** Publishes easy-to-read books, 4–7 years; chapter books, 5–10 years; and middle-grade titles, 8–12 years. Topics include Christianity, the Bible, and life skills.
- **Representative Titles:** *Baby Bible Stories about Jesus* by Robin Currie (0–3 years) offers age-appropriate stories accompanied by simple activities and hand motions. *Rescue in the Mayan Jungle* by Karla Warkentin (8–12 years) is about a mysterious stone capable of transporting Josh and his siblings back through time: part of the Time-Stone Travelers Series.

Submissions and Payment
Query with writing credits and market analysis of comparative products. Accepts photocopies and computer printouts. SASE. Response time and publication period vary. All books are written on a work-for-hire basis.

Editor's Comments
We are interested in writers who have a firm grip on what we publish. You are urged to review our catalogue and then review some of our titles before submitting. Note that many of our titles appear in series.

Falcon Publishing

246 Goose Lane
P.O. Box 480
Guilford, CT 06437

Acquisitions Editor

Publisher's Interests

This imprint of regional publisher the Globe Pequot Press specializes in books on the outdoors and recreation. Its list features titles on specific areas for such outdoor activities as hiking, biking, wildlife sightseeing, and water sports. Its children's books are devoted to subjects that relate to nature, the environment, and animals. It does not offer any fiction.
Website: www.globepequot.com

Freelance Potential

Published 150 titles in 2003: 3 were developed from unsolicited submissions, 90 were by agented authors, and 6 were reprint/licensed properties. Of the 150 titles, 60 were by authors who were new to the publishing house. Receives 100 queries each year.

- **Nonfiction:** Publishes chapter books, 5–10 years; middle-grade books, 8–12 years; and young adult books, 12–18 years. Topics include nature, animals, the environment, regional subjects, and history.
- **Representative Titles:** *Arctic Wild* by Lois Crisler is the story of two naturalists who spent 18 months in the Arctic, where their lives were touched by two wolf pups. *Wild Colorado* by Donna Lynn Ikenberry looks at the natural beauty found in the parks and preserves of Colorado and offers ideas on ways to enjoy these sights.

Submissions and Payment

Guidelines available. Query with synopsis, table of contents, and sample chapter. Accepts photocopies and computer printouts. SASE. Responds in 3 months. Publication in 1 year. Royalty.

Editor's Comments

We are a niche publisher focusing on nature and wildlife. Most of our material offers ideas for family fun that includes visits to the country's most beautiful natural wonders. Review our list before you consider sending a query.

Family Learning Association & ERIC/REC

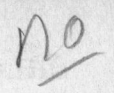

Suite 101
3925 Hagan Street
Bloomington, IN 47401

Director: Carl B. Smith

Publisher's Interests
This publisher focuses on educational material for use in the classroom as well as on related teacher resources, and books for parents. Some of the subjects regularly covered include study skills, character education, reading, writing, and cross-curricular themes.
Website: www.kidscanlearn.com

Freelance Potential
Published 20 titles in 2004: 1 was developed from an unsolicited submission and 5 were reprint/licensed properties. Of the 20 titles, 1 was by an unpublished writer. Receives 100 queries yearly.

- **Fiction:** Publishes easy-to-read books, 4–7 years.
- **Nonfiction:** Publishes easy-to read books, 4–7 years; story picture books, 4–10 years; chapter books, 5–10 years; and middle-grade books, 8–12 years. Also publishes professional development resources, research materials, and reference titles for educators. Features parenting and meeting leader guides, parent handouts, and Spanish and bilingual material. Topics include reading, writing, English, communications, and family and intergenerational literacy. Also offers interactive books with audio cassettes for family resource centers.
- **Representative Titles:** *Elementary Grammar: A Children's Resource Book* by Carl B. Smith includes guides to sentence structure, nouns and pronouns, verbs, and word study. *Phonics Plus Book A* by Carl B. Smith & Regina Ruff focuses on developing children's skills with recognizing the letters of the alphabet and the initial sounds in words.

Submissions and Payment
Query with table of contents, sample chapter, and market analysis. Accepts photocopies and computer printouts. SASE. Responds in 1 month. Publication in 1–2 years. Royalty, 6–10%. Flat fee.

Editor's Comments
Our goal is to be familiar with what teachers want to help them in their jobs and we look for materials that will meet these needs.

Farrar, Straus & Giroux

19 Union Square West
New York, NY 10003

Children's Editorial Department

Publisher's Interests
This well-known publisher offers fiction titles for children between the ages of three and eighteen. Occasionally they will publish a non-fiction work on a topic related to history, science, or nature, but these titles are few in number.
Website: www.fsgkidsbooks.com

Freelance Potential
Published 80 titles in 2004: 5 were developed from unsolicited submissions, 35 were by agented authors, and 5 were reprint/licensed properties. Of the 80 titles, 5 were by unpublished writers. Receives 1,000 queries, 6,000 unsolicited mss yearly.

- **Fiction:** Publishes easy-to-read books, 4–7 years; story picture books, 3–10 years; chapter books, 6–10 years; middle-grade novels, 8–12 years; and young adult books, 12–18 years. Genres include fantasy, humor, and contemporary fiction.
- **Nonfiction:** Publishes story picture books, 4–10 years; middle-grade books, 8–12 years; and young adult books, 12–18 years. Topics include history, science, and nature.
- **Representative Titles:** *Widget & The Puppy* by Lyn Rossiter McFarland and Jim McFarland (3–6 years) follows Widget, whose life is turned upside down when a stray puppy arrives. *Letting Go of Bobby James* by Valerie Hobbs (YA) chronicles the life of a young girl who is abandoned by her abusive husband.

Submissions and Payment
Guidelines available. Query for mss longer than 20 pages; send complete ms for shorter works. Accepts photocopies, computer printouts, and simultaneous submissions if identified. SASE. Responds in 2–3 months. Publication in 18–36 months. Royalty, 3–10% of list price, $3,000–$15,000.

Editor's Comments
Most of our accepted manuscripts come from agented authors, but we are willing to review excellent work from new writers as well.

Frederick Fell Publishers

Suite 305
2131 Hollywood Boulevard
Hollywood, FL 33020

Senior Editor: Barbara Newman

Publisher's Interests
Established in 1943, Frederick Fell Publishers concentrates primarily on spiritual and how-to books for adults and young adults. Guides to a wide range of issues, from self-promotion to hypnotism to tying knots, are a major part of its list.
Website: www.fellpub.com

Freelance Potential
Published 24 titles in 2004. Receives 4,000 queries yearly.

- **Fiction:** Publishes young adult books, 12–18 years. Genres include inspirational and religious fiction.
- **Nonfiction:** Publishes young adult books, 12–18 years. Topics include health and spirituality. Features how-to and self-help titles. Also publishes biographies and books about parenting, child care, business, science, and entertainment for adults.
- **Representative Titles:** *Help Your Child Excel in Math* by Margaret Berge & Philip Gibbons (parents) uses games and puzzles to illustrate how teaching and learning math can be enjoyable for both parents and children. *Angel Threads* by Robert J. Danzig (YA–Adult) presents inspirational stories that show the various ways angels have manifested themselves to people who were open to receiving them.

Submissions and Payment
Guidelines available. Query with résumé and marketing plan. Availability of artwork improves chance of acceptance. Accepts photocopies and simultaneous submissions if identified. SASE. Responds in 1 month. Publication in 9–12 months. Royalty.

Editor's Comments
Our commitment to excellence has made us one of the leading independent trade publishers in the U.S. Our backlist consists of over 1,500 books in 13 genres. Spiritual growth continues to be an area of interest. Our Know-It-All Guides™ cover a broad range of topics and we will consider adding to this list. Consult a catalogue to see what we like and which subjects have already been covered.

Ferguson Publishing

17th Floor
132 West 31st Street
New York, NY 10001

Editorial Director: Laurie Likoff

Publisher's Interests
This publisher offers career education and vocational resource materials for middle-school through college students and their guidance counselors. It also includes financial aid directories and handbooks on occupational outlooks.
Website: www.fergpubco.com and www.factsonfile.com

Freelance Potential
Published 35–45 titles (30 juvenile) in 2004: 2 were developed from unsolicited submissions and 10 were by agented authors. Of the 35–45 titles, 2 were by authors who were new to the publishing house. Receives 30 queries, 15 unsolicited mss yearly.

- **Nonfiction:** Published 30 young adult books, 12–18 years. Also publishes chapter books, 12–18 years. Topics include college planning, career awareness, and job training. Also publishes professional development titles and general reference books.
- **Representative Titles:** *Career Skills Library Set* (grades 5–8) helps students learn the technical skills and personal skills that are critical to success in any field. *Community Service for Teens* (grades 7–12) is a resource for students interested in volunteering that discusses the many benefits of volunteering, lists a variety of community service options, and includes a directory of organizations with volunteer opportunities.

Submissions and Payment
Guidelines available at website. Query with table of contents; or send complete ms with proposal. Accepts photocopies, computer printouts, email submissions to editorial@factsonfile.com, and simultaneous submissions if identified. Publication period varies. Work-for-hire and some royalty assignments.

Editor's Comments
We're looking for material from experienced writers on career exploration and general job skills for ages 12–18, and career guidance and development for ages 14 to adult.

Floris Books

15 Harrison Gardens
Edinburgh, EH11 1SH
Scotland
United Kingdom

Editor: Gail Winskill

Publisher's Interests

In 2001, this publisher acquired the Kelpies imprint, which produces contemporary Scottish fiction for readers age 9 to 12 and teen fiction for young adults. It features classic Kelpies titles, as well as original material by new authors.
Website: www.florisbooks.co.uk

Freelance Potential

Published 12 titles in 2004: 1 was developed from an unsolicited submission and 9 were by agented authors. Receives 150 unsolicited mss yearly.

- **Fiction:** Published 4 story picture books, 4–10 years; 6 middle-grade books, 8–12 years; and 2 young adult books, 12–18 years. Genres include contemporary, multicultural, and regional fiction; drama; and fantasy.
- **Representative Titles:** *Goldie at the Orphanage* by Martha Sandwall-Bergström (5–7 years) is about a little girl with flaxen hair who meets a new friend in the orphanage. *Hamish and the Fairy Gifts* by Moira Miller (8–11 years) is a humorous tale about an old lady and her trouble with the "wee folk."

Submissions and Payment

Guidelines available. Query or send complete ms. Agented submissions improve chance of acceptance. Does not accept nonfiction. Accepts photocopies. SASE. Responds to queries in 1 week; to mss in 3 months. Publication in 18 months. Royalty.

Editor's Comments

Although most of the original Kelpies books consist of some historical fiction, our research has found that there is more demand for books that encompass modern settings, contemporary situations, and recognizable characters to which today's readers can relate. Note that we do not accept submissions for picture books—the picture books you see in our catalogues have been co-produced with other European publishing houses.

Focus on the Family Book Development

8675 Explorer Drive
Colorado Springs, CO 80920

Submissions Editor: Mark Maddox

Publisher's Interests
The Focus on the Family nonprofit organization is dedicated to the preservation of the home. Its publishing imprint offers an extensive catalogue of books for all ages. All of its titles reflect Christian values. The company plans numerous changes in its publishing program over the next year which will be posted on the website.
Website: www.family.org

Freelance Potential
Published 50 titles (15 juvenile) in 2004: 8 were developed from unsolicited submissions and 5 were by agented authors. Of the 50 titles, 1 was by an unpublished writer and 8 were by authors who were new to the publishing house. Receives 100 queries yearly.

- **Fiction:** Publishes chapter books, 5–10 years; middle grade novels, 8–12 years; and young adult books, 12–18 years. Genres include religious and inspirational fiction.
- **Nonfiction:** Publishes easy-to-read books, 4–7 years; story picture books, 4–10 years; young adult books, 12–18 years. Topics include hobbies, crafts, current events, entertainment, religion, and social issues. Also offers self-help titles.
- **Representative Titles:** *Protecting Your Child in an X–R World* by Frank York & Jan LaRue (parents) offers a practical plan for keeping your children away from the dangers of pornography. *MomTime* by Lisa Whelchel (mothers) takes a humorous yet practical look at home schooling.

Submissions and Payment
Guidelines available. Query with outline/synopsis, résumé, and market analysis. Accepts photocopies, disk submissions (Microsoft Word/RTF), and email to maddoxmh@fotf.org. SASE. Responds in 1 month. Publication in 12–14 months. Payment policy varies.

Editor's Comments
Keep checking our website for updates on our changing needs in material. Most of our books are written on a work-for-hire basis.

Forest House Publishing Company

P.O. Box 13350
Chandler, AZ 85248

President: Dianne Spahr

Publisher's Interests
Forest House Publishing Company specializes in educational materials for use in the school and library markets. It features fiction and nonfiction for children up to the age of ten as well as bilingual titles and books in Spanish.
Website: www.forest-house.com

Freelance Potential
Published 12 titles (6 juvenile) in 2004. Receives 100 queries yearly.

- **Fiction:** Publishes concept, toddler, and early picture books, 0–4 years; easy-to-read books, 4–7 years; story picture books, 4–10 years; chapter books, 5–10 years; and middle-grade fiction, 8–12 years. Genres include contemporary and multicultural fiction; fairy tales; and adventure.
- **Nonfiction:** Publishes easy-to-read books, 4–7 years; and chapter books, 5–10 years. Topics include nature, animals, arts and crafts, special education, sign language, history, the environment, and ethnic and multicultural subjects.
- **Representative Titles:** *The Prince Who Wrote a Letter* by Ann Love (grades K–3) is about a young prince who is delighted to write his first letters of the alphabet, except that the King and Queen think he has written a real letter on his first day of kindergarten. *To Be a Wolf* (grades 3–6) is the story of a Pawnee Indian boy who befriends a wild wolf pup.

Submissions and Payment
Query with résumé. No unsolicited mss. Accepts photocopies and computer printouts. SASE. Responds in 6 months. Publication in 1 year. Royalty; advance. Flat fee.

Editor's Comments
We continue to look for nonfiction for our American history series, as well as fiction, especially mysteries, for older readers. The books we publish are designed to entertain children while educating them. Remember that we no longer accept unsolicited manuscripts.

Formac Publishing Company, Ltd.

5502 Atlantic Street
Halifax, Nova Scotia B3H 1G4
Canada

Senior Editor: Elizabeth Eve

Publisher's Interests
Established in 1973, this Canadian publisher offers fiction for early readers through young adults. Many of its titles feature the people, history, and culture of Canada.
Website: www.formac.ca

Freelance Potential
Published 20 titles (10 juvenile) in 2004: 4 were reprint/licensed properties. Of the 20 titles, 1 was by an unpublished writer and 1 was by an author who was new to the publishing house. Receives 80 queries yearly.

- **Fiction:** Publishes easy-to-read books, 4–7 years; chapter books, 5–10 years; and middle-grade books, 8–12 years. Genres include mystery, suspense, fantasy, adventure, humor, historical fiction, and stories about sports.
- **Nonfiction:** Publishes middle-grade books, 8–12 years. Topics include regional, multicultural, and ethnic subjects; sports; nature; and the environment.
- **Representative Titles:** *Billy Higgins Rides the Freights* by Gloria Montero (8–12 years) is the story of a young man who comes of age in the brutal years of Canada's Great Depression. *First Spring on the Grand Banks* by Bill Freeman (8–12 years) captures the life and struggles of fishermen and their families in an isolated Nova Scotia village; part of the Bains series.

Submissions and Payment
Guidelines available at website. Query with résumé, outline, and sample chapters. No unsolicited mss. Accepts photocopies, computer printouts, and simultaneous submissions if identified. SAE/IRC. Responds in 1–12 months. Publication in 1–2 years. Royalty.

Editor's Comments
Historical fiction for children remains a priority for us, as well as nonfiction books about the Canadian environment. Writers are encouraged to check the guidelines and products at our website.

Forward Movement Publications

2nd Floor
300 West Fourth Street
Cincinnati, OH 45202

Submissions Editor: Edward S. Gleason

Publisher's Interests
Forward Movement is a religious publisher affiliated with the Episcopal Church. Its list features both fiction and nonfiction for middle-grade readers. All of its fiction titles are based on Christian beliefs and its nonfiction covers topics related to spirituality and church history.
Website: www.forwardmovement.org

Freelance Potential
Published 30 titles in 2004: 10 were developed from unsolicited submissions. Of the 30 titles, 16–20 were by unpublished writers and 15 were by authors who were new to the publishing house. Receives 400 queries yearly.

- **Fiction:** Publishes middle-grade books, 8–12 years; and young adult books, 12–18 years. Features contemporary fiction with Christian themes.
- **Nonfiction:** Publishes middle-grade books, 8–12 years. Topics include meditation, spirituality, church history, and contemporary issues such as drug abuse and AIDS.
- **Representative Titles:** *The Gift of Life* is designed to lead young worshippers through the communion rite, as practiced by members of the Anglican Church of Canada. *Murder at Rainbow Falls* by Tommy Lovelace & Betty Streett follows the adventures of two boys who witness a murder on a church camping trip.

Submissions and Payment
Guidelines, catalogue, and sample pamphlet available ($1.65 postage, no SASE). Query with sample chapters. Accepts photocopies and computer printouts. SASE. Responds in 1 month. Publication period varies. Flat fee.

Editor's Comments
Our goal is to support our readers in their lives of prayer and faith. At this time we continue to seek submissions of material for our pamphlets, to be used in Sunday school classrooms.

Frances Foster Books

Farrar, Straus & Giroux
19 Union Square West
New York, NY 10003

Editor: Frances Foster
Associate Editor: Janine O'Malley

Publisher's Interests
This imprint of Farrar, Straus & Giroux offers literary fiction for readers of all ages up to young adult. A few nonfiction titles may also be found in its catalogue. Both hardcover fiction and paperback reprints are published by Frances Foster Books.
Website: www.fsgkidsbooks.com

Freelance Potential
Published 20 titles in 2004: 10 were by agented authors. Receives 100 queries, 12,000 unsolicited mss yearly.

- **Fiction:** Publishes early picture books, 0–4 years; story picture books, 4–10 years; chapter books, 5–10 years; middle-grade novels, 8–12 years; and young adult books, 12–18 years. Genres include contemporary, historical, and ethnic fiction; fantasy, adventure, and drama.
- **Nonfiction:** Publishes a few titles on historical subjects.
- **Representative Titles:** *Tiger on a Tree* by Anushka Ravishankar (3–6 years) follows the adventures of a tiger in India who is captured and then let go, only to lead a raucous chase. *The Blue Mirror* by Kathe Koja (YA) is a coming-of-age story about a teen who escapes from her not-so-happy real world into a world she creates through her drawings.

Submissions and Payment
Guidelines available. Query with 3 sample chapters and synopsis for novels. Send complete ms for picture books. Do not send original art. Accepts photocopies, computer printouts, and simultaneous submissions if identified. No email submissions. SASE. Responds in 3+ months. Publication in 2+ years. Royalty; advance.

Editor's Comments
We consider all of our titles to fall under the description of literary fiction—meaning that because of their universal themes, they will stand the test of time. We look for writers whose work will meet this definition with strong characters, intriguing plot lines, and lively stories.

A Difference in the World
Douglas Fehlen
Free Spirit Publishing

Founded by Judy Galbraith in 1983, Free Spirit Publishing has specialized in producing high-quality nonfiction materials for children, teens, parents, teachers, counselors, and others involved in the lives of children. The company, located in Minneapolis, Minnesota, publishes an award-winning list of books and learning materials, all of which support the publisher's mission to help children and teens succeed in life and make a difference in the world.

Acquisitions Assistant Douglas J. Fehlen reports that Free Spirit has a long list of topics they are interested in, including mental, social, and emotional health; life skills; school success; conflict resolution; careers; sex and sexuality; substance abuse; eating disorders; etiquette; teen legal rights; and abuse. Authors do not necessarily have to be expert in a particular content, Fehlen says, but "books on weightier topics (depression/suicide, anxiety, and abuse, for example) tend to be those where it's important to us to have an expert from the health field."

Fehlen sees the trend for formatted books—lists, guides, steps—continuing. Writers should query with résumé, outline, and two sample chapters.

(See listing for Free Spirit Publishing on following page)

Free Spirit Publishing

Suite 200
217 Fifth Avenue North
Minneapolis, MN 55401-1299

Acquisitions Editor: Douglas J. Fehlen

Publisher's Interests
Founded in 1983, Free Spirit Publishing offers books and learning materials for children, teens, educators, counselors, and parents. Its mission is to bring children of all ages the knowledge and self understanding needed to get through life successfully. It does not publish any fiction.
Website: www.freespirit.com

Freelance Potential
Published 22 titles (9 juvenile) in 2004: 11 were developed from unsolicited submissions and 2 were by agented authors. Receives 2,000 queries yearly.

- **Nonfiction:** Published 3 toddler books, 0-4 years; 6 easy-to-read books, 4-7 years; 8 young adult books, 12-18 years. Topics include family and social issues, stress management, character building, relationships, creativity, self awareness, and self-esteem. Also publishes titles for parents, teachers, youth workers, and child-care professionals on learning disorders, psychology, and gifted and talented education.
- **Representative Titles:** *The Power of Positive Talk* by Douglas Bloch (parents) helps children by teaching adults how to communicate successfully and to deliver the right message. *How Rude!* by Alex J. Packer (13+ years) is a guide to good behavior and manners for teens.

Submissions and Payment
Guidelines available. Query with résumé, outline, and 2 sample chapters. Accepts photocopies and computer printouts. SASE. Responds in 1-3 months. Publication in 1-3 years. Royalty; advance.

Editor's Comments
Our books are respected for their creative, practical, and solution-based focus. A number of topics for the coming year will get a serious look. Subjects of interest are: bullying, listening, body image, life skills, gifted education, diversity, media, character education, activism, and conflict resolution.

Samuel French, Inc.

45 West 25th Street
New York, NY 10010

Editor: Lawrence Harbison

Publisher's Interests
Samuel French features a variety of musicals—from Broadway hits and intimate reviews, to simple productions—all suitable for children and teen theater groups. It also offers theater resources and classroom guides for theater educators.
Website: www.samuelfrench.com

Freelance Potential
Published 50 titles (3 juvenile) in 2004. Of the 50 titles, 5 were by unpublished writers and 10 were by authors who were new to the publishing house. Receives 150 queries, 150 unsolicited mss yearly.

- **Fiction:** Publishes full-length and one-act plays, monologues, readings, and anthologies for theater groups of all ages. Genres include musicals and operettas, religious and holiday plays, and Shakespearean drama.
- **Nonfiction:** Publishes books and resource materials for theater teachers and directors. Topics include acting methods, direction, stage design, lighting, management, auditions, comedy, improvisations, and film production.
- **Representative Titles:** *Bridge to Terabithia* by Katherine Paterson & Stephanie S. Tolan is a powerful children's play about growing up in rural Virginia. *The Dangerous Christmas of Red Riding Hood* by Robert Emmett is a bubbly musical about a holiday party and the social problems of Lone T. Wolf.

Submissions and Payment
Guidelines available. Query or send complete ms. Accepts photocopies. SASE. Responds to queries in 1 week, to mss in 2–3 months. Publication in 1 year. Payment policy varies.

Editor's Comments
We are seeking the world's best plays to make them available to a range of producing groups. We are especially interested in plays, monologues, and audition materials that address the contemporary concerns of youth and teens.

Front Street Books

862 Haywood Road
Asheville, NC 28806

Editor: Joy Neaves

Publisher's Interests
This well known independent publisher offers fiction and nonfiction titles for children of all ages. It welcomes submissions for fiction, poetry, and nonfiction but is no longer accepting unsolicited picture book manuscripts.
Website: www.frontstreetbooks.com

Freelance Potential
Published 24 titles in 2004: 2 were developed from unsolicited submissions, 1 was by an agented author, and 2 were reprint/licensed properties. Of the 24 titles, 3 were by unpublished writers and 4 were by authors who were new to the publishing house. Receives 2,000 queries and unsolicited mss yearly.

- **Fiction:** Published 3 early picture books, 0–4 years; 3 story picture books, 4–10 years; 3 middle-grade books, 8–12 years; and 3 young adult books, 12–18 years. Genres include humor; adventure; fantasy; and multicultural, historical, contemporary, and science fiction.
- **Nonfiction:** Publishes young adult books, 12–18 years. Also publishes novelty books, educational titles, and poetry.
- **Representative Titles:** *Apple Island* by Douglas Evans follows a young boy's adventure to Apple Island, the home of all teachers. *The Wicked Witch Is at It Again* by Hanna Kraan features interlinked short stories that are set in a magical forest.

Submissions and Payment
Guidelines available at website. Query with sample chapter for nonfiction. Send complete ms for fiction under 100 pages, or 2 sample chapters for longer works. Accepts photocopies, computer printouts, and simultaneous submissions if identified. SASE. Responds in 3 months. Publication in 12–18 months. Royalty; advance.

Editor's Comments
We welcome all submissions that fit our niche, but since we publish a small list, we will only consider submissions that really stand out.

Fulcrum Publishing

Suite 300
16100 Table Mountain Parkway
Golden, CO 80403-1672

Submissions Editor: T. J. Baker

Publisher's Interests
Established in 1984, Fulcrum Publishing specializes in books and support material for teachers, librarians, parents, and children in elementary school and middle school. Its list includes titles that cover science, nature, multicultural studies, and Native American and Hispanic culture.
Website: www.fulcrum-books.com

Freelance Potential
Published 30 titles (2 juvenile) in 2004: 2 were by agented authors. Receives 250 queries, 1,500 unsolicited mss yearly.

- **Nonfiction:** Publishes story picture books, 4–10 years; chapter books, 5–10 years; and middle-grade books, 8–12 years. Topics include Native American culture, outdoor activities, history, the American West, natural history, and the environment. Also publishes educational activity books for educators and parents.
- **Representative Titles:** *The Crimson Elf* by Michael J. Caduto (grades 3 and up) is an anthology of Italian folk stories with gentle lessons. *Dog People: Native Dog Stories* by Joseph Bruchac (grades 3 and up) celebrates the ancient relationship between youngsters and dogs.

Submissions and Payment
Guidelines available. Query or send complete ms with résumé and competition analysis. Accepts photocopies, computer printouts, and simultaneous submissions if identified. SASE. Responds to queries in 1 month, to unsolicited mss in 2–3 months. Publication in 18–24 months. Royalty; advance.

Editor's Comments
Our goal is to obtain the best manuscripts from the best authors to achieve the finest quality products. Nonfiction titles on the environment and multicultural issues are important at this time. We would also like to see educational packages that include books, lesson plans, teacher's guides, and reproducible masters to assist teachers in preparing their students for assessment.

Laura Geringer Books

HarperCollins Children's Books
1350 Avenue of the Americas
New York, NY 10019

Publisher: Laura Geringer

Publisher's Interests
Laura Geringer Books is one of the newer imprints of HarperCollins Children's Books and specializes in picture books and literary fiction for middle-grade through young adult readers. It does not publish any nonfiction. As Laura Geringer Books approaches its tenth anniversary, it continues to publish innovative authors who "push the envelope" and set new standards of excellence.
Website: www.harperchildrens.com

Freelance Potential
Published 9 titles in 2004: all were by agented authors. Of the 9 titles, 1 was by an unpublished writer and 2 were by authors who were new to the publishing house. Receives 900 queries yearly.

- **Fiction:** Publishes easy-to-read books, 4–7 years; story picture books, 4–10 years; middle-grade books, 8–12 years; and young adult books, 12–18 years. Genres include adventure; mystery; contemporary, multicultural, and historical fiction; folklore, fantasy; humor; drama; and stories about nature.
- **Representative Titles:** *The Little Giant* by Sergio Ruzzier is the story of Angelino, a little giant who runs away from home and meets Osvaldo, who is exactly the same size. *Shakespeare's Daughter* by Peter W. Hassinger is the story of Susanna Shakespeare, who thinks her small town of Stratford-upon-Avon is much too quiet and sets off on an unpredictable adventure to London.

Submissions and Payment
Query. Prefers submissions from agented authors. Accepts photocopies. SASE. Responds in 2–10 weeks. Publication period and payment policy vary.

Editor's Comments
We are interested in picture books and quality middle-grade and young adult fiction. Please note that we will prefer to review submissions from authors with agents.

Gibbs Smith, Publisher

P.O. Box 667
Layton, UT 84040

Children's Book Editor: Melissa Barlow

Publisher's Interests
This family-owned publishing house features both nonfiction and fiction for children and adults. The company's mission is "to enrich and inspire humankind." The year 2004 marks the 35th anniversary of Gibbs Smith.
Website: www.gibbs-smith.com

Freelance Potential
Published 75 titles (9 juvenile) in 2004: 2 were by unpublished writers and 30 were by authors who were new to the publishing house. Receives 500 queries, 2,000 unsolicited mss yearly.

- **Fiction:** Publishes easy-to-read books, 4–7 years; and story picture books, 4–10 years. Genres include adventure, Westerns, humor, fantasy, folktales, and stories about animals, nature, and the environment.
- **Nonfiction:** Publishes activity books, 4–10 years. Features books about the outdoors.
- **Representative Titles:** *My Subway Ride* by Paul Dubois Jacobs and Jennifer Swender (4–8 years) spotlights the rhythm, beat, and energy of New York City's subways. *Snowflakes for All Seasons* by Cindy Higham is an activity book that shows children of all ages how to make paper snowflakes of all shapes and sizes.

Submissions and Payment
Guidelines available. Send complete ms for picture books. Query with outline and writing samples for nonfiction. Accepts photocopies, computer printouts, and simultaneous submissions if identified. SASE. Responds in 10–12 weeks. Publication in 1–2 years. Royalty; advance.

Editor's Comments
If you are not familiar with our titles, think smart, think stylish, think original. This description fits every book in our catalogue and is a description prospective writers should keep in mind when submitting a query to us. Activity books continue to top our wish list, and we always will consider stories set in the West.

Gifted Education Press

P.O. Box 1586
10201 Yuma Court
Manassas, VA 20108

Publisher: Maurice D. Fisher

Publisher's Interests

This small educational publisher specializes in curriculum materials to be used with gifted children ages ten to fifteen. Its titles cover a wide range of subjects including mathematics, language arts, and critical thinking. All of its authors are experts in their educational field.
Website: www.giftededpress.com

Freelance Potential

Published 4 titles (2 juvenile) in 2004: all were developed from unsolicited submissions. Receives 100 queries yearly.

- **Nonfiction:** Published 4 middle-grade books, 8–12 years. Also publishes educational resources for teachers and parents working with gifted students, and school administrators running gifted-education programs.
- **Representative Titles:** *Essential Chemistry for Gifted Students: Preparation for High School Chemistry* by Francis T. Sganga (grades 4–8) offers hands-on science lessons on such topics as candle chemistry and the electrical nature of elements. *Essential Mathematics for Gifted Students: Preparation for Algebra* by Francis T. Sganga (grades 4–8) features hands-on activities designed to introduce students to the basic concepts of geometry and trigonometry.

Submissions and Payment

Submit 1-page query only. No unsolicited mss. SASE. Responds in 3 months. Publication in 3 months. Royalty, 10%.

Editor's Comments

At this time we are especially interested in seeing submissions of science and math books for gifted children. Remember that all of the titles we publish are written by experts in their field of study. If you have not done so already, we suggest you visit our website and review some of our most recent publications. Familiarize yourself with the kind of approach we prefer, as well as to make sure that what we have published recently does not overlap with your ideas.

The Globe Pequot Press

825 Great Northern Boulevard
Helena, MT 59601

Executive Editor: Erin H. Turner

Publisher's Interests
With books for readers ages five to eighteen, this regional publisher focuses on material related to the history and historical figures of the West. It does not publish any fiction. Domestic and international travel guides for families make up a large part of its list.
Website: www.globepequot.com

Freelance Potential
Published 300 titles (25 juvenile) in 2004: 45 were developed from unsolicited submissions, 15 were by agented authors, and 15 were reprint/licensed properties. Of the 300 titles, 75 were by unpublished writers and 45 were by authors who were new to the publishing house. Receives 500–600 queries yearly.

- **Nonfiction:** Published 1 story picture book, 4–10 years; 15 middle-grade books, 8–12 years; and 10 young adult books, 12–18 years. Topics include animals, pets, history, nature, the environment, and regional subjects. Also publishes biographies.
- **Representative Titles:** *Fun with the Family in Connecticut* by Doe Boyle (families) features hundreds of ideas for day trips in the state; part of the Fun with Family series. *Day Trips in Columbus* by Sandra Gurvis (families) brings visitors hundreds of fascinating things to do in this Ohio city; part of the Day Trips series.

Submissions and Payment
Guidelines available on website. Query with clips. Accepts photocopies and disk submissions. Availability of artwork improves chance of acceptance. SASE. Responds in 3 months. Publication in 18 months. Royalty, 8–12%; advance, $500–$1,500.

Editor's Comments
We continue to seek submissions related to women in history, especially for our More Than Petticoats series. Each book chronicles the lives of historical women from a particular state who accomplished extraordinary things. Books on national parks are also high on our "want" list.

Goodheart-Willcox

18604 West Creek Drive
Tinley Park, IL 60477-6243

Editor, Family & Consumer Sciences: Teresa Dec

Publisher's Interests
Established in 1921, Goodheart-Willcox publishes innovative textbooks, supplements, and multimedia resources for school and individual training in the fields of family and consumer sciences, technical/trade vocational training, and career education.
Website: www.g-w.com

Freelance Potential
Published 50 titles in 2004. Receives 100+ queries yearly.

- **Nonfiction:** Publishes textbooks and how-to titles. Topics include life management, personal development, family living, child care, child development, parenting, consumer education, food and nutrition, housing and interiors, fashion and clothing, career education, and professional development. Also features instructor's guides, resource guides, and software.
- **Representative Titles:** *Children: The Early Years* by Celia Anita Decker (educators) is an authoritative look at children's developmental needs from the prenatal level through the school-age years. *Child Care Administration: Planning Quality Programs for Young Children* by Linda S. & Alan E. Nelson (child care specialists) describes what prospective directors need to know to start a child-care program in their community; includes management, leadership, and organizational strategies.

Submissions and Payment
Guidelines available. Query with résumé, outline, sample chapter, and list of illustrations. SASE. Responds in 2 months. Publication in 2 years. Royalty.

Editor's Comments
Our products are designed to train everyone from students to practicing professionals. Our books and supplements contain a wealth of information on the latest theories, techniques, and operations for our areas of interest. We are looking for material that has authoritative content, sound topic sequence, an abundance of illustrations, and appropriate readability.

Graphia

Houghton Mifflin Co.
222 Berkeley Street
Boston, MA 02116

Senior Editor: Eden Edwards

Publisher's Interests
Graphia, a new imprint of the Houghton Mifflin Company, publishes quality paperbacks aimed at today's teens. Its first list launched in the spring of 2004. This imprint offers titles by high-profile Houghton Mifflin authors along with the works of new writers. Graphia considers submissions of fiction, nonfiction, and poetry.
Website: www.graphiabooks.com

Freelance Potential
Published 10 titles in 2004: 5 were by agented authors. Receives 180–240 queries, 240–360 unsolicited mss yearly.

- **Fiction:** Publishes young adult books, 12–18 years. Genres include contemporary, historical, and science fiction; mystery; suspense; and humorous fiction.
- **Nonfiction:** Publishes young adult books, 12–18 years. Topics include history and multicultural and ethnic issues.
- **Representative Titles:** *48 Shades of Brown* by Nick Earls (YA) is a humorous novel that centers around a teenage boy's world of calculus, roommates, birds, and love. *Zazoo* by Richard Mosher (grades 7 and up) is the story of a young Vietnamese girl, raised by adoptive parents in France, and the events that unfold when a young man arrives in her small French village.

Submissions and Payment
Guidelines available. Query with outline and sample chapters for nonfiction. Send complete ms for fiction. Responds only if interested. Publication period varies. Royalty; advance.

Editor's Comments
The name Graphia, derived from the Greek word meaning "to write," signifies the quality literature that is the hallmark of this new line of books for teen readers. We look for submissions of solid literary quality. The works of older teenage writers are of interest to us, as long as they reflect the high quality we seek.

Graphic Arts Center Publishing Co.

P.O. Box 10306
Portland, OR 97296-0306

Executive Editor: Timothy W. Frew

Publisher's Interests
This mid-size publishing house specializes in material that reflects life in Alaska, the Northwest, Canada, and the Western states. Its children's list features regional fiction and nonfiction books.
Website: www.gacpc.com

Freelance Potential
Published 20 titles in 2004: 10 were developed from unsolicited submissions, 3 were by agented authors, and 5 were reprint/licensed properties. Of the 20 titles, 5 were by unpublished writers and 10 were by authors who were new to the publishing house. Receives 250 queries, 100 unsolicited mss yearly.

- **Fiction:** Publishes early picture books, 0–4 years; story picture books, 4–10 years; chapter books, 5–10 years; and young adult books, 12–18 years. Genres include historical fiction, folklore, suspense, and stories about animals, nature, and the environment.
- **Nonfiction:** Publishes early picture books, 0–4 years; story picture books, 4–10 years; middle-grade books, 8–12 years; and young adult books, 12–18 years. Topics include animals, geography, natural history, and humor. Also publishes biographies.
- **Representative Titles:** *Big-Enough Anna* by Pam Flowers & Ann Dixon (5+ years) is a story about a sled dog who perseveres on a journey across the top of the world. *Mr. Bob's Magic Ride in the Sky* by Karen Johnston (4–10 years) tells a story about a dog whose dream of flying comes true.

Submissions and Payment
Guidelines available. Query with clips for fiction; send complete ms for children's books. Accepts photocopies, disk submissions, and simultaneous submissions if identified. SASE. Responds in 2–4 months. Publication in 2 years. Payment policy varies.

Editor's Comments
We concentrate our children's list on books that have a regional focus on the northwestern and western U.S., as well as Alaska.

Greene Bark Press

P.O. Box 1108
Bridgeport, CT 06601-1108

Associate Publisher: Michele Hofbauer

Publisher's Interests
Targeting children ages three to nine, this publisher offers high-quality picture books that make learning fun as well as interactive, story-based CD-ROMs, educational toys, games, and videos. In addition, it offers guides for teachers as follow-up activities to story hour.
Website: www.greenebarkpress.com

Freelance Potential
Published 1 title in 2004: it was developed from an unsolicited submission. Receives 1,200 unsolicited mss yearly.

- **Fiction:** Publishes story picture books, 3-9 years. Genres include fantasy and mystery. Also offers teachers' guides, as well as titles on CD-ROM.
- **Representative Titles:** *Hands Are Not for Hitting* by Elizabeth Verdick (2-6 years) teaches children the good things hands can do, and ways to manage their anger. *The Wordless Counting Book* by Cindy Kosowsky (3-7 years) provides a handy introduction to the concept of numbers by using colors of the rainbow and simple pictures of various types of fruit.

Submissions and Payment
Guidelines available. Send complete ms with illustrations and story board. Accepts photocopies and simultaneous submissions if identified. SASE. Responds in 2-6 months. Publication in 12-18 months. Royalty, 10-15%.

Editor's Comments
We're looking for stories that are engaging and educational. Colorful, eye-catching pictures and text that sparks the imagination and motivates children to keep turning the pages are of interest to us. Because we want children to have fun reading while learning something, we offer a wide range of products that are selected to help kids grow in mind and spirit. Send us something new and exciting, that kids will want to read over and over again.

Greenhaven Press

Suite C
15822 Bernardo Center Drive
San Diego, CA 92127

Senior Acquisitions Editor: Chandra Howard

Publisher's Interests
Books written as series make up the list of this educational publisher that targets students in grades nine through twelve. Topics covered include world history, literary criticism, American history, and biography. All of its titles are written on a work-for-hire basis.
Website: www.gale.com/greenhaven

Freelance Potential
Published 180 titles in 2004. Of the 180 titles, 18 were by unpublished writers and 18 were by authors who were new to the publishing house. Receives 300 queries yearly.

- **Nonfiction:** Published 180 young adult books, 12–18 years. Features anthologies and books in series about history, contemporary social issues, world authors, and literary criticism. Also features biographies of famous history makers.
- **Representative Titles:** *Teen Decisions: Gangs* (YA) addresses the issue of gangs and how kids can avoid getting involved; part of the Teen Decisions series. *Writing Research Papers* (YA) features practical, concrete suggestions for preparing a paper—from pre-writing and research to final product.

Submissions and Payment
Guidelines available. Query acquisitions editor for guidelines. All work done on a work-for-hire basis. Response time varies. Publication in 1 year. Flat fee, varies.

Editor's Comments
We are interested in hearing from writers who have experience in writing educational materials. Once we accept you as a writer, you will receive specific instructions on how to proceed. Of utmost importance is original research, and attention to deadlines. Before querying, review our titles, specifically those in your area of interest. For the coming year, we will be looking for writers to work on titles related to social issues and current events. All of our titles are curriculum-based and written for students in grades nine through twelve.

Greenwood Publishing Group

88 Post Road West
Westport, CT 06881

Editorial Secretary: Julia Warner

Publisher's Interests
Greenwood Publishing Group offers reference titles, academic and general interest books, textbooks, titles for librarians and other professionals, and electronic resources.
Website: www.greenwood.com

Freelance Potential
Published 100 titles (50 juvenile) in 2004: 16 were by agented authors. Of the 100 titles, 5 were by unpublished writers and 25 were by authors who were new to the publishing house. Receives 10 queries, 10 unsolicited mss yearly.

- **Nonfiction:** Publishes reference books and high interest/low vocabulary titles, grades 6 and up. Topics include the social sciences, humanities, modern history, military studies, psychology, business, current events, social issues, international affairs, politics, the arts, and literature. Also publishes biographies and encyclopedias.
- **Representative Titles:** *A Student's Guide to Mental Health & Wellness* (YA) is a four-volume set of books that identifies and explains the history, people, and issues surrounding mental health. *Student Almanac of Native American History* (YA), a two-volume set, teaches students about the great Native American leaders and how Native Americans adapted to white culture in the twentieth century.

Submissions and Payment
Guidelines and catalogue available. Query with clips; or send complete ms with résumé. Accepts photocopies. Availability of artwork improves chance of acceptance. SASE. Responds in 2–4 weeks. Publication in 9 months. Royalty, varies. Flat fee.

Editor's Comments
We are seeking reference books for academic, school, and public libraries. We welcome proposals for projects appropriate for our publishing programs. Your prospectus should indicate the scope and organization of your project. Be sure to let us know whether a complete manuscript is available.

Group Publishing

P.O. Box 481
Loveland, CO 80539

Editorial Assistant: Kerri Loesche

Publisher's Interests
Group Publishing is a religious publisher whose mission is to help churches to help children, youth, and adults grow in their relationship with Jesus. It describes its resources as inspiring those "ah-ha moments in your ministry."
Website: www.grouppublishing.com

Freelance Potential
Published 15 titles in 2004: 1 was developed from an unsolicited submission. Of the 15 titles, 2 were by authors who were new to the publishing house. Receives 500+ queries yearly.

- **Nonfiction:** Publishes activity, how-to, and programming books. Features children's educational titles and books on special education, hobbies, crafts, games, and religion.
- **Representative Titles:** *Why Nobody Learns Much of Anything at Church: and How to Fix It* by Thom and Joani Schultz (educators) takes a hard-hitting look at education in church and offers practical solutions on how to improve the way your church educates. *The Humongous Book of Children's Messages* offers pastors over 100 messages on everything from church holidays to Bible stories.

Submissions and Payment
Guidelines available. Query with outline, book introduction, 2–3 sample chapters, and sample activities. Accepts photocopies, computer printouts, and simultaneous submissions if identified. SASE. Responds in 3–6 months. Publication period varies. Royalty, to 10%. Flat fee, varies.

Editor's Comments
We are always looking for good writers who know kids, understand active learning, and have the ability to write lessons that help kids apply the Bible to their lives. If you think you are one of these writers, evaluate your own submission just as we would by asking yourself if your book is original, practical, need-oriented, and easy to use. If you have a manuscript that meets these criteria, we'd like to see it.

Gryphon House

P.O. Box 207
Beltsville, MD 20704-0207

Editor-in-Chief: Kathy Charner

Publisher's Interests
Early childhood resources for teachers and parents are the specialty of this publishing house. Its list offers titles covering a wide range of topics relating to the development of children up to the age of eight. Some areas covered include language development, conflict resolution, and bilingual education.
Website: www.gryphonhouse.com

Freelance Potential
Published 12 titles in 2004: 2 were developed from unsolicited submissions and 1 was by an agented author. Of the 12 titles, 1 was by an unpublished writer and 6 were by authors who were new to the publishing house. Receives 150 queries yearly.

- **Nonfiction:** Publishes titles for parents and teachers working with children under the age of eight. Topics include art, math, science, language development, teaching strategies, conflict resolution, program development, and bilingual education.
- **Representative Titles:** *Art Across the Alphabet* by Kelly Justus Campbell (3–6 years) contains art-centered activities designed to reinforce letter recognition, pre-reading skills, and phonemic awareness. *Teachable Transitions* by Rae Pica (educators) features movement activities, games, fingerplays, chants, and songs—all related to turning transition times between planned activities into pleasurable moments.

Submissions and Payment
Guidelines available. Query with table of contents, introductory material, and 20–30 pages of activities. Accepts photocopies and computer printouts. SASE. Responds in 3–4 months. Publication in 1–2 years. Payment policy varies.

Editor's Comments
If you have an idea for a book, we want to hear about it. At Gryphon House we strive to make our books useful for teachers of all levels, as well as for parents. We believe that spending time with children is a valuable and fun thing to do. Our books reflect these beliefs.

Gulliver Books

Harcourt Trade Publishers
15 East 26th Street
New York, NY 10010

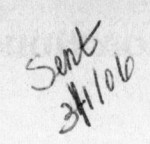

Editorial Director: Elizabeth Van Doren
Associate Editor: Kate Harrison

Publisher's Interests
This imprint of the well-known Harcourt Children's Books offers an extensive list of fiction and nonfiction titles for children of all ages. Gulliver Books accepts submissions only from agented authors, previously published writers, or members of the Society of Children's Book Writers and Illustrators.
Website: www.harcourtbooks.com

Freelance Potential
Published 23 titles in 2004: 1 was developed from an unsolicited submission and 13 were by agented authors. Of the 23 titles, 1 was by an unpublished writer and 1 was by an author who was new to the publishing house. Receives 500+ unsolicited mss yearly.

- **Fiction:** Publishes concept books, toddler books, and early picture books, 0–4 years; story picture books, 4–10 years; chapter books, 5–10 years; middle-grade books, 8–12 years; and young adult books, 12–18 years. Genres include adventure, and historical and contemporary fiction. Also publishes animal stories and poetry.
- **Nonfiction:** Publishes story picture books, 4–10 years. Topics include history, sports, nature, science, and the environment.
- **Representative Titles:** *Won't You Be My Kissaroo?* by Joanne Ryder (2–5 years) celebrates all the silly, slippery, snuggly kisses that make a day special. *Patience, Princess Catherine* by Carolyn Meyer (12+ years) is a historical novel about young Catherine of Aragon, future wife of King Henry VIII.

Submissions and Payment
Accepts submissions only from agented and previously published authors or members of SCBWI. SASE. Responds in 6–8 weeks. Publication in 2–4 years. Royalty; advance.

Editor's Comments
Children like to read about familiar situations and people, such as family, school, and friends, with a unique turn of events. Send us material young readers can identify with.

Hachai Publishing

156 Chester Avenue
Brooklyn, NY 11218

Submissions Editor: Devorah L. Rosenfeld

Publisher's Interests
Stories for Jewish children age two to six that convey traditional Jewish experiences in modern times are the specialty of this publisher. It also offers historical fiction and adventure stories for beginning readers that highlight faith and the relevance of Torah.
Website: www.hachai.com

Freelance Potential
Published 5 titles in 2004: 4 were developed from unsolicited submissions. Of the 5 titles, 3 were by unpublished writers and 3 were by authors who were new to the publishing house. Receives 600 unsolicited mss yearly.

- **Fiction:** Published 2 easy-to-read books, 4–7 years; 2 story picture books, 4–10 years; and 1 middle-grade book, 8–12 years. Genres include religious and historical fiction; folktales; and adventure.
- **Nonfiction:** Publishes concept books, 0–4 years; and story picture books, 4–10 years. Topics include Jewish holidays, mitzvos, and middos. Also publishes biographies.
- **Representative Titles:** *As Big As an Egg* by Rochel Sandman (3–6 years) is the story of a hungry young Russian boy who learns about giving when he contributes to the village mitzvah sack. *Light at the End of the Tunnel* by Joy Nelkin Wieder (7–10) is an exciting adventure in the City of David telling how the Jews outwitted the enemy by digging a water tunnel.

Submissions and Payment
Guidelines available. Send complete ms. Accepts photocopies. SASE. Responds in 2–6 weeks. Publication in 12–18 months. Flat fee.

Editor's Comments
We are dedicated to making storytime more meaningful by producing classic picture books with Jewish content. In addition to imparting the importance of good character traits, our stories are also tools for imparting a love of Hashem and a love of Judaism to the very youngest reader.

Hampton-Brown Books

26385 Carmel Rancho Boulevard
Carmel, CA 93923

Special Projects Coordinator

Publisher's Interests
Hampton-Brown provides educational materials for students, particularly those from diverse linguistic and cultural backgrounds. It is a leading publisher of English-as-a-Second-Language materials and high-interest, low-vocabulary books.
Website: www.hampton-brown.com

Freelance Potential
Published 200 titles (150 juvenile) in 2004: 100 were by agented authors and 100 were reprint/licensed properties. Of the 200 titles, some were by unpublished writers and most were by authors who were new to the publishing house. Receives 120 queries yearly.

- **Fiction:** Publishes early picture books, 0–4 years; easy-to-read books, 4–7 years; story picture books, 4–10 years; chapter books, 5–10 years; and middle-grade books, 8–12 years. Genres include fairy tales, folklore, drama, and contemporary and multicultural fiction.
- **Nonfiction:** Publishes early picture books, 0–4 years; easy-to-read books, 4–7 years; story picture books, 4–10 years; chapter books, 5–10 years; and middle-grade books, 8–12 years. Also publishes textbook anthologies on phonics, ESL, early literacy, dual-language programs, content-area reading, and homeschooling.
- **Representative Titles:** *Central Park* by Ann Morris (grade 3) is a commissioned selection for a literature anthology; part of the Avenues program. *Carlos Comes to Lakeside Elementary* (grades 3–5) uses a picture-dictionary approach to teach survival vocabulary, language function, and basic language patterns and structures.

Submissions and Payment
Query. No unsolicited mss. SASE. Responds in 3–6 months. Publication period varies. Flat fee.

Editor's Comments
We do not offer writers' guidelines, nor do we consider submissions of individual titles. As a provider of curriculum materials, we prefer to focus on the publication of complete educational programs.

Hampton Roads Publishing

1125 Stoney Ridge Road
Charlottesville, VA 22902

Editor-in-Chief: Frank DeMarco

Publisher's Interests
The goal of this publishing house is to produce quality metaphysical books that will make a difference in people's lives. It offers both fiction and nonfiction titles for readers between twelve and eighteen, as well as adult books. Parenting books may also be found in it catalogue. The publisher was founded in 1989.
Website: www.hamptonroadpub.com

Freelance Potential
Published 24 titles (4 juvenile) in 2004. Receives 1,000+ queries each year.

- **Fiction:** Publishes young adult books, 12-18 years. Genres include inspirational, visionary, and metaphysical fiction.
- **Nonfiction:** Publishes young adult books, 12-18 years. Topics include spirituality, metaphysics, and alternative medicine.
- **Representative Titles:** *Coping with Your Adolescent* by Larry Waldman (parents) offers ways that parents can cope with and guide their children through the rough times of adolescence. *Getting Rid of Ritalin* by Eduardo Castro & Robert W. Hill offers new research on A.D.D. and suggests that Ritalin be replaced by neurofeedback.

Submissions and Payment
Guidelines and catalogue available with SASE. Query with synopsis, chapter-by-chapter outline, and 1-2 sample chapters. Accepts photocopies, computer printouts, and simultaneous submissions if identified. SASE. Responds in 6 months. Publication in 18 months. Royalty, 10-20%; advance, $1,000.

Editor's Comments
We look for authors who can bring us ideas for the evolving human spirit. Be aware, though, that we and most publishers have an enormous number of proposals to read and that only the best will make the cut. Our niche is very specific, so before you send off your query, take the time to study our backlist and review some of our titles to be sure that your work and our needs are a good match.

Harbour Publishing

P.O. Box 219
Madeira Park, BC V0N 2H0

Editor: Shyla Seller

Publisher's Interests
Harbour publishes history, nature, and folklore books for children and adults on topics relating to British Columbia and the Pacific Northwest.
Website: www.harbourpublishing.com

Freelance Potential
Published 20 titles (1 juvenile) in 2004: 3 were developed from unsolicited submissions. Of the 20 titles, 1 was by an unpublished writer and 1 was by an author who was new to the publishing house. Receives 10–20 queries, 100+ unsolicited mss yearly.

- **Fiction:** Publishes young adult books, 12–18 years. Genres include contemporary, historical, multicultural, and regional fiction; adventure; folklore; folktales; ethnic fiction; and nature stories relating to the Pacific West Coast.
- **Nonfiction:** Publishes titles for adults. Topics include multicultural and ethnic issues, current events, history, social issues, geography, the environment, and biography.
- **Representative Titles:** *The Golden Pine Cone* by Catherine Anthony Clark (6+ years) is a classic adventure story of Native mythology, set in Kootenay, British Columbia. *Jason and the Sea Otter* by Joe Barber-Starkey contains beautifully illustrated tales of wonder and mystery for children of all ages.

Submissions and Payment
Guidelines available with 9x12 SASE. Query or send complete ms. Accepts photocopies. SASE. Responds in 6 months. Publication in 2 years. Royalty.

Editor's Comments
In a normal year, we usually publish about 20 new titles: 10 regional nonfiction, one children's title, two guidebooks, and one poetry anthology; the remainder could be artbooks, cookbooks, or how-to titles. You can see that competition for our children's book is keen, so send us your best original work about British Columbia.

Learning the Classics
Allyn Johnston
Harcourt Children's Books

With school and library budgets cut, it's tough to break into the hardcover early reader market. Nonetheless, Harcourt Children's Books holds its own with, among others, Cynthia Rylant's Mr. Putter and Tabby series, Keith Baker's Mr. and Mrs. Green books, and Molly Bang and Monika Bang-Campbell's Little Rat books. Editorial Director Allyn Johnston's enthusiasm for such terrific stories shines through.

Authors seeking a foothold in this competitive market should study the classics. "Read all the Mr. Putter and Tabby, Henry and Mudges, and Frog and Toads you can get your hands on. Lose yourself in them. Pay close attention to how the pacing, the timing, and the emotion work. You truly can learn a lot from these masters of the genre," Johnston says.

New authors must learn from these authors because these are the books their work will compete against. "I don't encourage writers to pursue the easy reader genre unless they are stunning at it because the books are so difficult to do well—and, as you hear over and over, because the market is so tough."

But authors who heed the lessons of the masters may indeed still find a home with Johnston and her staff. "Next year we're launching a funny, snappy, and moving new series by Erica Silverman about Cowgirl Kate and her horse Cocoa. And we're thrilled because Caldecott-Honor recipient and best-selling artist Betsy Lewin will be illustrating them, which will help them stand out in a crowded marketplace."

(See listing for Harcourt Children's Books on following page)

Harcourt Children's Books

Harcourt Trade Publishers
15 East 26th Street
New York, NY 10010

Submissions Editor

Publisher's Interests
Harcourt Children's Books produces fiction titles for its audience of young readers, which includes toddlers through young adults. Because it only publishes books of the highest quality, Harcourt will not consider freelance manuscripts unless they have been submitted through literary agents.
Website: www.harcourtbooks.com

Freelance Potential
Published 185 titles in 2004: all were by agented authors.

- **Fiction:** Publishes concept books, toddler books, and early picture books, 0–4 years; easy-to-read books, 4–7 years; story picture books, 4–10 years; chapter books, 5–10 years; middle-grade novels, 8–12 years; and young adult books, 12–18 years. Genres include mystery; fantasy; suspense; and contemporary, historical, and multicultural fiction. Also publishes poetry and stories about sports, nature, and the environment.
- **Representative Titles:** *Mr. Putter & Tabby Stir the Soup* by Cynthia Rylant (6–9 years) is the story of a man and his cat and a soup-making adventure with their neighbor's dog. *East* by Edith Pattou (12+ years) is a fantasy focusing on a young girl who is led by a mysterious white bear to a distant castle, where she solves a mystery and discovers her life's purpose.

Submissions and Payment
Accepts submissions from agented authors only. No simultaneous submissions. Responds to agents in 1 month. Publication in 2 years. Royalty; advance.

Editor's Comments
We receive thousands of submissions every year, but only a fraction of those are found to be acceptable for our high-quality list. If you do not have enough publishing credits to have acquired an agent, we are not the market for you. Your chances would be far better if you send your work to more approachable publishers.

Harcourt Religion Publishers

6277 Sea Harbor Drive
Orlando, FL 32887

Managing Editor: Sabrina Magnuson

Publisher's Interests
Harcourt Religion Publishers provides catechetical resources based on the teachings of the Catholic church for use in religious education classes, sacramental preparation programs, and vacation Bible schools. It is also a leading publisher of curriculum material that corresponds with the required and elective courses of Catholic high schools across the U.S.
Website: www.harcourtreligion.com

Freelance Potential
Published 30 titles in 2004: 2 were by unpublished writers and 4 were by authors who were new to the publishing house. Receives 30–35 queries yearly.

- **Nonfiction:** Publishes easy-to-read books, 4–7 years; chapter books, 5–10 years; middle-grade books, 8–12 years; and young adult books, 12–18 years. Topics include faith, catechism, education, Christian lifestyles, contemporary issues, prayer, worship, and family life.
- **Representative Titles:** *Catholics Believe* by Rev. Michael Savelesky & Rev. Dwayne Thoman (grade 9) uses discussion questions, activities, and stories to teach about faith, the Old Testament, the New Testament, the sacraments, and discipleship. *Justice and Peace* by Joseph Stoutzenberger (grades 11–12) provides a Catholic understanding of justice and examines Catholic teaching on issues related to peace.

Submissions and Payment
Query with outline, résumé, and 3 sample chapters. No unsolicited mss. Accepts photocopies, computer printouts, and simultaneous submissions if identified. SASE. Responds in 3–6 months. Publication in 1 year. Royalty. Flat fee.

Editor's Comments
Over the next three years, we will revise and expand our major programs to provide a more integrated approach to the faith needs of the whole parish, adults and families in particular.

Gripping Stories & Readability Combined
Anne Hoppe
HarperCollins Children's Books

HarperCollins's commitment to fine literature shows in its I Can Read series. "We are the only line of beginning readers to have Caldecott and Newbery Honor Medals awarded to our books," Executive Editor Anne Hoppe says. Notable titles come from authors Arnold Lobel, Katherine Paterson, Betsy Byars, Avi, and Emily Arnold McCully, and illustrators Maurice Sendak and Marc Simont.

Hoppe seeks manuscripts that combine the skills essential for top early readers. "A writer must create engaging stories with appealing characters," she says, "while working with certain challenges of vocabulary, style, and length."

Key to the process is word choice. "Authors should pay attention to their vocabulary. Think about each word," Hoppe says. "Is it easy to sound out or pick up from context? Is it a familiar part of most children's vocabulary? Is it a word they knew when they were five?"

Focus on vocabulary can come at the expense of story, however, and that's always a mistake. "It's deadly for an author to get too caught up in these concerns when trying to create a story!" Hoppe says.

Fascinating story is key. "Young readers struggling through each word need a compelling reason to turn every page," says Hoppe, "and the best way to achieve that is with the tension created through action and dialogue." Writers who combine compelling stories with accessible vocabulary and sentence structure may find a home within this award-winning tradition.

HarperCollins Children's Books

1350 Avenue of the Americas
New York, NY 10019

Executive Editor: Ruth Katcher

Publisher's Interests
Books for children of all ages appear on this publisher's list. It offers fiction in a wide variety of genres, but does not publish any nonfiction. Many of the books featured appear in series format.
Website: www.harperchildrens.com

Freelance Potential
Published 100 titles in 2004: 70 were by agented authors. Of the 100 titles, 4 were by unpublished writers and 12 were by authors who were new to the publishing house. Receives 1,080 queries, 700 unsolicited mss yearly.

- **Fiction:** Publishes easy-to-read books, 4–7 years; chapter books, 5–10 years; middle-grade novels, 8–12 years; and young adult books, 12–18 years. Genres include adventure, drama, fantasy, folklore, folktales, horror, humor, mystery, suspense, Westerns, contemporary, historical, multicultural, and science fiction. Also publishes stories about sports.
- **Representative Titles:** *How They Got Over* by Eloise Greengield (grades 3–6) discusses the connection of African Americans to the sea. *Don't Know Much about the Pioneers* by Kenneth C. Davis (grades 1–4) describes the everyday life of the pioneers who traveled the Oregon Trail.

Submissions and Payment
Catalogue available at website. Query with résumé and clips. SAE/IRC. Responds in 1 month. Publication in 18 months. Royalty, varies; advance, varies.

Editor's Comments
Unfortunately the volume of submissions we receive prevents us from reading unsolicited manuscripts or proposals. We will only review material that comes from agents. If you are a new writer, we suggest that you research the market carefully to make sure the publishers you choose are the best choice for reviewing your book or query. If you take the time to research publishers your chances may improve.

HarperCollins Children's Fiction

77-85 Fulham Palace Road
London W6 8JB
England

Submissions Editor

Publisher's Interests
This well-known division of HarperCollins Publishers, UK, publishes books across all ages from infants to teenagers, and from board books to teenage fantasy, including such classics as *The Hobbit* and *The Chronicles of Narnia*.
Website: www.harpercollins.co.uk

Freelance Potential
Published 100 titles in 2004: 70 were by agented authors. Of the 100 titles, 4 were by unpublished writers and 12 were by authors who were new to the publishing house. Receives 1,080 queries, 700 unsolicited mss yearly.

- **Fiction:** Published 10 easy-to-read books, 4–7 years; 40 chapter books, 5–10 years; 30 middle-grade novels, 8–12 years; and 15 young adult books, 12–18 years. Genres include adventure, drama, fantasy, folklore, folktales, horror, humor, mystery, suspense, Westerns, contemporary, historical, multicultural, and science fiction. Also publishes stories about sports.
- **Representative Titles:** *Cushie Butterfield—She's a Little Cow!* by Colin McNaughton is a story about a young cow who comes up with a novel method of being too "sick" to go to school. *Stealing Stacey* by Lynne Reid Banks (YA) follows a young British girl who suddenly finds herself transplanted from life in a dingy apartment in London to a home in the Australian outback.

Submissions and Payment
Catalogue available at website. Query with résumé and clips. SAE/IRC. Responds in 1 month. Publication in 18 months. Royalty, varies; advance, varies.

Editor's Comments
While we welcome submissions for all ages, we are especially interested in adding to our list of books for middle-grade readers. If you are new to us, please take the time to review our backlist. We are *not* HarperCollins Children's Books, that is another imprint.

Hayes School Publishing Company

321 Pennwood Avenue
Pittsburgh, PA 15221

President: Mr. Clair N. Hayes, III, Ph.D.

Publisher's Interests
This educational publisher caters to the school and library markets with a list that offers nonfiction for preschool through high school students. It covers a wide range of subjects including science, mathematics, language arts, reading, social studies, and geography. Reproducibles, student workbooks, and teacher guides are offered in all subject areas.
Website: www.hayespub.com

Freelance Potential
Published 50–60 titles in 2004: 2–3 were developed from unsolicited submissions. Of the 50–60 titles, 2–3 were by authors who were new to the publishing house. Receives 200–300 queries yearly.

- **Nonfiction:** Publishes educational resource materials, grades K–12. Topics include reading, vocabulary, language arts, math, music, mythology, art, social studies, and creative thinking.
- **Representative Titles:** *Diagramming Sentences* (grades 7–12) is a two-book series that examines the basics of grammar through the principles of sentence structure. *Reading about Famous Asian Americans* (grades 2–5) looks at the lives of notable figures in history including Bruce Lee, Maya Lind, and Ng Poon Chew.

Submissions and Payment
Guidelines available. Query with résumé, outline, table of contents, and sample pages. Accepts photocopies, computer printouts, and simultaneous submissions if identified. SASE. Responds in 2–3 weeks. Publication period varies. Flat fee.

Editor's Comments
At this time we are interested in reviewing queries for writers with expertise in the areas of Spanish and French language instruction, and standard testing components for use in grades K–8. The mission of this publishing house has always been to bring educators new ways to excite students about learning. Please remember that we do not publish any fiction.

Hazelden Foundation

P.O. Box 176
Center City, MN 55012-0176

Manuscript Coordinator

Publisher's Interests

Since its founding in 1949, Hazelden has worked to bring the world's leading experts on addiction and abuse into its fold. Its goal today is the same as it has always been: to help alcoholics and addicts. Its children's list features books for middle-grade and young adult readers.
Website: www.hazeldenbookplace.org

Freelance Potential

Published 100 titles in 2004: 60 were developed from unsolicited submissions and 5 were by agented authors. Receives 300 queries each year.

- **Nonfiction:** Publishes middle-grade books, 8–12 years; and young adult books, 12–18 years. Topics include alcohol and substance abuse, health, fitness, and social issues.
- **Representative Titles:** *Safe Dates* by Vangie Foshee, Ph.D. gets young people to think about how they want to be treated by a partner; what abusive dating relationships look like; and how to tell if they are in an abusive relationship. *Peer Helping Skills* by John DeMarco teaches skills to help train young adults to counsel their peers.

Submissions and Payment

Guidelines available. For catalogue, call 1-800-328-0098. Query with outline/synopsis, 3 sample chapters, and clips or writing samples. Accepts photocopies. SASE. Responds in 3 months. Publication in 12–18 months. Royalty. Flat fee.

Editor's Comments

Our mission remains the same: to bring solid, research-based material to children in kindergarten through twelfth grade, as well as books that will help families and communities deal with the issue of substance abuse and alcoholism. We look for writers who can bring our diverse audience material that will make a difference in their lives. Review our titles and catalogue and if you feel you are right for us, send us a strong, detailed query.

Health Press

P.O. Box 37470
Albuquerque, NM 87176

Editor: Kathleen Frazier

Publisher's Interests
Health Press publishes books on a wide variety of health topics, written by health care professionals for the layperson. Its catalogue incudes titles for children and adults on such topics as diet, nutrition, parenting, women's health, pet health, grief, and psychology. Many of its children's books strive to teach readers that it is OK to be different.
Website: www.healthpress.com

Freelance Potential
Published 4 titles (2 juvenile) in 2004: all were developed from unsolicited submissions and 1 was by an agented author. Receives 120 queries yearly.

- **Fiction:** Publishes concept books, 0–4 years; easy-to-read books, 4–7 years; middle-grade novels, 8–12 years; and young adult books, 12–18 years. All stories related to health subjects.
- **Nonfiction:** Publishes concept books, 0–4 years; easy-to-read books, 4–7 years; middle-grade books, 8–12 years; and young adult books, 12–18 years. Topics include health and health-related subjects.
- **Representative Titles:** *A Good Friend* by Ron Herron and Val J. Peter offers advice to help shy kids learn how to build friendships. *Blueberry Eyes* by Monica Driscoll Beatty addresses the many issues of eye treatment, including wearing glasses, eye patches, and undergoing eye surgery.

Submissions and Payment
Guidelines available at website. Query with brief synopsis, résumé, and 3 sample chapters. SASE. Response time varies. Publication period varies. Royalty.

Editor's Comments
Our primary interest is in reviewing queries on health topics that can teach children that health issues are a part of everyone's lives in one form or another. We are also interested in ideas that address special-needs children.

Heinemann

361 Hanover Street
Portsmouth, NH 03801-3912

Editorial Assistant: Melissa Wood

Publisher's Interests
Established in 1978, Heinemann Publishing specializes in professional development and resource books for teachers working with students in grades K–12. Topics covered include language arts, social studies, mathematics, and art education.
Website: www.heinemann.com

Freelance Potential
Published 90 titles in 2004. Receives 1,000+ queries yearly.

- **Nonfiction:** Publishes educational resource and multimedia materials for teachers and school administrators. Topics include math, science, social studies, art education, reading, writing, ESL, bilingual education, gifted and special education, early childhood, school reform, curriculum development, and the creative arts. Also publishes professional development and assessment materials.
- **Representative Titles:** *In Defense of Our Children* by Elaine M. Garan, Ph.D. (teachers) is designed in a question-and-answer format and helps readers think through the vital issues in education and parenting. *Becoming a Successful Urban Teacher* by Dave F. Brown (teachers) shares the stories of 13 successful urban educators from grades one through twelve.

Submissions and Payment
Writers' guidelines available. Query with résumé, proposal, outline, table of contents, and chapter summaries. Accepts photocopies, computer printouts, and email submissions to proposals@heinemann.com. SASE. Responds in 6–8 weeks. Publication in 10–12 months. Payment policy varies.

Editor's Comments
Our mission is to give a voice to those who share our respect for the professionalism and compassion of teachers and who support teachers' efforts to help children become literate, empathetic, and knowledgeable citizens. Most of our authors are educators who have spent extensive time in the field and can bring their experience to others.

Hendrick-Long Publishing Company

Suite D
10635 Tower Oaks
Houston, TX 77070

Vice President: Vilma Long

Publisher's Interests
Founded in 1969, Hendrick-Long is an educational publisher based in Texas. Most of its titles are concerned with some aspect of life in Texas or the Southwest. Its diverse list includes guidebooks to the Southwest, cookbooks, resource material, and books for children and young adults. Many of its titles are also produced in Spanish.
Website: www.hendricklongpublishing.com

Freelance Potential
Published 4 titles in 2004: 2 were developed from unsolicited submissions and 1 was by an agented author. Of the 4 titles, 1 was by an unpublished writer and 1 was by an author who was new to the publishing house. Receives 200+ queries yearly.

- **Fiction:** Publishes story picture books, 4–10 years; middle-grade novels, 8–12 years; and young adult books, 12–18 years. Genres include historical and regional fiction.
- **Nonfiction:** Publishes middle-grade books, 8–12 years; and young adult books, 12–18 years. Topics include geography, biography, animals, nature, and history.
- **Representative Titles:** *Camels for Uncle Sam* by Diane Yancey (9+ years) reveals the little-known fact that the U.S. military brought camels to the Southwest to be used as mounts in the dry terrain. *Trails of Tears* by Jeanne Williams (YA) offers the stories of Native American tribes forced from their homelands by the American government.

Submissions and Payment
Guidelines available. Query with outline/synopsis, résumé, table of contents, and 1–2 sample chapters. Accepts photocopies, computer printouts, and simultaneous submissions. SASE. Responds in 1–2 months. Publication in 18 months. Royalty; advance.

Editor's Comments
We continue to look for books for young adults, both fiction and nonfiction. While you need not be a native of the Southwest, your book must demonstrate indepth knowledge of its setting.

Heritage House

#6-356 Simcoe Street
Victoria, British Columbia V8V 1L1
Canada

Publisher: Rodger Touchie

Publisher's Interests
In business for more than 30 years, this Canadian publishing house is committed to publishing distinctive nonfiction works written by Canadian authors. Its list offers recreational guides, nature books, and special interest titles.
Website: www.heritagehouse.com

Freelance Potential
Published 19 titles in 2004: 4 were by unpublished writers and 6 were by authors who were new to the publishing house. Receives 100 queries yearly.

- **Nonfiction:** Publishes middle-grade books, 8–12 years. Topics include the environment, history, nature, and wildlife of western Canada; and the Royal Canadian Mounted Police. Also publishes activity books.
- **Representative Titles:** *Camping with Kids* by Jayne Seagrave (Families) covers all manner of topics related to exploring the outdoors with kids of all ages. *Tributes to the Scarlet Riders* compiled by Edgar Kuhn (all ages) is an anthology of verse written by individuals who served in the Mountie police force.

Submissions and Payment
Guidelines and catalogue available with 9x12 SAE/IRC. Query with sample illustrations. Accepts photocopies, computer printouts, and disk submissions (Microsoft Word or PageMaker). Availability of artwork improves chance of acceptance. SAE/IRC. Responds in 1 month. Publication in 8–10 months. Royalty.

Editor's Comments
We are looking for Canadian authors whose work celebrates the pioneer spirit of Canada and its many ethnic groups, or covers some aspect of the history of Western Canada. While we will consider non-Canadian authors, we publish far more work from Canadians. If you are new to the publishing house, we ask that you take the time to review our guidelines and website and read some of our books so you have a firm grasp of what works for us.

Heuer Publishing Company

Suite 200
211 First Avenue SE
Cedar Rapids, IA 52401

Editor: C. E. McMullen

Publisher's Interests
Heuer Publishing Company features a catalogue that includes plays for all ages as well as monologues, musicals and melodramas. It also offers a list of nonfiction titles related to the craft of theater. Many of its plays are performed in school and community theaters.
Website: www.hitplays.com

Freelance Potential
Published 15 titles in 2004: 14 were developed from unsolicited submissions and 1 was a reprint/licensed property. Of the 15 titles, 13 were by unpublished writers and 8 were by authors who were new to the publishing house. Receives 300 queries, 90+ unsolicited mss yearly.

- **Fiction:** Publishes middle-grade plays, 8–12 years; and young adult plays, 12–18 years. Genres include comedy, musicals, drama, suspense, mystery, and satire.
- **Nonfiction:** Publishes young adult books, 12–18 years. Features books on theater arts, stage production, auditions, and sound effects. Also offers theater resources.
- **Representative Titles:** *The Boarding House Reach* is a three-act comedy about a boy who would do almost anything to get a bicycle. *Finders Creepers* is a three-act comedy that follows the adventures of Wilbur Maxwell when he is invited to spend a weekend with his uncle, who is a mortician.

Submissions and Payment
Guidelines available. Query or send complete ms with synopsis, cast list, running time, and set requirements. Accepts photocopies and computer printouts. SASE. Responds in 2 months. Publication period varies. Royalty. Flat fee.

Editor's Comments
We specialize in plays and musicals for educational and community theaters and are always on the lookout for new playwrights. Most of the individuals performing the plays have little acting experience.

Holiday House

Sent 3-1-06

425 Madison Avenue
New York, NY 10017

Editor-in-Chief: Regina Griffin

Publisher's Interests
Targeting children of all ages, this publisher offers quality fiction and nonfiction books for the library and school market. It offers a variety of trade hardcovers including picture books, and young adult novels.
Website: www.holidayhouse.com

Freelance Potential
Published 52 titles in 2004: 4 were developed from unsolicited submissions and 16 were by agented authors. Receives 8,600 queries yearly.

- **Fiction:** Published 26 early picture books, 0–4 years; 8 easy-to-read books, 4–7 years; 2 story picture books, 4–10 years; 4 chapter books, 5–10 years; 12 middle-grade books, 8–12 years; and 4 young adult books, 12–18 years. Genres include humor, mystery, fantasy, humor, and historical and multicultural fiction.
- **Nonfiction:** Published 9 early picture books, 0–4 years; 2 easy-to-read books, 4–7 years; and 2 middle-grade books, 8–12 years. Topics include history, social issues, and science. Also publishes biographies.
- **Representative Titles:** *Punctuation Takes a Vacation* by Robin Pulver tells the story of students who discover just how difficult life can be when their punctuation marks decide to take a vacation. *In Defense of Liberty* by Russell Freedman examines the origins, applications, and challenges of the Bill of Rights.

Submissions and Payment
Guidelines available. Query only. SASE. Responds in 2 months. Publication period varies. Royalty; advance.

Editor's Comments
Send us a query for something lively and fresh. We are inundated with submissions and are accepting only a few. Please note that we are a small publisher that specializes in hardcovers, and do not publish activity books, coloring books, sticker books, or paperbacks. Middle-grade literary novels are of particular interest to us.

Henry Holt Books for Young Readers

115 West 18th Street
New York, NY 10011

Submissions Editor

Publisher's Interests
Henry Holt Books for Young Readers publishes original picture books, fiction, and nonfiction titles on a variety of topics for children of all ages, from pre-readers through young adults.
Website: www.henryholtchildrensbooks.com

Freelance Potential
Published 65 titles (64 juvenile) in 2004. Receives 2,000 unsolicited mss yearly.

- **Fiction:** Published 1 concept book and 4 early picture books, 0–4 years; 11 easy-to-read books, 4–7 years; 24 story picture books, 4–10 years; 2 chapter books, 5–10 years; 6 middle-grade books, 8–12 years; and 9 young adult books, 12–18 years. Genres include historical, multicultural, and ethnic fiction; adventure and nature stories; drama; and fantasy. Also publishes poetry.
- **Nonfiction:** Published 4 story picture books, 4–10 years; 1 chapter book, 5–10 years; and 2 middle-grade books, 8–12 years. Topics include history, multicultural and ethnic issues, nature, and the environment.
- **Representative Titles:** *Hunchback* by Randall Wright (10+ years) is a glorious adventure of castles, kings, and traitors, and the humble hunchback who saves them all. *American Moment* by Robert Burleigh (6–10 years) is an innovative picture book that puts readers right in the middle of 18 monumental events in American history.

Submissions and Payment
Guidelines and catalogue available with 9x12 SASE ($.80). Send complete ms. Accepts photocopies. SASE. Responds in 3–4 months. Publication period and payment policy vary.

Editor's Comments
Authors are invited to submit material for young readers. Ask yourself if a child you know would be interested in what you have written. Although we would like to comment specifically on each manuscript, the large volume of submissions we receive precludes this.

Honor Books

Cook Communications Ministries
4050 Lee Vance View
Colorado Springs, CO 80918

Product/Brand Manager

Publisher's Interests

The titles from Honor Books, written from a Christian perspective, are intended to encourage readers to grow closer to God and to experience love and grace. Its children's line of inspirational material ranges from novelty books for toddlers to lessons and devotionals for pre-teens.
Website: www.honorbooks.com

Freelance Potential

Published 15 titles in 2004: 1 was developed from an unsolicited submission and 3 were by agented authors. Of the 15 titles, 5 were by unpublished writers and all were by authors who were new to the publishing house. Receives 120 unsolicited mss yearly.

- **Nonfiction:** Publishes concept books, toddler books, and early picture books, 0–4 years; easy-to-read books, 4–7 years; story picture books, 4–10 years; and middle-grade books, 8–12 years. Also publishes activity, novelty, and board books, and titles in series. Features books with Christian themes.
- **Representative Titles:** *Happy Easter* is a collection of inspirational quotes, poems, stories, Scripture verses, and brief facts about the origins of Easter symbols. *A Simple Book of Prayers* by Kenneth & Karen Boa (3–5 years) includes one- or two-sentence prayers, backed by related Scripture verses, intended to release the burdens of the heart.

Submissions and Payment

Guidelines available. Send complete ms with interior sample spreads. Accepts simultaneous submissions if identified. Availability of artwork improves chance of acceptance. SASE. Responds in 3 months. Publication in 1–2 years. Royalty; advance. Flat fee.

Editor's Comments

Things are shifting here at Honor Books—we are changing direction editorially. By 2005 these changes should be in place, and we encourage you to check our website for the latest information.

Horizon Publishers

P.O. Box 490
50 South 500 West
Bountiful, UT 84001-0490

Submissions Editor: Dwayne Crowther

Publisher's Interests
This publisher offers books that target the Christian marketplace, and are directed to members of the Latter-day Saint faith, as well as the general public. Topics include marriage, family life, raising and teaching children, Bible studies, and comparative religions.
Website: www.horizonpublishersbooks.com

Freelance Potential
Published 15-20 titles in 2004: 8 were developed from unsolicited submissions. Receives 200 queries and unsolicited mss yearly.

- **Nonfiction:** Publishes activity and religious teaching books on the Mormon faith for children. Also publishes books about parenting, family life, social issues, crafts, outdoor life, and books that are of interest to scouts.
- **Representative Titles:** *Miracles for Michael* by JoAnn Arnold (all ages) is the story of how a boy's life changes when his mother is in an accident. It is fun to read and has a happy ending with numerous twists. *Planting Seeds of Faith* by Alison Palmer (teachers) offers lesson plans for primary-aged children that are based on the Gospel. Each plan includes a scriptural passage, song, learning activity, and lists teaching materials that are needed.

Submissions and Payment
Guidelines available. Query or send complete ms. Accepts photocopies and computer printouts. SASE. Responds to queries in 1-3 months, to mss in 4-5 months. Royalty, 8%; advance, $100-$500. Flat fee.

Editor's Comments
We look for wholesome, informative books, and learning activities geared towards children of the LDS faith, as well as books on cooking, gardening, and emergency preparedness. Material that will lift, inspire, inform, and entertain readers is always of interest to us. New writers are welcome to submit a query or manuscript.

Houghton Mifflin Children's Books

222 Berkeley Street
Boston, MA 02116

Editorial Assistant: Erica Zappy

Publisher's Interests
This privately-owned publishing company is committed to giving shape to ideas that educate, inform, and delight young readers of all ages. Its catalogue offers both fiction and nonfiction and the company has published some of today's best-loved children's authors.
Website: www.houghtonmifflinbooks.com

Freelance Potential
Published 100 titles in 2004: 50 were by unpublished writers and 10 were by authors who were new to the publishing house. Receives 15,000 queries yearly.

- **Fiction:** Publishes concept books, toddler books, and early picture books, 0–4 years; easy-to-read books, 4–7 years; chapter books, 5–10 years; middle-grade novels, 8–12 years; and young adult books, 12–18 years. Genres include historical and multicultural fiction; adventure, and humor.
- **Nonfiction:** Publishes early picture books, 0–4 years; middle-grade books, 8–12 years; and young adult books, 12–18 years. Topics include history, science, and biography.
- **Representative Titles:** *Ollie* by Olivier Dunrea is the story of two friends, Gossie and Gertie, who must wait patiently for their friend Ollie to hatch out of his egg. *A Cow's Alfalfa-Bet* by Woody Jackson (0–4 years) is a delightful book of the alphabet demonstrated through illustrations of Vermont cows.

Submissions and Payment
Guidelines available with SASE, at website, or by calling 617-351-5959. Send complete ms for fiction. Query with synopsis and sample chapters for nonfiction. Accepts photocopies and computer printouts. SASE. Responds in 3 months, but only if interested. Publication period varies. Royalty; advance.

Editor's Comments
As a leader in children's publishing, competition here is very high. Please note that we only respond if we are interested in your work.

Humanics

Suite 200
12 South Dixie Highway
Lake Worth, FL 33460

Acquisitions Editor

Publisher's Interests
Focusing on educational material, this publisher offers concept and activity books for children up to the age of six, as well as resource guides for their teachers.
Website: www.humanicslearning.com

Freelance Potential
Published 20 titles (5 juvenile) in 2004: 10–15 were developed from unsolicited submissions. Of the 20 titles, 3 were by unpublished writers and 6 were by authors who were new to the publishing house. Receives 500 queries yearly.

- **Nonfiction:** Publishes concept and toddler books, 0–4 years. Topics include crafts and hobbies. Also publishes titles for parents and educators.
- **Representative Titles:** *Fraid E. Cat* by Al Newman is the story of a cat that is afraid of the dark. It provides a fun opportunity to show children that there is nothing to fear when the lights go off. *The Planet of the Dinosaurs* by Barbara Carr tells the story of three young astronauts that take a trip to the Planet of the Dinosaurs and find dinosaurs in need of a place to live.

Submissions and Payment
Guidelines and catalogue available with 9x12 SASE ($.55 postage). Query with résumé, synopsis, and marketing plan. A one-time submissions fee of $50 is required with all submissions. Accepts photocopies, computer printouts, and disk submissions (Microsoft Word or WordPerfect). SASE. Responds in 3 months. Publication in 6 months. Royalty, 8%.

Editor's Comments
We offer practical, resourceful books and activities for parents and teachers. Topics related to parent involvement, parenting, science math, language arts, the infant and toddler years, and arts and crafts are of interest to us. Also, we like children's books that address developmental issues in a fun way.

Hunter House Publishers

P.O. Box 2914
Alameda, CA 94501-0914

Acquisitions Editor: Jeanne Brondino

Publisher's Interests
Contemporary health, family, and community issues are the focus of this publisher. Its list includes titles for general readers, health-care professionals, and educators at all levels.
Website: www.hunterhouse.com

Freelance Potential
Published 16 titles in 2004: 8 were developed from unsolicited submissions, and 8 were reprint/licensed properties. Of the 16 titles, 2 were by unpublished writers and 5 were by authors who were new to the publishing house. Receives 1,000 queries yearly.

- **Nonfiction:** Publishes resource titles for educators, parents, and social workers. Topics include violence prevention, self-respect, sexual abuse, friendship, and diversity. Also publishes activity books for children, 4+ years. Topics cover yoga, drama, dance, language arts, movement, and music.
- **Representative Titles:** *In Your Own Voice* by Bernard Selling (teachers) explains how to use life stories as a basis for teaching writing skills. *Days of Respect* by Ralph J. Cantor et al. (teachers) discusses ways to organize a school-wide violence prevention program to build respect and stop violence among students.

Submissions and Payment
Guidelines available. Query with résumé, overview, chapter by chapter outline, competitive analysis, and marketing ideas. Accepts computer printouts, and simultaneous submissions if identified. SASE. Responds in 3-4 months. Publication in 1-3 years. Royalty.

Editor's Comments
We are looking for comprehensive and up-to-date information presented in a clear and accessible manner. We have a growing line of books and workbooks that address topics such as violence prevention, disabilities, and human rights. Prospective titles for this area of interest should include clear explanations, activities and exercises, provocative insights, and practical theory.

John Hunt Publishing

46A West Street
New Alresford, Hants SO24 9AU
United Kingdom

Editor: John Hunt

Publisher's Interests
This publisher exclusively features nonfiction and all of its titles are religious; covering such topics as faith, family, and lifeskills. It also offers Bible stories for children. 5% self-, subsidy-, co-venture, or co-op published.
Website: www.o-books.net

Freelance Potential
Published 60 titles (15 juvenile) in 2004: 3 were developed from unsolicited submissions, 20 were by agented authors, and 5 were reprint/licensed properties. Of the 60 titles, 10 were by unpublished writers and 10 were by authors who were new to the publishing house. Receives 600 queries yearly.

- **Nonfiction:** Published 3 concept books, 0–3 years; 3 toddler books, 0–4 years; 4 early picture books, 0–4 years; 2 easy-to-read books, 4–7 years; 1 story picture book, 4–10 years; 2 middle-grade books, 8–12 years; and 6 young adult books, 12–18 years. Topics include religion, prayer, faith, family issues, and social issues. Also publishes Bible stories and educational titles.
- **Representative Titles:** *Woodland Bible Stories* by Linda & Alan Parry (3–7 years) offers Bible stories, told through the adventures of the animals living in Oaktree Wood. *Matt White Agent of God: Operation Family* by Andy Robb follows the adventures of a young boy as he goes looking for mysteries to solve.

Submissions and Payment
Query with clips. Accepts photocopies. SASE. Responds in 1 week. Publication in 18 months. Royalty. Flat fee.

Editor's Comments
Board books, activity books, and books for older readers are at the top of our wish list this year. For younger readers we want to see religious topics written in an entertaining way that will engage children. For older readers, books on the history, traditions, and beliefs of other faiths are welcome.

Illumination Arts

P.O. Box 1865
Bellevue, WA 98009

Editorial Director: Ruth Thompson

Publisher's Interests
The mission of this small publishing house is to produce books that will touch people's lives with illumination and transformation. Its children's list offers picture books for ages four through ten. All of Illumination Arts books feature enduring spiritual values, but are not based on organized religion.
Website: www.illumin.com

Freelance Potential
Published 4 titles in 2004: 3 were developed from unsolicited submissions and 1 was by an agented author. Of the 4 titles, 3 were by unpublished writers and 4 were by authors who were new to the publishing house. Receives 2,000 unsolicited mss yearly.

- **Fiction:** Published 4 story picture books, 4–10 years.
- **Representative Titles:** *Too Many Murkles* by Heidi Charissa Schmidt is a fantasy about a village invaded by strangers, and a young girl who learns that creatures who are different are not necessarily bad. *The Errant Knight* by Ann Tompert follows the adventures of a knight en route to serve his king whose true mission is to help those he meets along the way.

Submissions and Payment
Guidelines available. Send complete ms with sample illustrations. Accepts simultaneous submissions if identified. SASE. Response time, publication period, and payment policy vary.

Editor's Comments
The mission of our publishing program is to inspire the mind, touch the heart, and uplift the spirit. Please note that we are about inspiration, not religion. While we welcome submissions from writers familiar with our books, due to the overwhelming number of submissions we receive, we may be late in responding. If you do not send an SASE we will not respond.

Impact Publishers

P.O. Box 6016
Atascadero, CA 93423

Acquisitions Editor: Freeman Porter

Publisher's Interests
This family-owned publishing house is best known for its self-help books. Its editors seek material that will bring the best human service expertise to the widest possible audience. Its titles are designed for a general interest audience interested in one of the many topics that fall under the topic of self-help. It does not publish fiction.
Website: www.impactpublishers.com

Freelance Potential
Published 5 titles (1 juvenile) in 2004. Of the 5 titles, 2 were by unpublished writers and 2 were by authors who were new to the publishing house. Receives 750–1,000 queries yearly.

- **Nonfiction:** Published 1 middle-grade book, 8–12 years; and 1 young adult book, 12–18 years. Topics include social issues, marriage, mental health, self-esteem, creativity, relationships, social and emotional growth, parenting, popular psychology, and multicultural and ethnic issues.
- **Representative Titles:** *The Divorce Helpbook for Teens* by Cynthia MacGregor (YA) helps teens learn to talk to their parents about divorce. *Luck Is No Accident* by John D. Krumboltz, Ph.D. & Al S. Levin, Ed. helps individuals to learn how to create their own luck and make the best of it for success.

Submissions and Payment
Guidelines available. Query with résumé and sample chapters. Accepts photocopies, computer printouts, and simultaneous submissions if identified. SASE. Responds in 1–3 months. Publication in 1 year. Royalty; advance.

Editor's Comments
Our readers are laymen—not professionals. They are interested in finding books that will help them to better understand some aspect of their lives and to make conscious choices in difficult situations. Most of our authors are professionals working in human services who can speak to their audience in non-technical terms.

Imperial International

30 Montauk Boulevard
Oakdale, NY 11769

Editor-in-Chief: Laura Solimene

Publisher's Interests
This division of EDCON Publishing Group offers a unique selection of supplemental instruction material for grades pre-K through grade three. It focuses on specially designed products to improve reading and math skills.
Website: www.edconpublishing.com

Freelance Potential
Published 6 titles in 2004. Of the 6 titles, 3 were by unpublished writers and 3 were by authors who were new to the publishing house. Receives 100 unsolicited mss yearly.

- **Fiction:** Publishes easy-to-read books, 4–7 years; chapter books, 5–10 years; and middle-grade books, 8–12 years. Genres include science fiction, adventure, multicultural and ethnic fiction, and fairy tales. Also publishes hi/lo fiction, 6–18 years; and activity books, 6–12 years.
- **Nonfiction:** Publishes chapter books, 5–10 years; and young adult books, 12–18 years. Topics include reading comprehension, mathematics, science, and technology. Also publishes educational materials for homeschooling.
- **Representative Titles:** *Catch a Star with Reading* (K) introduces the concepts of shape, size, matching, sorting, reading comprehension, and following directions. *Critical Thinking* (grades 1–2) identifies thinking skills such as visual imagery, analogies, patterns, classifying, and sequencing.

Submissions and Payment
Guidelines available with 9x12 SASE ($1.35 postage). Send complete ms. Accepts photocopies and simultaneous submissions if identified. Submissions are not returned. Responds in 1–2 weeks. Publication in 6 months. Flat fee, $300–$1,000.

Editor's Comments
Hi/lo materials that grab the interest of remedial students are always a priority with us. Can you present a way to introduce and strengthen a math concept for young students?

All Manuscripts Treated Equally
Patience Camplair
Incentive Publications

Incentive Publications publishes teacher resource materials, targeted toward use with children in preschool through middle school, as well as students enrolled in English-as-a-Second-Language programs.

Editor Patience Camplair makes a point of saying that Incentive considers all manuscripts they receive at Incentive Publications equally: "There aren't really any tips for writers looking to break in with us. Our acceptance of a manuscript is determined by its quality." Because the primary criterion for Incentive is that freelancers can produce that high quality, Camplair says a teaching background isn't necessary for authors. It is important to note, however, that most of the writers who publish with Incentive do have solid teaching experience.

Incentive's guidelines for submissions are very straightforward. Writers are asked to send a letter of introduction (a cover letter), a table of contents for the proposed book, a sample chapter of the proposed book, and a self-addressed stamped envelope (large enough to hold your materials) and sufficient return postage. Editors at Incentive Publications make every effort to reply to submissions within six to eight weeks.

(See listing for Incentive Publications on following page)

Incentive Publications

3835 Cleghorn Avenue
Nashville, TN 37215

Editor: Patience Camplair

Publisher's Interests
Creative materials that meet the educational needs of students at all levels are the focus of this publisher. Incentive Publications develops books, videos, and classroom resources that help teachers, parents, and students master skills and realize their academic potential.
Website: www.incentivepublications.com

Freelance Potential
Published 30 titles in 2004: 12 were developed from unsolicited submissions. Of the 30 titles, 29 were by unpublished writers and 1 was by an author who was new to the publishing house. Receives 350 queries yearly.

- **Nonfiction:** Publishes early picture books, 0–4 years; chapter books, 5–10 years; middle-grade titles, 8–12 years; and young adult books, 12–18 years. Also publishes teachers resource materials. Topics include literacy, social awareness, science, arts and crafts, math, reading, and early learning.
- **Representative Titles:** *If You're Trying to Get Better Grades and Higher Test Scores, You've Gotta Have This Book* by Imogene Forte & Marjorie Frank (YA) provides students with the tools they need for academic success. *Romeo and Juliet Curriculum Guide* by Laura Maravilla (teachers, grades 7–9) helps students learn by relating current issues to Shakespearean themes.

Submissions and Payment
Guidelines available. Query with table of contents, outline/synopsis, and 1–3 sample chapters. Accepts photocopies and simultaneous submissions if identified. SASE. Responds in 4–6 weeks. Publication period varies. Royalty. Flat fee.

Editor's Comments
We are constantly faced with the challenge of finding new ways to meet the needs of students and teachers. We currently need more effective instructional and assessment materials, including kindergarten readiness books and middle-grade study resources.

Innovative Kids

18 Ann Street
Norwalk, CT 06854

Editorial Director: Don L. Curry

Publisher's Interests
Unique, interactive children's books that make reading fun and educational are the specialty of this publisher. It offers a variety of fiction and nonfiction material for children up to the age of 12.
Website: www.innovativekids.com

Freelance Potential
Published 30 titles in 2004: 2 were developed from unsolicited submissions. Of the 30 titles, 5 were by unpublished writers and 6 were by authors who were new to the publishing house. Receives 200 queries, 200 unsolicited mss yearly.

- **Fiction:** Publishes educational books, novelty books, and board books, 1–12 years. Genres include adventure, fairy tales, folklore, folktales, religious fiction, humor, and books about nature, the environment, and sports.
- **Nonfiction:** Publishes concept books and toddler books, 0–4 years; easy-to-read books, 4–7 years; story picture books, 4–7 years; and middle-grade books, 8–12 years. Topics include animals, pets, crafts, hobbies, geography, mathematics, nature, and the environment. Also publishes humor.
- **Representative Titles:** *Safari Sounds* by Susan Ring (4–8 years) takes readers on an African safari with hands-on learning. It offers vivid illustrations and real animal sounds. *Games for Brains* (7+ years) offers fact-filled reference books, games that reinforce learning, and science projects and activities on anatomy and space.

Submissions and Payment
Guidelines available at website. Query or send complete ms with dummies. Accepts photocopies. No ms will be returned. Responds in 4–6 months. Publication period and response time vary. Flat fee.

Editor's Comments
We are currently looking for more interactive, nonfiction books for children 12 and under. The material we publish makes learning fun for babies, preschoolers, beginning readers, and preteens.

International Reading Association

P.O. Box 8139
800 Barksdale Road
Newark, DE 19714-8139

Administrative Assistant: Michele Jester

Publisher's Interests

The publishing program of this company provides reading professionals worldwide with the best information available in reading research and practice. Its authors range from well-known educators in the field, to classroom teachers with successful programs, to doctoral students. The International Reading Program is a nonprofit organization.
Website: www.reading.org

Freelance Potential

Published 30 in 2004. Receives 100 queries yearly.

- **Nonfiction:** Publishes educational titles, research reports, and monographs. Topics include literacy programs, reading research and practice, language comprehension at all levels, and professional development.
- **Representative Titles:** *Promising Practices for Urban Reading Instruction* edited by Pamela A. Mason & Jeanne Shay Schumm (educators) features a collection of articles that show what has been working, and what has not, in urban classrooms—all based on the 10 children's literacy rights outlined in the IRA's policy statement. *Reciprocal Teaching at Work: Strategies for Improving Reading Comprehension* by Lori D. Oczhus (educators) presents an innovative teaching model that will help students in elementary and middle school classrooms to construct meaning from text by integrating reading comprehension strategies into three classroom settings.

Submissions and Payment

Guidelines available. Request a Publication Proposal Form before sending ms. Accepts photocopies. No simultaneous submissions. SASE. Response time, publication period, and payment policy vary.

Editor's Comments

Our goal is "teaching the world to read." To that end we are always interested in reviewing material from authors involved in teaching some aspect of literacy or reading.

JayJo Books

Guidance Channel Company
135 Dupont Street
P.O. Box 760
Plainview, NY 11803-0760

Editor-in-Chief: Sally Germain

Publisher's Interests
Working to provide books that build awareness of children with chronic conditions, JayJo Book features resources for healthcare professionals, social workers, school personnel, and families. All titles include a "Kids Quiz" for classroom interaction and a "Ten Tips for Teachers" guide.
Website: www.jayjo.com

Freelance Potential
Published 4 titles in 2004. Receives 120 queries yearly.

- **Fiction:** Publishes story picture books, 5–12 years. Features books on children's health issues and learning disabilities, including asthma, ADHD, diabetes, food allergies, cystic fibrosis, arthritis, Tourette Syndrome, autism, dyslexia, speech and hearing disorders, and Down's Syndrome.
- **Representative Titles:** *When Rufus Comes Home* by Kim Gosselin is a positive story about the diagnosis of diabetes, a little boy, and his special bear companion. *Taking Speech Disorders to School* by John E. Bryant helps children understand the causes and effects of speech disorders and how speech therapy can improve communication among friends and family.

Submissions and Payment
Guidelines available with #10 SASE ($.37 postage). Query. Accepts photocopies. SASE. Responds in 3 months. Publication in 2 years. Flat fee.

Editor's Comments
We are looking for simple, non-technical, colorful picture books that teach children about chronic illnesses and special needs. Easy to understand titles that help teachers, parents, and children cope with these issues in classroom, family, and social settings are needed for children age five to twelve. All submissions must be fun, entertaining, and informative for the reader.

Jewish Lights Publishing

P.O. Box 237
Sunset Farm Offices
Route 4
Woodstock, VT 05091

Submissions Editor

Publisher's Interests
This small publishing house prides itself on showcasing the work of writers at the forefront of spiritual thought. The books on its list are written for people of all faiths, and draw on Jewish wisdom and tradition to deal with the quest for faith. For the coming year its publishing program includes only two children's titles per year.
Website: www.jewishlights.com

Freelance Potential
Published 30 titles (2 juvenile) in 2004: 10 were developed from unsolicited submissions and 1 was by an agented author. Of the 30 titles, 9 were by unpublished writers and 12 were by authors who were new to the publishing house. Receives 500 queries, 700 unsolicited mss yearly.

- **Nonfiction:** Publishes toddler books, 0–4 years; easy-to-read books, 4–7 years; story picture books, 4–10 years; and young adult books, 12–18 years. Topics include religious and inspirational subjects and self-help.
- **Representative Titles:** *Because Nothing Looks Like God* by Lawrence and Karen Kushner (5–8 years) shows children the many ways God is with us every day. *Jerusalem of Gold* by Howard Schwartz (7+ years) offers young readers retellings of some of Judaism's best-loved stories and legends.

Submissions and Payment
Guidelines available. Query with résumé, table of contents, sample chapter, and marketing plan. Send complete ms for picture books. Accepts photocopies, computer printouts, and simultaneous submissions if identified. SASE. Responds in 4 months. Publication in 1 year. Payment policy varies.

Editor's Comments
If you are interested in submitting a proposal for a children's book to us, please be aware that we only plan to publish two per year in the future. Review our backlist and make sure your idea is new for us.

JIST Publishing

8902 Otis Avenue
Indianapolis, IN 46216-1033

Acquisitions Editor

Publisher's Interests
This publisher is known for its books, booklets, pamphlets, videos and games on the topics of career, job research, life skills, and character development. Its imprints JIST Life and KIDSRIGHTS are used by educators and other professionals working with children and tackle such topics as child abuse, domestic violence, character education, and parenting.
Website: www.jistlife.com; www.kidsrights.com

Freelance Potential
Published 40-50 titles in 2004: several were developed from unsolicited submissions. Receives 250 queries yearly.

- **Nonfiction:** Publishes textbooks, reference books, workbooks, assessment devices, pamphlets, videos, and software products. Topics include job search, career exploration, occupational information, life skills, character education, domestic and family violence, and child abuse.
- **Representative Titles:** *Becoming the Best Me* by Bob Orndorff (YA) is a workbook that helps teens develop good character traits and skills used in life and career. *Dealing with Bullies* (6-12 years) is a pamphlet dealing with what kinds of kids become bullies and how to keep them from bullying.

Submissions and Payment
Guidelines available at website. Query with résumé, outline/synopsis, and audience/market analysis. Accepts photocopies and computer printouts. SASE. Responds in 3-4 months. Publication in 1-2 years. Royalty, 8-10%.

Editor's Comments
While we will always consider submissions related to job search, career and occupational exploration, we are most interested in reviewing queries for our newer imprints of JIST Life and KIDSRIGHTS. The topics of child abuse and family violence continue to be top on our list of interests.

Journey Forth

1700 Wade Hampton Boulevard
Greenville, SC 29614-0060

Acquisitions Editor: Nancy Lohr

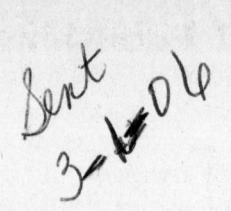

Publisher's Interests
Christian fiction, biographies, and nonfiction books for children and teens are offered by this division of Bob Jones University Press. Journey Forth is not currently accepting picture books.
Website: www.bjup.com

Freelance Potential
Published 10 titles in 2004: 1 was developed from an unsolicited submission, 1 was by an agented author, and 3 were reprint/licensed properties. Of the 10 titles, 1 was by an unpublished writer and 2 were by authors who were new to the publishing house. Receives 70 queries, 400 unsolicited mss yearly.

- **Fiction:** Published 2 easy-to-read books, 4–7 years; 3 chapter books, 5–10 years; 3 middle-grade books, 8–12 years; and 2 young adult books, 12–18 years. Genres include Christian living, mystery, historical and contemporary fiction, fantasy, animal adventure, and fictional biographies.
- **Nonfiction:** Publishes middle-grade books, 8–12 years; and young adult books, 12–18 years. Features Christian biographies.
- **Representative Titles:** *Jewel Cases* (YA) is a collection of mystery stories that keeps readers guessing. *Tales from Dust River Gulch* by Tim Davis (9–12 years) is a fanciful Western tale full of villains, vittles, robbers, and railroads.

Submissions and Payment
Guidelines available. Query with 5 sample chapters; or send complete ms. Accepts photocopies, computer printouts, and simultaneous submissions if identified. SASE. Responds in 3 months. Publication in 18–24 months. Royalty, negotiable. Flat fee.

Editor's Comments
Submissions for Christian fiction books should present clear scriptural applications and lessons. Standard fiction, although not overtly Christian, must offer a good story with Christian standards of thought, feeling, and action.

The Judaica Press

123 Ditmas Avenue
Brooklyn, NY 11218

Editor: Norman Shapiro

Publisher's Interests
Books that celebrate Jewish life and interests are featured in this publisher's catalogue, from children's titles that teach Jewish concepts to adult books and textbooks about the Torah.
Website: www.judaicapress.com

Freelance Potential
Published 15 titles (7 juvenile) in 2004: 10 were developed from unsolicited submissions and 3 were reprint/licensed properties. Of the 15 titles, 4 were by unpublished writers and 10 were by authors who were new to the publishing house. Receives 75 queries, 65 unsolicited mss yearly.

- **Fiction:** Publishes early picture books, 0–4 years; easy-to-read books, 4–7 years; story picture books, 4–10 years; and young adult books, 12–18 years. Genres include religious mystery and suspense, and religious fiction.
- **Nonfiction:** Publishes story picture books, 4–10 years. Topics include Jewish traditions, self-help issues, Bible stories, crafts, and hobbies.
- **Representative Titles:** *Facing the Music* by Eva Vogiel (YA) is a thoughtful account of a girl at a Jewish boarding school who desires a future different from the one expected of her. *Boruch Learns about Pesach* by Rabbi Shmuel Kunda (3–8 years) presents the customs and traditions of Pesach in a bright, lively format.

Submissions and Payment
Query with outline; or send complete ms. Accepts photocopies and computer printouts. Availability of artwork improves chance of acceptance. SASE. Responds in 3 months. Publication in 1–2 years. Royalty.

Editor's Comments
We seek books that enlighten, inspire, and educate our Jewish readers. Children's books geared for young readers that explain the tenets of the Jewish faith and how they relate to everyday living are needed. Send us material that children can understand.

Just Us Books

3rd Floor
356 Glenwood Avenue
East Orange, NJ 07017

Submissions Manager

Publisher's Interests
This independent publisher specializes in books that appeal to African American young adults between the ages of thirteen and sixteen. Most of the books on its list are fiction, but it does offer some nonfiction—particularly biographies. Each year, Just Us Books produces between four and eight new titles.
Website: www.justusbooks.com

Freelance Potential
Published 8 titles in 2004: 1 was developed from an unsolicited submission, 1 was by an agented author, and 3 were reprint/licensed properties. Of the 8 titles, 1 was by an unpublished writer and 5 were by authors who were new to the publishing house. Receives 1,000+ queries yearly.

- **Fiction:** Publishes story picture books, 4–10 years; and middle-grade books, 8–12 years. Genres include contemporary, multicultural, and historical fiction, adventure, and mystery.
- **Nonfiction:** Publishes middle-grade books, 8–12 years. Features biographies.
- **Representative Titles:** *Scientists, Healers, and Inventors* by Wade Hudson (9–12 years) chronicles the lives of such well-known figures as George Washington Carver and Dr. Daniel Hale Williams: part of the Black Heroes series. *A Blessing in Disguise* by Eleanora E. Tate (10+ years) follows the adventures of Zambia, a young girl from a small town, who is in search of fun and adventure.

Submissions and Payment
Guidelines available. Query with outline/synopsis. SASE. Responds in 3–4 months. Publication period varies. Royalty.

Editor's Comments
We are currently interested in chapter books and YA novels that will appeal to readers ages thirteen to sixteen and feature strong characterization and a well-developed story line. We will also review biographies. Keep in mind that we focus on African Americans.

Kaeden Books

P.O. Box 16190
Rocky River, OH 44116

Editor: Craig Urmston

Publisher's Interests
This educational publisher specializes in leveled books used for guided reading, early reading intervention, and independent reading. Its titles are geared for students reading at the level of readers between the ages of four and ten. It plans to expand its list of nonfiction to include titles for beginning readers.
Website: www.kaeden.com

Freelance Potential
Published 16 titles in 2004: all were developed from unsolicited submissions. Of the 16 titles, 2 were by unpublished writers and 10 were by authors who were new to the publishing house. Receives 1,500 unsolicited mss yearly.

- **Fiction:** Published 8 easy-to-read books, 0–4 years; and 8 story picture books. Also publishes early picture books.
- **Nonfiction:** Publishes easy-to-read books, 5–9 years. Topics include nature, mathematics, biography, science, and social studies.
- **Representative Titles:** *Can a Hippo Hop?* by Louise Todd introduces vocabulary used to describe the way animals move, complemented by realistic photography and illustrations. *Waking Up* helps children learn sequencing and recall by using shaking, wiggling, and twisting to try and wake up.

Submissions and Payment
Guidelines available at website. Send complete ms; no originals. Accepts photocopies and computer printouts. Responds only if interested. Publication period varies. Royalty. Flat fee.

Editor's Comments
In the coming year, we plan to begin publishing more nonfiction titles for beginning readers. Areas of interest to us include science, nature, biography, and history. Keep in mind that the subject matter should be suitable for students in kindergarten through grade three. If you are unsure of appropriate topics, you may want to review the school curriculum for the aforementioned grades.

Kar-Ben Publishing

Suite 2
11430 Strand Drive
Rockville, MD 20852

Submissions Editor: Madeline Wikler

Publisher's Interests
This publisher offers fiction and nonfiction books with Jewish themes for young children through high school. It is a division of Lerner Publishing Group.
Website: www.karben.com

Freelance Potential
Published 15 titles in 2004. Of the 15 titles, 1 was by an author who was new to the publishing house. Receives 300 queries, 250 unsolicited mss yearly.

- **Fiction:** Published 3 easy-to-read books, 4–10 years. Features Bible stories, holiday stories, life cycle stories, and folktalkes. Also publishes concept books, toddler books, and early picture books, 0–4 years; activity books, 4–7 years; and board books.
- **Nonfiction:** Published 2 toddler books, 0–4 years; 2 early picture books, 0–4 years; 1 easy to read book, 4–7 years, 3 story picture books, 4–10 years; 1 young adult book, 12–18 years. Also publishes family books; and activity books, 4–7 years.
- **Representative Titles:** *I Can Celebrate* Anne Eisenberg (1–4 years) is a book that encourages preschoolers to spin, whistle, and sing while they learn about Jewish customs. *The Hardest Word* by Jacqueline Jules (3–7 years) is about learning to say I am sorry.

Submissions and Payment
Guidelines available. Send complete ms. Accepts photocopies, computer printouts, and simultaneous submissions if identified. SASE. Responds in 3–5 weeks. Publication period varies. Royalty, 5–8%; advance $500–$2,000.

Editor's Comments
We're looking for books on topics related to interfaith families. Stories about the Jewish life cycle and multicultural families are always welcome. Before submitting your story, please make sure your characters are believable, and that there is enough action involved to catch and hold the reader's attention.

Key Curriculum Press

1150 65th Street
Emeryville, CA 94608

President & Editorial Director: Steve Rasmussen

Publisher's Interests
This educational publisher specializes in math textbooks, software, and supplemental materials for use in secondary and middle schools. All of the books in its catalogue conform to the standards of the National Council of Teachers of Mathematics.
Website: www.keypress.com

Freelance Potential
Published 35 titles in 2004. Receives 50 queries yearly.

- **Nonfiction:** Publishes textbooks, software, and supplemental materials for grades 6–12.
- **Representative Titles:** *Discovering Algebra* by Jerald Murdock et al. (grades 8–10) integrates the traditional algebra curriculum with statistics, data analysis, functions, geometry, probability, and trigonometry. *Precalculus and Trigonometry Explorations* by Paul A. Foerster (grade 11–college) helps students extend their understanding of key concepts in precalculus or trigonometry.

Submissions and Payment
Guidelines available on website. Query with résumé, prospectus, table of contents, and sample chapters. Accepts photocopies, computer printouts, disk submissions, and simultaneous submissions if identified. SASE. Responds in 2 months. Publication period varies. Royalty, 6–10%.

Editor's Comments
We welcome submissions of materials targeted primarily at secondary mathematics educators. We seek proposals and submissions whose pedagogy and mathematics content are sound and consistent with NCTM standards. While each project is handled in a manner suitable to its uniqueness, we strive to see certain standards and ideas expressed by all of our publications. As a prospective author, you can judge whether your material suits our editorial agenda by familiarizing yourself with the the guidelines and overview of our editorial procedure.

Key Porter Books

3rd Floor
70 The Esplanade
Toronto, Ontario M5E 1R2
Canada

Editorial Assistant: Janie Yoon

Publisher's Interests
Key Porter is a Canadian publisher known for its illustrated books for children. Its list includes both fiction and nonfiction titles for beginning readers, young adults, and their parents.
Website: www.keyporter.com

Freelance Potential
Published 90 titles (13 juvenile) in 2004: 6 were developed from unsolicited submissions, 63 were by agented authors, and 6 were reprint/licensed properties. Receives 200–250 queries yearly.

- **Fiction:** Publishes easy-to-read books, 4–7 years; story picture books, 4–10 years; chapter books, 5–10 years; and young adult books, 12–18 years. Genres include animal, nature, and environmental stories; folklore; and fairy tales. Also publishes anthologies.
- **Nonfiction:** Publishes story picture books, 4–10 years; middle-grade books, 8–12 years; and young adult books, 12–18 years. Topics include the environment, nature, natural history, health, and multicultural and ethnic issues. Also publishes parenting titles.
- **Representative Titles:** *Alligator Pie* by Dennis Lee is a collection of rhythmic stories and songs from classical Canadian childhood literature. *Ancient Adventures for Modern Kids* is a marvelous anthology of inspiring tales and fantastic stories from around the world and across the ages.

Submissions and Payment
Query with résumé, proposal, table of contents, and sample chapter or 20-page excerpt. SAE/IRC. Response time varies. Publication period and payment policy vary.

Editor's Comments
We continue to need fresh material that focuses on history, nature, animals, and the environment for children age four through teenagers. Our readers want hard-core information with a unique twist that keeps them reading. Send us books that will spark interest in a young reader.

Alfred A. Knopf Books for Young Readers

1745 Broadway
New York, NY 10019

Submissions Editor

Publisher's Interests
Alfred A. Knopf is a well-known imprint of Random House Children's Books, and features quality literature for preschool children through young adult readers in all formats, from board books to picture books to novels.
Website: www.randomhouse.com/kids

Freelance Potential
Published 50 titles in 2004: all by agented authors. Receives 4,000 unsolicited mss yearly.

- **Fiction:** Publishes picture books, 0–8 years; chapter books, 5–10 years; middle-grade novels, 8–12 years; and young adult books, 12–18 years. Genres include historical, contemporary, and multicultural fiction.
- **Representative Titles:** *A Necklace of Raindrops and Other Stories* by Joan Aiken contains eight imaginative, satisfying stories for bedtime reading. *Before We Were Free* by Julia Alvarez is an unforgettable story about adolescence, perseverance, and one girl's struggle to be free from a repressed life in the Dominican Republic. *What a Song Can Do* by Jennifer Armstrong is a compelling collection of stories that explore the impact of music on our lives, the depths music can reach in us, and the power it has to bind us together.

Submissions and Payment
Guidelines available. Accepts agented submissions only. Accepts photocopies, computer printouts, and simultaneous submissions if identified. SASE. Responds in 3 months. Publication in 1–2 years. Royalty; advance.

Editor's Comments
Our list of award-winning authors includes such well-known names as Leo Lionni and Roald Dahl. We consider manuscripts based on their artistic merit and literary quality. Before your agent submits your manuscript to us, please look at our website to get a feel for the type of books we publish. Note that we do not accept nonfiction titles.

Lark Books

67 Broadway
Asheville, NC 28801

Children's Book Editor: Joe Rhatigan

Publisher's Interests
In print for over 15 years, this publisher offers middle-grade readers, young adults, and adults books with easy-to-follow directions, and colorful pictures on a variety of crafts, as well as craft kits. Topics include fiber arts, ceramics, beading, and quilting.
Website: www.larkbooks.com

Freelance Potential
Published 60 titles (15 juvenile) in 2004: 10 were developed from unsolicited submissions and 5 were by reprint/licensed properties. Receives 250+ queries yearly.

- **Nonfiction:** Publishes middle-grade books, 8–12 years. Also publishes young adult books, 12–18 years. Topics include beading, book making, ceramics, doll making, fiber arts, knitting, crocheting, mosaics, nature crafts, paper, quilting, sewing, theater crafts, and weaving.
- **Representative Titles:** *Ceramics for Kids* by Mary Ellis (grades 8–12) offers brightly illustrated projects with detailed directions, and suggests inexpensive tools for children to make creative clay products. *Geography Fun* by Joe Rhatigan & Heather Smith (grades 8–12) presents over 50 illustrated geography projects, plus special informative sidebars to help parents answer kids' questions.

Submissions and Payment
Guidelines available at website. Prefers query with résumé, table of contents, introduction, 2–3 sample projects, and a description of artwork and illustrations. SASE. Response time varies. Publication period and payment policy vary.

Editor's Comments
Books about crafts and leisure activities are our focus. We publish both new and seasoned authors who have substantial expertise on the topic they are writing about. We want our books to be fun, so make sure your writing is friendly and upbeat. Send us a detailed query, and if we are interested—we'll ask you for a proposal.

Learning Horizons

1 American Road
Cleveland, OH 44144

Editorial Director: Bob Kaminski

Publisher's Interests
Established nearly 10 years ago, this educational publisher features home and classroom resources for children through grade six. Its books, games, and activities are designed by professional educators to provide parent and teachers with the information they need to give children a solid start.
Website: www.learninghorizons.com

Freelance Potential
Published 38 titles in 2004: all were assigned. Of the 38 titles, 14 who were by authors who were new to the publishing house. Receives 600 queries yearly.

- **Nonfiction:** Publishes toddler books, 2-3 years; and story picture books, 4-10 years. Features educational and informational titles and novelty and board books. Topics include math, language, science, social studies, holidays, nature, and the environment.
- **Representative Titles:** *Whales!* (4-9 years) tells how whales are born, what they eat, how they grow, how they communicate, and where they live; part of the Know-It-Alls® series. *Preschool Ultimate Skill Builder* (3-7 years) is a comprehensive workbook filled with teacher-approved activities designed to help children develop math and reading skills.

Submissions and Payment
Guidelines available. Query. SASE. Responds in 3-4 months. Publication in 18 months. Payment policy varies.

Editor's Comments
We're always looking for new ideas, especially in the areas of math and science, that will encourage parents to get involved with their child's learning. We know how important it is for children to develop a love of learning, and our hands-on learning materials are designed to excite, stimulate, and teach children in preschool though sixth grade. Please visit our website for a first-hand look at the types of materials we produce.

Learning Resources

380 North Fairway Drive
Vernon Hills, IL 60061

Editorial Director

Publisher's Interests
This publisher offers quality educational products that make learning exciting for all children. It covers math, science, early childhood, language products, and teacher resources.
Website: www.learningresources.com

Freelance Potential
Published 50 titles in 2004: Of the 50 titles, 5 were by authors who were new to the publishing house. Receives 25 queries yearly.

- **Nonfiction:** Publishes educational materials, manipulatives, workbooks, and activity books, pre-K–grade 6. Topics include language arts, phonics, math, science, geography, and nutrition. Also publishes teacher resources.
- **Representative Titles:** *Python Path Word Families Game* (grades 1 and up) encourages word recognition and reading confidence as kids move along a friendly snake path winning points for completing words. *Animal Classifying Cards* (grades K–6) allows students to have fun and learn about a range of wildlife from various regions. Early learners can do simple sorting and classifying while more advance students learn about animals.

Submissions and Payment
Catalogue available with 9x12 SASE ($3 postage). Query with résumé and writing samples. Accepts photocopies, computer printouts, and disk submissions. SASE. Responds in 6–12 weeks. Publication in 1–2 years. Flat fee.

Editor's Comments
We seek products that will benefit children as they grow and make learning a hands-on experience that is fun. We provide a wide variety of learning materials such as activity kits and books, board games, and manipulatives. If you are a professional in the educational field with a classroom idea that focuses on building skills through exploration, imagination, and fun, send us an overview, summary of the content, and the age group you are targeting.

Lee & Low Books

95 Madison Avenue
New York, NY 10016

Submissions Editor

Publisher's Interests
Lee & Low Books' mandate is to publish multicultural children's books that make a difference and that are culturally authentic. Its focus is on fiction and nonfiction picture books for children ages 2 to 12 that feature children/people of color.
Website: www.leeandlow.com

Freelance Potential
Published 20 titles in 2004: 2 were developed from unsolicited submissions and 4 were by agented authors. Of the 20 titles, 3 were by unpublished writers and 4 were by authors who were new to the publishing house. Receives 2,000 mss yearly.

- **Fiction:** Published 9 story picture books, 4–10 years; and 1 middle-grade novel, 8–12 years. Genres include historical, realistic, contemporary, multicultural, and ethnic fiction.
- **Nonfiction:** Published 4 story picture books, 4–10 years; and 1 middle-grade book, 8–12 years. Topics include people and multicultural issues.
- **Representative Titles:** *Ghosts for Breakfast* by Stanley Todd Terasaki (5–9 years) features a young boy and his father who solve the mystery of the "ghosts" seen by their neighbors. *Elizabeti's School* by Stephanie Stuve-Bodeen (4–7 years) follows a young girl named Elizabeti as she goes through her first day at school.

Submissions and Payment
Guidelines and catalogue available at website or with 9x12 SASE ($1.75 postage). Send complete ms. Accepts photocopies, computer printouts, and simultaneous submissions. SASE. Responds in 2–4 months. Publication in 1–2 years. Royalty; advance.

Editor's Comments
We have just celebrated our tenth year in publishing and continue with our original mission of bringing multicultural authors and books to the public. Both fiction and nonfiction for children ages six to twelve, middle-grade projects, and picture books are needed.

Legacy Press

P.O. Box 261129
San Diego, CA 92196

Editorial Director: Christy Scannell

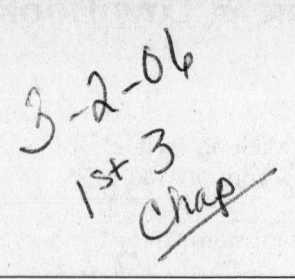

Publisher's Interests
Books that teach the Bible and promote Christian values for children age two to twelve are the focus of this Evangelical publisher. Its list includes fiction, nonfiction, devotionals, journals, and activity books.
Website: www.rainbowpublishers.com

Freelance Potential
Published 7 titles in 2004: all were developed from unsolicited submissions. Of the 7 titles, 1 was by an author who was new to the publishing house. Receives 240 unsolicited mss yearly.

- **Fiction:** Publishes series books, 2–12 years. Genres include contemporary religious and Christian fiction.
- **Nonfiction:** Publishes Evangelical-based books, 2–12 years. Topics include the Bible, religion, holidays, crafts, and hobbies. Also publishes activity books and devotionals.
- **Representative Titles:** *Escape from Camp Porcupine* (8–12) offers a story, devotions, and activities following the adventures of a group of Christian youths; part of The Ponytail Girls series. *Gotta Have God* (10–12 years) helps young men learn about God and how they can grow up to be strong Christian men.

Submissions and Payment
Guidelines and catalogue available with 9x12 SASE (2 first-class stamps). Query with table of contents and first 3 chapters. Accepts photocopies. SASE. Responds in 3 months. Publication in 6–36 months. Royalty, 8%+; advance, $500+.

Editor's Comments
We are looking for creative authors who relate well to the needs of the evangelical Christian market and are active participants in a Bible-believing church. We continue to need Christian nonfiction for preteens, and devotionals and activity books for all ages. Take a look at our "The Christian Girl's Guide to . . ." series for an idea of what our readers like.

Lerner Publishing Group

241 First Avenue North
Minneapolis, MN 55401

Submissions Editor: Jennifer Zimian

Publisher's Interests
Nonfiction that targets the school and library markets is found on the list of this educational publisher. For the coming years, it will only review submissions during the month of November. It publishes books for students from age four to eighteen.
Website: www.lernerbooks.com

Freelance Potential
Published 250 titles in 2004: 5 were developed from unsolicited submissions, 50 were by agented authors, and 12 were reprint/licensed properties. Of the 250 titles, 5 were by authors who were new to the publishing house. Receives 500 queries, 2,000 unsolicited mss yearly.

- **Nonfiction:** Publishes easy-to-read books, 4-7 years; chapter books, 5-10 years; middle-grade books, 8-12 years; and young adult books, 12-18 years. Topics include natural and physical science, current events, ancient and modern history, world cultures, and sports. Also publishes biographies.
- **Representative Titles:** *Cricketology* (grades 2-6) helps kids learn about the life cycle of crickets through experiments and activities; part of the Backyard Buddies series. *Bosnia* (grades 6-12) offers an unbiased look at history through maps, biographies, and recent history; part of the World in Conflict series.

Submissions and Payment
Guidelines and catalogue available with 9x12 SASE ($3.50 postage). Query with outline and sample chapter; or send complete ms with résumé. Accepts submissions only in November. Accepts photocopies, computer printouts, and simultaneous submissions if identified. SASE. Responds in 4-6 months. Publication period and payment policy vary.

Editor's Comments
We are seeking submissions of biographies of important, but not widely known, individuals and science topics that are written to appeal to boys.

Arthur A. Levine Books

Scholastic Press
557 Broadway
New York, NY 10012

Editorial Director: Arthur A. Levine

Publisher's Interests
Arthur A. Levine is one of several imprints of the award-winning Scholastic Press. This publisher features picture books, novels, and nonfiction titles for young readers, as well as poetry books and biographies for young adults.
Website: www.scholastic.com

Freelance Potential
Published 27 titles in 2004: 1 was developed from an unsolicited submission, 21 were by agented authors, and 11 were reprint/licensed properties. Of the 25 titles, 2 were by unpublished writers and 11 were by authors who were new to the publishing house. Receives 1,825 queries yearly.

- **Fiction:** Published 10 story picture books, 4–10 years; 1 middle-grade book, 8–12 years; and 15 young adult books, 12–18 years. Genres include multicultural fiction and poetry.
- **Nonfiction:** Published 1 concept book, 0–4 years. Also publishes picture books, 4–10 years; middle-grade books, 8–12 years; and young adult books, 12–18 years; and biographies.
- **Representative Titles:** *The Noisy Way to Bed* by Ian Whybrow (2–6 years) is a charming look at a small child's attempt to delay bedtime. *The Singer of All Songs* by Kate Constable (10+ years) is a novel about two young people and their efforts to save their enchanted land; part of the Chanters of Tremaris trilogy.

Submissions and Payment
Guidelines available. Query. Accepts complete ms from agented and previously published authors only. Accepts photocopies. SASE. Responds to queries in 2–4 weeks; to mss in 6–8 months. Publication in 18–24 months. Payment policy varies.

Editor's Comments
Make your query as original and individual as your book. Think of it as an opportunity to make an impression and introduce your work to readers who will enjoy what you've written.

Libraries Unlimited

88 Post Road West
Westport, CT 06881

Acquisitions Editor: Barbara Ittner

Publisher's Interests
Libraries Unlimited is an educational publisher specializing in quality bibliographies and books, library science textbooks, information science material, practical handbooks, monographs, and manuals for library educators, practicing librarians, and media specialists.
Website: www.lu.com

Freelance Potential
Published 75 titles in 2004: few were developed from unsolicited submissions. Of the 75 titles, 12 were by authors who were new to the publishing house. Receives 400 queries yearly.

- **Nonfiction:** Publishes curriculum titles. Features bilingual books, grades K–6; and activity books, grades K–12. Also features biographies, professional reference titles, gifted education titles, and regional books. Topics include science, mathematics, social studies, whole language, literature, and library connections.
- **Representative Titles:** *Blood, Bedlam, Bullets, and Badguys* by Michael B. Gannon (librarians) is a guide to the best and most popular titles in adventure and suspense fiction and their subgenres. *Cues: Choose, Use, Enjoy, Share* by Phyllis B. Leonard (librarians) is a model for educational enrichment through the school library media center.

Submissions and Payment
Guidelines available. Query with sample chapters, table of contents, and résumé; or send complete ms. Accepts photocopies, computer printouts, and simultaneous submissions if identified. SASE. Responds in 2–3 months. Publication in 10–12 months. Royalty.

Editor's Comments
We are always on the lookout for new material for educators by educators. In your proposal, please include information on the purpose of your book and your methodology. Explain why your book fits into the current market, and what, if any, are the competing titles.

Lillenas Publishing Company

2923 Troost Avenue
Kansas City, MO 64109

Drama Editor: Kimberly R. Messer

Publisher's Interests
This publishing house specializes in plays and sketches designed for use in church drama groups and by clergy who desire to minister using the dramatic arts. Its catalogue features material for all ages, from age 6 through adult.
Website: www.lillenasdrama.com

Freelance Potential
Published 50 titles (7 juvenile) in 2004. Receives 480 unsolicited mss yearly.

- **Fiction:** Publishes full-length and one-act plays, monologues, sketches, skits, recitations, puppet plays, and dramatic exercises, 6–18 years. Also publishes dramatic material on Christmas, Thanksgiving, Mother's Day, and other holiday themes.
- **Nonfiction:** Publishes theater resource materials. Topics include stage design, scenery, production techniques, and drama ministry.
- **Representative Titles:** *'Tis Better to Give* by Martha Bolton is the story of a young boy who learns the importance of giving during the holiday season. *Be Ye Thankful—Even for Your Vegetables* by Martha Bolton is about a boy who complains about his packed lunch until he gets a reminder that we ought to be thankful for the food we have.

Submissions and Payment
Guidelines available. Send complete ms with cast list, scene description, and prop list. Accepts computer printouts. SASE. Responds in 2–3 months. Publication period varies. Flat fee.

Editor's Comments
We never receive too many manuscripts, especially from serious playwrights. There is a need for work that fits into some, if not all of our classifications. We are interested in monologues, short prose, recitations for preschool, age five to seven, and eight to ten, and short sketches and skits, humorous, inspirational, or informative. We do receive scores of manuscripts, and reject many because they do not meet our needs.

Linnet Books

The Shoe String Press
2 Linsley Street
New Haven, CT 06473

President: Diantha C. Thorpe

Publisher's Interests

Linnet Books is a part of The Shoestring Press, founded in 1952. Its mission is to bring the best books with the latest information to the school and library markets. Its books cover a wide range of subjects and are targeted to students in grades six through twelve. Linnet Books does not publish any fiction.
Website: www.shoestringpress.com

Freelance Potential

Published 8 titles in 2004. Receives 500 queries yearly.

- **Nonfiction:** Publishes interdisciplinary books, memoirs, biographies, reference books, literacy companions, and multicultural children's publishing materials. Topics include social studies, natural history, folktales, storytelling, art, archaeology, and anthropology.
- **Representative Titles:** *Amphibians, Reptiles, and Their Conservation* by Marty Crump (grades 6 and up) explores the creatures in these families and why they are important to the world's ecology. *Beyond the Field Trip* by Uma Krishnaswami (teachers) offers ideas for projects that will extend the learning benefits of a class field trip.

Submissions and Payment

Query with 2 sample chapters. Accepts photocopies, computer printouts, and simultaneous submissions if identified. SASE. Responds in 4 months. Publication in 1 year. Royalty; advance.

Editor's Comments

For our teacher audience, we try to offer content that is user-friendly, written by experienced practitioners who have high standards, and strive to offer the very best. Editorially we are interested in books for children and those who work with children: folktales and folklore; historical narratives, oral histories, and other primary source materials; books about significant events as microcosms of historical or cultural influences; and science as an expression of culture. If you feel your writing is right for us, send us a detailed query that explains why you chose your subject and why you are qualified to write the book.

Linworth Publishing

Suite L
480 East Wilson Bridge Road
Worthington, OH 43085

Acquisitions Editor: Donna Miller

Publisher's Interests
Focusing on areas of school libraries, literature, and technology, this publisher offers resourceful information on topics related to professional development for media specialists and teachers working in kindergarten through high school.
Website: www.linworth.com

Freelance Potential
Published 20 titles in 2004: 10 were developed from unsolicited submissions. Receives 120 queries yearly.

- **Nonfiction:** Publishes books about school libraries, literature, and technology for media specialists and teachers, grades K–12. Also offers professional development books.
- **Representative Titles:** *Bringing Mysteries Alive for Children and Young Adults* by Jeanette Larson presents an introduction and a guide to using the various types of mysteries including true crime, detective stories, ghosts and gothics, and suspense. *Digital Storytelling: Creating an eStory* by Dusti D. Howell & Dianne K. Howell is an exciting teaching tool that includes tutorials with a step-by-step guide for building stories and creating digital videos, sounds, and images. Projects are easily adaptable for teacher and librarian collaboration.

Submissions and Payment
Catalogue and guidelines available at website. Query or send complete ms with 2 hard copies and IBM disk. Accepts email queries to linworth@linworthpublishing.com. SASE. Responds in 1 week. Publication in 6 months. Royalty.

Editor's Comments
We offer school librarians and teachers information to keep them up-to-date with the latest in resources and technology, and ways to enhance their professional development. Practical, informative material on application and technology, and managing a library media center is of interest to us. Your proposal should include the types of sources to be consulted and collection methods.

Lion Publishing

Mayfield House
256 Banbury Road
Oxford OX2 7DH
England

Editorial Secretary: Catherine Giddings

Publisher's Interests
Lion Publishing is a specialty publisher that features positive Christian books for children and adults. Its list includes fiction and nonfiction titles, as well as biographies of Christian personalities.
Website: www.lion-publishing.co.uk

Freelance Potential
Published 100 titles (85 juvenile) in 2004: 3 were developed from unsolicited submissions, and 30 were by agented authors. Of the 100 titles, 2 were by unpublished writers and 2 were by authors who were new to the publishing house. Receives 1,200 queries yearly.

- **Fiction:** Publishes concept books, toddler books, and early picture books, 0–4 years; easy-to-read books, 4–7 years; story picture books, 4–10 years; chapter books, 5–10 years; middle-grade books, 8–12 years; and young adult books, 12–18 years. Genres include adventure, fairy tales, folklore, and religious and inspirational fiction.
- **Nonfiction:** Publishes early picture books, 0–4 years; and easy-to-read books, 4–7 years; story picture books, 4–10 years, and middle-grade titles, 8–12 years. Topics include current events, health, fitness, history, humor, nature, the environment, religion, and social issues. Also publishes biographies.
- **Representative Titles:** *Bible Baddies* by Bob Hartman (8–11 years) is a gripping look at some of the Bible's worst villains. *The Best of the Night* by Steve Wood (6–8 years) follows a young gang of cats as they set out to find what has been terrorizing their neighborhood; part of The Courageous Cats' Club series.

Submissions and Payment
Guidelines available. Query with résumé. Accepts photocopies. SASE. Responds in 1 week. Publication period and payment vary.

Editor's Comments
Many of our readers have had little or no contact with a church, therefore you must avoid using Christian jargon. We favor Christian content that is presented naturally through the characters and plot.

Little, Brown and Company Books for Young Readers

1271 Avenue of the Americas
New York, NY 10020

Editor-in-Chief: Megan Tingley

Publisher's Interests
Children's literature in all genres and on various topics are offered by this well-known publisher. Little, Brown accepts submissions only from agented writers.
Website: www.lb-kids.com or www.lb-teens.com

Freelance Potential
Published 150 titles in 2004: all were by agented authors and 12 were reprint/licensed properties. Of the 150 titles, 1 was by an unpublished writer and 1 was by an author who was new to the publishing house. Receives 2,000 unsolicited mss yearly.

- **Fiction:** Publishes concept books, toddler books, and early picture books, 0–4 years; story picture books, 4–10 years; chapter books, 5–10 years; middle-grade books, 8–12 years; and young adult books, 12–18 years. Genres include contemporary and multicultural fiction; adventure; humor; mystery; suspense; and folktales. Also publishes poetry.
- **Nonfiction:** Publishes concept books, toddler books, and early picture books, 0–4 years; story picture books, 4–10 years; chapter books, 5–10 years; middle-grade books, 8–12 years; and young adult books, 12–18 years. Topics include family and social issues, nature, the environment, and crafts.
- **Representative Titles:** *America the Beautiful* by Katharine Lee Bates honors American strength and beauty with historical and contemporary illustrations. *Saying Goodbye to Lulu* by Corinne Demas (4–8 years) helps young readers come to terms with the loss of a pet, and shows how to honor a loved one while moving on.

Submissions and Payment
Accepts submissions through literary agents only. Send complete ms with author's qualifications and previous publications. Royalty, 5–10%.

Editor's Comments
We are currently considering agented submissions of picture books and middle-grade and young adult novels. Material must have high literary merit and touch on subjects of current relevance.

Little Simon

Simon & Schuster Children's Publishing Division
1230 Avenue of the Americas
New York, NY 10020

Editorial Department

Publisher's Interests
Little Simon, an imprint of Simon & Schuster Children's Publishing, offers novelty books for children from birth to age eight. Its list includes both fiction and nonfiction titles, and it specializes in interactive books, pop-up books, board books, lift-the-flap books, and bath books.
Website: www.simonsayskids.com

Freelance Potential
Published 65 titles in 2004: 20 were by agented authors and 15 were reprint/licensed properties. Receives 200 queries yearly.

- **Fiction:** Publishes concept, toddler, and board books, 0–4 years; and pop-up books, 4–8 years. Topics cover animals, holidays, trucks and automobiles, and the weather.
- **Representative Titles:** *Thanksgiving in the Barn* by Nadine Bernard Westcott (3–6 years) is a pop-up book about the barnyard animals who all pitch in and help Turkey celebrate Thanksgiving. *America the Beautiful* by Robert Sabuda (all ages) is a pop-up homage to America's most treasured anthem that features seven spreads based on the architectural and natural wonders of the United States.

Submissions and Payment
Query only. No unsolicited mss. Accepts agented submissions only. SASE. Responds in 6 months. Publication in 2 years. Royalty; advance. Flat fee.

Editor's Comments
Prospective writers should be familiar with novelty book formats. Our editors are always interested in ideas for innovative projects—note that we do not consider the usual type of picture books, chapter books, or young adult novels. Please take a look at some of the titles we have published to see if your material is appropriate. Unfortunately, due to the workload of our editorial staff, we cannot accept unsolicited manuscripts. If you are seeking publication, we recommend you have an agent represent you and your work.

Little Tiger Press

The Coda Centre
189 Munster Road
London SW6 6AW
United Kingdom

Editorial Department

Publisher's Interests
An imprint of Magi Publications, Little Tiger Press publishes picture books and novelty books for children up to the age of six. Its focus is on contemporary and innovative books that blend humor, drama, and imagination with educational and inspirational qualities.
Website: www.littletigerpress.co.uk

Freelance Potential
Published 20 titles in 2004.

- **Fiction:** Publishes concept books, toddler books, and early picture books, 0–4 years; and story picture books, 4–6 years. Genres include contemporary and humorous fiction. Also publishes animal stories, novelty books, and board books.
- **Nonfiction:** Publishes early picture books, 0–4 years; and story picture books, 4–6 years. Topics include animals, pets, nature, and the environment. Also publishes novelty and board books.
- **Representative Titles:** *The Very Lazy Lion* by Jack Tickle (3+ years) is a pop-up book of humorous rhymes about a lazy lion. *Laura's Secret* by Klaus Baumgart (3–7 years) is a story of how two young children cope with the bullies who make fun of their homemade kite.

Submissions and Payment
Guidelines available at website. Send complete ms. Accepts photocopies and computer printouts. SAE/IRC. Responds in 2 months. Publication period varies. Payment policy varies.

Editor's Comments
We want our books to be fun for parents as well as for their children. Our goal is to create books that offer laughter, comfort, learning, or exhilarating flights of imagination, and we're looking for new ideas and fresh styles from the best talent in writing and illustration. Please limit your manuscripts to 1,000 words, and note that we cannot comment on your work if we reject it.

Llewellyn Publications

P.O. Box 64383
St. Paul, MN 55164-0383

Acquisitions Editor: Megan C. Atwood

Publisher's Interests
Quality, well-written books about the paranormal, metaphysical topics, and the supernatural are featured by this publisher. It also offers fiction and nonfiction relating to alternative religions, astrology, and personal health.
Website: www.llewellyn.com

Freelance Potential
Published 12 titles in 2004: 4 were developed from unsolicited submissions, 3 were by agented authors, and 3 were reprint/licensed properties. Receives 520 queries, 420 unsolicited mss yearly.

- **Fiction:** Published 5 middle-grade books, 8–12 years; and 5 young adult books, 12–18 years. Genres include fantasy, mystery, science fiction, suspense, and fairy tales.
- **Nonfiction:** Published 2 young adult books, 12–18 years. Topics include the paranormal, New Age subjects, wicca, astrology, shamanism, parapsychology, and alternative religions. Also publishes self-help titles.
- **Representative Titles:** *Oh No! UFO!* by Linda Joy Singleton (8–12 years) is an upbeat novel about aliens and the supernatural that has a young girl concerned for her sister's welfare. *Tarot Kit for Kids* by Maria Shaw (YA) is a starter set that contains a basic guide to help teens use tarot cards responsibly and ethically.

Submissions and Payment
Guidelines available with #10 SASE ($.74 postage) or at website. Catalogue available at website. Send complete ms or query via email to childrensbooks@llewellyn.com. Accepts photocopies. SASE. Responds in 2–6 months. Publication in 1–2 years. Royalty, 10%.

Editor's Comments
We would like to see more material that introduces middle-grade and young adult readers to the paranormal and supernatural. Send us scary stories for teens and fiction about the occult; as well as nonfiction books on New Age ideas.

James Lorimer & Company

35 Britain Street
Toronto, Ontario M5A 1R7
Canada

Children's Book Editor: Hadley Dyer

Publisher's Interests
Fiction and nonfiction for children ages seven to fourteen is the specialty of this Canadian publisher. Its list includes titles about social issues in Canadian settings, and contemporary stories that reflect Canada's multicultural society.
Website: www.lorimer.ca

Freelance Potential
Published 20 titles (10 juvenile) in 2004: 2 were developed from unsolicited submissions and 2 were reprint/licensed properties. Of the 20 titles, 2 were by unpublished writers. Receives 96 queries each year.

- **Fiction:** Publishes easy-to-read books, 4–7 years; chapter books, 5–10 years; middle-grade books, 8–12 years; and young adult books, 12–18 years. Genres include mystery, suspense, fantasy, adventure, humor, and historical fiction.
- **Nonfiction:** Publishes easy-to-read books, 4–7 years; and middle-grade books, 8–12 years. Topics include multicultural subjects, nature, sports, and contemporary social concerns.
- **Representative Titles:** *Robyn Looks for Bears* by Hazel Hutchins is the story of a girl who can't find what she wants until she stops looking for it. *A Gift from Mooch* by Gilles Gauthier is a touching story of childhood loss, and how friendship helps to overcome it.

Submissions and Payment
Guidelines available. Canadian authors only. Query with outline/synopsis and 2 sample chapters. SASE. Responds in 4–6 months. Publication period varies. Royalty; advance.

Editor's Comments
Our first priority is good writing with believable characters, situations, and dialogue. We are currently seeking manuscripts for sports-themed juvenile fiction for children ages eight to twelve; and for edgy, contemporary novels for readers ages thirteen and up. We do not consider picture books, seasonal stories, or fantasy.

LTDBooks

Suite 301, Unit 1
200 North Service Road West
Oakville, Ontario L6M 2Y1
Canada

Editors: Dee Lloyd & T. K. Shells

Publisher's Interests

LTDBooks is accepting submissions again, but it will only consider electronic submissions. Any other type of submission will be automatically rejected. The publisher's list caters to young adult and adult readers and exclusively publishes fiction.
Website: www.ltdbooks.com

Freelance Potential

Published 25 titles (1 juvenile) in 2004: 5 were developed from unsolicited submissions. Of the 25 titles, 10 were by unpublished writers and 5 were by authors who were new to the publishing house. Receives 200 queries, 200 unsolicited mss yearly.

- **Fiction:** Published 1–3 young adult books, 12–18 years. Genres include suspense, horror, mystery, and stories about the paranormal.
- **Representative Titles:** *The Right Hand of Velachaz* by Rie Sheridan (YA) is a fantasy about a 12-year-old boy who finds himself on a quest to slay a dragon. *Lou Dunlop: Private Eye* by Glen Ebisch (YA) is the story of an average high school kid—average until a classmate disappears and he finds himself drawn into the mystery.

Submissions and Payment

Guidelines and sample contracts available at website. Query with synopsis. Accepts email submissions to editor@ltdbooks.com. Response time and publication period vary. Royalty, 30%.

Editor's Comments

We welcome new writers and invite them to submit their work based on our specific guidelines. We plan to publish ten new works each year and, unfortunately, if your query arrives in the wrong format it will not be reviewed. All fiction genres and subjects are welcome although we are especially interested in horror, mystery, and paranormal books. We are looking for authors who are interested in and excited about publishing their works in electronic format for the e-book reader. While we do offer paperback contracts these go only to a select number of our authors.

Keeping Readers in Mind
Lori Shein
Lucent Books

Lori Shein, Managing Editor, is proud of Lucent's long-standing reputation for publishing helpful books for teenagers. Successful titles in the Teen Issues series include *Teens and Drunk Driving, Teen Smoking,* and *Teen Alcoholism.* Shein also notes that The Other America series includes books about teen fathers, addicts, dropouts, disabilities. "And our longest-running series, the Overview series, also covers social issues that affect teens (although these books don't specifically focus on teens). Topics such as gangs, family violence, and eating disorders have done well."

Lucent also carries a Diseases and Disorders series, some of which titles apply to teens, such as acne, Attention Deficit Disorder, headaches, and diabetes.

Lucent publishes all of its books in series formats. Every series has a specific intent and its own specifications (length, back matter, etc.). Shein says, however, "We don't specify what each chapter must cover." Lucent guides its writers by providing sample books and Tables of Content in a given series.

Authors interested in writing for Lucent should contact Senior Acquisitions Editor Chandra Howard at Chandra.Howard@thomson.com. Howard gives authors information on what titles Lucent wants to assign and manuscript requirements. Lucent does not accept unsolicited manuscripts, single titles, or fiction.

"We really try to edit all of our books with our readers in mind," Shein concludes. "We try to think about what would interest them and what information they would need for reports or class discussion."

Lucent Books

Suite C
15822 Bernardo Center Drive
San Diego, CA 92127

Senior Acquisitions Editor: Chandra Howard

Publisher's Interests
Nonfiction titles produced for middle-grade and young adult readers make up the bulk of this educational publisher's list. Its titles cover a diverse range of subject matter, from sports, to history, health, and current events. While it welcomes queries, all of its books are produced on a work-for-hire basis.
Website: www.gale.com/lucent

Freelance Potential
Published 130 titles in 2004: 1 was by an agented author. Of the 130 titles, 7 were by unpublished writers and 20 were by authors who were new to the publishing house. Receives 200+ queries each year.

- **Nonfiction:** Published 130 middle-grade books, 8–12 years. Also publishes young adult titles. Topics include political, cultural, and social history; science; geo-politics; and current events.
- **Representative Titles:** *Anne Frank* is a biography based on the short life of this famous girl whose diary has become a powerful symbol of the injustices of war; part of the Heroes & Villains series. *Osama bin Laden* looks at the life of the mastermind behind the 9/11 attack on the World Trade Center; part of the Heroes & Villains series.

Submissions and Payment
Guidelines available. All books are written on a work-for-hire basis, by assignment only. Query with résumé and list of published work. Response time varies. Publication in 1 year. Flat fee, $2,500 for first book; $3,000 for subsequent books.

Editor's Comments
Our plans for the coming year include books on social issues, history, and humanities titles. If you have expertise in any of these subject areas we would like to hear from you. Keep in mind that all books are written as work-for-hire and follow a very specific format. All chapters must have a distinct theme and the work as a whole needs to develop through a running narrative.

Magination Press

750 First Street NE
Washington, DC 20002

Managing Editor: Darcie Johnston

Publisher's Interests
Magination Press is a speciality publisher offering self-help titles for children up to the age of 12, as well as a small number of books for younger readers. As an imprint of the American Psychological Association, all of the books it publishes are grounded in solid research. Topics covered include family issues, divorce, and illness.
Website: www.maginationpress.com

Freelance Potential
Published 10 titles in 2004: 8 were developed from unsolicited submissions and 1 was by an agented author. Of the 10 titles, 6 were by unpublished writers and 7 were by authors who were new to the publishing house. Receives 600 unsolicited mss yearly.

- **Fiction:** Published 2 easy-to-read books, 4–7 years; 2 story picture books, 4–10 years; and 4 chapter books, 5–10 years. Stories address psychological concerns and illnesses, family relationships, fears, and learning difficulties.
- **Nonfiction:** Published 1 story picture book, 4–10 years; and 1 chapter book, 5–10 years. Topics include grief, divorce, learning disabilities, and family issues.
- **Representative Titles:** *Jenny Is Scared!* by Carol Shuman, Ph.D. (4–8 years) helps children deal with the threats of violence and terrorism in the world today. *The Year My Mother Was Bald* by Ann Speltz (8–13 years) features a young girl's journal in which she describes her mother's battle with cancer.

Submissions and Payment
Guidelines and catalogue available with 10x13 SASE (2 first-class stamps). Send complete ms. Accepts photocopies and computer printouts. SASE. Responds in 1–6 months. Publication in 18–24 months. Royalty.

Editor's Comments
We are interested in clearly focused, specific concerns, both clinical and normal, as subject matter. Don't send us books on self-esteem.

Maple Tree Press Inc.

Suite 200
51 Front Street East
Toronto, Ontario M5E 1B3
Canada

Submissions Editor

Publisher's Interests

Formerly known as Owl Books, this Canadian publisher features a list for children up to the age of 12. It primarily publishes nonfiction in the areas of science, nature, and crafts, but also has a few fiction titles on its list. It almost exclusively publishes Canadian authors.
Website: www.mapletreepress.com

Freelance Potential

Published 10 titles in 2004. Receives 500+ queries, 1,000+ unsolicited mss yearly.

- **Fiction:** Published 1–2 story picture books, 4–10 years. Genres include contemporary fiction.
- **Nonfiction:** Published 4–8 middle-grade books, 8–12 years. Topics include science, nature, sports, and Canadian culture. Also publishes photo essays and concept books, 0–4 years.
- **Representative Titles:** *Gross Universe* by Jeff Szpirglas (8–12 years) talks about disgusting things in this humorous book that will delight youngsters; with topics that include scabs, mucus, and vomit. *How Baseball Works* by Keltie Thomas (8–12 years) takes a behind-the-scenes look at the physics of home runs, curve balls, and stolen bases.

Submissions and Payment

Send complete ms for fiction. Query with outline, sample chapter, and clips or writing samples for nonfiction. Accepts photocopies, computer printouts, and simultaneous submissions if identified. SAE/IRC. Responds in 2–3 months. Publication in 2 years. Royalty.

Editor's Comments

Please note that we rarely publish work from non-Canadian authors and accept little fiction. We do, however, welcome book ideas of all kinds for children between the ages of three and twelve. The submissions of most interest to us are nature and science—presented in a way that will engage young readers while teaching them something new. Keep in mind that topics that will appeal to both boys and girls are best suited for us.

Master Books

P.O. Box 726
Green Forest, AR 72638

Acquisitions Editor: Roger Howerton

Publisher's Interests
Creation-based books and materials are the focus of this Christian publisher. It features nonfiction books for children of all ages that emphasize the power and majesty of God.
Website: www.masterbooks.net

Freelance Potential
Published 16 titles (10 juvenile) in 2004: 1 was developed from an unsolicited submission. Receives 600 queries yearly.

- **Nonfiction:** Publishes middle-grade books, 8–12 years; and young adult books, 12–18 years. Also publishes concept books, early picture books, and novelty and board books, 0–4 years; easy-to-read and activity books, 4–7 years; and educational titles, 4–18 years.
  Topics include religion, science, technology, and animals. Also publishes biographies.
- **Representative Titles:** *The Ocean Book* by Frank Sherwin (12+ years) looks at life in the ocean and includes scriptural references where God speaks about the oceans; part of the Wonders of Creation series. *Westley, the Big Truck* by James McEwen is a fable about a young truck in trouble and the older, wiser truck that sets Westley firmly back on the road again.

Submissions and Payment
Guidelines and catalogue available with 9x12 SASE (5 first-class stamps). Query with clips. SASE. Responds in 3 months. Publication in 1 year. Royalty.

Editor's Comments
We are currently looking for books that meet the needs of Christian families and bring them balance. Prospective authors must honor our policy of "evolution-free" materials and write from a creation-based perspective. Our line of children's titles are scientifically educational and emphasize and acknowledge the Bible. We are also looking for animal stories with biblical themes.

Maval Publishing

567 Harrison Street
Denver, CO 80206

Editor: George Luder

Publisher's Interests
Established in 1992, Maval Publishing is a speciality publisher offering titles for children of all ages in both Spanish and English. Its list includes both fiction and nonfiction books. 30% self-, subsidy-, co-venture, or co-op published material.
Website: www.maval.com

Freelance Potential
Published 10 titles in 2004: all were developed from unsolicited submissions, 1 was by an agented author, and 1 was a reprint/licensed property. Of the 10 titles, 8 were by unpublished writers and 8 were by new authors. Receives 2,000 unsolicited mss yearly.

- **Fiction:** Publishes toddler books, 0–4 years; easy-to-read books, 4–7 years; story picture books, 4–10 years; middle-grade books, 8–12 years; and young adult books, 12–18 years. Genres include historical, religious, Western, multicultural, and ethnic fiction, adventure, folklore, fantasy, mystery, fairy tales, humor, and suspense. Also features stories about animals, pets, sports, nature, and the environment.
- **Nonfiction:** Publishes easy-to-read titles, 4–7 years; story picture books, 4–10 years; middle-grade books, 8–12 years; and young adult books, 12–18 years. Topics include animals and multicultural and ethnic subjects. Also publishes humor and biographies.
- **Representative Titles:** *Jim, The Heavy Cat* by Steve Simsich (2–8 years) is the story of an overweight cat who learns it is OK to be different. *Luna* by Jean Cumings (2–8 years) follows the life of a sea turtle.

Submissions and Payment
Guidelines available with 9x5 SASE ($.80 postage). Send ms with artwork (color prints or transparencies). Accepts simultaneous submissions. SASE. Responds in 4–6 months. Publication in 18 months. Royalty.

Editor's Comments
Children's books are a recent addition to our publishing program and therefore we are eager to review manuscripts for all ages.

Mayhaven Publishing

P.O. Box 557
803 Blackburn Circle
Mahomet, IL 61853

Editor: Doris Wenzel

Publisher's Interests
This publisher is dedicated to offering fiction and nonfiction books for children and young adult readers covering a variety of subjects by new and established authors. Each year it sponsors an award for fiction. 20% subsidy, or co-op published.
Website: www.mayhavenpublishing.com

Freelance Potential
Published 12 titles (6 juvenile) in 2004: all were developed from unsolicited submissions and 6 were by agented authors. Of the 12 titles, 10 were by unpublished writers and 12 were by authors who were new to the publishing house. Receives 3,000+ queries yearly.

- **Fiction:** Published 2 early picture books, 0–4 years; 1 easy-to-read book, 4–7 years; 1 chapter book, 5–10 years; 1 middle-grade book, 8–12 years; and 1 young adult book, 12–18 years. Genres include coming-of-age stories, adventure, humor, and historical fiction.
- **Nonfiction:** Publishes easy-to-read titles, 4–10 years; chapter books, 5–10 years; middle-grade books, 8–12 years; and young adult books, 12–18 years. Topics include nature, travel, cooking, history, and the West.
- **Representative Titles:** *Elbert Ein Swine Genius Pig* by Margaret Hollingsworth Clem (4–10 years) tells the story of a pig who solves a mystery for his friends. *Following the Raven* by Jenny Weaver (YA) is an adventurous book about a boy and his father who live in the woods in Alaska and follow a raven into the wilderness.

Submissions and Payment
Guidelines available. Query with 3 sample chapters. Accepts photocopies and computer printouts. SASE. Responds in 9–12 months. Publication in 12–18 months. Royalty; advance, varies.

Editor's Comments
We strive to reach a variety of readers with a variety of original titles. Our annual fiction contest offers writers a chance at publication and ongoing royalties.

Margaret K. McElderry Books

Simon & Schuster Children's Publishing Division
1230 Avenue of the Americas
New York, NY 10024

Vice President & Editorial Director: Emma D. Dryden
Senior Editor: Karen Wojtyla

Publisher's Interests
This imprint of Simon & Schuster publishes original hardcover books for children from pre-school age through young adult. Its catalogue includes picture books and middle-grade and young adult novels in a variety of genres.
Website: www.simonsayskids.com

Freelance Potential
Published 29 titles in 2004: 12 were by agented authors and 5 were foreign reprint/licensed properties. Of the 29 titles, 3 were by unpublished writers and 3 were by authors who were new to the publishing house. Receives 2,500 queries yearly.

- **Fiction:** Published 16 story picture books, 4–10 years; 6 middle-grade books, 8–12 years; and 4 young adult books, 12–18 years. Genres include historical fiction, folktales, fantasy, and humor. Also publishes poetry.
- **Nonfiction:** Published 2 story picture books, 4–10 years.
- **Representative Titles:** *Mayday! Mayday!* by Chris L. Demarest (4–10 years) is the true recounting of a dangerous rescue mission by the U.S. Coast Guard. *On Pointe* by Lorie Ann Grover (8–12 years) explores a girl's dream to be a professional ballet dancer as she considers her options for a future.

Submissions and Payment
Guidelines available. Query with résumé, outline/synopsis, and first three chapters for novels. No unsolicited mss. SASE. Responds in 1–2 months. Publication in 2–4 years. Royalty; advance.

Editor's Comments
We will take a look at material on a range of topics suitable for children. Make sure your idea can grab the interest of the reader, and consider the attention span and vocabulary of your audience. Nonfiction titles on contemporary issues and trends for older readers are of interest. We do not accept queries for textbooks, activity books, science fiction, or religious material.

Meadowbrook Press

5451 Smetana Drive
Minnetonka, MN 55343

General Submissions Editor

Publisher's Interests
This Midwest publishing house features a list that focuses on books for parents on such topics as pregnancy, baby and child care, party planning, and children's activities, as well as children's poetry. It publishes no children's fiction or picture books.
Website: www.meadowbrookpress.com

Freelance Potential
Publishes 10 titles in 2004. Of the 10 titles, 1 was by an unpublished writer and 3 were by authors who were new to the publishing house. Receives 200+ queries yearly.

- **Nonfiction:** Published concept books, 0–4 years; and middle-grade books, 8–12 years. Features activity, joke, and game books for children, as well as books on child care, parenting, and family activities for adults.
- **Representative Titles:** *Look Who's Talking* by Laura Dyer, M.C.D., (parents) offers advice on how to enhance a child's language development, starting at birth. *Getting Organized for Your New Baby* by Maureen Bard (parents) offers checklists, how-to's, and charts to help parents be prepared for the day the new baby comes home.

Submissions and Payment
Writers' guidelines available. Query. No unsolicited mss. Accepts photocopies, computer printouts, and simultaneous submissions if identified. SASE. Responds in 4 months. Publication in 2 years. Royalty; advance.

Editor's Comments
For the coming year, we are especially interested in queries for books on child care, from birth to age twelve; pregnancy; and childbirth. We take great pride in our ability to realize our books' full potential in the commercial marketplace. Given that, we are very particular about the books we choose to publish. The first step for new writers who want us to seriously look at their queries, is to follow our guidelines for submission to the letter.

Meriwether Publishing Ltd.

885 Elkton Drive
Colorado Springs, CO 80907

Submissions Editor

Publisher's Interests
One-act plays, adaptations, full-length plays, and material for speech contests are all found on this publisher's list, along with books and videotapes on theater subjects. It primarily caters to the educational market from middle school through college. A separate list of plays is also published for the church market.
Website: www.meriwetherpublishing.com

Freelance Potential
Published 60 titles in 2004: 50 were developed from unsolicited submissions and 9 were by agented authors. Of the 60 titles, 30 were by unpublished writers and 25 were by authors who were new to the publishing house. Receives 1,200 queries, 800 mss yearly.

- **Fiction:** Publishes middle-grade books, 8–12 years. Offers one-act and full-length dramas, musicals, comedies, folktales, and social commentaries, as well as dialogues and monologues.
- **Nonfiction:** Publishes theater reference books and how-to titles, 12–25 years. Topics include stage design, lighting techniques, theatrical makeup, theater games, and improvisation.
- **Representative Titles:** *The Complete Audition Book for Young Actors* by Roger Ellis (YA) offers a comprehensive guide to winning by enhancing acting skills. *More Theater Games for Young Performers* by Suzi Zimmerman (YA) features acting games designed specifically for young students.

Submissions and Payment
Guidelines available. Prefers query with outline/synopsis, and sample chapter. Will accept complete ms. Accepts photocopies and simultaneous submissions if identified. SASE. Responds in 4–6 weeks. Publication in 6 months. Royalty. Flat fee.

Editor's Comments
We continue to look for innovative manuscripts that relate to the craft of acting and will help students develop acting expertise while enhancing their love of theater.

Milet Publishing

6 North End Parade
London W1Y 05J
England

Editorial Director

Publisher's Interests
Milet publishes a vibrant and innovative range of artistic children's books that celebrate multiculturalism and multi-lingualism. Its titles feature a range of engaging, non-traditional themes.
Website: www.milet.com

Freelance Potential
Published 15 titles (14 juvenile) in 2004: 1 was developed from an unsolicited submission, and 2 were by agented authors. Of the 15 titles, 1 was by an unpublished writer, and 1 was by an author new to the publishing house. Receives 360 queries, 100+ unsolicited mss each year.

- **Fiction:** Published 12 toddler books, and 1 early picture book, 0–4 years; 1 easy-to-read book, 4–7 years; and 1 middle-grade book, 8–12 years. Genres include adventure; and contemporary, multicultural, and ethnic fiction.
- **Nonfiction:** Publishes Turkish language books, dictionaries, and literature guides for children and adults.
- **Representative Titles:** *How Bees Be* by Alison Boyle & Laura Hambleton tells how Queen Bee takes Little Bee aside and explains how grown-up bees work at the honey factory. *A Whole World* by A. Louchard & K. Couprie uses art to show the relation among the nature of things, how they are connected, and how we view them.

Submissions and Payment
Guidelines and catalogue available at website. Send complete ms for picture books; query with synopsis and sample text for all others. Accepts photocopies. SASE. Responds in 2 weeks. Publication in 12–18 months. Payment policy varies.

Editor's Comments
We are keen on new writers who offer a fresh, adventurous style. We focus mainly on picture books for younger children, but we also consider proposals aimed at older readers. Contemporary subjects, rather than historical or fantasy ideas, are needed.

Milkweed Editions

Sent 3-1-06

Suite 300
1011 Washington Avenue South
Minneapolis, MN 55415

First Reader: Elisabeth Fitz

Publisher's Interests
The books for young readers found on this publisher's list are high-quality novels targeting children between the ages of 8 and 13. Its books offer a wide range of genres—everything from science fiction to fantasy. Milkweed Editions also highlights fiction that shows a relationship to the world of nature.
Website: www.milkwood.org

Freelance Potential
Published 16 titles (3 juvenile) in 2004: 4 were developed from unsolicited submissions, 4 were by agented authors, and 1 was a reprint/licensed property. Of the 16 titles, 3 were by authors who were new to the publishing house. Receives 3,000 queries, 4,000 unsolicited mss yearly.

- **Fiction:** Publishes middle-grade titles, 8–12 years. Genres include historical, multicultural and ethnic fiction; and stories about nature.
- **Representative Titles:** *Parents Wanted* by George Harrar (8–13 years) follows the life of a troubled young boy who is sent to a foster home and how he learns to cope with a new set of parents. *Emma and the Ruby Ring* by Yvonne MacGrory (8–13 years) is set in Ireland in the 1880s and tells the adventures of an 11-year-old girl with a magic ring that doesn't grant wishes.

Submissions and Payment
Guidelines available. Query or send complete ms. Accepts photocopies and simultaneous submissions if identified. SASE. Responds to queries in 1 month; to mss in 1–6 months. Publication in 1 year. Royalty, 6.5% of list price; advance, varies.

Editor's Comments
We welcome submissions from writers who have previously published a book of fiction or nonfiction for either children or adults, or a minimum of three short pieces nationally distributed in commercial or literary journals. We lean towards contemporary stories but publish many genres. All of our titles embody humane values.

Mitchell Lane Publishers

P.O. Box 196
Hockessin, DE 19707

President: Barbara Mitchell

Publisher's Interests
Mitchell Lane is dedicated to providing quality nonfiction for middle-grade and young adult readers. It specializes in series biographies of well-known personalities in the fields of music, science, history, sports, and the fine arts. All material is written on a work-for-hire basis.
Website: www.mitchelllane.com

Freelance Potential
Published 63 titles (20 juvenile) in 2004. Of the 63 titles, 10 were by authors who were new to the publishing house. Receives 20 queries yearly.

- **Nonfiction:** Publishes chapter books, 5–10 years; middle-grade books, 8–12 years; and young adult books, 12–18 years. Topics include contemporary multicultural personalities, sports figures, entertainers, inventors, scientists, and political leaders.
- **Representative Titles:** *The Life and Time of John Philip Sousa* (grades 4–8) helps readers understand the accomplishments of one of the world's greatest composers; part of the Masters of Music series. *Randolph J. Caldecott and the Story of the Caldecott Medal* (grades 4–8) highlights the life of the famous children's illustrator and the award named for him.

Submissions and Payment
Assigned work only. Query with writing samples and résumé.
Flat fee.

Editor's Comments
We recently introduced three new series. Masters of Music: the World's Greatest Composers combines biographies with music, history, and culture. Great Achievement Awards features biographies of literary award-winners. Our revamped Blue Banner Biographies series covers contemporary media, music, and screen stars. We are also beginning a series of early chapter books designed for young readers in grades two and three.

Mondo Publishing

980 Avenue of the Americas
New York, NY 10018

Senior Editor: Susan Derkazarian

Publisher's Interests

Committed to providing high quality, exciting children's books, this publisher offers fiction, nonfiction, and sing-along music tapes. It also produces a line of research-based literacy materials for educational professionals.
Website: www.mondopub.com

Freelance Potential

Published 12 titles in 2004: 6 were developed from unsolicited submissions, 3 were by agented authors, and 1 was a print/licensed property. Of the 12 titles, 1 was by an unpublished writer and 9 were by authors who were new to the publishing house. Receives 400 unsolicited mss yearly.

- **Fiction:** Publishes easy-to-read books; story picture books; chapter books; and middle-grade books. Genres include fantasy, mystery, folktales, adventure, humor, stories about sports and science, and contemporary and historical fiction.
- **Nonfiction:** Publishes early picture books; story picture books; middle-grade books; and young adult books. Topics include science, nature, animals, the environment, language arts, history, music, crafts, and hobbies.
- **Representative Titles:** *Herbert Fieldmouse: Secret Agent* by Kevin O'Malley (6–12 years) tells the story of a mouse detective that is assigned the important job of delivering a top secret message for the queen. *America's Mountains* by Frank Staub (7–12 years) offers an introduction to spectacular mountains in America, including surprising facts and full-color photographs.

Submissions and Payment

Send complete ms. SASE. Response time varies. Publication in 1–3 years. Royalty, varies.

Editor's Comments

We are seeking fiction and nonfiction (including chapter books) for ages nine to twelve. All genres are welcome.

Moody Publishers

Moody Bible Institute
820 North LaSalle Boulevard
Chicago, IL 60610-3284

Acquisitions Coordinator

Publisher's Interests
Committed to producing inspirational fiction and nonfiction for children of all ages, this Christian publisher strives to spread the word of God through its publications.
Website: www.moodypublishers.org

Freelance Potential
Published 80 titles (20 juvenile) in 2004: 8 were by agented authors. Of the 80 titles, 1 was by an unpublished writer and 10 were by authors who were new to the publishing house. Receives 1,000+ queries and unsolicited mss yearly.

- **Fiction:** Publishes middle-grade books, 8–12 years; and young adult books, 12–18 years. Genres include adventure, Western, fantasy, mystery, suspense, and contemporary and historical fiction. Also publishes biblical fiction.
- **Nonfiction:** Publishes toddler books, 0–4 years; easy-to-read books, 4–7 years; story picture books, 4–10 years; and young adult books, 12–18 years. Topics include religion, social issues, and sports.
- **Representative Titles:** *Angels and Me* by Carolyn Nystrom is a carefully worded book that gives children straight, biblical answers about who angels are and what they do. *A Different Kind of Party* by Larry Burkett teaches children about generosity and discipline with their money, as they learn about the ways money they give to the church helps God's kingdom.

Submissions and Payment
Guidelines available. Query with résumé, outline/synopsis, and 3 sample chapters for fiction. Accepts nonfiction proposals through agents or manuscript services only. SASE. Responds in 2–3 months. Publication in 12–18 months. Payment policy varies.

Editor's Comments
We're looking for fascinating stories about people from history for middle-grade and young adult readers. Material must have a Christian slant. Unsolicited fiction must be sent through an agent only.

Moose Enterprise

684 Walls Side Road
Sault Ste. Marie, Ontario P6A 5K6
Canada

Publisher: Richard Mousseau

Publisher's Interests
Biographies, historical nonfiction and novels, humor, science fiction, adventure, and drama are just some of the kinds of books to be found on the list of Moose Enterprise. Its children's books are written for middle-grade and young adult readers.

Freelance Potential
Published 6 titles (4 juvenile) in 2004: all were developed from unsolicited submissions. Of the 6 titles, 6 were by authors who were new to the publishing house. Receives 180 queries yearly.

- **Fiction:** Publishes books for ages 10 and up. Genres include adventure, drama, fantasy, historical fiction, humor, horror, mystery, suspense, science fiction, and Westerns.
- **Nonfiction:** Publishes titles for ages 10–Adult. Topics include biography, history, and humor.
- **Representative Titles:** *A Mythical Land* by James Stanley Walters (8–12 years) follows the adventures of a young girl from the maritime coast of Canada as she travels to her mother's homeland of Ireland. *The Basement* by Tyler Barlow (YA–Adult) is the story of a young photographer who awakens to find himself a victim of kidnapping.

Submissions and Payment
Guidelines available. Query. SASE. Responds in 1 month. Publication in 1 year. Royalty, 10–30%.

Editor's Comments
We are a small Canadian house; our list is usually less than ten books per year. Because we are limited in the number of books we can take on each year, we look for writing that is new and fresh and will engage readers with a strong, plot-driven story. Our mission is also to promote and nurture new authors. As a small house, we work very closely with our authors and feel that the finished product that goes to press is the result of a strong collaboration between writer and editor. Review some of our titles at your local library and then send us a query that will convince us you should be part of our editorial family.

Morgan Reynolds Publishing

Suite 223
620 South Elm Street
Greensboro, NC 27406

Managing Editor: Angie DeCola

Publisher's Interests
This educational publisher features nonfiction titles that are written to complement the curriculum of elementary and secondary school classes. Its readers are aged ten to eighteen. Most of the books on its list are biographies that are combined as series.
Website: www.morganreynolds.com

Freelance Potential
Published 25 titles in 2004: 5 were developed from unsolicited submissions. Of the 25 titles, 5 were by authors who were new to the publishing house. Receives 400–500 queries, 300 mss yearly.

- **Nonfiction:** Published 12 middle-grade books, 8–12 years; and 12 young adult books, 12–18 years. Topics include history, music, science, business, feminism, and world events. Also features biographies.
- **Representative Titles:** *Let's Go! Let's Publish!* by Nancy Whitelaw (YA) is a biography of Katharine Graham, the famous publisher of the *Washington Post*; part of the Makers of the Media series. *Point of No Return* by Earle Rice Jr. (YA) relates the story behind the Tonkin Gulf Resolution and the Vietnam War; part of the First Battles series.

Submissions and Payment
Guidelines available. Query with outline and sample chapter; or send complete ms. Accepts photocopies, computer printouts, and simultaneous submissions if identified. SASE. Responds to queries in 1 month, to mss in 1–3 months. Publication in 12–18 months. Royalty; advance.

Editor's Comments
We are interested in biographies of world leaders, writers, explorers, innovators, artists, and scientists. While we will consider biographies of notables persons of today, we are not interested in books about movie stars, sports figures, or other individuals that fall under the umbrella of "pop culture." Please review our catalogue and take the time to read some of our books before you send us a query to ensure that your idea has not already been covered.

Mott Media ☆

112 East Ellen Street
Fenton, MI 48430

Vice President: Joyce Bohn

Publisher's Interests
This small educational publisher offers a list of nonfiction titles for readers age fourteen and up. Topics covered include mathematics, history, and religion. Many of its books are published as part of series. It plans to expand its publishing program over the next few years. Mott Media does not accept fiction submissions.
Website: www.mottmedia.com

Freelance Potential
Published 2 titles in 2004: 2 were assigned. Receives 48 queries each year.
- **Nonfiction:** Publishes middle-grade books, 8–12 years; and young adult books, 12–18 years. Topics include animals, history, humor, and religion. Also publishes biographies.
- **Representative Titles:** *The ABC's and All Their Tricks* by Margaret Bishop (teachers) is a phonics book that explains the rules behind the way words are spelled, as well as sample words to teach sound and spelling. *Language and Thinking for Young Children* by Ruth Beechick & Jeannie Nelson (teachers) features a wealth of language activities designed for use with children who do not yet read or are just beginning to read.

Submissions and Payment
Guidelines available. Query with outline and sample chapter; or send complete ms. Accepts photocopies, computer printouts, and simultaneous submissions if identified. SASE. Responds in 1–2 months. Publication in 6 months. Royalty; advance. Flat fee.

Editor's Comments
We have not published a large number of books in the last few years. We hope to increase our publishing efforts in the future, but have not yet decided on specific subject areas. However, we will consider queries on any curriculum-based subject that is appropriate for use with middle-grade and young adult students. Our motto is "classic curriculum: Yesterday's Values for Today's Child." Our interest is in methods that are based on successful implementation.

National Association for the Education of Young Children

1509 16th Street NW
Washington, DC 20036-1426

Publications Editor: Carol Copple

Publisher's Interests
This organization of early childhood teachers produces material that supports high-quality programs for children from birth through third grade. It also offers titles that serve the informational needs of parents of young children.
Website: www.naeyc.org

Freelance Potential
Published 5 titles in 2004: 3 were developed from unsolicited submissions and 1 was a reprint/licensed property. Of the 5 titles, 3 were by authors who were new to the publishing house. Receives 50 queries yearly.

- **Nonfiction:** Publishes educational materials for teachers, caregivers, and parents. Topics include professional development, family relationships, health, nutrition, assessment, language and literacy, social and emotional development, and violence prevention.
- **Representative Titles:** *Remote Control Childhood? Combating the Hazards of Media Culture* by Diane E. Levin (parents) discusses the downside of technology—the violence, stereotypes, commercialism, and no-brain entertainment that bombard today's kids. *Off to School: A Parent's-Eye View of the Kindergarten Year* by Irene Hannigan (parents) chronicles the hopes, challenges, fears, and joys of a mother and her son during his first year in school.

Submissions and Payment
Guidelines available. Query with outline and 3 sample chapters. Accepts photocopies and computer printouts. No simultaneous submissions. SASE. Responds in 1 month. Publication period varies. No payment.

Editor's Comments
If you have an idea for a book that would help others learn about the care and education of young children, we'd like to hear from you. Our goal is to help all who are trying to achieve healthy development and constructive education for the very young.

National Council of Teachers of English

1111 West Kenyon Road
Urbana, IL 61801-1096

Director of Book Publications: Zarina Hock

Publisher's Interests
The mission of the National Council of Teachers of English Books Program is to serve teachers, theorists, researchers, and administrators who work in English language arts, English education, and English studies. It does not publish any fiction. Many of its titles are developed from dissertations.
Website: www.ncte.org

Freelance Potential
Published 15 titles in 2004. Receives 150 queries yearly.

- **Nonfiction:** Publishes books for English and language arts educators working with students in grades K–12, as well as with college students. Topics include writing, reading, grammar, literature, diversity and society, poetry, censorship, media studies, technology, research, and teaching ideas.
- **Representative Titles:** *Valuing Language Study* by Yetta M. Goodman (teachers, grades K–8) offers teachers a rich language studies curriculum for use in elementary and middle school classrooms. *I Heard a Bluebird Sing* edited by Bernice E. Cullinan (teachers, grades K–6) features the best-loved poems by Aileen Fisher, as chosen by young readers.

Submissions and Payment
Guidelines available. Query with cover letter, formal proposal, chapter summaries, and table of contents. SASE. Responds in 1–2 weeks. Publication in 18 months. Royalty, varies.

Editor's Comments
We work very closely with our authors to ensure that each book published is the best it can be. Our publishing process is a lengthy one, tied to very specific steps. Therefore, we ask prospective authors to study our guidelines carefully and send us a detailed prospective before submitting a manuscript. In your proposal, tell us what makes your book special, why you have chosen to write it, and how the book will stand out from its competitors. This is your opportunity to tell us why your book is valuable to our readers.

National Geographic Society

Children's Books
1145 17th Street NW
Washington, DC 20036-4688

Submissions Editor: Susan Donnelly

Publisher's Interests
History and science books are the speciality of this well-known publisher. It offers nonfiction titles on a variety of topics for readers through the early teen years.
Website: www.nationalgeographic.com/books/kids_splash/

Freelance Potential
Published 24 titles in 2004: 1 was by an agented author and 2 were reprint/licensed properties. Of the 24 titles, 1 was by an unpublished writer and 4 were by authors who were new to the publishing house. Receives 100+ queries yearly.

- **Nonfiction:** Published 14 middle-grade books, 8–12 years; and 10 young adult books, 12–18 years. Topics include life, earth, and general science; American and world cultures and history; biography, animals, multicultural stories, and geography. Also publishes a few story picture books, 4–10 years.
- **Representative Titles:** *The Human Story* by Christopher Sloan (12+ years) uses expert commentary, in-depth discussion, and breathtaking artwork and photography to address the far-reaching questions surrounding human evolution. *High Hopes: A Photobiography of John F. Kennedy* by Deborah Heiligman (10+ years) celebrates the life and legacy of this young president.

Submissions and Payment
Query with outline and sample chapter. No unsolicited mss. Accepts photocopies and simultaneous submissions if identified. SASE. Responds in 1 month. Publication period varies. Flat fee.

Editor's Comments
Please note that we are not accepting any unsolicited manuscripts at this time. In general, we have no specific guidelines for submission. Generally, we are looking for manuscripts with a strong narrative voice and a strong story line that are well written and fit into the National Geographic publishing program. Our best guidelines for writers interested in our work are the titles found on our current list.

Naturegraph Publishers

P.O. Box 1047
3543 Indian Creek Road
Happy Camp, CA 96039

Managing Editor: Barbara Brown

Publisher's Interests
In the publishing business for more than 50 years, this company concentrates on covering natural history, the outdoor environment, and topics related to Native Americans. Its children's list features fiction and nonfiction for middle-grade and young adult readers.
Website: www.naturegraph.com

Freelance Potential
Published 3 titles in 2004: all were developed from unsolicited submissions. Of the 3 titles, 1 was by an unpublished writer and 1 was by an author who was new to the publishing house. Receives 400 queries yearly.

- **Fiction:** Publishes middle-grade novels, 8–12 years; and young adult books, 12–18 years. Genres include mythology, folktales, and Native American folklore.
- **Nonfiction:** Publishes middle-grade books, 8–12 years; and young adult books, 12–18 years. Topics include Native Americans, American wildlife, animals, the environment, crafts, hiking, and backpacking. Also publishes field guides for all ages.
- **Representative Titles:** *Alone in the Wilderness* by Hap Gilliland features a Native American boy who takes on a classroom challenge to spend three months alone in the wilderness. *Welcome to the Moon* by Robert Bruce Kelsey offers twelve expeditions to exciting lunar features.

Submissions and Payment
Guidelines available at website. Query with outline and 1–2 sample chapters. Accepts photocopies and computer printouts. SASE. Response time and publication period vary. Royalty.

Editor's Comments
Keep in mind that most of our titles are written for adults, and while we do feature books for middle-grade students, we are not interested in material for children under the age of 10. Nonfiction that connects to some aspect of native American tribes are of interest.

Neal-Schuman Publishers

Suite 2004
100 William Street
New York, NY 10038

Director of Publishing: Charles Harmon

Publisher's Interests
Neal-Schuman publishes books for librarians who work in either school or public libraries. It offers titles on library services; guides for Internet use by teachers, researchers, and information specialists; management; and funding. It does not publish fiction.
Website: www.neal-schuman.com

Freelance Potential
Published 36-40 titles (12-15 juvenile) in 2004. Receives 300 queries, 300 unsolicited mss yearly.

- **Nonfiction:** Publishes resource materials for school media specialists and public library librarians. Topics include curriculum support, the Internet, technology, literary skills, reading programs, collection development, reference needs, the first amendment, staff development, management, and communications.
- **Representative Titles:** *Connecting Kids and the Web: A Handbook for Teaching Internet Use and Safety* by Allen C. Benson (librarians) is a comprehensive multimedia guide designed specifically to teach kids to use Web resources effectively and safely. *A Core Collection for Young Adults* by Patrick Jones et al. (librarians) offers librarians an in-depth guide to the titles young adult readers are most likely to check out of the library.

Submissions and Payment
Guidelines available. Prefers query with résumé, outline, table of contents, and sample chapter. Will accept complete ms. Accepts photocopies and computer printouts. SASE. Responds to queries in 2 weeks, to unsolicited mss in 1-2 months. Publication in 10-12 months. Royalty.

Editor's Comments
Our readers are professional librarians and we are only interested in submissions that will fill their special needs. The Internet is always at the top of everyone's list, but it is also a topic covered frequently. Do your homework and research our published titles.

The New England Press

P.O. Box 575
Shelburne, VT 05482

Managing Editor: Christopher Bray

Publisher's Interests
The New England Press is a small regional publisher that produces books for readers of all ages. Nearly all of its titles have a connection to New England and it prefers working with authors who live in the region. Its children's books include both fiction and nonfiction titles for middle-grade through young adult readers.
Website: www.nepress.com

Freelance Potential
Published 4 titles in 2004: all were developed from unsolicited submissions. Of the 3 titles, 1 was by an unpublished writer and 2 were by new authors. Receives 300 queries yearly.

- **Fiction:** Published 1 middle-grade title, 8–12 years; and 1 young adult book, 12–18 years. Genres include regional and historical fiction set in Northern New England and Vermont.
- **Nonfiction:** Publishes middle-grade books, 8–12 years; and young adult books, 12–18 years. Topics include history, nature, and subjects related to Vermont. Also publishes biographies.
- **Representative Titles:** *Father by Blood* by Louella Bryant (YA) features a young woman who is the daughter of John Brown, and who must choose between her belief in her father's causes and his willingness to use violence to achieve them. *Cave of Falling Water* by Janice Ovecka is set in Vermont's Green Mountains and traces a growing relationship among three girls from different cultures who long for friendship.

Submissions and Payment
Query with sample chapter. SASE. Responds in three months. Publication in 18 months. Royalty.

Editor's Comments
We are particularly interested in historical fiction for young adults, and biographies about famous New Englanders. Since we are publishing a smaller list this year than last, we are very particular about the works we select. If you have a great story, it will help if you can also discuss why you think it will be a great story for our readers.

New Harbinger Publications

5674 Shattuck Avenue
Oakland, CA 94609

Acquisitions Editor: Tesilya Hanauer

Publisher's Interests
New Harbinger Publications specializes in step-by-step workbooks and companion titles that offer readers self-help techniques and exercises to cope with mental health and psychological issues.
Website: www.newharbinger.com

Freelance Potential
Published 40 titles (3 juvenile) in 2004: 10 were developed from unsolicited submissions and 10 were by agented authors. Of the 43 titles, 10 were by unpublished writers and 30 were by authors who were new to the publishing house. Receives 600 queries yearly.

- **Nonfiction:** Publishes self-help, psychology, and health books for lay persons and professionals. Topics include parenting, divorce, pregnancy, self-esteem, addictions, stress, depression, eating disorders, grief, and sexuality.
- **Representative Titles:** *Kid Cooperation* by Elizabeth Pantley (parents) offers practical skills to help parents stop yelling, nagging, and pleading, and get kids to cooperate. *The Stepparent's Survival Guide* by Suzen J. Ziegahn (parents) features a workbook to develop a plan for integrating a new family.

Submissions and Payment
Guidelines available. Query. Accepts photocopies and email submissions to acquisitions@newharbinger.com. SASE. Responds in 2–4 weeks. Publication in 1 year. Royalty, 10%.

Editor's Comments
We continue to look for self-help titles that help readers cope with a specific problem. We want a clear, simple, step-by-step approach that explains the problem and offers a concrete solution. Most of our books are double-targeted, meaning they are to be read by both a lay and professional audience. The best way to reach both types of readers is to write your book directly to the client with the issue you are addressing. Assume the reader knows absolutely nothing about the topic, and explain every step.

New Hope Publishers

P.O. Box 12065
Birmingham, AL 35201-2065

Manuscript Submissions

Publisher's Interests
As a member of the Evangelical Christian Publishers Association, this publisher provides books that equip Christian women and their families to grow in Christ and share his vision.
Website: www.newhopepubl.com

Freelance Potential
Published 24 titles in 2004: 2 were developed from unsolicited submissions, 4 were by agented authors, and 2 were reprint/licensed properties. Of the 24 titles, 4 were by unpublished writers and 12 were by authors who were new to the publishing house. Receives 40–50 queries, 300 unsolicited mss yearly.

- **Nonfiction:** Publishes inspirational and spiritual books for women and families. Topics include spiritual growth, women's issues, prayer, relationships, Christian living, and Bible studies.
- **Representative Titles:** *Tackling Rough Issues* by Fred Rogers et al. offers Christian responses to the hard issues children face, including violence, discipline, divorce, and special needs. *Cassie You're a Winner!* by Renée Kent is the story of an average girl who wants something special, and finds it through God.

Submissions and Payment
Guidelines available. Prefers proposal and sample chapter. Accepts query with outline or complete ms. Email submissions to New_Hope@wmu.org. SASE. Response time varies. Royalty. Flat fee.

Editor's Comments
Our books and Bible studies deal with real-life issues specific to Christian women—nurturing a child's faith, navigating the paths of adolescence, coping with the issues of young adults, and creating a Christian family. We need titles that help readers understand their role in God's plan and find a way to achieve that goal. Prospective writers are encouraged to familiarize themselves with our current products. Manuscripts are accepted on the basis of their adherence to our vision statement and marketability.

New Leaf Press

P.O. Box 726
Green Forest, AR 72638

Acquisitions Editor: Roger Howerton

Publisher's Interests
New Leaf Press is a non-denominational publishing house that features nonfiction books with a positive Christian message. Its list includes scholarly titles, children's books, and homeschooling materials with Christian themes.
Website: www.newleafpress.com

Freelance Potential
Published 21 titles (6 juvenile) in 2004: 2 were by agented authors, and 1 was a reprint/licensed property. Receives 600 queries yearly.

- **Nonfiction:** Published 2 early picture books, 0–4 years; and 4 young adult books, 12–18 years. Also publishes middle-grade books, 8–12 years. Topics include religion, current events, history, health and fitness, humor, nature and the environment, social issues, science, and technology.
- **Representative Titles:** *My Take-Along Bible* by Alice Joyce Davidson (4–8 years) is a durable board book of carefully chosen Bible stories retold in rhyme, with scriptural references. *Nightlights for Students* (12–18 years) features 30 stories of encouragement, anecdotes, scriptural passages, and quotations that tug at the heartstrings and bring chuckles to the end of the day.

Submissions and Payment
Guidelines and catalogue available with 9x12 SASE (5 first-class stamps). Query with cover letter, table of contents, synopsis, and sample chapter. Accepts photocopies and simultaneous submissions if identified. SASE. Responds in 3 months. Publication in 12–18 months. Royalty, 10% of net.

Editor's Comments
We like to see creation-based material that presents Christian principles at work in daily lives. Our children's titles are suitable for young readers, middle-grade students, and young adults. Our newest imprint, Balfour Books, presents a strong message that connects events in the Middle East with people everywhere.

Newmarket Press

15th Floor
18 East 48th Street
New York, NY 10017

Executive Editor: Keith Hollaman

Publisher's Interests
Newmarket Press was founded in 1981 and is an independent publisher that offers 15–20 titles each year in the areas of child care and parenting, psychology, nutrition, personal finance, self-help, and the performing arts. It does not publish any fiction.
Website: www.newmarketpress.com

Freelance Potential
Published 45 titles in 2004: most were by agented authors. Receives 1,200 queries yearly.

- **Nonfiction:** Publishes parenting and self-help books. Topics include child care, health, fitness, nutrition, sports, business, history, and multicultural and ethnic issues. Also publishes biographies.
- **Representative Titles:** *Baree: The Story of a Wolf-Dog* by James Oliver Curwood (YA) is an adventure story about a half-tame, half-wild wolf pup born of a dog father and a wolf mother who is accidentally separated from his parents and must learn to fend for himself in the Canadian wilderness. *The Bear* by James Oliver Curwood (YA) presents the story of a grizzly bear, a bear cub, and two hunters that must learn to come to terms with each other in the heart of the wilderness.

Submissions and Payment
Query with outline, table of contents, marketing information, clips, and author biography. Accepts photocopies. SASE. Responds in 1–3 months. Publication in 1 year. Royalty; advance.

Editor's Comments
While we do not have a specific set of guidelines for submissions to Newmarket Press, we suggest you include the following materials in most proposals: a concise, 1-page summary of your project and your writing credentials, a table of contents or list of topics you plan to address, specific marketing information on your book's competition and why your idea is different; and sample chapters that best illustrate your idea. As always, it's best to review some of our titles before you take the time to send in your submission.

New Society Publishers

P.O. Box 189
Gabriola Island, British Columbia V0R 1X0
Canada

Publisher: Christopher Plant

Publisher's Interests
New Society Publishers is a progressive publishing company specializing in books for those interested in environmental issues and ecological sustainability. It has been in business for almost a quarter of a century. It does not offer any fiction.
Website: www.newsociety.com

Freelance Potential
Published 20 titles in 2004: 6–8 were developed from unsolicited submissions, 2 were by agented authors, and 2 were reprint/licensed properties. Of the 20 titles, 8 were by unpublished writers and 16 were by authors who were new to the publishing house. Receives 300 queries yearly.

- **Nonfiction:** Publishes college guides and career resources for young adults. Also publishes titles on education systems, family issues, child development, sustainability, business practices, leadership, feminism, diversity, and community issues for adults.
- **Representative Titles:** *Storytelling to Encourage Caring and Healthy Families* by Allison M. Cox & David H. Albert provides powerful examples of the use of stories and storytelling to encourage healing. *Above All Be Kind* by Zoe Weil teaches parents how to raise their children to be humane and compassionate in their interactions with family and friends alike.

Submissions and Payment
Guidelines available. Query with proposal, table of contents, and sample chapter. SAE/IRC. Responds in 2–3 months. Publication in 1 year. Payment policy varies.

Editor's Comments
Our editorial goal is to publish books that help create a sustainable, more peaceful and just world through nonviolent action. We are interested in analyzing examples and situations, and developing theories and strategies for nonviolent social change. A large majority of our books are initiated by our staff.

New World Library

14 Pamaron Way
Novato, CA 94949

Submissions Editor

Publisher's Interests
Founded in 1977, this publisher offers inspirational and practical materials on spirituality, personal growth, and other related areas. It strives to challenge readers to improve the quality of their lives and the world in which they live.
Website: www.newworldlibrary.com

Freelance Potential
Published 35 titles (2 juvenile) in 2004: 1 was developed from an unsolicited submission, 34 were by agented authors, and 2 were from reprint/licensed properties. Of the 35 titles, 3 were by unpublished writers and 5 were by authors who were new to the publishing house. Receives 600 queries yearly.

- **Fiction:** Published 2 story picture books, 4–10 years. Genres include inspirational and religious fiction, and retellings of classic tales.
- **Representative Titles:** *The Chief's Blanket* by Michael Chanin (4–10 years) tells the story of a young girl who discovers the meaning of giving and receiving when she weaves her first chief's blanket. *Positively Mother Goose* by Julia Loomans (4–10 years) offers new versions of the classic nursery tales written to promote self-esteem, lifelong learning, and innovative thinking.

Submissions and Payment
Guidelines available at website. Query with 2 or 3 sample chapters, outline or table of contents, market assessment, and biographical information. SASE. Responds in 3 months. Publication period and policy vary.

Editor's Comments
We seek ideas for stories relating to spiritual growth and those that teach children how to deal with morality, conflict resolution, grief, stress, compassion, the value of self-esteem, and the importance of appreciating life. New writers are welcome to submit a query that offers an idea for a story that can make a positive impact on readers.

Nightwood Editions

RR #2
3692 Beach Avenue
Roberts Creek, British Columbia V0N 2W2
Canada

Editor: Shyla Seller

Publisher's Interests
Books on British Columbia, its history, nature, culture, and people, are the focus of this publisher. Its list includes several books for children age 4 to young adult.
Website: www.nightwoodeditions.com

Freelance Potential
Published 7–8 titles in 2004: 4 were by unpublished writers and 2 were by authors who were new to the publishing house.

- **Fiction:** Publishes Native British Columbian folklore and folktales for children. Also publishes history, natural history, and guide books for adults.
- **Representative Titles:** *Ch'Askin* is an engaging tale, told in the style of the oral tradition, of the thunderbird who comes to help the Sechelt people of the British Columbian coast. *Salmon Boy* by Donna Joe is a richly illustrated, compelling story that teaches the life cycle of the salmon and respect for the environment.

Submissions and Payment
Guidelines available. Catalogue available with 9x12 SASE. Query with paragraph summary, outline, and writing sample. Accepts photocopies. SASE. Responds in 3–6 months. Publication period varies. Royalty; advance.

Editor's Comments
At this time, poetry, native legends, and folktales of the Pacific Northwest and British Columbia make up the bulk of our editorial needs. We publish a few children's books each year; the majority of our titles are for adults. Our youth audience usually consists of children age two to eighteen. If we're interested in your query, you will hear from one of our editors in a few months. At that time you will be asked for more information on yourself, and we may make suggestions on how your manuscript can be revised to better suit our needs. Please note that this does not constitute a commitment to publish your work.

Nimbus Publishing Ltd.

P.O. Box 9166
3731 Mackintosh Street
Halifax, NS B3K 5M8
Canada

Managing Editor: Sandra McIntyre

Publisher's Interests
The largest publisher of English language books east of Ontario, Nimbus Publishing focuses on books that reflect the people and region of Atlantic Canada.
Website: www.nimbus.ns.ca

Freelance Potential
Published 30 titles (3 juvenile) in 2004: 15 were developed from unsolicited submissions. Of the 30 titles, 25 were by unpublished writers and 20 were by authors who were new to the publishing house. Receives 240 queries, 40 unsolicited mss yearly.

- **Fiction:** Published 2 story picture books, 4–10 years; and 1 middle-grade book, 8–12 years. Genres include historical, multicultural and regional fiction.
- **Nonfiction:** Publishes titles for young adults and adults. Topics include geography, history, humor, the environment, and regional, multicultural and ethnic fiction. Also publishes biographies.
- **Representative Titles:** *Joe Howe to the Rescue* by Michael Bawtree (9–13 years) is a historical story of the famous Nova Scotian, Joe Howe, and the adventures of his fictional printer boy. *Tommy's New Black Skates* by Garth Vaughan (4–8 years) is a wintery tale about a young boy's first pair of ice skates.

Submissions and Payment
Guidelines available. Query with outline and sample chapter; or send complete ms. Accepts photocopies, computer printouts, and simultaneous submissions if identified. SASE. Responds time varies. Publication in 12–24 months. Royalty; advance. Flat fee.

Editor's Comments
Most of our books are written by first-time authors from Atlantic Canada. We're looking for titles with a regional slant, and this year we are interested in minority voices, historical fiction, and nonfiction related to the region. We do not publish poetry, drama, or religious material and prefer letters of inquiry over manuscript submissions.

NL Associates

P.O. Box 1199
Highstown, NJ 08520

President: Nathan Levy

Publisher's Interests

NL Associates was founded by educator Nathan Levy to bring to print the best in teaching strategies for educators, as well as materials for parents, school districts, and business people. Its children's list includes nonfiction titles on critical thinking skills for use in grades 1–12.

Website: www.storieswithholes.com

Freelance Potential

Published 5 titles in 2004. Receives 10 queries, 10 unsolicited mss each year.

- **Nonfiction:** Publishes educational materials and activity books designed to help critical thinking skills, grades 1–12. Features books on special education and titles for parents and educators.
- **Representative Titles:** *Teaching Young Gifted Children in the Regular Classroom* by Smutny et al. (teachers) is designed to help teachers identify gifted children at an earlier age—thus bringing them to their full potential. *Thirty Three Multicultural Tales to Tell* by Pleasant DeSpain (all ages) features multicultural tales from many different countries.

Submissions and Payment

Query or send complete ms. Response time, publication period, and payment policy vary.

Editor's Comments

For more than twenty years, our focus has been on gifted education and critical thinking skills. We look for writers, familiar with our books, who have educational expertise to add to our list. Of special interest are activity books that are fun and engaging, while teaching logical thinking. We are interested in almost any topic covered by elementary and secondary schools, including language skills, mathematics, writing skills, and discussion skills. We will review both queries and unsolicited manuscripts but keep in mind that we are a small house and it may be some time before you hear back from us.

North Country Books

311 Turner Street
Utica, NY 13501

Publisher: Sheila Orlin

Publisher's Interests
This publisher produces high-quality books that explore regions in New York State. It includes books on history, nature, art and photography, biographies, and children's books, as well as regional field guides.

Freelance Potential
Published 7 titles (1 juvenile) in 2004: Of the 7 titles, 3 were by unpublished writers and 4 were by authors who were new to the publishing house. Receives 50-100 queries, 20-30 unsolicited mss each year.

- **Fiction:** Publishes story picture books, 4-10 years. Features folklore about New York State.
- **Nonfiction:** Publishes easy-to-read books, 4-7 years; and middle-grade books, 8-12 years. Also publishes biographies, field and trail guides, and art and photography books for adults.
- **Representative Titles:** *Children of the Longhouse* by Joseph Bruchac (7-12 years) is an exciting story that also offers an in-depth look at Native American life centuries ago. *Minnie the Mule* by Lettie A. Petrie (grades 4-8) tells the story of Captain Fairweather's daughter, Sarah, and her cousin, Jack, as they solve bank robberies along the Erie Canal with Minnie the Mule.

Submissions and Payment
Guidelines and catalogue available with 9x12 SASE ($2 postage). Query or send complete ms. Accepts photocopies. SASE. Responds to queries in 1-2 months, to mss in 6-12 months. Publication in 2-5 years. Royalty.

Editor's Comments
We primarily produce nonfiction with a focus on the following regions in New York State: the Adirondacks, Central and Northern New York, the Finger Lakes, the Hudson Valley, and the Catskills. Send us something new and exciting about New York State that will delight and educate our readers.

NorthWord Books for Young Readers

18705 Lake Drive East
Chanhassen, MN 55317

Submissions Editor

Publisher's Interests
Since 1989, NorthWord has been publishing books about animals and nature for the juvenile market, helping to educate children about the living world around them. 10% co-venture published material.
Website: www.northwordpress.com

Freelance Potential
Published 19 titles in 2004: 2 were developed from unsolicited submissions, 6 were by agented authors, and 5 were reprint/licensed properties. Of the 25 titles, 1 was by an unpublished writer and 6 were by authors who were new to the publishing house. Receives 500 queries, 400 unsolicited mss yearly.

- **Fiction:** Published 2 early picture books, 0–4 years; and 5 story picture books, 4–10 years. Genres include contemporary fiction with environmental themes.
- **Nonfiction:** Published 2 concept books and 4 toddler books, 0–4 years; 2 story picture books, 4–10 years; and 4 middle-grade books, 8–12 years. Topics include animals, hobbies, nature, the environment, wildlife, and natural history. Also publishes biographies.
- **Representative Titles:** *Friendships in Nature* by James Gary Hines II (5–8 years) explains the unique symbiotic relationships that exist between certain animals. *Everything Bug* by Cherie Winner (8–11 years) answers real questions from kids about the habitat, diet, and life cycle of insects.

Submissions and Payment
Submit queries and writing sample for nonfiction. Accepts complete ms for picture books. Accepts photocopies. SASE. Responds in 1–3 months. Publication in 2 years. Payment policy varies.

Editor's Comments
For 2005, we would like nonfiction series books about the natural world and nature for readers age four to ten. Send us picture books with the same themes, but no heavy-handed agendas or didactic treatments, please.

Novalis

Saint Paul University
223 Main Street
Ottawa, Ontario K1S 1C4
Canada

Commissioning Editor: Kevin Burns

Publisher's Interests

Founded in 1935, Novalis is a religious publishing house in the Catholic tradition. It is a part of St. Paul University in Ontario and publishes in the areas of liturgy, prayer, spirituality, personal growth, and religious education. Its catalogue features nonfiction for children of all ages.
Website: www.novalis.ca

Freelance Potential

Published 65 titles (5 juvenile) in 2004: 8 were developed from unsolicited submissions and 3 were by agented authors. Of the 65 titles, 12 were by unpublished writers and 12 were by authors who were new to the publishing house. Receives 150 queries, 100 unsolicited mss yearly.

- **Nonfiction:** Publishes early picture books, 0–4 years; story picture books, 4–10 years; and young adult books, 12–18 years. Topics include biography, history, and religion.
- **Representative Titles:** *Fergie Tries to Fly* by Nancy Cocks follows the adventures of Fergie the frog who tries to deal with all the problems of daily life, while jumping from one thing to another. *What You Will See Inside a Mosque* by Aisha Karen Khan (6–10 years) introduces young readers to the Muslim faith, worship, and religious life.

Submissions and Payment

Guidelines available. Query with clips. Accepts photocopies, disk submissions, and email to kburns@ustpaul.ca. No simultaneous submissions. SASE. Responds in 8 weeks. Publication in 12–18 months. Royalty; advance.

Editor's Comments

Our principal mission is to spread the good news of Jesus Christ and to connect it to contemporary culture. We want to see submissions that meet the daily challenges of life—even as times change. Please find the time to review our titles and website to make sure your work will fit our needs.

The Oliver Press

5707 West 36th Street
Minneapolis, MN 55416-2510

Editor: Denise Sterling

Publisher's Interests
The Oliver Press specializes in educational titles and biographies that cover contemporary and historical events and personalities for students in elementary grades through high school.
Website: www.oliverpress.com

Freelance Potential
Published 10 titles in 2004. Of the 10 titles, 1 was by an unpublished writer and 1 was by a author who was new to the publishing house. Receives 100 queries yearly.

- **Nonfiction:** Published 4 easy-to-read books, 4–7 years; and 6 young adult books, 12–18 years. Topics include current events, archaeology, astronomy, aviation, business, communications, law, government, the environment, medicine, meteorology, space, history, forensics, and genetics.
- **Representative Titles:** *Iraq and the Fall of Saddam Hussein* by Jason Richie (grade 5 and up) covers the conflict in Iraq and gives readers the background and history of Saddam Hussein. *How It Happens at the Candy Factory* by Jenna Andersen (grades 2–5) looks at how some of America's favorite candy is made and packaged; part of the How It Happens series.

Submissions and Payment
Guidelines available. Query with résumé, outline, and writing sample. Accepts photocopies, computer printouts, and simultaneous submissions if identified. SASE. Responds in 3–6 months. Publication in 1–2 years. Flat fee, $1,000.

Editor's Comments
We'd like to continue to add to our Business Builders series of biographies of entrepreneurs in specific industries such as fashion and broadcasting, and to our Innovators series, which consists of biographies of inventors, scientists, and technologists. We also need books about current events that can be discussed in grade five through grade twelve classrooms.

Orca Book Publishers

P.O. Box 468
Custer, WA 98240-0468

Publisher: Bob Tyrrell

Publisher's Interests
This regional publisher focuses on fiction books for children and teens, including picture books, chapter books, and young adult novels. All books are written by Canadian authors, and relate to Canadian history and culture.
Website: www.orcabook.com

Freelance Potential
Published 60–65 titles in 2004: 30 were developed from unsolicited submissions, 15 were by agented authors, and 2 were reprint/licensed properties. Receives 1,000 queries, 500 unsolicited mss yearly.

- **Fiction:** Publishes easy-to-read books, 4–7 years; story picture books, 4–10 years; chapter books, 5–10 years; middle-grade books, 8–12 years; and young adult books, 12–18 years. Genres include regional contemporary and historical fiction.
- **Representative Titles:** *Camels Always Do* by Lynn Manuel (4–8 years) is a historical fiction story about camels and the gold rush in British Columbia. *Flux* by Beth Goobie (12+ years) is a novel about alternate realities, experimental laboratories, and frightening conspiracies; written by a Canadian author.

Submissions and Payment
Canadian authors only. Guidelines available. Query with 2–3 sample chapters for novels; send complete ms for picture books. Accepts photocopies and computer printouts. SASE. Responds in 8–12 weeks. Publication in 18–24 months. Royalty, 10% split; advance.

Editor's Comments
We are currently seeking manuscripts for good picture books with credible characters, an engaging plot, and strong writing; contemporary stories and fantasy with compelling plots, a child protagonist, and a historical twist; and young adult fiction that takes its inspiration from historical subjects, but does not include a tedious history lesson. We accept material from Canadian authors only.

Orchard Books

Scholastic, Inc.
557 Broadway
New York, NY 10012-3999

Vice President/Editorial Director: Ken Geist

Publisher's Interests
This well-known children's publisher features books for all young readers. Its list offers picture books for infants, novels for middle-grade and young adult readers, and some nonfiction story picture books for ages four to ten. It is an imprint of Scholastic, Inc.
Website: www.scholastic.com

Freelance Potential
Published 25 titles in 2004: 3 were by unpublished writers. Receives 5,000 queries yearly.

- **Fiction:** Publishes concept books, toddler books, and early picture books, 0–4 years; story picture books, 4–7 years; chapter books, 5–10 years; and middle-grade novels, 8–12 years. Genres include historical, contemporary, and multicultural fiction; fairy tales; folktales; fantasy; humor; and stories about nature, animals, and sports.
- **Nonfiction:** Publishes story picture books, 4–10 years. Topics include history, nature, the environment, and social issues.
- **Representative Titles:** *Chief* by Chris Ganci (9+ years) is the true story of a firefighter who lost his life on 9/11, as told by his son. *Dinosaurumpus!* by Tony Mitton (3–6 years) is a rhyming book that will bring laughter to readers as they learn about a dinosaur who can shake, rattle, and roll.

Submissions and Payment
Guidelines available. Query only. No unsolicited mss. SASE. Responds in 3 months. Publication period varies. Royalty; advance.

Editor's Comments
As a well-known children's publisher, we feature the work of some of the best children's authors writing today. However, that does not mean we ignore new writers. We are searching for educational and captivating books that children can use to "leap into learning." Take the time to review some of our backlist titles before you send us a query and then send us your very best work.

Our Sunday Visitor

200 Knoll Plaza
Huntington, IN 46750

Acquisitions Editor

Publisher's Interests
This religious publisher produces a wide range of resources—from teen catechesis to parish programs—and markets its books primarily to parishes and schools as well as religious bookstores. Titles for children of all ages are found in its catalogue, but it does not publish any fiction.
Website: www.osv.com

Freelance Potential
Published 55 titles (6 juvenile) in 2004: 1 was developed from an unsolicited submission. Receives 1,300 queries each year.

- **Nonfiction:** Publishes concept books, 0–4 years; story picture books, 4–10 years; chapter books, 5–10 years; middle-grade books, 8–12 years; and young adult books, 12–18 years. Topics include family issues, parish life, church heritage, and the lives of saints.
- **Representative Titles:** *Penance and Reconciliation* by Joseph D. White, Ph.D. and Ana Arista White (educators) offers new ideas for preparing kids to come to Christ through the sacrament of reconciliation; part of the Teach It! series. *How to Celebrate Christmas As a Catholic* by Amy Welborn (all ages) offers practical ideas to help Catholics see beyond the material aspects of the holiday and focus on the real meaning of the season.

Submissions and Payment
Guidelines available. Query with résumé and sample chapter. Accepts photocopies, computer printouts, and simultaneous submissions if identified. SASE. Responds in 2–3 months. Publication in 1+ years. Royalty; advance. Flat fee.

Editor's Comments
As the nation's largest non-profit Catholic publishing company, we are committed to bringing Catholics everywhere the very best resources available. If you are interested in working with us, we welcome your proposal, but ask that you follow our guidelines to the letter. In addition make sure you know your book's market value.

The Overmountain Press

P.O. Box 1261
Johnson City, TN 37605

Managing Editor: Daniel Lewis

Publisher's Interests
Founded in 1970, this publisher offers children's picture books set in and about Southern Appalachia, as well as nonfiction books teaching Southern Appalachian history to readers in grades three through eight. It also offers adult fiction and nonfiction on the history of the region.
Website: www.overmountainpress.com

Freelance Potential
Published 25 titles (7 juvenile) in 2004: 3 were developed from unsolicited submissions, 3 were by agented authors, and 1 was a reprint/licensed property. Receives 500 queries each year.

- **Fiction:** Publishes early picture books, 0–4 years; middle-grade books, 8–12 years; and young adult books, 12–18 years. Genres include folklore, folktales, mystery, and regional fiction.
- **Nonfiction:** Publishes story picture books, 4–10 years; and chapter books, 5–10 years. Topics include Southern Appalachia.
- **Representative Titles:** *A Ducky Wedding* by Thelma Kerns (all ages) portrays wedding preparations from engagement to honeymoon through the experiences of Ducksann and her family in the town of Duckville. *Jeffrey the Jeep* by Bill N. Dingus (4–7 years) tells the story of a little jeep who dreams of being a firetruck, and is told he can never be one. He then becomes a hero when he takes firemen up a mountainside to put out a forest fire.

Submissions and Payment
Guidelines available at website or with 6x9 SASE ($.85 postage). Query with résumé and sample chapters; send complete ms for the History Series for Young Readers. Accepts photocopies and computer printouts. SASE. Responds in 2–3 months. Publication in 1 year. Royalty, 15%.

Editor's Comments
We accept regional titles only. It is helpful if you submit copies of illustrations with your work, as we like to see them together.

Richard C. Owen Publishers

P.O. Box 585
Katonah, NY 10536

Director of Children's Books: Janice Boland

Publisher's Interests
This small publishing house prides itself on producing top-quality educational titles for readers up to the age of ten. Its list includes both fiction and nonfiction titles. For younger readers, it focuses on stories that children can read alone. For older readers, it offers contemporary fiction as well as multicultural myths and folktales.
Website: www.RCOwen.com

Freelance Potential
Published 15 titles in 2004. Of the 15 titles, 12 were by unpublished writers and 12 were by authors who were new to the publishing house. Receives 1,000 queries, 1,000 unsolicited mss yearly.

- **Fiction:** Publishes easy-to-read books, 4–7 years; story picture books, 4–10 years; and chapter books, 5–10 years. Genres include mystery; humor; folktales, contemporary fiction; stories about animals and nature; and books about social, ethnic, and multicultural issues.
- **Nonfiction:** Publishes easy-to-read books, 4–7 years; story picture books, 4–10 years; and chapter books, 5–10 years. Topics include current events, geography, music, science, nature, and the environment. Also publishes resource materials, professional development titles, and parenting books.
- **Representative Titles:** *Jasper* (grades K–2) is a story about a mischievous monkey who knows the rules, but doesn't always obey them. *Books for Young Learners* by Margaret Mooney (teachers) provides in-depth knowledge of the stages of reading, writing, and oral language development.

Submissions and Payment
Guidelines available. Send complete ms. Accepts photocopies, computer printouts, and simultaneous submissions. SASE. Responds in 3–6 months. Publication period and payment policy vary.

Editor's Comments
We want to see manuscripts for books that will appeal to children in kindergarten through the third grade.

Pacific Educational Press

6365 Biological Sciences Road
Faculty of Education, University of British Columbia
Vancouver, British Columbia V6T 1Z4
Canada

Director: Catherine Edwards

Publisher's Interests
Pacific Educational Press is the publishing house of the Faculty of Education at the University of British Columbia. It is known for its textbooks for teacher education as well as professional resources for practicing teachers, especially in the area of language arts, social studies, multiculturalism, science, fine arts, and music. It books are used in elementary and high school classes.
Website: www.pep.educ.ubc.ca

Freelance Potential
Published 8 titles (1 juvenile) in 2004. Of the 8 titles, 1 was by an unpublished writer and 4 were by authors who were new to the publishing house. Receives 60 queries, 60 unsolicited mss yearly.

- **Fiction:** Publishes chapter books, 5–10 years; and middle-grade books, 8–12 years. Genres include historical and multicultural fiction.
- **Nonfiction:** Publishes middle-grade books, 8–12 years; and young adult books, 12–18 years. Also publishes books for teachers, grades K–12. Topics include mathematics, science, social studies, multicultural education, critical thinking, fine arts, and administration.
- **Representative Titles:** *The Reluctant Deckhand* by Jan Padgett (8–11 years) follows a young girl who learns to overcome her fear and become an expert deckhand on her mother's fishing boat. *The Golden Rose* by Dayle Campbell Gaetz (11+ years) traces the journey of a 14-year-old and her family in 1860 to their new home in Hope, British Columbia.

Submissions and Payment
Guidelines available. Query with résumé, outline, and 2 sample chapters. Accepts photocopies, computer printouts, and simultaneous submissions. SAE/IRC. Responds in 2–6 months. Publication in 10–18 months. Royalty.

Editor's Comments
We continue to seek submissions of mathematics texts and titles for teaching around the world. Visit our website before you submit here.

Pacific Press Publishing Association

1350 North Kings Road
Nampa, ID 83687

Acquisitions Editor: Tim Lale

Publisher's Interests
Pacific Press publishes books and periodicals with Christian themes for children and adults, including books with biblical and inspirational topics associated with the Seventh-day Adventist church.
Website: www.pacificpress.com

Freelance Potential
Published 32 titles in 2004. Of the 32 titles, 2 were by unpublished writers and 2 were by authors who were new to the publishing house. Receives 200+ queries yearly.

- **Fiction:** Publishes easy-to-read books, 4–7 years; chapter books, 5–10 years; middle-grade books, 8–12 years. Genres include adventure, mystery, and suspense.
- **Nonfiction:** Publishes easy-to-read books, 4–7 years; chapter books, 5–10 years; middle-grade books, 8–12 years. Topics include children and animals.
- **Representative Titles:** *Don't Let Your Heart Feel Funny* by Jerry & Kitty Thomas is about a little boy who mixes everything up, but his hilarious retelling of a favorite Bible story gets the right message across; part of the Mixed-Up Max series. *Petunia the Ugly Pug* by Heather Grovet teaches about self-acceptance and God's love.

Submissions and Payment
Guidelines available at website or with SASE. Query. Accepts photocopies, computer printouts, disk submissions, and email submissions to booksubmissions@pacificpress.com. SASE. Responds in 3 months. Publication in 6–12 months. Royalty. 6–12%; advance, to $1,500.

Editor's Comments
Many of our children's titles are published in a series. At this time, we are looking for juvenile books that teach family values and build character. Send us your idea for stories with Christian themes for children age four to fourteen, and picture books illustrating a Seventh-day Adventist belief for children age one to three.

Parenting Press, Inc.

P.O. Box 75267
Seattle, WA 98175-0267

Publisher: Carolyn Threadgill

Publisher's Interests
Parenting Press publishes books that teach practical life skills to children and to parents and teachers that care for them. Its titles emphasize skill-building information based on sound theory and everyday experiences.
Website: www.parentingpress.com

Freelance Potential
Published 4 titles (2 juvenile) in 2004. Of the 4 titles, 1 was by an unpublished writer and 2 were by authors who were new to the publishing house. Receives 480 queries yearly.

- **Fiction:** Published 2 toddler books, 0–4 years. Stories to build self-esteem and resolve conflict.
- **Nonfiction:** Publishes concept books, 0–4 years; and easy-to-read books, 4–7 years. Topics include emotions, loss, grief, child guidance, problem solving, personal safety, abuse, and conflict resolution.
- **Representative Titles:** *The Way I Feel* by Janan Cain (2–8 years) helps kids understand the concept of emotions and expressing their feelings with words. *It's My Body* by Lory Freeman (3–8 years) discusses personal boundaries and teaches young children to resist uncomfortable touches.

Submissions and Payment
Guidelines available. Query with outline and clips or writing samples. Accepts photocopies, computer printouts, and simultaneous submissions if identified. SASE. Responds in 2 months. Publication in 18–24 months. Royalty, 4–8% of net.

Editor's Comments
We are interested in books for young children that deal with contemporary social and behavioral issues in a nonjudgmental way, and that offer readers several options to a problem rather than just one solution. Our titles are short, easily understood, and can be used by people with a range of belief systems. All our material is field-tested prior to publication by a variety of people in different settings.

Paulist Press

997 Mcarthur Boulevard
Mahwah, NJ 07430

Children's Editor

Publisher's Interests
Paulist Press publishes ecumenical theology, Roman Catholic studies, and books on liturgy, spirituality, church history, and philosophy, as well as works on faith and culture.
Website: www.paulistpress.com

Freelance Potential
Published 9 titles (1 juvenile) in 2004. Receives 800 queries, 500 unsolicited mss yearly.

- **Fiction:** Publishes picture books, 2–5 years; middle-grade titles, 8–12 years; and young adult books, (12–18 years). Features contemporary and religious fiction with Catholic and Christian themes.
- **Nonfiction:** Publishes prayer books and books of blessings 5–8 years; and Catholic guidebooks, 5+ years. Also offers Catholic gift books and titles on Roman Catholic activities, traditions, and rituals.
- **Representative Titles:** *The Hurt* by Teddi Soleski (age 6–8) is a children's story about a boy whose feelings get hurt when his friend calls him a name. *A Walk Through Our Church* by Gertrud Mueller Nelson (5+ years) offer readers a reverent and educational tour of an empty church, teaching readers the names of its furnishings.

Submissions and Payment
Guidelines available at website. Send complete ms for very short submissions; query with summary and writing sample for longer works. SASE. Responds to queries in 2 weeks, to mss in 4 months. Publication in 2–3 years. Royalty, 8%; advance, $500.

Editor's Comments
The goal of our company is to publish quality books on Christian and Catholic themes. Although our publishing program is oriented toward adult-level nonfiction, we offer a growing selection of children's stories and activity books. All book ideas should be religious in nature, written for the Christian and Catholic market. We are especially interested in preschool picture books, middle-grade chapter books, and young adult biographies.

Peachtree Publishers

1700 Chattahoochee Avenue
Atlanta, GA 30318-2112

Submissions Editor: Helen Harriss

Publisher's Interests
Established in 1978, this independent publisher offers titles for readers of all ages. Fiction and nonfiction picture books, chapter books, middle-grade titles, and young adult books are all featured on its list.
Website: www.peachtree-online.com

Freelance Potential
Published 30 titles (26 juvenile) in 2004: 2 were developed from unsolicited submissions, 5 were by agented authors, and 9 were reprint/licensed properties. Of the 30 titles, 10 were by new authors. Receives 20,000 queries yearly.

- **Fiction:** Published 2 early picture books, 0–4 years; 6 story picture books, 4–10 years; 2 chapter books, 5–10 years; 3 middle-grade novels, 8–12 years; and 2 young adult books, 12–18 years. Genres include historical, regional, and multicultural fiction.
- **Nonfiction:** Published 2 early picture books, 0–4 years; 4 story picture books, 4–10 years; 2 chapter books, 5–10 years; and 3 midde-grade books, 8–12 years. Topics include nature and history.
- **Representative Titles:** *Anna Casey's Place in the World* by Adrian Fogelin (8–12 years) follows the life of a girl who must live in a foster home after the death of her parents. *The Night You Were Born* by Wendy McCormick (3–7 years) is a picture book that captures a family's joy at the birth of a new baby.

Submissions and Payment
Guidelines available. Send ms for works under 5,000 words. Query with résumé, outline, and 2–3 sample chapters for longer works. Accepts photocopies and computer printouts. No queries via fax or email. SASE. Responds in 4–6 months. Publication period varies. Payment policy varies.

Editor's Comments
We continue to seek submissions for children and young adults for both our fiction and nonfiction lists.

Pelican Publishing Company

P.O. Box 3110
Gretna, LA 70054-3110

Editorial Department

Publisher's Interests
The majority of the titles appearing on this publisher's list are either hardcover or trade paperback originals, but it also features a small percentage of reprints. Its catalogue offers children's fiction and nonfiction as well as regional history books and travel guides.
Website: www.pelicanpub.com

Freelance Potential
Published 85 titles (36 juvenile) in 2004: 30 were developed from unsolicited submissions, 5 were by agented authors, and 22 were reprint-licensed properties. Of the 85 titles, 10 were by unpublished writers and 35 were by authors who were new to the publishing house. Receives 6,500 queries, 3,500 unsolicited mss yearly.

- **Fiction:** Published 14 easy-to-read books, 4–7 years; 5 middle-grade books, 8–12 years; and 2 young adult books, 12–18 years. Genres include historical, regional, and holiday-related fiction.
- **Nonfiction:** Published 8 early picture books, 0–4 years; 6 easy-to-read books, 4–7 years; and 1 middle-grade book, 8–12 years. Topics include regional history and social commentary. Also publishes travel guides, cookbooks, biographies, and self-help books.
- **Representative Titles:** *Elijah's Tears* by Sydelle Pearl (5+ years) is an anthology of stories linked to Jewish holidays. *Nurse's Night Before Christmas* by David Davis (5–8 years) tells the story of a visit by St. Nick to a hospital where he spreads cheer among people who must work on the holiday.

Submissions and Payment
Guidelines available. Query with outline and clips or writing samples. Send complete ms for easy-to-read books only. Accepts photocopies. No simultaneous submissions. SASE. Responds in 3 months. Publication in 9–18 months. Royalty.

Editor's Comments
Right now we are focusing on developing biographies for children between the ages of five and eight.

Pembroke Publishers

538 Hood Road
Markham, Ontario, L3R 3K9
Canada

Submissions Editor: Mary Macchiusi

Publisher's Interests
This Canadian publisher offers teachers, librarians, and parents practical books that celebrate the joy of learning. Topics include classroom management, writing, reading, grammar, and other areas related to education.
Website: www.pembrokepublishers.com

Freelance Potential
Published 15 titles in 2004. Of the 15 titles, 3 were by unpublished writers and 3 were by authors who were new to the publishing house. Receives 50 queries each year.

- **Nonfiction:** Publishes chapter books, 5–10 years; and middle-grade titles, 8–12 years. Topics include history, science, and writing. Also publishes titles for educators about literacy, spelling, grammar, educational assessment, and school safety, as well as titles on home-school partnerships.
- **Representative Titles:** *Do I Really Have to Teach Reading?* by Cris Tovani (teachers) offers ideas for teachers to help students in grades 6–12 apply reading comprehension strategies in any subject and to any text. *Word Savvy: Integrating Vocabulary, Spelling, and Word Study* by Max Brand (teachers) presents new and innovative methods of integrating word learning into activities that will inspire students to learn new words.

Submissions and Payment
Guidelines available. Query with résumé, outline, and sample chapters. Accepts photocopies and simultaneous submissions if identified. SAE/IRC. Responds in 1 month. Publication in 6–24 months. Royalty.

Editor's Comments
We look for material that is practical and useful to teachers of all grade levels. Our readers turn to us to provide them with the motivational tools necessary for educating children. Make sure your information is up-to-date, and offers strategies and solutions.

Perfection Learning Corporation

10520 New York Avenue
Des Moines, IA 50322

Editorial Director, Books: Sue Thies

Publisher's Interests
Dedicated to meeting the educational needs of a diverse and changing world, Perfection Learning Corporation offers curriculum materials for use in preschool through high school classrooms. Its list also features books for reluctant readers, including chapter books, novels, myths and folktales, and informational books.
Website: www.perfectionlearning.com

Freelance Potential
Published 40 titles in 2004: 20 were developed from unsolicited submissions and 10 were reprint/licensed properties. Receives 500+ queries yearly.

- **Fiction:** Publishes hi/lo chapter books, 7–12 years; middle-grade novels, 10–14 years; and young adult books, 12–18 years. Genres include historical, contemporary, multicultural, ethnic, and science fiction; mystery; suspense; humor; folktales; and stories about sports.
- **Nonfiction:** Publishes hi/lo chapter books, 7–12 years; and middle-grade books, 10–14 years. Topics include language arts, reading skills, literature, drama, history, social studies, mathematics, science, sports, and multicultural issues. Also publishes on-level science and social studies titles, grades 3–6.
- **Representative Titles:** *Callie: A Great Gray Owl* by Bonnie Highsmith Taylor (grades 2–6) follows an owl from birth to maturity. *Chelsey and the Green-Haired Kid* by Carol Gorman (grades 5–8) is the story of two kids who think they have witnessed a murder.

Submissions and Payment
Guidelines available at website or with SASE. Query with outline and 2–3 sample chapters. Accepts photocopies, computer printouts, and simultaneous submissions if identified. SASE. Responds in 4 months. Publication in 1 year. Payment varies.

Editor's Comments
If you wish to submit a hi/lo or high-interest manuscript, either fiction or factual, please consult our detailed guidelines first.

Perigee Books

Penguin Group (USA), Inc.
375 Hudson Street
New York, NY 10014

Publisher: John Duff

Publisher's Interests
Perigee Books is an imprint of the well-known publisher, Penguin Group. Its list is devoted to books for parents, including self-help, how-to, and reference titles. It does not publish any fiction or children's books.
Website: www.penguin.com

Freelance Potential
Published 69 titles in 2004: 1 was developed from an unsolicited submission, 68 were by agented authors, and 3 were reprint/licensed properties. Receives 300+ queries yearly.

- **Nonfiction:** Publishes reference books for parents.
- **Representative Titles:** *The Gift of Learning* by Ronald Davis & Eldon M. Braun (parents) chronicles new methods for correcting ADD/ADHD, math, and handwriting problems. *How to Survive Your Husband's Midlife Crisis* by Pat Gaudette & Gay Courter (wives) offers tips on how to recognize the symptoms of and deal with a husband's midlife crisis.

Submissions and Payment
Query. Accepts photocopies and computer printouts. SASE. Responds in 3–4 weeks. Publication in 18 months. Royalty; advance.

Editor's Comments
We are always interested in hearing from authors who have a firm handle on the kinds of material that will spark our interest. In general we are primarily interested in self-help and how-to titles on subjects that will appeal to parents and caregivers. We cannot stress enough that children's books are not part of our publishing program. If you are new to us, take the time to review our catalogue. Then send us a query on your idea. We look for ideas that are innovative and on the cutting edge of the latest research and are of importance to parents. New writers who can send a query that offers us these characteristics will get a second look.

Peter Pauper Press

Suite 400
202 Mamaroneck Avenue
White Plains, NY 10601

Editorial Director: Nick Beilenson

Publisher's Interests
Up-beat gift books, journals, organizers, and activity journals with nuggets of wisdom and original aphorisms are the specialty of this publisher. Its material is suitable for middle-grade teenagers and young adults.
Website: www.peterpauper.com

Freelance Potential
Published 40 titles (4 juvenile) in 2004: 2 were developed from unsolicited submissions and 4 were by agented authors. Of the 40 titles, 2 were by unpublished writers and 4 were by authors who were new to the publishing house. Receives 150 queries yearly.

- **Nonfiction:** Published 4 activity journals, 7–13 years. Also publishes books, journals, and organizers for adults.
- **Representative Titles:** *Brainiacs Secret Agent* (8-13) is an activity journal that features secret messages, mysteries, mazes, and information on real spies of the past. *Mood Rings, Mood Swings, and Other Things* (7–13 years) is a journal for tweens and teens that includes quotations from movie, TV, and sports celebrities.

Submissions and Payment
Guidelines available with 9x12 SASE. Query with clips. Accepts photocopies and computer printouts. SASE. Responds in 2 weeks. Publication period varies. Flat fee.

Editor's Comments
Please note that we are not interested in poetry, short stories, novels, narrative nonfiction, or children's literature. We are most likely to consider up-beat material that focuses on a single theme or relationship, such as sisters, friendship, mothers, or teachers; or celebrates special occasions such as graduation, birthdays, holidays, or weddings. The material submitted for teen journals must be age-appropriate, and we do require that all material is original to you, the writer. You must be able to certify that you have the right to sell any quotes you include in your manuscript.

Philomel Books

Penguin Young Readers Group
345 Hudson Street
New York, NY 10014

Editor: Emily Heath

Publisher's Interests
Philomel is an imprint of Penguin Group (USA) and is devoted to young readers. Over the years, it has published the work of some of the best known children's authors, including Roald Dahl and Patricia Polacco. Both fiction and nonfiction for infants through young adult readers will be found on its current list and backlist of titles.
Website: www.penguingroup.com

Freelance Potential
Published 30–40 titles in 2004: 2 were developed from unsolicited submissions. Receives 1,500 queries yearly.

- **Fiction:** Publishes early picture books, 0–4 years; easy-to-read books, 4–7 years; story picture books, 4–10 years; chapter books, 5–10 years; middle-grade books, 8–12 years; and young adult books, 12–18 years. Genres include fantasy and contemporary, historical, multicultural, and science fiction. Also publishes poetry.
- **Nonfiction:** Publishes story picture books, 4–10 years; and young adult books, 12–18 years. Features biographies and first-person narratives.
- **Representative Titles:** *The Big Blue Spot* by Peter Horowitz (0–4 years) is an interactive book that teaches young children about colors as well as friendship. *Skeleton Key* by Anthony Horowitz (10–14 years) features Alex Ricter, a young James Bond, who saves the country from hijackers.

Submissions and Payment
Guidelines available with SASE. Query. Include outline/synopsis. No unsolicited mss. SASE. Responds in 1–2 months. Publication in 1–2 years. Royalty.

Editor's Comments
We are interested in seeing submissions for historical fiction, hi/lo titles, fantasy, and science fiction. Please note that we do not accept unsolicited manuscripts, only queries.

Phoenix Learning Resources

2nd Floor
25 3rd Street
Stamford, CT 06902

Executive Vice President: John A. Rothermich

Publisher's Interests
Phoenix Learning Resources specializes in fiction and textbooks for the library and school market. Its materials are used by students in kindergarten through grade twelve, students in English as a Second Language programs, and students in homeschooling programs.
Website: www.phoenixlearninggroup.com

Freelance Potential
Published 10 titles in 2004. Receives 40–50 queries, 25–30 unsolicited mss yearly.

- **Nonfiction:** Publishes textbooks and educational materials for pre-K–post-grade 12. Also publishes books for special and gifted education students, material for use with ESL students, reference books, and biographies. Topics include social studies, integrated language arts, reading, comprehension, language skills, math, and study skills.
- **Representative Titles:** *Presidents' Day* by Barbara deRupertis (grades 1–5) highlights the Presidents of the United States and the history behind Presidents' Day; part of the Holidays & Heroes series. *New Practice Readers* by Anderson et al. (grade 2 and up) is a reading comprehension program that features informative, grade-appropriate articles from across the curriculum

Submissions and Payment
Query or send complete ms with résumé. Accepts photocopies, computer printouts, and simultaneous submissions if identified. SASE. Responds in 1–4 weeks. Publication in 1–15 months. Royalty. Flat fee.

Editor's Comments
We need supplemental textbooks that address reading and language skills at all levels, from comprehension to written language arts. Math and science textbooks and workbooks for middle-grade students to help them understand basic concepts are also needed. Send us grade-appropriate, accessible material that helps students develop effective general study skills.

The Pilgrim Press

700 Prospect Avenue East
Cleveland, OH 44115-1100

Editorial Director: Kim M. Sadler

Publisher's Interests
The Pilgrim Press is an imprint of Local Church Ministries, and it publishes curriculum materials for use in church education. The company was founded in 1895. Pilgrim Press offers nonfiction titles for all ages and its audience includes both laypersons and clergy.
Website: www.pilgrimpress.com

Freelance Potential
Published 54 titles in 2004: 23 were developed from unsolicited submissions and 1 was by an agented author. Of the 54 titles, 1 was by an unpublished writer and 12 were by authors who were new to the publishing house. Receives 200+ queries and mss yearly.

- **Nonfiction:** Publishes educational titles of interest to religious educators, clergy, parents, and caregivers. Also publishes informational titles on religion, social issues, and multicultural and ethnic subjects.
- **Representative Titles:** *A Baby for Sarah* by Carol Wehrheim (0–4 years) is a Bible story picture book. *Dancing in the Aisle* by Rochelle Melander & Harold Eppley presents a collection of stories from the authors' personal experiences as parents, pastors, and friends of young children.

Submissions and Payment
Guidelines available. Query with table of contents, and sample chapters; or send complete ms. Accepts photocopies. SASE. Responds to queries in 6–8 weeks, to unsolicited mss in 2–3 months. Publication in 9–12 months. Flat fee for work-for-hire.

Editor's Comments
Our needs have not changed in the past year and we continue to be interested in submissions of books that investigate social issues as they relate to faith. We look for trade books as well as titles that will appeal to academics and members of the clergy. Topics of interest are religion, ethics, public policy, science, and gender and race relations in religion.

Piñata Books

Arte Público Press
452 Cullen Performance Hall
University of Houston
Houston, TX 77204-2004

Submissions Department

Publisher's Interests
Bilingual picture books for children and entertaining novels for young adults are included on this list of this publisher. It features titles that accurately reflect themes, characters, and customs unique to U.S. Hispanic culture.
Website: www.artepublicopress.com

Freelance Potential
Published 30 titles (12 juvenile) in 2004. Of the 30 titles, 2 were by unpublished writers and 2 were by authors who were new to the publishing house. Receives 2,000 queries and unsolicited mss yearly.

- **Fiction:** Published 6 story picture books, 4–10 years; 3 middle-grade books, 8–12 years; and 3 young adult novels, 12–18 years. Genres include contemporary fiction, drama, poetry, and anthologies.
- **Nonfiction:** Published 2 story picture books, 4–10 years. Also publishes young adult books, 12–18 years. Publishes autobiographies and biographies.
- **Representative Titles:** *Remembering Grandma* by Teresa Armas (3–7 years) is a poignant bilingual picture book that deals with the death of a grandparent. *Chiles for Benito* by Ana Baca (3–7 years) is story about a boy who grows an unusual chili plant that overtakes a New Mexico community.

Submissions and Payment
Guidelines and catalogue available at website. Query with sample chapter. Will accept complete ms for easy-to-read books. Accepts photocopies and computer printouts. SASE. Responds to queries in 2–4 months, to mss in 3–6 months. Publication in 2 years. Royalty.

Editor's Comments
We are committed to publishing books that accurately portray Hispanic culture in the United States. We are interested in submisssions that showcase contemporary and historic Hispanic literary creativity, arts, and culture, especially through bilingual Spanish/English picture books for young readers.

Pineapple Press

P.O. Box 3889
Sarasota, FL 34230

Executive Editor: June Cussen

Publisher's Interests
This regional publisher focuses on a wide range of topics related to Southern Florida. It offers both fiction and nonfiction titles for readers of all ages. Many of its titles are used as supplementary education resources in Florida schools.
Website: www.pineapplepress.com

Freelance Potential
Published 20 titles (5 juvenile) in 2004: 6 were developed from unsolicited submissions and 1 was by an agented author. Of the 20 titles, 2 were by unpublished writers and 8 were by authors who were new to the publishing house. Receives 800 queries yearly.

- **Fiction:** Published 1 chapter book, 5–10 years; 1 middle-grade book, 8–12 years; and 1 young adult book, 12–18 years. Genres include, folklore, mystery, science fiction, mythology, and historical fiction related to Florida.
- **Nonfiction:** Published 2 chapter books, 5–10 years; 2 middle-grade books, 8–12 years; and 3 young adult books, 12–18 years. Topics include sports and topics related to Florida.
- **Representative Titles:** *Hunted Like a Wolf* by Milton Meltzer tells the story of the Seminole War, one of the most important Native American wars. *The Gopher Tortoise* (10+ years) by Ray E. Ashton Jr. & Patricia S. Ashton explores the life and habitat of this animal found in the Southeastern U.S.

Submissions and Payment
Guidelines available at website. Query with clips, synopsis, and sample chapters for fiction. Query with table of contents and sample chapters for nonfiction. Accepts photocopies and simultaneous submissions if identified. SASE. Responds in 2 months. Publication in 12–18 months. Royalty.

Editor's Comments
As the titles on our newest list demonstrate, our mission continues to be to explore topics unique to our region.

Pioneer Drama Service

P.O. Box 4267
Englewood, CO 80155-4267

Assistant Editor: Lori Conary

Publisher's Interests
Pioneer Drama Service is a full service play-publishing, performance-licensing company. It offers musicals, full-length plays, children's plays, one-act plays, plays for special holidays, melodramas, and educational books and resources related to theater topics.
Website: www.pioneerdrama.com

Freelance Potential
Published 25+ titles in 2004: 8–10 were developed from unsolicited submissions and 10+ were by agented authors. Receives 300+ unsolicited mss yearly.

- **Fiction:** Publishes plays, 8+ years. Genres include comedy, mystery, fantasy, adventure, folktales, and musicals.
- **Nonfiction:** Publishes books about stage management, scene design, costumes, and acting techniques. Also offers monologue collections and scene books.
- **Representative Titles:** *Darius the Dragon* by Eleanor Harder is a children's play about a medieval dragon who is released into the 20th century by a bulldozer. *For the Love of a Worm* by Sally Passmore Watson follows the adventures of the magical Star Queen, who can only be seen by those who help others.

Submissions and Payment
Guidelines available. Query with synopsis and clips or writing samples; or send complete ms with résumé and proof of production. Accepts photocopies, computer printouts, and simultaneous submissions if identified. SASE. Responds to queries in 1 month, to mss in 4–6 months. Publication in 3–6 months. Royalty.

Editor's Comments
At Pioneer Drama Service our editors are on the lookout for new plays. As a full-service theater publishing company, our needs fall into a number of areas. A review of the catalogue at our website will give you an idea of the scope of our publishing efforts. If you are interested is submitting your material, please query first.

Pipers' Ash Ltd

Church Road, Christian Malford
Chippenham, Wiltshire SN15 4BW
UK

Manuscript Evaluation Desk

Publisher's Interests
The goal of this British publisher is to discover new, talented authors. Its list includes general fiction and nonfiction for children ages four to young adult.
Website: www.supamasu.com

Freelance Potential
Published 12 titles (2 juvenile) in 2004. Of the 12 titles, 10 were by unpublished writers and 11 were by authors who were new to the publishing house. Receives 1,000 queries yearly.

- **Fiction:** Publishes story picture books, 4–10 years; and chapter books, 5–10 years. Genres include contemporary and historical fiction, fairy tales, fantasy, folklore, mystery, and science fiction.
- **Nonfiction:** Publishes chapter books, 5–10 years; and young adult books, 12–18 years. Topics include animals, crafts, hobbies, and history. Also publishes biographies.
- **Representative Titles:** *Free-Wheeler* by Shay Wilson (5+ years) is the upbeat story of a little girl confined to a wheelchair, but who still has fun with her friends. *Flying Colours* by Alfred Tyson (10+ years) is a rip-roaring flying adventure for older readers that features dramatic real-life situations.

Submissions and Payment
Guidelines available. Short, 25-word query. Accepts email queries to pipersash@supamasu.com. Response time and publication period vary. Royalty, 10%.

Editor's Comments
In general, our readers are positive, articulate, and have a wide range of interests. Ultimately, they are the ones who decide what we should publish and we want books that inspire readers to greater things. Specifically, we need local histories, biographies that provide role models for young readers, contemporary short stories that present new angles on the world, and character-based novels that capture the history and spirit of our times.

Pitspopany Press

Suite 16D
40 East 78th Street
New York, NY 10021

Editor: Dorothy Tananbaum

Publisher's Interests
Established in 1993, this publisher focuses on books with Jewish themes for readers of all ages. Its goal is to reach young readers in all branches of Judaism.
Website: www.pitspopany.com

Freelance Potential
Published 14 titles in 2004: 6 were developed from unsolicited submissions, and 2 were by agented authors. Receives 30 mss yearly.

- **Fiction:** Published 3 toddler books, and 1 early picture book, 0–4 years; 2 easy-to-read books, 4–7 years; 2 story picture books, 4–10 years; 3 chapter books, 5–10 years; 1 middle-grade book, 8–12 years; and 2 young adult books, 12–18 years. Genres include historical, multicultural, and religious fiction; science fiction; mystery; adventure; and humor.
- **Nonfiction:** Publishes easy-to-read books, 4–7 years; story picture books, 4–10 years; chapter books, 5–10 years; middle-grade books, 8–12 years; and young adult books, 12–18 years. Topics include multicultural and ethnic issues, religion, fitness, sports, and history.
- **Representative Titles:** *Tali's Jerusalem Scrapbook* by Sylvia Rouss (6–9 years) is a moving story of the current situation in Israel as seen through the eyes of a child. *The Burning Light* by Betsey Ramsay (10–14 years) catches two time travelers in the adventure and heroism of the Hanukkah story.

Submissions and Payment
Catalogue and guidelines available at website. Send complete ms. Accepts photocopies and email submissions to pitspop@netvision.net.il. SASE. Responds in 3 months. Publication in 4–6 months. Royalty; advance.

Editor's Comments
We are seeking material for our children's list, including the series Jewish Supernatural Stories for Kids, Jewish Humor Stories for Kids, and Jewish Detective Stories for Kids.

Players Press

P.O. Box 1132
Studio City, CA 91614-0132

Editor: Robert W. Gordon

Publisher's Interests
Dramatic works for thespians and audiences of all ages, and textbooks on theater arts, film, and television are the mainstay of this theatrical publisher. It also features material for drama instructors.

Freelance Potential
Published 122 titles (72 juvenile) in 2004: 9 were developed from unsolicited submissions, and 2 were reprint/licensed properties. Of the 122 titles, 10 were by unpublished writers and 19 were by authors who were new to the publishing house. Receives 1,000–1,500 queries yearly.

- **Fiction:** Published 40 middle-grade plays, 8–12 years; and 20 young adult plays, 12–18 years. Genres include musicals, drama, and humor.
- **Nonfiction:** Published 8 middle-grade books, 8–12 years; and 4 young adult books, 12–18 years. Topics include audition technique, stage management, mime, makeup, clowning, acting methods, and costume design. Also publishes education titles for drama teachers.
- **Representative Titles:** *California Wax Museum* by Renon Blum (YA) is a full-length comedy about four students who visit a local wax museum. *Textbook of Stagecraft* by Richmond (theater educators) highlights the principles of acting for students, teachers, amateurs, and professionals.

Submissions and Payment
Guidelines available. Query with résumé, outline, synopsis, production flyer, program, tape of music for musicals, and reviews if available. Accepts photocopies. SASE. Responds in 3–6 weeks. Publication in 3–24 months. Royalty; 10% advance. Flat fee.

Editor's Comments
Strong, easily produced one-act and full-length plays for community groups continue to be a priority. Characters that can be played by either men or women of any age are easier to cast than a play with very specific character types. All material must be previously produced before we can consider it.

Pleasant Company Publications

8400 Fairway Place
Middleton, WI 53562-0998

Submissions Editor

Publisher's Interests
This well-known publisher offers fiction and nonfiction for middle-grade readers, particularly young girls. Many of its books originated as companions to American Girl dolls, and novels about these dolls continue to appear regularly. However, the company has continued to expand its fiction offerings to include contemporary fiction and to expand its list of nonfiction with activity books, advice titles, and books about the various interests of pre-teen girls.
Website: www.pleasantpublications.com

Freelance Potential
Published 50 titles in 2004: 2 were developed from unsolicited submissions.

- **Fiction:** Publishes middle-grade novels, 10+ years. Genres include mystery, and contemporary and historical fiction.
- **Nonfiction:** Publishes middle-grade books, 8–12 years Features advice books, activity books, and interactive CD-ROMS.
- **Representative Titles:** *Flying High, Pogo!* by Constance M. Foland (8–12 years) follows the adventures of Pogo, a young gymnast who gets an invitation to gymnastics camp and must find a way to pay for the camp. *A Ceiling of Stars* by Ann Howard Creel (8–12 years) is the story of a young homeless girl living on the streets of Denver who must decide to trust others and keep hope alive.

Submissions and Payment
Guidelines available. Prefers query; first chapter for fiction. Accepts complete ms. Accepts photocopies and simultaneous submissions if identified. SASE. Responds in 3–4 months. Publication period and payment policy vary.

Editor's Comments
At this time we continue to review submissions of contemporary fiction for middle-grade readers and stand-alone historical fiction for our AG fiction imprint. Please remember that we do not accept submissions for our American Girls books.

Polar Bear & Company

Brook Street
P.O. Box 311
Solon, ME 04979

Submissions Editor: Alex duHoux

Publisher's Interests
Books that highlight cultural diversity with sensitivity and humor are the focus of this small publishing company. Its list includes titles for adults and children. 40% co-venture published material.
Website: www.polarbearandco.com

Freelance Potential
Published 6 titles in 2004: all were developed from unsolicited submissions. Of the 6 titles, 5 were by unpublished writers and all were by authors who were new to the publishing house. Receives 50 queries yearly.

- **Fiction:** Published 2 chapter books, 5–10 years; and 4 young adult books, 12–18 years. Genres include contemporary, multicultural, and ethnic fiction; folklore; folktales; and mythology.
- **Nonfiction:** Publishes young adult books about contemporary social and cultural issues.
- **Representative Titles:** *Millicent the Magnificent* by Burton Hoffmann (grades 3–7) helps children appreciate the wonders of classical music by telling about a magical mockingbird that sings. *Martin McMillan and the Lost Inca City* by Elaine Russell (grades 5–8) follows a young teenager as he discovers a hidden temple, stolen treasure, an Inca princess, and a lost city.

Submissions and Payment
Guidelines available. Query for nonfiction; include outline/synopsis and sample chapter for fiction. Accepts photocopies, computer printouts, and simultaneous submissions if identified. SASE. Responds in 2–4 weeks. Publication in 1 year. Royalty.

Editor's Comments
Our mission is to rebuild America's cultural heritage with words and art. We want titles that make the mythology and lore of Native America come alive, as well as books that help young readers cope with social issues they encounter as they grow.

Polychrome Publishing Corporation

4509 North Francisco Avenue
Chicago, IL 60625-3808

Editorial Department

Publisher's Interests
Polychrome books promote racial, ethnic, cultural, and religious tolerance and understanding by teaching young readers about diverse cultural heritages. Its titles introduce multicultural characters and illustrate situations that all children can identify with.
Website: www.polychromebooks.com

Freelance Potential
Published 5 titles in 2004: 2 were developed from unsolicited submissions and 1 was by an agented author. Of the 5 titles, 3 were by authors who were new to the publishing house. Receives 1,000+ unsolicited mss yearly.

- **Fiction:** Publishes early picture books, 0–4 years; middle-grade books, 8–12 years; and young adult books, 12–18 years. Genres include adventure, contemporary, and historical fiction.
- **Nonfiction:** Publishes books about Asian American culture for families and educators.
- **Representative Titles:** *Almond Cookies & Dragon Well Tea* by Cynthia Chin-Lee (grades 1–4) is the story of two girls from different backgrounds who learn about each other's culture. *Char Siu Bao Boy* by Sandra S. Yamate (grades K–4) examines a boy's view of peer pressure to conform versus preserving his heritage.

Submissions and Payment
Guidelines available at website. Send complete ms with résumé. Accepts photocopies, computer printouts, and simultaneous submissions if identified. SASE. Responds in 3–6 months. Publication in 1–2 years. Royalty; advance.

Editor's Comments
We believe that children need a balanced multicultural education if they are to thrive in today's world. We need authentic multicultural material that offers children the tools they need to value and validate their own experiences and learn how to appreciate other cultures. Our editors are always interested in discovering the talents of new authors.

Portage & Main Press

100-318 McDermont Avenue
Winnipeg, Manitoba R3A 0A2
Canada

Submissions Editor: Jill Condra

Publisher's Interests
Books for teachers on educational topics that are based on school and provincial curriculums are the focus of this Canadian publisher. It specializes in classroom materials for kindergarten through college educators.
Website: www.portageandmainpress.com

Freelance Potential
Published 16 titles in 2004: 2 were developed from unsolicited submissions, and 14 were by agented authors. Of the 16 titles, 2 were by authors who were new to the publishing house. Receives 15 queries, 15 unsolicited mss yearly.

- **Nonfiction:** Published 16 educational resource and professional development titles for teachers, grades K–8. Topics include reading, spelling, math, assessment, literacy, ESL, school safety, social studies, peer mediation, and theater.
- **Representative Titles:** *Peer Mediation* by Hetty van Gurp (grades K–6) is a hands-on guide to developing a program for resolving conflict in elementary and middle schools. *Awakening Brilliance* by Pamela Sims (teachers) weaves true teacher-student experiences into a story that demonstrates how to look after the emotional and academic needs of students.

Submissions and Payment
Guidelines available with SAE/IRC ($.50 postage). Query with table of contents and 1 sample chapter; or send complete ms. Accepts photocopies and IBM disk submissions. SAE/IRC. Responds in 1–2 months. Publication in 6 months. Royalty, 8–12%.

Editor's Comments
At this time, we are interested in books and materials that offer new ideas and new activities for teaching elementary-age children. We need more information on assessment techniques, English as a Second Language programs, and programs that meet Canadian curriculum requirements.

PowerKids Press

29 East 21st Street
New York, NY 10010

Editorial Director: Joanne Randolph

Publisher's Interests
PowerKids Press is an imprint of the Rosen Publishing Group that features nonfiction guidance and curriculum-based books for children from pre-kindergarten through eighth grade. Its titles support assessment in the areas of history, social studies, science, and cultural diversity. The publisher is actively seeking new writers.
Website: www.powerkidspress.com

Freelance Potential
Published 130 titles in 2004: 25 were by unpublished writers and 25 were by authors who were new to the publishing house. Receives 500–1,000 queries yearly.

- **Nonfiction:** Publishes elementary educational materials, pre-K–grade 8. Topics include biography, geography, health, fitness, history, science, technology, self-help, sports, social issues, special education, and multicultural and ethnic subjects.
- **Representative Titles:** *English Colonies in the Americas* by Lewis K. Parker (grades 3–6) explores the early settlements of Europeans in the New World: part of the European Colonies in America series. *Water in the Atmosphere* by Isaac Nadeau (K–grade 5) explores the many ways water works in the earth's atmosphere: part of The Water Cycle series.

Submissions and Payment
Guidelines available. Query with outline and sample chapter. Accepts photocopies, computer printouts, and simultaneous submissions if identified. SASE. Responds in 3 months. Publication in 9–18 months. Royalty. Flat fee.

Editor's Comments
We are interested in reviewing queries for elementary school students and at this time we are actively seeking new writers who want to become part of our publishing family. We strongly urge prospective authors to review some of our titles before querying. We often must reject submissions because they are too similar to books already on our list.

Prometheus Books

59 John Glenn Drive
Amherst, NY 14228-2197

Editor-in-Chief: Steven L. Mitchell

Publisher's Interests
Prometheus Books publishes books, journals, and audio tapes for educational, professional, scientific, library, and popular markets. It presents authoritative and thoughtful works in many categories, including contemporary issues, popular adult and children's fiction and nonfiction, religious studies, and social science.
Website: www.prometheusbooks.com

Freelance Potential
Published 90–105 titles in 2004: 15–20 were developed from unsolicited submissions. Receives 300 queries, 400 unsolicited mss each year.

- **Nonfiction:** Publishes easy-to-read books, 4–7 years. Topics include social issues, health, sexuality, religion, critical thinking, and decision making.
- **Representative Titles:** *All Families Are Different* by Sol Gordon (7+ years) illustrates a variety of family situations to stimulate awareness and acceptance of differences, and stresses that children are loved by their families, whoever they may be. *It's Up to You...What Do You Do?* by Sandra McLeod Humphrey (6+ years) offers challenging situations and helps readers arrive at a well-reasoned conclusion.

Submissions and Payment
Guidelines available. Query or send complete ms with résumé and bibliography. Accepts photocopies, computer printouts, and simultaneous submissions if identified. Availability of artwork improves chance of acceptance. SASE. Responds in 2–3 months. Publication in 12–18 months. Payment policy varies.

Editor's Comments
We are committed to testing the boundaries of established thought and paving the way to new frontiers in philosophy and science. We would like to expand our children's list of titles to help young minds grow. Send us material that shows readers how to make the most of the diverse world they live in.

Publish America

P.O. Box 151
Frederick, MD 21705

Editorial Director: Miranda N. Prather

Publisher's Interests
This publisher features fiction and nonfiction titles for all ages that deal with overcoming personal challenges and hardships.
Website: www.publishamerica.com

Freelance Potential
Published 1,200 titles (58 juvenile) in 2004: 1,000 were developed from unsolicited submissions and 100 were by agented authors. Of the 1,200 titles, 900 were by unpublished writers and 500 were by new authors. Receives 1,200 unsolicited mss yearly.

- **Fiction:** Published 5 concept books, 5 toddler books, and 5 early picture books, 0–4 years; 4 easy-to-read books, 4–7 years; 3 chapter books, 5–10 years; 2 middle-grade books, 8–12 years; and 5 young adult books, 12–18 years. Genres include contemporary, historical, and multicultural fiction; fantasy; humor; and adventure..
- **Nonfiction:** 5 concept books, 5 toddler books, and 5 early picture books, 0–4 years; 4 easy-to-read books, 4–7 years; 3 chapter books, 5–10 years; 2 middle-grade books, 8–12 years; and 5 young adult books, 12–18 years. Topics include social issues, current events, history, ethnic concerns, and special education.
- **Representative Titles:** *Adam's Apples* by Terry James is a futuristic story about children who learn history by passing through a magic door. *An In Flew Enza* by Sherri Vollbracht Fuchs tells about growing up during World War I, and finding that not all enemies are in Europe.

Submissions and Payment
Guidelines and catalogue available. Query or send complete ms and biography. Accepts photocopies, disk submissions (Microsoft Word or WordPerfect). 9x12 SASE ($.99 postage). Responds to queries in 1–2 weeks; to mss in 1–2 months. Publication in 10–12 months. Royalty, 8–12%; advance.

Editor's Comments
We want to see the author's own experiences hidden in the book because these elements add spice to the writing.

Puffin Books

Penguin Putnam Books for Young Readers
345 Hudson Street
New York, NY 10014

Submissions Editor

Publisher's Interests
The list of this publisher features both fiction and nonfiction for children of all ages. All picture books and most of the titles for older readers are paperback reprints. It does publish a few paperback originals—specifically in the categories of young chapter books, easy-to-read titles, and lift-the-flap books.
Website: www.penguinputnam.com

Freelance Potential
Published 217 titles in 2004: 195 were reprint/licensed properties. Receives 100+ queries yearly.

- **Fiction:** Published 15 early picture books, 0–4 years; 15 easy-to-read books, 4–7 years; 40 story picture books, 4–10 years; 10 chapter books, 5–10 years; and 40 middle-grade novels, and 50 young adult novels, 12–18 years. Genres include historical fiction, science fiction, mystery, adventure, and romance.
- **Nonfiction:** Published 5 story picture books, 4–10 years; and 5 middle-grade books, 8–12 years. Topics include social issues and science.
- **Representative Titles:** *Things Will Never Be the Same* by Tomie dePaola (7+ years) follows a year in the life of a child in the year 1941 and offers his stories about the year and family events he experiences. *The President and Mom's Apple Pie* by Michael Garland (3+ years) takes place in 1909 and tells the story of President Howard Taft as he follows his nose to the best food on Main Street.

Submissions and Payment
Guidelines available. Query with outline/synopsis. Accepts computer printouts. SASE. Responds in 4–5 months. Publication in 12–18 months. Royalty, 2–6%.

Editor's Comments
Please note that we do not publish original picture books and such manuscripts will not be considered. We are currently interested in queries for young adult and middle-grade mysteries, and original young adult novels.

G. P. Putnam's Sons

345 Hudson Street
New York, NY 10014
Manuscript Editor

Publisher's Interests
Part of Penguin Group USA, G. P. Putnam's Sons is known for producing award-winning books by some of the most prominent authors of children's literature. Its list includes fiction for all age groups and nonfiction for readers up to the age of twelve.
Website: www.penguin.com

Freelance Potential
Published 45 titles in 2004: 2 were developed from unsolicited submissions. Of the 45 titles, 4 were by unpublished writers and 10 were by authors who were new to the publishing house. Receives 1,500 queries, 8,000 unsolicited mss yearly.

- **Fiction:** Publishes toddler books and early picture books, 0–4 years; story picture books, 4–10 years; chapter books, 5–10 years; middle-grade books, 8–12 years; and young adult books, 12–18 years. Also publishes novelty books. Genres include contemporary and multicultural fiction.
- **Nonfiction:** Publishes early picture books, 0–4 years; story picture books, 4–10 years; chapter books, 5–10 years; and middle-grade books, 8–12 years.
- **Representative Titles:** *Fireboat* by Maira Kalman (5+ years) is the true story of a retired New York City fireboat that was reinstated on September 11, 2001. *Santa Claustrophobia* by Mike Reiss (3+ years) is a tale about the chaos that ensues when Santa takes a vacation.

Submissions and Payment
Guidelines available. Send complete ms for picture books. Query with outline/synopsis and 2 sample chapters for chapter books. Accepts photocopies, computer printouts, and simultaneous submissions if identified. SASE. Responds in 2 months. Publication in 18–36 months. Royalty; advance.

Editor's Comments
Send us something that will grab our attention. We look for a strong voice, well-developed characters, and unusual plots or settings.

Quest Books

P.O. Box 270
Wheaton, IL 60189

Assistant Editor: Karen Schweizer

Publisher's Interests
All the material published by Quest Books is compatible with the philosophy of its affiliate, the Theosophical Society in America, an organization that upholds freedom of individual search and belief. It seeks to help people better understand themselves and each other by providing informative books on psychology, ecology, spiritual growth, and comparative religion.
Website: www.questbooks.net

Freelance Potential
Published 8-10 titles in 2004: 1 was developed from an unsolicited submission and 3 were by agented authors. Receives 6,000 queries each year.

- **Nonfiction:** Publishes young adult books, 12-18 years. Topics include alternative healing, development of creativity, transpersonal psychology, deep ecology, mythology, comparative religion, consciousness, spiritual evolution, ancient wisdom, mysticism, esoteric studies, and perennial philosophy.
- **Representative Titles:** *Frodo's Quest: Living the Myth in The Lord of the Rings* by Robert Ellwood interprets the epic fantasy's themes of higher consciousness, death and rebirth, and the triumph of good over evil. *Life: Your Great Adventure* by Felix Layton & Eunice Layton discusses theosophical concepts such as life after death, finding inner peace, and the meaning of existence.

Submissions and Payment
Guidelines available at website. Query with author biography, table of contents, introduction, and sample chapter. No unsolicited mss. SASE. Responds in 4-6 weeks. Publication period varies. Royalty; advance.

Editor's Comments
Although we don't publish books for children, our titles are of interest to young adults. Please do not submit fiction, poetry, or material that deals with channeling or personal psychic experiences.

Rainbow Publishers

P.O. Box 261129
San Diego, CA 92196

Editorial Director: Christy Scannell

Publisher's Interests
Sunday School teachers turn to Rainbow Publishers for its reproducible classroom books. All of its materials are designed to teach the Bible to children ages two to twelve. Crafts, games, puzzles, and other activities are part of most of its titles.
Website: www.rainbowpublishers.com

Freelance Potential
Published 11 titles (5 juvenile) in 2004: 4 were developed from unsolicited submissions and 7 were assigned. Of the 11 titles, 1 was by an author who was new to the publishing house. Receives 1,000 unsolicited mss yearly.

- **Fiction:** Publishes middle-grade books, 8–12 years. Genres include inspirational and religious fiction.
- **Nonfiction:** Publishes Christian educational resource materials, pre-K–grade 6. Topics include the Bible, religion, crafts, and hobbies. Also offers titles in series, 8+ years.
- **Representative Titles:** *Is Noah Missing the Boat?* (pre-K–grade 6) is written on 5 different reading levels and introduces readers to the well-known figures of the Bible; part of the Undercover Heroes of the Bible series. *Jesus Is My Friend* (1–3 years) features complete lessons followed by themed puzzles and crafts; part of the Instant Bible Lessons for Toddlers series.

Submissions and Payment
Guidelines and catalogue available with 9x12 SASE (2 first-class stamps). Query with table of contents and first 3 chapters. Accepts photocopies. SASE. Responds in 3 months. Publication in 1–3 years. Flat fee.

Editor's Comments
We specifically seek reproducible classroom resource books. Our publishing program does not ever publish children's fiction, poetry, or picture books. Most of our writers are teachers themselves and we prefer classroom-tested materials.

Raven Tree Press

Suite 306
200 South Washington Street
Green Bay, WI 54301

Editor: Amy Crane Johnson

Publisher's Interests
Specializing in a fresh approach to bilingual English/Spanish children's picture books since 2001, Raven Tree Press offers titles that capture the imagination of young readers and help introduce or strengthen a second language. 10% self-published.
Website: www.raventreepress.com

Freelance Potential
Published 10 titles in 2004: 9 were developed from unsolicited submissions. Of the 10 titles, 2 were by unpublished writers. Receives 1,200 unsolicited mss yearly.

- **Fiction:** Published 3 early picture books, 0–4 years; 5 easy-to-read books, 4–7 years; and 2 story picture books, 4–10 years. Genres include contemporary and multicultural fiction; drama; fairy tales; fantasy; folklore and folktales; humor; nature; and the environment.
- **Representative Titles:** *Mason Moves Away* by Amy Crane Johnson (grades 3 and up) explains the gentle balance between humans and wildlife, and shows that the changes that come with moving can be a good thing. *On the Banks of the Amazon* by Nancy Kelley Allen (grades 4 and up) transports readers to the lush, untamed world of the exotic Amazon rainforest.

Submissions and Payment
Guidelines and catalogue available at website. Send complete ms. Accepts photocopies and simultaneous submissions if identified. SASE. Responds in 2–4 months. Publication in 18–24 months. Royalty; advance.

Editor's Comments
We want bilingual titles that generate optimism, inspire self-growth, and provide a positive reading experience for our young audience. We are proud that many of our books feature first-time authors. New voices allow us to offer original material to the growing Hispanic and bilingual households in our country.

Rayve Productions Inc.

P.O. Box 726
Windsor, CA 95492

Editor: Barbara Ray

Publisher's Interests
In addition to titles for adults who are small-business entrepreneurs, counselors, history aficionados, and cooking enthusiasts, Rayve Productions offers a selection of illustrated books designed to delight and encourage young readers.
Website: www.rayveproductions.com

Freelance Potential
Published 5 titles in 2004: 2 were developed from unsolicited submissions. Of the 5 titles, 2 were by unpublished writers. Receives 100+ queries and unsolicited mss yearly.

- **Fiction:** Publishes easy-to-read books, 4–7 years; story picture books, 4–10 years; and chapter books, 5–10 years. Genres include historical, multicultural, and ethnic fiction; folktales; and adventure stories.
- **Nonfiction:** Publishes biographies and history books, 5 years–adult. Also publishes educational titles for teachers, children's counselors, and parents; cookbooks; and how-to books.
- **Representative Titles:** *The Laughing River* by Elizabeth Haze Vega is a folktale about a planned tribal attack that turns into a celebration of laughter and peace because of the Laughing River. *Night Sounds* by Lois G. Grambling describes the sounds a child hears while drifting off to sleep, from the cat purring on the bed to a train whistle in the distance; also available in a Spanish edition.

Submissions and Payment
Guidelines available. Query with résumé for adult books. Send complete ms for children's books. SASE. Responds in 6 weeks. Publication in 1 year. Royalty, 10%; advance, varies.

Editor's Comments
This year marks our return to reviewing submissions of children's books. We have won several national awards for publishing excellence, and we once again look forward to working with caring and gifted individuals who will present quality ideas and manuscripts.

Razorbill ☆

Penguin Young Readers Group
345 Hudson Street, 15th Floor
New York, NY 10014

Editorial Assistant: Margaret Wright

Publisher's Interests
Razorbill launched its first line of paperback and hardcover books in fall 2004 with eleven titles for pre-teens and young adults. This division of Penguin Young Readers Group offers contemporary commercial fiction titles both in series format and as stand-alone books.
Website: www.penguinputnam.com

Freelance Potential
Published 11 titles in 2004: 1 was by an agented authors. Receives 240 queries yearly.

- **Fiction:** Publishes middle-grade books, 8–12 years; and young adult books, 12–18 years. Genres include contemporary fiction, suspense, and science fiction.
- **Nonfiction:** Publishes middle-grade books, 8–12 years; and young adult books, 12–18 years. Topics include popular culture, media trends, and film and television.
- **Representative Titles:** *So Yesterday* by Scott Westerfield (12+ years) is an ultra-hip conspiracy thriller about teenage sleuth and the latest trends in consumerism. *The Big Empty* by J. B. Stephens (12+ years) is a two-part sci-fi novel about seven teens trying to put their life back together after a plague killed three quarters of the human race. *Break the Surface* by Daniel Parker & Lee Miller (12+ years) tries to uncover the reason behind the mysterious disappearance of a teenage girl; part of the Watching Alice series.

Submissions and Payment
Query. SASE. Response time and publication period vary. Advance. Flat fee.

Editor's Comments
As a relatively new publisher, we continue to seek the best and hottest fiction for readers age eight to eighteen. Send us your ideas for thoughtful coming-of-age books, thrilling mysteries, and mind-bending science fiction.

Red Deer Press

MacKimmie Library Tower, Room 813
2500 University Drive NW
Calgary, Alberta T2N 1N4
Canada

Children's Editor: Peter Carver

Publisher's Interests

Books by, about, or of interest to Canadians are produced by this publisher. It offers children's picture books, chapter books, young adult and teen fiction.
Website: www.reddeerpress.com

Freelance Potential

Published 18 titles (7 juvenile) in 2004: 1 was developed from an unsolicited submission and 3 were by agented authors. Of the 18 titles, 3 were by new authors. Receives 2,000 unsolicited mss yearly.

- **Fiction:** Publishes story picture books, 4–10 years; middle-grade books, 8–12 years; and young adult books, 12–18 years. Genres include regional and contemporary fiction, adventure, fantasy, mystery, suspense, drama, and multicultural and ethnic fiction.
- **Nonfiction:** Publishes family activity books, 4+ years. Features a nature series as well as field guides, biographies, and anthologies for adults.
- **Representative Titles:** *Anywhere But Here* by Adele Dueck (9–14 years) tells how a boring summer vacation turns into adventure when a young girl discovers stolen pesticides on her family's farm. *With a Silent Companion* by Florida Ann Town (14+ years) recounts the remarkable journey of Margaret Anne Bulkley, a young woman born in 19th century Ireland who became a surgeon disguised as a man.

Submissions and Payment

Canadian authors only. Guidelines and catalogue available with 9x12 SASE. Query with outline and 2 sample chapters. Accepts photocopies. SASE. Responds in 4–6 months. Publication in 2–3 years. Royalty.

Editor's Comments

At this time, we are currently not accepting any fiction and are only interested in exceptional children's nonfiction from Canadian authors. We prefer material from established writers with a demonstrable record of publishing success.

Renaissance House

9400 Lloydcrest Drive
Beverly Hills, CA 90210

Editor: Raquel Benatar

Publisher's Interests
This publisher and book packager specializes in educational and multicultural children's material. It offers picture books, middle-grade titles, and books for young adult readers in both Spanish and English.
Website: www.renaissancehouse.net

Freelance Potential
Published 12 titles in 2004: 1 was developed from an unsolicited submission. Of the 12 titles, 2 were by unpublished writers and 2 were by authors who were new to the publishing house. Receives 200 queries, 150 unsolicited mss yearly.

- **Fiction:** Published 5 story picture books, 4–10 years; 15 middle-grade books, 8–12 years. Genres include folklore, folktales, biographies, and stories with multicultural themes.
- **Nonfiction:** Published 8 middle-grade books, 8–12 years. Topics include animals and pets, and multicultural themes.
- **Representative Titles:** *Hob the Raven* by Teresa Donmauer tells the legend about the origin of corn and the tortilla. It features a girl who befriends a magic raven who shows her how to plant corn. *The Young Ollac* by Raquel Benatar is the story of a young peasant who visits a mysterious cave where he finds his ancestral roots. When faced with the Spirit of Nature, he chooses his cultural heritage and the wisdom of nature over wealth.

Submissions and Payment
Guidelines and catalogue available at website. Query or send complete ms. Prefers email submissions to submissions@laredopub.com. Place synopsis in the body of email or make a link to your site. SASE. Response time and publication period vary. Royalty.

Editor's Comments
We are seeking multicultural stories for a television animated series that targets the Hispanic community. We are also interested in titles dealing with Hispanic folktales and folklore.

Resource Publications, Inc.

Suite 290
160 East Virginia Street
San Jose, CA 95112

Publisher: William Burns

Publisher's Interests
This Christian publisher strives to help people reach their fullest potential, on both personal and professional levels, by providing leadership resources for those working with children in the areas of ministry and education.
Website: www.resourcepublications.com

Freelance Potential
Published 7 titles (3 juvenile) in 2004. Of the 7 titles, 1 was by an unpublished writer and 1 was by an author who was new to the publishing house. Receives 130–180 queries yearly.

- **Fiction:** Publishes young adult books, 12–18 years. Also publishes activity books and educational fiction for adults.
- **Nonfiction:** Publishes middle-grade books, 8–12 years; and young adult books, 12–18 years. Also features educational titles and books in series. Topics include religion, catechesis, liturgy, pastoral ministry, and books on special education.
- **Representative Titles:** *God Made All of Me: Activities for Young Children* by Jolynn Johanning (4-7 years) offers activities that help young children become aware of themselves and their relationship with God and their families. *Heartwaves: Daily Meditations for Children* by Mary S. Burnett (7–14 years) offers stories based on facts that introduce children to concepts such as setting boundaries and detaching in relationships.

Submissions and Payment
Guidelines and catalogue available with 9x12 SASE ($1.03 postage). Query with clips. SASE. Responds in 6–8 weeks. Publication in 9–18 months. Royalty, 8% of net.

Editor's Comments
We produce high-quality material that is designed to engage students so that they will be motivated to learn and grow. Ideas in the areas of liturgy, catechesis, pastoral ministry, and service that respond to the growing needs of our audience is of interest to us.

Rising Moon

2900 North Fort Valley Road,
P.O. Box 1389
Flagstaff, AZ 86001

Children's Editor: Theresa Howell

Publisher's Interests
Rising Moon is an imprint of Northland Publishing. It was founded in 1988 to publish Southwestern picture books and focuses on acquiring titles with wide appeal and universal themes for the national market. Its list features fiction books for elementary school children.
Website: www.northlandpub.com

Freelance Potential
Published 8 titles in 2004: 3 were developed from unsolicited submissions and most were by agented authors. Of the 8 titles, 2 were by unpublished writers and 2 were by authors who were new to the publishing house. Receives 100 queries, 1,800 mss yearly.

- **Fiction:** Publishes concept books; 0–4 years, and story picture books, 4–8 years. Genres include fairy tales, folklore, humor, and inspirational and multicultural fiction. Also publishes books about the American Southwest, activity books, novelty and board books, and bilingual Spanish/English books, 4–8 years.
- **Representative Titles:** *I Howl, I Grow* by Marcia Vaughan (1–5 years) is about the wide range of animals living in the desert habitat. *The Seed and The Giant Saguaro* by Jennifer Ward (4–8 years) is a rhyming book about all the desert elements and animals that help a seed grow into a saguaro cactus.

Submissions and Payment
Guidelines available. Accepts picture book submissions from agented and previously published authors only. Accepts queries and unsolicited mss for books with Southwest themes. SASE. Responds in 3 months. Publication in 1–2 years. Royalty, varies; advance, varies.

Editor's Comments
We are currently looking for picture books that relate to the Western and Southwestern United States.

Robins Lane Press

10726 Tucker Street
Beltsville, MD 20704

Acquisitions Editor

Publisher's Interests
Books on subjects that are of interest to today's parents are produced by this publisher. Topics that help support parents, provide guidance in making healthy family choices, and help them deal with the challenges that exist in daily life are offered.
Website: www.robinslane.com

Freelance Potential
Published 1 title in 2004: it was developed by an unpublished writer who was new to the publishing house. Receives 100+ queries, 20+ unsolicited mss yearly.

- **Nonfiction:** Publishes parenting titles that offer information and guidance for parents confronting complex issues of society, home and self; easy, practical parenting ideas; and activities that engender curiosity and creative play in children.
- **Representative Titles:** *"Mom, I Got a Tatoo!"* by Dr. Janet Irwin & Susanna deVries (parents) offers straightforward answers to parents' questions about teenage girls' behavior. Addresses serious issues such as tattoos, piercing, sexuality, cliques, and drugs and alcohol use. *The Simpler Family* by Christine Klein (parents) shows families how to make smart choices about the way they spend their time and money by offering strategies to help them increase their free time together, reduce stress on parents and children, and save money.

Submissions and Payment
Guidelines available. Query or send complete ms. SASE. Responds to queries in 4–6 weeks, to mss in 6–8 weeks. Publication in 9–12 months. Royalty; advance.

Editor's Comments
Our material provides parents with the help and guidance they need to be effective parents in today's changing world. We offer books that address topics such as balancing career and family time, building father-child relationships, and finding quality child care. Send us something that stands out from the rest.

Rocky River Publishers

P.O. Box 1679
Sheperdstown, WV 25443

Acquisitions Editor

Publisher's Interests
Since 1987, Rocky River Publishers has specialized in books that help children cope with the problems they face in contemporary society. It publishes fiction and nonfiction for juveniles and young adults, as well a several titles for parents and educators.
Website: www.rockyriver.com

Freelance Potential
Published 10 titles in 2004. Receives 240 queries, 720 unsolicited mss yearly.

- **Fiction:** Publishes toddler books, 0–4 years; easy-to-read books, 4–7 years; story picture books, 4–10 years; and young adult books, 12–18 years. Genres include contemporary, inspirational, and educational fiction.
- **Nonfiction:** Publishes middle-grade books, 8–12 years; and young adult books, 12–18 years. Topics include drug education, self-esteem, stress avoidance, youth safety, abuse, health, disabilities, and addiction. Also offers parenting resources.
- **Representative Titles:** *Buzzy Newton's Terrible Discovery* by Mary Alice Baumgardner is a delightful story with an important message that will encourage children to develop independent thinking skills. *Mac's Choice* by Debra Wert uses a caterpillar named Mat to teach about the dangers and consequences of using drugs.

Submissions and Payment
Guidelines available. Query or send complete ms. Accepts photocopies. Availability of artwork improves chance of acceptance. SASE. Response time varies. Publication in 9–18 months. Royalty; advance. Flat fee.

Editor's Comments
We are seeking books that offer creative ways to explain to young readers how to deal with the issues of stress, self-esteem, and violence prevention. We also need innovative approaches for parents, teachers, counselors, and child-care providers to assist children as they grow.

Ronsdale Press

3350 West 21st Avenue
Vancouver, British Columbia V6S 1G7
Canada

Submissions Editor: Veronica Hatch

Publisher's Interests
Ronsdale Press is a small Canadian house that publishes both adult and young adult books. Ronsdale does not publish any nonfiction for children. Its editors will only review the work of Canadian authors.
Website: www.ronsdalepress.com

Freelance Potential
Published 10 titles (2 juvenile) in 2004. Of the 10 titles, most were by unpublished writers and 5 were by authors who were new to the publishing house. Receives 2,000 queries, 1,970 mss yearly.

- **Fiction:** Published 1 middle-grade book, 8-12 years; and 1 young adult book, 12-18 years. Genres include Canadian historical fiction.
- **Nonfiction:** Publishes adult titles about economics, politics, and language, as well as biographies.
- **Representative Titles:** *Adrift in Time* by John Wilson (10-14 years) tells of a young boy who finds himself adrift in the Pacific Ocean in an open boat. *Jeannie and the Gentle Giants* by Luanne Armstrong (10-14 years) features a young foster girl who learns to love and trust through her friendship with two work horses.

Submissions and Payment
Canadian authors only. Guidelines available at website. Query with sample chapter; or send complete ms. Accepts photocopies and computer printouts. SASE. Responds in 1-2 months. Publication in 1 year. Royalty, 10%.

Editor's Comments
We are interested in reviewing quality historical fiction for young adults. New writers are welcome but remember that we only work with Canadian authors. We consider ourselves to be a literary publisher, which means we look for work that enhances the way we perceive the world. We also look for writing that shows the author has read widely in contemporary and earlier literature. It is always a good idea to review some of our books to make sure you aren't wasting your time or ours by sending an inappropriate submission.

50 Years of Knowledge & Guidance
Iris Rosoff
Rosen Publishing Group

Rosen Publishing has been providing teens with knowledge and guidance for over 50 years.

It is also one of the largest nonfiction publishers, putting out 500 titles a year. In fact, says Iris Rosoff, Editorial Director of the young adult division, Rosen has published so widely and successfully—"we've covered it all"—it has been diversifying into more curriculum-related areas such as social studies and science.

Like many nonfiction publishers, Rosen is quick to respond to national and world events and statistics. Recent series topics include random violence and terrorism. But Rosoff explains that the books aren't trendy, in the sense that they will go out of date quickly. "They're written so the books can have a long life."

Speaking of long life, Rosen regularly updates their books with new editions. Author Raymond M. Jamiolkowski revised his successful book, *Coping with an Emotionally Distant Father*, twice since it first appeared. It has also been translated into French, which shows that Rosen is aggressive about marketing subsidiary rights. Jamiolkowski's current books with Rosen include *Baby Doesn't Make the Man: Alternative Sources of Power and Manhood for Young Men*.

Since Rosen generates almost all of the book topics in-house, writers who wish to be considered for assignments should email Rosoff with résumé, writing credits, and a stated interest or experience in existing series topics. Rosoff will then pass qualified writers on to the appropriate series editors. Rosoff's email address is: irisr@rosenpub.com.

The Rosen Publishing Group

29 East 21st Street
New York, NY 10010

Editorial Director, YA Division: Iris Rosoff

Publisher's Interests
This major educational publisher has been publishing books for more than half a century. Its catalogue includes books for middle and high school students and teachers. It has recently added a new imprint, Rosen Central, developed especially for middle-school students—especially those who are reluctant readers. Topics covered include science, social issues, economics, violence prevention, ethics, guidance, and health. Rosen Publishing does not offer any fiction titles.
Website: www.rosenpublishing.com

Freelance Potential
Published 200 titles in 2004: 20 were by unpublished writers and 40 were by authors who were new to the publishing house. Receives 100 queries yearly.

- **Nonfiction:** Publishes chapter books, 5–10 years; middle-grade books, 8–12 years; and young adult books, 12–18 years. Topics include history, health, science, the arts, animals, sports, safety, and guidance.
- **Representative Titles:** *Hydropower of the Future: New Ways of Turning Water into Energy* by Allison Stark Draper (grades 7–12) discusses the topic of hydropower and what it can do in today's world: part of The Library of Future Energy series. *Uncle Tom's Cabin and the Abolitionist Movement* by Julie Carlson (grades 5–8) takes an in-depth look at America in the era of the Civil War.

Submissions and Payment
Query with outline and sample chapter. Accepts photocopies, computer printouts, and simultaneous submissions if identified. SASE. Responds in 3 months. Publication in 9 months. Royalty. Flat fee.

Editor's Comments
Our books are curriculum based and target middle-grade or young adult students. If you have something new to add to our catalogue, send us a query explaining your topic and why we should publish it.

Running Press Kids

125 South 22nd Street
Philadelphia, PA 19103-4399

Editor: Andra Serlin

Publisher's Interests
Running Press Kids specializes in innovative, hands-on, educational products for children from birth through the ninth grade. Although its main focus is educational nonfiction, it does have a small list of picture books.
Website: www.runningpress.com

Freelance Potential
Published 40 titles in 2004. Receives 800 queries yearly.

- **Nonfiction:** Publishes concept, toddler books, and early picture books, 0–4 years; story picture books, 4–10 years; and middle-grade books, 8–12 years. Features activity, puzzle, and discovery books. Topics include ancient history, geography, biology, nature, dinosaurs, fairy tales, magic, science, technology, and arts and crafts. Also publishes parenting titles.
- **Representative Titles:** *Mummies* by Jacqueline Dineen is an exploration kit that combines lessons in science, archaeology, and anthropology with the experience of building a mummy. *Big Book of Dinosaurs* by Robert Walters is an informative, illustrated guide to prehistoric creatures.

Submissions and Payment
Catalogue available. Send complete ms for picture books. Query with outline, table of contents, and synopsis for all other material. Accepts simultaneous submissions if identified. SASE. Responds in 2–3 months. Publication in 1–2 years. Advance, varies.

Editor's Comments
We are continually looking for unique products that combine learning and fun. Take a look at our line of "Kinesthetic Learning Tools," which uses movement and activity to help preschool children master basic concepts. We need interactive nonfiction titles; basic concept books for letters, numbers, opposites, and shapes; and beginning reading projects. As we grow, we expect to expand into more areas of juvenile publishing.

St. Anthony Messenger Press

28 W. Liberty Street
Cincinnati, OH 45202

Editorial Director: Lisa Biedenbach

Publisher's Interests
This religious press offers books that educate and inspire Catholic Christians of all ages. Its efforts help support the life, ministry, and charities of the Franciscan Friars of St. John Paul the Baptist Province. St. Anthony Messenger Press is no longer accepting submissions for children's books.
Website: www.americancatholic.org

Freelance Potential
Published 30 titles in 2004: 10 were developed from unsolicited submissions, 1 was by an agented author, and 3 were reprint/licensed properties. Of the 30 titles, 6 were by unpublished writers and 11 were by authors who were new to the publishing house. Receives 300 queries yearly.

- **Nonfiction:** Publishes story picture books, 4–10 years; middle-grade books, 8–12 years. Topics include the Christian community, prayer, scripture, spirituality, spiritual heroes, personal growth, faith, and the sacraments. Also publishes titles for adults.
- **Representative Titles:** *Spirit with Us* by Mary Cummins Wlodarski (11–14 years) features stories that explore the presence of the Holy Spirit in the Church, from the New Testament to today. *Seven Lonely Places, Seven Warm Places* by April Bolton gives young readers concrete examples of the seven deadly sins, the four cardinal virtues, and the three theological virtues.

Submissions and Payment
Guidelines available. Query with outline/synopsis. Accepts photocopies. No simultaneous submissions. SASE. Responds in 6–8 weeks. Publication in 1–2 years. Royalty, 10%; advance, $1,000.

Editor's Comments
We consider our editorial style to be *popular*, that is, easy to read, practical, and filled with examples. Through our publications we endeavor to evangelize and inform those who search for God and seek a richer Catholic life.

Saint Mary's Press

702 Terrace Heights
Winona, MN 55987-1320

Submissions Coordinator

Publisher's Interests
Saint Mary's Press is a nonprofit, Catholic publisher administered by the Christian Brothers Province. Its audience includes Christian youth between the ages of ten and nineteen and it offers material designed to share the Gospel of Jesus Christ with young people.
Website: www.smp.org

Freelance Potential
Published 20 titles (13 juvenile) in 2004: 2 were developed from unsolicited submissions and 1 was a reprint/licensed property. Receives 100+ queries, 100+ unsolicited mss yearly.

- **Nonfiction:** Publishes middle-grade books, 8–12 years; and young adult books, 12–18 years. Topics include spirituality, Christianity, and the Catholic faith. Also publishes titles for adults who minister to youth.
- **Representative Titles:** *A Promise in the Storm* by Nancy Marrocco (YA) helps teens learn to cope with grieving and dying with a focus on spirituality and eternal life. *Betsy's Up-and-Down Year* by Anne Pellowski (YA) follows a young girl through a year in which she learns how to deal with life's good and bad times.

Submissions and Payment
Guidelines available. Query with outline and sample chapter; or send complete ms. Accepts computer printouts, disk submissions (RTF files), and simultaneous submissions if identified. SASE. Responds to queries in 2 months, to mss in 2–3 months. Publication in 18 months. Royalty, 10%.

Editor's Comments
Our primary focus has evolved to target educators working with young adults in religious classes. We no longer publish any fiction. Our mission is to share the Gospel of Jesus Christ for the good of young people through materials that are both timely and yet focuses in the eternal lessons of faith. New writers are encouraged to review our books before they query or send a manuscript.

Sandcastle Publishing

1723 Hill Drive
P.O. Box 3070
South Pasadena, CA 91030

Acquisitions Editor

Publisher's Interests
Since 1990, Sandcastle Publishing has been developing books to introduce young people to the wonders of the performing arts, as well as to improve youth literacy. Its list includes both fiction and nonfiction titles, all related to the arts.
Website: www.childrenactingbooks.com

Freelance Potential
Published 3 titles in 2004: 1 was by an author who was new to the publishing house. Receives 750 queries, 500 unsolicited mss yearly.

- **Fiction:** Publishes story picture books, 3–8 years. Features 32-page read-aloud stories that include parts for children to act out. Also publishes collections of monologues and dramatic scenes.
- **Nonfiction:** Publishes young adult books, 12–18 years. Topics include acting and the dramatic arts.
- **Representative Titles:** *Sensational Scenes for Teens* by Chambers Stevens (YA) offers scene work for young people, designed to help them express their emotions. *24-Carat Commercials for Kids* by Chambers Stevens (YA) includes examples of successful résumés, headshot examples, and commercials for kids to practice.

Submissions and Payment
Guidelines available. Query with résumé. Send complete ms for early reader fiction. SASE. Responds in 2–3 months. Publication period and payment vary.

Editor's Comments
We are interested in quality nonfiction that will compliment our existing list of titles. Our commitment is to literacy as well as the performing arts and new ideas that incorporate the two in fun and lively ways are always of interest. We see hundreds of manuscripts and queries each year and often reject many simply because they do not fit our niche. Please take the time to carefully review our catalogue and some of our books before sending us your work.

Scarecrow Press

Suite 200
4501 Forbes Boulevard
Lanham, MD 20706

Acquisitions Editor

Publisher's Interests
Educational, scholarly, and professional books for secondary school librarians and media specialists are featured in the list of Scarecrow Press. It also offers reference titles, handbooks, and self-help books for young adults.
Website: www.scarecrowpress.com

Freelance Potential
Published 150–200 titles (25 juvenile) in 2004. Of the 150–200 titles, 60–80 were by authors who were new to the publishing house. Receives a large number of queries and unsolicited mss yearly.

- **Nonfiction:** Publishes handbooks and reference tools, bibliographies, historical dictionaries, library science monographs, and reference works. Topics include the humanities, history, social issues, music, and science.
- **Representative Titles:** *When Will I Stop Hurting?* by Edward Myers (YA) is a self-help guide for teenagers struggling with bereavement and the emotional difficulties it presents. *Opera for Everyone* by Jean Grundy Fanelli concentrates on the social, literary, musical, and artistic elements of opera.

Submissions and Payment
Guidelines available. Prefers query with résumé, table of contents, introduction, chapter summaries, and sample chapter. Accepts complete ms with curriculum vitae. Accepts photocopies, computer printouts, and simultaneous submissions if identified. SASE. Responds in 2 months. Publication in 6–12 months. Royalty, 8–15%.

Editor's Comments
We have a strong commitment to publishing intellectually important works. We seek proposals that represent new treatments of traditional topics, original scholarship in developing areas, and cogent syntheses of existing research. While we welcome unsolicited submissions, we prefer that you submit a proposal.

Scholastic Canada Ltd.

175 Hillmount Road
Marham, Ontario L6C 1Z7
Canada

The Editors

Publisher's Interests
This publisher offers a variety of fiction and nonfiction written by Canadian authors. It includes books for young children as well as young adults.
Website: www.scholastic.ca

Freelance Potential
Published 70 titles (69 juvenile) in 2004: 25 were by agented authors, and 10 were by reprint/licensed properties. Receives 1,500+ queries yearly.

- **Fiction:** Publishes story books, 4–10 years; chapter books, 5–10 years; middle-grade novels, 8–12 years; and young adult books, 12–16 years. Genres include adventure, mystery, suspense, humor, stories about sports, drama, and contemporary and historical fiction.
- **Nonfiction:** Publishes concept books and toddler books, 0–4 years; easy-to-read books, 4–7 years; and middle-grade books, 8–12 years. Topics include Canadian history, regional subjects, animals, technology, and sports. Also publishes activity books and biographies.
- **Representative Titles:** *Smelly Socks* by Robert Munsch (3–8 years) tells the humorous story of a young girl who loves her new socks so much, she refuses to take them off. *I Want to Go Home* by Gordon Korman (9–12 years) tells the story of a boy and his friend who plan and attempt to escape from camp.

Submissions and Payment
Accepts queries from Canadian authors only. Query with outline and table of contents; include résumé for nonfiction. Accepts photocopies and computer printouts. No simultaneous submissions. SASE. Responds in 3 months. Publication in 2 years. Payment policy varies.

Editor's Comments
We are seeking Canadian-themed nonfiction and reference materials for all age levels, as well as hockey fiction for ages three to eight. Remember, we only publish works from Canadian writers.

Scholastic Inc./Trade Paperback Division

555 Broadway
New York, NY 10012

Editorial Director/Trade Paperbacks: Craig Walker

Publisher's Interests
Scholastic Trade Books is an award-winning publisher of original children books. It lists includes paperback titles that educate, entertain, and motivate children and help them to understand the world around them.
Website: www.scholastic.com

Freelance Potential
Published 350–400 titles in 2004: all were by agented authors. Of the 350–400 titles, 52 were by authors who were new to the publishing house. Receives 250 queries, 150 unsolicited mss yearly.

- **Fiction:** Publishes picture books for all ages; and middle-grade novels, 8–11 years. Genres include science fiction, fantasy, adventure, mystery, and sports stories.
- **Nonfiction:** Publishes books for all ages. Topics include nature, science, and multicultural issues. Also publishes photo-essays and parenting titles.
- **Representative Titles:** *The Singer of All Songs* by Kate Constable is a novel about an enchanted land where music is magic and can control different powers. *Chasing Vermeer* by Blue Balliett is a puzzling adventure story about unexplained occurrences and an international scandal.

Submissions and Payment
Accepts submissions through agents, and queries from authors who have previously published with Scholastic Trade. SASE. Response time, publication period, and payment policy vary.

Editor's Comments
We recognize that literacy is the cornerstone of a child's intellectual, personal, and cultural growth. To that end, our mission is to instill the love of reading and learning for lifelong pleasure in children. Again this year, we are seeking middle-grade fiction that can be published in a series format. The stories must be original, with interesting plots and strong characters. Remember we prefer submissions through agents only.

Scholastic Press

557 Broadway
New York, NY 10012

Editorial Director: Elizabeth Szabla

Publisher's Interests
This children's division of Scholastic Inc. offers picture book fiction and nonfiction, as well as literary non-series or genre middle-grade and young adult fiction. Scholastic Press will consider material from agented or previously published authors only.
Website: www.scholastic.com

Freelance Potential
Published 50 titles (30 juvenile) in 2004: 43 were by agented authors. Receives 600+ queries yearly.

- **Fiction:** Publishes toddler books and early picture books, 0–4 years; easy-to-read books, 4–7 years; story picture books, 4–10 years; chapter books, 5–10 years; middle-grade books, 8–12 years; and young adult books, 12–18 years. Genres include contemporary and multicultural fiction, adventure, fantasy, humor, mystery, and sports.
- **Nonfiction:** Publishes early picture books, 0–4 years; easy-to-read books, 4–7 years; story picture books, 4–10 years; chapter books, 5–10 years; middle-grade books, 8–12 years; and young adult books, 12–18 years. Topics include history, nature, the environment, and multicultural and ethnic subjects. Also offers biographies.
- **Representative Titles:** *Math Fables* by Greg Tang (3–6 years) encourages readers to think about math basics in the most revolutionary of ways. *The King of Slippery Falls* by Sid Hite (YA) is a touching novel about the search for self and the power of belief.

Submissions and Payment
Guidelines and catalogue available at website. Agented queries only. SASE. Responds in 3–6 months. Publication in 12–24 months. Royalty; advance.

Editor's Comments
We are interested in subtly handled treatments of key relationships in a child's life, and unusual approaches to commonly dry subjects such as science, math, history, or biographies. Our readers want books to transport and entertain them.

Scholastic Professional Books

557 Broadway
New York, NY 10012-3999

Editorial/Production Coordinator: Adriane Rozier

Publisher's Interests
Scholastic Professional Books provides resource books for kindergarten through grade-eight educators, including language arts specialists, curriculum coordinators, and staff developers. It also offers resource titles for students.
Website: www.scholastic.com/professional

Freelance Potential
Published 120 titles in 2004: 8–10 were developed from unsolicited submissions. Receives 300–400 queries, 150–200 unsolicited mss each year.

- **Nonfiction:** Publishes titles for educators in grades pre-K through grade 8. Topics include teaching strategies, curriculum development, assessment, evaluation, cooperative learning, and classroom management. Also offers cross-curriculum and literature-based materials for teaching reading, language arts, literature, mathematics, science, social studies, and art. Also publishes dictionaries and encyclopedias.
- **Representative Titles:** *Inventors & Inventions* by Lorraine Hopping Egan (grades 4–8) offers cross-curriculum activities that teach students about the scientific method. *Fresh & Fun: Teeth* by Jacqueline Clarke (grades K–2) gives teachers creative ideas for teaching dental health.

Submissions and Payment
Guidelines available. Query with outline and 2 sample chapters; or send complete ms. Accepts photocopies, computer printouts, and simultaneous submissions if identified. SASE. Responds in 4 months. Publication in 12–14 months. Flat fee.

Editor's Comments
We welcome submissions from all educators and are looking for current, helpful, and inspiring ideas. We need practical activity books for teaching integrated language arts, science, math, social studies, and other areas; books on new ideas, strategies, and approaches to teaching; classroom resources for grade four through eight; and hands-on reference materials for all levels.

School Specialty Children's Publishing

2nd Floor
8720 Orion Place
Columbus, OH 43240

Submissions Editor

Publisher's Interests

Formerly listed as McGraw-Hill Children's Publishing, this publisher offers educational books including stories that stress the importance of reading, rhyming stories, and educational math books. It is currently looking for submissions for its Gingham Dog Press picture book imprint which specializes in picture books that feature rich language and distinctive illustrations.
Website: www.childrensspecialty.com

Freelance Potential

Published 420 titles (416 juvenile) in 2004: 1 was by an agented author. Receives 400 unsolicited mss yearly.

- **Fiction:** Published 5 early picture books, 0–4 years; 24 easy-to-read books, 4–7 years; 5 story picture books, 4–10 years; 11 chapter-books, 5–10 years; 11 young adult books, 12–18 years. Genres include fairy tales, folklore, folktales, and contemporary fiction. Also publishes board books, novelty books, activity books, books in series, and educational workbooks.
- **Representative Titles:** *Eleanor, Ellatony, Ellencake, and Me* by C. M. Rubin (3–8 years) tells the story of how a spunky kid comes up with a perfect nickname for herself. *Snug in Mama's Arms* by Angela Shelf Medearis (0–8 years) tells a soothing bedtime story that stresses the importance of a mother's loving embrace.

Submissions and Payment

Guidelines available. Send complete ms with list of published works. SASE. Response time, publication period, and payment policy vary.

Editor's Comments

Currently, we are not seeking nonfiction. We are pleased to offer imaginative and inspiring literature for young children and we invite published authors to submit manuscripts for picture books that meet our guidelines. We prefer to receive one manuscript at a time, from writers that have a publishing track record.

Scorpius Digital Publishing

P.O. Box 19423
Queen Anne Station
Seattle, WA 98109

Editor: Marti McKenna

Publisher's Interests
This electronic publisher offers juvenile and young adult readers a variety of fiction books including fantasy, science fiction, horror, and mystery. It produces books in electronic format only.
Website: www.scorpiusdigital.com

Freelance Potential
Published 20 titles (4 juvenile) in 2004: 5 were developed from unsolicited submissions and all were by agented authors. Of the 20 titles, 2 were by unpublished writers and 5 were by new authors. Receives 60+ queries each year.

- **Fiction:** Publishes story picture books, 4–10 years; middle-grade novels, 8–12 years; and young adult books, 12–18 years. Genres include fantasy, folklore, folktales, horror, mystery, suspense, science fiction, historical fiction, and fairy tales. Also publishes books in series, 12–18 years.
- **Nonfiction:** Publishes multicultural, ethnic, regional, and historical titles; self-help books; biographies; and photo-essays.
- **Representative Titles:** *Naming of Parts* by Tim Lebbon is a fantasy about a boy who wakes up in a new world of fear and uncertainty where everyone is acting strange, and he doesn't know why. *Ariel* by Steven R. Boyett follows the adventures of a young man and his mysterious and miraculous traveling companion on a dark and dangerous odyssey through a world where fantasy and reality have collided.

Submissions and Payment
Guidelines and catalogue available at website. Query. Accepts email submissions to submissions@scorpiusdigital.com. Responds in 1 month. Publication in 6 months. Royalty.

Editor's Comments
We look for quality stories written by professionals. Send us a query and synopsis that gives us a taste that excites us and has us asking for more.

Seedling Publications

20 West Kanawha Avenue
Columbus, OH 43214-1432

Submissions Editor: Lynn Salem

Publisher's Interests
Emergent readers are the target audience of this small publishing house. Established in 1991, Seedling Publications features a list of fiction and nonfiction books that are used in Guided Reading and Reading Recovery programs, as well as in independent reader programs.
Website: www.seedlingpub.com

Freelance Potential
Published 25 titles in 2004: 10 were developed from unsolicited submissions. Of the 25 titles, 4 were by authors who were new to the publishing house. Receives 400 unsolicited mss yearly.

- **Fiction:** Published 10 easy-to-read books, 4–7 years. Genres include adventure, fairy tales, stories about sports and nature, and humor.
- **Nonfiction:** Published 10 easy-to-read books, 4–7 years. Topics include science, nature, animals, mathematics, technology, and multicultural subjects.
- **Representative Titles:** *Crocodile's Smile* is written for emergent readers and features high-frequency words to help promote reading confidence; part of the Emergent Collection. *Snow Leopards* is designed to help young readers develop their fluency through an engaging story; part of the Fluent Collection.

Submissions and Payment
Send complete ms. Accepts photocopies, computer printouts, and simultaneous submissions if identified. SASE. Responds in 6 months. Publication in 1 year. Payment policy varies.

Editor's Comments
We are interested in manuscripts for beginning readers. All our books are produced in an 8-, 12-, or 16-page format and we will not review materials in any other format. All books run between 150 and 200 words and use natural language and supportive text. We do not accept manuscripts in rhyme, full-length picture books, poetry, or chapter books.

Silver Moon Press

Suite 622
160 Fifth Avenue
New York, NY 10010

Managing Editor: Hope Killcoyne

Publisher's Interests
Biographies of American heroes as well as historical fiction based on American history make up the list of this educational publisher. Its titles are curriculum-based for students in grades three through six.
Website: www.silvermoonpress.com

Freelance Potential
Published 3-4 titles in 2004: 2 were developed from unsolicited submissions. Of the 3-4 titles, 2 were by authors who were new to the publishing house. Receives 75-100 queries yearly.

- **Fiction:** Publishes chapter books, 5-10 years; and middle-grade books, 8-12 years. Genres include historical, multicultural, and ethnic fiction; adventure; mystery; folktales; and books about family issues.
- **Nonfiction:** Publishes chapter books, 5-10 years; and middle-grade books, 8-12 years. Topics include history, politics, geography, civil rights, ecology, nature, the environment, science, and technology. Also publishes biographies and test preparation materials for language arts and social studies.
- **Representative Titles:** *Empire Dreams* by Wendy Wax (8-12 years) is set in 1930 New York and is the story of one young girl's adventures in the city. *In The Hands of the Enemy* by Robert Sheely (8-12 years) takes place in Plymouth at the time of the landing of the *Mayflower* and the adventure of a young boy who strays from home.

Submissions and Payment
Guidelines available. Send complete ms with word count, chapter outline, and brief synopsis for first book of series. Query for stand-alone titles. Accepts computer printouts and simultaneous submissions if identified. SASE. Responds in 6-12 months. Publication period and payment policy vary.

Editor's Comments
We are interested in submissions for our nonfiction series. Send us a query that explores a significant event in an actual person's life. Include a detailed cover letter describing your research.

Silver Whistle

Harcourt, Inc.
15 East 26th Street
New York, NY 10010

Submissions Editor

Publisher's Interests
Established in 1997, this imprint of Harcourt, Inc. offers fiction for middle-grade and young adult readers, picture books for early readers, and nonfiction and biographies for all ages.
Website: www.harcourtbooks.com

Freelance Potential
Published 12 titles in 2004: 1 was developed from an unsolicited submissions and 11 were by agented authors. Receives 100–200 queries yearly.

- **Fiction:** Publishes early picture books, 0–4 years; easy-to-read books, 4–7 years; story picture books, 4–10 years; chapter books, 5–10 years; middle-grade books, 8–12 years; and young adult books, 12–18 years. Genres include inspirational and contemporary fiction and adventure stories.
- **Nonfiction:** Publishes early picture books, 0–4 years; and story picture books, 4–10 years. Also publishes biographies and books about history.
- **Representative Titles:** *The Mighty Asparagus* by Vladimir Radunsky (5–9 years) tells the tale of a mighty asparagus that grew in front of a king's castle and the trouble it was to remove it. *Heir Apparent* by Vivian Vande Velde (8–12 years) is a fantasy adventure that takes readers into a virtual reality game where a girl must avoid getting killed by finding a magic ring, a stolen treasure, and defeating barbarians and dragons.

Submissions and Payment
Not currently accepting unsolicited manuscripts. Query for nonfiction, biographies, and collections. SASE. Responds in 1 month. Payment policy varies.

Editor's Comments
We like to see thrilling adventures for young adults, and story books that make reading fun. Writing should involve the readers, have them eager to turn the page, and reflect the appropriate age group.

Simon & Schuster Books for Young Readers

1230 Avenue of the Americas
New York, NY 10020

Submissions Editor

Publisher's Interests
Picture books, fiction, and nonfiction books for beginning readers though young adults are offered by this well-known publisher. Its children's literature imprints include Atheneum, Margaret K. McElderry, and Aladdin Paperbacks, among others.
Website: www.simonsayskids.com

Freelance Potential
Published 75 titles in 2004: 60 were by agented authors. Receives 10,000 queries yearly.

- **Fiction:** Publishes toddler books and early picture books, 0–4 years; easy-to-read books, 4–7 years; story picture books, 4–10 years; chapter books, 5–10 years; middle-grade books, 8–12 years; and young adult books, 12–18 years. Genres include contemporary, historical, and multicultural fiction; mystery; fantasy; folklore; and fairy tales.
- **Nonfiction:** Publishes story picture books, 4–10 years; and middle-grade books, 8–12 years. Topics include social issues, science, nature, math, and history. Also publishes anthologies and biographies.
- **Representative Titles:** *Among the Barons* by Margaret Peterson Haddix (8–12 years) is a novel about the dangerous life of a third child in a society that allows only two children per family. *Clorinda* by Robert Kinerk (4–8 years) is a picture book about an imaginative cow who fulfills her dream of dancing in a ballet.

Submissions and Payment
Guidelines available. Query. No unsolicited mss. SASE. Responds in 2 months. Publication in 2–4 years. Royalty; advance.

Editor's Comments
Due to the overwhelming amount of material we receive each year, we will only accept queries, not manuscripts, however, you don't need to have an agent. This year, we continue to look for original, top-notch fiction for middle-grade and young adult readers. Topics of interest to this group include school and family issues, mysteries, and historical fiction.

Simon Pulse

Simon & Schuster
1230 Avenue of the Americas
New York, NY 10020

Submissions Editor

Publisher's Interests

This recent addition to the list of imprints from Simon & Schuster is designed for teens and young adult readers. It focuses on contemporary issues in its nonfiction titles and contemporary fiction. Many of its books have media tie-ins to popular teen television programs.
Website: www.simonsays.com

Freelance Potential

Published 50 titles in 2004: all were developed from unsolicited submissions. Of the 50 titles, 1 was by an unpublished writer and 3 were by authors who were new to the publishing house. Receives 1,000+ queries and unsolicited mss yearly.

- **Fiction:** Publishes middle-grade books, 8–12 years; and young adult books, 12–18 years. Genres include adventure, mystery, suspense, romance, fantasy, folktales, drama, horror, humor, and contemporary, inspirational, and ethnic and multicultural fiction.
- **Nonfiction:** Publishes middle-grade books, 8–12 years; and young adult books, 12–18 years. Topics include animals, pets, current events, entertainment, multicultural and ethnic subjects, technology, science, sports, and social issues. Also publishes biographies and self-help books.
- **Representative Titles:** *Dropping in with Andy Mac* by Andy Macdonald (YA) tells the life story of one of the world's top skateboarders. *Cheating Lessons* by Nan Willard Cappo (YA) follows a young girl who must uncover whether a community is involved in a scandal.

Submissions and Payment

Guidelines available. Only accepts queries from agents. SASE. Response time varies. Publication in 6–24 months. Payment varies.

Editor's Comments

We cannot stress enough that we will only accept queries from agented authors at this time. If you are a writer who is new to us, we suggest you review some of our series titles since working on an established series offers the best chance to have your work published.

Sleeping Bear Press

Suite 300
310 North Main Street
Chelsea, MI 48118

Acquiring Editor

Publisher's Interests
Based in Michigan, this small publishing house specializes in non-fiction, illustrated picture books, and regional books for children up to the age of 12. Its list incudes historical subjects, and series of alphabet books—some based on the states, others written around a specific state, and others based on animals.
Website: www.sleepingbearpress.com

Freelance Potential
Published 37 titles in 2004: 2 were developed from unsolicited submissions. Of the 37 titles, 14 were by unpublished writers and 10 were by authors who were new to the publishing house. Receives 1,500–2,000 unsolicited mss yearly.

- **Nonfiction:** Published 37 story picture books, 4–10 years.
- **Representative Titles:** *M Is for Melody: A Music Alphabet* by Kathy-jo Wargin (4 to 12 years) gives children music lessons while teaching them the alphabet. *My Teacher Likes to Say* by Denise Brennan-Nelson (4–10 years) brings young readers interpretations of maxims, idioms, proverbs, and clichés.

Submissions and Payment
Guidelines available at website. Send complete ms. SASE. Response time, publication period, and payment policy vary.

Editor's Comments
Our mission at Sleeping Bear Press is to continue to inspire and motivate readers with our Discover America State by State series and our Counting Your Way Across America series. We continue to expand and grow the number of titles found in our catalogue. We are always interested in hearing from new writers who have a firm grasp on what we look for in a submission. Review our catalogue before sending in your work and remember, as a small publisher, we often receive more manuscripts throughout the year than we could possibly publish, so make sure your material is a good fit for us.

Smith and Kraus

P.O. Box 127
Lyme, NH 03768

Submissions

Publisher's Interests
Smith and Kraus exclusively publishes materials related to theater and the dramatic arts, as well as plays, skits, and monologues for all ages. It features a series devoted to young actors up to the age of 22 and most of its works are performed in school and community theaters.
Website: www.smithkraus.com

Freelance Potential
Published 35 titles (3 juvenile) in 2004. Of the 35 titles, 2 were by unpublished writers and 3–4 were by authors who were new to the publishing house. Receives 240 queries yearly.

- **Nonfiction:** Publishes collections of plays, scenes, and monologues, grades K–12. Also offers instructional books for teachers; anthologies; collections of work by contemporary playwrights; translations; books on career development; and period and special interest monologues.
- **Representative Titles:** *Take a Bow!* by Nina Czitrom (grades preK–K) is a teacher's guide to successful drama lessons for the pre-school age group and explains four major types of drama. *Time on Fire* by Timothy Mason follows the lives of a group of New England young people and a young British officer in 1775, each of them caught up in the turbulence of the American Revolutionary War.

Submissions and Payment
Catalogue available. Query with résumé. Accepts photocopies, computer printouts, and simultaneous submissions if identified. SASE. Responds in 1 month. Publication in 1 year. Royalty; advance. Flat fee.

Editor's Comments
At this time we are interested in reviewing submissions for our upcoming anthologies and will no longer be publishing single plays. Our planned collections are: *Women Playwrights: The Best New Plays* and *New Playwrights: The Best New Plays*. We will continue to review material for our monologue and scene books.

Smooch ☆

Suite 2000
200 Madison Avenue
New York, NY 10016

Editor: Kate Seaver

Publisher's Interests
Established in 2003, this new publisher features contemporary teen fiction and paranormal titles about vampires, ghosts, and werewolves for girls age twelve to sixteen. Smooch is an imprint of Dorchester Publishing.
Website: www.smoochya.com

Freelance Potential
Published 12 titles in 2004: 6 were developed from unsolicited submissions, 6 were by agented authors, and 8 were reprint/licensed properties. Of the 12 titles, 2 were by unpublished writers and 8 were by authors who were new to the publishing house.

- **Fiction:** Published 12 young adult books, 12-18 years. Genres include contemporary fiction, horror, humor, fantasy, the paranormal, and romance.
- **Representative Titles:** *You Are So Cursed* by Naomi Nash (YA) is a humorous look at high school life through the eyes of a young witch, who learns the value of knowing who your true friends are. *Putting Boys on the Ledge* by Stephie Davis (YA) is the story of a teenage girl who finally finds three best friends and true love, despite the usual problems. *My Life As a Snow Bunny* by Kaz Delaney (YA) follows the snowy escapades of a girl and the mysterious Swiss guy she meets on the slopes.

Submissions and Payment
Guidelines and catalogue available at website. Query with synopsis and 2 chapters. Accepts photocopies. SASE. Responds in 3-8 months. Publication in 9-12 months. Payment policy varies.

Editor's Comments
Although romance and humor play a major role in our titles, stories should focus on the many issues teens face today, such as self-esteem, peer pressure, and social issues. We do not consider erotic material suitable for our young adult readers, so please do not include such material.

Soundprints/Studio Mouse

353 Main Avenue
Norwalk, CT 06851-1552

Editorial Assistant: Brian E. Giblin

Publisher's Interests
This small publisher focuses on producing nonfiction for readers up to the age of ten. Its titles appear in series and all deal with some aspect of nature and the environment. All of it titles approach their topics through an engaging story line based on solid research.
Website: www.soundprints.com

Freelance Potential
Published 50 titles in 2004: few were developed from unsolicited submissions and 25 were by agented authors. Of the 50 titles, 1 was by an author who was new to the publishing house. Receives 200 queries yearly.

- **Fiction:** Published 4 toddler books and 22 early picture books, 0–4 years; 10 easy-to-read books, 4–7 years; and 14 story picture books, 4–10 years. Also publishes books in series about nature, the environment, and animals; and multiculture and adventure stories.
- **Representative Titles:** *Red Otter at Autumn Lane* (pre-K–grade 2) follows a young family as its cubs learn to fend for themselves; part of the Smithsonian's Backyard series. *Triceratops Get Lost* by Dawn Bentley (pre-K–grade 2) follows a young dinosaur who, when he loses his herd, must defend himself against a Tyrannosaurus Rex; part of the Smithsonian's Prehistoric Pals series.

Submissions and Payment
Query with clips or writing samples. Accepts photocopies and computer printouts. SASE. Responds in 1 month. Publication period varies. Flat fee.

Editor's Comments
Our mission is to entertain young readers while at the same time, introducing them to new ideas and subjects. All of our work is based on solid research and is vetted by experts at the Smithsonian Institution. We only publish books as parts of series so we suggest you read a few titles that interest you and verify in advance that we are not currently planning to publish a book on your chosen topic.

Sourcebooks

Suite 139
1935 Brookdale Road
Naperville, IL 60563

Editorial Submissions

Publisher's Interests

The majority of titles on this publisher's list are nonfiction books for adults. Subjects include entertainment, history, sports, business, parenting, women's issues, health and beauty. In addition, it publishes a small variety of fiction.
Website: www.sourcebooks.com

Freelance Potential

Published 130 titles in 2004: 10 were developed from unsolicited submissions, 70 were by agented authors, and 5 were reprint/licensed properties. Receives 1,000 queries, 1,000 unsolicited mss each year.

- **Nonfiction:** Publishes self-help books. Topics include parenting, single parenting, family issues, childbirth, multicultural issues, and lifestyle issues.
- **Representative Titles:** *Motherhood without Guilt* by Debra Rosenberg uses a question-and-answer format to address the issues that cause a mother to feel bad about her mothering. *Moonslivers* by Kathy O'Dell supplies parents with a creative way to record their children's words. It includes blank cards and comes in a keepsake box for capturing and storing children's milestones as they grow.

Submissions and Payment

Guidelines and catalogue available. Query résumé, synopsis, table of contents, 2 sample chapters, and market anaylsis. Accepts photocopies, computer printouts, and simultaneous submissions if identified. SASE. Responds in 4–6 weeks. Publication in 1 year. Royalty, 6–15%.

Editor's Comments

We are always enthusiastically interested in developing the careers of authors. Well-written, informative books on parenting, child development, childbirth, and family issues are of interest to us. Send us a query on something that will show us you are as committed to success as we are.

The Speech Bin, Inc.

1965 25th Avenue
Vero Beach, FL 32960

Senior Editor: Jan J. Binney

Publisher's Interests
Fiction and nonfiction books for individuals of all ages who have communication disorders are the target audience for this special interest publisher. Also included on its list of titles are resource books and other materials for audiologists, speech-language professionals, occupational therapists, and other rehabilitation specialists.
Website: www.speechbin.com

Freelance Potential
Published 10 titles (no juvenile) in 2004: all were developed from unsolicited submissions. Of the 10 titles, 5 were by unpublished writers and 5 were by new authors. Receives 500+ queries yearly.

- **Fiction:** Publishes picture books, 4–10 years. Features stories that deal with stuttering, conversation, phonology, articulation, communication, and language skills.
- **Nonfiction:** Publishes concept books and early picture books, 0–4 years; story picture books, 4–10 years; and middle-grade books, 8–12 years. Topics include stuttering, phonology, articulation, and language skills. Also publishes textbooks and how-to titles for parents, speech pathologists, and occupational therapists.
- **Representative Titles:** *Bugaboo Words* by Noreen Briggs (all ages) helps individuals with immature patterns of speech tackle words that are difficult for them to say. *Tips for Teaching Infants & Toddlers* by Carol Weill et al. features multidisciplinary lessons that incorporate all five senses.

Submissions and Payment
Guidelines available with #10 SASE ($.37 postage); catalogue available with 9x12 SASE ($1.47 postage). Query with résumé and outline/synopsis. Accepts photocopies. No Internet queries. SASE. Responds in 1–2 months. Publication in 1 year. Royalty.

Editor's Comments
We would like to see more material written for professionals who work with individuals with communication disorders. Please keep in mind that we do not accept any material sent over the Internet.

Sports Publishing Inc.

804 North Neil
Champaign, IL 61820

Acquisitions Editor: Mike Pearson

Publisher's Interests
This specialty publisher is dedicated to developing information for the sports enthusiast in a way that enlightens, entertains, enriches, and educates its markets around the world. Its children's list targets middle-grade readers and includes both fiction and nonfiction.
Website: www.sportspublishinginc.com

Freelance Potential
Published 150 titles (10 juvenile) in 2004. Receives 50 queries each year.

- **Fiction:** Publishes middle-grade novels, 8–14 years. Features stories about sports and athletics.
- **Nonfiction:** Publishes middle-grade books, 8–14 years. Topics include auto racing, baseball, basketball, football, golf, and hockey. Also publishes biographies.
- **Representative Titles:** *ABC's: Albert's Gator Alphabet* by Marisol Novak & Mike Bianchi teaches young children their ABC's while it creates an early love of sports and a bond between parent and child. *Al McGuire* by Roger Jaynes profiles the man who has become one of the most successful coaches in the history of college basketball.

Submissions and Payment
Guidelines available. Query with outline, synopsis, 2–3 sample chapters, competition analysis, and résumé. Accepts photocopies, computer printouts, and email queries to mpearson@sagamore.com. SASE. Response time varies. Publication period and payment policy vary.

Editor's Comments
Our list has been growing seadily each year, and by 2003, we published more than 500 different sports titles. As we expand, we continue to be on the lookout for authors with a flare for sports writing. Almost any sport is of interest, but make sure to make sure your idea has not recently been covered by another title. A visit to our website will also help you understand what works best here.

Standard Publishing

8121 Hamilton Avenue
Cincinnati, OH 45231

Director, Family Resources: Diane Stortz
Director, Children's Ministry: Ruth Frederick

Publisher's Interests

This children's publisher specializes in evangelical books for readers from birth up to the age of twelve. All of its books have a strong biblical message. Standard Publishing usually publishes about 30 titles a year, one quarter of which one quarter are from freelancers.
Website: www.standardpub.com

Freelance Potential

Published 47 titles (2 juvenile) in 2004. Of the 47 titles, 1 was by an unpublished writer and 2 were by authors who were new to the publishing house. Receives 500 queries, 1,500 mss yearly.

- **Fiction:** Publishes concept books, 0–4 years; and story picture books, 4–10 years. Genres include religious fiction.
- **Nonfiction:** Publishes early picture, concept, and toddler books, 0–4 years; story picture books, 4–10 years; and young adult books, 12–18 years. Features activity books, coloring books, religious education titles, devotionals, and reference books as well as Bible study guides.
- **Representative Titles:** *Thankful Together* (4–10 years) by Holly Davis is the story of a mother squirrel and her child as they celebrate a day of thanks. *Hi God, Let's Talk about My Life* by Karen Ann Moore (8–12 years) addresses situations found in everyday life with devotions, biblical advice, and prayer starters.

Submissions and Payment

Guidelines available. Query with outline/synopsis and 1–2 sample chapters. Send complete ms for picture books only. Accepts photocopies, computer printouts, and simultaneous submissions if identified. SASE. Responds in 2–3 months. Publication in 18 months. Royalty. Flat fee.

Editor's Comments

Although most of our books are written on assignment, we welcome children's and tween books for birth to age 12, and young adult books for ages 13 to 22. Do not send any poetry, activity books, and stories about Bible people not based on recorded events.

Star Bright Books

Suite 2B
42-26 28th Street
Long Island City, NY 11101

Director of Marketing: Marie Bernard

Publisher's Interests
High-quality books for children of all reading abilities are produced by this independent publisher. Pre-readers and beginning readers make up half of its list. It also includes books in Spanish, and plans to produce more in other languages.
Website: www.starbrightbooks.com

Freelance Potential
Published 15–20 titles (13 juvenile) in 2004: 2 were developed from unsolicited submissions and 1 was by an agented author. Receives 360–480 queries, 240–360 unsolicited mss yearly.

- **Fiction:** Publishes concept books, toddler books, and early picture books, 0–4 years; easy-to-read books, 4–7 years; story picture books, 4–10 years; chapter books, 5–10 years; and middle-grade books, 8–12 years. Features multicultural and educational books. Also publishes board books.
- **Representative Titles:** *Backpack Baby* by Miriam Cohen (6 months–2 years) features a baby who shares his big secret with all the people he sees on the street, but readers don't find out what the secret is until the last page of the book—he has a new sibling. *The Seaweed Book* by Rose Treat (7–11 years) offers an absorbing introduction to the amazing world of seaweed. It explains how to collect, identify, preserve, and make gifts with seaweed.

Submissions and Payment
Guidelines available. Query or send complete ms. SASE. Response time and publication period vary. Royalty; advance.

Editor's Comments
Children will learn to love and read books early on if they are appealing, easy-to-read, and fun. We are interested in the following types of books: multicultural, inclusion, picture, educational, and board books for children ages 0–15 years. If you have an idea for something new and creative, send it to us. Be sure your writing style matches the age group you are targeting.

Starscape Books

175 Fifth Avenue
New York, NY 10010

Senior Editor, Children's/Young Adult: Susan Chang

Publisher's Interests
Starscape Books, an imprint of Tor Books, is devoted exclusively to publishing the very best in the genres of science fiction and fantasy for young readers.
Website: www.starscapebooks.com

Freelance Potential
Published 25 titles in 2004: 3 were developed from unsolicited submissions and 22 were by agented authors. Of the 23 titles, 2 were by unpublished writers and 3 were by authors who were new to the publishing house. Receives 400 queries yearly.

- **Fiction:** Publishes middle-grade books, 8–12 years; and young adult books, 12–18 years. Genres include science fiction, fantasy, and crossover novels with elements of romance, suspense, history, and religion.
- **Nonfiction:** Publishes middle-grade books, 8–12 years; and young adult books 12–18 years. Features general interest and how-to titles.
- **Representative Titles:** *A School for Sorcery* by E. Rose Sabin (YA) is a fantasy novel that takes readers to a teenage school for magic. *Briar Rose* by Jane Yolen (YA) is a powerful and heartwarming retelling of the classic, *Sleeping Beauty*.

Submissions and Payment
Guidelines available at www.tor.com. Send cover letter with synopsis and first 3 chapters. Accepts photocopies and computer printouts. No electronic or simultaneous submissions. SASE. Responds in 4–6 months. Publication in 18–24 months. Royalty; advance.

Editor's Comments
Please be sure to send the first three chapters of your book. It is difficult for us to get a sense of your book without them. A cover letter should be included with all submissions stating the genre of the submission and previous publications, if relevant. We carefully review each submission, so it may take several months for us to get back to you.

Starseed Press

P.O. Box 1082
Tiburon, CA 94920

Acquisitions: Jan Phillips

Publisher's Interests
This imprint of New World Library, established in 1984, is devoted to titles for children up to the age of 12. Its emphasis is on promoting positive values, nonviolence, and self-esteem.
Website: www.nwlib.com

Freelance Potential
Published 5 titles (2 juvenile) in 2004. Receives 1,500 queries yearly.

- **Fiction:** Publishes toddler and early picture books, 0–4 years; and story picture books, 4–10 years. Genres include inspirational fiction and books about nature, personal growth, and self-esteem.
- **Nonfiction:** Publishes parenting titles.
- **Representative Titles:** *Where Does God Live?* by Holly Bea (3–6 years) teaches children about God and heaven. *The Lovables in the Kingdom of Self-Esteem* by Diane Loomans (3–10 years) introduces children to the concept of self-esteem and helps them to find their own way to believe in themselves.

Submissions and Payment
Query. No unsolicited mss. No submissions via fax or email. SASE. Responds in 8–10 weeks. Publication in 6–18 months.

Editor's Comments
We continue to be interested in submissions for picture books for readers up to the age of ten. As a whole, our company believes in promoting personal growth, health and wellness, religion, and spiritutality. Without using an overtly religious tone, our material focuses on themes of nonviolence and self-esteem, and we are dedicated to instilling positive values in our young readers. If you think your book is right for us, make sure by reviewing our current catalogue, visiting our website, and taking a look at our recent children's titles to ensure that we are a good fit. As always, we will not consider any unsolicited manuscripts.

Stemmer House Publishers

4 White Brook Road
Gilsum, NH 03448

President: Ernest N. Peter

Publisher's Interests
This publisher presents a list of quality nonfiction books for young readers as well as adults. Topics include nature and science, geography, art, and cooking.
Website: www.stemmer.com

Freelance Potential
Published 5 titles (2 juvenile) in 2004: all were developed from unsolicited submissions. Of the 5 titles, 1 was by an unpublished author who was new to the publishing house. Receives 1,000 queries, 800 unsolicited mss yearly.

- **Nonfiction:** Publishes story picture books, 4–10 years. Also publishes easy-to-read books, 4–7 years; chapter books, 5–10 years; and middle-grade books, 8–12 years. Topics include natural history, art, music, and geography. Also publishes biographies and titles for adults.
- **Representative Titles:** *Ask Me If I'm a Frog* by Ann Milton (4–10 years) this nonfiction picture book compares the anatomy, social habits, and lifestyles of a pond frog with those of a small child. *The Hawaiian Coral Reef* by Katherine Orr explores the Hawaiian reefs, where some of the world's most richly colored animals live.

Submissions and Payment
Guidelines and catalogue available with 9x12 SASE ($.77 postage). Send complete ms for picture books. Query with outline/synopsis and 2 samples chapters for longer works. Accepts photocopies, computer printouts, and simultaneous submissions if identified. SASE. Responds in 2 weeks. Publication in 1–3 years. Royalty; advance.

Editor's Comments
We are seeking educational nonfiction on topics that will fascinate readers, and have them eager to turn the pages. Send us something new and exciting; uncover hidden treasures that children will love to explore. Please note that we do not accept fiction.

Sterling Publishing Company

387 Park Avenue South
New York, NY 10016-8810

Editorial Director: Frances Gilbert

Publisher's Interests
Sterling Publishers is one of the world's leading providers of nonfiction titles. Its children's list includes books on crafts, art, magic, and puzzles, as well as nature and animals.
Website: www.sterlingpub.com

Freelance Potential
Published 250 titles in 2004: 25 were developed from unsolicited submissions, 10 were by agented authors, and 50 were reprint/licensed properties. Of the 250 titles, 20 were by unpublished writers. Receives 500 queries yearly.

- **Nonfiction:** Publishes how-to, activity, and craft books, 0–14 years, and reference titles. Topics include art, animals, games, history, photography, puzzles and games, magic, gardening, woodworking, sports, and travel. Also publishes books for adults on home decor, health, religion, and science and nature.
- **Representative Titles:** *Found You, Little Wombat* by Angela McAllister & Charles Fuge is a board book about a wombat who gets too involved in a game of hide-and-seek. *I Know a Rhino* by Charles Fuge is a rhyming tale about a delightful menagerie of animals, with a little twist at the end.

Submissions and Payment
Guidelines available. Query with outline. Accepts photocopies, computer printouts, and simultaneous submissions if identified. SASE. Response time varies. Publication in 1 year. Royalty; advance.

Editor's Comments
Although we do not currently publish picture books, we are planning to do so in the near future. Books for children age four to ten that stress science and nature topics are usually needed, as are craft and project books with a hands-on approach to activities. Send us your idea for a nonfiction book that gets readers interested. Review our catalogue to see what we have published in the past—we rarely duplicate previously published topics.

Storytellers Ink Publishing Co.

P.O. Box 33398
Seattle, WA 98133-0398

Editor-in-Chief: Quinn Currie

Publisher's Interests
Storytellers Ink publishes books for children from preschool through middle school. Its mission is to teach children to love reading through exciting books about animals and the environment, which also instill in them compassion, justice, responsibility, and love of all living things.
Website: www.storytellers-ink.com

Freelance Potential
Published 1–3 titles in 2004. Receives 120 queries yearly.

- **Fiction:** Publishes adventure, folktales, fantasy, and multicultural and ethnic fiction, 2–12 years. Also features stories about animals, nature, and the environment.
- **Nonfiction:** Publishes biographies and books about animals, nature and the environment, and social issues. Features ethnic, multicultural, and bilingual titles.
- **Representative Titles:** *The Butterfly Garden* by Judith Levicoff (grade 3) is a true story about a boy who finds a butterfly egg and how he and his class get involved in helping it and other butterflies. *It Happened to Herbie* by Michaela Friends (grade 1) follows the adventures of a hedgehog who becomes separated from his family and encounters difficulties finding his way back home.

Submissions and Payment
Send complete ms. Accepts photocopies and simultaneous submissions if identified. SASE. Response time, publication period, and payment policy vary.

Editor's Comments
We are always interested in reviewing submissions of stories for young children. We want to see books that will help instill a love of reading in young people through exciting storylines, strong characters, and memorable narratives. Our list is a small one and we get far more submissions than we can publish, so if you think your book is right for us, take the time to make it the best it can be before sending it.

Sword of the Lord

P.O. Box 1099
Murfreesboro, TN 37133-1099

Editorial Department Supervisor: Dr. Terry Frala

Publisher's Interests
A fundamentalist Christian publisher, Sword of the Lord offers books and pamphlets that strictly follow the teachings of the Bible. All of the material it publishes stems from a conservative, rather than contemporary, Christian philosophy. Titles for children ages five through the teen years are included on its list. 10% self-, subsidy-, co-venture, or co-op published material.
Website: www.swordofthelord.com

Freelance Potential
Published 32 titles (3–4 juvenile) in 2004: 2 were developed from unsolicited submissions. Of the 32 titles, 3 were by unpublished writers and 4 were by authors who were new to the publishing house. Receives 120 queries, 50 unsolicited mss yearly.

- **Fiction:** Publishes story picture books, 4–10 years; middle-grade books, 8–12 years; and young adult novels, 12–18 years. Genres include adventure; humor; and inspirational, religious, and Western fiction. Also publishes educational fiction, 6–10 years; and series, 6–17 years.
- **Nonfiction:** Publishes biographies, humor, and religious titles for adults.
- **Representative Titles:** *Short People Need Tall Trees* by Ruth Scarff (5–10 years) retells the biblical story of Zacchaeus. *The Truth About Rock Music* by Hugh Pyle (YA) offers a conservative view of this topic.

Submissions and Payment
Guidelines available. Query or send complete ms. Accepts photocopies, computer printouts, and email to terryfrala@swordofthelord.com. SASE. Responds in 2–3 months. Publication period varies. Royalty, 10%.

Editor's Comments
Christian fiction for readers ages six through seventeen and Christian biographies for teens are of interest to us, as long as they are written from a conservative, fundamentalist perspective.

Tanglewood Press, LLC

P.O. Box 3009
Terre Haute, IN 47803

Acquistions Editor

Publisher's Interests
This publisher of fiction offers readers story picture books, chapter books, middle-grade books, and young adult books. It produces stories with great plots that respect kids' intelligence, savvy, and the issues with which they grapple. Genres include historical, adventure, humor, and mystery.
Website: www.tanglewoodbooks.com

Freelance Potential
Published 4 titles in 2004: 2 were developed from unsolicited submissions and 1 was by an agented author. Of the 4 titles, 2 were by unpublished writers and 3 were by authors who were new to the publishing house.

- **Fiction:** Published 3 story picture books, 4–10 years; 1 middle-grade book, 8–12 years; and 1 young adult book, 12–18 years. Genres include adventure, historical, humor, and mystery.
- **Representative Titles:** *Noah—A Cat Too Many* by Judith Neville (5–9 years) tells of Noah, a lonely and ill cat who wanders into a loving family who makes room for him. *Mystery at Blackbeard's Cove* by Audrey Penn (8–12 years) tells the tale of what happens in the Outer Banks in North Carolina when you mix an unruly group of youngsters, Blackbeard's ghost, hidden treasures, skeletons, the Bermuda triangle, and a hurricane together.

Submissions and Payment
Send complete ms. Accepts photocopies. SASE. Responds in 2 months. Publication in 12–18 months. Royalty; 10%.

Editor's Comments
We are a new publisher and are looking for humorous, original, kid-centric fiction, for ages 4–12. Send us something that will excite kids, and take them on an adventure. Make sure your plot and characters match the age range for which you are targeting. Please note that we do not publish nonfiction or "issue" books. Send us your manuscripts only, we do not accept queries.

Teacher Created Materials

P.O. Box 1040
Huntington Beach, CA 92647

Editor-in-Chief

Publisher's Interests
Resource books covering language arts, social studies, the arts, math, science, and technology, for early childhood, elementary, middle school, and high school classes, are offered by this publisher. In addition, it produces materials to help educators create stimulating learning environments such as, bulletin boards, stickers, name tags, and incentive charts.
Website: www.teachercreated.com

Freelance Potential
Published 200 titles in 2004. Receives 500 queries yearly.

- **Nonfiction:** Publishes workbooks and activity books, pre-K–grade 12. Topics include art, geography, history, social studies, science, mathematics, reading, phonics, spelling, writing, language arts, and technology. Also publishes teacher resource materials on student testing, gifted education, multiple intelligences, assessment techniques, professional development, classroom management, and reading plans.
- **Representative Titles:** *Nonfiction Strategies* (grades 1–3) offers lessons for students detailing how to read, write, discuss, research, remember, and listen to information to master comprehension skills. *Practice Makes Perfect* (grades K–4) provides activities to help students master skills in math, reading, writing, grammar, map reading, and penmanship.

Submissions and Payment
Guidelines available. Query with outline or table of contents, summary, and 10–12 sample pages. Accepts photocopies, computer printouts, and simultaneous submissions if identified. SASE. Responds in 1 year. Publication in 6–12 months. Flat fee.

Editor's Comments
We are always on the lookout for top-quality materials from experienced writers that offer new techniques to keep up with the growing trends and requests of educators.

Teaching & Learning Company

P.O. Box 10
1204 Buchanan Street
Carthage, IL 62321

Vice President of Production: Jill Day

Publisher's Interests
In print for over 10 years, this publisher offers teachers and parents creative ideas to educate, motivate, and encourage students. Its publishes material that covers subjects such as math, science, language arts, and social studies as well as resources for teachers.
Website: www.TeachingLearning.com

Freelance Potential
Published 35–40 titles in 2004: 3 were developed from unsolicited submissions and 1 was by an agented author. Receives 350 unsolicited mss yearly.

- **Nonfiction:** Publishes educational teacher resource materials for pre-K–grade 8. Topics include language arts, social studies, current events, biography, mathematics, computers, science, nature, the environment, animals, pets, holidays, arts and crafts, hobbies, multicultural and ethnic issues, and responsibility education. It also offers materials for gifted and special education classrooms.
- **Representative Titles:** *Four Square* (grades 1–3) offers a step-by-step approach that can be used with all forms of writing and will fit any reading or language program. *Presidential Elections* (grades 4–8) offers an easy and exciting way for students to learn about the election process. It provides timely, informative, and intriguing material.

Submissions and Payment
Guidelines available. Send complete ms. Accepts photocopies and computer printouts. SASE. Responds in 6–9 months. Publication in 1–3 years. Payment policy varies.

Editor's Comments
We're looking for a variety of creative ideas and activities for pre-kindergarten through eighth grade classrooms. Holiday and seasonal materials are always of interest to us. Please keep in mind that the writing we publish must reflect the diverse and culturally rich population we serve in the United States and Canada.

TEACH Services, Inc.

254 Donovan Road
Brushton, NY 12916

Editor: Wayne Reid

Publisher's Interests
Established in 1984, this company publishes nonfiction books for Seventh-day Adventist children and adults. Its list includes Christian study guides, early readers for young children, novels for young adults, and resources for ministers.
Website: www.teachservicesinc.com

Freelance Potential
Published 60 titles (20 juvenile) in 2004. Of the 60 titles, 17 were by authors who were new to the publishing house. Receives 200 queries yearly.

- **Nonfiction:** Publishes easy-to-read books, 4–7 years; story picture books, 4–10 years; chapter books, 5–10 years; middle-grade books, 8–12 years; and young adult books, 12–18 years. Topics include practical Christianity, Bible study, prayer, church history, health, and spiritual growth. Also publishes biographies, self-help titles, devotionals, and poetry.
- **Representative Titles:** *Guess Who Took the Battered-Up Bike?* by Raymond & Dorothy Moore follows a group of children as they face dilemmas and make choices that help readers set standards for their own lives. *Remarkable Influence* by Emilia Lopes (YA) is a set of stories that encourage young adults to pursue a good future following the paths of righteousness.

Submissions and Payment
Guidelines and catalogue available at website or with 9x12 SASE ($2 postage). Query. Accepts photocopies, IBM disk submissions, and simultaneous submissions if identified. SASE. Responds in 1 week. Publication in 6 months. Royalty; 10%.

Editor's Comments
Although all authors and publishers hope that their books will be successful, no one can guarantee a best-seller. Your manuscript will be reviewed by our publishing committee and evaluated to determine if it meets our publishing criteria.

Texas Tech University Press

P.O. Box 41037
Lubbock, TX 79409-1037

Editor-in-Chief: Judith Keeling

Publisher's Interests
Scholarly, historical fiction and nonfiction titles relating to the American West are the specialty of this publisher, as well as books on Texas history, Texana, folktales, and the Southwest. Its catalog includes books for young adults and middle-grade readers, as well as for adults.
Website: www.ttup.ttu.edu

Freelance Potential
Published 20 titles (4 juvenile) in 2004: 15 were developed from unsolicited submissions. Of the 20 titles, 7 were by unpublished writers and 16 were by authors who were new to the publishing house. Receives 300 queries yearly.

- **Fiction:** Published 2 middle-grade books, 8-12 years. Genres include historical and contemporary fiction, mystery, and suspense. Also publishes poetry and stories about the environment.
- **Nonfiction:** Published 2 middle-grade books, 8-12 years. Topics include the natural sciences, history, natural history, and the American West. Also publishes biographies and memoirs.
- **Representative Titles:** *Seeing the Elephant: Voices from the Oregon Trail* by Joyce Badgley Hunsaker (8-12 years) is a work of historical interpretation that tells the stories of those who traveled West in search of a better life. *The Long Way West* by Hershell H. Nixon (YA) is a coming-of-age tale about a young man who grapples with his dreams of conquering the American West.

Submissions and Payment
Guidelines available at website. Query with clips. Accepts photocopies. SASE. Responds in 1-2 months. Publication in 1 year. Royalty; 10%.

Editor's Comments
Our young adult list needs more titles on American history as it relates to the West. Historical fiction, biographies, and regional novels with national appeal are of special interest.

Third World Press

P.O. Box 19730
7822 South Dobson
Chicago, IL 60619

Editorial Director: Gwendolyn Mitchell

Publisher's Interests
For 35 years, Third World Press has published African American literature for children and adults that inspires and educates readers about the African American community.
Website: www.thirdworldpress.com

Freelance Potential
Published 20 titles in 2004. Of the 20 titles, several were by authors who were new to the publishing house. Receives 200 queries, 400 unsolicited mss yearly.

- **Fiction:** Publishes concept, toddler, and early picture books, 0–4 years; easy-to-read books, 4–7 years; story picture books, 4–10 years; chapter books, 5–10 years; middle-grade books, 8–12 years; and young adult books, 12–18 years. Features stories and novels about African, African American, and Caribbean life.
- **Nonfiction:** Publishes easy-to-read books, 4–7 years; story picture books, 4–10 years; chapter books, 5–10 years; middle-grade books, 8–12 years; and young adult books, 12–18 years. Topics include history, culture, and ethnic and multicultural issues.
- **Representative Titles:** *The Sweetest Berry on the Bush* by Nubia Kai (YA) features 19 pithy short stories for young teenagers. *Maud Martha* by Gwendolyn Brooks is a provocative novel about a spirited and idealistic black woman.

Submissions and Payment
Guidelines available. Prefers query with synopsis. Accepts complete ms in July only. Accepts photocopies, computer printouts, and simultaneous submissions if identified. SASE. Response time varies. Publication in 1 year. Royalty.

Editor's Comments
We are one of the nation's oldest independent publishers of African American literature. As such, we are committed to publishing books that foster African American economic and cultural awareness. Children's titles are especially needed at this time.

Charles C. Thomas Publisher Ltd.

2600 South First Street
Springfield, IL 62704

Editor: Michael P. Thomas

Publisher's Interests

In business since 1927, this publishing house has been a leading provider of titles in the biological and social sciences. It has always sought to address current needs for information. Recently, it has added titles on the behavioral sciences—education, special education, and rehabilitation—to its publishing program.
Website: www.ccthomas.com

Freelance Potential

Published 800+ titles in 2004: 600 were developed from unsolicited submissions. Receives 600 queries and unsolicited mss each year.

- **Nonfiction:** Publishes titles for educators, pre-K–grade 12. Topics include early childhood, elementary, secondary, and higher education; reading research and statistics; physical education and sports; special education; the learning disabled; teaching the blind and visually impaired; gifted and talented education; and speech and language pathology. Also offers parenting titles.
- **Representative Titles:** *Read This Book Before Your Child Starts School* by Miriam W. Lukken (parents) explains how parents can prepare their children for successful school experiences. *Making Our Schools More Effective* by Martin Patchen (teachers, parents) distills years of research into a comprehensive guide to the conditions that make schools more effective places of learning.

Submissions and Payment

Guidelines and catalogue available at website. Query or send complete ms. Accepts disk submissions. SASE. Responds in 1 week. Publication in 6–8 months. Royalty.

Editor's Comments

We promptly review all manuscripts submitted and welcome questions from potential authors who may need advice on presenting their material. Answers to general questions concerning the specifics of manuscript preparation may be found at our website.

Thompson Educational Publishing

Suite 200
6 Ripley Avenue
Toronto, Ontario M6S 3N9
Canada

Submissions Editor: Keith Thompson

Publisher's Interests
This publisher provides the Canadian and international market with undergraduate textbooks for use at colleges and universities, and supplementary texts for the social sciences and humanities. In addition, it offers author monographs.
Website: www.thompsonbooks.com

Freelance Potential
Published 7 titles in 2004: 1 was developed from an unsolicited submission. Of the 7 titles, 1 was by an unpublished writer. Receives 20 queries yearly.

- **Nonfiction:** Publishes undergraduate textbooks and single-author monographs for use in undergraduate education. Topics include social studies, sociology, social work, economics, communications, native studies, labor studies, and sports.
- **Representative Titles:** *Social Work in Canada* by Steven Hick provides an introduction to the key concepts and contemporary issues in social work in Canada. *Media and Minorities: Representing Diversity in a Multicultural Canada* by Augie Fleras & Jean Lock Kunz examines the representational basis of media-minority relations in Canada. In doing so, it hopes to advance the cause of Canada that is inclusive, equitable, workable, and fair.

Submissions and Payment
Guidelines available. Query with curriculum vitae and market analysis. Email submissions to publisher@thompsonbooks.com. SAE/IRC. Response time, publication period, and payment policy vary.

Editor's Comments
When submitting a query, make sure you address points such as: the subject and audience for which your book is intended, what makes your approach to the subject unique, the content of the course, what kind of student your text would be intended for, and the pedagogical devices you want to use in the text.

Tilbury House Publishers

2 Mechanic Street
Gardiner, ME 04345

Publisher: Jennifer Bunting

Publisher's Interests
Imaginative books that spark childrens' curiosity about the world around them and the people that inhabit it are offered by this publisher. Many of their publications feature user-friendly teacher's guides for classroom use.
Website: www.tilburyhouse.com

Freelance Potential
Published 2 titles in 2004: both were developed from unsolicited submissions; both were by unpublished writers who were new to the publishing house. Receives 450 queries yearly.

- **Fiction:** Published 1 middle-grade book, 8–12 years. Genres include multicultural and ethnic fiction, and stories about nature and the environment. Also publishes story picture books, 7–10 years.
- **Nonfiction:** Published 1 middle-grade book, 8–12 years. Topics include cultural diversity, ethnic issues, nature, the environment, history, and social studies. Also publishes teaching guides to accompany their titles.
- **Representative Titles:** *Say Something* by Peggy Moss (grades 2–6) is an engaging story that encourages children to help make bullying uncool. *The Goat Lady* by Jane Bregoli (grades 3–6) is the true story of an elderly woman who raises goats to help others, despite the pressure of her neighbors.

Submissions and Payment
Guidelines available. Prefers query with outline/synopsis and sample chapters. Accepts complete ms or partial ms with outline. Accepts photocopies and computer printouts. SASE. Responds in 1 month. Publication in 1 year. Royalty; advance, negotiable.

Editor's Comments
We want to see books that sow the seeds of kindness and understanding, and show how children can make a difference. Through our books, we hope young readers will build more respect, tolerance, and compassion into their lives.

Megan Tingley Books

Little, Brown and Company
1271 Avenue of the Americas
New York, NY 10020

Editor-in-Chief: Megan Tingley

Publisher's Interests

This imprint of Little, Brown and Company publishes children's titles in three general categories: picture books, middle-grade books, and young adult books, as well as some books for toddlers.
Website: www.lb-kids.com

Freelance Potential

Published 12 titles in 2004: all were by agented authors. Of the 12 titles, 1 was by an author new to the publishing house. Receives 600+ queries yearly.

- **Fiction:** Publishes toddler books, 0–4 years; story picture books, 4–10 years; middle-grade books, 8–12 years; and young adult books, 12–18 years. Genres include contemporary and multicultural fiction. Also publishes stories about holidays and music.
- **Nonfiction:** Publishes toddler books, 0–4 years; story picture books, 4–10 years; middle-grade books, 8–12 years; and young adult books, 12–18 years. Topics include multicultural and ethnic issues, crafts, and hobbies.
- **Representative Titles:** *Ruby and the Sniffs* by Michael Emberley (3–6 years) is the adventurous tale of a hip heroine who's not afraid to rise to a challenge. *House-Mouse Friends* by Ellen Jareckie (birth–3 years) is a rhyming story about five mischievous mice who befriend a slew of lovable animals.

Submissions and Payment

Accepts submissions by literary agents or those sent at the request of the editors only. No unsolicited mss or queries. Accepts photocopies. SASE. Responds in 2 months. Publication period varies. Royalty; advance.

Editor's Comments

This year, we are looking for fresh, new material in all formats, with a special interest in narrative and nonfiction humor, music, multicultural issues, the supernatural, and poetry. We continue to focus or editorial efforts on titles suitable for middle-grade and young adult readers.

Torah Aura Productions

4423 Fruitland Avenue
Los Angeles, CA 90058

Submissions Editor: Jane Golub

Publisher's Interests
This educational publisher features materials used for Jewish Sunday and after school programs. The books on its list include both fiction and nonfiction titles that are marketed by catalogue exclusively to educators. All of its books are either classroom texts or teacher education materials.
Website: www.torahaura.com

Freelance Potential
Published 10 titles in 2004. Receives 60 queries each year.

- **Fiction:** Publishes chapter books, 5–10 years; middle-grade novels, 8–12 years; and young adult books, 12–18 years. Genres include religious and inspirational fiction with Jewish themes.
- **Nonfiction:** Publishes story picture books, 4–10 years; chapter books, 5–10 years; middle-grade books, 8–12 years; and young adult books, 12–18 years. Topics include religion, history, current events, and family issues—all as they relate to Judaism. Also publishes books on Jewish law, prayer, and the Bible.
- **Representative Titles:** *Gabriel's Ark* by Sandra R. Curtis is the story of a family that helps a boy with special needs through his bar mitzvah experience. *The Passover Passage* by Susan Atlas (8–11 years) follows a young girl on a sailing trip where she learns about Passover on a ship, but also important lessons of freedom and family.

Submissions and Payment
Guidelines available. Query. No unsolicited mss. Accepts photocopies. SASE. Responds in 6 months. Publication in 18 months. Royalty, 10%.

Editor's Comments
Please note that for the time being, we will only be looking at queries rather than unsolicited manuscripts. Given that, we continue to look for unique books that will enlighten young readers about some aspect of Jewish faith or life, but at the same time keep them entertained.

Tor Books

175 Fifth Avenue
New York, NY 10010

Senior Editor, Children/Young Adults: Susan Chang

Publisher's Interests
This publishing house specializes in fantasy and science fiction for all ages. Its imprints Starscape and Tor Teen target young readers. In addition, it offers a nonfiction line that includes titles on crafts and science subjects.
Website: www.tor.com

Freelance Potential
Published 25 titles in 2003: 3 were developed from unsolicited submissions, 22 were by agented authors, and 10 were reprint/licensed properties. Of the 25 titles, 2 were by unpublished writers and 3 were by authors who were new to the publishing house. Receives 400 queries yearly.

- **Fiction:** Published 18 middle-grade books, 8–12 years; and 7 young adult books, 12–18 years. Genres include fantasy and science fiction.
- **Nonfiction:** Published 2 middle-grade books, 8–12 years; and 1 young adult book, 12–18 years. Features general interest and how-to titles, as well as books about science and crafts.
- **Representative Titles:** *Ender's Game* by Orson Scott Card (YA) is the first of a series of titles following two children on their adventures in a fantasy world. *Sister Light, Sister Dark* by Jane Yolen (YA) draws on folklore in telling a coming-of-age story about a young girl.

Submissions and Payment
Guidelines available at website. Query with synopsis and first 3 chapters Accepts photocopies and computer printouts. No electronic or simultaneous submissions. SASE. Responds in 4–6 months. Publication in 18–24 months. Royalty; advance.

Editor's Comments
Our main focus continues to be science fiction and fantasy for middle-grade and young adult readers. We'd also like to see more crossover novels with elements of romance, horror, mystery, suspense, history, or religion. Also welcome are general nonfiction submissions, especially narrative nonfiction.

Toy Box Productions

7532 Hickory Hills Court
Whites Creek, TN 37189

Submissions Editor

Publisher's Interests
Toy Box Productions is committed to the creation of quality read-along and audio interactive story books for children from age four through twelve. Its popular series include the Time Traveler Adventures series and its Bible stories for kids.
Website: www.crttoybox.com

Freelance Potential
Published 6 titles in 2004: all were assigned. Of the 6 titles, 1 was by an unpublished writer.

- **Fiction:** Publishes story picture books, 4–10 years; chapter books, 5–10 years; and middle-grade books, 8–12 years. Genres include Western, historical, and religious fiction.
- **Nonfiction:** Publishes story picture books, 4–10 years; and chapter books, 5–10 years. Topics include history and religion.
- **Representative Titles:** *Meet the Wright Brothers* follows Farley's Raiders as they travel back in time to visit the Wright Brothers and watch as the inventors experiment with flight. *George Washington Carver and the Great Peanut Adventure* finds the Raiders traveling back in time to meet one of the country's greatest educators and inventors to watch him solve the mystery of the peanut.

Submissions and Payment
Query with résumé and clips. All work is done on assignment. SASE. Accepts photocopies. Response time, publication period, and payment policy vary.

Editor's Comments
We are a niche publisher with very special needs. Our books are designed to help strengthen children's reading skills as they read along with our audiotapes. Authors with a firm grasp of the kind of material that works best for us and the ability to tell a story with an interesting plot and strong characters are always of interest. Take the time to review some of our recent titles and to visit our website before sending us your clips and résumé.

Tricycle Press

P.O. Box 7123
Berkeley, CA 94707

Project Editor: Abigail Samoun

Publisher's Interests
This small publisher features fiction and nonfiction titles for preschool through middle grade children. Its catalogue includes board books, picture books, novelty books, real life books, and literary novels.
Website: www.tenspeed.com

Freelance Potential
Published 22 titles in 2004: 7 were developed from unsolicited submissions and 1 was by an agented author. Of the 22 titles, 6 were by unpublished writers and 8 were by authors who were new to the publishing house. Receives 20,000 unsolicited mss yearly.

- **Fiction:** Published 5 concept books, and 5 toddler books, 0–4 years; 10 story picture books, 4–10 years; and 5 middle grade books, 8–12 years. Features books on nature, tolerance, and contemporary issues.
- **Nonfiction:** Published 1 story picture book, 4–10 years. Also publishes middle grade titles, 8–12 years. Topics include real life issues, mathematics, gardening, and cooking.
- **Representative Titles:** *Albie's Trip to the Jumble Jungle* by Robert Skutch (4–7 years) is the story of a boy who visits a wondrous land full of new kinds of animals. *Alice Yazzie's Year* by Ramona Maher (8+ years) is a story about the adventures of a young Navajo girl.

Submissions and Payment
Guidelines and catalogue available with 9x12 SASE ($1.02 postage). Send complete ms for picture books. Send 2–3 sample chapters for chapter books and longer nonfiction. Does not accept queries. Accepts photocopies, computer printouts, and simultaneous submissions if identified. SASE. Responds in 2–6 months. Publication period varies. Royalty; advance.

Editor's Comments
If you feel your idea is right for our company, send it to us and we will give it the attention it deserves. Remember that ultimately, your manuscript must speak for itself and demonstrate why it is special.

Tyndale House Publishers

351 Executive Drive
Carol Stream, IL 60188

Manuscript Review Committee

Publisher's Interests
The mission of this publisher is to "minister to the spiritual needs of people, primarily through literature consistent with biblical principles." Its Tyndale Kids imprint offers faith-building books, Bibles, and devotionals for toddlers through teens.
Website: www.tyndale.com

Freelance Potential
Published 300 titles (45 juvenile) in 2004: 1 was developed from an unsolicited submission and 44 were by agented authors. Receives 500 queries yearly.

- **Fiction:** Publishes middle-grade novels, 8–12 years; and young adult books, 12–18 years. Features fiction on general interest topics written from a Christian perspective.
- **Nonfiction:** Publishes concept and toddler books, 0–4 years; easy-to-read titles, 4–7 years; story picture books, 4–10 years; middle grade books, 8–12 years; and young adult books, 12–18 years. Features books about Christian faith. Also publishes parenting titles.
- **Representative Titles:** *Canyon Quest* by Jim Ware (10–14 years) is a mystery set in the Arizona desert; part of the Last Chance Detectives series. *The Growing Reader Book of Prayers* by Joy MacKenzie (4–8 years) teaches kids about different types of prayer, such as thanksgiving, praise, and petition.

Submissions and Payment
Guidelines available. Accepts work from agented authors, Tyndale authors, and authors introduced through other publishers only. Accepts email submissions to manuscripts@tyndale.com. SASE. Responds in 3 months. Publication period varies. Royalty; advance. Flat fee.

Editor's Comments
For the year ahead, we are most interested in seeing devotionals aimed at eight- to twelve-year-old children, as well as those written for young adults ages fifteen to nineteen.

Resources for All
Matt Mulder
Upstart Books, Highsmith Press

Upstart Books is an imprint of Highsmith Press and accepts unsolicited proposals and manuscripts and welcomes inquiries. According to Matt Mulder, Director of Publications, editors at Upstart develop some titles in-house and assign them to freelancers they've worked with before or to librarians or educators.

The company's primary interest is in resources that help media specialists, librarians, and teachers develop and stimulate reading interests, and facilitate library and information-seeking skills among youth (preschool through high school).

Mulder points to their website as the best source of information about current needs. He cautions that "writers should *not* submit children's or YA fiction." Upstart does look for "proposals or manuscripts for (1) creative reading activity books that can be used by children's and school librarians and teachers to stimulate reading among youth; (2) basic guides for teachers and librarians that offer instructional activities, lesson plans, and resources that develop library, information-seeking, and computer skills among youth; (3) guides to library-related resources on the Internet for youth: and (4) storytelling resources for children's librarians, teachers, and professional storytellers that feature interesting and easy-to-learn stories and storytelling techniques."

Upstart Books

P.O. Box 800
Fort Atkinson, WI 53538-0800

Publications Director: Matt Mulder

Publisher's Interests
Resources for teachers, librarians, and media specialists who work with children are the mainstay of this educational publisher. Its list also features books for children that reinforce library skills.
Website: www.highsmith.com

Freelance Potential
Published 15 titles in 2004: 15 were developed from unsolicited submissions. Of the 15 titles, 5 were by unpublished writers and 5 were by authors who were new to the publishing house. Receives 150 queries, 150 unsolicited mss yearly.

- **Nonfiction:** Publishes elementary and middle-grade books, 6–12 years. Also publishes educational resource materials for teachers and librarians, pre-K–grade 12. Topics include library skills, storytime, reading activities, and literature.
- **Representative Titles:** *Battle of the Books and More* by Sybilla Coot et al. (grades 5–8) is a guide for librarians for planning and implementing reading competitions that motivate children to read. *What Happened to Marion's Book?* by Brook Berg (pre-K–grade 2) teaches the proper way to care for books by telling about a hedgehog and her messy library book.

Submissions and Payment
Prefers query with outline or sample chapters for manuscripts for longer than 100 pages. Prefers complete ms for shorter works. Accepts photocopies and computer printouts. SASE. Responds in 2 months. Publication period varies. Royalty, 10–12%; advance.

Editor's Comments
We are currently looking for instructional activities, lesson plans, and resources that develop library, information technology, and computer skills for school-age children. We want to help librarians and teachers stimulate reading in their students. We are looking for story books that introduce research concepts, as well as guides to library-related resources on the Internet for middle-grade and high school students.

URJ Press

633 Third Avenue
New York, NY 10017

Editorial Director: Rabbi Haraerson

Publisher's Interests
Formerly known as UAHC Press, this publisher features high-quality Jewish educational materials for use in the home and school classroom. Its catalogue offers fiction and nonfiction books for preschool through adult readers.
Website: www.urjpress.com

Freelance Potential
Published 25 titles in 2004: some were developed from unsolicited submissions. Of the 25 titles, 5 were by authors who were new to the publishing house. Receives 200 queries, 600 mss yearly.

- **Fiction:** Publishes early picture books, 0–4 years; and story picture books, 4–10 years. Features stories based on Judaism and the Bible, and religious and historical fiction.
- **Nonfiction:** Publishes toddler and early picture books, 0–4 years; chapter books, 5–10 years; and young adult books, 12–18 years. Topics include Jewish history, holidays, the Holocaust, and Hebrew studies.
- **Representative Titles:** *CHAI: Early Childhood Parent Education* by the URJ Department of Lifelong Jewish Learning (families) helps parents address their questions on how to create a Jewish hone environment that will lead to a lifetime of meaningful affiliation.
A Candle for Grandpa by Joel Iskowitz is an is illustrated story that sensitively explains the Jewish views on death and funeral practices.

Submissions and Payment
Guidelines available. Query with résumé, outline and 2 sample chapters. Send complete ms for picture books. Accepts photocopies, computer printouts, and email submissions (queries only) to editor@urjpress.com. SASE. Response time and publication period vary. Royalty; advance.

Editor's Comments
At this time we will review materials for any age group that feature an educational approach to topics related to the Jewish faith and traditions.

UXL

27500 Drake Road
Farmington Hills, MI 48331-3535

Editorial Coordinator: Carol Nagel

Publisher's Interests
Specializing in reference materials, this imprint of Gale Group serves the informational needs of students and the general public in libraries, schools, and on the Internet. UXL offers books and CD-ROMs on a variety of educational topics.
Website: www.gale.com

Freelance Potential
Published 15 titles in 2004.

- **Nonfiction:** Publishes young adult books, 12–18 years. Topics include science, medicine, history, social studies, current events, multicultural issues, the arts, sports, and careers. Also publishes curriculum-based reference titles and encyclopedias.
- **Representative Titles:** *African Biography* (YA) is a three-volume set of more than 200 profiles of noteworthy current and historical African American writers, artists, and political leaders. *Arab American Biography* (YA) examines the contributions Arab Americans have made to the American community; includes biographical sketches of early pioneers and current personalities.

Submissions and Payment
Catalogue available at website. Query with résumé and writing samples. Accepts photocopies and computer printouts. No simultaneous submissions. SASE. Response time varies. Publication period varies. Flat fee.

Editor's Comments
We publish a comprehensive line of reference titles that make learning fun and help students get right to the point. We are known for the accuracy, breadth, and convenience of our information, which is available in several formats. Our editors are looking for submissions for reference products aimed at the school, public, or academic library markets. See our website for query procedures. Most commonly rejected ideas include submissions for non-reference products, or material that is highly specialized or technical.

J. Weston Walch, Publisher

321 Valley Street
Portland, ME 04104-0658

Editor-in-Chief: Susan Blair

Publisher's Interests
This company is known for its supplementary teaching aids for grades six through adult. It produces innovative titles, activity books, and workbooks that encourage learning at all levels.
Website: www.walch.com

Freelance Potential
Published 130+ titles (20 juvenile) in 2004: 13 were developed from unsolicited submissions. Of the 130 titles, 33 were by unpublished writers and 33 were by authors who were new to the publishing house. Receives 200 queries yearly.

- **Nonfiction:** Published 20 middle-grade books, 8–12 years. Also publishes young adult books, 12–18 years. Topics include reading, writing, vocabulary, grammar, geometry, algebra, critical thinking, world history, social science, chemistry, physics, money management, careers, and special education. Also offers resource materials for teachers and guidance counselors.
- **Representative Titles:** *Daily Warm-Ups Mythology* (grade 5) explores the legends and lore of Greek, Roman, and Norse gods, heroes, and monsters. *25 Low Cost Biology Investigations* by Joel Beller (grades 8–10) stimulates scientific inquiry with 25 high-interest, classroom-proven labs.

Submissions and Payment
Guidelines available. Query with résumé, outline, table of contents, and sample chapter. Accepts photocopies and simultaneous submissions if identified. SASE. Responds in 2–4 months. Publication period varies. Royalty. Flat fee.

Editor's Comments
As we continue to improve our product line, we are looking for standards-based materials teachers can use in their classrooms. English, math, and social studies remain a priority for our middle-grade and high school list, as well as practical, economical, and easy-to-use resource materials for guidance counselors.

Walker & Company

104 Fifth Avenue
New York, NY 10011

Submissions Editor

Publisher's Interests
Established in 1961, this house offers a small and select list of children's books. It currently publishes two lists a year, each with approximately ten picture books and two or three middle-grade or young adult titles.
Website: www.walkeryoungreaders.com

Freelance Potential
Published 38 titles in 2004: 4 were developed from unsolicited submissions, 14 were by agented authors, and 2 were reprint/licensed properties. Of the 38 titles, 3 were by unpublished writers and 9 were by authors who were new to the publishing house. Receives 6,000–8,000 queries and unsolicited mss yearly.

- **Fiction:** Published 2 toddler books and 2 early picture books, 0–4 years; 5 easy-to-read books, 4–7 years; 12 story picture books, 4–10 years; 8 middle-grade books, 8–12 years; and 2 young adult books, 12–18 years. Genres include historical and contemporary fiction.
- **Nonfiction:** Published 7 story picture books, 4–10 years. Topics include nature, history, biography, and social issues.
- **Representative Titles:** *Mama Love* by Kathy Mallat (2–6 years) addresses the issues of courage and friendship in this story of a young chimp and his mother. *Big Friends* by Margery Cuyler (4–8 years) is set in Eastern Africa and demonstrates that laughter can be a very good beginning for friendship.

Submissions and Payment
Guidelines available. Query with outline and 3–5 sample chapters. Send complete ms for picture books. Accepts photocopies, computer printouts, and simultaneous submissions. SASE. Responds in 3–4 months. Publication in 18–24 months. Royalty; advance.

Editor's Comments
We are dedicated to publishing new talent, but the competition here is rigorous. Our strongest need continues to be quality fiction for middle-grade and young adult readers.

Warner Press

P.O. Box 2499
1200 East Fifth Street
Anderson, IN 46018-9988

Senior Editor: Karen Rhodes

Publisher's Interests
Warner Press has been the publishing house for the Church of God for over one hundred years. Its mission is to continue to develop and produce materials for the Christian market. Its children's list offers Bible-based, activity books for ages 6 to 16.
Website: www.warnerpress.com

Freelance Potential
Published 5 titles (4 juvenile) in 2004: all were developed from unsolicited submissions. Of the 5 titles, 2 were by authors who were new to the publishing house. Receives 50 queries yearly.

- **Fiction:** Published 1 easy-to-read book, 4–7 years; and 1 story picture book, 4–10 years. Features religious fiction.
- **Nonfiction:** Published 1 easy-to-read book, 4–7 years; and 1 story picture book, 4–10 years.
- **Representative Titles:** *Missing Maggie* by Connie S. Owens is a story of one little boy's heartfelt loss; part of the Tender Topics series. *What Would Jesus Do?* (10+ years) offers 32 pages of puzzles, mazes, and activities based on the teachings of Jesus.

Submissions and Payment
Guidelines available. Query. Accepts photocopies. SASE. Responds in 3–6 months. Publication in 12–18 months. Flat fee.

Editor's Comments
We appreciate your interest in our publishing program, but before you send a submission, ask yourself the following questions: Do I have a personal knowledge of and involvement with the Scriptures? Have I received an honest appraisal of my work from a qualified writer? Have I prayed about submitting my material to Warner Press? If your answers to all three questions are yes, you are ready to submit your work and we will look forward to seeing it. In addition, please review some of our current children's titles. You will see that all our books are either 16 or 32 pages, mostly activity based, and rooted in the Bible's teachings.

WaterBrook Press

Suite 160
2375 Telstar Drive
Colorado Springs, CO 80920

Senior Editor: Ron Lee

Publisher's Interests
Books for Christian living and spiritual growth, fiction for adults and young adults, Bible study resources, and engaging children's books are produced by this division of Random House, Inc.
Website: www.waterbrookpress.com

Freelance Potential
Published 94 titles (2 juvenile) in 2004: 1 was developed from an unsolicited submission and 55 were by agented authors. Of the 94 titles, 3 were by unpublished writers and 3 were by authors who were new to the publishing house. Receives 1,000+ queries yearly.

- **Fiction:** Publishes easy-to-read books, 4–7 years; story picture books, 4–10 years; and middle-grade books, 8–12 years. Genres include inspirational and religious fiction.
- **Nonfiction:** Publishes young adult books, 12–18 years. Topics include Christianity and religion.
- **Representative Titles:** *Generation Ex* by Jen Abbas reports on the lifelong effects on the children caught in the crossfire of divorce. Written by an adult child of divorce, it helps readers understand the issues dealt with by children of divorced parents. *See How They Run* by Lorilee Craker offers a hilarious but practical guide to surviving, enjoying, and laughing your way through the busy and exhausting toddler years.

Submissions and Payment
Catalogue available with 9x12 SASE. Accepts queries submitted through literary agents only. No unsolicited mss. SASE. Responds in 4–6 weeks. Publication in 1 year. Payment policy varies.

Editor's Comments
We provide a wide variety of books that provide encouragement, support, and challenges to Christians' every day lives. Authors who can provide thought-provoking material that will bring readers to a renewed sense of faith and hope are welcome to submit a query, but it must be through a literary agent only.

Watson-Guptill

770 Broadway
New York, NY 10003

Senior Acquisitions Editor: Julie Mazur

Publisher's Interests
Watson-Guptill publishes high-quality nonfiction for early readers through adults. Its imprints include Billboard Books, Amphoto Books, Backstage Books, and Art Encounters.
Website: www.wgpub.com

Freelance Potential
Published 100 titles (15 juvenile) in 2005.

- **Fiction:** Publishes young adult books, 12–18 years. Topics include historical fiction.
- **Nonfiction:** Publishes story picture books, 4–10, easy-to-read books, 4–7 years; middle-grade books, 8–12 years; and young adult books, 12–18 years. Topics include crafts, fine art, and pop culture.
- **Representative Titles:** *Kids Draw Animals* by Christopher Hart (6–12 years) teaches children to draw many different animals. *His Song* by Elizabeth R. Rosenthal (YA–Adult) chronicals the musical journey of Elton John. *The Best of Sewing Machine Fun for Kids* by Lynda Milligan and Nancy Smith offers an introduction to sewing for children.

Submissions and Payment
Guidelines and catalogue available at website. Query with table of contents and sample chapters for nonfiction and YA fiction. Send complete ms for picture books. All submissions must include a brief author bio and description of marketing considerations. Accepts photocopies and computer printouts. SASE. Response time and publication period vary. Royalty; advance.

Editor's Comments
We are launching our Art Encounters series in the fall of 2004, and are actively seeking submissions. It is a historical fiction series based on the lives of famous artists. We are also looking for nonfiction books that have broad market appeal. Books for children should be well-researched and age-appropriate. Books for teens should be fun, lively, and involving.

Wayne State University Press

The Leonard N. Simons Building
4809 Woodward Avenue
Detroit, MI 48201-1309

Acquisitions Assistant: Annie Martin

Publisher's Interests
Focusing on scholarly publications about the Great Lakes region of Michigan, Wayne State University Press offers educational books that reflect the diversity of its audience.
Website: http://wsupress.wayne.edu/

Freelance Potential
Published 40 titles (3–5 juvenile) in 2004. Of the 40 titles, all were by unpublished writers and 20 were by authors who were new to the publishing house. Receives 180 queries yearly.

- **Nonfiction:** Publishes middle-grade books, 8–12 years. Topics include the art, architecture, and culture of Michigan; the history of the Upper Peninsula and the Great Lakes region; and historical Detroit personalities. Also publishes titles on Africana, art and culture, film and television, Judaica, labor, literature, automotive history, and speech pathology.
- **Representative Titles:** *The Outdoor Museum* by Marcy Heller Fisher (8+ years) explores the magic of Michigan's Marshall M. Fredericks museum through the eyes of two young friends. *Albert Kahn* by Roger Matuz (10+ years) is a biography of Detroit's famous architect at the dawn of the automobile age.

Submissions and Payment
Guidelines available. Query with résumé, clips, table of contents, and chapter-by-chapter outline. Accepts photocopies, computer printouts, and email to annie.martin@wayne.edu. SASE. Responds in 2–3 weeks. Publication in 15 months. Royalty, 7.5–10%.

Editor's Comments
Although our books are published for scholars, libraries, and the general public, we do have a small list of children's titles. We are seeking material for our Detroit Biography Series for Young Readers, which features biographies of men and women who contributed to the development of the city of Detroit and its surrounding area—local heroes from diverse backgrounds and all walks of life.

Weigl Educational Publishers Limited

6325 10th Street SE
Calgary, Alberta T2H 2Z9
Canada

Managing Editor: Lee Shenkman

Publisher's Interests

Curriculum-based titles for both Canadian and American students are found in this Canadian publisher's catalogue. It only publishes nonfiction and covers the subject areas of social studies, global issues, nature, and science. The books are designed for readers age five to young adult. Most of its titles are published as series.
Website: www.weigl.com

Freelance Potential

Published 112 titles in 2004: 3 were developed from unsolicited submissions and 51 were reprint/licensed properties. Of the 112 titles, 4 were by authors who were new to the publishing house.

- **Nonfiction:** Published 92 chapter books, 5–10 years; 16 middle-grade books, 8–12 years; and 4 young adult books, 12–18 years. Topics include social studies, history, science, nature, art, career guidance, and multicultural and ethnic issues.
- **Representative Titles:** *Memorial Day* (grades 1–3) explores some of the history and traditions of this holiday: part of the American Holidays series. *The Grand Canyon* (grades 4–6) traces the geography and history behind this natural wonder: part of the Natural Wonders series.

Submissions and Payment

Send résumé only. No queries or unsolicited mss. Accepts photocopies, computer printouts, and email to kara@weigl.com. SAE/IRC. Responds in 6 months. Publication in 2 years. Work-for-hire; fee paid on acceptance.

Editor's Comments

We are interested in writers who can tackle such topics as science, career guidance, life skills, and social studies. Books should be chapter books for readers age five to ten; middle-grade titles for ages eight to twelve; and young adult nonfiction. Please remember to send your résumé first.

Whitecap Books Ltd.

352 Lynn Avenue
North Vancouver, British Columbia V7J 2C4
Canada

Editor: Annmarie MacKinnon

Publisher's Interests
Whitecap Books publishes nonfiction titles on North American natural history, regional topics, and Canadian history for young and middle-grade readers, as well as fiction books that focus on nature, wildlife, and animals.
Website: www.whitecap.ca

Freelance Potential
Published 65 titles (10-15 juvenile) in 2004: 6 were developed from unsolicited submissions, 4 were by agented authors, and 17 were reprint/licensed properties. Of the 65 titles, 8 were by unpublished writers and 17 were by authors who were new to the publishing house. Receives 1,000 queries yearly.

- **Fiction:** Publishes story picture books, 4-10 years; chapter books, 5-10 years; and young adult titles, 12-16 years. Genres include contemporary fiction, adventure, and fantasy. Also publishes sports stories.
- **Nonfiction:** Publishes easy-to-read books, 4-7 years. Topics include Canadian history, natural history, the environment, science, and regional subjects.
- **Representative Titles:** *Digging Canadian Dinosaurs* by Rebecca L. Grambo (7-11 years) investigates the diverse species of dinosaurs that roamed prehistoric Canada. *Peak Survival* by Pam Withers (12-16 years) is a novel about four teens who find themselves stranded after an avalanche and must use their wits to survive.

Submissions and Payment
Guidelines available. Query with outline/synopsis, table of contents, and sample chapters. Accepts photocopies, computer printouts, and simultaneous submissions if identified. SAE/IRC. Responds in 2-3 months. Publication in 1 year. Royalty, negotiable; advance.

Editor's Comments
Our juvenile list is comprised of titles on a variety of natural subjects for children between the ages of four and sixteen. We still need material for quality picture books.

White Mane Publishing Company

P.O. Box 708
63 West Burd Street
Shippensburg, PA 17257

Acquisitions Department

Publisher's Interests
Historical fiction for middle-grade and young adult readers is the specialty of White Mane Kids, an imprint of White Mane Publishing. Stand-alone and series books feature accurate historical information in an engaging format. 10% self-, subsidy-, or co-op published material.

Freelance Potential
Published 14 titles in 2004: all were developed from unsolicited submissions. Receives 360 queries yearly.

- **Fiction:** Publishes middle-grade books, 8–12 years; and young adult books, 12–18 years. Genres include historical fiction.
- **Nonfiction:** Publishes young adult books, 12–18 years. Topics include history, the Civil War, the Salem witchcraft trials, the American frontier, slavery, and Pearl Harbor.
- **Representative Titles:** *The Irish Dresser* by Cynthia G. Neale (YA) is the saga of a teenage girl who dreams of satiating her hunger as her family struggles to survive the Irish Famine. *The Ghost Comes Out* by Shelley Sykes & Lois Szymanski (8–12 years) follows three boys who plant a garden, and dig up more than they bargained for; part of the Gettysburg Ghost Gang series.

Submissions and Payment
Guidelines available. Query. Accepts photocopies. SASE. Responds in 2–3 months. Publication in 12–18 months. Royalty.

Editor's Comments
We pride ourselves in providing children's titles that are both entertaining and educational, and we strive to give children a thirst for knowledge through the love of reading. We've been told our Young American series seems so realistic that readers get lost in the stories. Although most of our books relate to the American Civil War, we are also interested in other historical periods. Writers who can take a specific part of American history and bring it to life for our young readers are invited to send us a query.

Albert Whitman & Company

6340 Oakton Street
Morton Grove, IL 60053-2723

Editor-in-Chief: Kathleen Tucker

Publisher's Interests

Well known for its high-quality books, Albert Whitman & Company features titles for readers up to the age of 12. Its list includes fiction and nonfiction titles with books on serious topics such as dyslexia, as well as heart-warming, comedic tales of family and friendship.
Website: www.albertwhitman.com

Freelance Potential

Published 30 titles in 2004: 5 were by agented authors and 2 were by unpublished writers. Of the 30 titles, 2 were by unpublished writers and 8 were by new authors. Receives 300 queries, 4,500 mss each year.

- **Fiction:** Publishes early picture books, 0–4 years; chapter books, 5–10 years; and middle-grade books, 8–12 years. Genres include historical fiction, mystery, and humor.
- **Nonfiction:** Publishes early picture books, 0–4 years. Topics include family, ethnic and multicultural issues, and social issues.
- **Representative Titles:** *Armadilly Chili* by Helen Ketteman (5–8 years) is an adaptation of a classic folktale in which an armadillo named Billie gets all her friends together to make a pot of chili. *Doing Time Online* by Jan Siebold (9–12 years) follows young Michael who must chat online with a nursing home resident as punishment for a prank that injured an elderly woman.

Submissions and Payment

Guidelines available. Send complete ms for picture books. Send query and 3 sample chapters for novels and nonfiction. Indicate if package is query or ms. Accepts simultaneous submissions if identified. SASE. Responds to queries in 6 weeks, to mss in 3–4 months. Publication in 18–24 months. Royalty; advance.

Editor's Comments

Take a look at our catalogue and you will see that we publish a diverse list of books. Picture books, novels, and chapter books, as well as nonfiction are all of interest to us at this time.

Wiley Children's Books

John Wiley
111 River Street
Hoboken, NJ 07030

Editor: Kate Bradford

Publisher's Interests
Founded in 1807, Wiley has always been known for its books on scientific subjects. Today it continues to be known as a leading nonfiction publisher. Its children's list offers nonfiction titles for middle-grade and young adult students. Some of the topics covered are history, mathematics, science, environmental studies, and nature. Wiley also offers parenting titles and teacher resource materials.
Website: www.wiley.com/children

Freelance Potential
Published 20 titles (19 juvenile) in 2004: 2 were developed from unsolicited submissions and 3 were by agented authors. Receives 300 queries each year.

- **Nonfiction:** Publishes middle-grade books, 8–12 years; and 2 young adult books, 12–18 years. Topics include history, nature, science, arts and crafts, nature, mathematics, multicultural issues, and sports. Also offers biographies, activity books, books on parenting, and educational resources for teachers.
- **Representative Titles:** *Arithmetricks: 50 Easy Ways to Add, Subtract, Multiply, and Divide Without a Calculator* by Edward H. Julius is packed with ways to make math easier, while making it fun. *Teresa Weatherspoon's Basketball for Girls* by Teresa Weatherspoon is full of basketball secrets from this professional player.

Submissions and Payment
Guidelines available. Query with résumé, outline, sample chapter, artwork if applicable, and summary of primary market and competition. Accepts photocopies, computer printouts, and simultaneous submissions if identified. SASE. Responds in 1–3 months. Publication in 18 months. Royalty; advance.

Editor's Comments
We are always interested in new material that will enrich our list of books for students of all ages. Our goal is to publish innovative books that readers will find fun while they learn.

Williamson Publishing

P.O. Box 185
Charlotte, VT 05445

Editorial Director: Susan Williamson

Publisher's Interests
Williams Publishing is now an imprint of Ideals Publications, a division of Guideposts. They are dedicated to providing interactive and how-to books for children age three to fourteen.
Website: www.williamsonbooks.com

Freelance Potential
Published 8 titles in 2004. Of the 8 titles, 3 were by unpublished writers and 3 were by authors who were new to the publishing house. Receives 1,500 queries yearly.

- **Nonfiction:** Published 4 easy-to-read books, 3-7 years; and 4 middle-grade books, 8-14. Topics include math, science, geology, history, natural history, cooking, art, crafts, and multicultural subjects. Also publishes folktales.
- **Representative Titles:** *Math Adventures* by Ann McCallum (7-14 years) introduces some of the world's counting and number systems, and explores global solutions to computation and problem solving. *The Kids' Multicultural Craft Book* by Roberta Gould (8-14 years) features 50 creative ideas from 30 counties that help kids understand the customs and beliefs of other cultures.

Submissions and Payment
Query with outline and sample chapters. Accepts photocopies and computer printouts. SASE. Responds in 3-4 months. Publication in 12-18 months. Royalty; advance. Flat fee.

Editor's Comments
We pride ourselves in offering books that can make a difference in the lives of children. We currently need books in the areas of science, history, nature, and diversity for children ages three to fourteen, as well as insightful biographies for older readers. Send us ideas for books and materials that show kids how to learn by doing, creating, thinking, and expressing themselves.

Windward Publishing

3943 Meadowbrook Road
Minneapolis, MN 55426-4505

President: Alan E. Krysan

Publisher's Interests
Established in 1973, this publisher offers natural history books for adults and children on popular subjects including animals, science, nature, horticulture, agriculture, and recreation.
Website: www.finney-hobar.com

Freelance Potential
Published 10–12 titles (5 juvenile) in 2004. Receives 120+ queries, 90+ unsolicited mss yearly.

- **Nonfiction:** Publishes easy-to-read books, 4–7 years; story picture books, 4–10 years; chapter books, 5–10 years; middle-grade books, 8–12 years; and young adult books, 12–18 years. Topics include nature, shells, fishing, mammals, sharks, birds, and sports.
- **Representative Titles:** *The Magic of Sea Shells* identifies more than 80 shells through a story following three children at the seashore. *My Little Book of River Otters*, by Hope Irvin Marston is a delightful story about a new family of river otters, from the birth of a baby to their adventures in the exciting world around them.

Submissions and Payment
Query with publishing credits, synopsis, table of contents, introduction, and up to 3 chapters; or send complete ms with artwork. Accepts photocopies, computer printouts, and simultaneous submissions if identified. No electronic submissions. Availability of artwork improves chance of acceptance. Accepts 8x10 or 35mm B/W or color prints or transparencies, line art, and drawings, SASE. Responds in 8–10 weeks. Publication in 6–8 months. Royalty, 10% of net.

Editor's Comments
We continue to focus on natural history titles for children ages four to twelve. Our products are marketed to audiences in the southeast United States and the Caribbean, so send us materials suitable for readers in those areas. Books that tie a story in with educational details about a specific topic are welcome.

Wizards of the Coast

P.O. Box 707
Renton, WA 98057-0707

Editor: Nina Hess

Publisher's Interests
Wizards of the Coast is a well-known publisher of contemporary fantasy literature and shared-world fiction series books for young adults and adults. It also offers role-playing guides and games.
Website: www.wizards.com

Freelance Potential
Published 65 titles in 2004 (11 juvenile): 6 were developed from unsolicited submissions and 32 were by agented authors. Of the 65 titles, 16 were by unpublished writers and 19 were by authors who were new to the publishing house. Receives 500 queries yearly.

- **Fiction:** Published 11 middle-grade books, 8–12 years. Genres include adventure; science fiction; and medieval, mystical, heroic, and epic fantasy.
- **Nonfiction:** Publishes role-playing games and guidebooks for young adults and adults.
- **Representative Titles:** *Secret of the Spiritkeeper* by Matt Forbeck (8+ years) follows a group of young companions as they become members of the Order of the Knights of the Silver Dragon. *Temple of the Dragonslayer* by Tim Waggoner (10+ years) launches a new adventure series about friends who band together during the golden age of the Dragonlance world.

Submissions and Payment
Guidelines available. Query with 10-page writing sample. All work is assigned. Accepts photocopies and simultaneous submissions if identified. SASE. Responds in 4 months. Publication in 1 year. Payment policy varies.

Editor's Comments
This year, we would like to expand our listings to include fantasy for younger readers ages 8 to 12. Keep in mind that we do not always have openings for writers in all our book lines every year, and some years there are no openings at all. We are actively seeking new authors, but the competition is fierce.

Woodbine House

6510 Bells Mill Road
Bethesda, MD 20817

Acquisitions Editor: Nancy Gray Paul

Publisher's Interests
This publisher focuses exclusively on children's books relating to a disability. Its list includes children's picture books, as well as fiction and nonfiction chapter books for older children.
Website: www.woodbinehouse.com

Freelance Potential
Published 10–12 titles (2 juvenile) in 2004: 3 were developed from unsolicited submissions and 1 was by an agented author. Of the 10–12 titles, 2 were by unpublished writers and 4 were by new authors. Receives 1,000 queries, 600 unsolicited mss yearly.

- **Fiction:** Publishes early picture books, 0–4 years; story picture books, 4–10 years; chapter books, 5–10 years; middle-grade titles, 8–12 years; and young adult books, 12–18 years. All stories feature children with disabilities.
- **Nonfiction:** Publishes early picture books, 0–4 years; story picture books, 4–10 years. Topics include developmental disabilities such as autism, cerebral palsy, Down Syndrome, and others.
- **Representative Titles:** *Help Your Teenager Beat Depression* by Katharina Manassis and Anne Marie Levac (parents) helps families deal with teen depression by taking an active role in their child's treatment. *Teaching Math to People with Down Syndrome and Other Hands-on Learners* by DeAnna Horstmeier, Ph.D., (educators) is written for both parents and teachers and offers strategies for helping children with number concepts and computation.

Submissions and Payment
Guidelines available. Query with outline, 3 sample chapters, and clips. Accepts complete ms for picture books only. Accepts photocopies, computer printouts, and simultaneous submissions. SASE. Responds in 1–3 months. Publication in 1–2 years. Payment varies.

Editor's Comments
We prefer books that offer a conflict and resolution, rather than "what it's like to have" or "day in the life" type stories.

Workman Publishing Company

708 Broadway
New York, NY 10003-9555

Submissions Editor

Publisher's Interests
Workman Publishing is an independent publishing company that features adult and juvenile books as well as calendars. Its books for children target toddlers through middle-school readers and both fiction and nonfiction can be found on its current list. Parenting titles also make up a big part of its catalogue.
Website: www.workman.com

Freelance Potential
Published 50 titles (10 juvenile) in 2004: most were by agented authors. Of the 50 titles, 3 were by unpublished writers and 6 were by authors who were new to the publishing house. Receives 1,000 queries, 2,000 unsolicited mss yearly.

- **Fiction:** Publishes toddler books, 0–4 years; story picture books, 4–10 years; and board and novelty books. Features humor and books about nature.
- **Nonfiction:** Publishes concept and early picture books, 0–4 years; story picture books, 4–10 years; middle-grade books, 8–12 years; and young adult books, 12–18 years.
- **Representative Titles:** *1,400 Things for Kids to Be Happy About* by Barbara Ann Kipfer (4–7 years) covers important things in a child's world and what makes them so special. *10 Button Book* by William Accorsi (2–4 years) is an interactive counting book.

Submissions and Payment
Writers' guidelines available. Query with clips; or send complete ms with illustrations for fiction. Query with table of contents, outline/synopsis, sample chapters, and clips for nonfiction. Accepts photocopies and computer printouts. SASE. Responds in 6 weeks. Publication period varies. Royalty; advance.

Editor's Comments
If you can deliver strong writing, a unique approach to your subject, and intelligence in its conception and execution, we'd like to hear from you.

World Book

Suite 2000
233 North Michigan Avenue
Chicago, IL 60601

General Managing Editor: Paul Kobasa

Publisher's Interests
Since 1917, World Book has provided broad range of accurate and objective research materials for both children and adults. This publisher features award-winning encyclopedias, reference sources, and multimedia products for school and home.
Website: www.worldbook.com

Freelance Potential
Published 30 titles (15 juvenile) in 2004: 2 were reprint/licensed properties.

- **Nonfiction:** Publishes easy-to-read books, 4–7 years; middle-grade books, 8–12 years; and young adult books, 12–18 years. Topics include geography, history, languages, nature, science, health, social studies, and cultural studies. Also publishes biographies, activity books, reference books, and how-to titles; as well as multimedia educational products.
- **Representative Titles:** *Friends in the Wild* (grades 2–6) takes a look at how animals raise their young, find food and shelter, and defend themselves. *Young Scientist* (grades 3–8) uses environmental and conservation concerns to examine the world and work of the scientist, and introduce the scientific method to students.

Submissions and Payment
Catalogue available with 9x12 SASE. Query with outline or synopsis. No unsolicited mss. Accepts simultaneous submissions if identified. SASE. Responds in 1–2 months. Publication in 18 months. Payment rate and policy vary.

Editor's Comments
Our materials are written and produced to meet the highest quality standards in education. We are committed to improving our products in all formats to meet today's evolving reference and teaching needs. We would like to see print and multimedia materials that helps both educators and students. Take at look at our *Student Discovery Encyclopedia* for an idea of what we do best.

Wright Group/McGraw-Hill

Suite 400
1 Prudential Plaza
130 East Randolph Street
Chicago, IL 60601

Submissions Editor: Christine DeLuca

Publisher's Interests
In addition to fiction and nonfiction titles for students in preschool through grade six, this educational publisher also offers curriculum resources for teachers.
Website: www.wrightgroup.com

Freelance Potential
Published 225 titles in 2004: 30 were developed from unsolicited submissions, 30 were by agented authors, and 16 were reprint/licensed properties. Of the 225 titles, 35 were by authors who were new to the publishing house. Receives 300 queries, 200 unsolicited mss yearly.

- **Fiction:** Publishes easy-to-read books, 4–7 years; story picture books, 4–10 years; chapter books, 5–10 years; and middle-grade books, 8–12 years. Genres include contemporary, ethnic, and multicultural fiction; Westerns; adventure, fantasy, folklore; mystery; and science fiction.
- **Nonfiction:** Publishes easy-to-read books, 4–7 years; story picture books, 4–10 years; chapter books, 5–10 years; and middle-grade books, 8–12 years. Topics include nature, history, animals, crafts, multicultural and ethnic subjects, and biographies. Also publishes literacy and mathematics material for classroom use, as well as professional development titles for educators.
- **Representative Titles:** *Gear Up!* (grades K–2) is a guided reading series to develop phonemic awareness that includes lesson plans and activities. *Woodland Mysteries* (grades 2 and up) is a series of mysteries for delayed readers that strengthen comprehension and literacy.

Submissions and Payment
Accepts queries and unsolicited mss. Publication and payment policies vary.

Editor's Comments
We continue to seek research-based strategies and ideas that make teaching more effective at all grade levels. We are especially interested in guided reading programs.

XC Publishing

16006 19th Avenue Ct E
Tacoma, WA 98445

Editor: Cheryl Dyson

Publisher's Interests
Founded in 2000, XC Publishing is a new royalty-paying e-publisher, with the mission of helping new writers to find publishers for their books. It currently offers fiction for young adult and adult readers in a wide range of genres.
Website: www.xcpublishing.com

Freelance Potential
Published 6 titles in 2004: all were developed from unsolicited submissions. Of the 6 titles, 5 were by unpublished writers and all were by authors who were new to the publishing house. Receives 50 queries yearly.

- **Fiction:** Publishes young adult books, 12–18 years. Genres include fantasy, horror, mystery, suspense, romance, and science fiction. Also publishes adult titles.
- **Representative Titles:** *Rusalka Moon* by Cenizas de Rosas is the story of a young man who leaves his village and his sweetheart in order to fight for his country. *Queen of Diamonds* by Richard L. Graves follows the adventures of a top secret government "consultant" as he faces one of his toughest cases yet.

Submissions and Payment
Guidelines available. Query with clips or writing samples. Accepts photocopies, disk submissions, and email submissions to editor@xcpublishing.com. Availability of artwork improves chance of acceptance. SASE. Responds in 1 week. Publication in 4–6 months. Royalty, 40%.

Editor's Comments
We are currently accepting fiction submissions for the following categories: fantasy, science fiction, romance, mystery, and horror. We are particularly interested in cross-genre novels. New authors are encouraged to submit their manuscripts for consideration. We limit the number of titles we publish each year so that we may give them the attention and the promotion they deserve.

Zephyr Press

814 North Franklin Avenue
Chicago, IL 60610

Acquisitions Editor: Jerome Pohlen

Publisher's Interests
Zephyr Press was created in 1979 with the express purpose of helping students reach their full potential. It offers curriculum-based books in the areas of mathematics, social studies, literacy, and science, as well as teacher resource materials for use in kindergarten through twelfth-grade classrooms.
Website: www.zephyrpress.com

Freelance Potential
Published 10 titles in 2004: 4 were developed from unsolicited submissions and 3 were reprint/licensed properties. Receives 250 queries yearly.

- **Nonfiction:** Publishes educational titles for use in grades K–12. Topics include gifted education, multiple intelligences, brain-based learning, thinking skills, science, technology, history, mathematics, social studies, literacy, and character education.
- **Representative Titles:** *Building Moral Intelligence* by Michele Borba, (teachers) covers the seven essential virtues that teach kids to do the right thing. *Rachel Rude Rowdy* by Ginny Kalish (grades 2–6) is a novel with discussion questions and activities that serve as a basis for a character-education program.

Submissions and Payment
Guidelines and submissions packet available. Send completed submission packet, detailed outline, and sample chapter. Accepts photocopies and computer printouts. Availablity of artwork improves chance of acceptance. SASE. Responds in 3–6 months. Publication in 1–2 years. Royalty, varies.

Editor's Comments
We are always looking for innovative ideas and materials that will help teachers in their classrooms. Most of our books are written by experienced teachers and others who work with young children. Remember, you must send of a submission packet in order to be considered as a writer for us.

Additional Listings

We have selected the following publishers to offer you additional marketing opportunities. Most of these publishers have special submissions requirements or they purchase a limited number of juvenile titles each year.

For published authors, we include information about houses that produce reprints of previously published works. For writers who are proficient in foreign languages, we list publishers of foreign-language material. You will also find publishers who accept résumés only; who work with agented authors; or who usually accept unsolicited submissions, but due to a backlog, are not accepting material at this time.

As you survey these listings, you may find that a small regional press is a more appropriate market for your submission than a larger publisher. Also, if you are involved in education or are a specialist in a certain field, consider sending your résumé to one of the educational publishers—you may have the qualifications they are looking for.

Publishers who usually accept unsolicited submissions but were not accepting unsolicited material at our press time are designated with an ⊗. *Be sure to contact the publisher before submitting material to determine the current submissions policy.*

As you review the listings that follow, use the Publisher's Interests section as your guide to the particular focus of each house.

A & B Publishers Group

1000 Atlantic Avenue
Brooklyn, NY 11238

Managing Editor: Maxwell Taylor

Publisher's Interests
Striving to produce books that identify the diverse cultures of the world and encourage self-esteem, this publisher offers fiction and nonfiction for children and young adults. New writers have the best chance at publication with picture books and middle-grade books.

Freelance Potential
Published 16 titles (6 juvenile) in 2004: 8 were developed from unsolicited submissions and 2 were by agented authors. Of the 16 titles, 12 were by unpublished writers and 6 were by authors who were new to the publishing house. Receives 200 queries yearly.
Submissions and Payment: Query with sample chapters and table of contents. Accepts photocopies, computer printouts, and simultaneous submissions if identified. SASE. Responds in 2–3 months. Publication period varies. Royalty, 4–5%; advance, $500.

Abbeville Kids

Suite 500
116 West 23rd Street
New York, NY 10011

Editor: Susan Costello

Publisher's Interests
This imprint of the Abbeville Press, a company known for its books on art, brings readers up to the age of 12 a selection of illustrated fiction and nonfiction. Much of its list is devoted to books about famous artists and writers, both past and present. The company was established in 1947. 50% self-, subsidy-, co-venture, or co-op published material.
Website: www.abbeville.com

Freelance Potential
Published 20–25 titles in 2004. Receives 120 unsolicited mss yearly.
Submissions and Payment: Send complete ms with illustrations. Prefers agented authors. Accepts photocopies and computer printouts. SASE. Responds in 5 weeks. Publication in 18–24 months. Royalty; advance. Flat fee.

Abdo Publishing Company

Suite 622
4940 Viking Drive
Edina, MN 55435

Editor-in-Chief: Paul Abdo

Publisher's Interests
Educational materials that supplement the curriculum are the focus of this publishing house. Its materials are used in preschool through eighth grade classrooms and cover a wide range of topics. Its editors are interested in reviewing queries for history, sports, biographies, and geography at this time.
Website: www.abdopub.com

Freelance Potential
Published 230 titles in 2004: 23 were developed from unsolicited submissions. Of the 230 titles, 2 were by unpublished writers and 5 were by authors who were new to the publishing house. Receives 150 queries yearly.
Submissions and Payment: Query with résumé. No unsolicited mss. Response time varies. Publication in 1 year. Flat fee.

Abingdon Press

P.O. Box 801
201 8th Avenue South
Nashville, TN 37203

Editor: Peg Augustine

Publisher's Interests
This publisher is committed to producing high-quality, effective, religious publications. It offers books and non-print media including computer software and audio and video cassettes. It strives to produce religious literature that enriches church communities across the globe. 50% co-op published material.
Website: www.abingdonpress.com

Freelance Potential
Published 10 titles in 2004: all were developed from unsolicited submissions. Receives 600 queries yearly.
Submissions and Payment: Guidelines available. Query with outline. Accepts photocopies and email submissions to paugustine@umpublishing.org. SASE. Responds in 3 months. Publication in 2 years. Royalty; 5–10%. Flat fee, $1,000+.

Activity Resources Company

20655 Hathaway Avenue
Hayward, CA 94541

Editor: Mary Laycock

Publisher's Interests
For over 25 years, this publisher has offered teachers of kindergarten through grade nine the latest in books and activities for teaching mathematics. It strives to produce materials that provide a real understanding of math, such as hands-on manipulatives, books, and games that cover numbers, geometry, algebra, logic, statistics, measurement, probability, and discrete math.
Website: www.activityresources.com

Freelance Potential
Published 4 titles in 2004. Receives 25–30 queries yearly.
Submissions and Payment: Query with résumé, sample chapter, and bibliography. Accepts photocopies, computer printouts, and simultaneous submissions if identified. SASE. Responds in 2–4 weeks. Publication in 1 year. Royalty, varies.

Advocacy Press

402 E. Carillo
Santa Barbara, CA 93102

Curriculum Specialist: Luke Besner

Publisher's Interests
Advocacy Press is dedicated to providing learning materials to help children, pre-teens, teens, and young adults develop skills for constructive lives. It is interested in books that promote self-reliance and gender equality, and encourage realistic life and career planning. It also seeks picture books for younger readers that focus on character building and personal growth.
Website: www.advocacypress.com

Freelance Potential
Published 2 titles in 2004: both were assigned. Receives 500 unsolicited mss yearly.
Submissions and Payment: Guidelines available at website or with SASE. Send complete ms. Accepts photocopies. SASE. Responds in 1 month. Publication in 1 year. Royalty.

Alpha Publishing

P.O. Box 53788
Lafayette, LA 70505

Publisher: Mark Anthony

Publisher's Interests
Focusing on the critical issues of today and time-tested solutions, this publisher offers adult nonfiction books that address current social, ethical, political, educational, family, and moral issues. In addition, it produces a line of inspirational fiction for young adults. It seeks material that takes a fresh, insightful look at the real-life issues that affect us all.
Website: www.alphapublishingonline.com

Freelance Potential
Published 10–20 titles in 2004. Receives 2,000 queries yearly.
Submissions and Payment: Guidelines available. Query with 200- to 300-word proposal. No unsolicited mss. Accepts photocopies, computer printouts, and simultaneous submissions if identified. SASE. Responds in 3–4 months. Publication in 6–8 months. Royalty.

AMG Publishers

6815 Shallowford Road
Chattanooga, TN 37421

Editor: Dan Penwell

Publisher's Interests
AMG Publishers was established in 1962 and specializes in biblically-oriented books for children and adults including books on Christian living, family issues, single and divorce issues, devotionals, Bible study titles, and gift books. It plans a new line of young fiction and interested writers should consult the website for details.
Website: www.amgpublishers.com

Freelance Potential
Published 35 titles (12 juvenile) in 2004: 3–4 were developed from unsolicited submissions, 6 were by agented authors, and 2 were assigned. Receives 900–1,200 queries yearly.
Submissions and Payment: Guidelines available at website. Query. Accepts email queries to danp@amginternational.org. Response time and publication period vary. Royalty; advance.

Amirah Publishing

P.O. Box 541146
Flushing, NY 11354

Submissions Editor: Adam Emerick

Publisher's Interests
As the publishing arm of the Islamic Foundation of America, Amirah Publishing offers materials that further religious understanding of Islam. Textbooks, literature, and other educational materials for Islamic schools are included on its list, as well as fiction and nonfiction titles for young children through young adult readers, and curriculum guides and resources for Muslim educators.
Website: www.amirahpublishing.com

Freelance Potential
Published 3 titles (1 juvenile) in 2004. Of the 3 titles, 1 was by an unpublished writer. Receives 30 queries yearly.
Submissions and Payment: Query. Accepts email to amirahpbco@aol.com and simultaneous submissions if identified. SASE. Responds in 4–6 weeks. Publication in 4–6 months. Flat fee.

Aquila Communications Ltd.

2642 Diab Street
St. Laurent, Quebec H4S 1E8
Canada

President: Sami Kelada

Publisher's Interests
Aquila Communications publishes materials for French-as-a-Second Language classes. "Teacher-friendly" books for grades four through college level are offered on a variety of themes and styles, including mystery, humor, horror, and fantasy as well as creative nonfiction. Many titles also include audio cassettes and supplementary exercises; teacher's guides are sold separately. All submissions must be written in French.
Website: www.aquilacommunications.com

Freelance Potential
Published 14 titles in 2004. Receives 500 queries yearly.
Submissions and Payment: Guidelines available. Query with synopsis. Accepts photocopies. SAE/IRC. Responds in 1 month. Publication in 2–6 months. Royalty, 5%. Flat fee, $50–$500+.

Association for Childhood Education International

Suite 215, 17904 Georgia Avenue
Olney, MD 20832-2277

Director, Editorial Department: Anne Bauer

Publisher's Interests
Established in 1946, this publisher offers resource and reference books, videotapes, and audio cassettes that promote and support the education and development of children. It is currently seeking manuscripts that describe programs and practices for children from infancy through early adolescence, and address the current needs and rights of children.
Website: www.acei.org

Freelance Potential
Published 5 titles in 2004. Receives 120 unsolicited mss yearly.
Submissions and Payment: Guidelines available. Send complete ms. Accepts photocopies, computer printouts, and disk submissions (ASCII or Microsoft Word 5.0). SASE. Responds in 2 weeks. Publication in 1–3 years. Provides author's copies in lieu of payment.

Avocet Press

19 Paul Court
Pearl River, NY 10965

Editor: Cynthia Webb

Publisher's Interests
This small, independent publisher offers fiction in many genres, including historical fiction, contemporary fiction, mysteries, suspense, and poetry. It is currently interested in reviewing queries for books that will bring young adult and adult readers new, fresh stories that intrigue and inspire and are of the highest literary quality. New writers are encouraged to review published titles before querying with their ideas.
Website: www.avocetpress.com

Freelance Potential
Published 8 titles in 2004: 4 were developed from unsolicited submissions. Receives 2,400 queries yearly.
Submissions and Payment: Guidelines available at website. Query. SASE. Response time and publication period vary. Royalty; advance.

Avocus Publishing

4 White Brook Road
Gilsum, NH 03448

Editor: Craig Thorn

Publisher's Interests
Serving educators, this publisher offers books that focus on independent school life. Its publishes books about classroom teaching, individualized academic programs, and new challenges in the development of curricula. Books on parenting, chapter books, middle-grade books, and young adult titles are also produced.
Website: www.avocus.com

Freelance Potential
Published 4 titles in 2004: 1 was developed from an unsolicited submission and 3 were assigned. Receives 100+ queries, 72 unsolicited mss yearly.
Submissions and Payment: Guidelines and catalogue available at website. Query or send complete ms. SASE. Response time and publication period vary. Royalty; advance.

Azro Press

PMB 342
1704 Llano Street B
Sante Fe, NM 87505

Submissions Editor

Publisher's Interests
Established in 1997, this small publishing company features the work of authors and illustrators of the American Southwest. Azro Press offers illustrated children's books for ages two to six, easy readers for children five to eight, and novels for older readers.
Website: www.azropress.com

Freelance Potential
Published 5 titles in 2004: all were developed from unsolicited submissions. Of the 5 titles, all were by unpublished writers. Receives 1,000 queries and unsolicited mss yearly.
Submissions and Payment: Guidelines available. Query with résumé. Accepts photocopies and simultaneous submissions if identified. SASE. Responds to queries in 1 week, to mss in 3–4 months. Publication in 2 years. Royalty, 5%.

Ballyhoo Bookworks, Inc.

P.O. Box 534
Shoreham, NY 11786

Executive Editor: Liam Gerrity

Publisher's Interests
A variety of nonfiction crafts and how-to activity books for young children, as well as books for middle-grade readers are produced by this publisher. Due to a large increase in the volume of submissions, it is currently only accepting queries.

Freelance Potential
Published 4 titles in 2004: 2 were developed from unsolicited submissions and 2 were reprint/licensed properties. Receives 100 queries yearly.
Submissions and Payment: Guidelines available. Query with outline and 3 sample chapters for long works. Accepts photocopies, computer printouts, and simultaneous submissions if identified. SASE. Responds in 1 month. Publication in 12–18 months. Royalty; advance. Flat fee.

Bancroft Press ☆

P.O. Box 65360
Baltimore, MD 21209

Nonfiction Editor: Bruce Bortz
Fiction Editor: Elly Zupko

Publisher's Interests
Based in Baltimore, Maryland, Bancroft Press is a general interest publisher that seeks to produce high quality works of fiction and nonfiction. Established in 1995, its books target young adult and adult readers. It does not publish any children's titles. Its editors are interested in reviewing queries for mysteries, especially mysteries with a touch of humor.
Website: www.bancroftpress.com

Freelance Potential
Published 6 titles (5 juvenile) in 2004.
Submissions and Payment: Guidelines and catalogue available at website. Query with 4 or 5 chapters; or send complete ms. Accepts photocopies and computer printouts. SASE. Responds in 6 months. Publication period varies. Royalty, 8%; advance.

Barefoot Books Ltd.

124 Walcot Street
Bath BA1 5BG
United Kingdom

Submissions Editor

Publisher's Interests
Barefoot Books is an independent publisher that offers picture books and anthologies for children up to twelve years of age. Themes focus on independence of spirit, enthusiasm for learning, and acceptance of other cultures. It is interested in creative submissions that combine art and story that honor the diversity and multitude of traditional cultures of the world.
Website: www.barefoot-books.com

Freelance Potential
Published 10 titles in 2004.
Submissions and Payment: Guidelines available at website. Send complete ms with artwork if applicable. Accepts photocopies and computer printouts. SAE/IRC. Responds only if interested. Publication period and payment policy vary.

Barron's Educational Series

250 Wireless Boulevard
Hauppauge, NY 11788

Acquisitions Editor: Wayne Barr

Publisher's Interests
In addition to its well-known array of test preparation manuals and school directories, Barron's also offers an extensive line of children's fiction and nonfiction books, as well as parenting titles. 50% self-, subsidy-, co-venture, or co-op published material.
Website: www.barronseduc.com

Freelance Potential
Published 400 titles (100 juvenile) in 2004. Receives 1,000 queries, 600 unsolicited mss yearly.
Submissions and Payment: Guidelines available. Send complete ms with résumé for fiction. Query with résumé, table of contents, outline/synopsis, 2 sample chapters, and description of audience for nonfiction. SASE. Responds in to queries in 1–3 months, to mss in 6–8 months. Publication in 2 years. Royalty; advance. Flat fee.

Bay Light Publishing

P.O. Box 3032
Mooresville, NC 28117

Publisher: Charlotte Soutullo

Publisher's Interests
Established in 1998, Bay Light Publishing specializes in Christian books for the whole family, and is dedicated to helping children discover a Christ-centered life. It targets children between the ages of four and twelve, and includes story picture books and series titles. This year, Bay Light is interested in fun and meaningful titles with Christian themes.
Website: www.baylightpub.com

Freelance Potential
Published 2 titles in 2004: 2 were developed from unsolicited submissions. Receives 50 queries yearly.
Submissions and Payment: Query. Accepts photocopies and simultaneous submissions. SASE. Responds in 3-6 weeks. Publication in 1 year. Payment policy varies.

Baylor University Press

P.O. Box 97363
Waco, TX 76798-7363

Director: Carey C. Newman

Publisher's Interests
Baylor University Press publishes contemporary and historical scholarly works for college students in topics such as religion, ethics, archaeology, and the arts as they relate to Texas and the Southwest.
Website: www1.baylor.edu/BUPress/

Freelance Potential
Published 6 titles in 2004: 2 were developed from unsolicited submissions. Of the 6 titles, 3 were by unpublished writers and 3 were by authors who were new to the publishing house. Receives 120-180 queries yearly.
Submissions and Payment: Guidelines and catalogue available with 9x12 SASE or at website. Query. Accepts photocopies and IBM disk submissions. SASE. Responds in 1 month. Publication in 9 months. Royalty, 10%.

Alexander Graham Bell Association for the Deaf and Hard of Hearing

3417 Volta Place NW
Washington DC 20007-2778

Director of Publications: Elizabeth Quigley

Publisher's Interests
This publisher offers books, brochures, instructional materials, videos, CDs, and audiocassettes related to hearing loss. It offers nonfiction books on topics related to children and deafness including cochlear implants and using hearing aids to promote speech. In addition, it produces fiction titles and inspirational biographies for children with hearing loss. It seeks books in Spanish on a variety of topics related to deafness.
Website: www.agbell.org

Freelance Potential
Published 6 titles in 2004. Receives 10–15 unsolicited mss yearly.
Submissions and Payment: Guidelines available. Send up to 15 ms pages. Accepts computer printouts. SASE. Responds in 3 months. Publication in 9–16 months. Royalty, to 10%.

The Benefactory

P.O. Box 128
Cohasset, MA 02025

Creative Director

Publisher's Interests
Children's books with accompanying audiotapes, toys, or videocassettes that focus on animal welfare are offered by this small publishing house. Its products for children age four to ten are designed to foster an interest in animal protection and environmental preservation, motivate young readers to expand their abilities, encourage children to be creative, and initiate community involvement.
Website: www.readplay.com

Freelance Potential
No titles were published in 2004; publishing program will resume in 2005.
Submissions and Payment: Guidelines available. Most work is done on assignment. Query only. No unsolicited mss. SASE. Responds in 6–8 weeks. Publication in 2 years. Royalty; advance, 5%.

BePuzzled

University Games Corporation
2030 Harrison Street
San Francisco, CA 94110

General Manager: Connie Gee

Publisher's Interests
This imprint of the University Games Corporation specializes in puzzles that are linked to well-known mysteries that readers solve as they assemble the puzzles. Its material caters to young readers between the ages of seven and nine. New authors are strongly urged to review previously published puzzles/mysteries to get a firm grip on the unique products published by the company.
Website: www.areyougame.com

Freelance Potential
Published 15 titles (10 juvenile) in 2004: all were developed from unsolicited submissions. Receives 500 queries yearly.
Submissions and Payment: Guidelines available. Query with short mystery sample. Accepts computer printouts. SASE. Responds in 2 weeks. Publication in 1 year. Buys world rights. Flat fee.

Bick Publishing House

307 Neck Road
Madison, CT 06443

President: Dale Carlson

Publisher's Interests
Nonfiction titles for young adults are the focus of this publisher. Its list includes books on wildlife rehabilitation, science, ethics, philosophy, psychology, special needs, disabilities, meditation, life planning, and substance abuse.
Website: www.bickpubhouse.com

Freelance Potential
Published 2 titles in 2004: 1 was by an agented author. Receives 50–100 queries yearly.
Submissions and Payment: Guidelines and catalogue available with 9x12 SASE ($1 postage). Query with 3 chapters, outline/synopsis, table of contents, and author biography. Accepts photocopies. SASE. Responds in 2 weeks. Publication in 1 year. Royalty, 10% net; advance.

Blue Marlin Publications

823 Aberdeen Road
West Bay Shore, NY 11706

Publisher: Francine Poppo Rich

Publisher's Interests
Striving to publish and promote quality children's and young adult books, this independent publisher offers fiction and nonfiction books that make reading fun.
Website: www.bluemarlinpubs.com

Freelance Potential
Published 2 titles in 2004: 1 was developed from an unsolicited submission. Of the 2 titles, 1 was by an author who was new to the publishing house. Receives 250 unsolicited mss yearly.
Submissions and Payment: Send complete ms. Accepts photocopies and simultaneous submissions if identified. No email submissions, please. Availability of artwork may improve chance of acceptance. SASE. Responds in 6 weeks. Publication in 12–18 months. Royalty; advance.

Bollix Books   ☆

1609 West Callender Avenue
Peoria, IL 61606

Submissions Editor

Publisher's Interests
A publisher of fiction only, Bollix Books offers early picture books for children up to the age of four, story picture books for children ages four to ten, middle-grade novels, and young adult books. Its editors look for offbeat stories with literary quality, and stories that deal with social issues. Books that carry a moral or lesson are acceptable as long as the message is subtle. Contemporary, multicultural, and ethnic fiction are among the genres it seeks.
Website: www.bollixbooks.com

Freelance Potential
Published 4 titles in 2004.
Submissions and Payment: Guidelines and catalogue available at website. Query. Accepts email to editor@bollixbooks.com. SASE. Responds in 3 weeks. Publication period varies. Royalty; advance.

Books of Wonder

Room 806
16 West 18th Street
New York, NY 10011

Editor: Peter Glassman

Publisher's Interests
Books of Wonder publishes many of the Oz classics, including original L. Frank Baum titles, as well as those written by other authors. Gift book editions of classic children's stories are also offered by this publisher. At this time, Books of Wonder is interested only in submissions of books written in the style and tradition of L. Frank Baum for children ages eight to twelve.
Website: www.booksofwonder.com

Freelance Potential
Published several titles in 2004. Receives 30 unsolicited mss yearly.
Submissions and Payment: Guidelines available at website.
Send complete ms. Accepts photocopies and computer printouts. SASE. Responds in 6 months. Publication period varies. Royalty; advance.

BOW Books

P.O. Box 185848
Fort Worth, TX 76181

Editor: Jennifer Noland

Publisher's Interests
Targeting readers ages 3–12, this publisher offers picture books and chapter books, as well as audio books, and ancillary products. Led by Christian values, it produces material with a focus on the positive side of life. It is currently not accepting unsolicited manuscripts.
Website: www.bowbooks.com

Freelance Potential
Published 5 titles in 2004: 1 was developed from an unsolicited submission. Of the 5 titles, 1 was by an unpublished writer and 1 was by an author who was new to the publishing house.
Submissions and Payment: Guidelines and catalogue available with 6x9 SASE ($.55 postage). Query with information on intended audience, length, and author biography. SASE. Responds in 3 months. Publication in 18 months. Royalty. Flat fee.

Caddo Gap Press

PMB 275
3145 Geary Boulevard
San Francisco, CA 94118

Executive Editor: Alan H. Jones

Publisher's Interests
Caddo Gap Press publishes books and periodicals for college and university teachers and teacher educators. Its list includes books on the social foundations of education, teacher education, multicultural education, educational foundations and curriculum, science and museum education, and international education. Although most of its titles are related to teaching, it occasionally publishes titles on parenting strategies.
Website: www.caddogap.com

Freelance Potential
Published 2–3 titles in 2004. Receives 12 queries, 12 unsolicited mss yearly.
Submissions and Payment: Query or send complete ms. SASE. Response time and publication period vary. Royalty, 10%.

Calkins Creek Books ☆

815 Church Street
Honesdale, PA 18431

Submissions Editor: Jeanna DeLuca

Publisher's Interests
This new imprint of Boyds Mills Press targets the school and library markets. It features historical fiction and nonfiction for children ages 8–14, as well picture books with an emphasis on the events, people, and places in U.S. history. Materials on all aspects of American history, especially the Revolutionary War, pre-Civil War, and Civil War eras, are needed. It plans to enhance and expand upon some of the American history titles Boyds Mills Press has published.
Website: www.boydsmillspress.com

Freelance Potential
Plans to publish several books in 2005.
Submissions and Payment: Guidelines available. Send complete ms with detailed biography. Accepts photocopies. SASE. Response time and publication period varies. Royalty.

Camex Books

535 5th Avenue
New York, NY 10017

Submissions Editor: Victor Benedetto

Publisher's Interests
Camex Books publishes material for preschool through young adult readers, including novelty books, picture books, fairy tales, folktales, middle-grade mysteries and adventure stories, and young adult contemporary fiction and romance novels. It also features promotional titles, self-help books, special interest books, cookbooks, and celebrity biographies for adults. The editors at Camex Books request that all writers phone for submission instructions instead of sending material.

Freelance Potential
Published 20 titles in 2004 (12 juvenile).
Submissions and Payment: No queries or unsolicited mss. Editors prefer prospective writers call 212-682-8400 prior to submitting work. Publication in 6 months. Royalty; advance. Flat fee.

Carousel Press

P.O. Box 6038
Berkeley, CA 94706-0038

Publisher: Carole T. Meyers

Publisher's Interests
Travel in the United States and abroad is the focus of Carousel Press. Its catalogue includes international, national, and regional travel guides for weekend excursions, American zoos, camping in Europe, and European castle and manor hotels, as well as books of car games and travel activities for children. This publisher plans to continue expanding its list of guides for vacationers of all ages.
Website: www.carousel-press.com

Freelance Potential
Published 1 title in 2004. Receives 50 queries yearly.
Submissions and Payment: Query with table of contents and sample chapter. Accepts photocopies and computer printouts. SASE. Responds in 1 month. Publication in 1 year. Royalty; advance.

Chaosium

895 B Street #423
Hayward, CA 94541

Editor-in-Chief: Lynn Willis

Publisher's Interests
Founded in 1975 and later incorporated, Chaosium specializes in adventure stories, fiction, horror anthologies, and role-playing games for young adults and adults. Most material is based on the works of popular genre authors.
Website: www.chaosium.com

Freelance Potential
Published 12 titles in 2004. 6 were developed from unsolicited submissions and 4 were reprint/licensed properties. Of the 12 titles, 2 were by unpublished writers. Receives 40 queries yearly.
Submissions and Payment: Guidelines available. Query with summary and writing samples. Accepts photocopies and Macintosh disk submissions. SASE. Responds in 1–2 weeks. Publication in 1–2 years. Flat fee, $.03–$.05 per word.

Children's Story Scripts ⊗

2219 West Olive Avenue
PMB 130
Burbank, CA 91506

Editor: Deedra Bébout

Publisher's Interests
Targeting classroom teachers, this publisher offers exciting and motivating theatre-style scripts for children from kindergarten through eighth grade. Each script provides a positive story with a purpose that is designed to make learning fun while promoting reading fluency, problem solving, independent thinking, and self-confidence. Currently, it is not accepting unsolicited submissions.

Freelance Potential
Published 4 titles in 2004: all were developed from unsolicited submissions. Receives 500 unsolicited mss yearly.
Submissions and Payment: Guidelines available. Send SASE for updates in submissions policy.

Clark City Press

P.O. Box 1358
Livingston, MT 59047

Submissions Editor

Publisher's Interests
Clark City Press is committed to producing a small number of titles that deliver a unique message to the reader. Established in 1988, it features poetry, mysteries, short stories, novellas, children's classics, biographies, and autobiographies for older readers and adults. This small press prides itself on a publishing strategy that challenges traditional procedures and offers quality and integrity without compromise. All freelance work is by assignment only.
Website: www.clarkcitypress.com

Freelance Potential
Published 4–6 titles in 2004. Receives 24 queries yearly.
Submissions and Payment: All work is assigned. Query. No unsolicited mss. SASE. Responds in 2–3 weeks. Publication in 6 months. Payment policy varies.

Consortium Publishing

640 Weaver Hill Road
West Greenwich, RI 02817-2261

Chief of Publications: John M. Carlevale

Publisher's Interests
Books for educators and counselors are featured by this publisher. Material focuses on early education, counseling, substance abuse, intervention, and health and safety. 5% self-, subsidy-, co-venture, or co-op published material.

Freelance Potential
Published 20 titles in 2004: 2 were developed from unsolicited submissions and 1 was by an agented author. Of the 20 titles, 2 were by unpublished writers and 1 was by an author who was new to the publishing house. Receives 150 queries yearly.
Submissions and Payment: Guidelines available. Query or send complete ms with résumé. Accepts photocopies, computer printouts, and Macintosh disk submissions (Microsoft Word). SASE. Responds in 1–2 months. Publication in 3 months. Royalty.

Contemporary Books

Suite 900
130 East Randolph Street
Chicago, IL 60601

Submissions Editor: Betsy Lane

Publisher's Interests
Adult education, GED, and ESL textbooks for adult education schools, community colleges, and international education programs are offered by this division of McGraw-Hill. Its titles cover basic skills, math, reading, language, vocabulary, workplace issues and employability, and testing and assessment. Writers are encouraged to visit the website for current information.
Website: www.contemporarybooks.com

Freelance Potential
Published several titles in 2004. Receives 480 queries yearly.
Submissions and Payment: Guidelines available at website. Query with résumé, prospectus, table of contents, sample chapters, and market analysis. Accepts photocopies and disk submissions. SASE. Response time, publication period, and payment policy vary.

Continental Press

520 East Bainbridge Street
Elizabethtown, PA 17022

Vice President, Publications: Beth Spencer

Publisher's Interests
Educational materials for students in kindergarten through grade twelve classrooms are the focus of this publisher. It features textbooks, workbooks, and reproducibles on reading, language, math, and social studies, as well as teachers' resource materials on assessments, literacy, curriculum development, classroom planning, and special education.
Website: www.continentalpress.com

Freelance Potential
Published 50 titles in 2004: 2 were by authors who were new to the publishing house. Receives 50 unsolicited mss yearly.
Submissions and Payment: Guidelines available. Query or send complete ms. Accepts computer printouts. SASE. Responds in 2 months. Publication period and payment policy vary.

Cornerstone Press Chicago

939 West Wilson Avenue
Chicago, IL 60640

Fiction Editor: Libby Kahler
Nonfiction Editor: Chris Rice

Publisher's Interests
A variety of fiction and nonfiction books written with a Christian worldview for children and adults are produced by this publisher. It seeks exciting, compelling stories. Children's fiction is welcome.
Website: www.cornerstonepress.com

Freelance Potential
Published 1 title in 2004: it was developed from an unsolicited submission and it was by an author who was new to the publishing house. Receives 100+ mss yearly.
Submissions and Payment: Guidelines available at website. Send ms with author biography, synopsis, 3-5 sample chapters, description of book's audience, and estimated length. Accepts disk submissions and email to cspress@jpusa.org. SASE. Responds in 2 weeks. Publication period varies. Royalty, 10%.

Cottonwood Press

109-B Cameron Drive
Fort Collins, CO 80525

President: Cheryl Thurston

Publisher's Interests
English and language arts teachers use textbooks and activity books by Cottonwood Press in their classrooms. This publisher is seeking creative material for grades five through twelve.
Website: www.cottonwoodpress.com

Freelance Potential
Published 2 titles in 2004: 1 was developed from an unsolicited submission. Of the 2 titles, both were by unpublished writers who were new to the publishing house. Receives 50 queries, 70 unsolicited mss yearly.
Submissions and Payment: Guidelines available. Query with sample pages; or send complete ms. Accepts computer printouts and simultaneous submissions if identified. SASE. Responds in 1-4 weeks. Publication in 6-12 months. Royalty, 10%.

For the At-Risk & Reluctant
Lise Ragan
Course Crafters, Inc.

"We are always looking for good writers and editors of nonfiction, fiction, student, and teacher materials for preK-12," says Lise B. Ragan, President and CEO of Course Crafters. Teacher consultants are also needed. The company "develops materials for the educational (school) market, specifically for at-risk students and reluctant readers, and notably those children who are learning English as a second language —English language learners."

Ragan says, "Interested writers should submit a résumé and writing samples." But note that she also clarifies, "We do not typically accept unsolicited manuscripts, unless someone has developed a product that is particularly innovative and one that fits squarely within our publishing focus."

Materials may be emailed to jobs@coursecrafters.com. Additionally, the Course Crafters website lists current job opportunities and says they also hire freelance development content editors, consultants/reviewers, proofreaders, illustrators, book designers, copyeditors, translators, and project managers, and those interested in work with Course Crafters should "include a cover letter specifying the job you're interested in, whether you want a staff or freelance position, and the hours you have available each week. You can also send your résumé by regular mail."

(See listing for Course Crafters on following page)

Course Crafters, Inc.

44 Merimac Street
Newburyport, MA 01950

Editor

Publisher's Interests
Specializing in developing educational materials for students in English-as-a-Second language classes in kindergarten through high school and their teachers, this publisher offers high-quality student texts, supplementary materials, teacher's editions, and multimedia learning materials. It uses a vast network of freelance personnel and welcomes freelancers to contact them regarding job opportunities.
Website: www.coursecrafters.com

Freelance Potential
Published 12 titles in 2004. Of the 12 titles, 3 were by authors who were new to the publishing house.
Submissions and Payment: Guidelines available. Query with clips. Accepts photocopies and email to jobs@coursecrafters.com. SASE. Responds in 1 month. Publication in 1–2 years. Flat fee.

Creative Editions

123 South Broad Street
Mankato, MN 56001

Managing Editor: Aaron Frisch

Publisher's Interests
A variety of fun, exciting books for children of all ages is produced by this publisher, which is an imprint of The Creative Company. Its list includes quality fiction, nonfiction, picture books, and poetry on various topics. It is interested in unique stories that can capture the readers' attention through creative words and great illustrations, and spark their imaginations.

Freelance Potential
Published 5 titles in 2004: 3 were by agented authors. Receives 50 queries yearly.
Submissions and Payment: Query with 500-word sample from manuscript. Accepts photocopies and computer printouts. No simultaneous submissions. SASE. Responds in 4–6 months. Publication in 4 years. Royalty; advance.

Creative Education

123 South Broad Street
Mankato, MN 56001

Managing Editor: Aaron Frisch

Publisher's Interests
Story picture books, middle-grade books, and young adult books on animals, history, nature, and literature are produced by this publisher. Targeting libraries and schools, most of its material is used as resource material in the classroom.

Freelance Potential
Published 50 titles in 2004: 10-20 were developed from unsolicited submissions and 5 were by agented authors. Receives 100-150 queries yearly.
Submissions and Payment: Guidelines available. Query with manuscript sample. Accepts photocopies and computer printouts. No simultaneous submissions. SASE. Responds in 4-6 months. Publication in 4 years. Payment policy varies.

Creative Paperbacks

123 South Broad Street
Mankato, MN 56001

Managing Editor: Aaron Frisch

Publisher's Interests
An imprint of The Creative Company, this publisher offers readers in kindergarten through grade six high-quality fiction and nonfiction paperbacks. Genres include contemporary and historical fiction, adventure, and fantasy. Topics for nonfiction books include animals, entertainment, geography, history, science, and technology. It also produces biographies.

Freelance Potential
Published 10-12 titles in 2004: a few were reprint/licensed properties. Receives 1,200-1,800 queries yearly.
Submissions and Payment: Writers' guidelines available. Query with manuscript sample. Accepts photocopies and computer printouts. SASE. Responds in 4-6 months. Publication in 2-4 years. Payment rate varies.

Crossquarter Publishing Group

P.O. Box 8756
Santa Fe, NM 87504

Submissions Editor: Anthony Ravenscroft

Publisher's Interests
This small publishing group produces books, e-books, and information packages. Targeting both young adult and adult readers, it offers nonfiction topics such as biographies, autobiographies, health, spirituality, and multicultural issues, as well as science fiction.
Website: www.crossquarter.com

Freelance Potential
Published 4 titles (1 juvenile) in 2004. Of the 6 titles, 3 were by unpublished writers and 6 were by authors who were new to the publishing house. Receives 1,500 queries yearly.
Submissions and Payment: Writers' guidelines available at website. Query. Accepts photocopies and simultaneous submissions if identified. SASE. Responds in 2–3 months. Publication in 9 months. Royalty; 5–10%.

Delmar Learning

Executive Woods
5 Maxwell Drive
Clifton, NY 12065

Acquisitions Editor: Erin O'Connor

Publisher's Interests
Books, software, and video cassettes for education professionals and early childhood education students appear on the list of this publisher. Its titles cover topics such as child development, child-care programs, children's activities, teaching methods, early learning, and professional care-giving.
Website: www.earlychilded.delmar.com

Freelance Potential
Published 25–30 titles in 2004. Receives 120 queries yearly.
Submissions and Payment: Guidelines available. Query with résumé, description of project, detailed outline, and sample chapters. Accepts photocopies, computer printouts, and simultaneous submissions if identified. SASE. Responds in 1 month. Publication in 2 years. Payment policy varies.

Different Books

3900 Glenwood Avenue
Golden Valley, MN 55422

Editor: Roger Hammer

Publisher's Interests
Children's books that feature heroes and heroines with disabilities are produced by this publisher. It is interested in stories for early elementary readers—grades pre-K–6.

Freelance Potential
Published 5 titles in 2004: 4 were developed from unsolicited submissions and 1 was by an agented author. Of the 5 titles, 4 were by unpublished writers who were new to the publishing house. Receives 100 queries, 10,000 unsolicited mss yearly.
Submissions and Payment: Guidelines available. Query or send complete send ms. Accepts photocopies and computer printouts. No simultaneous submissions. SASE. Responds to queries in 1 week, to mss in 2 months. Publication in 1 year. Royalty. Flat fee for each new printing.

Displays for Schools

1825 NW 22nd Terrace
Gainesville, FL 32605

Manager: Sherry DuPree

Publisher's Interests
Established in 1976, this educational publisher supplies public and private educators with useful and instructive materials that promote learning. Its list focuses on books for kindergarten through grade twelve students and their teachers, concentrating on history, religion, writing, and reading, as well as biographies and self-help titles. It will consider original material that has been tested and utilized in a teaching situation.
Website: www.displaysforschools.com

Freelance Potential
Published 2 titles (1 juvenile) in 2004. Receives 180 queries yearly.
Submissions and Payment: Guidelines available. Query with outline/synopsis, sample chapters, and a brief biography. SASE. Responds in 2 months. Publication in 4–24 months. Royalty, 10%.

Dog-Eared Publications

P.O. Box 630863
Middleton, WI 53562-0863

Publisher: Nancy Field

Publisher's Interests
This publisher offers nature books for middle-grade readers. It strives to make learning fun and exciting by offering nonfiction, mysteries, and hands-on activities that promote development of cognitive thinking skills, problem solving, and an appreciation of wild things and wild places. It welcomes engaging, interactive material on science and nature topics.
Website: www.dog-eared.com

Freelance Potential
Published 1 title in 2004. Receives 100 queries yearly.
Submissions and Payment: Query with outline/synopsis. Prefers email queries to field@dog-eared.com. Accepts photocopies and computer printouts. SASE. Response time varies. Publication period varies. Royalty; advance.

Domhan Books

Suite 514
9511 Shore Road
Brooklyn, NY 11209

Young Adult Editor

Publisher's Interests
Domhan Books publishes fiction and nonfiction for middle-grade and young adult readers.
Website: www.domhanbooks.com

Freelance Potential
Published 50 titles (20 juvenile) in 2004: 48 were developed from unsolicited submissions and 12 were by agented authors. Of the 50 titles, 25 were by unpublished writers and 25 were by new authors. Receives 500+ queries, 1,500+ unsolicited mss yearly.
Submissions and Payment: Guidelines and catalogue available at website or with 9x12 SASE ($.55 postage). Query with clips. Accepts disk submissions (RTF or ASCII). SASE. Responds to queries in 1–2 weeks, to mss in 6 months. Publication in 6 months. Royalty, 30–50% net.

E & E Publishing

Suite 227
1001 Bridgeway
Sausalito, CA 94965

Submissions Editor: Eve Bine-Stock

Publisher's Interests
Paperback books and e-books for children age three to eight are the mainstay of this publisher. It is interested in receiving submissions for picture books with memorable characters and touching or amusing stories. It does not accept young adult material.
Website: www.eandegroup.com/publishing

Freelance Potential
Published 12 titles in 2004. Of the 12 titles, 9 were by authors who were new to the publishing house.
Submissions and Payment: Send complete ms for picture books; query for longer works. Prefers email to eandegroup@eandegroup.com. Accepts photocopies and computer printouts. SASE. Responds in 1 week. Publication period and payment policy vary.

Eastgate Systems

134 Main Street
Watertown, MA 02472

Acquisitions Editor: Elin Sjursen

Publisher's Interests
Fiction and nonfiction hypertext—interlinked, interactive material specifically written to be read on the computer with pictures, sound, and video—is the specialty of Eastgate Systems. It also offers stand-alone hypertext on disk and CD-ROMs.
Website: www.eastgate.com

Freelance Potential
Published 10 titles in 2004: all were developed from unsolicited submissions. Receives 25 unsolicited mss yearly.
Submissions and Payment: Guidelines available at website. Send complete ms. Accepts disk submissions, CD-ROMs, URL submissions to dgreco@eastgate.com, and simultaneous submissions if identified. SASE. Responds in 4–6 weeks. Publication in 1 year. Royalty, 15%; advance.

Encounter Books

Suite 330
665 3rd Street
San Francisco, CA 94107-1951

Acquisitions Editor: Steve Wiley

Publisher's Interests
Nonfiction books for young adults and adults that offer a new perspective on ideas that challenge morality and imaginations are offered by this publisher. Topics include history, religion, education, public policy, and politics.
Website: www.encounterbooks.com

Freelance Potential
Published 20 titles (2 juvenile) in 2004: 1 was developed from an unsolicited submission and 15 were by agented authors. Receives 2,400 queries, 600 unsolicited mss yearly.
Submissions and Payment: Guidelines available at website. Accepts manuscripts through literary agents only. No email submissions. SASE. Response time varies. Publication period varies. Advance: one-third at signing, one-third when received, one-third at publication.

ESP Publishers, Inc.

5200 South Jules Verne Court
Tampa, FL 33611

Editor: Dan Brooks

Publisher's Interests
This educational publisher specializes in "yearbooks," which are workbooks for public school, private school, and homeschooled students. Each book contains the entire basic skills curriculum for a given grade level, from kindergarten through grade seven. Each yearbook includes vocabulary and achievement tests and answers.
Website: www.espbooks.com

Freelance Potential
Published 100–150 titles in 2004: all were by agented authors. Receives 24 queries, 4 unsolicited mss yearly.
Submissions and Payment: Query or send complete ms. Accepts photocopies, computer printouts, and simultaneous submissions if identified. SASE. Responds in 1 week. Publication period and payment policy vary.

ETC Publications

700 East Vereda del Sur
Palm Springs, CA 92262

Senior Editor: Richard W. Hostrop

Publisher's Interests
This educational publisher produces reference books for teachers and school administrators along with educational titles for students in elementary school through high school.

Freelance Potential
Published 3 titles in 2004: 1 was developed from an unsolicited submission. Of the 3 titles, 1 was by an unpublished writer and 1 was by an author who was new to the publishing house. Receives 50+ queries yearly.
Submissions and Payment: Query with 2 sample chapters. No unsolicited mss. Accepts photocopies, computer printouts, and simultaneous submissions if identified. Availability of artwork improves chance of acceptance. SASE. Responds in 1 month. Publication in 9 months. Royalty, 5–15%.

Excelsior Cee Publishing

P.O. Box 5861
Norman, OK 73070

Publisher: J. C. Marshall

Publisher's Interests
Nonfiction books for young adults and adults, including biographies, inspirational books, humor, titles on family history and personal philosophy, self-help books, writing texts, and poetry are the focus of this publisher. Established in 1989, Excelsior Cee is especially interested in how-to books on genealogy.
Website: www.excelsiorcee.com

Freelance Potential
Published 12 titles in 2004: 6 were developed from unsolicited submissions. Receives 1,500+ queries yearly.
Submissions and Payment: Query with synopsis; include sample chapter for longer works. Accepts photocopies, computer printouts, and simultaneous submissions if identified. SASE. Responds in 6 weeks. Publication in 6 months. Payment policy varies.

Exclamation! Publishers

P.O. Box 664
Phoenixville, PA 19460

President & Publisher: Denise E. Heap

Publisher's Interests
This small publisher focuses on titles that open doors to the world of discovery, where heroism triumphs celebrity and honesty outranks legend. Its list includes historical fiction; creative, well-documented nonfiction; and poetry for both children and adults.
Website: www.deheap.com

Freelance Potential
Published 8 titles (4 juvenile) in 2004: 2 were developed from unsolicited submissions. Of the 8 titles, 5 were by authors who were new to the publishing house. Receives 250 queries yearly.
Submissions and Payment: Guidelines available at website. Query with author biography or résumé. No unsolicited ms. Accepts email to dheap@deheap.com (no attachments). Responds in 4–6 weeks. Publication period varies. Royalty, 15%.

The Feminist Press

The Graduate Center
365 5th Avenue
New York, NY 10016

Publisher: Jean Casella

Publisher's Interests
The Feminist Press is a nonprofit educational publishing organization dedicated to eliminating gender stereotypes in schools and literature. It offers biographies of female role models, books with multicultural and international themes, and titles for parents about raising successful female children.
Website: www.feministpress.org

Freelance Potential
Published 15 titles in 2004: 2 were by agented authors, and 2 were reprint/licensed properties. Receives 800 queries yearly.
Submissions and Payment: Guidelines available at website. Query via email (200 words or less) to jcasella@gc.cuny.edu; include "submissions" in subject line. Responds in 3–4 months. Publication period varies. Royalty; advance.

Fiesta City Publishers

P.O. Box 5861
Santa Barbara, CA 93150-5861

President: Frank E. Cooke

Publisher's Interests
Musical plays, as well as books on cooking, music, song writing, and musical instruments for middle-grade students and young adults are offered by this publisher. It is always on the lookout for unique, well-written material and is especially interested in how-to nonfiction books, fiction, and musicals. If you have an idea for something that is new and creative, submit a query.

Freelance Potential
Published 2 titles in 2004. Of the 2 titles, 1 was by an unpublished writer and 1 was by an author who was new to the publishing house. Receives 80 queries yearly.
Submissions and Payment: Query with clips or writing samples. Accepts photocopies and simultaneous submissions if identified. SASE. Responds in 1–2 months. Publication period varies. Royalty.

Finney Company

3943 Meadowbrook Road
Minneapolis, MN 55426

Editor: Alan E. Krysan

Publisher's Interests
Targeting young adult and adult readers, this publisher specializes in publishing career materials that fit the needs of today's career and development programs. It offers textbooks, videotapes, computer software, and various instructional kits. Its Hobart imprint offers books on agrilurual and technical subjects.
Website: www.finney-hobar.com

Freelance Potential
Published 4–6 titles (4 juvenile) in 2004: 1 was developed from an unsolicited submission. Receives 240 queries, 240 unsolicited mss each year.
Submissions and Payment: Guidelines available at website. Query or send complete ms. SASE. Response time varies. Publication period varies. Royalty, 10% of net.

Fondo de Cultura Economica USA

2293 Verus Street
San Diego, CA 92154

Submissions Editor: Ignacio de Echevarria

Publisher's Interests
This publisher supplies Spanish-language books to schools, libraries, universities, and bookstores throughout the United States. Fiction and nonfiction picture books, middle-grade titles, and young adult books for Latin American readers are included in its catalogue.
Website: www.fceusa.com

Freelance Potential
Published 40 titles in 2004: 5 were developed from unsolicited submissions and 35 were by agented authors. Receives 300 queries each year.
Submissions and Payment: Query with résumé. Accepts photocopies, computer printouts, and disk submissions. Availability of artwork improves chance of acceptance. SASE. Responds in 6 months. Publication in 6 months. Royalty; advance. Flat fee.

Franklin Watts

Scholastic Inc.
90 Sherman Turnpike
Danbury, CT 06816

Acquisitions Editor

Publisher's Interests
Franklin Watts, a division of Scholastic Inc., has long been known for its curriculum-based titles on topics covered in the middle grades through the high school years. All of its titles target the school and library markets and it publishes no fiction.
Website: www.scholastic.com

Freelance Potential
Published 300 titles in 2004: 5 were developed from unsolicited submissions and 20 were by agented authors. Of the 300 titles, 8 were by unpublished writers and 13 were by authors who were new to the publishing house. Receives 1,000+ queries yearly.
Submissions and Payment: Query with résumé, outline, and sample chapters. No unsolicited mss. SASE. Responds in 3–5 weeks. Publication period and payment policy vary.

Gefen Publishing House

12 New Street
Hewlett, NY 11557-2012

Editor: Ilan Greenfield, Jr.

Publisher's Interests
Headquartered in Jerusalem, this publisher distributes its own titles, as well as those of other Israeli publishers. Its list includes a selection of children's books on Jewish culture, folklore, and Israel.
Website: www.israelbooks.com

Freelance Potential
Published 20 titles (4 juvenile) in 2004: most were developed from unsolicited submissions. Of the 20 titles, most were by authors who were new to the publishing house. Receives 240 queries, 100+ unsolicited mss yearly.
Submissions and Payment: Guidelines available. Query or send compete ms. Accepts photocopies, computer printouts, and simultaneous submissions if identified. SASE. Response time, publication period, and payment policy vary.

David R. Godine, Publisher

9 Hamilton Place
Boston, MA 02108

Editorial Department

Publisher's Interests
This award-winning, independent publisher offers a variety of high-quality original fiction and nonfiction books for young readers of all ages. It is interested in picture books, chapter books, and young adult novels. Genres include history, poetry, fables, folktales, mystery, literature, humor, art, nature, travel, gardening, and contemporary fiction. It strives to identify the best work and to produce it in the best way possible.
Website: www.godine.com

Freelance Potential
Published 30 titles (2 juvenile) in 2004: 10 were by agented authors, and 20 were reprint/licensed properties. Receives 1,000 queries yearly.
Submissions and Payment: Guidelines available at website. Query. No unsolicited mss. Publication period and payment policy vary.

Greenwillow Books

HarperCollins Children's Books
1350 Avenue of the Americas
New York, NY 10019

Editorial Department

Publisher's Interests
Greenwillow Books, an imprint of HarperCollins Children's Books, publishes picture books, fiction for young readers of all ages, and nonfiction primarily for children under seven years of age. Its list includes contemporary fiction, animal stories, and nonfiction books on nature and animals.
Website: www.harperchildrens.com

Freelance Potential
Published 60 titles in 2004: 11 were developed from unsolicited submissions. Of the 60 titles, 12 were by authors who were new to the publishing house. Receives 5,500 queries, 8,000+ unsolicited mss yearly.
Submissions and Payment: Not accepting queries or unsolicited mss at this time.

Groundwood Books

Suite 500, 720 Bathurst Street
Toronto, Ontario M5S 2R4
Canada

Manuscript Acquisitions

Publisher's Interests
With a mandate to publish high-quality, character-driven fiction for children of all ages, Groundwood Books seeks contemporary, multicultural, and ethnic stories. It avoids genre fiction such as thrillers and mysteries, and stories with an obvious message or moral. At this time, it is not reviewing unsolicited picture book manuscripts.
Website: www.groundwoodbooks.com

Freelance Potential
Published 25 titles in 2004. Of the 25 titles, 5 were by authors who were new to the publishing house.
Submissions and Payment: Guidelines and catalogue available at website. Query with synopsis and sample chapters. Accepts photocopies and computer printouts. No simultaneous submissions. SASE. Responds in 2–4 months. Publication period varies. Royalty; advance.

Harcourt Canada Ltd.

55 Horner Avenue
Toronto, Ontario M8Z 4X6
Canada

Vice-President of Publishing: Melanie Myers

Publisher's Interests
For over 100 years, this educational publisher has offered quality educational resources for use in Canadian classrooms. Subjects include science, language arts, social studies, English, math, and music. The curriculum-based products target children in kindergarten through grade 12.
Website: www.harcourtcanada.com

Freelance Potential
Published 60 titles (40 juvenile) in 2004: all were by agented authors and 10 were reprint/licensed properties. Of the 60 titles, 8 were by authors new to the publishing house. Receives 100 queries yearly.
Submissions and Payment: Query. No unsolicited mss. SAE/IRC. Responds in 6–12 months. Publication period varies. Payment policy varies.

Harvard Common Press

535 Albany Street
Boston, MA 02118

Executive Editor: Pamela Hoenig

Publisher's Interests
Quality trade books are produced by this small independent publisher. It specializes in cookbooks, parenting and child-care books, and, on occasion, it offers health and beauty books.
Website: www.harvardcommonpress.com

Freelance Potential
Published 12 titles in 2004: 7 were by agented authors. Of the 12 titles, 2 were by unpublished writers and 9 were by authors who were new to the publishing house. Receives 1,200 queries yearly.
Submissions and Payment: Guidelines and catalogue available at website. Query with résumé, outline, 1–2 sample chapters, and market analysis. Accepts photocopies, computer printouts, and simultaneous submissions if identified. SASE. Responds in 1–3 months. Publication period varies. Royalty, 5%; advance, $1,500+.

Hodder Children's Books

338 Euston Road
London NW1 3BH
United Kingdom

The Reader

Publisher's Interests
Hodder Children's Books is a prize-winning British publisher that offers fiction for children and young adults. It is not currently accepting unsolicited material for consideration. Check website for updates in its submissions policy.
Website: www.hodderheadline.co.uk

Freelance Potential
Published 500 titles in 2004: 10 were developed from unsolicited submissions, 200 were by agented authors, and 20 were reprint/licensed properties. Receives 3,000 queries, 2,000 unsolicited mss yearly.
Submissions and Payment: Not currently accepting unsolicited manuscripts or queries.

Holloway House Publishing Group

8060 Melrose Avenue
Los Angeles, CA 90046

Submissions Editor: Neal Colgrass

Publisher's Interests
Established in 1960, this publisher offers biographies of outstanding African American role models for young adults. It assigns most of its books, but will consider submissions for its Black American series.
Website: www.hollowayhousebooks.com

Freelance Potential
Published 12 titles in 2004: 2 were developed from unsolicited submissions. Of the 12 titles, 10 were by unpublished writers and all were by authors who were new to the publishing house. Receives 500+ queries, 100 unsolicited mss yearly.
Submissions and Payment: Guidelines available. Query with résumé or send ms. Accepts photocopies, computer printouts, and disk submissions. SASE. Responds to queries in 3 weeks, to mss in 3 months. Publication period and payment policy vary.

Hyperion Books for Children

14th Floor
114 5th Avenue
New York, NY 10011

Vice President of Publishing: Brenda Bowen

Publisher's Interests
A variety of outstanding nonfiction and fiction titles for children of all ages are produced by this publisher. An imprint of the Walt Disney Company, it offers board books, picture books, chapter books, and young adult and middle-grade novels. It does not accept unsolicited submissions and suggests new writers turn to the Society of Children's Book Writers for information on publishers, and how to locate a reputable literary agent.
Website: www.hyperionbooksforchildren.com

Freelance Potential
Published 240 titles (215 juvenile) in 2004: all were by agented authors.
Submissions and Payment: Guidelines and titles available at website. Accepts manuscripts through literary agents only.

I B Publications

P.O. Box 5123
South Murwillumbah 2484
Australia

Director: David Vickers-Shand

Publisher's Interests
The philosophy and teachings of Rudolf Steiner are the focus of this Australian publisher's list. 25% self-, subsidy, co-venture, or co-op published material
Website: www.immortalbooks.com.au

Freelance Potential
Published 5 titles in 2004: 1 was developed from an unsolicited submission and 2 were reprint/licensed properties. Of the 5 titles, 3 were by unpublished writers and 3 were by authors who were new to the publishing house. Receives 5–6 unsolicited mss yearly.
Submissions and Payment: Catalogue available at website. Send complete ms. Accepts email submissions to info@immortalbooks.co.au (Microsoft Word). Artwork improves chance of acceptance. Responds in 3–4 weeks. Publication in 3–6 months. Payment policy varies.

InQ Publishing Co.

P.O. Box 10
North Aurora, IL 60542

Editor: Jana Fitting

Publisher's Interests
Books, games, and activity books that educate and inform compose the list of this specialty publisher. It offers titles on health, safety, and genealogy for children, as well as a special line of materials for babysitters and day care providers. This publisher is interested in how-to books and accompanying products that cover topics not usually found in other publications.
Website: www.inqbooks.com

Freelance Potential
Published 2 titles in 2004: Receives 50 queries each year.
Submissions and Payment: Catalogue available at website. Query with writing samples. No unsolicited mss. Accepts photocopies. SASE. Responds in 6 weeks. Publication in 18 months. Payment policy varies.

InterVarsity Press

P.O. Box 1400
Downers Grove, IL 60515

Editor: Elaine Whittenhall

Publisher's Interests
This publisher features Christian books, academic and theological material, reference titles, and Bible studies written and used by professional educators. Although it no longer publishes books for children, it does offer a limited number of parenting titles with a Christian viewpoint. InterVarsity Press is interested in material that encourages readers to become better Christians.
Website: www.ivpress.com

Freelance Potential
Published 20 titles in 2004. Receives 750 queries yearly.
Submissions and Payment: Guidelines and catalogue available at website. Query with résumé, chapter-by-chapter summary, and 2 sample chapters. SASE. Responds in 12 weeks. Publication in 2 years. Payment policy varies.

Iron Crown Enterprises

112 Goodman Street
Charlottesville, VA 22902

Managing Editor

Publisher's Interests
For over 20 years, this publisher has produced fantasy role-playing, board, miniature, and collectible card games and puzzles for young adults and adults. Its primary focus is on non-electric, table top, role-playing games. Check its website for detailed submission guidelines before submitting a query.
Website: www.ironcrown.com

Freelance Potential
Published 6 titles in 2004. Receives 10–20 queries yearly.
Submissions and Payment: Guidelines available. Query with outline/synopsis and writing samples. Accepts computer printouts, disk submissions, and email queries to ozmar_ice@yahoo.com. SASE. Responds in 6 months. Publication in 6–12 months. Royalty; 2–6%; advance, $100. Flat fee, $500–$1,500.

January Productions

116 Washington Avenue
Hawthorne, NJ 07506

Creative Director: Barbara Peller

Publisher's Interests
Serving libraries and schools, this publisher offers a variety of educational materials for students in kindergarten through eighth grade; with the majority being high-interest/low-reading level students. It offers stimulating activities and products such as books, videos, filmstrips, CD-ROMS, and games. Educational material that is motivational and exciting is of interest here.
Website: www.awpeller.com

Freelance Potential
Receives 100 queries, 50 unsolicited mss yearly.
Submissions and Payment: Catalogue available at website. Prefers query with outline/synopsis. Accepts complete ms with résumé. Accepts photocopies. SASE. Response time and publication period vary. Flat fee, $325–$375.

Jump at the Sun

114 5th Avenue
New York, NY 10011

Submissions Editor

Publisher's Interests
This imprint of Disney Enterprises celebrates the African American experience with books that invite children to embrace the beauty of African American culture. It is interested in novelty books, picture books, middle-grade novels, and historical fiction that highlights cultural diversity. Jump at the Sun accepts only agented queries.
Website: www.hyperionbooksforchildren.com

Freelance Potential
Published 50 titles in 2004: most were by agented authors. Receives 240 queries yearly.
Submissions and Payment: Catalogue available at website. Accepts queries from agents only. Accepts photocopies. SASE. Responds in 1–3 months. Publication in 2 years. Royalty; advance.

Kingfisher

215 Park Avenue South
New York, NY 10003

Submissions Editor

Publisher's Interests
Children of all ages enjoy a variety of nonfiction books produced by this award-winning publisher. An imprint of Houghton Mifflin Company, it specializes in illustrated nonfiction, but also offers anthologies, Spanish-language titles, series titles, and a small number of picture books. Topics include animals, history, geography, science, the environment, food, and myths and legends. Please note that it accepts submissions from literary agents only.
Website: www.houghtonmifflinbooks.com/kingfisher

Freelance Potential
Published 60 titles in 2004: all were by agented authors.
Submissions and Payment: Catalogue available with 9x12 SASE (5 first-class stamps). All work is assigned by publisher. Accepts agented submissions only. No unsolicited mss.

Kodiak Media Group

P.O. Box 1029-A
Wilsonville, OR 97070

Marketing Director: Rhonda Grabenhorst-Pachl

Publisher's Interests
Nonfiction educational books for parents, teachers, and other professionals working with hearing-impaired and deaf children are produced by this publisher. It offers insight into issues relating to deaf culture, education, and children. The majority of its work is done in-house, but it does accept queries from writers who are experts in the field.

Freelance Potential
Published 2 titles in 2004. Receives 10 queries, 10 unsolicited mss each year.
Submissions and Payment: Query or send complete ms. Accepts photocopies, computer printouts, and simultaneous submissions if identified. SASE. Responds in 1 month. Publication period varies. Royalty, negotiable.

Wendy Lamb Books ☆

1745 Broadway
New York, NY 10019

Editor: Wendy Lamb

Publisher's Interests
Wendy Lamb Books is an imprint of the well-known publisher Random House, offering a list of approximately 10 to 15 new titles, fiction and nonfiction, each year. Its books are read by young adults and adults. Topics covered include history, multicultural and ethnic subjects, adventure fiction, humor, mystery, suspense, and multicultural and ethnic fiction.
Website: www.randomhouse.com

Freelance Potential
Published 10–15 titles in 2004.
Submissions and Payment: Query with age group and publishing credits. Accepts photocopies, computer printouts, and disk submissions (Microsoft Word). SASE. Responds in 6 weeks. Publication period and payment policy vary.

LangMarc Publishing

P.O. Box 90488
Austin, TX 78709-0488

Submissions Editor

Publisher's Interests
LangMarc Publishing was established in 1991 in San Antonio, Texas, as a trade publisher of inspirational and educational books targeting the Christian market. Its primary audience is young adults and it is interested in reviewing both fiction and nonfiction queries. All submissions should be written from a positive point of view, and feature ideas that are important to young adults today. Nonfiction that offers sound, practical, faith-based solutions, to problems teens face in their everyday lives are an on-going need.
Website: www.langmarc.com

Freelance Potential
Published 4 titles (1 juvenile) in 2004.
Submissions and Payment: Query. Response time varies. Publication in 9 months. Payment policy varies.

Leadership Publishers Inc.

P.O. Box 8358
Des Moines, IA 50301-8358

Editor/Owner: Dr. Lois Roets

Publisher's Interests
This specialty publisher offers educational materials for gifted and high-ability students, as well as reference books for parents and educators who work with them. Leadership Publishers selects titles based on their marketability and potential for use in elementary and middle-grade settings.

Freelance Potential
Published 2 titles in 2004. Receives 10 queries yearly.
Submissions and Payment: Send for guidelines and catalogue (SASE with 2 first-class stamps) prior to submission. After receipt of guidelines, query with table of contents, outline, and 2 sample chapters. Accepts photocopies and computer printouts. No simultaneous submissions. SASE. Responds in 2 months. Publication in 6–12 months. Royalty, 10%. Flat fee.

Learning Links Inc.

2300 Marcus Avenue
New Hyde Park, NY 11042

Chairman: Joyce Friedland

Publisher's Interests
Established in 1980, this publisher offers teacher's study guides to accompany instruction of classic literature for grades one through twelve. It is seeking writers who have worked on teacher's manuals, or have written other study guides. Query only—it does not accept unsolicited manuscripts.
Website: www.learninglinks.com

Freelance Potential
Published 25 titles in 2004: 6 were developed from unsolicited submissions, and 19 were assigned. Of the 25 titles, 4 were by unpublished writers and 3 were by authors who were new to the publishing house. Receives 24 queries yearly.
Submissions and Payment: Guidelines available. Query. Responds in 1 week. Publication in 3 months. Flat fee.

LifeSong Publishers

P.O. Box 183
Somis, CA 93066

Editor: Laurie Donahue

Publisher's Interests
LifeSong Publishers features Christian titles for adults and children. Its list includes workbooks, manuals, and study guides to prepare teens, junior high school, and senior high school students for various church-related milestones. It is interested in authors that are ministry oriented and are willing to promote their work. Subsidy publishing will be considered in certain cases.
Website: www.lifesongpublishers.com

Freelance Potential
Published 4 titles in 2004. Receives 48 queries, 24 unsolicited mss each year.
Submissions and Payment: Catalogue available at website. Query or send complete ms. SASE. Response time varies. Publication period varies. Royalty, 10% of net.

Little Blue Works

P.O. Box 28
Port Orchard, WA 98366

Editor: Cris DiMarco

Publisher's Interests
Entertaining and educational books for children and young adults are produced by this publisher. It seeks books that are timeless, rather than the next "hot thing." Submissions must follow its five-step process. Check its website for details.
Website: www.windstormcreative.com

Freelance Potential
Published 2–5 titles in 2004: most were developed from unsolicited submissions. Receives 6,000 queries yearly.
Submissions and Payment: Guidelines available at website. Query with 1-page synopsis. Submissions that do not indicate a website visit will be returned. SASE. Response time and publication period vary. Royalty, 10–15%.

Living the Good News

Suite 400
600 Grant Street
Denver, CO 80203

Editorial Management Team

Publisher's Interests
Living the Good News is a non-denominational publisher dedicated to helping readers share in God's word. It offers a list of titles for all ages and focuses on material for use in Christian education programs and curriculums.
Website: www.livingthegoodnews.com

Freelance Potential
Published 30 titles in 2004: 5 were developed from unsolicited submissions. Of the 30 titles, 1 was by an unpublished writer. Receives 150 queries yearly.
Submissions and Payment: Query with sample chapter. Accepts photocopies, computer printouts, Macintosh disk submissions, and simultaneous submissions if identified. SASE. Responds in 2 months. Publication in 2 years. Royalty.

Lobster Press

Suites C & D, 1620 Sherbrooke Street West
Montreal, Quebec H3H 1C9
Canada

Assistant Editor: Karen Li

Publisher's Interests
Well-written picture books, early chapter books, and young adult fiction and nonfiction are produced by this publisher. It is currently interested in young adult material. Please send a query only. It is not accepting unsolicited manuscripts.
Website: www.lobsterpress.com

Freelance Potential
Published 11 titles (4 juveniles) in 2004: 8 were developed from unsolicited submissions, 2 were by agented authors, and 2 were reprint/licensed properties. Of the 11 titles, 3 were by unpublished writers and 6 were by authors who were new to the publishing house.
Submissions and Payment: Guidelines available at website. Query only—not accepting unsolicited mss at this time.

The Love and Logic Press

2207 Jackson Street
Golden, CO 80401-2300

Publisher

Publisher's Interests
This independent publishers features material based on the "Love and Logic" method of child rearing. Its philosophy is based on developing responsible kids by teaching them how to take responsability in the real world. It offers an extensive product list based on its philosophy, including books, videos, audiocassettes, and training programs for parents and educators.
Website: www.loveandlogic.com

Freelance Potential
Published 10 titles in 2004. Receives 30 queries yearly.
Submissions and Payment: Query with proposal or outline. Accepts photocopies, computer printouts, and simultaneous submissions if available. SASE. Responds in 1 month. Publication in 18 months. Royalty, 5–7%.

The Lutterworth Press

P.O. Box 60
Cambridge CB12 NT
United Kingdom

Managing Editor: Adrian Brink

Publisher's Interests
More than 200 years old, this British publisher is known for its high-quality books for children and adults, with a particular emphasis on moral values. It publishes approximately 30 titles a year and rejects many more simply because they are not suitable in subject matter as outlined in the company's guidelines. Interested authors are urged to include a detailed market analysis with each query.
Website: www.lutterworth.com

Freelance Potential
Published 10 titles in 2004.
Submissions and Payment: Guidelines available at website. Query with outline/synopsis and 1–2 sample chapters. Availability of artwork improves chance of acceptance. SAE/IRC. Responds in 2 months. Publication period varies. Royalty.

MacAdam/Cage

Suite 550
155 Sansome Street
San Francisco, CA 94104

Editor: Pat Walsh

Publisher's Interests
Established in 1998, MacAdam/Cage is primarily a publisher of adult literary fiction and narrative nonfiction. It does not publish any children's titles however, many of its titles also appeal to a young adult audience.
Website: www.macadamcage.com

Freelance Potential
Published 30 titles in 2004: 15 were developed from unsolicited submissions and 15 were by agented authors. Receives 6,000 queries each year.
Submissions and Payment: Guidelines and catalogue available at website or with SASE ($2.21 postage). Query with clips. Accepts photocopies. SASE. Responds in 4–5 months. Publication period and payment policy vary.

Mage Publishers

1032 29th Street NW
Washington, DC 20007

Submissions Editor: Amin Sepehri

Publisher's Interests
This small independent publisher was founded in 1985. It specializes in books about Persian culture and history and offers a catalogue that includes books for both adults and children. The company was founded in 1985.
Website: www.mage.com

Freelance Potential
Published 3-4 titles in 2004: 1 was developed from an unsolicited submission. Of the 3-4 titles, 1 was by an author who was new to the publishing house. Receives 50 queries, 25 unsolicited mss yearly.
Submissions and Payment: Guidelines available at website. Query or send ms. Availability of artwork improves chance of acceptance. Accepts photocopies and computer printouts. SASE. Responds in 1-3 months. Publication in 9-15 months. Royalty; advance.

Marlor Press

4304 Brigadoon Drive
St. Paul, MN 55126

Editorial Director: Marlin Bree

Publisher's Interests
Books about boating and travel are the specialty of this small niche publishing house. While most of its catalogue is devoted to adult titles, it does offer activity books for children between the ages of four and twelve, as well as family travel guides and travel journals. Submissions for activity books continue to be needed, but keep in mind that Marlor Press does not publish any fiction.

Freelance Potential
Published 2 titles in 2004: one was developed from an unsolicited submission and was by an unpublished writer. Receives 100+ queries yearly.
Submissions and Payment: Query with market analysis. No unsolicited mss. Accepts photocopies and computer printouts. SASE. Response time varies. Publication in 1 year. Royalty, 8-10% of net.

Marsh Media

8025 Ward Parkway Plaza
Kansas City, MO 64112

Submissions Editor: Joan K. Marsh

Publisher's Interests
Established in 1969, Marsh Media was founded as a developer of educational filmstrips specializing in health and guidance. Since then, it has expanded its catalogue to include books on personal development in the areas of respect, family, friendship, personal power, self-control, trust, risk-taking, and responsibility. Writers interested in submitting may now find guidelines at the website and are encouraged to review them before querying.
Website: www.marshmedia.com

Freelance Potential
Published 1 title in 2004. Receives 12 queries yearly.
Submissions and Payment: Guidelines and catalogue available at website. Query with résumé. SASE. Response time, publication period, and payment policy vary.

Miles Kelly Publishing

Bardfield Centre, Great Bardfield
Essex CM7 4SL
United Kingdom

Submissions Editor

Publisher's Interests
Miles Kelly Publishing was founded in 1996 and now has more than 360 books in its catalogue. Its focus is on nonfiction for children between ages four and fourteen and novelty books, reference books, and activity titles are found on its list. Topics covered include history, mathematics, geography, nature, the environment science, technology, and animals. Fiction and poetry are also published here. 20% co-published material.
Website: www.mileskelly.net

Freelance Potential
Published 100 titles (90 juvenile) in 2004.
Submissions and Payment: Guidelines available at website. Query with clips. SAE/IRC. Response time varies. Publication period varies. Flat fee.

The Millbrook Press

2 Old New Milford Road
Brookfield, CT 06804

Editorial Director: Jean Reynolds

Publisher's Interests
The goal of Millbrook Press has always been to produce exceptional children's books. Each manuscript it accepts for publication receives individual and personal care to ensure the highest standard of quality. For approximately one year Millbrook had suspended its publishing program, but it plans to be back in business in 2005. As in the past, it will continue to seek nonfiction titles appropriate for schools and public libraries—no fiction.
Website: www.millbrookpress.com

Freelance Potential
Plans to resume publishing (1 or more titles) in 2005.
Submissions and Payment: Guidelines available at website. Query with résumé, outline, and sample chapter. SASE. Responds in 6–8 weeks. Publication in 12–18 months. Royalty; advance. Flat fee.

Mirrorstone Books

P.O. Box 707
Renton, WA 98057

Submissions: Nina Hess

Publisher's Interests
This new series imprint from Wizards of the Coast, a well-known publisher of shared-world series, publishes fiction for middle-grade and young adult audiences. Genres includes adventure, contemporary, drama, fantasy, mystery, and science fiction. Work is done on assignment only. It seeks authors who can write cinematically.
Website: www.mirrorstonebooks.com

Freelance Potential
Published 8 titles in 2004: 4 were by agented authors. Receives 30–40 queries yearly.
Submissions and Payment: Writers' guidelines available at website. Query with sample chapter and a résumé. All work is done by assignment only. Responds in 12–18 weeks. Publication period varies. Royalty; advance.

Modern Publishing

155 East 55th Street
New York, NY 10022

Editorial Director: Kathy O'Hehir

Publisher's Interests
Targeting children ages two through ten, this publisher specializes in the publication of licensed and non-licensed titles in a variety of formats including: activity and board books, storybooks, educational books, and novelty books.
Website: www.modernpublishing.com

Freelance Potential
Published 300 titles in 2004: 10–15 were developed from unsolicited submissions. Receives 75 queries and unsolicited mss yearly.
Submissions and Payment: Guidelines available. Query with outline/synopsis; or send complete ms. Accepts photocopies and simultaneous submissions if identified. Availability of artwork improves chance of acceptance. SASE. Responds in 2 months. Publication period varies. Royalty, by arrangement. Flat fee. Work-for-hire.

Morning Glory Press

6595 San Haroldo Way
Buena Park, CA 90620-3748

President: Jeanne Lindsay

Publisher's Interests
Resources for pregnant teens and teen parents are the specialty of this publisher. Morning Glory Press also offers award-winning novels and nonfiction titles for young adults about contemporary social issues and problems, child development, abuse, life skills, teen fathers, and personal relationships. Its editors are interested in materials for at-risk teens and the educators and social workers who help them.
Website: www.morningglorypress.com

Freelance Potential
Published 5 titles in 2004. Receives 100 queries yearly.
Submissions and Payment: Query. Accepts photocopies. SASE. Responds in 1–3 months. Publication in 6–8 months. Royalty; advance, $500.

Mountain Meadow Press

P.O. Box 447
Kooskia, ID 83539

Submissions Editor

Publisher's Interests
Since 1983, this midwestern publisher has offered regional travel books and titles on Pacific Northwest history and culture for adults. It also offers several books and various materials about the Pacific Northwest for students in homeschooling programs. Although Mountain Meadow Press does not accept unsolicited manuscripts, it will consider queries for original material it deems appropriate for its publishing program.

Freelance Potential
Published 1 title in 2004. Receives 6 queries and unsolicited mss each year.
Submissions and Payment: Catalogue available. Query only. No unsolicited mss. Accepts photocopies and computer printouts. SASE. Responds in 3 months. Publication period varies. Royalty.

Mount Olive College Press

634 Henderson Street
Mount Olive, NC 28365

Acquisitions Editor: Pepper Worthington

Publisher's Interests
The culture, people, history, and wildlife of North Carolina are featured in books published by this regional publisher. It is interested in imaginative, inspirational middle-grade children's stories that offer educational value.

Freelance Potential
Published 3 titles (1 juvenile) in 2004: 1 was developed from an unsolicited submission. Of the 3 titles, 2 were by authors who were new to the publishing house. Receives 500+ queries, 400 unsolicited mss yearly.
Submissions and Payment: Guidelines available. Query with outline/synopsis and 3 sample chapters; or send complete ms. Accepts photocopies and computer printouts. SASE. Responds in 6–12 months. Publication in 1 year. Payment policy varies.

Munchweiler Press

P.O. Box 2529
Victorville, CA 92393-2529

Publisher: Ted Lish

Publisher's Interests
Established in 1999, this small house publisher offers quality picture books for young readers ages four through eight. It is open to all styles, especially humorous stories with a moral. Currently, it is not accepting submissions of young adult or adult titles, and it only accepts queries. Check its website for updates.
Website: www.munchweilerpress.com

Freelance Potential
Published no new titles in 2004. It will resume publishing in 2005. Receives 20–30 queries yearly.
Submissions and Payment: Guidelines available. Query. No unsolicited mss. Accepts email queries to publisher@munchweilerpress.com. SASE. Responds in 2 months. Publication in 1 year. Royalty, 5%. Flat fee.

National Geographic Books for Children

1145 17th Street NW
Washington DC 20036-4688

Editorial Assistant: Susan Donnelly

Publisher's Interests
Well known for its fascinating nonfiction books, this imprint of the National Geographic Society targets readers ages four through young adult. Its list includes adventure, history, geography, animals, culture, exploration, nature, science, and reference books. Currently, it is not accepting unsolicited submissions.
Website: www.nationalgeographic.com/books/kids.splash

Freelance Potential
Published 25 titles in 2004: 3 were developed from unsolicited submissions, 2 were by agented authors, and 12 were assigned. Of the 25 titles, 3 were by unpublished writers and 15 were by authors who were new to the publishing house.
Submissions and Payment: Not accepting queries or unsolicited manuscripts at this time.

National Resource Center for Youth Services

College of Continuing Education, University of Oklahoma
4502 East 41st Street, Tulsa, OK 74135

Marketing Manager: Rhoda Baker

Publisher's Interests
Self-esteem, substance abuse, depression, and sexuality are some of the topics covered by this publisher for social service professionals and at-risk teenagers.
Website: www.nrcys.ou.edu

Freelance Potential
Published 2 titles (1 juvenile) in 2004: 1 was developed from an unsolicited submission. Of the 2 titles, 1 was by an unpublished writer and 1 was by an author who was new to the publishing house. Receives 50 queries yearly.
Submissions and Payment: Guidelines available. Query with outline and 1–3 sample chapters. Accepts computer printouts and disk submissions. SASE. Responds in 1–3 months. Publication in 8–18 months. Royalty.

Natural Heritage Books

P.O. Box 95, Station O
Toronto, Ontario M4A 2M8
Canada

Editor: Jane Gibson

Publisher's Interests
This publisher offers quality fiction and nonfiction titles for middle-grade readers that focus on the history, heritage, and culture of Canada. It welcomes Canadian stories by new and aspiring authors.
Website: www.naturalheritagebooks.com

Freelance Potential
Published 14 titles (2 juvenile) in 2004: 7 were developed from unsolicited submissions, 2 were by agented authors, and 1 was a reprint/licensed property. Of the 14 titles, 5 were by unpublished writers and 6 were by authors who were new to the publishing house. Receives 100+ queries yearly.
Submissions and Payment: Guidelines available. Query with clips or writing samples. Accepts photocopies. SAE/IRC. Responds in 2–3 months. Publication in 1–2 years. Royalty; advance.

New Canaan Publishing Company

P.O. Box 752
New Canaan, CT 06840

Editor

Publisher's Interests
This small, independent publisher offers Christian books for children and adults, as well as educational fiction and nonfiction titles for readers ages six to fourteen. It is especially interested in material that helps children to study on their own.
Website: www.newcanaanpublishing.com

Freelance Potential
Published 4 titles in 2004. Of the 4 titles, 2 were by unpublished writers and 3 were by authors who were new to the publishing house.
Submissions and Payment: Guidelines available. Query with synopsis; or send complete ms. Accepts photocopies and computer printouts. SASE. Responds in 10–12 months. Publication period and payment policy vary.

Nomad Press

P.O. Box 875
Route 5 South
Norwich, VT 05055

Acquisitions Editor: Lauri Berkenkamp

Publisher's Interests
Nomad Press is a small, independent publisher that offers practical, comprehensive titles for adults. It seeks humorous how-to books on parenting topics relating to teens and young adults. Nomad Press will not consider fiction.
Website: www.nomadpress.net

Freelance Potential
Published 10 titles in 2004: 1 was developed from an unsolicited submission. Of the 10 titles, 4 were by authors who were new to the publishing house. Receives 100+ unsolicited mss yearly.
Submissions and Payment: Guidelines available at website. Send complete ms. Accepts photocopies and disk submissions. SASE. Responds in 1–3 months. Publication in 6–18 months. Royalty. Flat fee.

North-South Books

Suite 1901
875 6th Avenue
New York, NY 10001

Submissions Editor

Publisher's Interests
This international company publishes simultaneous editions of its fiction and nonfiction books in 15 countries and in seven languages. It is the English-language imprint of Nord-Süd Verlag, and produces translations of books and new titles. Targeting children from birth to age 10, it offers early toddler, early picture, easy-to-read, story picture, and chapter books. Genres include adventure, mystery, nature, fairy tales, folklore, fantasy, and multicultural. Please note that submissions are accepted through literary agents only.
Website: www.northsouth.com

Freelance Potential
Published 30 titles in 2004: all were by agented authors.
Submissions and Payment: Accepts mss through literary agents only. Royalty; advance.

OnStage Publishing

214 East Moulton Street NE
Decatur, AL 35601

Senior Editor: Dianne Hamilton

Publisher's Interests
At this time, fiction of interest to middle-grade boys is the priority of this publisher. It also offers nonfiction books for beginning and young adult readers.
Website: www.onstagebooks.com

Freelance Potential
Published 5 titles in 2004: 4 were developed from unsolicited submissions and 1 was by an agented author. Of the 5 titles, 3 were by unpublished writers and 3 were by authors who were new to the publishing house. Receives 900 unsolicited mss yearly.
Submissions and Payment: Guidelines available with 9x12 SASE (3 first-class stamps). Send complete ms for fiction. Accepts photocopies. SASE. Responds in 6–8 weeks. Publication in 1–2 years. Royalty, varies; advance, varies.

Our Child Press

P.O. Box 4379
Philadelphia, PA 19118

President: Carol Perrott

Publisher's Interests
Fiction and nonfiction titles about parenting and adoption for children and their families are the specialty of this small publisher. 50% self-, subsidy-, co-venture, or co-op published material.
Website: www.ourchildpress.com

Freelance Potential
Published 2 titles in 2004: 1 was developed from an unsolicited submission and 1 was a reprint/licensed property. Of the 2 titles, 1 was by an unpublished writer. Receives 50 queries, 35 unsolicited mss yearly.

Submissions and Payment: Guidelines available. Query with outline/synopsis; or send complete ms. Accepts photocopies and computer printouts. SASE. Responds in 1–3 months. Publication in 1 year. Royalty.

Pacific View Press

P.O. Box 2657
Berkeley, CA 94702

Acquisitions Editor: Pam Zumwalt

Publisher's Interests
This publisher offers a variety of multicultural nonfiction and literature for children ages eight to twelve. It produces engaging books with a focus on the culture and history of China, Japan, the Philippines, Mexico, and other countries in the Pacific Rim.
Website: www.pacificviewpress.com

Freelance Potential
Published 2 titles in 2004: 1 was developed from unsolicited submissions. Of the 2 titles, 1 was by an unpublished writer. Receives many queries yearly.

Submissions and Payment: Guidelines available. Query with outline and sample chapter. Accepts photocopies and computer printouts. SASE. Responds in 1 month. Publication period varies. Royalty, 8–10%; advance, $500–$1,000.

Parachute Press

Suite 302
156 5th Avenue
New York, NY 10010

Submissions Editor

Publisher's Interests
Parachute Press is a book packager that specializes in horror fiction for middle-grade readers. It also offers all levels of children's picture books and easy-to-read chapter books, as well as young adult novels and nonfiction.
Website: www.parachutepublishing.com

Freelance Potential
Published 100 titles (80 juvenile) in 2004: 10 were developed from unsolicited submissions, and 50 were by agented authors.
Submissions and Payment: Work-for-hire guidelines available with SASE. Send résumé and 1- to 5-page writing sample. Accepts unsolicited mss from literary agents only. No simultaneous submission. Accepts photocopies. SASE. Response time varies. Publication in 9 months. Flat fee, $3,000–$4,000.

Parkway Publishers

P.O. Box 3678
Boone, NC 28607

President: Rao Aluri

Publisher's Interests
Fiction and nonfiction topics relating to North Carolina's high country are the focus of this regional publisher. It is interested in local legends and folktales for young readers.
Website: www.parkwaypublishers.com

Freelance Potential
Published 20 titles (2 juvenile) in 2004: 18 were developed from unsolicited submissions and 2 were reprint/licensed properties. Of the 20 titles, 5 were by unpublished writers and 15 were by authors who were new to the publishing house. Receives 25 unsolicited mss yearly.
Submissions and Payment: Send complete ms. Accepts photocopies, computer printouts, and IBM disk submissions (Microsoft Word). SASE. Responds in 2–6 weeks. Publication in 6–12 months. Royalty, 10%.

Paws IV Books

Suite 400
119 South Main Street
Seattle, WA 98104

Editor

Publisher's Interests
This regional publisher specializes in fiction and nonfiction titles on the wilderness, wildlife, and culture of the American West Coast. Its list includes books for children ages four to ten. Paws IV Books currently seeks picture books about Alaska, as well as wilderness adventures for older readers, and books on multicultural issues that are pertinent to the region.
Website: www.sasquatchbooks.com

Freelance Potential
Published 4 titles in 2004. Of the 4 titles, 2 were by authors who were new to the publishing house. Receives 50 unsolicited mss yearly.
Submissions and Payment: Send complete ms with résumé and clips. SASE. Responds in 4 months. Publication period varies. Royalty; advance.

Pearson Learning Group

135 South Mount Zion Road
P.O. Box 2500
Lebanon, IN 46052

V.P. Publisher: Celia Argiriou

Publisher's Interests
This educational publisher features supplemental material for grades pre-K to twelve, including bilingual products, phonics and assessment materials, and programs for special needs and ESL students. It also offers cross-curriculum titles for math, computer technology, literature, and science.
Website: www.pearsonlearning.com

Freelance Potential
Published 50 titles in 2004: 1 was developed from an unsolicited submission and 1 was a reprint/licensed property. Of the 50 titles, 1 was by an unpublished writer. Receives 30 queries yearly.
Submissions and Payment: Query with résumé and writing sample. SASE. Response time, publication period, and payment policy vary.

Peartree

P.O. Box 14533
Clearwater, FL 33766

Submissions Editor: Barbara Birenbaum

Publisher's Interests
Now in its 20th year, this publisher seeks titles for readers in grades two through five. It is interested in adventure, animal stories, safety, contemporary fiction, and high-interest/low-vocabulary books. Peartree prefers authors interested in promoting their own books. 50% subsidy-published material.

Freelance Potential
Published 4 titles in 2004: 4 were developed from unsolicited submissions. Of the 4 titles, 1 was by an unpublished writer. Receives 50–75 queries, 25 unsolicited mss yearly.
Submissions and Payment: Query or send complete ms. Accepts photocopies and computer printouts. Availability of artwork improves chance of acceptance. SASE. Responds in 6–8 weeks. Publication in 1 year. Payment policy varies.

Peel Productions

P.O. Box 546
Columbus, NC 28722-0546

Editor: Susan DuBosque

Publisher's Interests
Peel Productions is a small, tightly focused publisher that concentrates on series titles that help children explore their world and develop their language skills. It is interested in books for its how-to-draw series for budding artists ages eight to fourteen, as well as additions to its riddle series about nature, science, school, animals, and the alphabet for beginning readers. Peel Productions will also consider material for new series.
Website: www.peelbooks.com

Freelance Potential
Published 4–5 titles in 2004. Receives 1,500 queries yearly.
Submissions and Payment: Query. No unsolicited mss. Accepts photocopies. SASE. Response time varies. Publication period varies. Royalty, 11% of net sales.

Penguin Books Canada Limited

Suite 300, 10 Alcorn Avenue
Toronto, Ontario M4V 3B2
Canada

The Editorial Department

Publisher's Interests
Penguin Books will only consider the works of Canadian authors, and submissions through literary agents. Its juvenile list includes fiction titles for middle-grade through young adults, as well as several historical nonfiction titles. Prospective authors are encouraged to look at *The Canadian Writer's Guide* for information on the publishing process.
Website: www.penguin.ca

Freelance Potential
Published 88 titles (14 juvenile) in 2004: all were by agented authors.
Submissions and Payment: Canadian authors only. Send complete ms. Accepts submissions from literary agents only. SASE. Responds in 1 month. Publication in 1–2 years. Royalty, 8–10%.

Perspectives Press, Inc.

P.O. Box 90318
Indianapolis, IN 46290-0318

Editor: Pat Johnston

Publisher's Interests
Established in 1982, this publisher offers nonfiction titles relating to infertility issues. It is interested in decision-making material on reproductive health education, adoption information, infertility, and lifestyle and family-building alternatives.
Website: www.perspectivespress.com

Freelance Potential
Published 3 titles (1 juvenile) in 2004: all were developed from unsolicited submissions. Of the 3 titles, 1 was by an author who was new to the publishing house. Receives 300 queries yearly.
Submissions and Payment: Guidelines available at website. Query with résumé and outline. No unsolicited mss. Accepts photocopies and computer printouts. Responds in 1 month. Publication in 9–18 months. Royalty, 5–15%.

Piano Press

P.O. Box 85
Del Mar, CA 92014-0085

Editor: Elizabeth C. Axford

Publisher's Interests
Short stories, poems, and essays on music-related topics of interest to children are the specialty of this small press. Its next anthology will be published in the fall of 2005.
Website: www.pianopress.com

Freelance Potential
Published 5 titles in 2004: 3 were developed from unsolicited submissions. Of the 5 titles, 3 were by authors who were new to the publishing house. Receives 150 queries 250 unsolicited mss yearly.
Submissions and Payment: Guidelines available. Query for fiction and nonfiction; send complete ms for poetry. Accepts photocopies, computer printouts, disk submissions (Microsoft Word), and email submissions to pianopress@aol.com (no attachments). SASE. Responds in 2–4 months. Publication in 1 year. Royalty.

Pippin Press

Gracie Station, Box 1347
229 East 85th Street
New York, NY 10028

Publisher: Barbara Francis

Publisher's Interests
Pippin Press is a small publisher that specializes in historical fiction for children ages seven to eleven, childhood memoirs for readers age eight to twelve, and engaging nonfiction for six- to twelve-year old children. It is interested in material on recent immigrants from Russia and Central and South America.

Freelance Potential
Published 5 titles in 2004: 3 were developed from unsolicited submissions. Of the 5 titles, 3 were by unpublished writers and 3 were by authors who were new to the publishing house. Receives 1,000 queries yearly.
Submissions and Payment: Guidelines available. Prefers query. Accepts unsolicited mss. SASE. Responds in 3 months. Publication in 1–2 years. Royalty; advance.

The Place in the Woods

3900 Glenwood Avenue
Golden Valley, MN 55422-5302

Editor & Publisher: Roger Hammer

Publisher's Interests
Targeting the multicultural market, this publisher produces books for children ages four and up. It offers adventurous and positive, uplifting stories that teach children about diversity, and that it is okay to be different. It is currently seeking stories on Asian American history.

Freelance Potential
Published 2 titles in 2004: both were developed from unsolicited submissions and both were by unpublished writers. Receives 100 queries, 300 unsolicited mss yearly.
Submissions and Payment: Guidelines available. Query or send complete ms. Accepts computer printouts. No simultaneous submissions. SASE. Responds in 1–4 weeks. Publication in 18 months. Royalty. Flat fee.

Playhouse Publishing

1566 Akron-Peninsula Road
Akron, OH 44313

Submissions Editor

Publisher's Interests
This publisher strives to find imaginative new ways to encourage children to read. It offers a variety of fun, educational books that appear under one of its three imprints for young children. Check guidelines for information.
Website: www.playhousepublishing.com

Freelance Potential
Published 15 titles in 2004: all were assigned; 6 were by previously unpublished authors.
Submissions and Payment: Query with writing sample or résumé. Accepts email queries only to webmaster@playhousepublishing.com (no attachments). Accepts simultaneous submissions if identified. Responds in 2 months. Publication in 1 year. Flat fee. Work-for-hire.

Playwrights Canada Press

Suite 230, 215 Spadina Avenue
Toronto, Ontario M5T 2C7
Canada

Editorial Coordinator: Betony Main

Publisher's Interests
The Playwrights Canada Press is formerly part of Playwrights Union of Canada. It will consider queries for dramatic works, one-act plays, and musicals for adults and children written by Canadian citizens or landed immigrants. Plays must have had at least one professional production in the past 10 years.
Website: www.playwrightscanada.com

Freelance Potential
Published 20 titles (1 juvenile) in 2004: 1 was developed from an unsolicited submission. Receives 10–15 queries yearly.
Submissions and Payment: Canadian authors only. Query with synopsis. Accepts computer printouts and simultaneous submissions if identified. SASE. Responds in 6–12 months. Publication in 5 months. Royalty.

Prep Publishing

1110½ Hay Street
Fayetteville, NC 28305

Submissions Editor: Frances Sweeney

Publisher's Interests
Established in 1994, Prep Publishing features Christian fiction and nonfiction titles for young adults and adults. It offers books on Christian ethics, business, and career development, as well as general interest titles.
Website: www.prep-pub.com

Freelance Potential
Published 7 titles in 2004: all were developed from unsolicited submissions. Of the 7 titles, 5 were by new authors. Receives 5,000 queries, 1,000 unsolicited mss each year.
Submissions and Payment: Guidelines and catalogue available. Query with synopsis; or send complete ms with $225 reading fee. Accepts photocopies. SASE. Responds in 3 months. Publication in 18 months. Royalty, 15%.

Pruett Publishing Company

Suite A-9
7464 Arapahoe Road
Boulder, CO 80303-1500

Editor: Jim Pruett

Publisher's Interests
Nonfiction books on the history, nature, and outdoor recreational activities in the western region of the Rocky Mountains are offered by this publisher. It targets children in grades four through twelve.
Website: www.pruettpublishing.com

Freelance Potential
Published 12 titles in 2004. Of the 12 titles all were by unpublished writers and 8 were by authors who were new to the publishing house. Receives 300 queries, 300 unsolicited mss yearly.
Submissions and Payment: Guidelines available. Query or send complete ms. Accepts photocopies, computer printouts, and simultaneous submissions if identified. SASE. Responds to queries in 2 weeks, to mss in 1–2 months. Publication period varies. Royalty, 10–12%; advance, to $1,000.

Quartz Editions ☆

112 Station Road
Edgware HA8 7BJ
United Kingdom

Publisher: Susan Pinkus

Publisher's Interests
Highly illustrated titles with international appeal are the preference of this British book packager. Quartz Editions specializes in putting together books and selling rights for foreign language editions. Although it rarely publishes material from an unsolicited manuscript, it will consider submissions of pre-school picture books, texts for teaching English, junior high school science and math books, and books about health, hobbies, pets, dinosaurs, and wild animals.

Freelance Potential
Published 2 titles in 2004.
Submissions and Payment: Send complete ms. Accepts photocopies. SASE. Responds in 2 months. Publication in 1 year. Payment policy varies.

Quixote Press

1854 345th Avenue
Wever, IA 52658

President: Bruce Carlson

Publisher's Interests
Targeting the general population, this small press features fiction and nonfiction for adults, as well as children of all ages. It seeks middle-grade and young adult stories.

Freelance Potential
Published 50 titles in 2004: 25–30 were developed from unsolicited submissions, and 5 were reprint/licensed properties. Of the 50 titles, 48 were by unpublished writers and 25 were by authors who were new to the publishing house. Receives 200–300 queries, 100–150 unsolicited mss yearly.
Submissions and Payment: Query or send complete ms. Accepts photocopies, computer printouts, and simultaneous submissions if identified. SASE. Responds in 1 week. Publication in 2–24 months. Royalty.

Rainbow Books

P.O. Box 430
Highland City, FL 33846-0430

Editorial Director: Betsy Lampe

Publisher's Interests
Middle-grade biographies about prominent role models, how-to titles, and books on coping skills are needed by Rainbow Books.
Website: www.rainbowbooksinc.com

Freelance Potential
Published 20 titles in 2004: all were developed from unsolicited submissions. Of the 20 titles, 10 were by unpublished writers and 20 were by authors who were new to the publishing house. Receives 200 queries, 100 unsolicited mss yearly.
Submissions and Payment: Guidelines available. Prefers complete ms with author biography. Accepts query with word count, table of contents, and author biography. Accepts photocopies, computer printouts, and simultaneous submissions. SASE. Responds in 6 weeks. Publication in 1 year. Royalty, 6%+; advance.

Raincoast Books

9050 Shaughnessy Street
Vancouver, British Columbia V6P 6E5
Canada

Editorial Department

Publisher's Interests
This Canadian book publisher and distributor produces a wide range of fiction and nonfiction for both children and adults. Children's nonfiction topics include science, sports, and natural history. Young adult topics include contemporary and historical fiction.
Website: www.raincoast.com

Freelance Potential
Published 30 titles (8 juvenile) in 2004. Receives 2,000 queries each year.
Submissions and Payment: Canadian authors only. Guidelines available at website. Query with outline and/or synopsis. Accepts photocopies and computer printouts. No electronic submissions. SASE. Responds in 2–4 months. Publication period varies. Royalty; advance.

Rand McNally

8255 North Central Park
Skokie, IL 60076

Editorial Director: Laurie Borman

Publisher's Interests
The well-known mapmaker Rand McNally features a line of retail and educational books targeting children ages four to young adult. Its list includes activity books, travel games, atlases, reference books, and maps for home and school. All freelance writing for Rand McNally is done on a for-hire basis; this publisher will not accept unsolicited manuscripts. Prospective writers are invited to submit their résumé.
Website: www.randmcnally.com

Freelance Potential
Published 8 titles in 2004: all were written with some freelance assistance.
Submissions and Payment: Send résumé only. All work is done on assignment.

It's All About the Reader
Shana Corey
Random House

Random House gears its Step into Reading series for early readers of all levels, from pre-reading preschoolers who know the alphabet through confident readers who are ready for chapter books.

"Early readers can be difficult to write because they can't be about the writer. They have to be about the audience and the audience's needs," says Assistant Editorial Director Shana Corey. "While we want to tell exciting, unique, and engaging stories, we have a commitment to our readers to provide them with successful reading experiences so that they'll develop confidence in their abilities."

Some authors find this limiting. "Many authors see the short, simple sentences that early readers require as obstacles," Corey explains, "but for writers with a talent for early readers those short simple sentences can develop a very catchy, readable rhythm and pace and become a kind of poetry in their own right."

The best authors also acknowledge the role of the illustrator. "In Step into Reading, especially the early steps, the illustrations need to be very literal to the text so that kids struggling over the words can use the illustrations as visual cues to help them decode the text," Corey says.

Authors should take time to perfect their craft. "We're booked through mid-2006, so we're not taking unsolicited manuscripts," says Corey. "As a rule though, we look for both nonfiction and fiction, and the younger the better." She is confident that those with a knack for this type of book will find publishers excited to work with them.

(See listing for Random House Children's Publishing on following page)

Random House Children's Books

61-63 Uxbridge Road
Ealing, London W5 5SA
United Kingdom

Editorial Assistant: Lucy Walker

Publisher's Interests
Ranked among the top five children's publishers in the UK, this juvenile division of the Random House Group Ltd., which includes The Bodley Head, Jonathan Cape, Corgi, Doubleday, David Fickling Books, Hutchinson, and Red Fox, produces top quality fiction and nonfiction books for all reading levels. It offers picture books, chapter books, middle-grade titles, and young adult novels. Genres for fiction include adventure, animal stories, mystery, and fantasy. At this time, it is only accepting submissions from literary agents.
Website: www.kidsatrandomhouse.co.uk

Freelance Potential
Published 200 titles in 2004. Receives 2,000–3,000 queries yearly.
Submissions and Payment: Accepts submissions from agented authors only. Publication in 1–2 years. Royalty; advance.

Random House Children's Publishing

1745 Broadway
New York, NY 10019

Submissions Editor

Publisher's Interests
This well-known publisher features quality literature for preschool children through young adults. It is interested in all formats, from board books and picture books to novels and series titles, and will consider both fiction and nonfiction material. Random House accepts only agented submissions.
Website: www.randomhouse.com

Freelance Potential
Published 375 titles in 2004. Receives 5,000 queries yearly.
Submissions and Payment: Guidelines available. Accepts queries from agented authors only. Query with writing sample or partial ms. Accepts photocopies, disk submissions, and simultaneous submissions if identified. SASE. Responds in 1 month. Publication in 1 year. Royalty; advance.

Redbird Press

P.O. Box 11441
Memphis, TN 38111

Submissions Editor: Virginia McLean

Publisher's Interests
Redbird Press is a small publishing house that produces books on the people and history of foreign countries. Its titles for children ages six to twelve combine text, photographs, and drawings by children to allow readers to fully explore the culture of different countries; as well as an audio tape, which lets readers experience the sound of the language.

Freelance Potential
Plans to resume publishing 1 or more titles in 2005. Receives 30 queries yearly.
Submissions and Payment: Query with outline/synopsis and clips or writing samples. Accepts photocopies, computer printouts, and simultaneous submissions if identified. SASE. Response time, publication period, and payment policy vary.

Redleaf Press

10 Yorkton Court
St. Paul, MN 55117

Submissions Editor: Kathy Kolb

Publisher's Interests
This publisher offers a variety of early childhood education resources that support child care professionals and parents. Material must be developmentally appropriate, based on sound theory and research, and support cultural diversity in child development.
Website: www.redleafpress.org

Freelance Potential
Published 12 titles in 2004. Of the 12 titles, 3 were by unpublished writers and 5 were by authors who were new to the publishing house. Receives 24 queries yearly.
Submissions and Payment: Guidelines available. Query with résumé, outline, table of contents, and writing samples. SASE. Responds in 3 months. Publication in 6–9 months. Payment policy varies.

Red Wheel/Weiser/Conari Press

4th Floor
368 Congress Street
Boston, MA 02210

Editorial Acquisitions: Pat Bryce

Publisher's Interests
Three imprints are produced by this publisher: Red Wheel, which publishes self-help and inspirational books; Conari Press, which offers topics on parenting, spirituality, and personal growth; and Weiser books, which publishes books on esoteric topics.
Website: www.redwheelsweiser.com

Freelance Potential
Published 100 titles in 2004: 20 were developed from unsolicited submissions, 10 were by agented authors, and 1 was a reprint/licensed property. Receives 500 queries yearly.
Submissions and Payment: Guidelines available. Query with outline, résumé, table of contents, and 3 sample chapters. Accepts photocopies and simultaneous submissions if identified. SASE. Responds in 3 months. Royalty; advance.

River City Publishing

1719 Mulberry Street
Montgomery, AL 36106

Editor: Ashley Gordon

Publisher's Interests
This publisher emphasizes Southern writers and stories about the South. Its children's list includes picture books and young adult novels. 5% self-, subsidy-, co-venture, or co-op published material.
Website: www.rivercitypublishing.com

Freelance Potential
Published 12 titles in 2004: 2 were developed from unsolicited submissions, 1 was by an agented author, and 1 was a reprint/licensed property. Of the 12 titles, 10 were by authors who were new to the publishing house. Receives 1,000 queries yearly.
Submissions and Payment: Guidelines available. Query with sample chapters. Accepts photocopies, computer printouts, disk submissions, and simultaneous submissions. SASE. Responds in 1–6 months. Publication in 1 year. Royalty; advance, $1,000–$5,000.

Riverfront Books

7825 Telegraph Road
Bloomington, MN 55438

Project Manager: Joan Berge

Publisher's Interests
Riverfront Books is a new publisher that has recently begun offering fiction series picture books for preschool to age eight children. It is looking for imaginative storytellers who feel they can write series books around a specific Riverfront-owned character. Themes to consider include contemporary and historical fiction, adventure, fantasy, animals, history, humor, nature, the environment, family, social issues, and school. Prospective authors are invited to submit their their résumés.

Freelance Potential
Published 26 titles in 2004.
Submissions and Payment: Query with résumé. Accepts simultaneous submissions if identified. Accepts photocopies. SASE. Responds in 4 months. Publication in 18 months. Flat fee.

Salina Bookshelf

Suite 130
1254 West University Avenue
Flagstaff, AZ 86001

Publisher: Eric Lockard

Publisher's Interests
Children's books that portray the traditional language and culture of the Navajo people are produced by this publisher. It is interested in picture books and fiction for children ages 6–12 years old.
Website: www.salinabookshelf.com

Freelance Potential
Published 7 titles (5 juvenile) in 2004: 2 were developed from unsolicited submissions and 1 was by a reprint/licensed property. Of the 7 titles, 1 was by an unpublished writer and 4 were by authors who were new to the publishing house. Receives 75 queries each year.
Submissions and Payment: Send ms. Accepts photocopies, computer printouts, and disk submissions (Adobe Acrobat). SASE. Responds in 3 weeks. Publication in 1 year. Royalty and advance varies.

Sandlapper Publishing

1281 Amelia Street
Orangeburg, SC 29115

Managing Editor: Amanda Gallman

Publisher's Interests
Educational titles about the history and culture of South Carolina is the specialty of this regional publisher. It seeks to add middle-grade historical biographies to its juvenile list.
Website: www.sandlapperpublishing.com

Freelance Potential
Published 4 titles (2 juvenile) in 2004: all were developed from unsolicited submissions. Of the 4 titles, 2 were by unpublished writers and 2 were by authors who were new to the publishing house. Receives 150 queries yearly.
Submissions and Payment: Guidelines available. Query with résumé, outline/synopsis, 3 sample chapters, and bibliography. Accepts photocopies and computer printouts. SASE. Responds in 2 months. Publication in 2 years. Royalty.

Sandpiper Paperbacks

222 Berkeley Street
Boston, MA 02116

Editor: Hannah Rodgers

Publisher's Interests
This imprint of Houghton Mifflin publishes paperback reprints of contemporary and mainstream fiction and humorous novels for middle-grade readers, as well as biographies and books on history for young adults.
Website: www.houghtonmifflinbooks.com

Freelance Potential
Published 35 titles in 2004: all were reprint/licensed properties. Receives 100 queries, 200 unsolicited mss each year.
Submissions and Payment: Guidelines available with SASE. Query with sample chapter; or send complete ms. Accepts photocopies, computer printouts, and simultaneous submissions if identified. SASE. Responds to queries in 3–8 weeks, to mss in 3–5 months. Publication period and payment policy vary.

Sasquatch Books

Suite 400
119 South Main Street
Seattle, WA 98104

The Editors

Publisher's Interests
Founded in 1986, this publisher offers books from the Pacific Northwest, Alaska, and California. Topics include travel, food and wine, gardening, nature, photography, and regional history. It also produces early picture books, easy-to-read books, and story picture books. All material must be regional.
Website: www.sasquatchbooks.com

Freelance Potential
Published 32 titles (4 juvenile) in 2004: all were by agented authors. Receives 200+ unsolicited mss yearly.
Submissions and Payment: Guidelines available at website. Send complete ms. Accepts photocopies and computer printouts. No electronic submissions. SASE. Responds in 1-3 months. Publication period and payment policy vary.

School Zone Publishing

P.O. Box 777
1819 Industrial Drive
Grand Haven, MI 49417

Editor

Publisher's Interests
School Zone Publishing Company is a publisher of elementary educational products. Its catalogue includes workbooks, flash cards, games, mats, posters, and CD-ROMs. Its goal is to bring teachers working with students in kindergarten through grade 4 the best tools available to supplement school curriculum in teaching basic learning skills. Most of its authors are teachers with extensive classroom experience.
Website: www.schoolzone.com

Freelance Potential
Published 5 titles in 2004: 4 were by agented authors. Receives 100 queries yearly.
Submissions and Payment: Query with résumé and writing samples. No mss. Response time and publication period vary. Flat fee.

Scott Foresman

1900 East Lake Avenue
Glenview, IL 60025

Editor: Derek Everette

Publisher's Interests
This well-known educational publisher features nonfiction for elementary school students, as well as resource materials for teachers and parents. Its catalogue offers titles on the subjects of reading, language arts, science, mathematics, music, and social studies. Potential writers should have a firm grasp of school curricula.
Website: www.scottforesman.com

Freelance Potential
Published 1,000 titles in 2004: Of the 1,000 titles, 50 were by authors who were new to the publishing house. Receives 350 queries yearly.
Submissions and Payment: Query with résumé, outline, and sample chapters. Accepts photocopies and computer printouts. SASE. Responds in 2 months. Publication in 1–3 years. Royalty. Flat fee.

Seaburn Publishing

P.O. Box 2085
Astoria, NY 11103

President: Tyra Mason

Publisher's Interests
The children's books produced by Seaburn center around contemporary topics that explore such issues as cultural diversity, nature, and the environment. African American, Greek, Ibo, and Spanish titles also appear on its list. Seaburn authors are asked to be available for workshops, school presentations, and bookstore events.
Website: www.seaburn.com

Freelance Potential
Published 20 titles (6 juvenile) in 2004: 2 were developed from unsolicited submissions and 1 was by an agented author. Receives 120 queries yearly.
Submissions and Payment: Guidelines available. Query. Accepts photocopies and computer printouts. SASE. Responds in 1 month. Publication in 4 months. Royalty.

Seal Press

Suite 375
300 Queen Anne Avenue North
Seattle, WA 98109

Editorial Department

Publisher's Interests
This small West Coast publisher features a list of fiction and nonfiction by women writers. Founded more than a quarter of a century ago, Seal Press is an imprint of the Avalon Publishing Group. Its mission is to present groundbreaking books that are suited for use in the classroom, as well as topics related to parenting. Prospective writers are encouraged to visit the website and review the company's existing titles before sending a query.
Website: www.sealpress.com

Freelance Potential
Published 22 titles in 2004. Receives 100 queries yearly.
Submissions and Payment: Query. SASE. Responds in 6–8 months. Publication period and payment policy vary.

Second Story Press

Suite 301, 720 Bathurst Street
Toronto, Ontario M5S 2R4
Canada

Editor

Publisher's Interests
This small Canadian feminist press offers a mix of fiction, nonfiction, and children's books on many diverse and varied aspects of women's and girls' lives. It prides itself on featuring books that challenge, inform, stimulate, and entertain.
Website: www.secondstorypress.on.ca

Freelance Potential
Published 5 titles in 2004.
Submissions and Payment: Canadian authors only. Guidelines available at website. Query or send complete ms for children's books. Query with outline and sample chapter for adult fiction and nonfiction. Accepts photocopies and computer printouts. SASE. Responds in 4–6 months. Publication period varies. Royalty; advance.

Shen's Books

40951 Fremont Boulevard
Fremont, CA 94538

Owner: Renee Ting

Publisher's Interests
Established in 1985, this specialty publisher offers a select list of children's fiction and nonfiction focusing on cultures and legends from countries around the world. Most of its books target readers between age four and ten.
Website: www.shens.com

Freelance Potential
Published 2 titles in 2004: 1 was by an unpublished writer and both were by authors who were new to the publishing house. Receives 50 unsolicited mss yearly.
Submissions and Payment: Send complete ms. Accepts computer printouts, disk submissions (Microsoft Word), and simultaneous submissions if identified. SASE. Responds in 6–12 months. Publication in 18 months. Payment policy varies.

Silver Dolphin Books

5880 Oberlin Drive
San Diego, CA 92121

Submissions Editor

Publisher's Interests
Silver Dolphin publishes activity, novelty, and educational nonfiction books for preschoolers to twelve-year-old readers. It is interested in ideas for highly interactive formats, such as its Inventor's Handbooks series and Discovery Plus series titles. Material should be boldly illustrated, educational, and entertaining.
Website: www.silverdolphinbooks.com

Freelance Potential
Published 55 titles in 2004: most were reprint/licensed properties. Receives 50+ unsolicited mss yearly.
Submissions and Payment: Guidelines available. Query only. No unsolicited mss. Availability of artwork improves chance of acceptance. SASE. Responds in 1 month. Publication period and payment policy vary.

Siphano Picture Books

Regent's Place, 338 Euston Road
London NW1 3BT
England

Editor

Publisher's Interests
This publisher targets three- to seven-year-old children with its imaginative picture books that feature humorous situations and appealing characters. It looks for manuscripts 300 to 700 words in length that are appropriate for picture-book formats.
Website: www.siphano.com

Freelance Potential
Published 10 titles in 2004. Of the 10 titles, 2 were by unpublished writers and 2 were by authors who were new to the publishing house. Receives 100 queries yearly.
Submissions and Payment: Guidelines available at website. Query with clips. Accepts email to info@siphano.com and simultaneous submissions if identified. SASE. Responds in 2–3 months. Publication in 6 months. Payment policy varies.

Smallfellow Press

Suite 320
1180 South Beverly Drive
Los Angeles, CA 90035

Manuscript Acquisitions: Claudia Sloan

Publisher's Interests
Launched by the founders of the publishing company of Price Stern Sloan, Smallfellow Press produces board books for toddlers, story picture books for children ages four to ten, and young adult fiction. Novelty books are also included on its list, and humorous stories, especially those that are informative as well as entertaining, are among the genres it seeks. This publishing company's goal is to display the same enthusiasm and creative thinking that made Price Stern Sloan a publishing success story.
Website: www.smallfellow.com

Freelance Potential
Published several titles in 2004.
Submissions and Payment: Catalogue available at website. Query. Response time, publication period, and payment policy vary.

Small Horizons

P.O. Box 669
Far Hills, NJ 07931

Publisher: Dr. Joan S. Dunphy

Publisher's Interests
Teachers, parents, and professionals who work with youth use books from this publisher to help children deal with stress, depression, self-esteem, anger, divorce, and peer pressure issues.
Website: www.newhorizonpressbooks.com

Freelance Potential
Published 12 titles (2 juvenile) in 2004: 11 were developed from unsolicited submissions, 6 were by agented authors. Receives 100+ queries yearly.
Submissions and Payment: Guidelines available. Query with résumé, outline, 2 sample chapters, and market comparison. Accepts photocopies and computer printouts. Availability of artwork improves chance of acceptance. SASE. Responds in 3 months. Publication period varies. Royalty, 7.5% of net; advance.

Smith and Kraus Books for Kids

P.O. Box 127
Lyme, NH 03768

Publisher: Marisa Smith

Publisher's Interests
Plays, monologues, skits, acting guides, and other topics related to theater are the mainstay of this imprint of theater publisher Smith and Kraus. Its children's list offers plays and nonfiction material suitable for children in kindergarten through grade twelve. Picture books for four- to eight-year-old readers, and chapter books for 10- to 14-year-old readers are also found in its catalogue.
Website: www.SmithKraus.com

Freelance Potential
Published 35 titles (11 juvenile) in 2004.
Submissions and Payment: Query with résumé for fiction. Query with outline for nonfiction. Accepts photocopies, computer printouts, and simultaneous submissions. SASE. Responds in 2 months. Publication in 1 year. Royalty; advance. Flat fee.

Soho Press

853 Broadway
New York, NY 10003

Submissions Editor: Laura Hruska

Publisher's Interests
This fiction publisher is currently interested in seeing submissions of literary and juvenile fiction, including fantasy and Westerns.
Website: www.sohopress.com

Freelance Potential
Published 35 titles in 2004: 8 were developed from unsolicited submissions, 6 were by agented authors, and 19 were reprint/licensed properties. Of the 35 titles, 5 were by unpublished writers and 12 were by authors who were new to the publishing house. Receives 2,400 queries yearly.
Submissions and Payment: Guidelines available. Prefers query with first 3 chapters and outline. Accepts complete ms. All finished mss should be 60,000+ words. Accepts photocopies. SASE. Responds in 6 weeks. Publication in 12-15 months. Royalty; advance.

Southern Early Childhood Association

P.O. Box 55930
Little Rock, AR 72215-5930

Executive Director: Glenda Bean

Publisher's Interests
The Southern Early Childhood Association is a regional organization committed to promoting quality care and education for young children and their families. Established in 1948, its titles cater to preschool, kindergarten, and primary teachers.
Website: www.southernearlychildhood.org

Freelance Potential
Published 2 titles in 2004: 1 was developed from an unsolicited submission and both were by unpublished writers. Receives 4 unsolicited mss yearly.
Submissions and Payment: Guidelines available. Send 4 copies of complete ms. Accepts disk submissions (WordPerfect or Microsoft Word). SASE. Responds in 4 months. Publication in 9-12 months. No payment.

Stiles-Bishop Productions Inc.

12652 Killion
Valley Village, CA 91607

Editor: Kathryn Bishop

Publisher's Interests
This small publisher brings children between the ages of four and ten, a series of 36-page books based on well-known fairy tales. The titles are developed from the company radio program for children and their families. It has recently expanded into the area of feature films and has cut back on the number of books published. There were no new titles in 2004, and none are scheduled for publication in 2005, but it continues to review queries for future publication at this time.

Freelance Potential
Plans to resume publishing in 2005.
Submissions and Payment: Query. Artwork improves chance of acceptance. Accepts photocopies and computer printouts. SASE. Responds in 2 weeks. Publication in 6 months. Royalty. Flat fee.

Story Time Stories That Rhyme

P.O. Box 416
Denver, CO 80201

Founder: A. Doyle

Publisher's Interests
This small, unique publishing house was founded in 1989. Its mission is to bring young readers elementary and middle school books that will not only educate them, but entertain them as well. All of its titles are written in rhyme. Topics covered include history, language, art, nature, math, science, business, and food. It continues to call for queries related to nature and the environment from writers who have a firm grasp of the company's unique style.
Website: www.storytimestoriesthatrhyme.com

Freelance Potential
Published 3 titles in 2004. Receives 250 queries yearly.
Submissions and Payment: Guidelines available. Query. No unsolicited mss. Accepts photocopies and computer printouts. SASE. Response time varies. Publication period and payment policy vary.

Success Publications

3419 Dunham Road
Warsaw, NY 14569

Submissions Editor: Dana Herbison

Publisher's Interests
Success Publications offers nonfiction how-to titles for middle-grade students and young adults on crafts and hobbies, as well as self-help books and informational titles.

Freelance Potential
Published 6 titles (2 juvenile) in 2004: 4 were developed from unsolicited submissions and 2 were by agented authors. Of the 6 titles, 2 were by unpublished writers and 4 were by authors who were new to the publishing house. Receives 200 unsolicited mss each year.
Submissions and Payment: Guidelines available. Send complete ms. Accepts photocopies. SASE. Availability of artwork improves chance of acceptance. Responds in 2 weeks. Publication in 3 months. Payment policy varies.

Sunburst Technology

400 Columbus Avenue
Valhalla, NY 10595

Vice President, Software: David Wolff

Publisher's Interests
Multimedia products on guidance and health topics for students in kindergarten through twelfth grade are found in the catalogue of Sunburst Technology. Its list also includes products on the subjects of social studies, the Internet, science, language arts, mathematics, and creativity.
Website: www.sunburst.com

Freelance Potential
Published 50 titles in 2004: 1 was developed from an unsolicited submission. Receives 150 queries yearly.
Submissions and Payment: Query with résumé and writing samples. Accepts product concept proposals and accompanying graphics. SASE. Responds in 3–6 weeks. Publication period and payment policy vary.

Teachers & Writers Collaborative

5 Union Square West
New York, NY 10003-3306

Editor: Christina Davis or Christopher Edgar

Publisher's Interests
Teachers & Writers Collaborative was founded in 1967 by a group of writers and teachers who believed that writers could make a unique contribution to the teaching of writing. Its list includes books on oral history, creative nonfiction, and fiction writing. Queries for all age groups are welcome.
Website: www.twc.org

Freelance Potential
Published 3 titles in 2004: 3 were reprint/licensed properties. Receives 224 queries yearly.
Submissions and Payment: Query with résumé, outline, market analysis, and sample chapter. Accepts photocopies and computer printouts. SASE. Responds in 6 months. Publication in 18 months. Royalty; advance.

Thistledown Press

633 Main Street
Saskatoon, Saskatchewan S7H 0J8
Canada

Submissions Editor: Allen Forrie

Publisher's Interests
This small house only publishes works by Canadian authors. It has recently expanded its list to include more short fiction and novels as well as more young adult fiction. Other than literary criticism, it does not publish nonfiction.
Website: www.thistledown.sk.ca

Freelance Potential
Published 12 titles (5 juvenile) in 2004: 2 were developed from unsolicited submissions and 4 were by agented authors. Of the 12 titles, 3 were by unpublished writers and 5 were by authors who were new to the publishing house. Receives 600 queries yearly.
Submissions and Payment: Canadian authors only. Guidelines and catalogue available. Query with outline and sample chapter. SASE. Responds in 1 week. Publication in 3 months. Royalty.

Touchwood Editions

Suite 6, 356 Simcoe Street
Victoria, British Columbia V8V 1L1
Canada

Acquisitions Editor

Publisher's Interests
Touchwood Editions is one of three imprints under the umbrella of The Heritage Group. It focuses on history, biography, architecture, design, and topics related to ships and the sea. Its audience includes young adults and adults. As a Canadian publisher, its primary interest for the coming year is submissions related to Western Canada. The company has also recently expanded its fiction list.
Website: www.touchwoodeditions.com

Freelance Potential
Published 7 titles (1 juvenile) in 2004.
Submissions and Payment: Guidelines available. Query with synopsis, table of contents, 2–3 sample chapters, and word count. SAE/IRC. Response time varies. Publication period and payment policy vary.

TowleHouse Publishing

1312 Bell Grimes Lane
Nashville, TN 37207

Editor: Mike Towle

Publisher's Interests
Founded by a veteran sportswriter, this nonfiction publisher is now entering its fifth year of business. Submissions for books on almost any sport are of interest, particularly those in new areas as it grows its list. New writers are encouraged to visit the website first, to get a grasp of the type of material that will have the best chance of getting published here.
Website: www.towlehouse.com

Freelance Potential
Published 9 titles in 2004: 3 were developed from unsolicited submissions, 6 were assigned. Receives 600 queries yearly.
Submissions and Payment: Query with outline and 2 sample chapters. Accepts photocopies. SASE. Response time varies. Publication period varies. Royalty; advance.

Tradewind Books Ltd.

1809 Maritime Mews
Vancouver, British Columbia V6H 3W7
Canada

Submissions Editor: R. David Stephens

Publisher's Interests
Established in 1994, this Canadian book publisher produces a variety of middle-grade fiction and easy-to-read books.
Website: www.tradewindbooks.com

Freelance Potential
Published 5 titles in 2004: 1 was developed from an unsolicited submission. Of the 5 titles, 1 was by an unpublished writer and 4 were by authors who were new to the publishing house. Receives 1,000 queries, 1,500 unsolicited mss yearly.
Submissions and Payment: Query with résumé and sample chapter for fiction. Send ms with résumé for nonfiction. All submissions must include an indication that authors have read a selection of the publisher's works. Accepts photocopies. SAE/IRC. Responds in 3 months. Publication in 3 years. Royalty; advance.

Turtle Books

Suite 525
866 United Nations Plaza
New York, NY 10017

Submissions Editor: John Whitman

Publisher's Interests
Illustrated English and Spanish children's books for ages two to ten are the specialty of this publisher. Its goal is to bring readers the highest quality in all its titles. The company is interested in receiving manuscripts of stories that will work well as illustrated books.
Website: www.turtlebooks.com

Freelance Potential
Published 1 title in 2004: it was developed from an unsolicited submission and was by an unpublished writer. Receives 1,000+ unsolicited mss yearly.
Submissions and Payment: Send complete ms. Accepts photocopies and computer printouts. SASE. Response time varies. Publication in 1 year. Royalty; advance.

Turtle Press

P.O. Box 290206
Whethersfield, CT 06129-0206

Editor: Cynthia Kim

Publisher's Interests
This specialty publisher features books on martial arts, health, and fitness. Training manuals for teachers of martial arts and guides for parents of prospective students are included in its catalogue, as well as instructional titles on various aspects of martial arts and self-defense for adults.
Website: www.turtlepress.com

Freelance Potential
Published 8 titles in 2004: 3 were developed from unsolicited submissions. Of the 8 titles, 1 was by an unpublished writer and 2 were by authors who were new to the publishing house. Receives 400–500 queries yearly.
Submissions and Payment: Guidelines available. Query. SASE. Responds in 2–3 weeks. Publication period and payment policy vary.

Twenty-First Century Books

2 Old New Milford Road
Brookfield, CT 06804

Editorial Director: Jean Reynolds

Publisher's Interests
The publishing program of Twenty-First Century Books had been suspended temporarily and it produced no titles in 2004. This year, it plans to resume publishing nonfiction titles for young adults that supplement the school curriculum. In the past, this publisher has considered material submitted through literary agents only, but at this time unagented authors are welcome to query.
Website: www.millbrookpress.com

Freelance Potential
Plans to resume publishing (1 or more titles) in 2005.
Submissions and Payment: Guidelines available at website. Query with outline, sample chapters, and publishing history. Accepts simultaneous submissions if identified. SASE. Responds in 2 months. Publication in 1–2 years. Royalty; advance.

Twenty-Third Publications

P.O. Box 180
185 Willow Street
Mystic, CT 06355

Submissions Editor: Gwen Costello

Publisher's Interests
A wide range of nonfiction and fiction on topics relating to catechetical aids for catechists and teachers; pastoral books, and personal spirituality are offered by this publisher. It is currently seeking young adult and adult books on spiritual growth.
Website: www.twentythirdpublications.com

Freelance Potential
Published 42 titles (4 juvenile) in 2004: 20 were developed from unsolicited submissions.
Submissions and Payment: Guidelines available at website. Send complete ms. Accepts photocopies, computer printouts, disk submissions (Microsoft Word), and email submissions to gcostello@twentythirdpublications.com. SASE. Response time, payment rate, and payment policy varies.

Two Lives Publishing

P.O. Box 736
Ridley Park, PA 19078

Editor: Bobbi Combs

Publisher's Interests
Two Lives Publishing is a publisher of children's books for children of gay, lesbian, bisexual, and transgendered families. Its mission is to portray such children in positive, loving ways throughout well-written picture books and stories.
Website: www.twolives.com

Freelance Potential
Published 2 titles in 2004: both were developed from unsolicited submissions. Of the 2 titles, both were by new authors. Receives 30 unsolicited mss yearly.
Submissions and Payment: Guidelines available. Send ms. Accepts photocopies, disk submissions, and email submissions to bcombs@twolives.com. SASE. Responds in 2 months. Publication in 3 years. Royalty, 5%; advance, $500–$1,000.

Unity House

Unity School of Christianity
1901 NW Blue Parkway
Unity Village, MO 64065-0001

Editor: Michael Maday

Publisher's Interests
Spiritual books for young adults and children that express the Unity philosophy and principles, practical Christianity, and/or metaphysics are produced by this publisher. Currently, it is not publishing children's books. Check its website for updates.
Website: www.unityworldhq.org

Freelance Potential
Published 15 titles (1 juvenile) in 2004: 1 was developed from an unsolicited submission. Of the 15 titles, most were by unpublished writers and most were by authors who were new to the publishing house. Receives 450 queries yearly.
Submissions and Payment: Guidelines available by mail and at website. Query. SASE. Responds in 6–8 weeks. Publication in 11 months. Royalty.

Viking Children's Books

Penguin Young Readers Group
345 Hudson Street
New York, NY 10014

Associate Editor, Fiction: Catherine Frank
Executive Editor, Nonfiction: Tracy Gates

Publisher's Interests
Since 1933, this children's imprint has brought readers of all ages, preschool through young adult, quality hardcover titles of both fiction and nonfiction. It is now accepting unsolicited submissions again, after a brief hiatus.
Website: www.penguin.com

Freelance Potential
Published 76 titles in 2004. Receives 3,000 queries and mss yearly.
Submissions and Payment: Guidelines available at website. Submit complete ms for picture books. For longer fiction, submit outline with 3 sample chapters. Query with outline and 1 sample chapter for nonfiction. Accepts photocopies and computer printouts. SASE. Response time varies. Publication period varies. Royalty, 2–10%; advance, negotiable. Flat fee.

Visual Education Corporation

Building #4
14 Washington Road
Princeton, NJ 08550

Acquisitions Editor: Jean Elkin

Publisher's Interests
Established in 1969 this publisher offers a list of textbooks, school library and reference titles, and ancillary books for students in kindergarten through twelfth grade. It does not publish any fiction. All work is assigned and unsolicited manuscripts that are received will be returned unopened. The company also offers custom-tailored titles for nonfiction projects related to school curriculums as well as titles on research, writing, and editing.

Freelance Potential
Published 12-15 titles in 2004: all were assigned. Of the 12-15 titles, 5 were by authors who were new to the publishing house.
Submissions and Payment: All work is assigned. Guidelines available. Query with résumé and clips. SASE. Response time and publication period vary. Flat fee.

Windstorm Creative ☆

P.O. Box 28
Port Orchard, WA 98366

Senior Editor: Cris DiMarco

Publisher's Interests
Timeless fiction that celebrates youth is the specialty of this pro-child publisher. Its books include fiction and nonfiction titles that advocate tolerance.
Website: www.windstormcreative.com

Freelance Potential
Published 100-200 titles (50-100 juvenile) in 2004: all were developed from unsolicited submissions. Of the 100-200 titles, 10-20 were by unpublished writers and 50-100 were by authors who were new to the publishing house. Receives 1,000-2,000 queries yearly.
Submissions and Payment: Guidelines and submission form available at website. Query with chapter by chapter synopsis. Accepts photocopies. SASE. Responds in 1-3 months. Publication in 18 months. Royalty, 15%. Flat fee.

Windswept House Publishers

P.O. Box 159
Mt. Desert, ME 04660

Manuscript Editor

Publisher's Interests
Children's picture books, young adult novels, and adult fiction are produced by this small, independent publisher. Genres include adventure, mystery, sports, and historical fiction. Focusing on Maine, it specializes in quality books that cover topics on the environment, conservation, history, culture, nature, wildlife, and the people of the region. 50% co-venture.
Website: www.booknotes.com/windswept

Freelance Potential
Published 3 titles in 2004. Of the 3 titles, 2 were by authors who were new to the publishing house.
Submissions and Payment: Guidelines available with SASE. Query. No unsolicited mss. SASE. Response time varies. Publication and payment policy vary.

Winslow Publishing

P.O. Box 38012, 550 Eglinton Avenue West
Toronto, Ontario M5N 3A8
Canada

President & Publisher: Michelle West

Publisher's Interests
Since 1981, this publisher has featured craft books, how-to titles, and craft supplies. Its products are sold through direct mail. Although many of its titles are commissioned, Winslow Publishing is interested in submissions of craft books for children age five to ten. Freelance writers with original, age-appropriate projects are encouraged to query with any available artwork.
Website: www.winslowpublishing.com

Freelance Potential
Published 2 titles in 2004. Receives 40 queries yearly.
Submissions and Payment: Query with sample illustrations. Availability of artwork improves chance of acceptance. Simultaneous submissions if identified. SAE/IRC. Responds in 2 weeks. Publication in 2–3 months. Flat fee.

Wordware Publishing

Suite 200
2320 Los Rios Boulevard
Plano, TX 75074

Chief Operations Officer: Tim McEvoy

Publisher's Interests
This regional publisher specializes in educational materials designed to help prepare students for the Texas state and district exams. Its list features software, workbooks, and curriculum-based nonfiction titles for use in grades three through twelve. Wordware Publishing was established in 1987.
Website: www.wordware.com

Freelance Potential
Published 25 titles in 2004: 1 was by an agented author. Of the 25 titles, 4 were by unpublished writers. Receives 100+ queries yearly.
Submissions and Payment: Guidelines available. Query with résumé. Accepts photocopies, computer printouts, disk submissions, and simultaneous submissions if identified. SASE. Responds in 6 weeks. Publication in 1 year. Royalty.

YMAA Publication Center

4354 Washington Street
Rosindale, MA 02131

Director: David Ripianzi

Publisher's Interests
This small specialty publisher offers a list of titles on subjects related to advanced martial arts and Asian health. While its titles target the adult market, many are read by young adults as well.
Website: www.ymaa.com

Freelance Potential
Published 6 titles (2 juvenile) in 2004: all were developed from unsolicited submissions. Of the 6 titles, 3 were by authors who were new to the publishing house. Receives 72 queries, 240 mss yearly.
Submissions and Payment: Guidelines and catalogue available with 6x9 SASE ($1 postage) or at website. Query with clips or send complete ms. Accepts photocopies. Availability of artwork improves chance of acceptance. SASE. Responds in 1–3 months. Publication in 12–18 months. Royalty, 10%.

Contests and Awards

Selected Contests & Awards

Whether you enter a contest for unpublished writers or submit your published book for an award, you will have an opportunity to have your book read by established writers and qualified editors. Participating in a competition can increase recognition of your writing and possibly open more doors for selling your work. If you don't win and the winning entry is published, try to read it to see how your work compares with its competition.

To be considered for the contests and awards that follow, your entry must fulfill all of the requirements mentioned. Most are looking for unpublished article or story manuscripts, while a few require published works. Note special entry requirements, such as whether or not you can submit the material yourself, need to be a member of an organization, or are limited in the number of entries you can send. Also, be sure to submit your article or story in the standard manuscript submission format.

For each listing, we've included the address, the contact, a description, the entry requirements, the deadline, and the prize. In some cases, the 2005 deadlines were not available at press time. We recommend that you write to the addresses provided and ask for an entry form and the contest guidelines, which usually specify the current deadline.

American Book Cooperative Children's Picture Book Competition

11010 Hanning Lane
Houston, TX 77041-5006

Description
Open to writers living in the U.S. and over the age of 21, this competition is sponsored by the American Book Cooperative. Ten finalists are chosen by the judges and then posted on the ABC website for others to vote on the winner. The competition accepts original, unpublished manuscripts only.
Website: www.americanbookcooperative.org
Length: No length limit.
Requirements: No entry fee. Limit 5 entries per competition. Critique sheets on each entry are available by request with SASE after July 1. Accepts photocopies and computer printouts. Manuscripts will not be returned. Guidelines available at website.
Prizes: Winner receives publication of their manuscript along with a marketing plan and initial PR launch.
Deadline: April.

Atlantic Writing Competition

Writers' Federation of Nova Scotia
1113 Marginal Road
Halifax, Nova Scotia B3H 4P7
Canada

Description
Open to writers in the Atlantic provinces of Canada, this annual competition accepts entries in the categories of novel, short story, poetry, writing for children, and magazine/article essay. It accepts previously unpublished, original work only.
Website: www.writers.ns.ca
Length: Varies for each category.
Requirements: Entry fees: novel category, $25; all other categories, $15. WFNS members receive a $5 discount on entry fees. Published authors may not enter the competition in the genre in which they have been published. Limit one entry per category. Accepts photocopies and computer printouts. Guidelines available at website.
Prizes: First- through third-place winners in each category receive cash awards ranging from $50 to $250.
Deadline: August 1.

The Boston Globe-Horn Book Awards

Suite 200
56 Roland Street
Boston, MA 02129

Description
Established in 1967, the *Boston Globe-Horn Book* Awards honor excellence in literature for children and young adults. Winners are selected in three categories: picture book; fiction and poetry; and nonfiction. Eligible books must be published in the U.S. during the year preceding the contest.
Website: www.hbook.com/bghb.html
Length: No length requirements.
Requirements: No entry fee. Publishers may submit up to 8 books from each of their juvenile imprints. Guidelines available at website.
Prizes: Winner receives $500 and an engraved silver bowl. Honor books may also be named.
Deadline: May 15 of each year.

Marilyn Brown Novel Award

Association of Mormon Letters
125 Hobble Creek Canyon
Springville, UT 84663

Description
Open to all writers, this competition accepts previously unpublished novel entries about or for Mormons celebrating the religion. The Marilyn Brown Novel Award is presented every other year.
Website: www.aml-online.org
Length: No length limits.
Requirements: No entry fee. Author's name should not be included on manuscript. Include an envelope with author's name, address, and phone number inside and title of entry written on envelope. Include an SASE for return of manuscript. Guidelines and further information available at website.
Prizes: Winner receives a cash prize of $1,000.
Deadline: July 1, 2006.

CIPA National Writing Contest

Colorado Independent Publishers
5476 Mosquito Pass Drive
Colorado Springs, CO 80917

Description
The purpose of this contest is to provide new writers with an opportunity to show their work to experienced authors and publishers and receive feedback on how their work fits into the publishing market. The competition is open to all writers and accepts nonfiction entries in the categories of children's books, business, self-help, health, and cookbooks.
Website: www.cipabooks.com
Length: To 20 pages.
Requirements: Entry fee, $25. Send 3 copies of each entry. All entries must include a cover letter that lists the title, category, author's name, and contact information.
Prizes: First-place winners in each category receive a cash award of $100 and membership in CIPA.
Deadline: January 15.

CNW/FFWA Florida State Writing Competition

CNW/FFWA
P.O. Box A
North Stratford, NH 03590

Description
Open to all writers, this annual competition presents awards in 11 categories including children's literature short story, children's nonfiction, novel chapter, nonfiction book chapter, and poetry.
Website: www.writers-editors.com
Length: Varies for each category.
Requirements: Entry fees vary for each category. Multiple entries are accepted, as long as each entry is accompanied by an entry fee. Use paper clips only. Author's name must not appear on manuscript. Send an SASE for complete contest guidelines, specific category information, and official entry form, or visit the website.
Prizes: First through third prizes will be awarded in each category. Winners receive cash awards ranging from $50 to $100.
Deadline: March 15.

The Dana Awards

Mary Elizabeth Parker
7207 Townsend Forest Court
Browns Summit, NC 27214-9634

Description
Presented in the categories of novel, short fiction, and poetry, the Dana Awards are held annually. It accepts original, unpublished entries with clear, well-developed themes that are written in a style that exhibits a love of language and a mastery of the craft of writing.
Website: www.danaawards.com
Length: Lengths vary for each category.
Requirements: Entry fees: One short story or five poems, $10; novel entries, $20. Multiple submissions are accepted. Email danaawards@pipeline.com with questions regarding the contest. Guidelines and entry forms available at website.
Prizes: Winner in each category receives a cash prize of $1,000.
Deadline: October 31.

Delacorte Dell Yearling Contest ☆

Delacorte Press/Random House, Inc.
1745 Broadway, 9th Floor
New York, NY 10019

Description
Open to residents of the U.S. and Canada who have not yet published a middle-grade novel, this competition will be held annually. It looks to encourage the writing of contemporary or historical fiction set in North America for readers ages 9 to 12.
Website: www.randomhouse.com
Length: 96- to 160-typewritten pages.
Requirements: No entry fee. Limit 2 entries per competition. Accepts photocopies and computer printouts. No simultaneous submissions or foreign-language translations. Include a brief plot summary and cover letter. Include an SASE for return of manuscript. Guidelines available at website.
Prizes: Winner receives a book contract including an advance of $7,500 and a cash prize of $1,500.
Deadline: June 30.

Delacorte Press Contest for a First Young Adult Novel

Delcorte Press/Random House, Inc.
1745 Broadway, 9th Floor
New York, NY 10019

Description
Open to writers in the U.S. and Canada who have not yet published a young adult novel, this annual competition looks to encourage quality writing of contemporary fiction for young adults.
Website: www.randomhouse.com
Length: 100- to 244-typewritten pages.
Requirements: No entry fee. Limit 2 entries per competition. Accepts photocopies and computer printouts. No simultaneous submissions or foreign-language translations. Include a brief plot summary and cover letter. Include an SASE for return of manuscript. Guidelines available at website.
Prizes: Winner receives a book contract including an advance of $7,500 and a cash prize of $1,500.
Deadline: December 31.

Dragonfly Spirit Writing for Children Short Story Contest ☆

331 Elmwood Drive, Suite 4 #261
Moncton, New Brunswick E1A 7Y1
Canada

Description
Sponsored by *Dragonfly Spirit*, this competition is open to writers who have not yet been published in the children's and young adult genre. Its goal is to give first-time authors a chance to be heard.
Website: www.dragonflyspirit.com
Length: To 2,000 words.
Requirements: Entry fee, $7. Accepts photocopies and complete manuscripts. No cover letter necessary. Manuscripts will not be returned. Include target age range of entry. Writers' guidelines available at website.
Prizes: First-place winner receives a cash prize of $225. Second- and third-place winners will receive $50 and $25, respectively. Winning entries will be published on the *Dragonfly Spirit* website.
Deadline: September 30. Winners will be announced on December 31.

The Barbara Karlin Grant

The Society of Children's Book Writers and Illustrators
8271 Beverly Boulevard
Los Angeles, CA 90048

Description
Established to recognize and encourage the work of aspiring picture book writers, this grant is available to members of SCBWI who have not yet published a picture book. Original short stories, nonfiction, or re-tellings of fairy tales, folktales, or legends are eligible.
Website: www.scbwi.org
Length: 8 pages.
Requirements: No entry fee. Requests for applications may be made beginning October 1 of each year. Instructions and complete guidelines are sent with application forms.
Prizes: Cash grants of $1,500 and $500 are awarded in each of the 5 categories.

Milkweed Prize for Children's Literature

Milkweed Editions
1011 Washington Ave. South, Suite 300
Minneapolis, MN 55415-1246

Description
Milkweed Editions is looking for high-quality manuscripts for readers ages 8 to 13 for its children's book publishing program. Manuscripts should embody humane values, and contribute to cultural understanding. It is open to authors who have previously published a book of fiction or a minimum of three short stories.
Website: www.milkweed.org
Length: 90–200 typewritten pages.
Requirements: No entry fee. Entries must have been accepted for publication by Milkweed during the calendar year by a writer not previously published by Milkweed. Picture books and collections of stories are not eligible. All entries must follow Milkweed's usual children's manuscript guidelines.
Prizes: Winners receive a $10,000 cash advance on royalties.
Deadline: Ongoing.

National Children's Theatre Festival Competition

Actors' Playhouse at the Miracle Theatre
280 Miracle Mile
Coral Gables, FL 33134

Description
In its tenth year, this contest invites the submission of original scripts for musicals to be judged by a distinguished panel from both professional and academic theatre. All entries should target the 3-to-12 age group, but plays that are appealing to both children and adults are preferred.
Website: www.actorsplayhouse.org
Length: Running time, 45–60 minutes.
Requirements: Entry fee, $10 per submission. Accepts photocopies and computer printouts. Multiple submissions are accepted. Include an SASE for return of manuscript. Guidelines available at website.
Prizes: Winner receives a cash prize of $500 and a full production of their play.
Deadline: August 1.

Newbery Medal Award

American Library Association
50 East Huron
Chicago, IL 60611

Description
Awarded by the Association for Library Service to Children, a division of the American Library Association, this award is presented annually to an author who has made a distinguished contribution to literature for children. Citizens or residents of the U.S. are eligible.
Website: www.ala.org
Length: No length limit.
Requirements: No entry fee. Multiple submissions are accepted. All entries must have been published in the year preceding the contest. Guidelines available at website.
Prizes: The Newbery Medal is awarded to the winner. Honor books may also be named.
Deadline: December 31.

New Voices Award

Lee & Low Books
95 Madison Avenue
New York, NY 10016

Description
Lee & Low Books, the award-winning publisher of multicultural books for children, sponsors this award. It is presented annually for a picture book manuscript by an author of color. The contest is open to U.S. residents who have not published a children's picture book. All entries should target children ages 2 through 10 and may be either fiction or nonfiction.
Website: www.leeandlow.com
Length: To 1,500 words.
Requirements: No entry fee. Limit 2 entries per competition. Accepts computer printouts. Guidelines available at website.
Prizes: Winner receives a cash grant of $1,000 and a standard publishing contract from Lee & Low Books.
Deadline: Manuscripts are accepted between May 1 and October 31.

Ursula Nordstrom Fiction Contest ☆

HarperCollins Children's Books
1350 Avenue of the Americas
New York, NY 10019

Description
Open to U.S. writers over the age of 21 who have not been previously published, this annual first-fiction contest is named for the legendary children's editor. It looks to encourage new talent in the writing of innovative and challenging middle-grade fiction. All entries must be suitable for children ages 8 to 12.
Website: www.harpercollins.com
Length: 100 to 300 pages.
Requirements: No entry fee. Limit one entry per competition. Accepts photocopies and computer printouts. Include an SASE for return of manuscript. Guidelines available at website.
Prizes: Winner receives a book contract for a hardcover edition, a $7,500 advance, and a $1,500 cash award.
Deadline: Entries will be accepted between March 15 and April 15 only.

NWA Novel Contest

National Writers Association
3140 S. Peoria Street #295
Aurora, CO 80014

Description
Encouraging the development of creative skills, this award is presented annually by the National Writers Association. It accepts previously unpublished novel entries in any genre.
Website: www.nationalwriters.com
Length: To 100,000 words.
Requirements: Entry fee, $35. Accepts photocopies and computer printouts. Include an SASE for return of manuscript. If entrants would like their manuscripts critiqued, please note this on the entry form. Guidelines and entry form available at website.
Prizes: First-place winners receive $500. Second- and third-place winners receive $250 and $150, respectively. Fourth- through tenth-place winners receive a book and an honor certificate.
Deadline: April 1.

Once Upon a World Book Award

Museum of Tolerance
1399 S. Roxbury Drive
Los Angeles, CA 90035-4709

Description
The mission of this award is to support and perpetuate the values and mandate of the Simon Wiesenthal Center & Museum of Tolerance by honoring children's books targeting the 6 to 10 age group. Entries should deal with the issues of tolerance, diversity, human understanding, and social justice. Entries may be fiction, nonfiction, or poetry.
Website: www.wiesenthal.com/library/award.cfm
Length: No length limit.
Requirements: No entry fee. All entries must have been published in the year preceding the contest. A nomination form must accompany each submission. Guidelines and nomination form available at website.
Prizes: Winners receive a cash award of $1,000.
Deadline: April.

Pacific Northwest Writers Association Literary Contests

PNWA
P.O. Box 2016
Edmonds, WA 98020-9516

Description
Held annually, these contests are sponsored by the Pacific Northwest Writers Association and present awards in several categories including juvenile/young adult novel; nonfiction book; juvenile memoir; and short story. The competition accepts original, previously unpublished material only.
Website: www.pnwa.org
Length: Varies for each category.
Requirements: Entry fee, $35 for members; $45 for non-members. Multiple entries are accepted. Accepts photocopies and computer printouts. All entries must include an official entry form. Submit 2 copies of each entry. Guidelines and category information available at website.
Prizes: Winners receive cash awards ranging from $150 to $600.
Deadline: February.

Pikes Peak Writers Conference Annual Contest

Angel Smits, Contest Coordinator
P.O. Box 63114
Colorado Springs, CO 80962

Description
Encouraging emerging authors to focus on producing a marketable manuscript, this contest is held each year. It accepts manuscripts in several categories including children's, young adult, mystery, historical fiction, creative nonfiction, and contemporary romance.
Website: www.pikespeakwriters.org
Length: Lengths vary for each category.
Requirements: Entry fee, $25 ($40 entry fee includes a manuscript critique). Accepts photocopies and computer printouts. All entries must be accompanied by an entry form, a cover letter, and two copies of manuscript. Guidelines available at website.
Prizes: First-place winner in each category receives $100. Second-place winner in each category receives $50.
Deadline: November 1.

Skipping Stones Awards

Skipping Stones Awards
P.O. Box 3939
Eugene, OR 97403

Description
This competition focuses on multicultural awareness and honors exceptional contributions to ecological and multicultural education. Books, magazines, and educational videos are considered in each of the four categories: Ecology & Nature, Educational Videos, Multicultural & International, and Teaching Resources.
Website: www.efn.org/~skipping
Length: No length requirements.
Requirements: Entry fee, $50. Multiple entries are accepted. Send 4 copies of each book and magazine entry; 2 copies of each video. Only entries produced in the preceding calendar year are eligible.
Prizes: Cash prizes are awarded to first- through fourth-place winners. Winning entries are reviewed in *Skipping Stones*.
Deadline: January 15.

Kay Snow Writing Contest

Willamette Writers
Suite 5A
9045 SW Barbour Blvd
Portland, OR 97219-4027

Description
The Kay Snow Writing Contest presents awards in several categories including juvenile short story or article, fiction, nonfiction, and student writer. Held annually, it accepts original, unpublished material only.
Website: www.willamettewriters.com
Length: Lengths vary for each category.
Requirements: Entry fee, $10 for members; $15 for non-members. Submit 3 copies of each entry. Author's name must not appear on manuscript. Request complete contest guidelines or visit website for additional information.
Prizes: Cash prizes ranging from $50 to $300 are awarded in each category. A Liam Callen award will also be presented to the best overall entry with a cash prize of $500.
Deadline: May 15.

Southwest Writers Contests

Southwest Writers Workshop
Suite 106
8200 Mountain Road NE
Albuquerque, NM 87110

Description
The Southwest Writers Workshop presents writing contests in several categories including middle-grade novel, young adult novel, children's picture book, and nonfiction book. It looks to recognize, encourage, and honor excellence in writing.
Website: www.southwestwriters.org
Length: Lengths vary for each category.
Requirements: Entry fee, $29 for members; $39 for non-members. Submit 2 copies of each entry. Each entry must be accompanied by an official entry form. Author's name should appear on the entry form only. Multiple entries are accepted. All entries must be typed. Send an SASE for complete contest guidelines and official entry form, or visit the website.
Prizes: Cash prizes ranging from $75–$100.
Deadline: May 1.

Tall Tales Press Hidden Talents Short Story Contest

20 Tuscany Valley Park NW
Calgary, Alberta T3L 2B6
Canada

Description
This annual contest offers writers a chance to gain the experience that publishers demand. It accepts manuscripts in several categories for both adult and young adult writers and accepts previously unpublished work only.
Website: www.talltalespress.com
Length: To 5,000 words.
Requirements: Entry fees, $10 for adults; $5 for junior categories. Multiple entries are accepted. All entries must be accompanied by an official entry form. Guidelines and entry forms available at website.
Prizes: Winners and honorable mentions receive cash prizes ranging from $10 to $500 and possible publication.
Deadline: May 31.

Peter Taylor Prize for the Novel

Knoxville Writers Guild
P.O. Box 2565
Knoxville, TN 37901-2565

Description
This competition is open to both published and unpublished writers living in the U.S. Held annually, it looks to identify, promote, and publish novels of high literary quality.
Website: www.knoxvillewritersguild.org
Length: 40,000 words minimum.
Requirements: Entry fee, $20. Multiple submissions are accepted provided that each is accompanied by an entry fee. Entries must be on standard white paper. Manuscripts will not be returned. Include an SASE for contest results.
Prizes: The prize includes a $1,000 cash award, publication of the novel by the University of Tennessee Press, and a standard royalty contract.
Deadline: Entries must be postmarked between February 1 and April 30.

Work-in-Progress Grants

The Society of Children's Book Writers and Illustrators
8271 Beverly Boulevard
Los Angeles, CA 90048

Description
SCBWI presents 5 grants annually to assist children's book writers in the completion of a project. Grants are awarded in the categories of General Work-in-Progress; Contemporary Novel for Young People; Nonfiction Research; and Unpublished Author.
Website: www.scbwi.org
Length: 750-word synopsis and writing sample from the entry that is no longer than 2,500 words.
Requirements: No entry fee. Requests for applications may be made beginning October 1 of each year. Instructions and complete guidelines are sent with application forms.
Prizes: Cash grants of $1,500 and $500 are awarded in each of the 5 categories.

Paul Zindel First Novel Award

Hyperion Books for Children
P.O. Box 6000
Manhasset, NY 11030-6000

Description
This award is presented annually for the best contemporary or historical fiction for readers ages 8 to 12 that is set in the United States and that reflects the diverse ethnic and cultural heritage of the country. The competition is open to all writers living in the U.S. who have not yet published a novel.
Website: www.hyperionbooksforchildren.com
Length: 100- to 240-typewritten pages.
Requirements: No entry fee. Limit two entries per competition. Accepts photocopies and computer printouts. Include an SASE for return of manuscript. Guidelines available at website.
Prizes: Winner receives a book contract and an advance against royalties of $7,500 and a cash prize of $1,500.
Deadline: April 30.

Zoo Press Award for Short Fiction

Zoo Press
P.O. Box 22990
Lincoln, NE 68542

Description
This annual contest is sponsored by Zoo Press. Open to all writers, it accepts previously unpublished, original entries of collections of short fiction.
Website: www.zoopress.org
Length: Collections must total 40,000 words.
Requirements: Entry fee, $25 per entry. Multiple entries are accepted under separate cover. Accepts computer printouts. All entries must include a cover letter. Manuscripts will not be returned. Guidelines available at website.
Prizes: Winning entry will be published by Zoo Press and winner receives a $5,000 advance against royalties.
Deadline: February 14.

Indexes

2005 Market News

New Listings ☆

Harry N. Abrams Books for Young Readers
American Book Cooperative Children's Picture Book Competition
Amulet Books
A.R.E. Publishing, Inc.
Ave Maria Press
Bancroft Press
Bloomsbury Children's Books
Boardwalk Books
Bollix Books
Brown Barn Books
Buster Books
Calkins Creek Books
CIPA National Writing Contest
Darby Creek Publishing
Delacorte Dell Yearling Contest
Dorchester Publishing
Dragonfly Spirit Writing for Children Short Story Contest
E & E Publishing
Egmont Children's Books
Floris Books
Laura Geringer Books
Graphia
Groundwood Books
Harbour Publishing
Wendy Lamb Books
Lion Publishing
Little Tiger Press
Maple Tree Press Inc.
Milet Publishing
Mirrorstone Books
Moose Enterprise
Mott Media
Nightwood Editions
Nimbus Publishing
Ursula Nordstrom Fiction Contest
Pikes Peak Writers Conference Annual Contest
Pipers' Ash Ltd.
PowerKids Press
Quartz Editions
Raincoast Books
Raven Tree Press
Razorbill
Riverfront Books
School Specialty Children's Publishing
Second Story Press
Smallfellow Press
Smooch
Starscape Books
Tanglewood Press, LLC
Twenty-Third Publications
URJ Press
Watson-Guptill
Windstorm Creative
Paul Zindel First Novel Award
Zoo Press Award for Short Fiction

2005 Market News

Deletions/Name Changes

Africa World Press: Unable to locate
All About Kids Publishing: Removed; status uncertain
Amsco School Publications: No response
ATL Press: Unable to locate
Blushing Rose Publishing: Unable to locate
The Boxwood Press: Unable to locate
The Brookfield Reader: Unable to locate
Chronicle Books: No response
I. E. Clark Publications: No response
The Colonial Williamsburg Foundation: No longer publishing material for children
Crocodile Books, USA: Ceased publication
Focus Publishing: Publishes only adult Bible studies
Good Year Books: Imprint sold
Halstead Press: No response
ImaJinn Books: Ceased publication
Interlink Publishing Group: No response
Jalmar Press/Innerchoice Publishing: Imprint sold
Kidszip Ltd: No response
Lightwave Publishing, Inc: Not using freelancers
Lion Books: Unable to locate
McGraw-Hill School Division: See listing for **School Specialty Children's Publishing**
MightyBook: No response
Modern Learning Press: Merged with **Educators Publishing Service**
Thomas More Publishing: See **Ave Maria Press**
Morehouse Publishing: No response
Owl Books: See **Maple Tree Press Inc.**
Pearson Education Canada: Merged into **Penguin Canada**
Prima Publishing: Division closed
Pro Lingua Associates: Changing publishing priorities
Raintree Publishers: No response
Roaring Brook Press: Status uncertain
Scholastic Book Group: No response
Shining Star Publications: Unable to locate
Starry Puddle Publishing: No response
Teachers College Press: No response
Tortoise Press: No response
UAHC Press: See **URJ Press**
VGM Career Books: Unable to locate
Zig Zag Children's Books: See **Chrysalis Books**
Zino Press Children's Books: Not publishing children's material
Zonderkidz: Unable to locate

Category Index

To help you find the appropriate market for your query or manuscript, we have compiled a selective index of publishers according to the types of books they currently publish.

If you don't find a category that exactly fits your material, try a broader term that covers your topic. For example, if you have written a middle-grade biography, look through the list of publishers for both Middle-Grade (Nonfiction) *and* Biography. If you've written a young adult mystery, look under Mystery/Suspense *and* Young Adult (Fiction). Always check the publisher's listing for explanations of specific needs.

For your convenience, we have listed all of the categories that are included in this Index.

Activity Books
Adventure
Animals/Pets
Bilingual (Fiction)
Bilingual (Nonfiction)
Biography
Board Books
Canadian Publishers
Chapter Books (Fiction)
Chapter Books (Nonfiction)
Concept Books
Contemporary Fiction
Crafts/Hobbies
Current Events
Drama
Early Picture Books (Fiction)
Early Picture Books (Nonfiction)
Easy-to-Read (Fiction)
Easy-to-Read (Nonfiction)
Education/Resource Material
Fairy Tales
Fantasy
Folklore/Folktales
Geography
Gifted Education
Health/Fitness
High-Interest/ Low-Vocabulary
Historical Fiction
History (Nonfiction)
Horror
How-to
Humor
Inspirational Fiction
Language Arts
Mathematics
Middle-Grade (Fiction)
Middle-Grade (Nonfiction)
Multicultural/ Ethnic (Fiction)
Multicultural/Ethnic (Nonfiction)
Mystery/Suspense
Nature/ Environment
Parenting
Photo Essays
Picture Books (Fiction)
Picture Books (Nonfiction)
Plays
Reference Books
Regional (Fiction)
Regional (Nonfiction)
Religious (Fiction)
Religious (Nonfiction)
Romance
Science Fiction
Science/Technology
Self-Help
Series
Social Issues
Social Sciences
Special Education
Sports (Fiction)
Sports (Nonfiction)
Story Picture Books (Fiction)
Story Picture Books (Nonfiction)
Toddler Books (Fiction)
Toddler Books (Nonfiction)
Travel
Western
Young Adult (Fiction)
Young Adult (Nonfiction)

Activity Books

Absey and Company	81
Accord Publishing	82
Augsburg Books	95
Ballyhoo Books, Inc.	446
The Benefactory	449
Carson-Dellosa Publishing Company	127
Chicago Review Press	133
Childswork/Childsplay	137
Christian Ed. Publishers	140
Christian Focus Publications	141
Chrysalis Children's Books	143
Cottonwood Press	458
Creative Learning Press	155
Dandy Lion Publications	163
May Davenport, Publishers	165
Didax	172
Dog-Eared Publications	464
Dover Publications	177
Edupress	185
Evan-Moor Educational Publishers	191
Forest House Publishing Company	201
Fulcrum Publishing	209
Gibbs Smith, Publisher	211
Greene Bark Press	217
Group Publishing	220
Heritage House	238
Honor Books	242
Humanics	245
Hunter House Publishers	246
Iron Crown Enterprises	477
Kar-Ben Publishing	262
Leadership Publishers Inc.	480
Learning Horizons	267
Learning Resources	268
Legacy Press	270
Libraries Unlimited	273
Marlor Press	485
Master Books	288
Modern Publishing	488
NL Associates	316
Paulist Press	329
Pleasant Company Publications	345
Rainbow Publishers	355
Rand McNally	504
Resource Publications, Inc.	361
Rising Moon	362
Robins Lane Press	363
Running Press Kids	368
Sterling Publishing Company	396
Story Time Stories That Rhyme	518
Teacher Created Materials	400
Tricycle Press	412
Warner Press	420

Adventure

Action Publishing	84
Aquila Communications Ltd.	443
Atheneum Books for Young Readers	94
A/V Concepts Corporation	96
Bethany House	107
BOW Books	452
Breakwater Books	118
Brown Barn Books	120
Camex Books	454
Clarion Books	144
Coteau Books	151
Covenant Communications	152
Creative Paperbacks	461
Crossway Books	160
May Davenport, Publishers	165
Denlinger's Publishers	169
Dover Publications	177
Down East Books	178
Dutton Children's Books	180
Focus on the Family Book Development	200
Formac Publishing Company Ltd.	202
Frances Foster Books	204
Gibbs Smith, Publisher	211
Gulliver Books	222
Hachai Publishing	223
Harbour Publishing	226
Innovative Kids	253
Just Us Books	260
Wendy Lamb Books	479
Little, Brown and Company	278
Lobster Press	483
MacAdam/Cage	484
Margaret K. McElderry Books	291
Milet Publishing	294
Mirrorstone Books	487
Modern Publishing	488
Moody Publishers	298
Moose Enterprise	299
Pioneer Drama Service	341
Playhouse Publishing	500

549

Random House Children's Books	506	Mott Media	301
Random House Children's Publishing	506	Mount Olive College Press	489
		National Geographic Society	304
Rayve Productions Inc.	357	North-South Books	493
Red Deer Press	359	NorthWord Books for Young Readers	318
River City Publishing	508		
Riverfront Books	509	OnStage Publishing	493
Scholastic Canada Ltd.	373	Pipers' Ash Ltd.	342
Seedling Publications	379	Pleasant Company Publications	345
Silver Moon Press	380	Quartz Editions	502
Soundprints/Studio Mouse	387	Quest Books	354
Storytellers Ink Publishing Co.	397	Random House Children's Publishing	506
Tanglewood Press, LLC	399		
Turtle Press	523	Renaissance House	360
Viking Children's Books	525	Riverfront Books	509
Whitecap Books Ltd.	425	The Rosen Publishing Group	367
		Running Press Kids	368
Animals/Pets		Seedling Publications	379
Abdo Publishing Company	440	Silver Dolphin Books	514
Harry N. Abrams Books for Young Readers	80	Soundprints/Studio Mouse	387
		Storytellers Ink Publishing Co.	397
Benchmark Books	105	Tilbury House Publishers	407
The Benefactory	449	Windward Publishing	430
Buster Books	122		
Capstone Press	125	**Bilingual (F)**	
Charlesbridge	130	Children's Book Press	134
Children's eLibrary	135	Cricket Books	158
Chrysalis Children's Books	143	Fondo de Cultura Economica USA	470
Creative Editions	460		
Creative Education	461	Renaissance House	360
Creative Paperbacks	461	Rising Moon	362
Creative With Words Publications	157	Salina Bookshelf	509
		Turtle Books	522
Darby Creek Publishing	164		
Dover Publications	177	**Bilingual (NF)**	
Falcon Publishing	194	Abingdon Press	440
Gibbs Smith, Publisher	211	Aquila Communications Ltd.	443
Graphic Arts Center Publishing Co.	216	Bebop Books	103
		Chrysalis Children's Books	143
Gulliver Books	222	Contemporary Books	457
Hendrick-Long Publishing Company	237	Corwin Press	150
		Encore Performance Publishing	189
Henry Holt Books for Young Readers	241	Family Learning Assn./ERIC/ REC Press	195
Journey Forth	258	Fondo de Cultura Economica USA	470
Kingfisher	478		
Learning Horizons	267	Forest House Publishing Company	201
Little Tiger Press	280		
Master Books	288	Gryphon House	221
Maval Publishing	289	Hampton-Brown Books	224
Miles Kelly Publishing	486	Heinemann	236

Incentive Publications	252
Kingfisher	478
Libraries Unlimited	273
Mitchell Lane Publishers	296
Pearson Learning Group	496
Portage & Main Press	348
Renaissance House	360
Salina Bookshelf	509
Scott Foresman	512
Star Bright Books	392
Storytellers Ink Publishing Co.	397

Biography

Absey and Company	81
Aladdin Paperbacks	85
Avisson Press	98
Alexander Graham Bell Assn. for the Deaf	449
Blue Marlin Publications	451
Camex Books	454
Capstone Press	125
Chicago Review Press	133
Christian Focus Publications	141
Clark City Press	456
Creative Paperbacks	461
Crossquarter Publishing Group	462
Eerdmans Books for Young Readers	186
Encounter Books	466
Enslow Publishers, Inc.	190
Excelsior Cee Publishing	467
The Feminist Press	468
Franklin Watts	470
Greenhaven Press	218
Hendrick-Long Publishing Company	237
Holloway House Publishing Group	474
Houghton Mifflin Children's Books	244
Journey Forth	258
Just Us Books	260
Lerner Publishing Group	271
Libraries Unlimited	273
Linnet Books	275
Lucent Books	285
Mage Publishers	485
The Millbrook Press	487
Mitchell Lane Publishers	296
Mondo Publishing	297
Moose Enterprise	299

Morgan Reynolds Publishing	300
Mott Media	301
National Geographic Books for Children	490
North Country Books	317
Novalis	319
The Oliver Press	320
OnStage Publishing	493
Paulist Press	329
Piñata Books	339
PowerKids Press	349
Random House Children's Publishing	506
Rayve Productions Inc.	357
Ronsdale Press	365
Sandlapper Publishing	510
Simon Pulse	383
Sports Publishing Inc.	390
Stemmer House Publishers	395
Storytellers Ink Publishing Co.	397
Sword of the Lord	398
Teaching & Learning Company	401
TEACH Services, Inc.	402
Touchwood Editions	521
Toy Box Productions	411
Twenty-First Century Books	523
Two Lives Publishing	524

Board Books

Abingdon Press	440
Bess Press	106
Chrysalis Children's Books	143
Honor Books	242
John Hunt Publishing	247
Hyperion Books for Children	475
Innovative Kids	253
Kar-Ben Publishing	262
Alfred A. Knopf Books for Young Readers	265
Little Simon	279
Little Tiger Press	280
Master Books	288
Playhouse Publishing	500
Rising Moon	362
Silver Dolphin Books	514
Smallfellow Press	515
Standard Publishing	391
Star Bright Books	392
Warner Press	420
Workman Publishing Company	433

551

Canadian Publishers

Annick Press	92
Beach Holme Publishing	102
Boardwalk Books	113
Borealis Press Limited	114
Breakwater Books	118
Coteau Books	151
Creative Bound	153
Formac Publishing Company Ltd.	202
Harcourt Canada Ltd.	473
Heritage House	238
Key Porter Books	264
James Lorimer & Company	282
LTDBooks	283
Maple Tree Press Inc.	287
Natural Heritage Books	491
Orca Book Publishers	321
Pembroke Publishers	332
Penguin Books Canada Limited	498
Playwrights Canada Press	501
Raincoast Books	504
Red Deer Press	359
Ronsdale Press	365
Scholastic Canada Ltd.	373
Second Story Press	513
Thistledown Press	520
Thompson Educational Publishing	406
Touchwood Editions	521
Tradewind Books Ltd.	522

Chapter Books (F)

Absey and Company	81
Alef Design Group	87
Ambassador-Emerald International	90
Bantam Books for Young Readers	101
Bethany House	107
Bloomsbury Children's Books	111
BOW Books	452
Candlewick Press	124
Christian Focus Publications	141
Clarion Books	144
Coteau Books	151
Cricket Books	158
Darby Creek Publishing	164
Denlinger's Publishers	169
Dial Books for Young Readers	171
Dorling Kindersley	176
Eakin Press	181
Educators Publishing Service	184
Egmont Children's Books	187
Faith Kidz	193
Farrar, Straus & Giroux	196
The Feminist Press	468
Formac Publishing Company Ltd.	202
Frances Foster Books	204
Graphic Arts Center Publishing Co.	216
Hachai Publishing	223
Hampton-Brown Books	224
HarperCollins Children's Books	231
HarperCollins Children's Fiction	232
Henry Holt Books for Young Readers	241
Hodder Children's Books	474
Holiday House	240
Hyperion Books for Children	475
Imperial International	250
Journey Forth	258
Alfred A. Knopf Books for Young Readers	265
Lion Publishing	277
Mayhaven Publishing	290
Mondo Publishing	297
New Canaan Publishing Company	492
North-South Books	493
Orca Book Publishers	321
Orchard Books	322
The Overmountain Press	324
Richard C. Owen Publishers	325
Pacific Educational Press	326
Pacific Press Publishing Association	327
Parachute Press	495
Paulist Press	329
Peartree	497
Philomel Books	336
Pipers' Ash Ltd.	342
Polychrome Publishing Corporation	347
Publish America	351
Puffin Books	352
G. P. Putnam's Sons	353
Random House Children's Books	506
Rayve Productions Inc.	357
Red Deer Press	359
Scholastic Canada Ltd.	373
Shen's Books	514
Silver Whistle	381

Simon & Schuster Books for Young Readers	382
Smith and Kraus Books for Kids	516
Soundprints/Studio Mouse	387
Star Bright Books	392
Tanglewood Press, LLC	399
Third World Press	404
Torah Aura Productions	409
Tricycle Press	412
Turtle Press	523
Whitecap Books Ltd.	425
Albert Whitman & Company	427
The Wright Group/McGraw-Hill	435

Chapter Books (NF)

Abdo Publishing Company	440
Alef Design Group	87
Behrman House	104
Benchmark Books	105
Blackbirch Press	109
Breakwater Books	118
Candlewick Press	124
Carolrhoda Books	126
Children's Press	136
Critical Thinking Company	159
Crown Books for Young Readers	161
Discovery Enterprises	173
Facts On File	192
Faith Kidz	193
Falcon Publishing	194
Family Learning Assn./ERIC/ REC Press	195
The Feminist Press	468
Ferguson Publishing	198
Formac Publishing Company Ltd.	202
Fulcrum Publishing	209
Harcourt Religion Publishers	229
Hodder Children's Books	474
John Hunt Publishing	247
Hyperion Books for Children	475
Imperial International	250
Incentive Publications	252
Lerner Publishing Group	271
Lobster Press	483
Marlor Press	485
Meadowbrook Press	292
Mitchell Lane Publishers	296
Mondo Publishing	297
National Geographic Society	304
New Canaan Publishing Company	492

Our Sunday Visitor	323
Pacific Press Publishing Association	327
Paulist Press	329
Pembroke Publishers	332
Perfection Learning Corporation	333
Pipers' Ash Ltd.	342
Pitspopany Press	343
The Rosen Publishing Group	367
Silver Moon Press	380
Smith and Kraus Books for Kids	516
Standard Publishing	391
Stemmer House Publishers	395
TEACH Services, Inc.	402
Torah Aura Productions	409
Toy Box Productions	411
Tricycle Press	412
Turtle Press	523
URJ Press	416
Windward Publishing	430

Concept Books

Atheneum Books for Young Readers	94
Augsburg Books	95
Boyds Mills Press	115
Broadman & Holman Publishers	119
Cartwheel Books	128
Charlesbridge	130
Children's Press	136
Chrysalis Children's Books	143
Cook Communications Ministries	148
Covenant Communications	152
Crown Books for Young Readers	161
Dial Books for Young Readers	171
DiskUs Publishing	174
Dorling Kindersley	176
Dutton Children's Books	180
Egmont Children's Books	187
Gifted Education Press	212
Greenwillow Books	472
Hachai Publishing	223
Harcourt Children's Books	228
HarperCollins Children's Books	231
Honor Books	242
Houghton Mifflin Children's Books	244
Humanics	245

553

Just Us Books	260	Graphia	215
Kar-Ben Publishing	262	Greenwillow Books	472
Little, Brown and Company	278	Groundwood Books	472
Little Simon	279	Harcourt Children's Books	228
Master Books	288	HarperCollins Children's Fiction	232
The Millbrook Press	487	Journey Forth	258
North-South Books	493	Just Us Books	260
Orchard Books	322	Alfred A. Knopf Books for Young Readers	265
Our Sunday Visitor	323	Lee & Low Books	269
Philomel Books	336	Arthur A. Levine Books	272
Playhouse Publishing	500	Little Tiger Press	280
Rising Moon	362	MacAdam/Cage	484
School Specialty Children's Publishing	377	Maple Tree Press Inc.	287
Seaburn Publishing	512	Milet Publishing	294
Silver Dolphin Books	514	Mirrorstone Books	487
The Speech Bin, Inc.	389	Moody Publishers	298
Standard Publishing	391	Morning Glory Press	488
Third World Press	404	Orca Book Publishers	321
Megan Tingley Books	408	Orchard Books	322
Tricycle Press	412	Richard C. Owen Publishers	325
Two Lives Publishing	524	Parachute Press	495
Tyndale House Publishers	413	Perfection Learning Corporation	333
Viking Children's Books	525	Piñata Books	339
Walker and Company	419	Pleasant Company Publications	345
Workman Publishing Company	433	Publish America	351
		G. P. Putnam's Sons	353
Contemporary Fiction		Raincoast Books	504
Aladdin Paperbacks	85	Razorbill	358
Amulet Books	91	Red Deer Press	359
Annick Press	92	Riverfront Books	509
Barron's Educational Series	447	Saint Mary's Press	370
Beach Holme Publishing	102	Sandpiper Paperbacks	510
Bethany House	107	Silver Whistle	381
A & C Black Publishers	110	Simon Pulse	383
Boardwalk Books	113	Smooch	386
Bollix Books	451	Texas Tech University Press	403
Carolrhoda Books	126	Megan Tingley Books	408
Cavendish Children's Books	129	Turtle Books	522
Christian Focus Publications	141	Two Lives Publishing	524
Coteau Books	151	Whitecap Books Ltd.	425
Creative Paperbacks	461		
Cricket Books	158	**Crafts/Hobbies**	
Crossway Books	160	Ballyhoo Books, Inc.	446
Darby Creek Publishing	164	Creative Teaching Press, Inc.	156
Dorchester Publishing	175	Evan-Moor Educational Publishers	191
Farrar, Straus & Giroux	196	Focus on the Family Book Development	200
Floris Books	199		
Forward Movement Publications	203		
Laura Geringer Books	210		

Forest House Publishing Company	201	Meriwether Publishing Ltd.	293
Group Publishing	220	Mirrorstone Books	487
Humanics	245	North-South Books	493
Lark Books	266	OnStage Publishing	493
Legacy Press	270	Piñata Books	339
The Millbrook Press	487	Pioneer Drama Service	341
Naturegraph Publishers	305	Players Press	344
Pleasant Company Publications	345	Playwrights Canada Press	501
Quartz Editions	502	Saint Mary's Press	370
Quixote Press	503	Sandcastle Publishing	371
Rainbow Publishers	355	Smith and Kraus	385
Sterling Publishing Company	396	Smith and Kraus Books for Kids	516
Success Publications	519		
Teaching & Learning Company	401		
Tor Books	410		
Watson-Guptill	422		
Wiley Children's Books	428		
Williamson Publishing	429		
Winslow Publishing	527		
World Book	434		

Early Picture Books (F)

Harry N. Abrams Books for Young Readers			80
Accord Publishing			82
Action Publishing			84
Atheneum Books for Young Readers			94
Augsburg Books			95
Bantam Books for Young Readers			101
Bess Press			106
Beyond Words Publishing			108
Bloomsbury Children's Books			111
Blue Marlin Publications			451
Blue Sky Press			112
Bollix Books			451
Boyds Mills Press			115
Breakwater Books			118
Cartwheel Books			128
Charlesbridge			130
Cook Communications Ministries			148
Covenant Communications			152
Dial Books for Young Readers			171
Dorling Kindersley			176
Down East Books			178
Eakin Press			181
E & E Publishing			465
Egmont Children's Books			187
Frances Foster Books			204
Gulliver Books			222
Hachai Publishing			223
Hampton-Brown Books			224
Harcourt Children's Books			228
HarperCollins Children's Books			231
Holiday House			240
Houghton Mifflin Children's Books			244
Incentive Publications			252

Current Events

Alpha Publishing	442
Facts On File	192
Focus on the Family Book Development	200
Lerner Publishing Group	271
MacAdam/Cage	484
New Leaf Press	310
Publish America	351
Random House Children's Publishing	506
Sandpiper Paperbacks	510
Teaching & Learning Company	401
UXL	417

Drama

Baker's Plays	100
Boardwalk Books	113
Borealis Press Limited	114
Boynton/Cook Publishers	116
Children's Story Scripts	455
Contemporary Drama Service	147
Dramatic Publishing	179
Encore Performance Publishing	189
Floris Books	199
Samuel French, Inc.	207
Heuer Publishing Company	239
Hunter House Publishers	246
Lillenas Publishing Company	274

The Judaica Press	259	Down East Books	178
Kar-Ben Publishing	262	E & E Publishing	465
Lee & Low Books	269	Free Spirit Publishing	206
Lion Publishing	277	Gulliver Books	222
Little, Brown and Company	278	Honor Books	242
Little Tiger Press	280	John Hunt Publishing	247
Lobster Press	483	Kar-Ben Publishing	262
The Lutterworth Press	484	Learning Horizons	267
Maple Tree Press Inc.	287	Lion Publishing	277
Margaret K. McElderry Books	291	Little Blue Works	482
Milet Publishing	294	Little Tiger Press	280
Mondo Publishing	297	Maple Tree Press Inc.	287
Orchard Books	322	Master Books	288
The Overmountain Press	324	National Geographic Books for Children	490
Philomel Books	336		
Playhouse Publishing	500	North-South Books	493
Polychrome Publishing Corporation	347	Novalis	319
		Peachtree Publishers	330
Puffin Books	352	G. P. Putnam's Sons	353
G. P. Putnam's Sons	353	Sandpiper Paperbacks	510
Random House Children's Books	506	Scholastic Press	375
		Silver Dolphin Books	514
Raven Tree Press	356	Silver Whistle	381
Riverfront Books	509	Siphano Picture Books	515
Sandpiper Paperbacks	510	The Speech Bin, Inc.	389
Scholastic Press	375	URJ Press	416
Silver Whistle	381	Albert Whitman & Company	427
Simon & Schuster Books for Young Readers	382	Workman Publishing Company	433
Siphano Picture Books	515	**Easy-to-Read (F)**	
Star Bright Books	392	Abbeville Kids	439
Starseed Press	394	Abingdon Press	440
Megan Tingley Books	408	Harry N. Abrams Books for Young Readers	80
Two Lives Publishing	524		
Walker and Company	419	Augsburg Books	95
Albert Whitman & Company	427	Azro Press	445
		Bantam Books for Young Readers	101
Early Picture Books (NF)		Bay Light Publishing	448
Abdo Publishing Company	440	Bebop Books	103
Aladdin Paperbacks	85	Alexander Graham Bell Assn. for the Deaf	449
Bloomsbury Children's Books	111		
Blue Marlin Publications	451	BePuzzled	450
Buster Books	122	Bethany House	107
Cartwheel Books	128	BOW Books	452
Concordia Publishing House	146	Boyds Mills Press	115
Continental Press	457	Cavendish Children's Books	129
Cook Communications Ministries	148	Clear Light Publishers	145
		Cook Communications Ministries	148
Covenant Communications	152	Creative Teaching Press, Inc.	156
Dial Books for Young Readers	171		
Didax	172	Critical Thinking Company	159

Jonathan David Publishers	166	School Specialty Children's Publishing	377
Dial Books for Young Readers	171		
DiskUs Publishing	174	Seedling Publications	379
Dutton Children's Books	180	Simon & Schuster Books for Young Readers	382
Eakin Press	181		
E & E Publishing	465	Star Bright Books	392
Educators Publishing Service	184	Story Time Stories That Rhyme	518
Eerdmans Books for Young Readers	186	Tradewind Books Ltd.	522
		Tricycle Press	412
Egmont Children's Books	187	Viking Children's Books	525
Faith Kidz	193	Whitecap Books Ltd.	425
Family Learning Assn./ERIC/ REC Press	195	The Wright Group/McGraw-Hill	435
Farrar, Straus & Giroux	196	**Easy-to-Read (NF)**	
Formac Publishing Company Ltd.	202	Abbeville Kids	439
Laura Geringer Books	210	Abingdon Press	440
Hampton-Brown Books	224	Harry N. Abrams Books for Young Readers	80
Hampton Roads Publishing	225		
HarperCollins Children's Books	231	Action Publishing	84
HarperCollins Children's Fiction	232	Azro Press	445
		Bebop Books	103
Hodder Children's Books	474	Blackbirch Press	109
Journey Forth	258	Boyds Mills Press	115
The Judaica Press	259	Broadman & Holman Publishers	119
Kaeden Books	261		
Kar-Ben Publishing	262	Buster Books	122
Little Blue Works	482	Carolrhoda Books	126
Little, Brown and Company	278	Cartwheel Books	128
Living the Good News	482	Cavendish Children's Books	129
Lobster Press	483	Children's Press	136
The Lutterworth Press	484	Chrysalis Children's Books	143
Magination Press	286	Concordia Publishing House	146
Maple Tree Press Inc.	287	Creative Teaching Press, Inc.	156
Margaret K. McElderry Books	291	Jonathan David Publishers	166
Mondo Publishing	297	Dial Books for Young Readers	171
North-South Books	493	Discovery Enterprises	173
Richard C. Owen Publishers	325	Dorling Kindersley	176
Pacific Press Publishing Association	327	E & E Publishing	465
		Eerdmans Books for Young Readers	186
Paws IV Books	496		
Peartree	497	Faith Kidz	193
Pelican Publishing Company	331	Family Learning Assn./ERIC/ REC Press	195
Philomel Books	336		
Playhouse Publishing	500	Forest House Publishing Company	201
Polar Bear & Company	346		
Puffin Books	352	Free Spirit Publishing	206
Quixote Press	503	Harcourt Religion Publishers	229
Raven Tree Press	356	HarperCollins Children's Books	231
Rayve Productions Inc.	357	Hodder Children's Books	474
River City Publishing	508	Honor Books	242
Scholastic Press	375	Jewish Lights Publishing	256

557

Kaeden Books	261	Avocus Publishing	445
Lerner Publishing Group	271	Barron's Educational Series	447
Lion Publishing	277	Behrman House	104
Living the Good News	482	Alexander Graham Bell Assn.	
Master Books	288	for the Deaf	449
Mayhaven Publishing	290	The Benefactory	449
Meadowbrook Press	292	Bess Press	106
Modern Publishing	488	Blackbirch Press	109
Mondo Publishing	297	A & C Black Publishers	110
The Oliver Press	320	Boynton/Cook Publishers	116
OnStage Publishing	493	Breakwater Books	118
Pacific Press Publishing		The Bureau for At-Risk Youth	121
Association	327	Butte Publications	123
Paws IV Books	496	Caddo Gap Press	453
Pitspopany Press	343	Capstone Press	125
Prometheus Books	350	Carson-Dellosa Publishing	
Redbird Press	507	Company	127
Scholastic Press	375	Childswork/Childsplay	137
Seaburn Publishing	512	Child Welfare League of America	139
Seedling Publications	379	Christian Ed. Publishers	140
Silver Dolphin Books	514	Christopher-Gordon Publishers	142
Stemmer House Publishers	395	Concordia Publishing House	146
Story Time Stories That Rhyme	518	Consortium Publishing	456
TEACH Services, Inc.	402	Contemporary Books	457
Third World Press	404	Continental Press	457
Tradewind Books Ltd.	522	Corwin Press	150
Tricycle Press	412	Cottonwood Press	458
Tyndale House Publishers	413	Course Crafters	460
UXL	417	Creative Education	461
Watson-Guptill	422	Creative Learning Press	155
Weigl Educational Publishers		Creative Teaching Press, Inc.	156
Limited	424	Critical Thinking Company	159
Whitecap Books Ltd.	425	CSS Publishing Company	162
Williamson Publishing	429	Dandy Lion Publications	163
Windward Publishing	430	Dawn Publications	168
World Book	434	Delmar Learning	462
		Didax	172
Education/		Discovery Enterprises	173
Resource Material		Displays for Schools	463
Absey and Company	81	Dover Publications	177
Activity Resources Company	441	Dramatic Publishing	179
Advocacy Press	441	Educational Ministries	183
ALA Editions	86	Educators Publishing Service	184
Alef Design Group	87	Edupress	185
Alpha Publishing	442	Encore Performance Publishing	189
Amirah Publishing	443	Encounter Books	466
A.R.E. Publishing, Inc.	93	Enslow Publishers, Inc.	190
Association for Childhood		ESP Publishers, Inc.	466
Education Int'l	444	ETC Publications	467
A/V Concepts Corporation	96	Evan-Moor Educational	
Ave Maria Press	97	Publishers	191

Exclamation! Publishers	468	Neal-Schuman Publishers	306
Family Learning Assn./ERIC/		New Canaan Publishing	
REC Press	195	Company	492
Ferguson Publishing	198	New Society Publishers	312
Finney Company	469	NL Associates	316
Franklin Watts	470	Pacific Educational Press	326
Free Spirit Publishing	206	Pearson Learning Group	496
Samuel French, Inc.	207	Peartree	497
Front Street Books	208	Pembroke Publishers	332
Fulcrum Publishing	209	Phoenix Learning Resources	337
Gifted Education Press	212	Piano Press	499
Goodheart-Willcox	214	The Pilgrim Press	338
Group Publishing	220	Pioneer Drama Service	341
Gryphon House	221	The Place in the Woods	500
Hampton-Brown Books	224	Portage & Main Press	348
Harcourt Canada Ltd.	473	PowerKids Press	349
Harcourt Religion Publishers	229	Prometheus Books	350
Hayes School Publishing		Quartz Editions	502
Company	233	Redleaf Press	507
Hazelden Foundation	234	Resource Publications, Inc.	361
Heinemann	236	Rocky River Publishers	364
Heuer Publishing Company	239	St. Anthony Messenger Press	369
Humanics	245	Sandcastle Publishing	371
Hunter House Publishers	246	Scarecrow Press	372
Imperial International	250	Scholastic Professional Books	376
Incentive Publications	252	School Specialty Children's	
Innovative Kids	253	Publishing	377
International Reading		School Zone Publishing	511
Association	254	Scott Foresman	512
InterVarsity Press	476	Silver Dolphin Books	514
January Productions	477	Small Horizons	516
JIST Publishing	257	Smith and Kraus	385
Kaeden Books	261	Southern Early Childhood	
Key Curriculum Press	263	Association (SECA)	517
Kodiak Media Group	479	The Speech Bin, Inc.	389
Leadership Publishers Inc.	480	Story Time Stories That Rhyme	518
Learning Horizons	267	Sunburst Technology	519
Learning Resources	268	Sword of the Lord	398
Libraries Unlimited	273	Teacher Created Materials	400
Linnet Books	275	Teachers & Writers	
Linworth Publishing	276	Collaborative	520
The Love and Logic Press	483	Teaching & Learning Company	401
Marsh Media	486	Charles C. Thomas, Publisher	405
Master Books	288	Thompson Educational	
Modern Publishing	488	Publishing	406
Morgan Reynolds Publishing	300	Toy Box Productions	411
Mountain Meadow Press	489	Upstart Books	415
National Assn. for the Educ.		URJ Press	416
of Young People	302	Visual Education Corporation	526
National Council of Teachers		J. Weston Walch, Publisher	418
of English	303	Warner Press	420

559

Weigl Educational Publishers Limited	424
Williamson Publishing	429
Woodbine House	432
Wordware Publishing	528
The Wright Group/McGraw-Hill	435
Zephyr Press	437

Fairy Tales

Baker's Plays	100
Beyond Words Publishing	108
Blue Sky Press	112
Books of Wonder	452
Camex Books	454
Charlesbridge	130
Children's eLibrary	135
Creative Editions	460
Creative With Words Publications	157
Dover Publications	177
Henry Holt Books for Young Readers	241
Innovative Kids	253
Key Porter Books	264
Llewellyn Publications	281
The Lutterworth Press	484
Mage Publishers	485
Modern Publishing	488
North-South Books	493
Orchard Books	322
Pipers' Ash Ltd.	342
Playhouse Publishing	500
Raven Tree Press	356
Rising Moon	362
Seedling Publications	379
Stiles-Bishop Productions Inc.	518

Fantasy

Accord Publishing	82
Action Publishing	84
Aquila Communications Ltd.	443
Atheneum Books for Young Readers	94
A/V Concepts Corporation	96
Bloomsbury Children's Books	111
Books of Wonder	452
Chaosium	455
Children's eLibrary	135
Contemporary Drama Service	147
Creative Paperbacks	461
Creative Teaching Press, Inc.	156

Cricket Books	158
DAW Books	167
Denlinger's Publishers	169
Domhan Books	464
Dover Publications	177
Farrar, Straus & Giroux	196
Floris Books	199
Formac Publishing Company Ltd.	202
Frances Foster Books	204
Laura Geringer Books	210
Gibbs Smith, Publisher	211
Greene Bark Press	217
Harcourt Children's Books	228
Holiday House	240
I B Publications Pty Ltd	475
Llewellyn Publications	281
LTDBooks	283
Margaret K. McElderry Books	291
Milkweed Editions	295
Mirrorstone Books	487
Moody Publishers	298
Moose Enterprise	299
Pioneer Drama Service	341
Random House Children's Books	506
Random House Children's Publishing	506
Raven Tree Press	356
Red Deer Press	359
Riverfront Books	509
Saint Mary's Press	370
Scholastic Inc./Trade Paperback Division	374
Scholastic Press	375
Scorpius Digital Publishing	378
Smooch	386
Storytellers Ink Publishing Co.	397
Tor Books	410
Whitecap Books Ltd.	425
Wizards of the Coast	431
XC Publishing	436

Folklore/Folktales

Harry N. Abrams Books for Young Readers	80
Advocacy Press	441
Baker's Plays	100
Blue Marlin Publications	451
Blue Sky Press	112
Books of Wonder	452
Camex Books	454
Clarion Books	144

Contemporary Drama Service	147	Didax	172
Creative Editions	460	Eakin Press	181
Creative Teaching Press, Inc.	156	ESP Publishers, Inc.	466
Creative With Words Publications	157	Hendrick-Long Publishing Company	237
Jonathan David Publishers	166	Innovative Kids	253
Denlinger's Publishers	169	Kingfisher	478
Dover Publications	177	Learning Resources	268
Eldridge Publishing	188	Miles Kelly Publishing	486
Fulcrum Publishing	209	National Geographic Books for Children	490
Laura Geringer Books	210	National Geographic Society	304
Gibbs Smith, Publisher	211	Nimbus Publishing	315
Graphic Arts Center Publishing Co.	216	PowerKids Press	349
Harbour Publishing	226	Running Press Kids	368
Henry Holt Books for Young Readers	241	Teacher Created Materials	400
Innovative Kids	253	World Book	434
Kar-Ben Publishing	262		
Key Porter Books	264	**Gifted Education**	
Margaret K. McElderry Books	291	Avocus Publishing	445
Meriwether Publishing Ltd.	293	Continental Press	457
Naturegraph Publishers	305	Corwin Press	150
Nightwood Editions	314	Creative Learning Press	155
North-South Books	493	Dandy Lion Publications	163
The Overmountain Press	324	Free Spirit Publishing	206
Richard C. Owen Publishers	325	Gifted Education Press	212
Pineapple Press	340	Heinemann	236
Pioneer Drama Service	341	Leadership Publishers Inc.	480
Pipers' Ash Ltd.	342	Libraries Unlimited	273
Playhouse Publishing	500	National Council of Teachers of English	303
Polar Bear & Company	346	NL Associates	316
Raven Tree Press	356	Phoenix Learning Resources	337
Rayve Productions Inc.	357	Teacher Created Materials	400
Redbird Press	507	Teaching & Learning Company	401
Renaissance House	360	Charles C. Thomas, Publisher	405
Rising Moon	362	Zephyr Press	437
Salina Bookshelf	509		
Scorpius Digital Publishing	378	**Health/Fitness**	
Shen's Books	514	Bick Publishing House	450
Smith and Kraus	385	Branden Books	117
Storytellers Ink Publishing Co.	397	The Bureau for At-Risk Youth	121
Turtle Books	522	Capstone Press	125
		Chelsea House Publishers	132
Geography		Corwin Press	150
Abdo Publishing Company	440	Creative Bound	153
Capstone Press	125	Crossquarter Publishing Group	462
Children's Press	136	ESP Publishers, Inc.	466
The Creative Company	154	Frederick Fell Publishers	197
Creative Learning Press	155	Greenwood Publishing Group	219
Creative Paperbacks	461	Harvard Common Press	473

561

Health Press	235	Creative Paperbacks	461
Hunter House Publishers	246	Cricket Books	158
InQ Publishing Co.	476	Crossway Books	160
New Harbinger Publications	308	May Davenport, Publishers	165
New Leaf Press	310	Denlinger's Publishers	169
Newmarket Press	311	Discovery Enterprises	173
New World Library	313	Ebooksonthe.net	182
Perigee Books	334	Exclamation! Publishers	468
Pitspopany Press	343	Focus on the Family Book Development	200
Pleasant Company Publications	345	Frances Foster Books	204
Prometheus Books	350	Front Street Books	208
The Rosen Publishing Group	367	Graphia	215
Sunburst Technology	519	Graphic Arts Center Publishing Co.	216
TEACH Services, Inc.	402	Gulliver Books	222
Charles C. Thomas, Publisher	405	Hachai Publishing	223
Turtle Press	523	Harbour Publishing	226
Twenty-First Century Books	523	Harcourt Children's Books	228
UXL	417	Holiday House	240
		Journey Forth	258
High-Interest/ Low-Vocabulary		Jump at the Sun	478
Abdo Publishing Company	440	Lee & Low Books	269
A/V Concepts Corporation	96	LTDBooks	283
A & C Black Publishers	110	Maval Publishing	289
Enslow Publishers, Inc.	190	Margaret K. McElderry Books	291
Hampton-Brown Books	224	Milkweed Editions	295
January Productions	477	Moody Publishers	298
Richard C. Owen Publishers	325	Moose Enterprise	299
Perfection Learning Corporation	333	The New England Press	307
The Rosen Publishing Group	367	Nimbus Publishing	315
The Wright Group/McGraw-Hill	435	Orca Book Publishers	321
		Orchard Books	322
Historical Fiction		Pacific Educational Press	326
Aladdin Paperbacks	85	Peartree	497
Ambassador-Emerald International	90	Pelican Publishing Company	331
Atheneum Books for Young Readers	94	Perfection Learning Corporation	333
		Philomel Books	336
Avocet Press	444	Pineapple Press	340
Barron's Educational Series	447	Pleasant Company Publications	345
Beach Holme Publishing	102	Publish America	351
Bethany House	107	Puffin Books	352
Blue Marlin Publications	451	Raincoast Books	504
Blue Sky Press	112	Rayve Productions Inc.	357
Branden Books	117	Riverfront Books	509
Breakwater Books	118	Ronsdale Press	365
Calkins Creek Books	453	Saint Mary's Press	370
Carolrhoda Books	126	Scholastic Press	375
Cavendish Children's Books	129	Shen's Books	514
Clear Light Publishers	145	Silver Moon Press	380
Coteau Books	151	Starscape Books	393

Tanglewood Press, LLC	399	Houghton Mifflin Children's	
Touchwood Editions	521	Books	244
Toy Box Productions	411	Kaeden Books	261
Turtle Books	522	Wendy Lamb Books	479
URJ Press	416	Lerner Publishing Group	271
Watson-Guptill	422	Linnet Books	275
White Mane Publishing		Lucent Books	285
Company	426	Mage Publishers	485
Albert Whitman & Company	427	Miles Kelly Publishing	486
		Moose Enterprise	299
History (NF)		Morgan Reynolds Publishing	300
Absey and Company	81	Mott Media	301
Advocacy Press	441	National Geographic Books for	
Avisson Press	98	Children	490
Ballyhoo Books, Inc.	446	National Geographic Society	304
Behrman House	104	Natural Heritage Books	491
Benchmark Books	105	The New England Press	307
Calkins Creek Books	453	New Leaf Press	310
Capstone Press	125	Nimbus Publishing	315
Charlesbridge	130	North Country Books	317
Chelsea House Publishers	132	Novalis	319
Creative Education	461	The Oliver Press	320
Creative Learning Press	155	OnStage Publishing	493
Creative Paperbacks	461	Pacific View Press	494
Creative Teaching Press, Inc.	156	Parkway Publishers	495
Crown Books for Young Readers	161	Paws IV Books	496
Darby Creek Publishing	164	Pembroke Publishers	332
Jonathan David Publishers	166	Penguin Books Canada Limited	498
Discovery Enterprises	173	Pipers' Ash Ltd.	342
Displays for Schools	463	Pitspopany Press	343
Dover Publications	177	Pruett Publishing Company	502
Eakin Press	181	Raincoast Books	504
Encounter Books	466	Random House Children's	
Enslow Publishers, Inc.	190	Publishing	506
ESP Publishers, Inc.	466	Rayve Productions Inc.	357
ETC Publications	467	Riverfront Books	509
Facts On File	192	The Rosen Publishing Group	367
Falcon Publishing	194	Sandlapper Publishing	510
Forest House Publishing		Silver Moon Press	380
Company	201	Sourcebooks	388
Fulcrum Publishing	209	Texas Tech University Press	403
Graphia	215	Tilbury House Publishers	407
Greenhaven Press	218	Touchwood Editions	521
Greenwood Publishing Group	219	Twenty-First Century Books	523
Gulliver Books	222	UXL	417
Hendrick-Long Publishing		Viking Children's Books	525
Company	237	Weigl Educational Publishers	
Henry Holt Books for Young		Limited	424
Readers	241	White Mane Publishing	
Heritage House	238	Company	426
Holiday House	240	Wiley Children's Books	428

Williamson Publishing	429	Buster Books	122
Windswept House Publishers	527	Cavendish Children's Books	129
Windward Publishing	430	Covenant Communications	152
World Book	434	Creative With Words	
Zephyr Press	437	Publications	157
		May Davenport, Publishers	165

Horror

		Eldridge Publishing	188
A/V Concepts Corporation	96	Encore Performance Publishing	189
Chaosium	455	Excelsior Cee Publishing	467
HarperCollins Children's		Formac Publishing Company Ltd.	202
Fiction	232	Front Street Books	208
LTDBooks	283	Gibbs Smith, Publisher	211
Moose Enterprise	299	HarperCollins Children's Fiction	232
Parachute Press	495	Innovative Kids	253
Smooch	386	LangMarc Publishing	480
XC Publishing	436	Little, Brown and Company	278
		The Lutterworth Press	484

How-to

		Maval Publishing	289
Ballyhoo Books, Inc.	446	Mayhaven Publishing	290
Charles River Media	131	Moose Enterprise	299
Chicago Review Press	133	Mott Media	301
Creative Learning Press	155	Nimbus Publishing	315
Dramatic Publishing	179	Nomad Press	492
Excelsior Cee Publishing	467	Parachute Press	495
Frederick Fell Publishers	197	Pippin Press	499
Fiesta City Publishers	469	Quixote Press	503
Goodheart-Willcox	214	Random House Children's	
Group Publishing	220	Publishing	506
InQ Publishing Co.	476	River City Publishing	508
InterVarsity Press	476	Riverfront Books	509
Legacy Press	270	Scholastic Canada Ltd.	373
Meriwether Publishing Ltd.	293	Smallfellow Press	515
Peel Productions	497	Tanglewood Press, LLC	399
Perigee Books	334	Albert Whitman & Company	427
Players Press	344	Workman Publishing Company	433
Running Press Kids	368		
Smith and Kraus Books for Kids	516	**Inspirational Fiction**	
Starscape Books	393	Alpha Publishing	442
Sterling Publishing Company	396	Bay Light Publishing	448
Success Publications	519	Bethany House	107
Tor Books	410	Beyond Words Publishing	108
Winslow Publishing	527	BOW Books	452
World Book	434	Denlinger's Publishers	169
		Ebooksonthe.net	182

Humor

		Eerdmans Books for Young	
Accord Publishing	82	Readers	186
Annick Press	92	Faith Kidz	193
Aquila Communications Ltd.	443	Frederick Fell Publishers	197
Bancroft Press	446	Focus on the Family Book	
Blue Marlin Publications	451	Development	200
Breakwater Books	118	Hampton Roads Publishing	225

Illumination Arts	248	Teacher Created Materials	400
The Judaica Press	259	J. Weston Walch, Publisher	418
LangMarc Publishing	480	The Wright Group/McGraw-Hill	435
National Resource Center for Youth Services	491		

Mathematics

Pacific Press Publishing Association	327	Activity Resources Company	441
Rainbow Publishers	355	Benchmark Books	105
Rising Moon	362	Carson-Dellosa Publishing Company	127
Seaburn Publishing	512	Cartwheel Books	128
Starseed Press	394	Christopher-Gordon Publishers	142
Torah Aura Productions	409	Creative Learning Press	155
WaterBrook Press	421	Creative Teaching Press, Inc.	156
		Critical Thinking Company	159

Language Arts

		Dandy Lion Publications	163
Boynton/Cook Publishers	116	Didax	172
Butte Publications	123	Edupress	185
Carson-Dellosa Publishing Company	127	Evan-Moor Educational Publishers	191
Christopher-Gordon Publishers	142	Greenwood Publishing Group	219
Cottonwood Press	458	Gryphon House	221
Creative Learning Press	155	Harcourt Canada Ltd.	473
Critical Thinking Company	159	Hayes School Publishing Company	233
Edupress	185	Heinemann	236
Evan-Moor Educational Publishers	191	Imperial International	250
Gryphon House	221	Kaeden Books	261
Hampton-Brown Books	224	Key Curriculum Press	263
Harcourt Canada Ltd.	473	Learning Horizons	267
Hayes School Publishing Company	233	Learning Resources	268
Imperial International	250	Libraries Unlimited	273
Incentive Publications	252	Miles Kelly Publishing	486
International Reading Association	254	The Millbrook Press	487
January Productions	477	Modern Publishing	488
Learning Links Inc.	481	Mount Olive College Press	489
Learning Resources	268	Pacific Educational Press	326
Linworth Publishing	276	Phoenix Learning Resources	337
Modern Publishing	488	Scholastic Professional Books	376
National Council of Teachers of English	303	Scott Foresman	512
Pacific Educational Press	326	Simon & Schuster Books for Young Readers	382
Pembroke Publishers	332	Sterling Publishing Company	396
Phoenix Learning Resources	337	Sunburst Technology	519
Portage & Main Press	348	Teacher Created Materials	400
Scholastic Professional Books	376	Teaching & Learning Company	401
Scott Foresman	512	Twenty-First Century Books	523
Silver Moon Press	380	J. Weston Walch, Publisher	418
Southern Early Childhood Association (SECA)	517	Wiley Children's Books	428
		Williamson Publishing	429
		The Wright Group/McGraw-Hill	435
		Zephyr Press	437

565

Middle-Grade (F)

Publisher	Page
Abbeville Kids	439
Harry N. Abrams Books for Young Readers	80
Action Publishing	84
Aladdin Paperbacks	85
Ambassador-Emerald International	90
Amulet Books	91
Annick Press	92
Atheneum Books for Young Readers	94
Augsburg Books	95
Avocus Publishing	445
Azro Press	445
Baker Book House Company	99
Bantam Books for Young Readers	101
Barefoot Books Ltd.	447
Bay Light Publishing	448
Beach Holme Publishing	102
Bethany House	107
Bloomsbury Children's Books	111
Blue Sky Press	112
Bollix Books	451
Boyds Mills Press	115
Branden Books	117
Calkins Creek Books	453
Candlewick Press	124
Carolrhoda Books	126
Cavendish Children's Books	129
Child Welfare League of America	139
Christian Focus Publications	141
Clarion Books	144
Contemporary Drama Service	147
Cook Communications Ministries	148
Coteau Books	151
Cricket Books	158
Crossway Books	160
Darby Creek Publishing	164
Denlinger's Publishers	169
Different Books	463
Discovery Enterprises	173
Domhan Books	464
Dorling Kindersley	176
Down East Books	178
Dutton Children's Books	180
Eakin Press	181
Eastgate Systems	465
Educators Publishing Service	184
Eerdmans Books for Young Readers	186
Egmont Children's Books	187
Faith Kidz	193
Farrar, Straus & Giroux	196
The Feminist Press	468
Floris Books	199
Fondo de Cultura Economica USA	470
Formac Publishing Company Ltd.	202
Forward Movement Publications	203
Frances Foster Books	204
Front Street Books	208
Laura Geringer Books	210
David R. Godine, Publisher	471
Greenwillow Books	472
Groundwood Books	472
Gulliver Books	222
Hampton-Brown Books	224
Hampton Roads Publishing	225
Harcourt Children's Books	228
HarperCollins Children's Books	231
HarperCollins Children's Fiction	232
Hyperion Books for Children	475
Imperial International	250
Just Us Books	260
Key Porter Books	264
Alfred A. Knopf Books for Young Readers	265
Arthur A. Levine Books	272
Lion Publishing	277
Living the Good News	482
Llewellyn Publications	281
Lobster Press	483
The Lutterworth Press	484
Magination Press	286
Maple Tree Press Inc.	287
Mayhaven Publishing	290
Margaret K. McElderry Books	291
Meadowbrook Press	292
Meriwether Publishing Ltd.	293
Milet Publishing	294
Milkweed Editions	295
Mirrorstone Books	487
Moody Publishers	298
National Geographic Society	304
Natural Heritage Books	491
Naturegraph Publishers	305

New Canaan Publishing Company	492	Viking Children's Books	525
The New England Press	307	Walker and Company	419
Newmarket Press	311	White Mane Publishing Company	426
Nimbus Publishing	315	Albert Whitman & Company	427
OnStage Publishing	493	Woodbine House	432
Orca Book Publishers	321	The Wright Group/McGraw-Hill	435
Orchard Books	322		
The Overmountain Press	324	**Middle-Grade (NF)**	
Richard C. Owen Publishers	325	Abbeville Kids	439
Pacific Educational Press	326	Abdo Publishing Company	440
Pacific Press Publishing Association	327	Harry N. Abrams Books for Young Readers	80
Pacific View Press	494	Action Publishing	84
Parachute Press	495	Advocacy Press	441
Peachtree Publishers	330	Alef Design Group	87
Pelican Publishing Company	331	Ambassador-Emerald International	90
Penguin Books Canada Limited	498	Amulet Books	91
Perfection Learning Corporation	333	A/V Concepts Corporation	96
Philomel Books	336	Ave Maria Press	97
Piñata Books	339	Avocus Publishing	445
Pippin Press	499	Baker Book House Company	99
Pleasant Company Publications	345	Ballyhoo Books, Inc.	446
Polar Bear & Company	346	Behrman House	104
Publish America	351	Benchmark Books	105
Puffin Books	352	Bess Press	106
G. P. Putnam's Sons	353	Beyond Words Publishing	108
Rainbow Publishers	355	Blackbirch Press	109
Random House Children's Books	506	Blue Marlin Publications	451
Razorbill	358	Blue Sky Press	112
Renaissance House	360	Boyds Mills Press	115
Ronsdale Press	365	Breakwater Books	118
Saint Mary's Press	370	Buster Books	122
Sandpiper Paperbacks	510	Calkins Creek Books	453
Scholastic Canada Ltd.	373	Candlewick Press	124
Scholastic Inc./Trade Paperback Division	374	Capstone Press	125
Scorpius Digital Publishing	378	Cavendish Children's Books	129
Second Story Press	513	Chelsea House Publishers	132
Silver Moon Press	380	Chicago Review Press	133
Silver Whistle	381	Children's Press	136
Sports Publishing Inc.	390	Chrysalis Children's Books	143
Star Bright Books	392	Clear Light Publishers	145
Starscape Books	393	Creative Education	461
Sword of the Lord	398	Critical Thinking Company	159
Tanglewood Press, LLC	399	Crown Books for Young Readers	161
Texas Tech University Press	403	Darby Creek Publishing	164
Torah Aura Productions	409	May Davenport, Publishers	165
Tor Books	410	Jonathan David Publishers	166
Toy Box Productions	411	Didax	172
Unity House	525	Different Books	463

Discovery Enterprises		Llewellyn Publications	281
Dog-Eared Publications	173	Lobster Press	483
Dorling Kindersley	464	Lucent Books	285
Dutton Children's Books	176	Magination Press	286
Eastgate Systems	180	Maple Tree Press Inc.	287
Ebooksonthe.net	465	Meadowbrook Press	292
Eerdmans Books for Young	182	Mitchell Lane Publishers	296
Readers		Mott Media	301
Enslow Publishers, Inc.	186	National Geographic Books for	
ETC Publications	190	Children	490
Facts On File	467	National Geographic Society	304
Faith Kidz	192	Natural Heritage Books	491
Falcon Publishing	193	Naturegraph Publishers	305
Family Learning Assn./ERIC/	194	New Canaan Publishing	
REC Press		Company	492
Farrar, Straus & Giroux	195	The New England Press	307
The Feminist Press	196	New Leaf Press	310
Ferguson Publishing	468	North Country Books	317
Fiesta City Publishers	198	NorthWord Books for Young	
Fondo de Cultura	469	Readers	318
Economica USA		The Oliver Press	320
Forward Movement	470	Our Sunday Visitor	323
Publications		Pacific Educational Press	326
Franklin Watts	203	Pacific Press Publishing	
Free Spirit Publishing	470	Association	327
Front Street Books	206	Pacific View Press	494
Fulcrum Publishing	208	Parkway Publishers	495
Hampton Roads Publishing	209	Peartree	497
Harcourt Religion Publishers	225	Pelican Publishing Company	331
Hazelden Foundation	229	Pembroke Publishers	332
Hendrick-Long Publishing	234	Perigee Books	334
Company		Pineapple Press	340
Heritage House	237	Pippin Press	499
Honor Books	238	Pitspopany Press	343
Houghton Mifflin Children's	242	Players Press	344
Books		Pleasant Company Publications	345
Hunter House Publishers	244	Polar Bear & Company	346
John Hunt Publishing	246	Pruett Publishing Company	502
Hyperion Books for Children	247	Rainbow Books	503
Impact Publishers	475	Rainbow Publishers	355
Incentive Publications	249	Razorbill	358
Journey Forth	252	Renaissance House	360
Just Us Books	258	The Rosen Publishing Group	367
Key Curriculum Press	260	St. Anthony Messenger Press	369
Key Porter Books	263	Saint Mary's Press	370
Lark Books	264	Sandpiper Paperbacks	510
Legacy Press	266	School Specialty Children's	
Lerner Publishing Group	270	Publishing	377
Arthur A. Levine Books	271	Second Story Press	513
Little, Brown and Company	272	Silver Dolphin Books	514
Living the Good News	278	Silver Moon Press	380
	482		

568

Simon & Schuster Books for Young Readers	382	Frances Foster Books	204
		Gefen Publishing House	471
The Speech Bin, Inc.	389	Laura Geringer Books	210
Sports Publishing Inc.	390	Groundwood Books	472
Starscape Books	393	Hachai Publishing	223
Stemmer House Publishers	395	Harbour Publishing	226
Success Publications	519	HarperCollins Children's Fiction	232
TEACH Services, Inc.	402		
Texas Tech University Press	403	Imperial International	250
Third World Press	404	Jump at the Sun	478
Megan Tingley Books	408	Just Us Books	260
Torah Aura Productions	409	Alfred A. Knopf Books for Young Readers	265
Tyndale House Publishers	413		
Upstart Books	415	Wendy Lamb Books	479
UXL	417	Lee & Low Books	269
Walker and Company	419	James Lorimer & Company	282
Watson-Guptill	422	Maval Publishing	289
Weigl Educational Publishers Limited	424	Milet Publishing	294
		Milkweed Editions	295
White Mane Publishing Company	426	Nimbus Publishing	315
		Orchard Books	322
Wiley Children's Books	428	Richard C. Owen Publishers	325
Williamson Publishing	429	Pacific Educational Press	326
Windward Publishing	430	Peartree	497
World Book	434	Perfection Learning Corporation	333
Zephyr Press	437		
		Philomel Books	336
Multicultural/Ethnic (F)		Piñata Books	339
A&B Publishers Group	439	The Place in the Woods	500
Abingdon Press	440	Polar Bear & Company	346
Amirah Publishing	443	Polychrome Publishing Corporation	347
Beach Holme Publishing	102		
Bebop Books	103	G. P. Putnam's Sons	353
Beyond Words Publishing	108	Rayve Productions Inc.	357
Bloomsbury Children's Books	111	Renaissance House	360
Bollix Books	451	Rising Moon	362
Borealis Press Limited	114	River City Publishing	508
Brown Barn Books	120	Salina Bookshelf	509
Carolrhoda Books	126	Scholastic Press	375
Children's Book Press	134	Shen's Books	514
Children's eLibrary	135	Silver Moon Press	380
Clear Light Publishers	145	Soundprints/Studio Mouse	387
Cricket Books	158	Star Bright Books	392
Jonathan David Publishers	166	Storytellers Ink Publishing Co.	397
Domhan Books	464	Third World Press	404
Educators Publishing Service	184	Tilbury House Publishers	407
Encore Performance Publishing	189	Megan Tingley Books	408
The Feminist Press	468	Turtle Books	522
Floris Books	199	Two Lives Publishing	524
Fondo de Cultura Economica USA	470		

Multicultural/Ethnic (NF)

A&B Publishers Group	439
Advocacy Press	441
Amirah Publishing	443
Amulet Books	91
Avisson Press	98
Bebop Books	103
Benchmark Books	105
Borealis Press Limited	114
Branden Books	117
The Bureau for At-Risk Youth	121
Caddo Gap Press	453
Carson-Dellosa Publishing Company	127
Chelsea House Publishers	132
Children's Book Press	134
Children's eLibrary	135
Clear Light Publishers	145
Jonathan David Publishers	166
Dawn Publications	168
Domhan Books	464
Eakin Press	181
Enslow Publishers, Inc.	190
Facts On File	192
The Feminist Press	468
Forest House Publishing Company	201
Gefen Publishing House	471
Graphia	215
Greenwood Publishing Group	219
Holloway House Publishing Group	474
Wendy Lamb Books	479
Lee & Low Books	269
Arthur A. Levine Books	272
Linnet Books	275
James Lorimer & Company	282
Lucent Books	285
National Geographic Books for Children	490
Natural Heritage Books	491
Newmarket Press	311
The Oliver Press	320
The Pilgrim Press	338
Pitspopany Press	343
The Place in the Woods	500
Polychrome Publishing Corporation	347
PowerKids Press	349
Redbird Press	507
Renaissance House	360
Seedling Publications	379
Small Horizons	516
Sourcebooks	388
Storytellers Ink Publishing Co.	397
Tilbury House Publishers	407
Turtle Press	523
Twenty-First Century Books	523
Weigl Educational Publishers Limited	424
Albert Whitman & Company	427
Wiley Children's Books	428
Williamson Publishing	429
Windswept House Publishers	527

Mystery/Suspense

Aladdin Paperbacks	85
Amulet Books	91
Aquila Communications Ltd.	443
Atheneum Books for Young Readers	94
Avocet Press	444
Baker's Plays	100
Bancroft Press	446
Beach Holme Publishing	102
BePuzzled	450
Bloomsbury Children's Books	111
Boardwalk Books	113
Branden Books	117
Brown Barn Books	120
Camex Books	454
Carolrhoda Books	126
Cavendish Children's Books	129
Coteau Books	151
Covenant Communications	152
May Davenport, Publishers	165
Domhan Books	464
Down East Books	178
Formac Publishing Company Ltd.	202
Laura Geringer Books	210
Graphia	215
Greene Bark Press	217
Groundwood Books	472
Harcourt Children's Books	228
Heuer Publishing Company	239
Holiday House	240
The Judaica Press	259
Just Us Books	260
Wendy Lamb Books	479
Llewellyn Publications	281
LTDBooks	283
The Lutterworth Press	484

Maval Publishing	289	The Globe Pequot Press	213
Mirrorstone Books	487	Graphic Arts Center	
Moody Publishers	298	Publishing Co.	216
Moose Enterprise	299	Greenwillow Books	472
The Overmountain Press	324	Greenwood Publishing Group	219
Richard C. Owen Publishers	325	Gulliver Books	222
Parachute Press	495	Hendrick-Long Publishing	
Perfection Learning		Company	237
Corporation	333	Henry Holt Books for Young	
Pineapple Press	340	Readers	241
Pioneer Drama Service	341	Heritage House	238
Pleasant Company Publications	345	Kingfisher	478
Puffin Books	352	Learning Horizons	267
Random House Children's		Lerner Publishing Group	271
Books	506	Arthur A. Levine Books	272
Random House Children's		Little Tiger Press	280
Publishing	506	The Lutterworth Press	484
Razorbill	358	Maple Tree Press Inc.	287
Sandlapper Publishing	510	Maval Publishing	289
Scholastic Canada Ltd.	373	Miles Kelly Publishing	486
Scholastic Inc./Trade Paperback		Milkweed Editions	295
Division	374	Naturegraph Publishers	305
Starscape Books	393	The New England Press	307
Tanglewood Press, LLC	399	New Leaf Press	310
Texas Tech University Press	403	North Country Books	317
Two Lives Publishing	524	NorthWord Books for Young	
Albert Whitman & Company	427	Readers	318
XC Publishing	436	Peartree	497
		Polar Bear & Company	346
Nature/Environment		Raincoast Books	504
Aladdin Paperbacks	85	Sandlapper Publishing	510
Amulet Books	91	Sasquatch Books	511
Ballyhoo Books, Inc.	446	Scholastic Inc./Trade Paperback	
The Benefactory	449	Division	374
Bick Publishing House	450	Seedling Publications	379
Blackbirch Press	109	Soundprints/Studio Mouse	387
Boyds Mills Press	115	Starseed Press	394
Children's eLibrary	135	Stemmer House Publishers	395
Clark City Press	456	TEACH Services, Inc.	402
Creative Editions	460	Texas Tech University Press	403
Creative Education	461	Tilbury House Publishers	407
Creative With Words		Tradewind Books Ltd.	522
Publications	157	Weigl Educational Publishers	
Crossquarter Publishing Group	462	Limited	424
Dawn Publications	168	Whitecap Books Ltd.	425
Dog-Eared Publications	464	Wiley Children's Books	428
ESP Publishers, Inc.	466	Windswept House Publishers	527
Falcon Publishing	194	Windward Publishing	430
Forest House Publishing		Workman Publishing Company	433
Company	201		
Gibbs Smith, Publisher	211		

Parenting

Advocacy Press	441
Alef Design Group	87
Alpha Publishing	442
Alyson Publications	88
AMG Publishers	442
Association for Childhood Education Int'l	444
Ave Maria Press	97
Avocus Publishing	445
Behrman House	104
Butte Publications	123
Caddo Gap Press	453
Capstone Press	125
Carousel Press	454
Chicago Review Press	133
Childswork/Childsplay	137
Creative Bound	153
Crossway Books	160
Dawn Publications	168
Excelsior Cee Publishing	467
Frederick Fell Publishers	197
Free Spirit Publishing	206
Gifted Education Press	212
Goodheart-Willcox	214
Gryphon House	221
Harvard Common Press	473
Hazelden Foundation	234
Horizon Publishers	243
Humanics	245
John Hunt Publishing	247
InQ Publishing Co.	476
InterVarsity Press	476
LifeSong Publishers	481
Living the Good News	482
The Love and Logic Press	483
Magination Press	286
Meadowbrook Press	292
Morning Glory Press	488
New Hope Publishers	309
Newmarket Press	311
New Society Publishers	312
New World Library	313
Nomad Press	492
Our Child Press	494
Parenting Press, Inc.	328
Peachtree Publishers	330
Perigee Books	334
Perspectives Press, Inc.	498
Redwheel/Weiser/Conari Press	508
Resource Publications, Inc.	361
Robins Lane Press	363
Sasquatch Books	511
School Zone Publishing	511
Seal Press	513
Small Horizons	516
Soho Press	517
Sourcebooks	388
The Speech Bin, Inc.	389
Success Publications	519
Sword of the Lord	398
Teaching & Learning Company	401
Charles C. Thomas, Publisher	405
WaterBrook Press	421
Woodbine House	432

Photo Essays

Jump at the Sun	478
Running Press Kids	368
Scholastic Inc./Trade Paperback Division	374

Picture Books (F)

Abbeville Kids	439
Absey and Company	81
Azro Press	445
Baker Book House Company	99
Barefoot Books Ltd.	447
Beyond Words Publishing	108
Calkins Creek Books	453
Camex Books	454
Candlewick Press	124
Cavendish Children's Books	129
Children's eLibrary	135
Clarion Books	144
Clear Light Publishers	145
Creative Editions	460
Cricket Books	158
Dutton Children's Books	180
Fondo de Cultura Economica USA	470
Front Street Books	208
David R. Godine, Publisher	471
Greenwillow Books	472
Hodder Children's Books	474
Hyperion Books for Children	475
Illumination Arts	248
Jump at the Sun	478
Alfred A. Knopf Books for Young Readers	265
Little Blue Works	482
Mondo Publishing	297

Munchweiler Press	490	Quartz Editions	502
NorthWord Books for Young Readers	318	Salina Bookshelf	509
		Smith and Kraus Books for Kids	516
Paulist Press	329	Standard Publishing	391
Peachtree Publishers	330	Tricycle Press	412
Pippin Press	499	Viking Children's Books	525
Puffin Books	352		
Quartz Editions	502	**Plays**	
River City Publishing	508	Baker's Plays	100
Riverfront Books	509	Children's Story Scripts	455
Salina Bookshelf	509	Discovery Enterprises	173
Scholastic Inc./Trade Paperback Division	374	Dramatic Publishing	179
		Eldridge Publishing	188
Shen's Books	514	Encore Performance Publishing	189
Siphano Picture Books	515	Fiesta City Publishers	469
Smith and Kraus Books for Kids	516	Samuel French, Inc.	207
The Speech Bin, Inc.	389	Heuer Publishing Company	239
Standard Publishing	391	Lillenas Publishing Company	274
Tricycle Press	412	Meriwether Publishing Ltd.	293
Albert Whitman & Company	427	Pioneer Drama Service	341
Windswept House Publishers	527	Players Press	344
		Playwrights Canada Press	501
Picture Books (NF)		Smith and Kraus	385
Abbeville Kids	439	Smith and Kraus Books for Kids	516
Azro Press	445		
Baker Book House Company	99	**Reference Books**	
Barefoot Books Ltd.	447	ALA Editions	86
Beyond Words Publishing	108	Association for Childhood Education Int'l	444
Calkins Creek Books	453		
Candlewick Press	124	Barron's Educational Series	447
The Creative Company	154	Borealis Press Limited	114
Dawn Publications	168	The Bureau for At-Risk Youth	121
Dutton Children's Books	180	Displays for Schools	463
Fondo de Cultura Economica USA	470	Dramatic Publishing	179
		Family Learning Assn./ERIC/ REC Press	195
Greenwillow Books	472		
Hampton Roads Publishing	225	Ferguson Publishing	198
Henry Holt Books for Young Readers	241	Greenhaven Press	218
		Greenwood Publishing Group	219
Houghton Mifflin Children's Books	244	International Reading Association	254
Illumination Arts	248	InterVarsity Press	476
Jump at the Sun	478	JIST Publishing	257
Kingfisher	478	Leadership Publishers Inc.	480
Little Blue Works	482	Libraries Unlimited	273
The Lutterworth Press	484	Lillenas Publishing Company	274
Modern Publishing	488	Linnet Books	275
Mondo Publishing	297	Meriwether Publishing Ltd.	293
New Leaf Press	310	Miles Kelly Publishing	486
Peachtree Publishers	330	Mountain Meadow Press	489
Pembroke Publishers	332	National Geographic Society	304

Neal-Schuman Publishers	306	Libraries Unlimited	273
New Society Publishers	312	James Lorimer & Company	282
Novalis	319	Mountain Meadow Press	489
Our Sunday Visitor	323	Mount Olive College Press	489
Perigee Books	334	Natural Heritage Books	491
School Specialty Children's Publishing	377	The New England Press	307
		The Overmountain Press	324
Sterling Publishing Company	396	Pacific View Press	494
UXL	417	Parkway Publishers	495
Visual Education Corporation	526	Paws IV Books	496
Workman Publishing Company	433	Pelican Publishing Company	331
		Pineapple Press	340

Regional (F)

		Pruett Publishing Company	502
Ambassador-Emerald International	90	Redbird Press	507
		Red Deer Press	359
Bess Press	106	Sandlapper Publishing	510
Chicago Review Press	133	Sasquatch Books	511
Cornell Maritime Press	149	Scholastic Canada Ltd.	373
Coteau Books	151	Texas Tech University Press	403
Down East Books	178	Tilbury House Publishers	407
Floris Books	199	Wayne State University Press	423
Graphic Arts Center Publishing Co.	216	Windswept House Publishers	527

Religious (F)

Harbour Publishing	226	Alef Design Group	87
James Lorimer & Company	282	Amirah Publishing	443
The New England Press	307	Augsburg Books	95
Nightwood Editions	314	Baker Book House Company	99
Nimbus Publishing	315	Bay Light Publishing	448
Orca Book Publishers	321	Broadman & Holman Publishers	119
The Overmountain Press	324		
Paws IV Books	496	Christian Ed. Publishers	140
Peachtree Publishers	330	Christian Focus Publications	141
Pelican Publishing Company	331	Cook Communications Ministries	148
Pineapple Press	340		
Red Deer Press	359	Crossway Books	160
Sasquatch Books	511	Educational Ministries	183
Turtle Books	522	Eerdmans Books for Young Readers	186
Windswept House Publishers	527		
		Eldridge Publishing	188

Regional (NF)

		Encore Performance Publishing	189
Azro Press	445	Faith Kidz	193
Bess Press	106	Frederick Fell Publishers	197
Cornell Maritime Press	149	Focus on the Family Book Development	200
Down East Books	178		
Falcon Publishing	194	Forward Movement Publications	203
The Globe Pequot Press	213		
Graphic Arts Center Publishing Co.	216	Samuel French, Inc.	207
		Gefen Publishing House	471
Hendrick-Long Publishing Company	237	Hachai Publishing	223
Heritage House	238	Innovative Kids	253

574

The Judaica Press	259	Jonathan David Publishers	166
LangMarc Publishing	480	DiskUs Publishing	174
Legacy Press	270	Displays for Schools	463
LifeSong Publishers	481	Eerdmans Books for Young Readers	186
Living the Good News	482		
Maval Publishing	289	Focus on the Family Book Development	200
Moody Publishers	298		
New Canaan Publishing Company	492	Forward Movement Publications	203
Pacific Press Publishing Association	327	Gefen Publishing House	471
		Group Publishing	220
Paulist Press	329	Hachai Publishing	223
Peartree	497	Harcourt Religion Publishers	229
Playhouse Publishing	500	Horizon Publishers	243
Prep Publishing	501	John Hunt Publishing	247
Quixote Press	503	I B Publications Pty Ltd	475
Rainbow Publishers	355	InterVarsity Press	476
Saint Mary's Press	370	Jewish Lights Publishing	256
Starscape Books	393	The Judaica Press	259
Sword of the Lord	398	Legacy Press	270
Torah Aura Productions	409	LifeSong Publishers	481
Toy Box Productions	411	Living the Good News	482
Twenty-Third Publications	524	Master Books	288
URJ Press	416	Mott Media	301
Warner Press	420	Mount Olive College Press	489
WaterBrook Press	421	New Hope Publishers	309
		New Leaf Press	310
Religious (NF)		Novalis	319
Absey and Company	81	The Oliver Press	320
ACTA Publications	83	Our Sunday Visitor	323
Alef Design Group	87	Pacific Press Publishing Association	327
Ambassador Books	89		
Ambassador-Emerald International	90	The Pilgrim Press	338
		Prep Publishing	501
AMG Publishers	442	Prometheus Books	350
Amirah Publishing	443	Publish America	351
A.R.E. Publishing, Inc.	93	Quest Books	354
Ave Maria Press	97	Rainbow Publishers	355
Baker Book House Company	99	Resource Publications, Inc.	361
Baylor University Press	448	St. Anthony Messenger Press	369
Behrman House	104	Saint Mary's Press	370
Broadman & Holman Publishers	119	Standard Publishing	391
		Sword of the Lord	398
Christian Ed. Publishers	140	TEACH Services, Inc.	402
Christian Focus Publications	141	Torah Aura Productions	409
Concordia Publishing House	146	Toy Box Productions	411
Cook Communications Ministries	148	Twenty-Third Publications	524
		Tyndale House Publishers	413
Cornerstone Press Chicago	458	WaterBrook Press	421
Crossway Books	160		
CSS Publishing Company	162		

Romance
Camex Books	454
Creative With Words Publications	157
Darby Creek Publishing	164
Domhan Books	464
LTDBooks	283
Parachute Press	495
Smooch	386
Starscape Books	393
XC Publishing	436

Science Fiction
Amulet Books	91
Atheneum Books for Young Readers	94
A/V Concepts Corporation	96
Bloomsbury Children's Books	111
Crossquarter Publishing Group	462
DAW Books	167
Ebooksonthe.net	182
Graphia	215
Llewellyn Publications	281
LTDBooks	283
Mayhaven Publishing	290
Mirrorstone Books	487
Moose Enterprise	299
Perfection Learning Corporation	333
Pineapple Press	340
Pipers' Ash Ltd.	342
Scholastic Inc./Trade Paperback Division	374
Scorpius Digital Publishing	378
Tor Books	410
Wizards of the Coast	431
XC Publishing	436

Science/Technology
Abdo Publishing Company	440
ALA Editions	86
Ballyhoo Books, Inc.	446
Benchmark Books	105
Bick Publishing House	450
Blackbirch Press	109
Boyds Mills Press	115
Caddo Gap Press	453
Carson-Dellosa Publishing Company	127
Cartwheel Books	128
Charles River Media	131
Chelsea House Publishers	132
Children's eLibrary	135
Children's Press	136
Christopher-Gordon Publishers	142
Corwin Press	150
The Creative Company	154
Creative Education	461
Creative Learning Press	155
Creative Paperbacks	461
Critical Thinking Company	159
Dandy Lion Publications	163
Dog-Eared Publications	464
Dover Publications	177
Edupress	185
ESP Publishers, Inc.	466
Evan-Moor Educational Publishers	191
Facts On File	192
Frederick Fell Publishers	197
Greenwood Publishing Group	219
Gryphon House	221
Hampton Roads Publishing	225
Harcourt Canada Ltd.	473
Hayes School Publishing Company	233
Heinemann	236
Houghton Mifflin Children's Books	244
Imperial International	250
Incentive Publications	252
Kaeden Books	261
Kingfisher	478
LangMarc Publishing	480
Learning Resources	268
Libraries Unlimited	273
Linworth Publishing	276
Lobster Press	483
Maple Tree Press Inc.	287
Master Books	288
Miles Kelly Publishing	486
The Millbrook Press	487
Morgan Reynolds Publishing	300
National Geographic Books for Children	490
Neal-Schuman Publishers	306
The Oliver Press	320
Pembroke Publishers	332
Phoenix Learning Resources	337
Portage & Main Press	348
PowerKids Press	349
Raincoast Books	504

Random House Children's Publishing	506	Mount Olive College Press	489
Razorbill	358	National Resource Center for Youth Services	491
The Rosen Publishing Group	367	New Harbinger Publications	308
Running Press Kids	368	Newmarket Press	311
Scholastic Inc./Trade Paperback Division	374	Parenting Press, Inc.	328
		Perigee Books	334
Scholastic Professional Books	376	PowerKids Press	349
Scott Foresman	512	Quest Books	354
Seedling Publications	379	Rainbow Books	503
Silver Dolphin Books	514	Redwheel/Weiser/Conari Press	508
Simon & Schuster Books for Young Readers	382	Robins Lane Press	363
		Scorpius Digital Publishing	378
The Speech Bin, Inc.	389	Small Horizons	516
Sterling Publishing Company	396	Sourcebooks	388
Sunburst Technology	519	Starseed Press	394
Teacher Created Materials	400	Megan Tingley Books	408
Teaching & Learning Company	401	Turtle Press	523
Texas Tech University Press	403	Unity House	525
Tor Books	410		
Twenty-First Century Books	523	**Series**	
UXL	417	Abdo Publishing Company	440
Viking Children's Books	525	Action Publishing	84
J. Weston Walch, Publisher	418	Ambassador-Emerald International	90
Weigl Educational Publishers Limited	424	Bay Light Publishing	448
		Books of Wonder	452
Wiley Children's Books	428	Charles River Media	131
Williamson Publishing	429	Chelsea House Publishers	132
Windward Publishing	430	Children's Press	136
World Book	434	Cook Communications Ministries	148
Zephyr Press	437		
		DAW Books	167
Self-Help		The Feminist Press	468
A&B Publishers Group	439	Greenhaven Press	218
Ave Maria Press	97	Holloway House Publishing Group	474
The Bureau for At-Risk Youth	121		
		Honor Books	242
Camex Books	454	Innovative Kids	253
Consortium Publishing	456	Jump at the Sun	478
Creative Bound	153	Kingfisher	478
DiskUs Publishing	174	Legacy Press	270
Ebooksonthe.net	182	Lucent Books	285
Excelsior Cee Publishing	467	Mitchell Lane Publishers	296
Frederick Fell Publishers	197	Novalis	319
Free Spirit Publishing	206	Pearson Learning Group	496
Hazelden Foundation	234	Peel Productions	497
Hunter House Publishers	246	Rainbow Publishers	355
Jewish Lights Publishing	256	Resource Publications, Inc.	361
Llewellyn Publications	281	Sleeping Bear Press	384
Magination Press	286	Soundprints/Studio Mouse	387
Marsh Media	486		

Sword of the Lord 398
Unity House 525

Social Issues
Alyson Publications 88
Alexander Graham Bell Assn.
  for the Deaf 449
A & C Black Publishers 110
Branden Books 117
Broadman & Holman
  Publishers 119
Charlesbridge 130
Children's Book Press 134
Childswork/Childsplay 137
Consortium Publishing 456
Creative Teaching Press, Inc. 156
Crown Books for Young Readers 161
Different Books 463
Ebooksonthe.net 182
Encounter Books 466
Enslow Publishers, Inc. 190
Facts On File 192
Forward Movement Publication 203
Free Spirit Publishing 206
Front Street Books 208
Greenhaven Press 218
Greenwood Publishing Group 219
Hazelden Foundation 234
Hunter House Publishers 246
Jewish Lights Publishing 256
LangMarc Publishing 480
Lerner Publishing Group 271
James Lorimer & Company 282
Lucent Books 285
The Lutterworth Press 484
National Resource Center for
  Youth Services 491
New Harbinger Publications 308
New Leaf Press 310
The Oliver Press 320
Our Child Press 494
Parenting Press, Inc. 328
Perigee Books 334
The Pilgrim Press 338
The Place in the Woods 500
PowerKids Press 349
Prometheus Books 350
Quest Books 354
Rainbow Books 503
Redwheel/Weiser/Conari Press 508
Robins Lane Press 363
Scott Foresman 512
Small Horizons 516
Thompson Educational
  Publishing 406
UXL 417
Walker and Company 419
Windstorm Creative 526
Woodbine House 432

Social Sciences
Barefoot Books Ltd. 447
Benchmark Books 105
The Bureau for At-Risk Youth 121
Chicago Review Press 133
Critical Thinking Company 159
Edupress 185
ESP Publishers, Inc. 466
Evan-Moor Educational
  Publishers 191
Facts On File 192
Harcourt Canada Ltd. 473
Hayes School Publishing
  Company 233
Heinemann 236
John Hunt Publishing 247
Impact Publishers 249
Incentive Publications 252
Linnet Books 275
The Love and Logic Press 483
Magination Press 286
The Millbrook Press 487
New Society Publishers 312
Phoenix Learning Resources 337
Portage & Main Press 348
Scholastic Professional Books 376
Storytellers Ink Publishing Co. 397
Sunburst Technology 519
Thompson Educational
  Publishing 406
Tilbury House Publishers 407
Twenty-First Century Books 523
J. Weston Walch, Publisher 418
Weigl Educational Publishers
  Limited 424
World Book 434

Special Education
Avocus Publishing 445
Alexander Graham Bell Assn.
  for the Deaf 449
Bick Publishing House 450

The Bureau for At-Risk Youth	121	Creative With Words		
Butte Publications	123	Publications		157
Childsworld/Childsplay	137	Crown Books for Young Readers		161
Continental Press	457	Gulliver Books		222
Dandy Lion Publications	163	Lucent Books		285
Displays for Schools	463	The Millbrook Press		487
Educators Publishing Service	184	National Geographic Books		
Forest House Publishing		for Children		490
Company	201	Newmarket Press		311
Free Spirit Publishing	206	OnStage Publishing		493
Group Publishing	220	Pineapple Press		340
Heinemann	236	Pitspopany Press		343
Incentive Publications	252	Raincoast Books		504
International Reading		The Rosen Publishing Group		367
Association	254	Sourcebooks		388
JayJo Books	255	Sports Publishing Inc.		390
Kaeden Books	261	Texas Tech University Press		403
Kodiak Media Group	479	Charles C. Thomas, Publisher		405
Leadership Publishers Inc.	480	Thompson Educational		
National Council of Teachers		Publishing		406
of English	303	TowleHouse Publishing		521
NL Associates	316	Turtle Press		523
Perigee Books	334	Twenty-First Century Books		523
Phoenix Learning Resources	337	UXL		417
Publish America	351	Wiley Children's Books		428
Resource Publications, Inc.	361	YMAA Publication Center		528
The Speech Bin, Inc.	389			
Teaching & Learning Company	401	**Story Picture Books (F)**		
Charles C. Thomas, Publisher	405	Abbeville Kids		439
J. Weston Walch, Publisher	418	Abingdon Press		440
Woodbine House	432	Absey and Company		81
The Wright Group/McGraw-Hill	435	Action Publishing		84
Zephyr Press	437	Advocacy Press		441
		Aladdin Paperbacks		85
Sports (F)		Alef Design Group		87
Darby Creek Publishing	164	Augsburg Books		95
Parachute Press	495	Baker Book House Company		99
Scholastic Inc./Trade Paperback		Bantam Books for Young Readers		101
Division	374	Bay Light Publishing		448
Seedling Publications	379	Bess Press		106
Sports Publishing Inc.	390	Bethany House		107
Turtle Press	523	Blue Marlin Publications		451
Whitecap Books Ltd.	425	Blue Sky Press		112
		Bollix Books		451
Sports (NF)		Borealis Press Limited		114
Branden Books	117	BOW Books		452
Chelsea House Publishers	132	Branden Books		117
Children's Press	136	Broadman & Holman Publishers		119
The Creative Company	154	Carolrhoda Books		126
Creative Editions	460	Charlesbridge		130
		Children's Book Press		134

Child Welfare League of America	139
Clarion Books	144
Clear Light Publishers	145
Covenant Communications	152
Creative Editions	460
Creative Education	461
Crossway Books	160
May Davenport, Publishers	165
Jonathan David Publishers	166
Dial Books for Young Readers	171
Eerdmans Books for Young Readers	186
Egmont Children's Books	187
Floris Books	199
Frances Foster Books	204
Fulcrum Publishing	209
Laura Geringer Books	210
Gibbs Smith, Publisher	211
Graphic Arts Center Publishing Co.	216
Greene Bark Press	217
Hampton-Brown Books	224
Hampton Roads Publishing	225
Harcourt Children's Books	228
HarperCollins Children's Books	231
Henry Holt Books for Young Readers	241
Hodder Children's Books	474
Holiday House	240
The Judaica Press	259
Just Us Books	260
Key Porter Books	264
Lee & Low Books	269
Arthur A. Levine Books	272
Lion Publishing	277
Little Tiger Press	280
Lobster Press	483
Magination Press	286
Maval Publishing	289
Mayhaven Publishing	290
Margaret K. McElderry Books	291
Mondo Publishing	297
National Geographic Society	304
Nimbus Publishing	315
North Country Books	317
North-South Books	493
OnStage Publishing	493
Orca Book Publishers	321
Peartree	497
Philomel Books	336
Piñata Books	339
Pipers' Ash Ltd.	342
Puffin Books	352
G. P. Putnam's Sons	353
Raven Tree Press	356
Rayve Productions Inc.	357
Red Deer Press	359
Rising Moon	362
Ronsdale Press	365
Sandcastle Publishing	371
Scholastic Canada Ltd.	373
Scholastic Press	375
School Specialty Children's Publishing	377
Scorpius Digital Publishing	378
Silver Whistle	381
Simon & Schuster Books for Young Readers	382
Siphano Picture Books	515
Smallfellow Press	515
Small Horizons	516
Soundprints/Studio Mouse	387
Star Bright Books	392
Stiles-Bishop Productions Inc.	518
Tanglewood Press, LLC	399
Third World Press	404
Tilbury House Publishers	407
Megan Tingley Books	408
Toy Box Productions	411
Viking Children's Books	525
Walker and Company	419
Warner Press	420
Woodbine House	432
Workman Publishing Company	433
The Wright Group/McGraw-Hill	435

Story Picture Books (NF)

Abbeville Kids	439
Abingdon Press	440
Augsburg Books	95
Baker Book House Company	99
The Benefactory	449
Bess Press	106
Beyond Words Publishing	108
Blackbirch Press	109
Blue Marlin Publications	451

Broadman & Holman Publishers	119	TEACH Services, Inc.	402
		Tilbury House Publishers	407
Cartwheel Books	128	Megan Tingley Books	408
Charlesbridge	130	Torah Aura Productions	409
Children's Book Press	134	Toy Box Productions	411
Children's Press	136	Tricycle Press	412
Chrysalis Children's Books	143	Tyndale House Publishers	413
Concordia Publishing House	146	Walker and Company	419
Covenant Communications	152	Watson-Guptill	422
Creative Education	461	Windward Publishing	430
Crown Books for Young Readers	161	Workman Publishing Company	433
CSS Publishing Company	162		
Dawn Publications	168	**Toddler Books (F)**	
Dial Books for Young Readers	171	Abingdon Press	440
Down East Books	178	Blue Sky Press	112
Eakin Press	181	Cartwheel Books	128
Egmont Children's Books	187	Chrysalis Children's Books	143
Family Learning Assn./ERIC/ REC Press	195	Crossway Books	160
		Dial Books for Young Readers	171
Fulcrum Publishing	209	DiskUs Publishing	174
Hachai Publishing	223	Dorling Kindersley	176
Holiday House	240	Educational Ministries	183
Honor Books	242	Egmont Children's Books	187
The Judaica Press	259	Farrar, Straus & Giroux	196
Key Porter Books	264	Greenwillow Books	472
Learning Horizons	267	Harcourt Children's Books	228
Lee & Low Books	269	HarperCollins Children's Books	231
Arthur A. Levine Books	272	Houghton Mifflin Children's Books	244
Lion Publishing	277		
Little, Brown and Company	278	Kar-Ben Publishing	262
Little Tiger Press	280	Lee & Low Books	269
Maval Publishing	289	Lion Publishing	277
National Geographic Society	304	Little, Brown and Company	278
NorthWord Books for Young Readers	318	Little Simon	279
		Little Tiger Press	280
Novalis	319	Milet Publishing	294
Our Sunday Visitor	323	Playhouse Publishing	500
The Overmountain Press	324	Polychrome Publishing Corporation	347
Richard C. Owen Publishers	325		
Parenting Press, Inc.	328	G. P. Putnam's Sons	353
Peachtree Publishers	330	School Specialty Children's Publishing	377
Pitspopany Press	343		
St. Anthony Messenger Press	369	Simon & Schuster Books for Young Readers	382
Scholastic Press	375		
Simon & Schuster Books for Young Readers	382	Soundprints/Studio Mouse	387
		Star Bright Books	392
Sleeping Bear Press	384	Starseed Press	394
The Speech Bin, Inc.	389	Third World Press	404
Standard Publishing	391	Megan Tingley Books	408
Stemmer House Publishers	395	Workman Publishing Company	433
Sterling Publishing Company	396		

581

Toddler Books (NF)

Abingdon Press	440
Augsburg Books	95
Broadman & Holman Publishers	119
Cartwheel Books	128
Charlesbridge	130
Chicago Review Press	133
Cook Communications Ministries	148
Crown Books for Young Readers	161
DiskUs Publishing	174
Dorling Kindersley	176
Egmont Children's Books	187
Greenwillow Books	472
Honor Books	242
Humanics	245
John Hunt Publishing	247
Jewish Lights Publishing	256
Kar-Ben Publishing	262
Learning Horizons	267
The Millbrook Press	487
Orchard Books	322
Running Press Kids	368
School Specialty Children's Publishing	377
Seaburn Publishing	512
Silver Dolphin Books	514
Standard Publishing	391
Tyndale House Publishers	413
URJ Press	416

Travel

Abdo Publishing Company	440
Carousel Press	454
Chelsea House Publishers	132
Fulcrum Publishing	209
The Globe Pequot Press	213
Leadership Publishers Inc.	480
Marlor Press	485
Rand McNally	504
Sasquatch Books	511

Western

Domhan Books	464
Ebooksonthe.net	182
Gibbs Smith, Publisher	211
HarperCollins Children's Fiction	232
Moody Publishers	298
Renaissance House	360

Turtle Books	522

Young Adult (F)

A&B Publishers Group	439
Harry N. Abrams Books for Young Readers	80
Absey and Company	81
Action Publishing	84
Advocacy Press	441
Aladdin Paperbacks	85
Alpha Publishing	442
Ambassador-Emerald International	90
Amirah Publishing	443
Amulet Books	91
Annick Press	92
Atheneum Books for Young Readers	94
A/V Concepts Corporation	96
Avocet Press	444
Avocus Publishing	445
Bancroft Press	446
Bantam Books for Young Readers	101
Beach Holme Publishing	102
Bethany House	107
Bloomsbury Children's Books	111
Blue Sky Press	112
Boardwalk Books	113
Bollix Books	451
Borealis Press Limited	114
Boyds Mills Press	115
Breakwater Books	118
Brown Barn Books	120
Camex Books	454
Carolrhoda Books	126
Chaosium	455
Christian Focus Publications	141
Clarion Books	144
Clear Light Publishers	145
Contemporary Drama Service	147
Coteau Books	151
Course Crafters	460
Covenant Communications	152
Creative Editions	460
Cricket Books	158
Crossquarter Publishing Group	462
Darby Creek Publishing	164
May Davenport, Publishers	165
DAW Books	167
Discovery Enterprises	173

DiskUs Publishing	174	The Overmountain Press	324
Domhan Books	464	Parachute Press	495
Dorchester Publishing	175	Peachtree Publishers	330
Down East Books	178	Penguin Books Canada Limited	498
Dutton Children's Books	180	Philomel Books	336
Eastgate Systems	465	Piñata Books	339
Ebooksonthe.net	182	Pineapple Press	340
Farrar, Straus & Giroux	196	Polar Bear & Company	346
Frederick Fell Publishers	197	Polychrome Publishing	
Floris Books	199	Corporation	347
Focus on the Family Book		Publish America	351
Development	200	Puffin Books	352
Fondo de Cultura		G. P. Putnam's Sons	353
Economica USA	470	Random House Children's	
Formac Publishing Company Ltd.	202	Books	506
Frances Foster Books	204	Razorbill	358
Front Street Books	208	Red Deer Press	359
Laura Geringer Books	210	Resource Publications, Inc.	361
David R. Godine, Publisher	471	River City Publishing	508
Graphia	215	Ronsdale Press	365
Graphic Arts Center		Sandpiper Paperbacks	510
Publishing Co.	216	Scholastic Canada Ltd.	373
Greenwillow Books	472	Scorpius Digital Publishing	378
Groundwood Books	472	Seaburn Publishing	512
Hampton Roads Publishing	225	Second Story Press	513
Harbour Publishing	226	Silver Whistle	381
HarperCollins Children's Books	231	Simon Pulse	383
HarperCollins Children's		Smallfellow Press	515
Fiction	232	Smooch	386
Henry Holt Books for Young		Starscape Books	393
Readers	241	Sword of the Lord	398
Journey Forth	258	Tanglewood Press, LLC	399
The Judaica Press	259	Third World Press	404
Key Porter Books	264	Thistledown Press	520
Wendy Lamb Books	479	Torah Aura Productions	409
LangMarc Publishing	480	Tor Books	410
Arthur A. Levine Books	272	Touchwood Editions	521
LifeSong Publishers	481	Twenty-Third Publications	524
Lion Publishing	277	Viking Children's Books	525
Little Blue Works	482	Walker and Company	419
Llewellyn Publications	281	WaterBrook Press	421
Lobster Press	483	Watson-Guptill	422
Margaret K. McElderry Books	291	White Mane Publishing	
Meriwether Publishing Ltd.	293	Company	426
Mirrorstone Books	487	Windswept House Publishers	527
Moody Publishers	298	Wizards of the Coast	431
Naturegraph Publishers	305	XC Publishing	436
The New England Press	307		
Newmarket Press	311	**Young Adult (NF)**	
OnStage Publishing	493	A&B Publishers Group	439
Orca Book Publishers	321		

Harry N. Abrams Books for Young Readers	80	Focus on the Family Book Development	200
Alef Design Group	87	Fondo de Cultura Economica USA	470
Ambassador-Emerald International	90	Forward Movement Publications	203
Amirah Publishing	443	Franklin Watts	470
Amulet Books	91	Front Street Books	208
Annick Press	92	Graphia	215
Avisson Press	98	Greenhaven Press	218
Avocus Publishing	445	Hampton Roads Publishing	225
Bancroft Press	446	Hazelden Foundation	234
Bantam Books for Young Readers	101	Hendrick-Long Publishing Company	237
Baylor University Press	448	Holiday House	240
Behrman House	104	Holloway House Publishing Group	474
Bess Press	106		
Beyond Words Publishing	108	Houghton Mifflin Children's Books	244
Bick Publishing House	450		
Blackbirch Press	109	John Hunt Publishing	247
Boardwalk Books	113	Hyperion Books for Children	475
Branden Books	117	Impact Publishers	249
Capstone Press	125	Imperial International	250
Charles River Media	131	Iron Crown Enterprises	477
Chelsea House Publishers	132	Jewish Lights Publishing	256
Chicago Review Press	133	Journey Forth	258
Clear Light Publishers	145	Key Curriculum Press	263
Contemporary Drama Service	147	Key Porter Books	264
Cornerstone Press Chicago	458	Wendy Lamb Books	479
Course Crafters	460	LangMarc Publishing	480
Creative Editions	460	Lark Books	266
Creative Education	461	Lerner Publishing Group	271
Critical Thinking Company	159	Arthur A. Levine Books	272
Crossquarter Publishing Group	462	LifeSong Publishers	481
Crown Books for Young Readers	161	Little Blue Works	482
CSS Publishing Company	162	Little, Brown and Company	278
Didax	172	Llewellyn Publications	281
Different Books	463	Lucent Books	285
Domhan Books	464	Magination Press	286
Dorling Kindersley	176	Mayhaven Publishing	290
Dutton Children's Books	180	The Millbrook Press	487
Eastgate Systems	465	Mitchell Lane Publishers	296
Ebooksonthe.net	182	Morgan Reynolds Publishing	300
Enslow Publishers, Inc.	190	Mott Media	301
ETC Publications	467	National Geographic Books for Children	490
Facts On File	192		
Falcon Publishing	194	National Resource Center for Youth Services	491
Farrar, Straus & Giroux	196		
Frederick Fell Publishers	197	Naturegraph Publishers	305
Ferguson Publishing	198	The New England Press	307
Fiesta City Publishers	469	New Harbinger Publications	308
Finney Company	469		

New Leaf Press	310
Nimbus Publishing	315
Novalis	319
The Oliver Press	320
Our Sunday Visitor	323
Pacific Educational Press	326
Parkway Publishers	495
Peachtree Publishers	330
Perfection Learning Corporation	333
Perigee Books	334
Peter Pauper Press	335
Piñata Books	339
Pipers' Ash Ltd.	342
Pitspopany Press	343
Players Press	344
Polar Bear & Company	346
Pruett Publishing Company	502
Publish America	351
Quest Books	354
Razorbill	358
Resource Publications, Inc.	361
The Rosen Publishing Group	367
Saint Mary's Press	370
School Specialty Children's Publishing	377
Seaburn Publishing	512
Second Story Press	513
Simon Pulse	383
Standard Publishing	391
Starscape Books	393
Success Publications	519
TEACH Services, Inc.	402
Third World Press	404
Touchwood Editions	521
TowleHouse Publishing	521
Twenty-First Century Books	523
Twenty-Third Publications	524
Tyndale House Publishers	413
Unity House	525
URJ Press	416
Walker and Company	419
Watson-Guptill	422
Weigl Educational Publishers Limited	424
White Mane Publishing Company	426
Wiley Children's Books	428
Windward Publishing	430
World Book	434
YMAA Publication Center	528

Publisher and Contest Index

If you do not find a particular publisher, turn to page 547 for a list of deletions and name changes.

★ indicates a newly listed publisher or contest

A

A&B Publishers Group	439
Abbeville Kids	439
Abdo Publishing Company	440
Abingdon Press	440
★ Harry N. Abrams Books for Young Readers	80
Absey and Company	81
Accord Publishing	82
ACTA Publications	83
Action Publishing	84
Activity Resources Company	441
Advocacy Press	441
Aladdin Paperbacks	85
ALA Editions	86
Alef Design Group	87
Alpha Publishing	442
Alyson Publications	88
Ambassador Books	89
Ambassador-Emerald International	90
★ American Book Cooperative Children's Picture Book Competition	53
AMG Publishers	442
Amirah Publishing	443
★ Amulet Books	91
Annick Press	92
Aquila Communications Ltd.	443
★ A.R.E. Publishing, Inc.	93
Association for Childhood Education Int'l	444
Atheneum Books for Young Readers	94
Atlantic Writing Competition	531
Augsburg Books	95
A/V Concepts Corporation	96
★ Ave Maria Press	97
Avisson Press	98
Avocet Press	444
Avocus Publishing	445
Azro Press	445

B

Baker Book House Company	99
Baker's Plays	100
Ballyhoo Books, Inc.	446
★ Bancroft Press	446
Bantam Books for Young Readers	101
Barefoot Books Ltd.	447
Barron's Educational Series	447
Bay Light Publishing	448
Baylor University Press	448
Beach Holme Publishing	102
Bebop Books	103
Behrman House	104
Alexander Graham Bell Assn. for the Deaf	449
Benchmark Books	105
The Benefactory	449
BePuzzled	450
Bess Press	106
Bethany House	107
Beyond Words Publishing	108
Bick Publishing House	450
Blackbirch Press	109
A & C Black Publishers	110
★ Bloomsbury Children's Books	111
Blue Marlin Publications	451
Blue Sky Press	112
★ Boardwalk Books	113
★ Bollix Books	451
Books of Wonder	452
Borealis Press Limited	114
The Boston Globe-Horn Book Awards	532
BOW Books	452
Boyds Mills Press	115
Boynton/Cook Publishers	116
Branden Books	117
Breakwater Books	118
Broadman & Holman Publishers	119
★ Brown Barn Books	120
Marilyn Brown Novel Award	532

586

Entry	Page
The Bureau for At-Risk Youth	121
★ Buster Books	122
Butte Publications	123

C

Entry	Page
Caddo Gap Press	453
★ Calkins Creek Books	453
Camex Books	454
Candlewick Press	124
Capstone Press	125
Carolrhoda Books	126
Carousel Press	454
Carson-Dellosa Publishing Company	127
Cartwheel Books	128
Cavendish Children's Books	129
Chaosium	455
Charlesbridge	130
Charles River Media	131
Chelsea House Publishers	132
Chicago Review Press	133
Children's Book Press	134
Children's eLibrary	135
Children's Press	136
Children's Story Scripts	455
Childswork/Childsplay	137
Child Welfare League of America	139
Christian Ed. Publishers	140
Christian Focus Publications	141
Christopher-Gordon Publishers	142
Chrysalis Children's Books	143
★ CIPA National Writing Contest	533
Clarion Books	144
Clark City Press	456
Clear Light Publishers	145
CNW/FFWA Florida State Writing Competition	533
Concordia Publishing House	146
Consortium Publishing	456
Contemporary Books	457
Contemporary Drama Service	147
Continental Press	457
Cook Communications Ministries	148
Cornell Maritime Press	149
Cornerstone Press Chicago	458
Corwin Press	150
Coteau Books	151
Cottonwood Press	458
Course Crafters	460
Covenant Communications	152
Creative Bound	153
The Creative Company	154
Creative Editions	460
Creative Education	461
Creative Learning Press	155
Creative Paperbacks	461
Creative Teaching Press, Inc.	156
Creative With Words Publications	157
Cricket Books	158
Critical Thinking Company	159
Crossquarter Publishing Group	462
Crossway Books	160
Crown Books for Young Readers	161
CSS Publishing Company	162

D

Entry	Page
The Dana Awards	534
Dandy Lion Publications	163
★ Darby Creek Publishing	164
May Davenport, Publishers	165
Jonathan David Publishers	166
DAW Books	167
Dawn Publications	168
★ Delacorte Dell Yearling Contest	534
Delacorte Press Contest for a First Young Adult Novel	535
Delmar Learning	462
Denlinger's Publishers	169
Dial Books for Young Readers	171
Didax	172
Different Books	463
Discovery Enterprises	173
DiskUs Publishing	174
Displays for Schools	463
Dog-Eared Publications	464
Domhan Books	464
★ Dorchester Publishing	175
Dorling Kindersley	176
Dover Publications	177
Down East Books	178
★ Dragonfly Spirit Writing for Children Short Story Contest	535
Dramatic Publishing	179
Dutton Children's Books	180

E

Entry	Page
Eakin Press	181
★ E & E Publishing	465
Eastgate Systems	465
Ebooksonthe.net	182

587

Educational Ministries	183
Educators Publishing Service	184
Edupress	185
Eerdmans Books for Young Readers	186
★ Egmont Children's Books	187
Eldridge Publishing	188
Encore Performance Publishing	189
Encounter Books	466
Enslow Publishers, Inc.	190
ESP Publishers, Inc.	466
ETC Publications	467
Evan-Moor Educational Publishers	191
Excelsior Cee Publishing	467
Exclamation! Publishers	468

F

Facts On File	192
Faith Kidz	193
Falcon Publishing	194
Family Learning Assn./ ERIC/REC Press	195
Farrar, Straus & Giroux	196
Frederick Fell Publishers	197
The Feminist Press	468
Ferguson Publishing	198
Fiesta City Publishers	469
Finney Company	469
★ Floris Books	199
Focus on the Family Book Development	200
Fondo de Cultura Economica USA	470
Forest House Publishing Company	201
Formac Publishing Company Ltd.	202
Forward Movement Publications	203
Frances Foster Books	204
Franklin Watts	470
Free Spirit Publishing	206
Samuel French, Inc.	207
Front Street Books	208
Fulcrum Publishing	209

G

Gefen Publishing House	471
★ Laura Geringer Books	210
Gibbs Smith, Publisher	211
Gifted Education Press	212
The Globe Pequot Press	213
David R. Godine, Publisher	471

Goodheart-Willcox	214
★ Graphia	215
Graphic Arts Center Publishing Co.	216
Greene Bark Press	217
Greenhaven Press	218
Greenwillow Books	472
Greenwood Publishing Group	219
★ Groundwood Books	472
Group Publishing	220
Gryphon House	221
Gulliver Books	222

H

Hachai Publishing	223
Hampton-Brown Books	224
Hampton Roads Publishing	225
★ Harbour Publishing	226
Harcourt Canada Ltd.	473
Harcourt Children's Books (See also Gulliver Books, Harcourt Canada Ltd., Silver Whistle)	228
Harcourt Religion Publishers	229
HarperCollins Children's Books (See also Laura Geringer Books, Greenwillow Books, HarperCollins Children's Fiction)	231
HarperCollins Children's Fiction	232
Harvard Common Press	473
Hayes School Publishing Company	233
Hazelden Foundation	234
Health Press	235
Heinemann	236
Hendrick-Long Publishing Company	237
Heritage House	238
Heuer Publishing Company	239
Hodder Children's Books	474
Holiday House	240
Holloway House Publishing Group	474
Henry Holt Books for Young Readers	241
Honor Books	242
Horizon Publishers	243
Houghton Mifflin Children's Books	244

(See also Clarion Books, Graphia, Kingfisher, Sandpiper Paperbacks)
Humanics 245
Hunter House Publishers 246
John Hunt Publishing 247
Hyperion Books for Children 475

I

I B Publications Pty Ltd 475
Illumination Arts 248
Impact Publishers 249
Imperial International 250
Incentive Publications 252
Innovative Kids 253
InQ Publishing Co. 476
International Reading Association 254
InterVarsity Press 476
Iron Crown Enterprises 477

J

January Productions 477
JayJo Books 255
Jewish Lights Publishing 256
JIST Publishing 257
Journey Forth 258
The Judaica Press 259
Jump at the Sun 478
Just Us Books 260

K

Kaeden Books 261
Kar-Ben Publishing 262
The Barbara Karlin Grant 536
Key Curriculum Press 263
Key Porter Books 264
Kingfisher 478
Alfred A. Knopf Books for Young Readers 265
Kodiak Media Group 479

L

★ Wendy Lamb Books 479
LangMarc Publishing 480
Lark Books 266
Leadership Publishers Inc. 480
Learning Horizons 267
Learning Links Inc. 481
Learning Resources 268
Lee & Low Books 269
Legacy Press 270
Lerner Publishing Group 271
Arthur A. Levine Books 272
Libraries Unlimited 273

LifeSong Publishers 481
Lillenas Publishing Company 274
Linnet Books 275
Linworth Publishing 276
★ Lion Publishing 277
Little Blue Works 482
Little, Brown and Company 278
Little Simon 279
★ Little Tiger Press 280
Living the Good News 482
Llewellyn Publications 281
Lobster Press 483
James Lorimer & Company 282
The Love and Logic Press 483
LTDBooks 283
Lucent Books 285
The Lutterworth Press 484

M

MacAdam/Cage 484
Mage Publishers 485
Magination Press 286
★ Maple Tree Press Inc. 287
Marlor Press 485
Marsh Media 486
Master Books 288
Maval Publishing 289
Mayhaven Publishing 290
Margaret K. McElderry Books 291
McGraw-Hill Publishing (See School Specialty Children's Publishing, The Wright Group/McGraw-Hill)
Meadowbrook Press 292
Meriwether Publishing Ltd. 293
Miles Kelly Publishing 486
★ Milet Publishing 294
Milkweed Editions 295
Milkweed Prize for Children's Literature 536
The Millbrook Press 487
★ Mirrorstone Books 487
Mitchell Lane Publishers 296
Modern Publishing 488
Mondo Publishing 297
Moody Publishers 298
★ Moose Enterprise 299
Morgan Reynolds Publishing 300
Morning Glory Press 488
★ Mott Media 301
Mountain Meadow Press 489
Mount Olive College Press 489
Munchweiler Press 490

N

National Assn. for the Educ.
  of Young People   **302**
National Children's Theatre
  Festival Competition   **537**
National Council of Teachers
  of English   **303**
National Geographic Books
  for Children   **490**
National Geographic Society   **304**
National Resource Center for
  Youth Services   **491**
Natural Heritage Books   **491**
Naturegraph Publishers   **305**
Neal-Schuman Publishers   **306**
Newbery Medal Award   **537**
New Canaan Publishing
  Company   **492**
The New England Press   **307**
New Harbinger
  Publications   **308**
New Hope Publishers   **309**
New Leaf Press   **310**
Newmarket Press   **311**
New Society Publishers   **312**
New Voices Award   **538**
New World Library   **313**
★ Nightwood Editions   **314**
★ Nimbus Publishing   **315**
  NL Associates   **316**
Nomad Press   **492**
★ Ursula Nordstrom Fiction
  Contest   **538**
North Country Books   **317**
North-South Books   **493**
NorthWord Books for Young
  Readers   **318**
Novalis   **319**
NWA Novel Contest   **539**

O

The Oliver Press   **320**
Once Upon a World Award   **539**
OnStage Publishing   **493**
Orca Book Publishers   **321**
Orchard Books   **322**
Our Child Press   **494**
Our Sunday Visitor   **323**
The Overmountain Press   **324**
Richard C. Owen Publishers   **325**

P

Pacific Educational Press   **326**
Pacific Northwest Writers
  Association Literary
  Contests   **540**
Pacific Press Publishing
  Association   **327**
Pacific View Press   **494**
Parachute Press   **495**
Parenting Press, Inc.   **328**
Parkway Publishers   **495**
Paulist Press   **329**
Paws IV Books   **496**
Peachtree Publishers   **330**
Pearson Learning Group   **496**
Peartree   **497**
Peel Productions   **497**
Pelican Publishing Company   **331**
Pembroke Publishers   **332**
Penguin Books Canada
  Limited   **498**
Penguin Group USA
  (See Dial BFYR, Dutton
  Children's Books, Penguin
  Books Canada Limited,
  Perigee Books, Philomel
  Books, Puffin Books, G. P.
  Putnam's Sons, Razorbill,
  Viking Children's Books)
Perfection Learning
  Corporation   **333**
Perigee Books   **334**
Perspectives Press, Inc.   **498**
Peter Pauper Press   **335**
Philomel Books   **336**
Phoenix Learning Resources   **337**
Piano Press   **499**
★ Pikes Peak Writers Conference
  Annual Contest   **540**
The Pilgrim Press   **338**
Piñata Books   **339**
Pineapple Press   **340**
Pioneer Drama Service   **341**
★ Pipers' Ash Ltd.   **342**
Pippin Press   **499**
Pitspopany Press   **343**
The Place in the Woods   **500**
Players Press   **344**
Playhouse Publishing   **500**
Playwrights Canada Press   **501**
Pleasant Company
  Publications   **345**
Polar Bear & Company   **346**
Polychrome Publishing
  Corporation   **347**
Portage & Main Press   **348**
★ PowerKids Press   **349**

Prep Publishing	501
Prometheus Books	350
Pruett Publishing Company	502
Publish America	351
Puffin Books	352
G. P. Putnam's Sons	353

Q

★ Quartz Editions	502
Quest Books	354
Quixote Press	503

R

Rainbow Books	503
Rainbow Publishers	355
★ Raincoast Books	504
Rand McNally	504
Random House (See Bantam BFYR, Crown BFYR, Alfred A. Knopf BFYR, Wendy Lamb Books, Random House Children's Books, Random House Children's Publishing)	
Random House Children's Books	506
Random House Children's Publishing	506
★ Raven Tree Press	356
Rayve Productions Inc.	357
★ Razorbill	358
Redbird Press	507
Red Deer Press	359
Redleaf Press	507
Redwheel/Weiser/Conari Press	508
Renaissance House	360
Resource Publications, Inc.	361
Rising Moon	362
River City Publishing	508
★ Riverfront Books	509
Robins Lane Press	363
Rocky River Publishers	364
Ronsdale Press	365
The Rosen Publishing Group	367
Running Press Kids	368

S

St. Anthony Messenger Press	369
Saint Mary's Press	370
Salina Bookshelf	509
Sandcastle Publishing	371
Sandlapper Publishing	510
Sandpiper Paperbacks	510
Sasquatch Books	511
Scarecrow Press	372
Scholastic Canada Ltd.	373
Scholastic Inc. (See Blue Sky Press, Cartwheel Books, Children's Press, Franklin Watts, Arthur A. Levine Books, Orchard Books, Scholastic Canada Ltd., Scholastic Inc./Trade Paperback Division, Scholastic Press, Scholastic Professional Books)	
Scholastic Inc./Trade Paperback Division	374
Scholastic Press	375
Scholastic Professional Books	376
★ School Specialty Children's Publishing	377
School Zone Publishing	511
Scorpius Digital Publishing	378
Scott Foresman	512
Seaburn Publishing	512
Seal Press	513
★ Second Story Press	513
Seedling Publications	379
Shen's Books	514
Silver Dolphin Books	514
Silver Moon Press	380
Silver Whistle	381
Simon & Schuster Books for Young Readers	382
Simon & Schuster Children's Publishing Division (See Aladdin Paperbacks, Atheneum BFYR, Little Simon, Margaret K. McElderry Books, Simon & Schuster BFYR, Simon Pulse)	
Simon Pulse	383
Siphano Picture Books	515
Skipping Stones Awards	541
Sleeping Bear Press	384
★ Smallfellow Press	515
Small Horizons	516
Smith and Kraus	385
Smith and Kraus Books for Kids	516
★ Smooch	386
Kay Snow Writing Contest	541
Soho Press	517
Soundprints/Studio Mouse	387
Sourcebooks	388
Southern Early Childhood Association (SECA)	517

Southwest Writers Contests	542		Upstart Books	415
The Speech Bin, Inc.	389		★ URJ Press	416
Sports Publishing Inc.	390		UXL	417
Standard Publishing	391			
Star Bright Books	392		**V**	
★ Starscape Books	393		Viking Children's Books	525
Starseed Press	394		Visual Education	
Stemmer House Publishers	395		Corporation	526
Sterling Publishing Company	396		**W**	
Stiles-Bishop Productions Inc.	518		J. Weston Walch, Publisher	418
Storytellers Ink Publishing Co.	397		Walker and Company	419
Story Time Stories That Rhyme	518		Warner Press	420
Success Publications	519		WaterBrook Press	421
Sunburst Technology	519		★ Watson-Guptill	422
Sword of the Lord	398		Wayne State University Press	423
			Weigl Educational Publishers Limited	424
T			Whitecap Books Ltd.	425
Tall Tales Press Hidden Talents Short Story Contest	542		White Mane Publishing Company	426
★ Tanglewood Press, LLC	399		Albert Whitman & Company	427
Peter Taylor Prize for the Novel	543		Wiley Children's Books	428
Teacher Created Materials	400		Williamson Publishing	429
Teachers & Writers Collaborative	520		★ Windstorm Creative	526
Teaching & Learning Company	401		Windswept House Publishers	527
TEACH Services, Inc.	402		Windward Publishing	430
Texas Tech University Press	403		Winslow Publishing	527
Third World Press	404		Wizards of the Coast	431
Thistledown Press	520		Woodbine House	432
Charles C. Thomas, Publisher	405		Wordware Publishing	528
Thompson Educational Publishing	406		Work-in-Progress Grants	543
Tilbury House Publishers	407		Workman Publishing Company	433
Megan Tingley Books	408		World Book	434
Torah Aura Productions	409		The Wright Group/ McGraw-Hill	435
Tor Books	410			
Touchwood Editions	521		**XYZ**	
TowleHouse Publishing	521		XC Publishing	436
Toy Box Productions	411		YMAA Publication Center	528
Tradewind Books Ltd.	522		Zephyr Press	437
Tricycle Press	412		★ Paul Zindel First Novel Award	544
Turtle Books	522		★ Zoo Press Award for Short Fiction	544
Turtle Press	523			
Twenty-First Century Books	523			
★ Twenty-Third Publications	524			
Two Lives Publishing	524			
Tyndale House Publishers	413			

U

Unity House   525